FEMALE ERASURE

FEMALE ERASURE

WHAT YOU NEED TO KNOW ABOUT GENDER POLITICS' WAR
ON WOMEN, THE FEMALE SEX AND HUMAN RIGHTS

Ruth Barrett, Anthology Editor

TidalTimePublishing, LLC

www.femaleerasure.com

FEMALE ERASURE
What You Need To Know About Gender Politics' War on Women, the Female Sex and Human Rights

Anthology Editor: Ruth Barrett
Copy Editor: Kate Victory Hannisian

Tidal Time Publishing, LLC
Pacific Palisades, CA, U.S.A.
www.tidaltimepublishing.com
Copyright © 2016, Tidal Time Publishing, LLC. First edition. All Rights Reserved.

ISBN: 0997146702
IBSN: 9780997146707
Library of Congress Control Number: 2016910692
Tidal Time Publishing, Lebec, CA
Cover Art and Design by Claudia Kunin ©2016
Interior Design: CreateSpace

"The First Sex: In the Beginning We Were All Created Female", by Monica Sjöö and Barbara Mor, from THE GREAT COSMIC MOTHER, copyright © 1985. (HarperCollins). Reprinted by permission of the publisher. Monica Sjöö's original pamphlet, *The Ancient Religion of the Great Cosmic Mother of All*, was distributed in Great Britain in 1975.

"A Creed For Free Women", by Elsa Gidlow, from SAPPHIC SONGS – EIGHTEEN TO EIGHTY, copyright ©1982, and published in Druid Heights Books. Reprinted by permission of the author's estate.

"Mother", by Patricia Monaghan, from SEASONS OF THE WITCH: POETRY AND SONGS TO THE GODDESS, Third Edition. Copyright © 2004. Reprinted by permission of the author's estate. All Rights Reserved.

The name of Tidal Time Publishing, LLC honors Mary Daly (1928 – 2010), wordsmith and feminist theologian. Tidal Time is "Elemental Time, beyond the clocking/clacking of clonedom; Wild Time; Time that cannot be grasped by the daily man-dated world; Time of Wicked Inspiration/genius" (Mary Daly, Wickedary, P 96.).

Endorsements

In different voices, this compendium of articles shows how transgenderism is erasing the reality of what it means to be a woman. There are some marvelous essays in Female Erasure that make this book the recent go-to analysis of gender identity as "an inherently misogynist idea." Read the writings by medical and psychological professionals who tell us about the wrongs their professions have inflicted on transitioners, including children; the accounts of women caught in the vicious cycle of transitioning and the stories of young lesbians pressured to be ABF (Anything But Female); and the narratives of wives of men who would be women, wives who learned the hard way that "women are [not] actually real to these men." These are only a few of the meaningful essays in this anthology that address the current travesty of gender identity orthodoxy.

~ Janice G. Raymond is Professor Emerita of Women's Studies and Medical Ethics, University of Massachusetts and author of The Transsexual Empire: the Making of the She-Male.

As the liberal/postmodern dogma of transgender politics becomes the norm in more and more social and intellectual spaces, it gets harder to ask crucial questions, let alone offer a critique, of the sex/gender politics of that movement. Coming from a variety of philosophical/spiritual backgrounds, in a variety of literary styles, this is an impressive collection. All the writers in Female Erasure share a crucial commitment to rejecting patriarchy, which opens up space for the blunt, honest talk we need. Waving away these feminists' questions and critiques with demands for "inclusion" won't magically answer the questions or respond to the critiques. As a man who has come to understand sex/gender politics through radical feminism,

I hope readers will not back away from the fight against institutionalized male dominance. Neither liberal individualism nor postmodern posturing offer much hope in the struggle against patriarchy.

~ Robert Jensen, author of The End of Patriarchy: Radical Feminism for Men

If you believe that women, including those who have been sexually assaulted by males, should not be forced against their will to share their most vulnerable spaces with males, this book is for you. If you believe that reality exists and is more important than ideology, this book is for you. If you believe that if a little boy likes dolls, he is a little boy who likes dolls and should be loved as he is; and that a little girl who likes working on cars is a little girl who likes working on cars and should be loved as she is, then this book is for you. On the other hand, if you think there's something wrong with little boys who like dolls and little girls who like cars, and these children need medical intervention, then you really need this book, because it will help bring reality into the discussion. This courageous book lays out how the transgender narrative and phenomenon are an end point of patriarchy's hatred of women, the body, sexuality, and the living planet; and how it is the end point of patriarchy's valuing of what we think about reality over reality itself. But brave women (and some men) are opposing this erasure of women and of material reality. With truth and reality on our side, how can we not prevail?

~ Derrick Jensen, author of Endgame, The Myth of Human Supremacy, and A Language Older Than Words

ABOUT THE COVER

IN MY INTRODUCTION to the anthology, I suggest that origins of female erasure in Western culture were propagated by the framing myth of Adam and Eve, and continues to affect a majority of people on our planet, regardless of whether an individual practices a religion based on this mythology.

The cover image is intentionally complex and multi-layered in its meanings. This classical image of Eve in the Garden of Eden is consistent with her portrayals in Renaissance art as a white European female. Our understanding of genetics today confirming human origins evolving out of Africa, the original "Eve" would surely have been a dark skinned female. Clearly the image does not represent all women in our glorious diversity of color and size. There is a double meaning intended in the cover image as the "white" Eve in the Renaissance portrayal has already been erased of her African origins, and continues to disappear even as she reaches for the fruit from the Tree of Knowledge.

In the Genesis II myth, a male God gives Adam, the first man, the power to name all the creatures of the earth, including Eve, the first woman. Adam is given the power by God to name her, and thus given power *over* the female sex, and given the power to *define* the very nature of woman. The male's empowerment by God to name the female is intentional and significant. The woman does not name, and thus define, herself. Her nature is literally man-made. The power of naming is a magical act with cultural significance. The power to name, and thus define ourselves, has been historically usurped from women, and over time we have forgotten that we ever had this power to begin with. Female erasure continues to be propagated through gender identity politics today and continuing efforts to define and enforce oppressive gender constructs on the female sex.

The cover for this anthology was created as a gift from my oldest and dearest friend, renowned photographic artist Claudia Kunin.

DEDICATION

In deepest gratitude to my beloved mother, Florence Bienenfeld (1929-2016), who taught me how to tend, advocate, and protect what is sacred. Mom, you raised an Amazon.

To Chava, Mother of the Living, and her older sister Lillith, who were willing to risk the loss of a man-made "paradise" for full female autonomy.

To Mary Daly and Andrea Dworkin (of blessed memory), Janice Raymond and Sheila Jeffreys for refusing to be silenced and for speaking out on behalf of all of us.

To the workers, craftswomen, workshop presenters, performers, attendees, Lisa Vogel and staff of The Michigan Womyn's Music Festival, who for 40 years provided the space for us to vision and experience the possibilities of female sovereign space to celebrate, educate, debate, and empower our diverse female tribes.

To our Granddaughters and Great Granddaughters. May you be blessed with the wisdom of your ancestors and foremothers, and remain courageous to claim and revel in your embodied female power.

ACKNOWLEDGEMENTS

THIS ANTHOLOGY WAS made possible through the energetic and financial support of the women and men, (including some trans allies), who generously donated to the fundraising campaign. You give me hope without end. Thank you.

To the anthology contributors for trusting me to bring their authentic voices to the readers of this book.

I simply could not have accomplished this project with out the assistance of Karen Cayer. Your dedication and enthusiasm for this endeavor paired with your patience, and impossible countless hours of internet support, website creations and troubleshooting, enabled me to do what I do best. Thank you, Sister!

Thanks to Kate Victory Hannisian of Blue Pencil Consulting for your publishing guidance and good humor with the spelling idiosyncrasies.

Thanks to Sara St. Martin Lynne, for the promotional video for the crowd funding campaign and your amazing way with words.

Thanks to Temple Ardinger for the awesome logo your created for Tidal Time Publishing LLC, to Wolfgang Nebmaier for your insights and activism with Vajra Ma, to Claudia Kunin for your generosity and brilliant artistry, and to Lierre Keith for your support in weaving several of the contributors into this book.

Thanks to Deb Posner, Sabine Ehrenfeld, Edna Myers, and all of the Priestesses who hold Her form.

And to my beloved, Falcon River, for your courage in surviving the oppression of gender-conformity to create a wonder-filled life, and for loving me through the numerous challenges of this project.

TABLE OF CONTENTS

A Note About Language

The language to describe persons who transition in their gender-identity is continually in flux. Legal terms for persons who transition usually use "MTF" or "FTM". Continuing to use these terms is to agree and propagate the fallacy that individuals are actually able to change their biological sex, which is impossible. That said, I have not told the contributors to use the same words to describe persons who gender-identify as the other biological sex. Contributors to this anthology use a variety of different terms, including the examples, "M2T", "M-T (male to trans) or "F2T" or "F-T" (female to trans), indicating the biological sex of that individual while not propagating the illusion that while an individual can attempt to alter their external presentation with surgery and/or hormones, no one can actually change their biology.

Some contributors use various spellings to describe biological females such as "wombyn", "wimmin" and "womyn" to express and emphasis female biology and autonomy.

FOREWORD

by Germaine Greer

HOW MANY SEXES are there? Most human societies have been organized on the principle that there are two, male and female. Some have allowed that there were individuals who did not fit securely into either category. In some hunter-gatherer societies if males begin to outnumber females, selected males will be required to live as females and carry out their essential work, except for child-bearing which will be understood to be beyond their capacity. Such strategies do not themselves challenge the notion that the sexes are two; indeed they should probably be understood to reinforce it. Nevertheless, the commonly-accepted idea of the twoness of sex is mistaken. Intersex is real and relatively common. Though the majority of humans will have either two X chromosomes or an X and a Y, many will have been born with different numbers and different combinations and many more will have their genes express themselves in unexpected ways.

When obstetricians encounter evidence of disorders of sexual development in newborns they almost invariably schedule sex assignment surgery, so that the parents will be able to present their children as what is regarded as 'normal'. In a recent decision the European Commission ruled that such operations on newborns are unethical and that intersex children should be allowed to develop without interference until they are of an age to decide whether they want to be boy or girl or neither.

Against this background we have to consider the case of males who 'know' that they have been born in the wrong body. Some, but by no means all, medical professionals will be happy to make the wrong body right by removing male sex organs so, by destroying sex, to reassign gender. Gender is not the same as sex; if I call my car 'Susan' I am assigning it a gender. If we make a distinction between 'male' and 'masculine' and between 'female' and 'feminine', as common sense suggests we should, we are distinguishing between sex and gender. If we treat both sex and gender as if they were the same thing, we are sowing confusion, which is what we've got.

Males have as much right to be resentful of the demands of masculinity as females have of the demands of femininity. What doesn't make sense is that anyone should interpret such unease as evidence that the man who feels it feels it because he is really a woman. The myriad women who refuse to pretend to be forever young, beautiful and submissive, don't think that the fit is bad because they're female, but because they're grown-up people.

The irony of gender-reassignment is that it reinforces essentialist notions of sex as binary. Seekers after gender-reassignment are of all ages, and their needs may be defined in different ways. However, in the case of a man who has lived with all the advantages of maleness and apparent masculinity into middle age, and then claims that he has been convinced of his fe-maleness all along, some protest would seem to be in order. In the UK a condition of gender reassignment used to be, and may be still, the annulment of any marriage between the acceptor and a spouse of the assumed 'opposite' sex. When a marriage is annulled it is assumed never to have happened. Faithful wives are strumpeted, legitimate children bastardized.

If a man who sincerely believes that he is female, marries a woman who has no reason to believe that he is not male, he is surely acting in bad faith and she should have a case against him. Such a man's wife and children know him better than anyone else, probably better than he knows himself, but they are not allowed to challenge him. No one, certainly no woman, is allowed to question his femaleness.

Men who adopt femininity may believe that they are achieving femaleness, but female-ness is a tougher destiny than they can know or guess. Femaleness is demanding and painful, whether at menarche, menstruation, childbed or menopause, and born women have no choice but to deal with it. Painted faces, depilated bodies, hair extensions and pumped up tits are available to all human beings. Femininity is a de-sexed masquerade. Men can be as good at it and better than women, but that does not make them women.

INTRODUCTION

"As I considered the power of myth, it became increasingly difficult to avoid questioning the influential effects that the myths accompanying the religions that worship male deities had upon my own image of what it meant to be born a female, another Eve, progenitress of my childhood faith."[1]

~ MERLIN STONE (1931 – 2011)

THIS BOOK IS an invitation to consciousness.

Female Erasure: What You Need to Know About Gender Politics' War on Women, the Female Sex and Human Rights, is an anthology that celebrates female embodiment while exposing the current trend of gender identity politics as a continuation of female erasure and silencing as old as patriarchy itself. Weaving together diverse voices bearing convergent and interrelated threads of thoughts and experiences, this anthology explores deeper issues of misogyny, violence, and sexism disguised today as progressive politics.

When the mass media pays increasing attention to the topic of gender and transgender politics, the deeper issues and implications for women and children need to be addressed courageously. When it is promoted as progressive to accept males who gender-identify as women as actually being female, many people are confused and afraid to ask questions. Female erasure is being enacted in a variety of ways, where even the words "women" and "female" are redefined to no longer refer to a group of human beings who are the source of human life and who, as a class, are treated as inferior to males worldwide. Advocates of gender stereotypes disseminated as "gender identity" managed to advance the idea that how one "feels" about oneself is more important than the physical reality of his or her body. As a consequence, the subjective psychological notion or "feeling" of a male person "being" a woman has gained legal standing superior to the objective and biological reality of being a female human in a male-dominated world. While everyone is entitled to their personal sense of identity, what often goes unexamined is the contextual influences and cultural norms (including enforced gender stereotypes) that informs consciously or unconsciously how a person arrives at their sense of personal identity. Promoters of gender-identity ideology and politics avoid discussing the vast differences in sex-based biology— biological facts that cannot be changed by behavior, clothing, surgery, or hormones.

Transgender activists dismiss biological sex differences as irrelevant, while suppressing critical conceptual examinations of gender itself, ignoring the history of female class oppression, enforcement, male domination, sexual violence, personal suffering, and social and economic inequality. Female erasure is being enacted through changing laws that have provided sex-based protections. Language that refers to women as a distinct class or that refers to female biology has been purposely removed or reframed to include biological males.

We are being told that we must accept without question or concern that males who identify as transgendered are to be considered equivalent to females in every way. Today, only the social and cultural construction of one's self-identity matters. Disregarding the fact that the excuse for the oppression of females *is* our biology, the issues around gender and gender identity have eclipsed the still unaddressed issues of sexism and its expressions of violence in the everyday lives of countless women and girls throughout the world.

Children as young as four years old are being diagnosed as transgender and given hormone blockers by age nine. The health risks to our children and adolescents have not been studied, yet a lucrative industry has emerged to "serve" and "support" confused and well-meaning parents, pointing them in only one psychiatric and medical industry direction. Concerns about sterilization and a lifetime of dependence on pharmaceuticals and with no long-term studies of the health impact, are silenced. Young lesbians and gay boys can be "normalized" by transitioning them. The possibility that homophobia is playing out in this issue seems to be too taboo to discuss.

We are in a new era of witch burning, except that today, the fire is that of media and propaganda, with trans activists and their supporters suppressing any information that contradicts their goals and silencing their critics through oppressive tactics. Some of our contributors have been fired from teaching positions at universities; some have been blacklisted; others threatened with physical harm, rape, even death—all because they have questioned or challenged the idea that the cultural construct of gender should supplant biological sex. Others have been de-platformed as speakers at universities for expressing what should be a matter of common sense: that women, many of whom have been sexually assaulted by males, should have the right to shower, bathe, sleep, or organize free from the presence of males.

How old is this latest face of female erasure and silencing? When did male subordination of women begin and take root, and how is this strategy of erasure showing up today? To begin to understand how we got here, we must look backward to the time when ancient female-centered cultures transitioned to male-centered hierarchies. This transition is found in women's own suppressed history where males began to silence and erase female origins with new mythologies.

Origin myths are the primary paradigms of a culture. According to the pre-historical archeological record, at the beginning of human experience there were cultures where a primary goddess was worshipped and the female body was venerated. Women were considered to be reflections of a wise female Creator through whom all creation emerged, was sustained, protected by, and returned to in death. Within this paradigm there is evidence of greater equality between the sexes, and women held positions of authority religiously, politically, and socially. In these cultures, women were warriors, mothers, priestesses, merchants, and leaders. Can we imagine what life might have been like for women and girls who lived in a society where their female body was held as sacred? This paradigm of Goddess and female-centered cultures pre-dated patriarchal history by tens of thousands of years.

Western civilization is largely based on the biblical myth from Genesis II, where Eve, the first woman, is created from male origins. Eve, who acted upon her own curiosity for knowledge, has been held responsible religiously and historically for the fall of humanity. As daughters of Eve, women inherited her legacy of defiance as well as the consequences of her disobedience. Similarly, Pandora, the first woman on earth in Greek mythology, opens the forbidden box that unleashes illnesses and hardships upon humanity. In both origin myths, female disobedience of divine male authority was what released evil into the world and became the justification of man's divine right to define woman, and rule over woman and nature. The physical and spiritual worlds that had once been united were separated. New male-centered religions placed spirit outside and above the material world. I propose that the usurping of women's power in culture and religion was propagated by this patriarchal myth and many others, and continues to affect a majority of people on our planet regardless of whether and individual practices a religion based on this mythology.

Myths explain and reinforce the cosmic order and hierarchy of human beings with one another and in the natural world. In other words, why things are the way they are - from why the moon hangs in the sky, to why human beings are here on earth at all. The myth of Eve reflects the cultural transition from earlier Goddess and female-centered civilizations to God and male-centered hierarchies. The strategy of patriarchy was to supplant any earlier knowledge of the Goddess by destroying physical evidence of Her worship, giving Her attributes to male gods, and eventually replacing Her priestesses with priests. The female body became property and children were taught a new mythology that affirmed women's subordinate status in all aspects of society.

How does this five-thousand-year-old origin myth, upon which our own civilization is based, consciously and unconsciously inform the way we understand ourselves and one another in the "natural" order of a male-defined and male-centered hierarchy of value? And how does our place as female or male human beings in this order continue to influence the politics of sex and gender today? Myths become the paradigm, the worldview that a society orders itself around, a frame around an inherited reality that becomes the context for our lives. How does the myth of Eve continue to shape our personal and collective consciousness, whether we are religious, spiritual, secular or humanist?

The concerted effort over millennia to propagate a paradigm that institutionalizes male-centered reality has resulted in the almost complete annihilation of Her presence and the earlier status of female sovereignty from our collective human memory. Female erasure is and has been the essential tool used throughout history to ensure the success and continuation of patriarchal values. We all live inside this frame of female denigration to the extent that we are blind to it, both women and men alike. We can't see the forest for the trees. Enacting this myth is an unconscious habit for most of us. The feminist movement of the 1970s and 1980s fought for and won some basic human rights for women, and succeeded in undoing female erasure by shining a light on women in history, uncovering original truths of women's religious leadership in the ancient world, and bringing awareness of how the dominant culture oppresses females worldwide. The backlash to these advancements today comes with a new face of female erasure by a new generation contributing to its own erasure.

Today, female erasure is men organizing to shut down feminist conferences. Today, female erasure is a full-scale media attack that ended the longest-standing female-centric gathering in the world. Today, female erasure is a young woman dieting her own body to death. Today, female erasure is the defunding of any resources that focus on female-specific services like battered women's shelters and rape crisis centers. Female erasure is taking place today on college campuses where young women are afraid to discuss or make any specific reference to their female anatomy or biological functions for fear of offending or hurting the feelings of males who gender-identify as women. Female erasure today is the number of journalists being harassed to the point where they fear for their physical safety and therefore stop writing about these issues or choose to do so anonymously. Female erasure is changing the words "pregnant woman" to "pregnant individual" in the Midwives Alliance of North America's core competencies document, and changing "mother" to "birthing parent." Female erasure is the 2015 Olympics eligibility policy change where under the new guidelines, any male can compete in women's events with no legal gender change and no medical treatment whatsoever. On the basis of his declaration alone, it is enough that he believes himself to possess a "female" personality or mentality, and his testosterone levels must remain in the lower range of typical male levels for the duration of one year. Female erasure is the female photographer who recently took a lighthearted family photo wherein the mother and the daughter posed with duct tape over their mouths while the father and the son gave satisfied smiles at the camera while holding a sign that said "peace on earth."

One of the most recently pervasive sources of female silencing and erasure has come from a seemingly surprising source, the progressive left. We have always had our eyes on the theocratic right, as it has called for the defunding, limiting or even criminalizing of women's access to reproductive autonomy. Many of us left male-dominated religions that deny the sacredness of the female body and deny women and girls the right to fully participate in rites and leadership of their communities. We expect corporations to profit from their marketing of impossible beauty standards for women. We did not expect that trans activists and so-called progressive politicians would advance gender politics by denying, restricting, or abolishing hard-won female autonomous spaces and services in the personal and public sphere as if there was no longer a need for them. Physical safety from male violence for both females and transgender individuals is a basic human right. It is revealing that concerns for physical safety has only been addressed by trans activists in either/or terms, while dismissing female concerns for our safety as "bigotry." We assert our right to freely discuss both/and solutions that can provide safety for both transgender individuals *and* assure that same safety for everyone else.

Currently in nineteen US states, with no objective proof required, self-identification as a woman is the only requirement to grant a man legal access to intimate female spaces, overriding female rights to privacy in all public accommodations including clinics, hospitals, bathhouses, swimming pools, gymnasiums and other spaces. While it is well-documented that physical and sexual violence against women and girls is on the rise globally, so-called progressives and the transgender lobbyists are acting to silence, disrupt, and legislate against our ability to name, gather and address the issues of our own oppression. This complete disregard of everyday female subordination in order to benefit the estimated 0.3 - 0.5% of males who define themselves as women further proves that the oppression of the female sex was the foundation upon which our society was built and continues to operate. The progressive left is perpetuating one of the basic tenets of Genesis II, that women can only be defined within a paradigm of male authority.

To speak of and fearlessly investigate what it is to be female in this postmodern patriarchal culture is widely regarded as nothing short of heresy. I am deeply disturbed by the hostility, intimidation, and bullying directed at anyone (including some trans allies) who dares to question or voice concerns about these issues. This anthology would not have been necessary if information and personal experiences were not being censored, silenced, or suppressed. Those who have responded with vitriol to the creation of this book have only demonstrated the very reason why this anthology became necessary.

There are growing numbers of people (trans included), and regardless of their positions on these issues, who cannot support the silencing and suppression of information that helps inform and contribute to a deeper understanding of these issues. The values of a democratic society are demonstrated when diverse ideas or points of view are encouraged, critically examined, and respectfully debated. These values include the right to life, liberty, and the pursuit of happiness; and where diversity of culture, ethnicity, race, lifestyle and belief is desirable and beneficial for a pluralistic society. These values enrich us all when exploring different points of view is encouraged, and where critical thinking and curiosity about another's experience is rewarded in mutual understanding. A truly progressive society whose empathetic moral values of equality for all of its citizens has the capacity to ensure rights and safety without removing the rights to safety from other oppressed people within its care.

This anthology's intention is to promote critical thinking, respectful dialogue, and help to answer the forbidden questions: "Who made this up, and whose cause does it ultimately serve?" This anthology encourages readers to consider how and why our female bodies matter, and how our bodies and socialization inform our everyday lives. Contributors shed light on how the language of gender identity politics has been purposely used to reframe and replace specifically biology-based realities, reinforcing the destructive hierarchy that objectifies and harms women and children. Some contributors connect the momentum of female erasure to the ways we treat our Mother Earth. Others share their personal struggles with being gender nonconforming women, with some sharing their journeys from living as transmen and their choice to de-transition. Some discuss political struggles and triumphs arising from providing female-centered spiritual spaces, reclaiming their female bodies as a source of power and significance, and why it is so important for all of us to consider asking deeper questions about how misogyny, violence, and sexism are being enacted in this issue.

Contributors to this anthology come from a wide variety of backgrounds in terms of race, class, religion, sexual orientation, and age (ranging from twenty to eight-three years old), and live in the United States, South Africa, Australia, Canada, and the United Kingdom. They are lesbian feminists, political and spiritual feminists, heterosexual-womanist women, mothers, scholars, attorneys, poets, medical and mental health providers, university educators, environmentalists, and women who chose to de-transition, all providing perspectives that are ignored, silenced, vilified, or underrepresented in the popular media and disregarded in discussions promoting legal protections for transgender persons at the expense of women and girls. Some contributors wrote under pseudonyms to keep their teaching jobs in universities or to protect their children from harassment. The content is presented in a variety of writing styles, including personal stories, essays, articles, poetry, current studies, and research.

The anthology contributors want radical societal change - freedom from oppressive gender roles and stereotypes of "femininity" and "masculinity", not by erasing the reality of biological sex. We want a world where the ideal of diversity is not abused to oppress and erase fifty-one percent of humanity. We want a world in which everyone's biological reality is honored, our sacred bodies are celebrated, and where sex-based violence and enforced gender roles become obsolete.

In weaving this anthology together, I have had the honor of connecting with brilliant women who have responded to the current trend of gender politics' war on women, the female sex, and human rights. I did not require that the contributors be in agreement with one another on all nuances of this topic in order to contribute to this book. While our personal experiences and views may differ, together we are in agreement that we must demonstrate our right to speak out, educate, and raise legitimate concerns. It has been a joy to introduce these contributors to other communities who are now woven together by our resistance to this new face of the same age-old misogyny attempting to disguise itself as progressive politics. This project would not have been possible without their courage and insights, and for their willingness to participate, I am deeply thankful.

This book is an invitation to consciousness.

By shining the spotlight on sex and gender politics today, we demonstrate the continuation of female erasure, as old as the creation of patriarchy. We invite you to eat of the forbidden fruit of knowledge, and with this knowledge have the courage to speak out, be visible, and take action.

The tide is beginning to turn, with a new wave of awareness rising. Courage is gaining momentum. It is to this great rising that we offer our voices to all hearing ears.

Ruth Barrett, Editor and Project Weaver
With special thanks to Sara St. Martin Lynne, who labored with me to midwife this Introduction.

---

[1] Merlin Stone, *The Paradise Papers: Suppression of Women's Rites,* London: Virago Limited in association with Quartet Books, 1976, p. 21.

The concept of gender (with its associated stereotypes) was created and then enforced by the dominant culture to advance its agenda, to oppress or elevate you, to sell you stuff, and so on. But however many gender stereotypes have been created, surely every human being has at least one character expression or performs some activity that does not fit a gender stereotype. It follows that each person's gender is actually unique. There are over seven billion human beings on the planet. Therefore, there have to be over seven billion genders. No one is special if we are all unique. When you think outside the gender identity frame, the concept of gender disappears because it is irrelevant to our uniqueness.

~ RUTH BARRETT

SECTION ONE

BIOLOGICAL ERASURE BY GENDER IDEOLOGY

GYN-OCIDE REVISITED

Because I feel that I am a woman, therefore you must treat me as if I actually am, otherwise you are transphobic. As I insist on participating as a woman in your groups, gatherings, or spaces you also must forgo discussing anything about your female socialization, female anatomy, or female functions because it hurts my feelings. It hurts my feelings because I was neither socialized as a girl nor am I capable of experiencing what the female body experiences from cradle to grave. But if you speak about this I am then reminded that I am not female, and therefore not really a woman. My experience of feeling like a woman must not be invalidated by your experiences of being a woman, therefore I will shame you for being female, teach you in university to estrange your body from your mind, make your distinct physicality and oppression that is specific to your sex irrelevant in the laws of the land or anything that names our differences until there is only the mind. Now only how I think about your body is real. Mind over body. Mind over matter. Spirit over matter/mater/mother. A woman is anyone who says they are a woman. My word is now more real than your mitochondrial DNA. Accept that by my word, you really don't exist.

~RUTH BARRETT

Women do not decide at some point in adulthood that they would like other people to understand them to be women, because being a woman is not an 'identity'. Women's experience does not resemble that of men who adopt the 'gender identity' of being female or being women in any respect. The idea of 'gender identity' disappears biology and all the experiences that those with female biology have of being reared in a caste system based on sex.

~ SHEILA JEFFREYS, *GENDER HURTS*

CHAPTER 1

THE FIRST SEX: IN THE BEGINNING, WE WERE ALL CREATED FEMALE

Monica Sjöö and Barbara Mor

*Anthology Editor's Introduction: This opening chapter is re-published from Great
Cosmic Mother: Rediscovering the Religion of the Earth, from 1975. These foremothers of the Women's Spirituality Movement provide a context for the evolution of biological sex long before gender stereotypes were propagated and enforced
in patriarchal cultures and religions. We begin this anthology at the beginning,
where the female is centered in culture and religion as the primal Matrix.*

IN THE BEGINNING...WAS a very female sea. For two-and-a-half billion years on earth, all life-
forms floated in the womb-like environment of the planetary ocean – nourished and protected
by its fluid chemicals, rocked by the lunar-tidal rhythms. Charles Darwin believed the menstrual cycle originated here, organically echoing the moon-pulse of the sea. And, because this
longest period of life's time on earth was dominated by marine forms reproducing parthenoge-
netically, he concluded that the female principle was primordial. In the beginning, life did not
gestate within the body of any creature, but within the ocean womb containing all organic life.
There were no specialized sex organs; rather, a generalized female existence reproduced itself
within the female body of the sea.[1]

Before more complex life forms could develop and move onto land, it was necessary to
miniaturize the oceanic environment, to reproduce it on a small and mobile scale. Soft, moist
eggs deposited on dry ground and exposed to air would die; life could not move beyond the
water-hugging amphibian stage. In the course of evolution, the ocean – the protective and
nourishing space, the amniotic fluids, even the lunar-tidal rhythm – was transferred into the
individual female body. And the penis, a mechanical device for land reproduction, evolved.

The penis first appeared in the Age of Reptiles, about 200 million years ago. Our archetypal association of the snake with the phallus contains, no doubt, this genetic memory.

This is a fundamental and recurring pattern in nature: Life is a female environment in which the male appears, often periodically, and created by the female, to perform highly specialized tasks related to species reproduction and a more complex evolution. *Daphnia,* a freshwater crustacean, reproduces several generations of females by parthenogenesis; the egg and its own polar body mate to form a complete set of genes for a female offspring. Once annually, at the end of the year's cycle, a short-lived male group is produced; the males specialize in manufacturing leathery egg cases able to survive the winter. Among honeybees the drone group is produced and regulated by the sterile daughter workers and the fertile queen. Drones exist to mate with the queen. An average of seven drones per hive accomplish this act each season, and then the entire male group is destroyed by the workers. Among whiptail lizards in the American Southwest, four species are parthenogenetic; males are unknown among the desert grassland, plateau, and Chihuahua whiptails, and have been found only rarely among the checkered whiptails.

Among mammals, even among humans, parthenogenesis is not technically impossible. Every female egg contains a polar body with a complete set of chromosomes; the polar body and the egg, if united, could form a daughter embryo. In fact, ovarian cysts are unfertilized eggs that have joined with their polar bodies, been implanted in the ovarian wall, and started to develop there.

This is not to say that males are an unnecessary sex. Parthenogenesis is a cloning process. Sexual reproduction, which enhances the variety and health of the gene pool, is necessary for the kind of complex evolution that has produced the human species. The point being made here is simply that, when it comes to the two sexes, one of us has been around a lot longer than the other.

In *The Nature and Evolution of Female Sexuality*, Mary Jane Sherfey, M.D., described her discovery in 1961 of something called the inductor theory. The inductor theory stated that "All mammalian embryos, male and female, are anatomically female during the early stages of fetal life."[2] Sherfey wondered why this theory had been buried in the medical literature since 1951, completely ignored by the profession. The men who made this herstory-making discovery simply didn't want it to be true.

Sherfey pioneered the discussion of the inductor theory; and now, with modifications based on further data, its findings are accepted as facts of mammalian – including human – development. As Stephen Jay Gould describes it, the embryo in its first eight weeks is an "indifferent" creature, with bisexual potential. In the eighth week, if a Y-chromosome-bearing sperm fuses with the egg, the gonads will develop into testes, which secrete androgen, which in turn induces male genitalia to develop. In the absence of androgen, the embryo develops into a female. There is a difference in the development of the internal and external genitalia, however. For the internal genitalia – the fallopian tubes and ovaries, or the sperm-carrying ducts – "the early embryo contains precursors of both sexes." In the presence or absence of androgen, as one set develops, the other degenerates. With the external genitalia, "the different organs of male and female develop along diverging lines from the *same* precursor." This means, in effect, that the clitoris and the penis are the same organ, formed from the same tissue. The labia majora and the scrotum are one, indistinguishable in the early embryonic stages; in the presence of androgen "the two lips simply grow longer, fold over and fuse along the midline, forming the scrotal sac."

Gould concludes: "The female course of development is, in a sense, biologically intrinsic to all mammals. It is the pattern that unfolds in the absence of any hormonal influence. The male route is a modification induced by secretion of androgens from the developing testes."[3]

The vulnerability of the male newcomer within the female environment is well known. Vaginal secretions are more destructive to the Y-bearing sperm. The mortality rate is higher among neonate and infant males. Within the womb the male fetus, for the first two months, is protected by being virtually indistinguishable from a female. After that, it must produce large amounts of the masculinizing hormone in order to define itself as male, to achieve and to maintain its sexual identity. For all we know the Near Eastern myths upon which our Western mythologies are built, those which portray the young god or hero battling against a female dragon, have some analog here, *in utero*, where the male fetus wages a kind of chemical war against rebecoming female.

For now, it is enough to say that "maleness" among mammals is not a primary state, but differentiates from the original female biochemistry and anatomy. The original libido of warm-blooded animals is female, and the male – or maleness – is a derivation from this primary female pattern. Why, then, did the medical men, the scientists, take longer to figure out this basic biological fact than it took them to split the atom? And why, once this fact was noted, did they turn around and bury it in professional silence for ten years, until a woman dug it up again? Why indeed.

For about two thousand years of Western history, female sexuality was denied; when it could not be denied it was condemned as evil. The female was seen as divinely designed to be a passive vessel, serving reproductive purposes only. In one not-too-ancient dictionary, "clitoris" was defined as a "rudimentary organ," while "masculinity" equaled "the Cosmic generative force"…! With Freud, female sexuality was not so much "rediscovered" as pathologized. Freud dismissed the clitoris as an undeveloped masculine organ and defined original libido as male. Clitoral eroticism was reduced to a perverse neurosis. Even after Master's and Johnson's laboratory studies were published in *Human Sexual Response* in 1966, their findings were not integrated into psychoanalytical theory. In Mary Jane Sherfey's research during that period, she found not one work of comparative anatomy that described – or even mentioned – the deeper-lying clitoral structures; yet every other structure of the human body was described in living detail. Even today, with our relative sophistication of 1987, we are frequently whistled at by magazine headlines that promise breathless articles announcing the discovery of new "spot" – a G-spot, an X-spot – located within the vagina. Within all these new "spots" exists the old wistful desire to deny the existence of the clitoris as a trigger-organ of female orgasm.

Why? There is the generalized, traditional fear of female sexuality. Further, there is discomfort with the similarity, with the common origin, of the female clitoris and the male penis. Women are used to hearing the clitoris described as an "undeveloped penis"; men are not used to thinking of the penis as an overdeveloped clitoris. Finally, and most seriously, there is a profound psychological and *institutional* reluctance to face the repercussions of the fact that the female clitoris is the only organ in the human body whose purpose is exclusively that of erotic stimulation and release. What does this mean? It means that for the human female, alone among all earth's life-forms, sexuality and reproduction are not inseparable. It is the male penis, carrier of both semen and sexual response, that is simultaneously procreative and erotic. If we wanted to reduce one of the sexes to a purely reproductive function, on the basis of its anatomy (we don't), it would be the male sex that qualified for such a reduction, not the female. Not the human female.

But these are only biological facts. These are only biological realities. As we know, facts and realities can be, and are, systematically ignored in the service of established ideologies. Throughout the world today virtually all religious, cultural, economic and political institutions stand, where they were built centuries ago, on the solid foundation of an erroneous concept. A concept that assumes the psychic passivity, the creative inferiority, and the sexual secondariness of women. This enshrined concept states that men exist to create the human world, while women exist to reproduce humans. Period. If we argue that data exists – not solely biological, but archaeological, mythological, anthropological, and historical data – which refutes the universality of this erroneous concept, we are told to shut up; because something called "God" supports the erroneous concept, and that's all that matters. That's the final word.

Throughout the world, throughout what *we* know of history, something called "God" has been used to support the denial, the condemnation, and the mutilation of female sexuality. Of the female sex, ourselves. Today, in parts of Africa – predominantly among African Muslims, but also among African Christians and Jews[4], and some tribal beliefs – young girls are still subjected to clitoridectomy. This surgery, often performed by older women with broken glass or knives, excises the clitoris, severing the nerves of orgasm; the operation is intended to force the girl to concentrate on her vagina as a reproductive vessel. Infibulation, a more thorough operation, removes the labia minora and much of the labia majora; the girl is then closed up with thorns or required to lie with her legs tied together until her entire vaginal orifice is fused shut, with a straw inserted to allow passage of urine and menstrual blood. On the wedding night the young woman is slit open by a midwife or her husband; further cutting and reclosing is performed before and after childbirth. Complications from these surgeries are numerous, including death from infection, hemorrhage, inability to urinate, scar tissue preventing dilation during labor, painful coitus, and infertility due to chronic pelvic infection. In 1976 an estimated 10 million women were involved with this operation.[5] And something called "God" justified it; a "God" who supposedly created young girls as filthy sex maniacs who must then be mutilated to turn them into docile breeders.

The word "infibulation" comes from the Latin *fibula*, meaning a "clasp." Those civilized Romans, great highway builders, also invented the technology of fastening metal clasps through the prepuces of young girls to enforce chastity. This practice was copied by Christian crusaders during the early Middle Ages in Europe; they locked up their wives and daughters in metal "chastity belts" and then took the keys with them while they were gone – often for many years – fighting for "God" in the Near East.

And, lest through hypocrisy and racism we dismiss these practices as merely "barbaric" or "ancient," we must recall that clitoridectomies were performed in the last century on young girls and women in both Europe and America. This surgery, very popular with nineteenth-century Victorians, was inflicted on any female considered to be "oversexed," or as a punishment for masturbation, or as a cure for "madness." These determinations were all made by male relatives, male physicians, and male clerics, and the women involved had no legal say in the matter.

These are extreme examples of the repression and mutilation of female sexuality, always sanctioned, however remotely and dishonestly, by something called "God." All the other repressions and mutilations – of the body, of the mind, of the soul, of our experienced female selves – are so well known and documented that they need no numeration at this point; we can all make our own lists. The point is this: Wherever repression of female sexuality, and of the female sex, exists – and, at the present writing, this is everywhere on earth – we find the same underlying assumptions. These are ontological assumptions – assumptions made at the very root of things, about the nature of life itself. They are (1) that the world was created by a male deity figure, or God; (2) that existing world orders, or cultures, were made by and for men, with God's sanction; (3) that females are an auxiliary sex, who exist to serve and populate these male world orders; (4) that autonomous female sexuality poses a wild and lethal threat to these world orders, and therefore must be controlled and repressed; and finally (5) that God's existence as a male sanctions this repression. The perfect circularity, or tautology, of these assumptions only helps to bind them more securely around the human psyche. That they are as erroneous as they are universal seems to pose no problem to their upholders. After all, wherever we go on earth, every intact institution – religious, legal, governmental, economic, military, communications, and customs – is built on the solid slab of these assumptions. And that's a pretty entrenched error.

In the post-World War II United States – as well as in Europe and most of the world generally – we've gone through a secularizing period in which some of these assumptions have been loosened up, and even been made to crumble, under questioning. But now the backlash is upon us. Today, spokespeople for various fundamentalist religious beliefs use modern media to broadcast a very old idea: that female sexuality – i.e., feminists, and feminist demands for abortion, contraception, reproductive autonomy, childcare, equal pay, psychological integrity – constitutes a threat to "our civilization"; and this amount to a "blasphemy against God." Whores of Babylon, Darwin's Theory of Evolution, and the "menace of world communism" all somehow get subliminally mixed up in this feminist threat – for some very good historic and psychological reasons, which we will explore later. For now, it is enough to say that "God" and "civilization" are loaded concepts (loaded with dynamite!) that can always be brought in to end an argument that cannot otherwise be refuted. Or, for those who don't lean too heavily on "God," or who major in "civilization," you can always quote an anthropologist!

For, just as established religions assume the maleness of God, just as Freud and psychoanalysis assumed the maleness of libido, so have the social sciences – and in particular anthropology – assumed the generic maleness of human evolution. Both popular and academic anthropological writers have presented us with scenarios of human evolution that feature, almost exclusively, the adventures and inventions of man the hunter, man the toolmaker, man the territorial marker, and so forth. Woman is not comprehended as an evolutionary or evo-lutionizing creature. She is treated rather as an auxiliary to a male-dominated evolutionary process; she mothers him, she mates him, she cooks his dinner, she follows around after him picking up his loose rocks. *He evolves*, she follows; *he evolutionizes*, she adjusts. If the book jackets don't give us pictures of female Homo sapiens being dragged by the hair through 2 or 3 million years of he-man evolution, we are left to assume this was the situation.

This, despite the known fact that among contemporary and historic hunting-and-gathering people, as among our remote hunting-and-gathering ancestors, 75 percent to 80 percent of the group's subsistence comes from the women's food-gathering activities. This, despite the known fact that the oldest tools used by contemporary hunters and gatherers, and the oldest, most primal tools ever found in ancient sites, are women's digging sticks. This, despite worldwide legends that cite women as the first users and domesticators of fire. This, despite the known fact that women were the first potters, the first weavers, the first textile-dyers and hide-tanners, the first to gather and study medicinal plants – i. e., the first doctors – and on and on. Observing the linguistic interplay between mothers and infants, mothers and children, and among work-groups of women, it is easy to speculate on the female contribution to the origin and elaboration of language. That the first time measurements ever made, the first formal calendars, were women's lunar-markings on painted pebbles and carved sticks is also known. And it is thoroughly known that the only "God-image" ever painted on rock, carved in stone, or sculpted in clay, from the Upper Paleolithic to the Middle Neolithic – and that's roughly 30,000 years – was the image of a human female.

In 1948 *The Gate of Horn* was published in Britain; in 1963 it was published in America, retitled *Religious Conceptions of the Stone Age.* In this pioneering work, archaeologist and schol-ar G. Rachel Levy showed the unbroken continuity of religious images and ideas descending from the Cro-Magnon peoples of the Upper Paleolithic period in Ice Age Europe, through the Mesolithic and Neolithic developments in the Near East, and down to our own historical time. As Levy noted, these early people are lost to us in the mists of time; but their primal visions, images, and gestalts of human experience on this planet still resonate in our psyches, as well as in our historic religious-ontological symbols. These Early Stone Age people "bequeathed to all humanity a foundation of ideas upon which the mind could raise its structures."[6] And what were these primal human images and ideas? The cave as the female womb; the mother as a pregnant earth; the magical fertile female as the mother of all animals; the Venus of Laussel standing with the horn of the moon upraised in her hand; the cave as the female tomb where

11

life is buried, painted blood red, and awaiting rebirth. Levy shows the continuity of these images and symbols through the Late Neolithic Near Eastern rites and mythologies, and their endurance 30,000 years later in "modern" religions. In Christianity, for example, with its central image of the birth of the sacred child, in a cave-like shelter, surrounded by magic animals; and, especially in Catholicism, the icon of the great mother who stands on the horned moon and awaits the rebirth of the world.

The evidence leaves no doubt that these images *were* at the origins of what we call human psychological and spiritual expression. Levy's book is a masterpiece; it received great praise upon both its British and American publications; and has since been virtually bypassed and ignored by the anthropological-archaeological-academic establishments. Why? Because her evidence is irrefutable. It shows with clarity – and in the solidity of stone and bone – that the first 30,000 years of *Homo sapiens'* existence was dominated by a celebration of the female processes: of the mysteries of menstruation, pregnancy, and childbirth; of the analogous abundance of the earth; of the seasonal movement of animals and the cycles of time in the Great Round of the Mother. *The Gate of Horn* is as close as we can come to reading the "sacred book" of our early human ancestors. And it confirms what too many people do not want to know: that the first "God" was female.

Since Levy wrote, the tendency has been to relegate these Old Stone Age and Neolithic images to the psychological realm – they've become "archetypes of the unconscious" and so forth, while anthropological writers proper, both academic and popular, continue to explain physical, real human development solely in terms of the experiences of the male body in hunting, aggression, and toolmaking. Thus the female images – which are there, and cannot be denied – are sideswiped, reduced to "the subjective," "the mythic realms"; and thus the first 30,000 years of our human history is denied to us, relegated to a "mind trip" or "psychological software." Even among feminists, in recent years, there has arisen doubt that these images and symbols might be anything but "mythology" – i. e., unrealities.

To approach our human past – and the female God – we need a wagon with at least two wheels: one is the mythical-historical-archaeological; the other is the biological-anthropological. A strong track has already been laid down for the mythical-historical-archaeological wheel; milestones along that track, along with G. Rachel Levy's great work, are J. J. Bachofen's *Myth, Religion and Mother-Right*, Robert Briffault's *The Mothers*, Helen Diner's *Mothers and Amazons*, Jessie Weston's *From Ritual to Romance*, Robert Graves's *The White Goddess*, O. G. S. Crawford's *The Eye Goddess*, Sibylle von Cles-Reden's *In the Realm of the Great Goddess*, Michael Dames's

Silbury Treasure and *Avebury Cycle*, Marija Gimbutas's *The Goddesses and Gods of Old Europe*; and most recently Elizabeth G. Davis's *The First Sex*; Merlin Stone's *When God Was a Woman* and *Ancient Mirrors of Womanhood*; Phyllis Chesler's *Women and Madness* and *About Men*; Adrienne Rich's *Of Woman Born*; Mary Daly's *Beyond God the Father, Gyn-Ecology*, and *Pure Lust*; Susan Griffin's *Woman and Nature*; Anne Cameron's *Daughters of Copper Woman* – and many many more, including the richly useful *Women's Encyclopedia of Myths and Secrets* by Barbara G. Walker.

The other side of our wagon – the biological-anthropological side – has almost no wheel and no track; not because there is no important place to go in that direction, but because the physical-cultural anthropologists are off somewhere else, busily mapping the evolution of Tarzan. There is no body of anthropological work based on the evolution of female biology. With rare exceptions, there have been no attempts whatsoever to study the evolution of human physiology and cultural organization – from prehominid to "modern man" – from the perspective of the definitive changes undergone by the female in the process of that evolution. Popular books on this subject, by Lionel Tiger, Desmond Morris, *et al.,* are invariably male-oriented, treating the evolution of the female as sex object only, from monkey-in-heat to hot bunny. One delightful exception is Elaine Morgan's *The Descent of Woman*: during 12 million years of dry Pliocene, Morgan speculates, the female prehominid took to the oceans, surviving in the warm and food-filled coastal waters – and during this experience underwent a sea-change from knuckle-walking, rear-sex primate to upright human sexual body, to which the male primate responded by becoming man. Morgan argues convincingly that the human species survived the long Pliocene drought through the cooperation and social invention of the evolving hominid females in their adaptation to the sea; academic "experts" ignore this theory, but they have no other explanation for our Pliocene survival, for our successful evolution from ape to human during this difficult period, or for the many ways in which our human bodies resemble the bodies of sea mammals, rather than primates.

In *The Time Falling Bodies Take to Light*, historian William Irwin Thompson points out that early human evolution occurred in three critical stages: (1) *hominization*, in which our primate bodies became human, not only in walking upright and freeing the hands, but specifically in our sexual characteristics and functions; (2) *symbolization*, in which we began using speech, marking time, painting and sculpting images; and (3) *agriculturalization*, in which we domesticated seeds and began control of food production. And, as Thompson writes, all three stages were initiated and developed by the human female.[7] The symbol-making and agricultural stages have been studied, and the origination role of women in these stages is known; it is sexual hominization which, as yet, has barely been explored.

Why? Why indeed. Because sexual hominization is almost exclusively the story of the human female. The mechanics and anatomy of male sexuality, after all, haven't changed greatly since the primates made love. The revolution in human sexuality – the revolution that made us human – resulted from evolutionary changes that occurred in the female body. These changes were not primarily related to mammalian reproduction, but to human sexual relationship. No one knows the order in which they occurred, but taken together, as an evolved cluster of sexual characteristics, they constitute a truly radical sexual metamorphosis undergone by the human female:

- *Elimination of the estrus cycle, and development of the menstrual cycle*, meant that women were not periodically in heat, but capable of sexual activity at any time. Pregnancy could occur during a part of the cycle; but for most the cycle sex could happen without necessarily resulting in pregnancy. Among all other animals, the estrus cycle determines that copulation always results in pregnancy, and has no other than a reproductive purpose.
- *Development of the clitoris and evolution of the vagina* meant a greatly enhanced sexuality and orgasmic potential in human females compared to all other animals.
- *The change from rear to frontal sex,* we can imagine, created an enormous change in relations between the sexes; frontal sex means a prolonged and enhanced lovemaking period, and what might be called the personalization of sex. The emotion-evoking role of face-to-face intercourse in the development of human self-consciousness has yet to be evaluated (she turned around and looked him in the eye: and there was light!)
- *Development of breasts* added to woman's potential for sexual arousal; further, combined with frontal sex, no doubt the female's maternal and social feelings were also now aroused by the personal lover, whose body was now analogous to the infant's body at her breast.

As Thompson points out, such radical changes in the female body alone were enough to trigger the hominization of the species. Human beings, with these changes, became the only creatures on earth for whom copulation occurs – can occur, anytime – for nonreproductive purposes. Human sex thus became a multipurpose activity. It can happen for emotional bonding, for social bonding, for pleasure, for communication, for shelter and comfort, for personal release, for escape – as well as for reproduction of the species. And this is one of the original and major, determining differences between humans and all other animals, birds, reptiles, insects, fishes, worms…for whom copulation exists only and solely for species reproduction.

<u>The human race has been definitely shaped by the evolution/revolution of the female body into a capacity for nonreproductive sex.</u>

This is not just a physical fact. It is a cultural, religious, and political fact of primary significance.

Many feminists today are unsure whether studies of evolutionary biology, or of religious mythology, can have political relevance for contemporary women. We believe that nothing could be more politically relevant than knowing why we got where we are now, by seeing how we got here, and where we began.

In the beginning, the first environment for all new life was female; the physical/emotional/spiritual body of the mother, and the communal body of women – young girls, grown women, older women – working together. When hunting-and-gathering people move, the infant is carried bound close to the mother's body; when they settle, the women form an "inner circle" campsite of women and children. The socialization process begins here.

Human culture is marked by a strengthening and prolongation of the relation between mothers and offspring. For its first year the human child is virtually an "embryo" outside the womb, extremely vulnerable and totally dependent. Female group behavior – the cooperative care-sharing among mothers and children, older and younger women, in the tasks of daily life – emerges from the fact of this prolonged dependence of the human child on the human female for its survival. Males help - but they also leave; the male body comes and goes, but the female presence is constant. Females train, discipline, and protect the young; beyond infant care, the maintenance and leadership of the entire kin-group is the task of women. The female animal is always on the alert, for on her rests the responsibility no only of feeding the young, but of keeping the young from being food for others. She is the giver and also the sustainer of beginning life. Among humans, males help with protection and food acquisition; but it is the communal group of females that surrounds the child, in its first four to six years of life, with a strong physical, emotional, traditional, and linguistic presence. And this is the foundation of social life and human culture.

The popular image of early human society as being dominated – indeed created – by sexist male hunters and ferocious territorial head-bangers just doesn't hold water. If the first humans had depended solely on despotic and aggressive male leaders, or on several males in chronic, ritualistic contention for power – human society would never have developed. Human culture could never have been invented. The human presence on earth would never have evolved.

The fact is that it was from this first inner circle of women – the campsite, the fire-site, the cave, the first hearth, the first circle of birth – that human society evolved. As hominids evolved into Paleolithic *Home sapiens*, and then into settled and complex Neolithic village people on the time-edge of "civilization," these tens of thousands of years of human culture were shaped and sustained by communities of creative, sexually and psychically active women – women who were inventors, producers, scientists, physicians, lawgivers, visionary shamans, artists. Women who were also the Mothers – receivers and transmitters of terrestrial and cosmic energy.

We have to understand how and why these ancient millennia of womancultures have been buried – ignore, denied, passed off as "mythology" or "primitive prehistoric origins" – by Western male historians who insist (and often really believe) that "real history" began *only about five thousand years ago* – with the relatively recent institutions of patriarchy.

---

[1] Helen Diner, *Mothers and Amazons: The First Feminine History of Culture*, Anchor Books A893, Garden City: Anchor Pr., Doubleday, 1973.

[2] Mary Jane Sherfey, *The Nature and Evolution of Female Sexuality,* New York: Vintage Books, 1973.

[3] Stephen Jay Gould, *Hen's Teeth and Horse's Toes,* New York: Norton, 1994.

[4] Note added by anthology editor from an article by Talia Lavin in The Guardian, Sept. 9, 2013– "Though there is nothing in Jewish religious sources requiring female genital mutilation (FGM), among Ethiopian Jews the practice does seem to have been common — though it was likely for cultural, not religious reasons. A study published in The Israel Journal of Psychiatry and Related Sciences reports: "In Ethiopia, FGM is universal among Christian, Muslim and Jewish groups. All women interviewed reported that FGM was universal in Ethiopia, but none intended to continue this practice with their daughters." "Female genital surgery is hardly performed in Israel and women express no desire to continue this practice," wrote Hebrew University professor Shalva Weil in an article about Ethiopian Jewish women."

[5] Fran P. Hosken, Women's International Network News 2, no. 1, January 1976: 30-44.

6 G. Rachel Levy, Religious Conceptions of the Stone Age, and Their Influence Upon European Thought New York: Harper & Row, 1963, p.70.

7 William Irwin Thompson, *The Time Falling Bodies Take to Light: Mythology, Sexuality, and the Origins of Culture*, New York: St. Martin's Griffin, 1996.

CHAPTER 2

THE END OF GENDER: REVOLUTION, NOT REFORM

Rachel Ivey

Gender is not an individual choice, it is not a natural state, and it is not just an idea. Don't settle for reform – strive for revolution, and the abolition of gender.

~ RACHEL IVEY

MY NAME IS Rachel and I was a teenage liberal. I'm twenty-three years old, and graduated with a women's studies minor from a pretty typical women's studies program at a mainstream university. As I exited adolescence, my liberalism started to fall apart. It was a gradual process. It took me a while to weed out that liberalism from my activist practice, and the liberal view of gender was the last part to go. I want to talk about why liberal ideology, especially in terms of gender, is so compelling, particularly to younger people.

As a feminist activist, I've had a lot of conversations about gender, from both the liberal and radical perspectives. Each conversation is different, but I've developed a kind of standardized approach to beginning them. If I feel like I need to bring up the topic of gender, or if someone else is tending towards the topic of gender, I have to stop them right there before we go any further and ask: "What is your definition of gender?" If I don't understand your definition of gender and you don't understand my definition of gender, you can bet your bottom dollar that conversation is not going to be productive. If you're using two different definitions of gender you're not even speaking the same language when it comes to feminism. That's the core of it. It took me a while to figure that out. And I think I'm still figuring it out because I'm still having those conversations.

I'm going to frame this comparison within the personal shift that I experienced with regard to my definition of gender. Characterizing these two broad definitions of gender can seem very simple on the surface, but I don't want to stay on the surface. I want to break down what "liberal" and "radical" mean in terms of this definition. I want to discuss the implications of these definitions in terms of the material effect that they have on women's lives. I also want to talk about some of the "lightbulb" moments, the personal experiences I've had that shifted my definition of gender.

Let's begin with the liberal definition: Gender (often referred to as "gender identity") is a personal, individual quality possessed by each person. Gender identity is the subjective perception by an individual of their position on a spectrum between "masculine" and "feminine." Gender is performed outwardly through choice of markers or symbols as in demeanor, body language, aesthetic choices like hair, clothing, presence or absence of makeup, and choice of pronoun. These outward markers are what govern whether others regard you as male or female. Each person has an innate gender identity which is independent of their biological sex (male, female, intersex). Sex and gender are not necessarily connected.

In the liberal definition, the oppression associated with gender is that it's a rigid binary system. It forces every person to identify as either a man or a woman (not neither, both at once, something in between or something else entirely) and punishes anyone who doesn't conform. This oppresses both men and women, especially those who don't fully identify with the prescribed model for their gender. From this it follows that in the liberal view, resistance to gender oppression looks like women and men rejecting the binary system, identifying as "gender outlaws" (e.g., genderqueer or trans) and demanding recognition for a range of gender identities. In this definition, ideally, gender is turned from a binary to a spectrum. The two ends of the binary get stretched out, and we can see some more options in between.

In contrast, when viewed through a radical lens, gender is not an innate part of our identities. It is a hierarchical system which maintains the subordination of females as a class to males through force. Gender is a material system of power that uses violence and psychological coercion to exploit female labor, sex, reproduction, and emotional support for the benefit of males.

Gender is not natural or voluntary, since women are not naturally subordinate and no one chooses to be subordinated. Biological sex is a physical feature of each person, and those deemed female upon birth are socialized by the culture into femininity. In this definition, femininity is recognized as a set of stereotypes amounting to ritualized displays of submission. Radical feminists work to organize to overthrow male power and thus the entire gender system. For radical feminists, the ideal number of genders would be zero. Instead of stretching out those binaries so there's a spectrum in between, this definition advocates for the abolition of that system of domination and oppression. Without patriarchy there would be no need for gender.

I don't think these two definitions of gender have anything to do with each other. I think they use the same word to describe two contradictory definitions.

On the liberal side, gender is seen as a personal individual quality, and thus politically neutral. The individual is held up as so sacred in our "pull yourself up by your bootstraps" culture that it's not politically correct to criticize or investigate anyone's idea of gender. This individualism makes it difficult in discussions to draw connections between how we see gender individually and the class issues that affect material reality.

The individualism inherent to liberalism can be seen in other movements as well. For instance, within liberal environmentalism this comes out as the supposed ability of individuals to effect change just by changing themselves. "I'm going to buy something different, I'm going to wear hemp clothing, I'm going to reduce my personal carbon footprint and that's going to help get rid of this system, or change this system, that's causing environmental destruction in the first place."

The logical conclusion of that line of thinking is "withdrawalism." If we just move ourselves out of that system entirely then we're not contributing to it at all. The problem with that is just because you're supposedly not contributing to it, doesn't necessarily mean you're contributing to the dismantling of it. The same line of thinking appears to manifest within the current rhetoric around gender.

Judith Butler coined the term "gender outlaw," which is a really attractive idea when you're a teenage liberal because it purports to put that power in your own hands. If I just stop conforming, personally, to these systems or to these attributes that are connected to these systems, then the system will wither and die without me, right? Or, at least I can personally escape the effects of it if I just don't enact it in my own life. Again, a "gender outlaw" is someone who abandons the gender stereotypes and the gender symbols that are traditional for their biological sex, and adopts those that are assigned to the other sex.

I do want to be very clear that I don't really care how someone dresses. I don't really care how they cut their hair or whether they wear makeup. Other radical feminists and I are not out to police personal lifestyle and appearance choices. But I do have a problem with the idea that nonconforming is always a meaningful political act of resistance in and of itself. However, as a teenage liberal, I found this really attractive because it left it all up to me. If I wanted to escape gender, I could do it. But in reality, it wasn't all up to me. And the idea that it is all up to me is as insulting as it is preposterous because no one, including me, would ever choose a role that involves constant sexual harassment, the ubiquitous threat and in my case occasional enactment of male violence, and the certainty growing up, the conviction that you were meant for exploitation, erasure, silence, but never personhood. I don't think any of us think that anyone would *choose* that.

However, when I was younger, the idea that I could change my outlook on life or change my own perceptions to escape what feminine socialization was doing to me was really too tempting to resist. I understand why younger women are really attracted to that, but I was wrong. And I was wrong because gender is not an individual choice and there was not something wrong with me. Gender is class oppression of females. In order to be an outlaw, there has to be a law. In the case of gender outlaws, that law is patriarchy, that system of values and that law is the class oppression of females. In order for gender "outlawism" to make sense, there has to be a majority in order for that minority to exist.

And that majority is "cis" women, of which I count myself one. Or, more accurately, I don't, because I think that term is oppressive to females on multiple levels. "Cis" describes female people who have capitulated, in the liberal view, to enacting femininity. "Cis" women are seen as enacting the feminine role that we're supposed to enact, and liberal feminists and trans activists say we're privileged because of that. I don't think it's a privilege to be socialized into a role, called "femininity" that encodes subordination so deeply in your identity that you don't call it subordination, you call it your nature, your religion, your culture.

Lierre Keith has noted: "It's become popular in some activist circles to embrace notions from postmodernism, and that includes the idea that gender is somehow a binary. Gender is not a binary. It is a hierarchy. It is global in its reach, it is sadistic in its practice, and it is murderous in its completion. Just like race, and just like class. Gender demarcates the geopolitical boundaries of patriarchy which is to say, it divides us in half. That half is not horizontal — it is vertical. And in case you missed this part, men are always on top."[1]

For radical feminists, gender itself is oppression. In a world without oppression, gender could not exist. Gender *is* sex-based oppression of female people, who as a class are systematically oppressed for the benefit of male people. The purpose of gender is to facilitate the exploitation of female people. For radical feminists, gender is the chain, and patriarchy is the ball, and it's cuffed to the ankle of every female person born. That socialization is not so easily escaped: if you have a TV, you're exposed to it. If you know men who have been socialized into this culture, it's there. If you have a mother who was socialized as feminine, it's there. And that's what makes it a class issue.

I could not escape gender by changing myself because changing my appearance did not change the fact that I was socialized into the sex class called "women" against my will. The fear and desperation that comes from that is not something that someone would choose, and it was not my fault. But even after I realized that, it took me a few years to hold my head up when I walked, and most days I still have to put conscious effort toward it. So when people postulate that gender is individual, that my individual identity involves walking like you're about to be kicked, or holding your head down when you speak that's offensive. No one chooses that identity; no one is innately subordinate.

It's not a coincidence that 91% of those who are raped are female, and 99% of the perpetrators are male. It's not a coincidence that stereotypically feminine shoes make it hard to run away. It's taboo to acknowledge that females are socialized from birth onward into a subordinate sex class for whom exploitation by males is so ingrained into the social norms that we can't recognize it any more. That it's become a "choice," that it's become our "identity." It's taboo within mainstream liberal feminism to address the fact that males are socialized from birth onward into a privileged sex class that feeds on violation and subordination of not only women, but as all of you can recognize, of the oceans, of the earth, of life itself.

Those who hold the radical view of gender are experiencing an escalating backlash. Lierre Keith said: "I have been fighting about this since 1982, and think 'transphobic' is a ridiculous word. I have no strange fear of people who claim to be 'trans.' I deeply disagree with them, as do most radical feminists."[2]

Try this on: I am a rich person stuck in a poor person's body. I've always enjoyed champagne rather than beer, and always knew I belonged in first class not economy, and it just feels right when people wait on me. My insurance company should give me a million dollars to cure my Economic Dysphoria.

Or how about this: I am really Native American. How do I know? I've always felt a special connection to animals, and started building tepees in the backyard as soon as I was old enough. I insisted on wearing moccasins to school even though the other kids made fun of me and my parents punished me for it. I read everything I could on native people, started going to powwows and sweat lodges as soon as I was old enough, and I knew that was the real me. And if you bio-Indians don't accept us trans-Indians, then you are just as genocidal and oppressive as the Europeans.

Gender is no different. It is a class condition created by a brutal arrangement of power.

In conversations I've had on this issue I've often asked why, with a conception of gender that centers transgenderism, do liberals find the idea of being transracial to be so different? Transracial as an idea analogous to "transgender" is the idea that if someone could be "born in the body" of the "wrong" sex, that they could also be born into the body of the "wrong" race/skin color. This idea is offensive because it *is* appropriation. Would a white person wearing clothing traditionally/stereotypically associated with individuals of another race mean that they are transracial? Would identifying more strongly with the culture of another racial group indicate that someone is transracial? No, of course not. Without the cultural background, including the oppression and abuse that goes along with being part of a marginalized racial class, someone claiming transracialism is obviously appropriating the experiences of others. Gender is no different.

On the liberal side, gender is idealist.

The idea that consciousness is everything leads to an activist practice that's focused on changing people's minds, as though oppression were a mistake that could be corrected if we could just explain well enough to our oppressors.

Rape is not just an idea. Again, there's a reason why 91% of rape victims are female, and 99% of the perpetrators are male. If she's lucky, the survivor of rape will be one of the 2% whose case actually goes to trial. Ninety-seven percent of men who rape never see a day in jail. These are not ideas; they are material reality.

For radical feminists, gender is maintained through force. Gender is a material system of power that uses violence and psychological coercion to exploit female labor, sex, reproduction, and emotional support for the benefit of men. Rape culture, right along with female poverty, lack of education, and the trafficking of our bodies, is maintained through material structures. Not through people's ideas. Gender is a system of power that uses violence and psychological coercion to maintain the oppression of females, not to just control our ideas about it, but to control actual physical reality.

Kourtney Mitchell writes: "It is important to understand what it means to view racial oppression in the context of class analysis. Whiteness is a class experience, and not based in biological reality. But that does not mean one can just decide to stop being white, just like I cannot decide to stop being a man as long as the dominant culture classes me as a man. As long as you are classed as white, you will continue to benefit from white privilege. This is what allies need to remember."[3]

If you put this in the context of gender oppression, it is just as true. This is what allies need to remember.

As someone socialized into femininity, I will always have to think about my posture so that I'm not hiding. I will have to speak extra-loud most of the time in order to counteract the social forces that tell me not to speak at all. None of that will change just because I decide it should. Gender is a system of stereotypes that works to maintain a system of domination and material exploitation.

Andrea Dworkin writes: "Woman is not born; she is made. In the making, her humanity is destroyed. She becomes symbol of this, symbol of that; mother of the earth, slut of the universe; but she never becomes herself because she is forbidden to do so."[4] For female people, this is the reality of the construction of gender: that it is not escapable. Just because it's constructed doesn't mean that it can be deconstructed at will. It doesn't mean that it can be deconstructed individually. It will take collective power to dismantle it.

Through my work, I met an adolescent girl who had been subject to assault and abuse by men for much of her life. She had short hair when we met; she then cut it a little shorter and asked me to use the pronoun "he," which I did. I didn't really think very deeply about it at the time. If you had asked me why she did that, I would have said that she was expressing her innate gender identity. But I don't believe that anymore.

One of the reasons I don't believe that is because one day in class, I asked all of my students to draw a picture of what they thought they deserved, what they wanted their lives to be like in the future.

The class drew a lot of different things, but I kept that one student's drawing for a really long time. In one corner she drew what was clearly a girl's face. It had pink lipstick, a pink bow in the hair, tears running down the face, and a big X through it. Underneath it she wrote words she thought described being a girl. She wrote "pain," "fear," and "rape." In the other corner she drew another face that looked a lot like her. It had short, brown hair, no makeup or accessories, and the face was smiling. And underneath it she wrote "confident," "happy," and "safe." Underneath the drawings she wrote: "If I wasn't a girl, I wouldn't have been raped. If I wasn't a girl, I wouldn't be scared. If I wasn't a girl..."

I kept that drawing for a while, because I didn't really understand it right away. It took time for the implications to sink in. I don't bring up this example to try to convey that every person who describes themselves as trans does so because of the type of horrific abuse that she endured. I do it to assert that being socialized into femininity *is* abuse. She did what she could to escape it at that time. As much as I want that for her, I know that she cannot erase the reality of what gender socialization did to her no matter how short she cut her hair, and no matter what name she used.

Gender is anything but natural. She was not born with a feminine brain or a masculine brain, but she was born with a female body and in this culture that means she's considered less human than members of the sex class "men." It's no wonder to me that she wanted to escape that oppression of female socialization by rejecting her femaleness, but just as men cannot erase the privilege of being raised in the dominant sex class, women cannot simply choose to erase the oppression of being socialized into femininity. In the radical view, gender is not a natural part of our identities – it is socially constructed for the purpose of maintaining and reproducing male supremacy.

Catharine MacKinnon writes: "In a society in which equality is a fact, not merely a word, words of racial or sexual assault and humiliation will be nonsense syllables."[5]

In the radical feminist view, the word "gender," along with the sex-class system based on subordination and domination that the word signifies, will cease to have meaning when male supremacy is dismantled.

This piece was adapted from a lecture given by the author in March 2012.

[1] Lierre Keith, speaking at Radfem Reboot 2012.

[2] Ibid.

[3] Kourtney Mitchell, "Our Experiences Matter: On White Privilege and Backlash," *Deep Green Resistance News Service*, March 5, 2013, http://dgrnewsservice.org/civilization/white-supremacy/kourtney-mitchell-our-experiences-matter-on-white-privilege-and-backlash/.

[4] Andrea Dworkin, *Pornography: Men Possessing Women*, New York: Plume, 1989.

[5] Catharine A. MacKinnon, "Only Words.pdf," http://14.139.206.50:8080/jspui/bitstream/1/2651/1/MacKinnon,%20Catharine%20A.%20-%20Only%20Words.pdf.

CHAPTER 3

THE DIFFERENCE BETWEEN SEX AND
GENDER AND WHY IT MATTERS

Kathy Scarbrough

WOMEN'S LIBERATION IS the goal of our movement. Feminists identify male **power** as a major impediment to women's freedom. This inequality in power holds back all women—white women, woman of color, lesbians, rich and poor women, women of the imperialist countries as well as women also suffering from neocolonialism. The impartial interest in the "genders" (however many genders you believe may exist), suggests that there is nothing special about the position of women in society. Gender is a step backward toward the old saw that men and women are equally oppressed. And that's just not true, its one of many ploys used to maintain male power.

The way that cultural expectations based on sex pervade everything we do and everywhere we go has been examined in great detail. Gender is a result of culture, and can be changed dramatically or even abolished completely. A woman spoke at a 2013 conference[1] organized by Redstockings in New York City about how such expectations based on sex were *opposed* in revolutionary China. She testified that she grew up *unaware* that she was a female child because at the time the differences between girls and boys were minimized. They were just children playing with a variety of toys and participating in a variety of activities. Promoting the idea that there is a continuum of human behavior that does not correlate with sex makes *meaningless* the concept of multiple genders.

To present this idea of a continuum in graphic form, consider that most intellectual and behavioral traits are characterized by what is known as a normal curve:

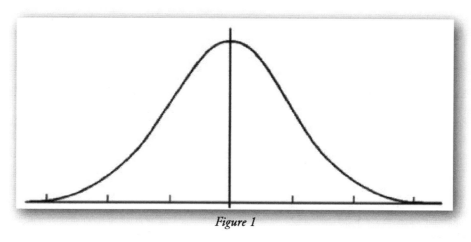

Figure 1

For a trait like artistic ability, for instance, this curve demonstrates how some people will be very good at drawing (one extreme) or have very poor abilities (the other extreme), but most of us fall somewhere in the middle. Similar distributions are formed when you look at math ability or verbal ability or the love of sparkles or almost any other human behavioral characteristic you can name. Indeed, distributions of math ability according to sex have been studied extensively. In spite of what male supremacists might claim, the male and female distributions for math ability overlap extensively:

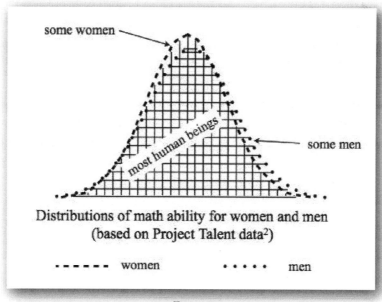

Figure 2

The overlap of horizontal and vertical lines in *Figure 2* indicated the math ability of most people, whether male or female. That is, there is no large difference in mathematical ability according to sex; most of us would fall in the area of overlap between women and men. There would be only a tiny sliver that remains uniquely lined vertically and a tiny sliver that remains uniquely lined horizontally, indicating very small differences between women and men for this trait.

Besides the material reality of one's sex, the idea of a *psychological* sense of one's sex, or "gender identity" is tossed around by people like it is a well-established scientific fact. On the contrary, this is a rather controversial notion. To believe in gender identity you have to believe that one can perceive one's own sex separate from the material reality of one's body. And, importantly, one has to believe that female brains are substantially different than male brains. Several recent books[3, 4, 5, 6] have lambasted the biased research leading many to conclude that we humans are born with either female "pink brains" or male "blue brains." Thus, gender identity itself is a fiction. Yet the idea of brain sex persists. One should ask who benefits from the idea that male and female brains are substantially different from one another.

Alternatively, if you start from the premise that our brains are fundamentally similar, let's consider how we get the perception of our own sex, our so-called "gender identity." It starts at birth when your parents dress you in pink or blue and treats your hair differently. It continues as people around you tell you that you are a boy or a girl. Have you noticed how common this is, particularly for young children under the age of 5 years? I have to make a conscious effort to stop participating in this acculturation of young children, it almost seems like a reflex. For many girls and boys, this communication comes in the form of "you can't do that because you are a girl, or you can't dress that way because you are a boy." Or, "you are such a pretty girl" and "thatta boy!" As we continue to develop physically, the reality of *menstruation* for female adolescents and *ejaculation* for male adolescents provides our brains with potent *evidence* of our sex and adds to our "gender identity". But all we are really doing is acknowledging the material reality of sex.

Gender is derived from, and depends on sex. This can cause confusion about the difference between the two. Focusing on gender tends to *elevate* and *invigorate* physical differences between the sexes and downplays our common humanity. Genderists today are what we used to call *essentialists* back in the 1960s and 70s: they believe that women's "nature" (that is, brain function) is inherently different than man's "nature."

BIOLOGICAL SEX

Biological sex, on the other hand, is about reproduction of the species– egg and sperm meeting to initiate the growth of a new individual. These gametes are how biologists define sex (egg is the female gamete and sperm is the male gamete). I know its fashionable to decry the binary, but sorry, we're stuck with just eggs and sperm when it comes to sex. There are only two types of gametes and there are no intermediate forms. Gonads (ovaries and testes) and gametes don't get mismatched in the natural world because the gamete is dependent on the gonad for its maturation. This means that there are no examples of human beings born with an ovary that produces sperm or vice versa. However, there are known conditions where people don't produce either gamete. And some small percent of human beings are born with an amalgam of the ovary and testis, neither gonad, or one of each. However, I know of no cases where a human being makes both functional eggs and functional sperm. Human beings make one or the other, or neither. This is material reality.

THE FEMINIST VIEW OF CHILDBEARING

Gonads and gametes are what biologists call primary sex characteristics. Most female human beings also have wombs and vaginas, we are the ones who menstruate and gestate. Menstruation, pregnancy, labor and delivery are *not* aspects of "gender expression," they are part of the material reality of having a female body. Pregnancy, labor and delivery take a physical toll, and removes women at least temporarily, from conventional productive forces of the economy. The subordination of women is rooted in the exploitation of this difference of reproductive labor. Women's liberation should therefore concern itself with sex. It is a travesty for groups concerned with women's reproduction to get confused about the politics of gender and sex. The Midwives Association of North America (MANA) recently erased the word 'woman' from their Core Competencies in favor of 'pregnant individual' and 'birthing parent'. Because MANA doesn't recognize this right wing attack on feminism and the fight against male supremacy, MANA actually promotes a parity that does not exist in reality making it more difficult to name and engage the real issues surrounding the male supremacist approach to pregnancy and birthing.

To recognize the sexual dimorphism involved in reproducing the human race does not make me an essentialist— it is *not* the same as saying that male and female brains and talents and interests are fundamentally different from one another. It is not elevating the class of female humans because of the importance of childbearing. It is not fighting for my "identity" as a woman, nor running away from it. It is fighting for the inherent worth and dignity of human beings while at the same time recognizing biological reality. This recognition of material reality means we feminists might press for some altered work rules for some jobs during the 3rd trimester of pregnancy. A women's liberation demand might also include getting some kind of *compensation* for the socially important work of childbearing. What that compensation might look like needs to be discussed, but the political point is that childbearing is not just a individual "family" issue, its a collective issue because societies require a reproductive rate high enough to replace aging workers. Other women's liberation demands have always included separating the childbearing from childrearing. Some women may choose to be a stay-at-home parent but this shouldn't be mandatory and it should be recognized that staying at home has *never* been an option for many, many women. Surely we mothers should not be *penalized* in hiring, promotion, seniority in the workplace etc., as we are now. These different demands arise from the simple recognition of the unequal division of labor involved in reproducing the human species, nothing more.

"Gender" can be viewed as the social signal for either being among the class of humans who bodies produce offspring or, alternatively, being among the class of humans who have a much more circumscribed role in the reproduction of the species– the role of the sperm provider. This is what "gender expression" was all about historically: the way we dress, wear our hair, groom ourselves was all about differentiating humanity depending on their sex. Male power depends on being able to distinguish women from men. In this sense, the mixing up of these gender tags is a good thing.

In a very few instances it makes sense to rely on gender instead of sex. Dr. Anne Fausto-Sterling makes the point that humankind shows more variation in genitalia than "stereotypically male" and "stereotypically female[3]. People born with ambiguous genitalia might actually need to *choose* whether they will represent themselves in the conventional world as man or woman until such a time when this no longer matters. Therefore, *gender* might provide an occasionally useful flexibility regarding *sex*.

Gender and Hormones

In her book *Sex Itself*[6] Sarah Richardson emphasizes human commonalities by showing that both men and women make both estrogens (female "sex" hormone) and androgens (male "sex" hormone). The differences between women and men in hormone secretion have always been over emphasized in our culture. Richardson even questions the description of these potent regulatory chemicals as "sex" hormones.

Over-emphasis of the hormonal differences between women and men leads to nasty jokes (and guilty secrets) about the physical attributes of aging women. When estrogen secretion by the ovary decreases significantly after menopause, the effect of our natural androgens becomes more obvious. Many a woman has agonized about beard hairs sprouting from her chin or the darkening of hair on the upper lip. We pluck and bleach and shave often without questioning the conventional notion that this hair is somehow unfeminine. Or we pluck and bleach and shave with full consciousness of doing it to get along more easily as an older woman in sexist society. Indeed, this age-related change *is* "unfeminine" because femininity itself is fictitious! These changes may be unfeminine but they do not stand in opposition to *femaleness*. Both women and men secrete estrogens and androgens—we are more alike than we are different. Here's a complementary example of this truth: it has been discovered recently that *male* fertility is dependent on the response to *both* hormones. Without estrogen action, men are infertile[7]. This fact again stresses our common humanity.

Today, our "self-representation" as male or female doesn't have to correspond to our chromosomes, sex organs or even whether we produce eggs or sperm. One unacknowledged way the word gender is commonly used is this: gender refers to our perception of someone *else's* sex. Our notion of whether a person is a man or a woman is detected by the existence of what biologists call *secondary sex characteristics,* those anatomical features that typically appear at puberty.

Looking at a person you can't tell if they have testes or ovaries but you can often immediately see whether they have breasts or beard hair. Secondary sex characteristics are *controlled* by estrogens and androgens, the hormones secreted mainly by the gonads. As we've seen, women and men respond to both kinds of hormones. Therefore the currently fashionable cross-sex ingestion of steroid hormones—although probably bad for one's health—can introduce some gender ambiguity. That is, biological male humans can grow breasts and biologically female humans can grow beard hair. These hormones are powerful and can be used to alter one's gender *but not* one's sex. That is, taking hormones cannot change the fact that you've grown an ovary containing eggs or a testis. [Note: when men take estrogen they stop producing sperm but they've already grown a penis and testes and those structures remain.]

Brain Sex and Hormone Secretion

Human brains *are* mostly alike but there is one small *functional* difference between male and female brains related to the continuation of the species. A tiny part of the evolutionarily old, non-conscious female brain creates a reproductive rhythm and the corresponding part of male brains don't. A physiologically important difference between the brains of the sexes is the network of a very few nerve cells, located in a brain area known as the hypothalamus, that produce menstrual cycles in women.

In women, the hypothalamus responds to estrogens and drives elevated blood levels of a pituitary gland hormone called luteinizing hormone once a month. These short term elevated levels of hormone stimulate ovulation. This cyclic pattern of pituitary hormone secretion ends before menopause in women (indeed it may be among the causes of menopause). Men secrete the very same pituitary hormones in very similar concentrations but the *pattern* of secretion is constant, not cyclic. Again, emphasizing our common humanity it should be noted that luteinizing hormone is essential for male reproduction too—specifically for testosterone secretion and sperm production. We've seen that both men and women can respond to estrogens. Jordan-Young's book *Brainstorm*[5] reminded me that there is some evidence in primates that feeding animals estrogens can cause their pituitaries to mimic the pattern of luteinizing hormone secretion observed during the normal menstrual cycle. So maybe it is possible for men who take estrogens to experience this hormone pattern as well. Whether there would be any other physiological effects of this pattern of hormone secretion in men is completely unknown.

Recently there has been a lot of hoopla from the proponents of the theory of "brain sex" regarding a gene called SRY, the so-called "testis determining factor". SRY is normally located on the Y chromosome and so isn't usually expressed in female human beings, who typically have no Y chromosome. Its action is very important during fetal life for the development of testes. Recently its been discovered that SRY is expressed in the brain, and this evidence has been used to argue that the brain is sexed. However, this gene is structurally similar to many that are expressed in both sexes, and its presence in male humans might be redundant. In addition, many genes are expressed in several different tissues in the body and they don't serve the same function in each tissue. For example, serotonin is made in the brain where it has gained public awareness as being somehow involved in cases of depression and other "mood" disorders. But serotonin is also secreted by a type of white blood cell where it functions in the process of blood clotting, and serotonin is secreted in the gut where it promotes the mixing of intestinal contents during digestion. When the SRY gene is expressed in the early embryo it has a role in the formation of the testes but this does not mean that it is important in "masculin-izing" the brain in any meaningful way. There is absolutely no evidence SRY affects something as complex as human behavior.

THE SOCIAL CONSTRUCTION AND DESTRUCTION OF GENDER

So where does this leave us? Gender is socially constructed, and social forces can also *confuse* self-identity, particularly in cases where people don't fit cultural norms. Conventional "girl" or "boy" behavior (and even body type) doesn't fit *many* people. Why not simply conclude that the culturally defined categories "feminine" and "masculine" are the problem?

Collective action is required to fight battles against socially constructed notions of femi-nine and masculine; it is difficult and maybe impossible to wage this battle successfully as an individual. Certain individuals may make the personal decision that they can't wait for that new day to dawn. But let us be clear—the decision to change one's gender is a personal one. It is not a political act that confronts the behavioral constraints following from the construction of masculinity and femininity. A personal decision to change one's appearance to reduce fric-tion in life doesn't help the struggle against the power differential between men and women. Indeed, it can be argued that the transgender movement embraces, supports and props up current notions of feminine and masculine and the unequal position of women and men in society at the same time that it gives *some individuals* needed relief from the condemnation of not meeting conventional gender expectations.

Getting rid of gender would be a step forward for everyone. And by abolishing gender we don't mean that it will no longer be possible to distinguish women from men (although a lot more ambiguity might be present), it just means that the *significance* of gender will cease. The significance of sex for the continuation of the human species will remain. Full women's libera-tion requires an attack on all biases based on sex but it should be understood that menstrua-tion, pregnancy and childbirth are not artificial biases; these are material realities of women's lives and necessary for the continuation of the species. Women need to organize together to fight male power in all realms, including the way that reproduction is regarded in sexist society.

THE ROLE OF SEPARATISM IN FIGHTING MALE POWER

To fight male power over women requires strategy. One useful strategy is called "Separate to Integrate"[8]. This means we need separate all-female women's liberation organizations to build a power base for women. Our overarching *demand* is, however, an end to the artificial division of labor and power based on sex and the integration of men and women in society where our differences are appreciated but not used to construct hierarchies. The struggle for women's liberation requires an all-female group because there are many conflicts of interest between women and men. But the goal is to stop defining people by their sex. I'm a scientist, a teacher, and a political activist who also happens to be a mother. My sex is only one of several identity tags that describe me. We simply cannot organize against male power with men in the room. Just as people of color cannot organize against white power with white people in the room and we cannot organize against the injustices we suffer as workers when the bosses are in the room. Frederick Douglass said famously, " Power concedes nothing without a demand. It never did and it never will. "[9] Women, people of color, workers need to meet with those who experience problems similar to their own to generate those demands for equal power.

Separatism is a strategy, not the desired outcome. Integration *with* equality is the goal of feminists. Women of color often find themselves in the uncomfortable position of needing to raise their "feminist flag" in male-female mixed groups working on racial oppression, and their "black power flag" when working in mixed race groups of women. Poor women of any race find that they need to raise the issues of class in both women's liberation groups and in groups organizing against racial oppression. Some women of color have concluded that they need their own separate groups. When we participate in separate groups we should ask ourselves whether we are meeting separately as an oppressed class determined to gain power, or are we actually going along with male supremacist/racist/classist segregation where oppressed people are excluded and "kept in their place"? Is the separate group allowed to exist, perhaps even funded by the establishment, because it doesn't challenge the status quo? We need to be aware of situations when separatism is a symbol of powerlessness (for example, ladies auxiliaries) rather than a base for power.

Sometimes separatism is simply personal. Lesbians need a place to meet and enjoy each other's company. Women may choose individually to withdraw temporarily into all female spaces to get some respite from the constant barrage of sexist objectification we face everyday in the world. But this should be recognized as a personal act, and not a political solution to our problems.

Acquiescing to male supremacy or withdrawing from it are *not* the only alternatives. Radical feminists fight male supremacy. We fight for a new society organized on the basis of equality for women, for people of color, for lesbians and gays as well as for workers and the poor and unemployed. Radical feminists seek freedom for all oppressed groups, but the feminist fights specifically to make sure women are included, not overlooked or relegated to some kind of secondary status.

How then does one analyze common instances of separatism we see around us today? Are they needed to fight male supremacy, or reactionary elements of sexist society, or simply personal? The separation of women and men in some religious organizations is a reactionary element of sexist society. What about separate sports teams for girls and boys, women and men? Clearly women had been kept out of sports and discriminated against within sport. The fact that Title IX of the 1972 Education Amendments became famous for leveling the playing field for women in sport is testimony to that history of discrimination. In just a few decades women have become stronger, faster and much better athletes. It is interesting to speculate about a time when the need for separate athletic teams might disappear.

What about separate toilet facilities? We don't practice this separatism at home, why is it essential in public accommodations? The answer to that question is, at least in part, due to the threat of male violence. Of course there's lots of male violence occurring at home but "stranger danger" has always had a much stronger hold on our collective imaginations. Public bathrooms are often dangerous for homosexual men as well. We can view the demands of the transwomen for access to women's toilets through the lens of the threat of male supremacist violence. But feminists have rightly pointed out that the perspective of female humans needs to be taken into account on an equal basis. Today any man can put on a dress, self-identify as a woman and demand access to women's toilet or shower facilities. This is a real problem. Luckily, the solution is fairly simple. All public bathrooms should become secure individual gender-neutral rooms. The fact that this idea is ridiculed is a measure of how little importance is placed on female human's continued need for security from male predators. When a train derails and people are hurt, we as a society pay for expensive upgrades to security; the American Disability Act required extensive reconstruction of bathrooms, entrances and many other alterations to public buildings. Changing public bathrooms to accommodate both women and transwomen should be similarly prioritized. This would have the added benefit of putting infant diaper changing tables in areas where fathers can access them equally. Although these changing tables are more available than they used to be, there are still many places where accessibility to them continues to be a measure of conventional gender expectations.

One of the first cases where female separatism was challenged was the case of the Michigan Women's Music Festival. Indeed, the transgender community played a large role in the festival's demise. Was this separatism needed? Certainly female musicians have been discriminated against in the male dominated world and many women found it a wonderful personal respite from male supremacy. Set up originally for cultural expression, it never really was a power base for feminist organizing. Its rather apolitical cultural separatism led to problems from the start. Many women needed/wanted to bring their children along. The question of what to do with male children[10] roiled the organization long before transwomen crashed the party.

CONCLUSION

Sex matters for the continuation of the species and also because the oppression of women is built on the material reality of the unequal division of reproductive labor. Our understanding of this root of male supremacy informs our efforts to gain power for all women. Gender is dispensable; indeed, the very notion of femininity and masculinity is oppressive.

---

[1] Shulamith Firestone Women's Liberation Memorial Conference on What is to Be Done, Redstockings of the Women's Liberation Movement, 2013. https://womenwhatistobedone.wordpress.com.

[2] Studies of a Complete Age Group- Age 15. M.F. Shaycroft, J. T. Dailey, D. B. Orr, C. A. Neyman, S. E. Sherman, Project Talent Office, University of Pittsburgh, Pittsburgh, PA 1963.

[3] *Sexing the Body.* Fausto-Sterling, Anne, Basic Books, 2000.

[4] *Delusions of Gender: How Our Minds, Society and Neurosexism Create Difference,* Fine, Cordelia, W. W. Norton & Co., 2010.

[5] *Brainstorm: The Flaws in the Science of Sex Differences,* Jordan-Young, Rebecca M., Harvard University Press, 2010.

[6] *Sex Itself: The Search for Male and Female in the Human Genome,* Richardson, Sarah S., University of Chicago Press, 2013.

[7] Estrogen action and male fertility: Roles of the sodium/hydrogen exchanger-3 and fluid reabsorption in reproductive tract function. Qing Zhou, Lane Clarke, Rong Nie, et al. Proceedings of the National Academy of Sciences, 98:24, 14132-14137, 2001.

[8] "Separate to Integrate," by Barbara Leon in *Feminist Revolution: An Abridged Edition with Additional Writings*, Redstockings of the Women's Liberation Movement, Random House, 1978.

[9] "If There is No Struggle, There is No Progress," Frederick Douglas, from a speech, 1857. http://www.blackpast.org/1857-frederick-douglass-if-there-no-struggle-there-no-progress. Accessed 3/7/16.

[10] A separate camp with activities throughout the day for boys was created on the festival grounds.

CHAPTER 4

FEMALE ERASURE, REVERSE SEXISM, AND THE CISGENDER THEORY OF PRIVILEGE

Elizabeth Hungerford

INTRODUCTION TO CIS

CIS IS A Latin prefix, traditionally unused in common parlance. Over the past decade, however, cis has become a popular way to describe the contours of modern gender theory. The compound term "cisgender" has even been making its way into traditional dictionaries. Formalization by institutional recognition represents the increasing importance of this new concept to our modern lexicon and shared understanding of gender.

The *Oxford Dictionary* defines cisgender as:

> Denoting or relating to a person whose sense of personal identity and gender corresponds with their birth sex. Compare with transgender.[1]

The *Merriam-Webster Dictionary* defines cisgender as:

> Of, relating to, or being a person whose gender identity corresponds with the sex the person had or was identified as having at birth.[2]

Other definitions of cisgender might read that a person's gender identity "matches with"[3] or is "consistent with," rather than "corresponds with" their sex at birth. The important point is that the prefix cis is being used to refer to a harmonious relationship between two things. As applied to the concept of gender, cisgender purports to describe a naturally unproblematic relationship between a person's gender identity and their birth sex.

In a strictly descriptive sense, cisgender may seem like a perfectly harmless concept. One might even assume that feminists and trans theorists equally support the idea because it recognizes a distinction between sex and gender (identity) such that a connector term is both coherent and necessary. Following from the basic concept of being cisgender, however, is a novel theory of gender itself. As I will show, this theory does not supplement, but actually contradicts and replaces, well-established feminist knowledge about gender and the machinations of sex-based inequality between men and women.[4]

The simplicity of the term *cis + gender* masks the very serious conceptual reversals it represents to feminism, to legal interpretation, and to materialist analyses of oppression in general. Instead of wrestling with the complex ways that deeply felt psychological connections between body and identity– specifically that of gender– are socially constructed,[5] the cis theory of gender operates from the belief that human relationships with gender and identity can be known *a priori*.[6] Gender identity can therefore be meaningfully separated from social influence (and reduced to a biological process). The theory further conceives of social privilege and oppression on the axis of gender in a wholly new way: as phenomena driven by subjective identification with gender. Cis theory of gender denies the lived experiences of millions of women who despise the social role "woman," instead framing non-trans women's gender identity as a privilege. The theory is blind to how these seemingly benign "gender identities" operate as a hierarchy of social roles and interactions whose end game is the unequal distribution of power and resources between male and female humans. This essentialist, ahistorical assessment of gender identity short-circuits women's ability to recognize themselves as oppressed by sex-based gender roles. It denies us use of the language and concepts necessary to describe women's specific exploitation *as women*.[7]

CIS ESSENTIALISM

One of the first things you will notice about cisgender is that it's positioned as a foil to the concept of transgender. Occasionally, a person might describe themselves as neither cisgender nor transgender,[8] but you absolutely cannot be *both*. That wouldn't make any sense. Cis and trans are opposites, mutually exclusive categories.[9] Like man and woman, cis and trans constitute a binary. Cis/trans is the new gender binary.

Humans' entire relationship to gender is roughly describable and reducible to either cisgender or transgender.

At this point you might wonder about the status of late transitioners–- transwomen such as Caitlyn Jenner or former boxing promoter Kellie Maloney, for example. In order to explain how the cis/trans binary plays out in cases of late-transitioning transgender people, trans activists explain their theory of gender as follows: despite having lived for decades under close public scrutiny as successful men who sired children, these people were always transgender and never cisgender.[10] To put a finer point on it, they were always "women" even when they were entirely unrecognizable as such, including to themselves.

The gender identity of a trans person is their personal destiny. It is a journey of internal discovery and revelation that transcends the limits of the physical body. Social and/or medical transition is the process by which the authentic self makes its grand entrance.

In order to be conceptually useful as the opposite of transgender, cisgender conceives of non-trans gender identities as a similar kind of personal inevitability. Where transgender people are destined to become "themselves" through social or physical transition, cisgender people already are "themselves." The cis theory of gender uncritically accepts that the gender identities of the overwhelming majority of female humans – to be generous, let's say ninety percent– just happen to be uniformly feminine and well-described by the social role "woman." Women are thus rebranded ciswomen. The theory must further accept that male humans' gender identities overwhelmingly manifest – again, say, close to ninety percent – as masculine "men" with a social role conveniently complimentary to females' "woman." Men are rebranded cismen. The cis theory of gender takes a shallow assessment of what appears normal or accepted, and interprets it as natural and good.

Gender identity is not under human control, but it is universally human. That is, to be human is to have a gender identity.[11]

This is essentialism.

CISGENDER ESSENTIALISM AND OPPRESSION

The essentialism of the cis/trans gender theory is a political problem. It is a problem for women as persons oppressed by their gender assignment: girl/woman. It is also a problem for feminism's ability to explain women's collective social position relative to men. How can women understand their own oppression if gender identity is natural and originates inside of us? A theory of gender that insists the social identity "woman" reflects anyone's authentic self fails to consider quite a lot about the mechanics of oppression.

The cis theory of gender does not wrestle with the fact that half of the world's humans, now known as ciswomen, are oppressed on the basis of the *assumed* connection between their birth sex and their identification with gender – female, feminine, woman – relative to the other half of the world's humans – male, masculine, man. The body is the single variable in the social classification process directing female bodies to be treated as "girls" and male bodies to be treated as "boys." Female humans are debased and exploited specifically because of the assumption that they could, would, or should embody particular personality characteristics socially coded as belonging to girls and women. Patterns of this assumption are played out again and again on the terrain of female bodies: sex-selective female infanticide, rape culture, compulsory motherhood, billions of hours of unpaid domestic labor, and even the "glass ceiling" in business and government. These wildly diverse examples of harm to women are all rooted in a conscious or unconscious belief in the presence of a natural connection between female bodies and their abilities or social worth. So-called ciswomen are materially harmed by their gender assignment.

By indulging gender essentialism, cis/trans theory cannot avoid making an implicit claim about the patriarchal status quo: it is as natural as cis people's gender identities. Indeed, to question the cisgender man/woman binary would be to throw the conceptual legitimacy of gender identity as a reflection of authentic self into question. As a result, the cis/trans theory of gender cannot and does not address the glaringly obvious problem that females are oppressed *as women.*

If gender identity is humans' destiny rather than a social construct, then the cis/trans binary offers women nothing from which to launch a logical attack against our gender-based oppression. The great weight of history has already conspired to demonstrate that female humans are weaker and less rational than male humans. The seemingly organic arrangements of man/woman, husband/wife, father/daughter are traditionally framed as benevolent protection of women by men. Without any counter-explanation for these hierarchies, and like all other forms of gender essentialism, the cis/trans theory of gender provides dangerous ideological cover for the continuation of male supremacist social structures.

More importantly, if identification with the ritualized submission of femininity is ciswomen's destiny, women cannot understand *themselves* as anything but unavoidably complicit in their own oppression. Women's alleged failure to be assertive in the workplace, for example, is now easily explained away as a charming and inevitable byproduct of women's authentic selves. Cisgender women might be advised to compensate for their little identity challenge by simply learning to *lean in,*[12] you know, like cisgender men do. It is not unfair stereotypes about women's (in)competence or the institutional devaluation of female labor,[13] but ciswomen's gender identity that hinders them on their path to professional success and equality.

Rather than pinpointing and deconstructing the complex web of external forces that create impossible double standards for women,[14] cisgender theory completely ignores women's lower social status relative to men. It does not account for or even recognize that the gendered characteristics of power and authority are incompatible with being womanly.[15] By failing to account for the negative effects of gender on half of the world's humans, the cis/trans binary functions as anti-feminist victim blaming. For if gender is "natural," it cannot be named as a cause of the oppression of women.

CISWOMEN'S GENDER IDENTITIES AND THE PSYCHOLOGY OF OPPRESSION

The cis theory of gender also fails to take on the psychology of oppression. It erroneously assumes that any person who does not want to transition is perfectly happy with their assigned gender at birth. Those humans who fail to stage a very specific kind of public performance – the act of *transitioning* – are assumed to affirmatively embrace the gender assigned to them at birth.

Yet gender's imprint on the identities of female humans cannot be measured by their apparent assimilation to being "girls" and "women." Women's internalization of gender identity and gender roles has been analyzed endlessly by feminist and political theorists of all kinds. Over a century and a half ago John Stuart Mill (in collaboration with his wife Harriet Taylor Mill, whose intellectual contributions were subsumed under her husband's name precisely because of gender roles) put it plainly in "The Subjection of Women":

> All causes, social and natural, combine to make it unlikely that women should be collectively rebellious to the power of men. … All men, except the most brutish, desire to have, in the woman most nearly connected with them, not a forced slave but a willing one, not a slave merely, but a favorite. They have therefore put everything in practice to enslave their minds.[16]

This passage highlights the importance of psychological control as a tool of domination. It is undeniable that some women are willing to participate in the structures of our own oppression. Radical feminist Andrea Dworkin's *Right-Wing Women* is all about this.[17] Liberal feminist Betty Friedan's *The Feminine Mystique* describes the quiet desperation of women suffering under the crushing weight their own conformity to women's sex-specific social positions as wives and mothers.[18] These very different but very classic feminist texts, along with many others, have helped women understand how identification with gender is externally constructed;

how we relate to the sex-based social roles expected of us; and why we might come to embrace practices or behaviors that ultimately serve to harm us.

Adopting the values of the oppressor is a well-documented coping skill of people who are debased and essentialized.[19,20] Feminists know that women are not unique in internalizing their own subjugation:

> Coerced assimilation is in fact one of the *policies* available to an oppressing group in its effort to reduce and/or annihilate another group. This tactic is used by the U.S. government, for instance, on the American Indians.[21]

Similarly, women have been subtly and not-so-subtly groomed to take joy or pride in the superficial social rewards of gender conformity. The target characteristics of the female gender role–to be passive, people pleasing, and self-blaming–increase the likelihood of eventual assimilation. Women who did not internally identify with femininity but who were willing to do whatever it took to fit in, to suffer in silence, to pretend forever; of women who grudgingly resigned themselves to their social role under threat of violence or social ostracization; these women are not part of the cis/trans theory of gender identification.

CISGENDER PRIVILEGE AND THE POLITICS OF INTERNAL IDENTITY

It gets worse. After establishing a hard distinction between cisgender people and transgender people, the cis/trans theory of gender is extended to claim that cisgender people experience a special type of privilege. *Cisgender privilege.*

According to the online encyclopedia, Wikipedia:

> In 2010, the term cisgender privilege appeared in academic literature, defined as the "set of unearned advantages that individuals who identify as the gender they were assigned at birth accrue solely due to having a cisgender identity."[22]

These "unearned advantages" accrue to cismen and ciswomen as a result of the alleged psychological comfort/ease they experience between their body and the gender they were assigned at birth. By contrast, we are asked to consider the extreme psychological distress transgender people report about being perceived as their assigned gender at birth. In other words, trans people's unique emotional struggle against the gender others *assume* them to be explains how they are marginalized on the axis of gender, and cisgender people are privileged.[23]

Gender nonconforming appearance or behavior is not a shield to the alleged benefits of cis privilege. This can be demonstrated by the fact that gender nonconforming lesbians and gay men are also said to benefit from cisgender privilege.[24] It is not merely that one does not want to or refuses to behave in accordance with her assigned gender. Being privileged or marginalized on the cis/trans axis of gender requires more than simple nonconformity.

To take the example of misgendering, it is thought that transgender people are more deeply and more justifiably injured by misgendering than cisgender people are. In a 2014 keynote address at the Creating Change conference of the National Gay and Lesbian Taskforce, actress and trans activist Laverne Cox claimed that misgendering a trans person–specifically, to call a transwoman a man– is an act of violence.[25] It's not just insulting to the trans person, it's an act of violence. Yet the only difference between a misgendered transwoman and a gender nonconforming woman who is frequently mistaken for a man is their respective gender identities. The first is trans and the second is cis. They both identify as women, but only one "woman's" experience is akin to violence. Measuring gender-based harm by internal reactions to external experiences is essentialist and individualist. If cisgender people's internal identities render them categorically privileged over transgender people, the cis theory of gender and privilege presents a wholly new way of conceiving of how social hierarchies are created and enforced.

A Structural Analysis of Cis Privilege and Trans Oppression

First, as an internal sense of self, gender identity is invisible. Whether a person is transgender or cisgender is not readily knowable by external observers. Some transgender people "pass," meaning that they do not appear transgender to the casual eye. Some cisgender people are gender nonconforming such that they appear as if they might identify as transgender. If your external appearance does not match your internal identity, you will be treated according to your appearance, not your identity. This is precisely how and why "misgendering" happens to both cis and trans people. Where transgender and cisgender status are easily confused, neither can be a reliable determinant of group-based privilege (or oppression).

Marilyn Frye's classic essay about oppression explains that:

[Oppression] has not to do with individual talent or merit, handicap or failure; it has to do with your membership in some category understood as a "natural" or "physical" category. The "inhabitant" of the "cage" is not an individual but a group, all those of a certain category. If an individual is oppressed, it is in virtue of being a member of a group or category of people that is systematically reduced, molded, immobilized. Thus, to recognize a person as oppressed, one has to see that individual *as* belonging to a group of a certain sort.[26]

In the terms of Frye's analysis, solidifying the categories of cisgender and transgender do not allow one "to see [the] individual as belonging to a group of a certain sort." There is no externally coherent unifying characteristic of an internal identity. This makes it impossible for trans people to constitute a group that can be "systematically reduced, molded, and immobilized."

Second, privilege and oppression must be measured by assessing socio-structural conditions that exploit bodies, labor, and minds. In attempt to align the concept of cisgender privilege with more commonly understood forms of privilege, "cis privilege" checklists in the style of Peggy McIntosh's iconic "White Privilege Knapsack" have proliferated on the internet.[27] The problem with this analogy is that there is no legal or economic history of class-based exploitation and exclusion by cisgender people of transgender people to support this inversion of concepts.

For example, the labor of transgender people has not been structurally exploited by cisgender people. There is no systemic immobilization or pattern of resource extraction from transgender people that benefits cisgender people. There is no global slave trade in transgendered people that is controlled by cisgender people. By contrast, there is and/or has been a global slave trade of black and brown people by white people, and of female people by male people; sometimes both at once. Unpaid physical, domestic, sexual, and reproductive labor are collected from individuals belonging to the oppressed group; money and power accumulate in the hands of individuals belonging to the oppressor group. But none of these economic arrangements are defined by a power differential between cisgender people over transgender. Transgender people have certainly been victimized by these same forms of labor exploitation and resource extraction, but it is not *because* they are internally transgendered. It is *because* they are objectively black, brown, female, young, sick, disabled, or otherwise vulnerable to exploitation.

Transgender people have not been owned by cisgender people as a matter of generational practice. By contrast, there have been centuries of ownership of black or brown people by white people and of females by males (see marriage). There were, and still are, legally binding contracts that reduce certain kinds of bodies to private property that can be bought and sold. None of these contractual forms have been constructed for the purpose of naming "transgender" bodies the private property of "cisgender" people.

Transgender people have not been legally denied the right to vote, to own property, or to be formally educated by cisgender people. There are no laws currently or historically that prohibit transgender-identifying people from these fundamental rights. By contrast, the histories of the United States and many other countries are littered with laws explicitly prohibiting or limiting the rights of female people and black or brown people from voting, from owning property, and from being publicly educated.

The cis/trans theory of gender significantly diverges from all previous theories of power and politics. It proposes that privilege and oppression are meted out according to internal identity, rather than a history of legal and economic exploitation by one clearly definable group against another clearly definable group. The new gender binary completely reorders our understanding of privilege and oppression on the axis of gender.

REVERSE SEXISM

The cis/trans theory of gender does not describe class based inequality between men and women; males and females, respectively. Instead, cis/trans identity politics reimagines gender as a struggle between transgender people and cisgender people. Equalizing the status of cismen and ciswomen relative to trans people, cisgender people take on the collective status of oppressor under the new gender hierarchy. This position of superiority was previously occupied by males on the axis of gender. The new oppressors are both male and female, men and women, but they are all cis. The oppressed class is comprised of transgender people. Transgender people now represent the subordinate position on the axis of gender previously occupied by females. Members of the gender-oppressed group may be male or female, but they are all trans.

The cis/trans gender binary thus describes a mechanism whereby females may oppress males on the axis of gender. And it all makes perfect sense to cis/trans theorists because the females are cisgender and the males are transgender.[28] This is not radical social theory; it is reverse sexism. It erases the material and psychological history of exploitation and oppression that females have endured at the hands of males, continuing into the present.

In this theory, the sexed body is irrelevant to the new gender order; gendered socialization from birth is irrelevant. Internal gender identity is the only relevant criteria for consideration.

According to the cis/trans theory of gender, internal identity must be must be acknowledged and protected at all costs.

THE CIS THEORY OF GENDER AS LAW

As I was in process of writing this article, the Unites States Department of Justice (DOJ) and the Department of Education (DOE) released significant guidance about the application of "gender identity" to Title IX's prohibition on sex discrimination.[29] Without ever using the word cis or cisgender, this groundbreaking directive adopts the basic logic of the cis/trans theory of gender theory by redefining sex according to the concept of internal identity:

> The Departments treat a student's gender identity as the student's sex for purposes of Title IX and its implementing regulations. This means that a school must not treat a transgender student differently from the way it treats other students of the same gender identity.[30]

"Students of the same gender identity" can be read here as "cisgender students" to the same effect. Just as the cis/trans binary inverts the axis of gender from male over female to cisgender over transgender, so too does this novel legal interpretation of sex discrimination. Individuals are not similarly situated by sex, but by gender identity. Rather than differential treatment of males versus females, the legal meaning of sex becomes chiefly concerned with treatment on the basis of a newly articulated but statutorily undefined concept: *gender identity*. This reordering of concepts closely mirrors the cis/trans theory of gender's insistence that transgender people are oppressed relative to cis people.

The guidance continues:

> Under Title IX, a school must treat students consistent with their gender identity even if their education records or identification documents indicate a different sex.[31]

Here, the plain meaning of sex is directly supplanted by gender identity. Gender identity must be honored – not in addition to, but *regardless of* physical, legal, and experiential sex.

The newly established legal primacy of identity over bodies becomes glaringly obvious in the context of sex-segregated spaces. Yet a quick reading of Title IX's supporting regulations show that certain forms of sex segregation are not considered discriminatory if comparable facilities are offered to "students of the other sex." Specifically:

§ 106.33   Comparable facilities.
A recipient may provide separate toilet, locker room, and shower facilities on the basis of sex, but such facilities provided for students of one sex shall be comparable to such facilities provided for students of the other sex.[32]

The recent DOJ and DOE guidance seems to ignore or contradict this regulation to the extent that enforcement of sex segregation as previously allowed may be considered newly discriminatory when challenged by a student alleging to have a sex-discordant internal gender identity. Preventing sex discrimination now requires schools to realign their treatment of students according to gender identity, regardless of sex. In other words, *cisgender students* are the standard by which the treatment of transgender students must be judged. For example, if there is a difference in physical sex between two parties (male and female), but their gender identities are the same (both girl/woman or boy/man), previously justified sex segregation under Section 106.33 is no longer allowed. The legal dominance of gender identity thus demands that sex segregation be compromised in furtherance of gender identity parity, such that "students of the same gender identity" are treated equally.

In the same way that the essentialism of cis/trans gender theory makes it impossible for women to understand their oppression as anything but a natural reflection of their innate gender identities, this guidance makes it impossible for concerns about this new arrangement to be heard:

A school's Title IX obligation to ensure nondiscrimination on the basis of sex requires schools to provide transgender students equal access to educational programs and activities even in circumstances in which other students, parents, or community members raise objections or concerns. As is consistently recognized in civil rights cases, the desire to accommodate others' discomfort cannot justify a policy that singles out and disadvantages a particular class of students.[33]

All potential concerns and objections are equated with frivolous "discomfort" that cannot be accommodated. As if the DOJ and the DOE, in all of their infinite wisdom about the shifting sands of gender theory, have already considered then disposed of every conceivable protest. No request to return to sex segregation as previously allowed under section 106.33 will be heard. Objections are preemptively silenced by this guidance.

Again, female humans who might report that their experiences identifying with their assigned gender are oppressive and traumatic must be ignored. Girls who do not want to share sex-segregated space with male-bodied people must be dismissed as intolerant and old-fashioned: *"As is consistently recognized in civil rights cases, the desire to accommodate others' discomfort cannot justify a policy that singles out and disadvantages a particular class of students."* By decree of the federal government, female students' objections to the infiltration of the oppressor class (males) into lawfully sex-segregated spaces have no standing. Transgender-identifying males cannot be thought of as members of the oppressor class; they are marginalized (transgender) girls who are being treated differently than "other students of the same gender identity" (cisgender girls).

The guidance formalizes the cis theory of gender and its frustratingly myopic view of gender as a freely chosen internal identity. This is why it attempts to preempt all interpretations of sex discrimination that would reference the body or the lived experience of gender socialization. Acknowledging either would undermine the essentialism required to maintain gender as nothing more than an internal identity.

CONCLUSION

The cis/trans gender binary replaces decades, maybe centuries, of feminist analysis in favor of radically altering the axis of gender. While feminism recognizes gender essentialism as the ideology that enables male supremacy, cis/trans theory reduces gender to a revelatory expression of individual existential destiny. Female-oriented concerns about bodies and the reification of sex-based social roles are shoved aside so that the new hierarchy of cisgender versus transgender may be installed.

Instead of challenging the ideological and structural foundations of power disparities between male humans and female humans, the cis/trans binary's intense focus on self-perception closes down all material, historical, and socialization-based analyses of gendered hierarchies. Its simplistic essentialism cannot handle context-based criticisms of gender or identity. The cis/trans theory of gender neglects to consider the psychology of coerced assimilation; the invisibility of internal identity, the embodied reality of the sex, and the institutionalized supports of law and industry that undergird similar claims to class-based privilege and exploitation.

As a result, this reconceptualization of gender fails to offer either a practical or a theoretical improvement in our understanding of the politics of oppression. It provides no insight into and no explanation for the violence and exploitation women as a group experience at the hands of men as a group. Worse than harmless impotence, however, it inverts the axis of gender such that females can be privileged over males while cismen and ciswomen become gendered equals.

Because cis/trans theory reduces the concept of gender to a disembodied mind-state, it becomes impossible for women to talk about being born into a female body as a gendered experience. It becomes impossible for females to articulate how internalizing femininity is both harmful and artificially constructed without insulting or undermining transgender identities. If the cis/trans theory of gender identity is enforceable per recent guidance from the DOJ and DOE, it will successfully undermine the plain meaning of sex under Title IX. Sex segregation will become mere "gender identity" segregation. Sex discrimination will become "gender identity" discrimination. The cis/trans theory of gender represents a reversal of both concepts and progress towards the liberation of women from the shackles of socially constructed gender. It is a Trojan horse.

---

[1] *Oxford Dictionary* definition of "cisgender." Accessed May 1, 2016, http://www.oxforddictionaries.com/us/definition/american_english/cisgender.

[2] *Merriam-Webster Dictionary* definition of "cisgender." Accessed May 1, 2016, http://www.merriam-webster.com/dictionary/cisgender.

[3] Urban Dictionary defines "cis" as *Short for 'cisgender' (opposite of 'transgender'), used to describe someone whose gender identity matches their anatomical gender at birth.* Accessed March 23, 2016, http://www.urbandictionary.com/define.php?term=cis.

[4] The term "woman" is defined in this essay as the *political class* women, historically constructed and socially intended to describe adult female humans. As a practical matter, it includes every person who was socialized from birth to embody the gendered role (girl).

[5] Cordelia Fine, *Delusions of Gender: How Our Minds, Society, and Neurosexism Create Difference.* New York: W.W. Norton, 2010.

[6] "*A priori* justification is a type of epistemic justification that is…independent of experience." Stanford Encyclopedia of Philosophy. Accessed June 8, 2016. http://plato.stanford.edu/entries/apriori/#WhaSorProPriJusKno

[7] Fine, cited above in Note 5.

[8] For example, see "agender" and "nonbinary" identities.

[9] Sunnivie Brydum, "The True Meaning of the Word 'Cisgender' It's not complicated: Cisgender is the opposite of transgender," *The Advocate*, July 31 2015. Accessed March 24, 2015, http://www.advocate.com/transgender/2015/07/31/true-meaning-word-cisgender

[10] Paris Lees, "Caitlyn Jenner: a life-affirming, provocative and downright fabulous *Vanity Fair* cover," *The Guardian*, June 2, 2015. Accessed May 1, 2016, http://www.theguardian.com/tv-and-radio/2015/jun/01/caitlyn-jenner-vanity-fair-cover-life-affirming. "Caitlyn, like Kellie, has always been a woman. Yes, even when they were 'fathering' children. Gender is what's inside – and for Caitlyn, finally on the outside too."

[11] This is also reflected in the claim that one's "right to exist" is being denied whenever the concept of gender identity is challenged. People refusing to engage in discussion about gender identity have said, "we will not debate our right to exist." Here, gender is considered essential to human existence.

[12] Sheryl Sandberg, *Lean In: Women, Work, and the Will to Lead*. New York: Alfred A. Knopf, 2013.

[13] Fabian Ochsenfeld, "Why Do Women's Fields of Study Pay Less? A Test of Devaluation, Human Capital, and Gender Role Theory," *European Sociological Review*, (2014) 30 (4): 536-548. doi: 10.1093/esr/jcu060

[14] Jessica Valenti, *He's a Stud, She's a Slut, and 49 Other Double Standards Every Woman Should Know*. Seal Press, 2008.

[15] In 1989, the Supreme Court of the United States recognized the impossible double standard of gender in the workplace when it opined: "An employer who objects to aggressiveness in women but whose positions require this trait places women in an intolerable and impermissible Catch-22: out of a job if they behave aggressively and out of a job if they do not. Title VII lifts women out of this bind." Price Waterhouse v. Hopkins (490 U.S. 228, 251).

16 John Stuart Mill, "The Subjection of Women." London, 1869.

17 Andrea Dworkin, *Right-Wing Women*. Perigee Trade, 1983.

18 Betty Friedan, *The Feminine Mystique*. New York: Norton, 1963.

19 Carl Ratner, *Macro Cultural Psychology: A Political Philosophy of Mind*. New York: Oxford University Press, 2011.

20 Eileen L. Zurbriggen, "Objectification, Self-Objectification, and Societal Change," in *Journal of Social and Political Psychology*, 2013, Vol. 1(1), doi:10.5964/jspp.v1i1.94

21 Accessed online May 30, 2016, http://jspp.psychopen.eu/article/view/94/html

22 Marilyn Frye, "Oppression," in *The Politics of Reality*. Trumansburg, NY: The Crossing Press, 1983, p. 8.

23 Wikipedia entry for "cisgender." Accessed March 24, 2016, https://en.wikipedia.org/wiki/Cisgender.

24 Sam Dylan Finch, "130+ Examples of Cis Privilege in All Areas of Life for You to Reflect On and Address" in *Everyday Feminism,* February 29, 2016. http://everydayfeminism.com/2016/02/130-examples-cis-privilege/]

25 Vanessa Vitiello Urquhart, "I'm a Butch Woman. Do I Have Cis Privilege?" *Slate* on-line magazine, December 26, 2014. Accessed May 1, 2016, http://www.slate.com/blogs/outward/2014/12/26/do_butch_lesbians_have_cisgender_privilege.html.

26 Speech accessed online August 2, 2016: http://thinkprogress.org/lgbt/2014/01/31/3235351/laverne-cox-loving-trans-people-revolutionary-act/

27 Marilyn Frye, "Oppression," *The Politics of Reality*, Trumansburg, NY: The Crossing Press, 1983, p. 7-8.

[28] For example, see, https://www.google.com/url?sa=t&rct=j&q=&esrc=s&source=web&cd=4&ved=0ahUKEwjw2fDBk5rNAhUBGx4KHbptAJ8QFgg0MAM&url=https%3A%2F%2Fnew.oberlin.edu%2FdotAsset%2F2012181.pdf&usg=AFQjCNEK-38SteLnf8yngD9ky7T0TzttUw&sig2=RKysX3fwD6DoBo-aStlKfg.

[29] Another incoherent paradox of the cis/trans gender binary is, on the one hand, that "transwomen are women" exactly the same as all other women; any suggestion to the contrary is transphobia. On the other hand, in order for cisgender women to have gendered privilege over transwomen, we must simultaneously acknowledge that cis and trans women are different.

[30] "Dear Colleague Letter on Transgender Students" issued by the US Department of Justice Civil Rights Division and the US Department of Education Office for Civil Rights, dated May 16, 2016. Accessed on June 5, 216: https://www.justice.gov/opa/pr/us-departments-justice-and-education-release-joint-guidance-help-schools-ensure-civil-rights

[31] Ibid, p. 2.

[32] Ibid, p. 3.

[33] Legal Code of Federal Regulations: 34 C.F.R. §106.33. http://www2.ed.gov/policy/rights/reg/ocr/edlite-34cfr106.html

[34] "Dear Colleague Letter," page 2. Cited above in Note 28.

CHAPTER 5

TRANSGENDER RIGHTS: THE ELIMINATION OF THE HUMAN RIGHTS OF WOMEN

GallusMag

Removing the legal right of women to organize politically against sex-based oppression by males

Removing the legal right of women to assemble outside the presence of men

Removing the legal right of women to educational programs created for women outside the presence of men

Eliminating data collection of sex-based inequalities in areas where females are underrepresented

Elimination of sex-based crime statistics

Eliminating athletic programs and sports competition for women and girls

Removing the legal right of women to be free from the presence of men in areas of public accommodation where nudity occurs

Elimination of grants, scholarships, board and trustee designations, representative positions, and affirmative programs for women

Removing the legal right of women to create reproductive clinics, rape crisis services, support groups, or any organizations for females

Eliminating media and all public discourse specific to females

Removal of the right of journalists to report the sex, and history, of subjects

Eliminating the legal right of lesbians to congregate publicly

Elimination of lesbian-specific organizations and advocacy groups

Removing the legal right of women to free speech related to sex roles and gender

Elimination of the legal right of women to protection from state-enforced sex-roles (appearance/behavior/thought)

Elimination of the legal right of girls to protection from state-enforced sex-roles in public education

Elimination of the patient right of dependent females to hospital/facility bed assignments separate from males

Elimination of the right of dependent females to prefer female providers for their intimate personal care requirements

Elimination of the human right of female prisoners under state confinement to be housed separately from male prisoners

Unlike any other "social justice" venture in history, Transgender Rights are unique in that they are completely based on eliminating the human rights of women. Transgender Rights are the "right" to eliminate the human rights of women. But how can such a relatively small group eliminate the legal human rights of half of the human race? Because the transgender politic is an anti-female politic, and as such receives blanket support from all male sectors who profit from the elimination of human rights for females: the state, the conservative politic, the liberal politic, the gay politic, the "queer" politic, academia, business, commerce, media.

Originally published July 11, 2013 gendertrender.wordpress.com. Used with permission.

CHAPTER 6

TRANSGENDER EQUALITY VERSUS WOMEN'S EQUALITY: A CLASH OF RIGHTS?
WRITTEN EVIDENCE SUBMITTED BY SHEILA JEFFREYS TO THE UK TRANSGENDER EQUALITY INQUIRY, OCTOBER 14, 2015

Sheila Jeffreys

Anthology Editor's Introduction: The Women and Equalities Committee was appointed by the UK House of Commons on 3 June 2015 to examine the expenditure, administration and policy of the Government Equalities Office (GEO) and associated public bodies on the issue of transgender equality. The Committee has the same powers as other departmental select committees, but has been established only until the end of the current Parliament. The Women and Equalities Committee report on Transgender Equality makes over 30 recommendations in a wide range of policy areas. The committee calls on the Government to take action to ensure full equality for trans people, emphasizing the need to update existing legislation; provide better services, especially in the National Health Service; and improve confidence in the criminal justice system. An inquiry was launched with a call for individuals and organizations to submit oral or written evidence on issues of transgender equality. This is Sheila Jeffreys' written evidence to the inquiry.

EXPERTISE:

I AM THE author of a number of influential books, book chapters and scholarly articles on transgenderism including the 2014 book Gender Hurts: a feminist analysis of the politics of transgenderism (Routledge). Gender Hurts has been featured on Woman's Hour in the UK and in The New Yorker, The Nation, Village Voice, and numerous other media outlets. See also my article 'The Politics of the Toilet: a feminist analysis of the 'degendering' of a women's space' (2014)

http://www.sheilajeffreys.com/wp-content/uploads/2014/08/toilet-article. pdfpublished- version.pdf (http://www.sheilajeffreys.com/wp-content/uploads/2014/08/toilet-article.pdfpublished-version.pdf)

TRANSGENDER EQUALITY VERSUS WOMEN'S EQUALITY: A CLASH OF RIGHTS?

SUMMARY:

- The submission argues that any discussion of transgender equality should consider the ways in which such equality might violate women's equality rights.
- The submission argues that men who transgender should be not be treated in law and policy as if they are women if such treatment enables them to gain access to spaces set aside to ensure women's dignity, security and right to organize as a specific rights bearing group, such as women's refuges, women's toilets, women's prisons, women only political groups and activities.
- The submission requests that ensuring women's equality rights in relation to women's spaces should inform the committee's deliberations and that a policy guideline aimed at protecting such spaces should be drawn up.

1. Transgender equality rights:

This submission supports legislation and policy that seeks to prevent discrimination against persons who transgender. All persons should have rights of employment and access to services irrespective of how they choose to dress or present themselves in public. It supports the rights of those in a category called 'transgender' to protection from discrimination in the exercise of their proclivities. Gender is not the same as sex. Women require protection as a sex, as it is on the basis of and through their sex that women are discriminated against and suffer disadvantage. Women do not occupy low status on the basis of their 'gender', i.e. aspects of appearance and behavior, but on the basis of sex. The protection of a category of men to express their 'gender' should not conflict with women's right to protection from discrimination as persons of the female sex.

2. Omission of women's interests in this inquiry:

Despite the fact that this committee's name specifically references women, women's equality rights are not included in the terms of reference for this inquiry. The inquiry does not refer to the effect that 'equality' for men who transgender might have upon women's equality. Women's and feminist groups are generally not invited to contribute to consultations on transgender rights as if they would have nothing relevant to say, despite the fact that men may, under the idea of transgender equality gain the right to be recognized in law as 'women'. Women are the 'absent referent', not officially referred to, despite the fact that it is 'women' that the majority of those persons who wish to express their 'gender rights' seek to emulate. In this submission I have taken the liberty of writing from the point of view of the category of persons, women, whose interests are usually omitted from consideration in relation to this issue.

3. Clash of rights:

i. The demand for transgender equality may create a 'clash of rights' in which the rights demanded by one group of people can substantially endanger the rights of another group (Sniderman, Fletcher, Russell and Tetlock, 1997). In a clash of rights some adjudication has to be made as to whether the group involved in the rights demand that compromises the rights of another group, can be accommodated in human rights norms.

ii. In the case of the campaign for transgender equality the main category of persons seeking rights are persons of the male sex, that is, those responsible for the violation of women's rights to, for example, live free from violence and the threat of death, to freedom of movement and expression, to freedom from discrimination (Romito, 2008). These male persons do not generally just claim that they are disadvantaged in their own right as members of the category 'transgender', but that they actually are physically members of the female sex, women, as in the demand by male bodied transgenders that they should be able to enter spaces such as toilets, set aside for women. A most serious clash of rights is likely to occur when members of one rights-bearing category claim to actually be members of another category.

iii. A clash of rights occurs also when members of one rights-bearing category, persons who transgender, promote ideas and practices which are recognized in international law as harmful to the equality of another group. Persons who transgender do not change their biological sex but follow the norms in outward appearance that are called in human rights terms 'gender stereotypes'. The promotion within the politics of transgenderism of the idea that an essential 'gender' exists and that the appropriate 'gender' for persons of the female sex is represented in particular forms of clothing and mannerisms creates a clash with the rights of women. In international law gender stereotypes are recognized as being in contradiction to the interests of women. The importance attributed to the elimination of these stereotypes is exemplified in the wording of the United Nations Convention on the Elimination of All forms of Discrimination against Women (CEDAW), which feminists advocated for throughout the 1970s until its promulgation in 1979. Article 5 of CEDAW calls upon States Parties, to **'take all appropriate measures' to 'modify the social and cultural patterns of conduct of men and women, with a view to achieving the elimination of prejudice and customary and all other practices which are based on the idea of the inferiority or the superiority of either of the sexes or on stereotyped roles for men and women'** (United Nations, 1979: Article 5). 'Stereotyped roles' are, according to feminist critics of the practice, the very foundation and sine qua non of transgenderism, and the notion of 'gender identity' (see Jeffreys, 2014). The promotion of such stereotypes by men who transgender is harmful to women's equality and this could be seen as a reason why 'transgender equality' inevitably conflicts with women's rights.

4. Why men who transgender should not have access to women's spaces:

i. Men who transgender should not have access to women's spaces because they do not change their biological sex and do not become female. Moreover, the majority of these male-bodied persons (85%) retain their genitalia (Transgender Law Centre, 2005). There is no requirement in UK legislation such as the 2004 Gender Recognition Act, that recognition as transgender must involve hormonal or surgical treatment. Thus male persons who access women's spaces may be physically attired and express their gender identity only through the assumption of feminine stereotypes, i.e. gender, in their appearance.

ii. The behavior of men who transgender towards women resembles the behavior of men who do not transgender in respect of male pattern violence i.e. some male-bodied transgenders, like their non- transgendering counterparts, have a pattern of violent practices towards women such as murder, rape, sexual harassment. The linked website provides a collection of newspaper accounts of sexual violence against women and girls by men who transgender: https://outofmypantiesnow.wordpress.com/2013/10/28/when-is-90-not-substantially-all/ (https://outofmypantiesnow.wordpress.com/2013/10/28/when-is-90-not-substantially-all/) The response from transgender rights campaigners is sometimes that the men who are violent are not genuine transgenders, but since transgenderism is not a biological condition but a mental one, adjudication of genuineness is not possible. Increasing numbers of those who have transgendered are deciding that they have made a mistake and engaging in 'detransition', which reveals that the mental condition can be temporary and evanescent. A google search reveals 19,600 pages of resources for persons who seek to detransition.

5. Women's spaces: Three varieties of spaces deliberately segregated to protect women's dignity and security will be considered here: women's refuges, women's toilets and women's prisons.

i.   **Women's refuges:** Women's refuges were established to create a place of refuge for women who have suffered violence from men. From their inception the majority of refuges have sought to offer women spaces where they are not forced to interact with men in order to enable them to recover from the trauma they have suffered. Unfortunately, as a result of the campaign for transgender equality, refuge provision for women is increasingly being opened up to men who 'identify' as women through the adoption of stereotyped feminine accouterments. Some of these men have histories of violence against women and media reports of court cases involved rape by such persons is starting to emerge. In a Canadian case a man called Christopher Hambrook was found guilty of sexually assaulting 'four vulnerable females between the ages of five and 53 in Montreal and Toronto over the past 12 years' in two shelters for homeless women and women escaping domestic violence (Pazzano, 2014). He accessed the shelters by claiming to identify as a woman called 'Jessica'. Clear dangers arise when women residents are forced to share bathrooms and bedrooms with violent men who profess to have gender identities.

ii. **Women's toilets:** Women's toilets constitute spaces in which women are particularly vulnerable and for this reason, to protect women's dignity and safety, they have tended to be segregated ever since women's rights campaigners in the nineteenth century demanded such provision. As a result of campaigns for transgender equality, men who cross-dress and transgender are increasingly gaining the right to access women's toilets.

There are a quite surprising number of cases in which men wearing women's clothing have been arrested for engaging in behavior in women's toilets that harms women. This webpage provides information and links to numerous occasions on which men dressed in stereotyped women's clothing have engaged in sexual violence in women's bathrooms/toilets: https://gendertrender.wordpress.com/2011/05/28/men-love-the-ladies-restroom-transgender- edition/ (https://gendertrender.wordpress.com/2011/05/28/ men-love-the-ladies-restroom- transgender-edition/) l The range of acts they engage in includes secret photographing of women using the toilets and showers, making audio recordings of women urinating or defecating, peeping at women from adjacent stalls or under stall dividers, demanding that women recognize them as women and becoming aggressive if women do not, luring children into women's toilets in order to assault them, and sexual assault. In a British case, a man dressed up as a 'mannequin with a mask and a wig' to enter a cubicle in the women's toilets in a shopping mall, where he 'performed' an unspecified 'sexual act' (Ninemsn staff, 2011). The 22-year-old man told police he 'found the sound of women on the toilet sexually exciting'. The man had filmed women's feet from beneath cubicle doors on his mobile phone, and recorded the sound of a flushing toilet.

iii. **Women's prisons:** Women's prisons are spaces in which women are confined and unable to escape unwanted attention from males. The fact that women may have to share cells and shower facilities with men who are seeking to transgender could be seen as an extra layer of punishment. Male prisoners in western countries are using human rights laws successfully to gain access to transgender treatment at public expense in prison, and the right to then transfer to the women's estate. These men are often precisely those who are most violent and dangerous to women's safety, having been convicted of grave crimes including the murder of women. In 2009, an appeal from an unnamed, violent male prisoner in the UK to be moved to a women's prison was successful. The petitioner in this case was found guilty in 2001 of the manslaughter of his male lover who was strangled with a pair of tights, allegedly for refusing to fund the murderer's sex change surgery. He was sentenced to five years imprisonment. Five days after his release he attempted to rape a female stranger and was sent back to prison (Allen, 2009). The man's lawyer told the court that the crimes were all linked to desperation to become a woman'. The judge declared that 'her (sic) continued detention in a male prison is in breach of her rights under Article 8 [the right to private and family life] under the European Convention on Human Rights'. The notion of human rights is trivialized thereby. In response to the judgment, new guidelines were issued for the treatment of prisoners seeking gender reassignment in UK prisons in March 2011, which enabled prisoners to have treatment and to be located in women's prisons. Unfortunately, there seems to be no acknowledgement here of the more serious and pressing right of women to avoid being compulsorily housed with violent men.

CONCLUSION

Persons of one biological sex who consider that they have a 'gender identity' stereotypically associated with the other sex do suffer discrimination and need protection. A problem arises, however, when 'gender' and 'sex' are confused, to the extent that male-bodied persons gain a right to enter spaces set aside for women. In such a case a clash of rights is created. Persons who wish to express a gender identity not usually stereotypically associated with their biological sex need to be accommodated in ways that protect them, but do not conflict with the rights of women.

RECOMMENDATIONS:

That the protection of women's rights to dignity and security and to separate women's spaces should be an underlying principle guiding the deliberations and recommendations of this committee. That the committee should establish a guideline that ensures such protection.

REFERENCES

Allen, Vanessa (2009, 5 September). Transsexual killer and attempted rapist wins 'human rights' battle to be moved to women's prison. London: The Daily Mail. http://www.dailymail. co.uk/news/article-1211165/Transexual-prisoner-wins-High-Court-battle-moved-womens-jail. html

(http://www.dailymail.co.uk/news/article-1211165/Transexual-prisoner-wins-High-Court-battle- moved-womens-jail.html)

Jeffreys, Sheila (2005). Beauty and Misogyny: harmful cultural practices in the west. London: Routledge. Jeffreys, Sheila (2014). Gender Hurts: a feminist analysis of the politics of transgenderism. London: Routledge.

Ninemsn Staff (2011, 18 April). Man dressed as mannequin found in mall toilet. Australia: Nine News. http://news.ninemsn.com.au/world/8238380/man-dressed-as-mannequin-found-in-mall-toilet

Pazzano, Sam (2014, 15 February). A sex predator's sick deception. Toronto Sun. http://www.torontosun.com/2014/02/15/a-sex-predators-sick-deception

Romito, Patrizia (2008). A Deafening Silence. Hidden Violence against Women and Children. Bristol: The Policy Press.

Transgender Law Centre (2005). Peeing in Peace: a Resource Guide for Transgender Activists and Allies. San Francisco Transgender Law Centre. 20 August 2015

http://data.parliament.uk/writtenevidence/committeeevidence.svc/evidencedocument/women-and-equalities-committee/transgender-equality/written/19512.html

Republished by permission of the author.

CHAPTER 7

AN AFRICAN-AMERICAN WOMAN REFLECTS ON THE TRANSGENDER MOVEMENT

Nuriddeen Knight

SUPPORTERS OF TRANSGENDER ideology believe that they are freeing people from restrictive understandings of gender. In reality, the more our society tries to free itself from gender stereotypes, the more it becomes enslaved to them. By saying that people can be born in a body of the wrong gender, transgender activists are saying there is a set of feelings that are only allocated to women and another set for men.

My parents never bought *Cinderella*, *The Little Mermaid*, or *Snow White*. They weren't stories told in our house or movies played on our TV. There was no Princess Tiana then, but my parents only showed us films with "colored" princesses: Mulan (Asian), Pocahontas (Native American), and Jasmine (Arab). We also loved the African animals of *The Lion King*. We never idealized whiteness in our house. None of this was done overtly, though it may have been intentional. Only in retrospect did I realize the kind of tacit self-love my parents were embedding in us.

Still, it wasn't enough. Around the age of thirteen, I realized that the world was telling me that light skin and "good hair" were better, skinny was better, and whiteness was better. In fleeting moments, I wished I could be white. I begged my mom to straighten my hair, and she did. I went through sometimes unreasonable means to lose weight, and I tried to keep my somewhat light skin out of the sun.

If I had gone to my parents begging them to be white, I think they might have laughed, cried, comforted me, and worried what they did wrong as parents. But what if I had told them not only that I wanted to be white but that I actually *was* white? What if I had declared that the race of my body simply didn't match that of my mind? I think they would've been deeply troubled.

THE BLUEST EYE

The famous Toni Morrison book, *The Bluest Eye*, parallels this idea. The main character, Pecola, is a dark-skinned girl who desperately wants blue eyes. By the end of the story, she *has* blue eyes—or at least, she believes that she does. We, as the readers, don't applaud this. In fact, by the end of the novel, we think Pecola has lost her mind. We know that it's not really blue eyes she wants, she wants something much deeper—love, acceptance, respect, honor . . . the intangible human desires we all crave but are not equally given. We know that she has not received this, but instead is a victim of perpetual abuse, and there is no easy solution to her problems.

But what if it *were* really possible for me to become white or for Pecola to acquire blue eyes? Would that be the end of the story—the happily ever after? Would changing our physical appearance magically erase all our issues of self-esteem and self-worth?

No, of course not. The eyes and the skin color were never the problem: racism and abuse were. We would only be putting a Band-Aid on the real issue. The many men and women who "passed" as white during America's shameful Jim Crow era may have gained the social privileges bestowed by being white, but they also lost their heritage, their family ties, and their integrity, thanks to the lie they were forced to tell every single day.

RACE, SEX, AND GENDER

But what if, instead of wanting to be white, I wanted to be a man? What if, instead of crying to my parents that I was really a white person, I told them that I was really a man and that I desperately wanted to change my body to match my mind? If, in this scenario, you think that my parents should applaud my courage, accept my new gender identity, and run to the nearest surgeon, please ask yourself: "Why?"

There's no doubt that race and sex are two very different issues. Race is a social construct invented during the era of slavery. Before the European enslavement of Africans, there were no united "black people" in Africa, and there were no united "white people" in Europe. Thanks to slavery, the labels of black and white became a convenient way to continue oppression, but they are a relatively new way of identifying one's self.

But sex is not a human invention. Yes, gender roles are culturally created. Still, that does not erase the fact that every human being (except intersex individuals, who represent a tiny percentage) is born with a distinctive set of physical and biological attributes that constitute them as male or female. That is a truth that cannot be erased with time.

Self-Love as a Virtue

When we want to be something other than our true authentic selves, that is self-hate. A black person who wants to be white is practicing self-hate, and so is a man who wants to be a woman or a woman who wants to be a man. We live in a climate of incredible self-absorption, but we won't encourage people to love the body they're in? We tell women to love their curves and love their age and love the skin they're in but we won't tell them (and men) to love the sex of their bodies?

We cry out about the horrors of female genital mutilation, yet we allow the practice in our backyard. We ignore the cries of patients who wake up from surgery full of remorse. We ignore their suffering and delude them with the promise of quick fixes and instant happiness. At *The Federalist,* Stella Morabito quotes a man who, upon waking up from his surgery thought, "What have I done? What on earth have I done?"[1]

Eerily, in his *Vanity Fair* interview, Jenner echoes this man as he recalls his own thoughts after his ten-hour face feminization surgery: "What did I just do? What did I just do to myself?"[2] Another post-op patient says in an online forum, "I am grieving at how I have mutilated my body." Here at *Public Discourse,* Walt Heyer has written about the regret he experienced after his sex-change surgery.[3]

We are playing a dangerous game. A man or a boy whose penis has been surgically removed can't go back in time and return to his God-given nature. What if we spent the money we spend on surgery and drugs on therapy and learning self-love? We should be teaching a message of self-acceptance instead of buying into the latest surgeries or believing we're born in the wrong body.

The Slavery of Freedom

Paradoxically, the more our society tries to free itself from gender stereotypes, the more it becomes enslaved to them. By saying that people can be born in a body of the wrong gender, transgender activists are saying there is a set of feelings that are only allocated to women and another set for men. Therefore, they believe, those who feel things that do not conform to their sex's acceptable set of feelings must outwardly change their gender to match their mind.

Why are we colluding with narrow ideas of femininity or masculinity? What does it mean to "feel" like a woman? Should we question that idea as much as we have questioned ideas of a "woman's place" or a "man's role"? When did we come to accept the idea of "gendered thoughts" or "gendered feelings"?

As a linguistic student of Arabic, I recently learned that women and men are not opposite so much as they are complementary. The idea that one could feel *opposite* from one's biological gender is actually nonsensical, linguistically and in reality. Men and women are different, but not so categorically that one can feel as though he or she were the other. We are full human beings, free to think as we wish without questioning our authenticity as men or as women.

"Bruce lives a lie. *She* is not a lie," says Bruce Jenner in his interview with Diane Sawyer. Bruce, now Caitlyn, Jenner, told Sawyer that he has a "soul of a woman," that he spent his life "running away from who I was." At the time of that interview, Jenner's voice and appearance are strikingly different from what they have been in the past, but not drastically enough to give the illusion of being female. Admittedly, Jenner looks much more feminine on the cover of *Vanity Fair*. Still, if he chooses to go through gender "reassignment" surgery, he will not become a woman but merely an illusion of one. As Dr. Paul McHugh, former psychiatrist-in-chief for Johns Hopkins Hospital, has written, "'Sex change' is biologically impossible. People who undergo sex-reassignment surgery do not change from men to women or vice versa. Rather, they become feminized men or masculinized women."

People opposed to the transgender movement are often accused of being bigots. In truth, I—like many others—harbor no hate for people who suffer from gender identity disorder. Rather, I feel deep compassion and concern for them in their suffering. As someone in the field of psychology, I hope we can one day find a more holistic, less invasive means to treat this disorder. However, I will concede that I find something quite insulting about the entire phenomenon. It is an insult to the other sex to think that by "dressing like them," "talking like them," or claiming to "feel like them," you can therefore *be* them. Being a man is about more than wearing a suit, and being a woman is about more than putting on makeup. If we feel confined in our bodies, perhaps it is not our bodies we should try to correct but our spirits we should reconnect with.

Originally published in Public Discourse, a collection of essays from The Witherspoon Institute, editors Serena Sigillito and Ryan T. Anderson, June 4th, 2015. Re-published with permission.

---

1 http://thefederalist.com/2014/11/11/trouble-in-transtopia-murmurs-of-sex-change-regret/

2 http://www.vanityfair.com/hollywood/2015/06/caitlyn-jenner-bruce-cover-annie-leibovitz

3 http://www.thepublicdiscourse.com/2015/04/14905/

CHAPTER 8

FEMALE ERASURE: A SAMPLER

Ava Park

I HAVE THE pleasure and, yes, the pain of running one of a very few fully functioning brick-'n-mortar goddess temples in the modern world. A poster I saw years ago showed a grizzled old cowhand, bullet hole in his hat, dirty face beaten from a hard ride on a long trail, the caption reading: "Well, they's just a whole lotta things they purty much failed to mention when I first signed on with this outfit."

Insert Ava in flowing gold robes instead of jeans, leafy little goddess crown instead of cowboy hat (yes, a few bullet holes in that crown by now!), and I could say "purty much" the same thing. There are a "whole lotta things" I didn't know I was getting into when twelve years ago I blithely said to my best friend, Marcy, "Hey, let's have a goddess temple!"

Note: I will use the phrase "people with penises" in this essay without a shred of sarcasm, but simply as an accurate descriptor of a group of human beings.

Since I was a little girl, there has always been a person with a penis telling me what I could and could not do with my body, my mind, and my life. This is the essence of erasure … of self, of agency, of freedom to create one's life as one chooses.

The concepts of "female erasure" and "patriarchal reversal" are related. A patriarchal reversal is the "erasing of truth" by turning reality on its head, asking you to accept as real that craziness; and in so doing, also requiring that you "forget" the original truth, and instead incorporate seamlessly into your thinking the new lie. It is the first order of business in the very profitable business of breaking and controlling a populace.

My favorite patriarchal reversal, heard all over the world every day, is: "Coke it's the real thing!" Coke is not the real thing. Coke is a toxic brew of stolen water, sugar and chemicals, sold at appalling profit. Water is the real thing … or perhaps mother's milk. Either way …

68

Erased: honoring of Mother's gift of nourishment in favor of a fake, overpriced, health-ruining substitute by a corporation run mostly by people with penises.

Female erasures and reversals of reality are everywhere. They are the murky sea in which humans now swim, the oppressive air we have sucked for centuries. My father was the first person with a penis who attempted to erase the idea of my own female bodily sovereignty. When you're five and you're "daddy's little girl," daddy is god … but then I turned eleven and came into my first moon.

My mother had been taught by her mother that menstruation was a "curse," so she was quite progressive when she told me that this "coming into womanhood" – the physical evidence of the very identity of the adult human female — "was no big deal." She meant well, but the message I received was: "Being a woman in this world is a trivial matter; you are of no particular consequence."

Erased: the knowing that I as a female could have any importance in life.

She explained the practical matters of handling the inconvenience of being female. In a woman-honoring culture, being female would not be "inconvenient," but we say "sanitary pads" and "feminine hygiene" because, in this culture, Woman's menstrual blood is considered so dirty that it must be cleaned up so we may all be "sanitary" and "hygienic."

Erased: the original, ancient wisdom that Woman's blood is holy, sacred, clean honored as the place from which all human life comes.

Seeing my first tampon commercial, I asked my mother if I might have those instead of pads, so, you know, I could keep swimming, horseback riding and generally continuing to live my life during my period. *"I'll have to ask your father,"* she answered.

"Whaat!?"

Up until this point in my short little life, I had assumed that I "owned" my body. Now at age eleven I realized the shocking truth: my body, including my vagina and the decisions about what could be inserted into it, clearly belonged not to me and not even to my mother but rather to the person in the house with a penis. He ended up refusing permission, because, you know … "Ethel, she might not be a virgin after that!"

This was the first time I experienced what I would now refer to as "sacred rage." *My dad owned my female body!* That opening "down there" was a receptacle for *his* wishes. My own wishes were of no importance. The person with the penis was the decider of the possibilities the female vagina might experience.

Erased: the wants, needs, and desires of a young girl about how she might live as a female in her own body.

In my first act of civil disobedience to my pa (penis authority?), I begged a tampon from a girlfriend, and, secretly, alone in the bathroom, feeling like some kind of first-time criminal, taught myself how to use it. My defiant refusal to tell my mother what I'd done (telling my father was altogether too terrifying a thought!) was my first conscious lie. I had always been a straightforward child; having now to choose between honesty and owning my own body was just the first of the many impossible choices between truth-telling and bodily sovereignty that I as a female human would be forced to make throughout my life.

Erased: a young girl's natural integrity.

My family lived on Guam, and we helped to build the first Episcopalian church on that tiny island. In that church, and in every other, it was assumed that god was male. No other option was ever presented. My father (despite my complaints, let me assure you, a good-hearted man) and I studied the major world religions together, every one centered on a male god.

Erased: some 250,000 years (at least) **of Goddess veneration on the planet.**

Once, at school recess, we kids were given an "Indian Chief" costume with full-feathered headdress. I claimed it, proud to play the role of the tribe's chief. But the boys *and* the girls demanded: "Take that off! Only boys can be chiefs!"

Erased: a young girl's idea of herself as a leader.

The erasure was all around me, daily, in every conversation, in every TV ad and sitcom, in every teacher's teaching, in what I was allowed to wear, to say, to think, in my father's words … and in my mother's, too. Because female erasure was literally everywhere, I, like a fish swimming in water, could not see what was all around me. "Water? What water?" I absorbed through osmosis the regular pronouncements of the person in the house with a penis, chiefly:

"Act like a lady," which meant: be clean, be quiet, keep your legs together, show no negative feelings, be pleasant, smile, do not disagree with anything, be conscious constantly of other people's feelings. If your feelings appear to cause discomfort in anyone, particularly people with penises, suppress them immediately because your female feelings are of the least importance of all.

Erased: a young girl's free, outspoken, unself-conscious Maiden Self.

For my mother, there was the almost-daily comment from my father: "Don't get to be more trouble than you're worth!" This was always said "jokingly," but the silent fear in Mom's eyes told me everything I needed to know. This was no joke. She was part of the family, but permitted to remain only on my father's sufferance. The teaching was clear: *at his whim, the person with a penis had the power to eliminate from our family the person with a womb and vagina.* Oh … *I* had a womb and vagina. When I grew up, this would apply to "female me," as well.

Erased: a young girl's confidence in the female's secure and rightful place as Queen of the family.

The incredible patriarchal reversal here was this: it was *my father* who was *"the trouble"* … always spending our money foolishly, never paying the bills, always dragging us to hell-and-gone for buried treasure never found. If not for my blessed, steady, sensible mother hiding pennies from him, we would have been homeless and hungry half the time.

From as early as I can remember, perhaps age four, I was occasionally molested by people with penises — male babysitters, strangers on playgrounds, next-door neighbors, or men driving by in grocery store parking lots, masturbating, intending for me to see, waiting for the sexual thrill my shocked little face would give them.

Erased: a little girl's trust in men — both strangers *and* those she knew well.

In school, my history textbooks were about men: men making war, men being kings, men inventing stuff. Clearly, it was the people with penises who created the world as we knew it.

Erased: women from history.

As a young woman, I continued to study the major religions and philosophies, all still male-centric! I kept spiritually seeking because none seemed satisfying. They were all dried out, no joy, no juice. So … on to the next one. A single male, all alone on his throne, a god with a penis but no womb, has no Shakti, no life power. I had no idea I was searching for what, in my culture, had been …

Erased: The Great Mother, Queen of Heaven and Earth, and All Between and Beyond.

In my twenties, working as an office assistant, my first three employers made it clear that, to keep my job, I would have to "sleep with them." Be assured: there was no "sleeping" involved.

Erased: a young woman's clarity of thinking, of knowing what is actually happening, by classic patriarchal tactics of confusion and misnaming.

At first I resisted, but eventually a girl's gotta eat and pay the rent … so …

Erased: a young woman's ability to work and simply survive without being forced into sex slavery.

I worried about pregnancies that I did not want. Birth control was unreliable and legal abortions nearly impossible to obtain. Four decades later, women are still begging legislators, mostly people with penises, to make abortion available.

Erased: women's sovereignty over their own bodies.

Through my thirties, I weighed a hundred pounds and was, like every other woman I knew, trying to drop a couple more. Right now, at the supermarket checkout stand is a magazine to "help women get in shape." It is called *Zero Belly*. That's right. Zero. There is nothing less than "zero." Cultural obsession with female thinness has apparently reached its ultimate logical conclusion. Most women with no body fat cannot menstruate or become pregnant.

Erased: literally the entire natural female body, female fertility, not to mention females' daily pleasure and comfort in our own bodies.

During my entire working career, I was paid far less than males of my age doing the same job.

Erased: a woman's objective worth as an employee.

In the corporate world, I encountered many people with penises who thrust upon me (yes, I meant to say that) their "need" for my body, usually with some version of the phrase: "See (pointing to penis) what you do to me!" The people with penises were telling me, "The current condition of *my* body is somehow *your* fault and your responsibility to deal with." I complained about this to my mother and grandmother. They both laughed out loud. "Oh, we've heard that a million times!" Women being faulted for "what we do to men" is generational, going on for millennia.

Erased: men's responsibility for their own erections.

Fast-forward to the nineties; angry, and searching for a god I could believe in, I take off for Egypt and meet Sekhmet, Lioness Goddess, "Mother of Fierce Compassion." Thus began my formal studies of Goddess and women's spirituality. I learned that for my entire life I as a female had, in nearly every way, been …

Erased.

And I've been in a state of sacred rage ever since.

The Mother is the Creatrix of Life, the one who, through Her passion and creative powers, births life, then nurtures that life with unconditional love and giving. My friend, Vajra Ma, says, "Love is unconditional, but relationships are not." The Queen is the Architect of Life, the one with a vision for a life lived well. It is She Who has a plan for The Mother's creativity—which, to prevent the abuse of The Mother, must include boundaries instituted for the benefit of all life.

The Queen's life-affirming boundaries prevent the life-denying dominator from stealing what he wants. For men to dominate women, Woman's boundaries, one by one, must be eliminated. For patriarchy to exist, since it is The Queen in Woman Who maintains boundaries, it is The Queen in Woman Who must be crushed. Her ancient stories of good, strong women leading the people to peace, prosperity, and justice are erased by fairy tales teaching little girls and boys alike, "The Queen is evil." Where there is craziness in a culture—as is surely the case in America—be certain that the boundary-holding Queen archetype has been deliberately both denied and demonized in that culture.

Erased: Woman as Queen, holding good boundaries for the benefit of all life.

Father dead, no husband, and self-employed, there was no longer any "person with a penis" telling me what to do. Or so I thought. "Hey, let's start a goddess temple!"

So there I am at City Hall, applying for a business permit for a church called The Goddess Temple of Orange County. Here's how the meeting with the councilmembers, each one a person with a penis, went:

Councilman #1: *"Goddess Temple? Is this a joke?"*
Ava: "No. I am applying for a license to do business in this city."
Councilman #2: *"Is this a massage parlor?"*
Ava: "No, this is a religious organization for the veneration of Goddess."
Councilman #3: *"Goddess? There is no goddess … "*
Councilman #4: *"… so you cannot have a goddess temple."*
Councilman #5: *"Application denied."*

Erased: my religion. My spirituality. My human history …
… and their human history, too, come to think of it.

With persistence plus a bit of magic, we obtained our permit and began Sunday Goddess Services for women. Men told us that we couldn't have spiritual worship services that did not include them. "Exclusionary!" "Spirituality is for everyone!" Politely ("Don't piss off the men!"), we explained that our form of spirituality was grounded in, irrevocably tied to and expressed through our female bodies and Blood Mysteries, in the physical powers of menstruation, conception, gestation, giving birth, lactation, and menopause. Since much of our spiritual service consisted of women sharing the feelings and experiences that are a direct result of these powers of the female body, males, without these powers, were not able to participate in the same way.

"Well, you don't need to talk about those things to talk about god."

Erased: the very essence and nature of our women's spirituality.

The women working together to run our temple are called "priestesses." When answering the question, "What do you do?" with "I am a priestess," they are often met with confusion or even outright derisive laughter. "Priestess! What's a priestess?" Everyone knows what a priest is … but a *priestess*?

Erased: the very title of Woman's spiritual power and leadership on earth.

Time passed, we evolved. Our women's congregation voted to keep three of the four monthly Sunday Services for women only and have one mixed spiritual service a month to which they could bring their male family members and friends. It made sense to have a place in our spirituality where males could learn to replace dominator-model conditioning with the peace, power, and beauty of Goddess values, where they could enjoy that rarest of spiritual spaces in modern society, a space that holds the nearly-erased reality:

Woman is the Lifegiver of humanity; She does not bow to a male god, but honors The Great Mother of All, of which She is the human embodiment on earth.

Here is where we get to the point of the phrase *"people with penises."* People with penises called men had already told us that we were wrong to have women-only circles. But now a different group of people, also with penises, who called themselves "women," came to say that our women-only circles were great — "you definitely should keep men out!" but the problem, they told us, was that our definition of "Woman" was *"wrong."* I well remember an encounter in my office with a forceful person (with a penis) demanding entry: "We are women, too, dammit!"

"Do you have the potential to experience the Blood Mysteries of Woman? Of menstruation, conception, gestation, giving birth, lactation, menopause? Can you share in the understanding of and speak to any one of these aspects of female spirituality expressed in physical form and add a voice of experience to our circle with authority and wisdom?"

"No, but I am a woman nonetheless. Because I say I am."

Erased: the very essence of what humanity has always understood Woman to be, the carrier of life, the Holder of The Sacred Blood Mysteries for Humanity.

I would enjoy hearing myself called by the title "doctor." I've read a lot about medicine. I imagine I would make a very fine doctor. But I do not call myself "doctor." I do not have the training, experiences, and history of a doctor. I have not paid the life price to be a doctor. It is in no way a personal insult to me to deny me the right to use "doctor" on my resume. It is simply the educational reality of my life. Putting on a white coat and stethoscope would not make me a doctor. Claiming "doctor" on my resume would constitute fraud.

There are now people with penises who wish to use the title "Woman." They would enjoy hearing themselves called "Woman." They've observed and read about what it means to be a woman. They imagine they would make a very fine woman. But they do not have the biology, the experiences, the Blood Mysteries of Woman; they have not paid the life price to be a woman. It is no personal insult to them to deny them that title. It is simply the biological reality of their lives. Applying this culture's "artifacts" of Woman long hair and painted fingernails, makeup, dresses, high heels, breast implants, and "feminizing" face surgery does not make them Woman. For a person with a penis, claiming "Woman" constitutes fraud.

"But would you reduce 'Woman' to mere biology? Woman is so much more than that!" This is "code" for "Woman is what we, the people with penises, determine it is." If Woman can be defined as anything one wishes, if Woman is a mental construct, an idea in your head, an emotional feeling in your consciousness, then we come full-circle to a three-thousand-year-old Greek patriarchal reversal of reality: the myth of the god Zeus "birthing" Goddess Athena from a cleft in his forehead. "Believe our lie: our male god, the one with a penis, has "thought" your Goddess into existence." The male god created a male in his image, and then "birthed" from the rib of that male the second sex, the female. "Believe our lie: male came first; male then creates female."

In this construct, since Woman is man's creation, it follows that Her identity shall also be decided by him. Her very body belongs to him … just as it was decided by my father for me at age eleven. A man in a white coat can put any body on an operating table and, with his will, his intellect and his knife, "make" it into "a woman."

Erased: woman as creator of life—replaced with the patriarchal reversal of "male as birther."

Every day we see more erasing of Woman, She with womb, vagina and Blood Mysteries:

- Bake sales may not have vulva-shaped cupcakes because it is insulting to the "women who do not have vulvas."

- Eve Ensler's *Vagina Monologues* is cancelled as offensive to "women who do not have vaginas."
- Penises are called "ladysticks."
- Major feminist speakers are deplatformed at universities for holding different points of view.
- Annual women's gatherings, enjoyed for decades, are ended due to pressure from people with penises.
- A person with a penis is chosen "Woman of the Year" by Glamour Magazine, November, 2015.
- Lesbian and gay teenagers — indeed, the freedom of childhood itself to explore and evolve its own nature-are erased because gender non-conforming children are convinced by confused professionals and parents that *they must be trans.*

Erased: sanity, common sense, clarity of thought.

We are now asked to use the terms "birthing individual" and "breeder."

Erased: the ancient, honored title of "mother."

Our one mixed circle a month is a good thing and we continue to hold it. Our Temple's male members are gentle, honoring and kind human beings, sitting in circle respectfully, speaking thoughtfully. In spite of that, something still happens: when people with penises are present, the people with vaginas censor their natural speech. Trained to have little to no Queen, most of the vagina people are not comfortable leading the penis people, or even simply confidently expressing their natural selves in front of them.

A documentary on "trans teenagers" shows a group of teenage girls having a sleepover the discussion being of first periods, sex, and fear of unwanted pregnancy. One of the teenagers is a person with a penis. Big-hearted and inclusive (and trained to have no boundaries —"don't be unpleasant!"), the girls had accepted him and his chosen designation as "girl."

As the actual girls chatter animatedly about all these issues so important to them, issues directly related to their specifically female bodies, the person with a penis looks on, silent, frowning. Suddenly, the group of girls becomes aware of his feelings. "Oh, we have to stop talking about these things because our girlfriend cannot participate and it makes her sad." Classic "Overgiving Mother" – these young girls had already fully absorbed patriarchal training that demands that females willingly relinquish their own needs in favor of the "needs" of the one person in the room with a penis.

Erased: "girl talk"—a flippant term which is "code" for the tender beginnings of females enjoying sisterhood, sharing and learning about their own bodies in circle with one another.

This is precisely what happens at The Temple in Sunday Services. The one Sunday a month where men are welcome (and they are most definitely welcome), the women do not speak as freely. The circle "feels" very different from the free, funny, vulnerable and outspoken circles of "women only."

Is this the fault of the men present? No. Not at all. *They are good men.* Rather, it is the broken nature of women's spirits, spirits crushed in patriarchy. We women are trained to *erase ourselves* before we say anything that may make a male angry or uncomfortable, including speaking of menstruation and other female bodily functions, because, rather than honor these functions as sacred, the majority of men in our culture have been taught that these things are *"distasteful" and we women know that.*

Erased: women's free speech about their own bodily experience.

Sometimes when women visit The Goddess Temple for the first time and are suddenly surrounded by abundant, beautiful imagery honoring the female body, they burst into tears, and say they do not know why they are crying.

I know why.

They are crying for their erased lives.

Yes, there was a lot I didn't know when I signed on to this goddess temple outfit ... but I offer what I have learned:

- The terms "Woman," "women," "female," and "mother" are related and rightfully belong to those persons who are born with wombs and vaginas, and who have the potential to experience the aforementioned Blood Mysteries.

- Women need to hold Woman-only space, yes, because women in a dominator-model society need a place to speak freely to recover from oppression and erasure ... but even more importantly because ...
- A circle of people born with wombs and vaginas is magical in a way that cannot be quantified scientifically.
- The womb is not a "hole" in the body. It is an organ with many as-yet-little-understood physical and spiritual powers, one of which is that it is a sacred portal to other realities.
- Forcing women's circles to accept people with penises on a regular, permanent basis would inevitably change the subtle spiritual nature of those circles in ways not now fully understood.

The body of Woman carries a spiritual power all Her own, but one that She offers freely to the world, just as She offers Her children to the world. We need both: we need mixed spiritual circles where all come together in oneness, honoring each other and all forms that are birthed from Woman, and we need Woman-only circles for women to come together to remember our own mysteries. As we do so, we women empower ourselves to serve humanity as Good Queens instituting life-affirming boundaries for all the people we birth, including those with penises, that our world may enjoy peace, prosperity and justice.

The Great Mother gives birth to all diverse forms, and the primary form of humanity is female. Most now know that all humans are female first in the womb; some then later become male. The deepest truth is that males are simply a wonderful natural variation of the original form of female; males are a "type" of female.

It is yet another patriarchal reversal to hold people with penises as "the standard" by which other human forms are compared. "Female" is actually the original, all-inclusive standard for humanity. Even our language acknowledges this reality. The word "she" includes "he," but "he" does not include "she." "Female" includes "male," but "male" does not include "female." "Goddess" includes "god," but "god" does not include "Goddess."

So we may well ask: Which form is the form of oneness and inclusion?

She, female, Goddess.

But some are attempting now to rename women ... because people with penises have long had the power to identify who and what we are allowed to be ... "cis women" ... the old metaphysical term "womb-man" ... or even the newest, laughable-if-wasn't-so-horrifying "non males." People with penises have stolen so very much from people with vaginas for so many thousands of years. Our title, "Woman," has been vilified, mocked and decried for millennia, but up until now, it has always been ours.

The people with penises referred to today as "trans" have been hideously brutalized by patriarchal culture for generations. Queenly women of leadership must guide humanity to end this terrible crime. But we do not rectify it by giving away our name and allowing people with penises to lay claim to it. We do not fix this by blurring all boundaries in the confused manner of an Overgiving Mother and letting others have what they demand because we are afraid they will be upset otherwise. We must not now hand over to people with penises the one thing that has always been ours: our very name, "Woman."

With all this talk of "erasure," the reality is that the biological and spiritual truth of Woman cannot actually *be* erased. Sure, men may concoct test-tube babies absent the body of Woman, but those poor creatures, having never heard their mother's heartbeat, will no doubt be dysfunctional in some essential way we cannot now predict. Sure, men may create very realistic robot sex dolls, but that collection of plastic parts, wiring and computer chips will never be able to offer what men indeed, all humanity needs: *Shakti,* the ineffable and numinous life energy that Woman holds in Her sacred female body. Man cannot create woman. Only Goddess can do that.

Through thousands of years of crushing oppression, there has remained the Lineage of Woman, a through line of ancient wisdom and power carried in our female bodies, passed down woman to woman. Aware people with penises clearly understand, peaceably accept, and rightly honor this reality. Many things can be erased: our women's spoken and written words, our contributions to history, our right to vote for our own leaders, our ability to control our own bodies. Yes, all this can be erased, but as long as Woman's body exists, somehow our goddess temples will live (with or without permits!) and our wisdom will stand because we are the origination of human life itself. Many things are in marked in pencil and can be erased. Woman's body is the Reality that is inked permanently on the pages of Life, because Her body *is* Life itself.

Try as they might, those who we have birthed can never really erase us because *they need our bodies.* All human forms have come out of "She of the womb and vagina," out of the earthly embodiment of Goddess that is called "Woman." A sane society honors the female, The Mother, who gives everything to continue the generations. No one is *"born in the wrong body."* Rather, it is the patriarchal mindset with its fake, constructed little boxes of gender that is mistaken. Let The Queen in Woman bring the clarity that rights this wrong for all of us. All humans are worthy of respect. All are sacred.

Woman is the Founder of Life, the embodiment of Goddess on earth.

Let Woman be rightfully honored for Her creation of Life.

Let no one try to falsely claim Her powers or usurp Her title.

Let Her peacefully meet in Sacred Space for Her own purposes, purposes which ultimately benefit all.

Bow down in reverence, for it is She Who made you.

Rest easy in the knowing that, no matter the bodily form She gave you, you are most assuredly Her sacred creation.

CHAPTER 9

MY DISSERVICE TO MY TRANSGENDER PATIENTS

Kathy Mandigo, M.D.

I AM PACKING up my stuff to move, and I came across a folder of work-related papers. One item was a card I had forgotten I had, but as soon as I opened it, I remembered it and the sender. It was a card of thanks from a transgendered patient, a lesbian who transitioned to a man, expressing appreciation for my help in her* journey to become the man she felt she was.

*(While I used to accede to my patients' chosen pronouns, I now use the biologically appropriate one.)

I saw this patient at a youth clinic (patients under 26), and she was usually accompanied by her girlfriend. She had been seen and assessed and started on treatment at the Gender Dysphoria Clinic that ran at the time in a local hospital. I initiated nothing, merely administered the testosterone injections they prescribed.

I watched my patient change: she gained weight and muscle, developed a lower voice, sprouted facial hair, and described increasing sex drive and aggressiveness. I remember feeling comfortable that this patient seemed very grounded and confident, and I did not feel manipulated in our interactions, which helped me feel comfortable to administer the injections.

I saw this patient in the mid or late 1990's, I don't exactly remember, and as I recall, she was the first transgendered patient I had seen. I was less than ten years into medical practice and hadn't been taught anything about transgenderism in medical school. I was young and naive and trusted science. There was no science about transgenderism. What was I to do?

With the growing criticism of medicine and physicians as paternalistic, we were encouraged to listen better to our patients, to their expressed realities. Although we did not take the Hippocratic oath in our medical school, we did still attend to the tenet of first do no harm, but I had no idea how to weigh the risks and benefits of attempts at gender transition. I didn't have a personal opinion then about transgenderism, and professionally I felt an obligation to try to meet my patients where they were, rather than where I was. I wasn't willing to diagnose transgenderism, but if the team of proclaimed professionals at the Gender Dysphoria Clinic had made such an assessment, I was willing to be the family doctor who provided follow-up.

A few years later, a pilot project clinic was opened within one of the community health centers in our city, a clinic specifically for queer patients. We staffed our clinic with as many queer providers as we could find. We expected a flood of queer patients alienated from the traditional medical system; those whom we actually saw were mostly alienated transgender patients, who either had not been accepted for gender transition by the Gender Dysphoria Clinic (often for psychological reasons) or were unable to tolerate the long assessment process of the Gender Dysphoria Clinic (again, often for psychological reasons).

As I recall, all of these patients were men wanting to transition to being women, and, as I recall, all of them struck me as psychologically unwell, as manifested in their behaviors. I remember thinking that there was an atmosphere of coercion among the staff in which it was uncool to question the validity of the patients' desires and expressed gender identity. Any psychological disturbance was often attributed to the patient's suffering of living their life in the "wrong" gender.

I remember often feeling that these patients tried to intimidate me into giving them what they wanted, that they often assumed outraged insult if I asked questions (how dare I enquire, presumably doubting them), that if I did not give them what they wanted they exploded into enraged diatribes and stormed off. I felt very uncomfortable with them and it was challenging to try to do my job and not react to their anger.

The pilot project did not last long, as there were few patients, other than this handful of disaffected transgendered patients. It may have been that, because the clinic operated on Monday afternoons, more well-adjusted patients were likely working and unable to access the clinic. It may have been that most queer patients by that time felt comfortable accessing the health care they wanted. Those questions were never asked to sort out whether it was lack of accessibility or lack of need.

Over the next years, I did not see many transgendered patients, until recently, and with most of them disproportionately appearing among the demographic of mentally ill and addicted in our city.

One patient came to my private office, a lesbian who was transitioning to a male, under the care of a gender specialist of some sort. (The Gender Dysphoria Clinic had ended, I wasn't clear why. I believe this was effected under the guise of rhetoric that all doctors ought to provide this care rather than it being relegated to a specialty clinic, but I expect there were other politics at play. Disturbingly, what has been opened is a transgender clinic within the provincial children's hospital.)

She came to my office telling me that she had heard I was a great doctor and that I specialized in transgender issues.

I immediately felt I was being manipulated with a big buttering-up job, and I said this was not true, I was neither a great doctor nor a transgender specialist. My guard was up. I expected this patient read me as a dyke, though I never disclosed, and over subsequent visits, this patient continued to try to be my pal, with an overly-friendly us-two-dykes demeanor, like we were butchly comrades, as though she was forgetting that she believed she was a he.

Over time, I discovered the patient had been withholding unflattering information from me that would have sped up diagnoses of her other issues. I increasingly felt she was attempting to manipulate me with her excessively friendly behavior, and then pressure me with her sense of what my obligations were (e.g. that I should provide a letter of support for her to have the gender on her birth certificate changed, when in fact this was her specialist's responsibility, as the diagnosing physician, a responsibility that he had fulfilled, despite the patient's claims and demands to me).

I tried to be professional, to mind the boundaries (e.g. not provide personal information, not collude in the play of friendship), and I administered the testosterone injections her specialist had prescribed, until the patient's girlfriend felt comfortable to take over. I held this ground, and eventually the patient tired of me, undoubtedly disappointed and disparaging, and left my practice.

Another patient I saw in my other, public health work, was a man transitioning to a female. What I was told by a nurse of the patient's story, of what clinics he had attended and who his doctors were, was all over the map, which made me suspicious about what the "facts" were and that I had to verify anything he said.

When I saw him, he began by being all girl-friend-y with me, like we were two girls together in this crazy world, behavior I assumed he had seen and adopted as how women get what they want (had he ever read me wrong! he was mimicking behavior without having the years of lived experience by which a women learns, if so inclined, when to use that tactic).

As I asked questions about his health background, he became uncomfortable that my questions were revealing inconsistencies in his story (suggesting to me psychological problems), and he got angry and leaned forward into my personal space and flashed me that "you fucking cunt" look.

All women know that look. This was the same look I remembered getting from the patients I saw at the pilot project clinic, but I didn't know then what to call it, what it was. Now, after so many more years of life experience, I knew exactly what it was: it is a look that men give women to dismiss and devalue and intimidate; it is not a look that women give women (they dismiss and devalue and intimidate in other ways, often by being passive-aggressively haughty).

I was better able, after the years in practice, to hold my ground, and I calmly told him that his angry tone and demeanor were making me uncomfortable and he had to calm down or the visit would be over. He denied being angry, but continued to have the angry tone of voice and body language that goes with that look, part of the package of male power tactics.

I stood my ground and repeated that he was making me uncomfortable. Eventually he settled, I gave him the (non-gender-related) prescription he had come for, and we terminated the visit. I saw him a second time some weeks later, and he did not flare into anger. Whether he was having a better day or had learned to camouflage and control himself better, I do not know.

These experiences, of seeing more men wanting to transition than women, of seeing almost all of the transitioning patients behave in stereotypical gendered ways (their biological gender behaviors flashing through their assumed gendered behaviors) and out of these behaviors try to manipulate me (rather than being able to discuss the situation openly and honestly), seeing more of these transitioning men settling among the mentally unwell in the most disenfranchised neighborhood, and especially seeing the transgender men continue to exhibit male aggressive behaviors, has convinced me that most, if not all, transgender patients are not in the wrong body but have mental health problems, problems they believe can be fixed if they get in the right body.

At the beginning of my years of practice, with my youth and inexperience, I thought I had an obligation to follow the patient. Now I believe that I failed these patients, and that I have a superseding obligation to tell the truth to my patients. I regret every testosterone injection I gave, every estrogen prescription I refilled, and every time I colluded with my patients in their gender delusion. I regret not speaking up to my colleagues and to my patients, instead giving in to the coercion I felt to go along rather than dare to question. I regret not having had the courage to ask questions to get to the story beneath the gender dysphoria story, to find out why my patients had ever been made to feel there was anything wrong with them in the first place. I want to tell the women that we need them as women, and especially as lesbians; I want to tell the men that no amount of medicalization will make them women. Women may have an easier time of masquerading as men, but as long as every man has within him the "you fucking cunt" look, no man can ever masquerade as a women.

That first patient's composure stands out from my subsequent experiences with transgender patients. Surely it helped her navigate the Gender Dysphoria Clinic. Was she truly of a different nature, or had she, with her relative youth, not accumulated distorting grievances? After finding that card, I tried to look her up. I wanted to ask if she was still grateful for transitioning, if she was still as happy to be living her life as the man she believed she was, if she still believed she was a man. I could not find her, at least not under his name.

Republished with permission from Radfem Repost, August 11, 2015

CHAPTER 10

EXILES IN THEIR OWN FLESH: A PSYCHOTHERAPIST SPEAKS

Lane Anderson

I AM A licensed psychotherapist. I'm writing this post on my last day at a teen health clinic, where I've seen patients and their families for nearly a decade. In the past year especially, it's become increasingly clear to me that I cannot uphold the primary value of my profession, to do no harm, without also seriously jeopardizing my standing in the professional community. It's a terrible and unfortunate conflict of interest. I've lost much sleep over the fact that, for a significant portion of my clients and their parents, I am unable to provide what they profess to come to me seeking: sound clinical judgment. Increasingly, providing such judgment puts me at risk of violating the emergent trans narrative which—seemingly overnight and without any explanation or push-back of which I am aware—has usurped the traditional mental health narrative.

When I am suddenly and without warning discouraged from exploring the underlying causes and conditions of my patients' distress (as I was trained to do), and instead forced to put my professional stamp of approval upon a prefab, one-size-fits-all narrative intended to explain the complexity of my patient's troubles, I feel confused. It's as if I am being held hostage. No longer encouraged or permitted to question, consider or discuss the full spectrum of my patient's mental health concerns, it has occurred to me that I am being used, my meager professional authority commandeered to legitimize a new narrative I may or may not wish to corroborate. It's been perilous to simply admit to not fully understanding it all—let alone *disagree* with the trans narrative. There was no training or teaching. I was just suddenly told that some of my patients thought they were trapped in the wrong body and that was that. After much soul searching, I felt I had no choice but to remove myself from this crippling work setting. Being told to exercise my clinical judgment with some clients, while ignoring it with others, made me feel like a fraud.

Throughout my career, I have come to my work with these thoughts in mind: that life is complex, that people are complex. But in one way or another, most people tend to balk at that kind of ambiguity. I try to assist people in flexing a little, try to help them find ways to manage life's gray areas, and the occasional distress that comes from simply being conscious. But at the end of the day, I couldn't deny it was a little weird for me to go on believing I could effectively teach others to be less rigid, more free people facing their lives head on, when I myself, their humble guide, was being exploited, tongue-tied by a new party line.

There are so many complex forces, from many different realms, coming into play with this trans wave. Most people are completely unaware of these intersecting interests. Unfortunately the culture war has done a number on the concept of critical thinking. I have considered myself liberal my entire adult life, and I still am. But for a long time I couldn't find anyone questioning this trans explosion who wasn't on the far right. It made me feel like only conservatives were allowed to think, to consider this issue, but ultimately their thoughts were rendered meaningless due to their branding by the culture war. It's essential that left-leaning people model critical thinking for the masses in this regard.

It's important to link people like us together, who have been silenced, so we can resume contact with our critical thinking skills and reduce our growing sense of self-doubt. Divide and conquer is best accomplished through silencing, through calling into question those who speak out. There is so much of this attached to the trans movement. Even just *wondering* about a profound concept such as transgender is labeled "transphobic". What I think has happened is that people are now phobic about their own gut responses to life. We are being systematically separated from our own intuition. This is fatal for a civilization, I think. Not that our intuition always tells the truth with a capital T, but it is a critical piece of who we are. Without it, we remain profoundly directionless, and more susceptible to coercion of all types.

What frightens me most about the trans movement is that the establishment has gotten involved and is leading it. I think that's really weird. Clearly they are benefiting from it financially. So sad. It disturbs me to see how giddy my former medical director is to be part of this growing craze. We used to treat kids with mental health problems, but now it's all about validating their emergent and shifting identities. As professionals, if we don't loudly prioritize their identities as being the most important thing about them (and identities do shift constantly in kids and teens), we risk coming across as unsupportive and even immoral. Identity development has always been a teen task, but in the past it wasn't necessarily supposed to become a lifestyle, or colonize the entirety of your existence.

Our world is in a profound state of flux. We can't begin to comprehend what the Internet has done to how we see ourselves. People are looking for ways to belong, ways to understand who they are in place and in time. They are looking to reduce the anxiety that comes when too much change happens all at once. I try and look at trans folks as people who are seeking to answer the new questions that have emerged in this early 21st century. I have been trying to find a way to understand their urges to detach from their bodies, to undo that feeling of exile they experience in their own flesh. We all want to get back to ourselves; it is our duty to reconnect with those weighty parts that inevitably sink to the depths of us, the parts too heavy to remain on the surface of our lives.

From what I can see, the age-old human task to reclaim that which has gone missing appears to be manifesting with great prominence in the trans community. The problem is this: we all look for shortcuts to finding the lost treasure. It's human nature to resist the long and serpentine journey to our own sense of personal truth. In our fear, in our self-doubt, we calculate the risk and often decide it is preferable to be shown what another person—a "helping professional" or an activist—bills as a sure thing, a direct path to what we sense we lack. We all, on some level, hold a childlike fantasy that someone else has figured it out and can provide us a direct map to ourselves. And that's what the trans narrative does. It promises to guide the follower to their essential, authentic self. But this, unfortunately, doesn't happen, because the essential self, whatever that is, is not created from another's road map, but can only be comprised of the trails we forge ourselves.

What saddens me the most is the way children are being trained to think their parents do not love them if mom and dad don't jump aboard the trans train. To me, this is a brutal aspect of a near- dictatorship being foisted on everyone. The kids are too young to see that there are no other people who will have their backs, throughout life with lasting devotion, in the unique way their families will. They think these new friends they've made online understand them perfectly. And in believing this unquestioningly, they find themselves lulled by the frictionless experience delivered most powerfully by group thinking.

Of course, I'm describing the pull of all cults; that deep human desire to be known through and through and through. The cult experience seeks to end the frustration that naturally comes when we mature and begin to see ourselves as separate beings. In our separateness, we must do the hard work of truly learning to know another. Group thinking reduces the fear that comes when we are unsure if we will be located by another, when we remain unable to locate *ourselves*.

Cults and closed narratives neutralize and tame what we see as the unknown. I think somebody needs to put a refresher out there on the cult mindset and group thinking. People seem to have forgotten that we are all very easily influenced by each other. Carl Elliot wrote about this in relation to body dysmorphic disorder (people wanting to amputate their own limbs because they dis-identify with them) in the *Atlantic*, "A new way to be mad."[1]

One common trait I've noticed in nearly all the trans kids I've met has been their profound sense of being different, and too alone. They often have had little success with making friends, or what I would call contact with "the other." Because of their psychic isolation, they are prime targets for group think narratives. But in addition to looking for a way to belong, they are also craving protection and the stamp of legitimacy, perhaps because they feel a profound lack of it.

Now that the government and medical communities are involved in the creation of who trans folks are, this class of individuals have finally found their safe havens. Now, rather than being merely invisible and awkward, they have been transformed into veritable leaders of a revolution. Now, rather than cower in the shadows, they have commandeered the narratives of others into a similar dark and brooding place where they once were. The tables, as they lived and viewed them, have now turned.

It's got to be dizzying for these formerly "ugly ducklings" to find themselves at the center of a flock of swans. To become a part of the movement, to finally be seen and found as whole, alive, and most importantly, *wanted*, all they have to do is renounce the very bodies in which they feel they have been imprisoned. In doing so, the promised payoff is very big, for they have finally found a way to render mute all those who once discounted and disbelieved them. Through silencing others who threaten them, they have unearthed a means of silencing their own self-hate. Rather than being afraid of themselves, they make others fear what they have become.

Psychologically these interpersonal tactics would once upon a time have been categorized as immature, "primitive" defenses erected by an undifferentiated self that cannot see the self or others as whole creatures. But as I witness it in my own practice, this is the basic thinking underlying the psychology of the trans narrative. In her recent blog post, "My Disservice to My Transgender Patients," Dr. Kathy Mandigo talks about feeling threatened by some of her MTF patients. Many of the trans kids I've worked with will joke about how they and their friends are dictators, "masters of the universe!" I find that clinically significant. This is something toddlers do when they are first discovering they are separate from their rulers (parents). Rather than fear the parent, they seek to control the parent, exert their will on the parent and co-opt the parent's power as their own. In doing this they hide from view their terror at facing their own powerlessness. Ideally, the child will gradually outgrow this urge to control, will gradually relinquish the dictatorial need to create safety through controlling the external realm. When that happens, we say it is a sign of maturity. As our own sense of agency grows, we are better able to forfeit the habit of controlling others. We also begin to feel guilt at the idea of controlling others, as we begin to see them as separate from us, 3D human beings instead of mere props on our psychic stage.

Unfortunately some people have a hard time making this shift. They get stuck or addicted to manipulating their external environment, and will continue to create inner safety through the constant and relentless work of controlling others. Last week in a team meeting, our medical director said he was meeting with a girl who identifies as FTM to discuss top surgery and testosterone treatment. Apparently, according to the director, the girl's mom is slowing down the process of transition. Bad mom, right? The director added that the girl's mom told her that *9 out of 9 of her daughter's friends also identify as FTM.*

At this point I couldn't hold my tongue any longer. I said, "Can we not be honest and see that we are dealing with a trend?" Of course, everyone else at the table was mute. Considering I'm leaving my post, I felt bold enough to say that I found it infuriating we couldn't discuss this topic clinically. More silent colleagues (except their eyes were wide as if they wanted me to keep talking and taking the risk for them). I said that what we were doing as a medical community was potentially very harmful, and made mention of some of the videos I'd watched featuring transmen who decided to go off testosterone. The medical director prides himself in providing special services for those patients he deems unjustly marginalized by society. But he can't see how the medical community has become complicit in the oppression he earnestly seeks to remedy.

A large part of the problem comes with the revolution in health care. More and more, we are giving people the power to define their own treatments. This is good in many ways, but the trans movement is using this moment, and is actively recruiting young, psychologically undefined and frightened people to push their agenda through the medical community. It's clearly not that difficult to do. These kids are just pawns. That's how it looks to me anyway. The trans community needs more converts so that the narrative becomes more cohesive. I'm guessing the push for this comes from a need to further cohere so they will have more members to fully cement a fragile, constructed reality.

We—people who don't identify as trans—are the external realm that must be controlled to bring the trans community the inner peace they now lack. But they don't get that they will never find calm or strength this way. You cannot find yourself through coercing others. You cannot extinguish your fears by turning from them. The trans community must face their own fears, face themselves and their own demons. They can't wipe out their fear that they are not really transitioning by censoring the thoughts and expressions of others. If they believe they are trans, they shouldn't need to spend so much effort foisting that belief on others.

The fact that they do dictate to others is to me diagnostic of their very condition. They are uncertain about who and what they are. No sin in that. That's human. The transgression comes in refusing to accept this uncertainty, and in sacrificing the lives and consciences of others to nullify your own self-doubt.

First published August 22ⁿᵈ, 2015 by 4ᵗʰ Wave Now. Republished with permission.

---

[1] Carl Elliot, *A New Way To Be Mad*, The Atlantic, December 2000 Issue.

CHAPTER 11

IN THE ABSENCE OF THE SACRED: THE MARKETING OF MEDICAL TRANSGENDERISM AND THE SURVIVAL OF THE NATURAL CHILD

Jennifer Bilek and Mary Ceallaigh

INTRODUCTION

THIS ARTICLE IS an attempt to provide an overview that encourages critical thinking and action towards an Ethics of Integrity with regards to the new industry that has emerged to "diagnose" and "treat" children who are gender nonconforming. The past two years in Western industrial culture have seen a surge of media focused on the medical transgenderism of adults, and along with it, a newly normalized pathologizing of large numbers of children as "trans kids" requiring highly invasive medical treatments. The innately fluid identities of children once simply considered the healthy expression of childhood's magical, diverse personality that guides their learning (and challenges parents) are now being labeled "transgender" rather than being correctly perceived by adults as either a transitory phase of child development or a possible cry for help that requires psychosocial therapies for mind-body integration.

In a complete reversal of previously established psychosocial approaches to child development and healing of mental disorders via dramatic play, sandbox therapy, logo therapy, art therapy, body-based modalities, and the addiction recovery movement - the dissociation of children's minds from their bodies is being enabled to a staggering degree by a strategically poised contingent of the medical industry. This reversal rewarding adult collusion in altering children's bodies with permanently invasive "solutions" for issues that reside in children's psyches and family dynamics are now being promoted as the new social ethics. Instead of helping children and families express, develop, and/or recover themselves by non-invasive means, the unacknowledged adult and cultural pathos are being reflected back to us by these children. Invoked by the iteration of "gender atypical" or "gender nonconforming" as a starting place, the cascade of sequences leading to medical transgenderism is being embraced by some parents and authority figures as the "new normal" of childhood - according to digital media at least.

This deeply conservative course of action, informed by postmodern transhumanist[1] values, begins with puberty-blocking medications that hijack children's glandular systems and keep them in a prepubescent state (no doubt of interest to pedophiles), followed by prescriptive hormonal manipulations to actively mimic the opposite sex as well as cosmetic surgeries that carry extreme risks, side effects, and lifelong, ecologically unsustainable dependencies. Medical transgenderism encompasses the performance of superficial stereotypes of the opposite sex and the hatred of the natural body; and the pursuit of a chemically-altered body is being viewed as a valid and worthwhile dream for these children to aspire towards. Instead of the staggeringly *huge* range of other possible childhood passions and dreams that might carry their hearts and souls beyond performance-of-self, such dreams are increasingly being portrayed as old-fashioned or boring to the highly individualist, sedentary, privileged and/or traumatized children in what is a high-tech "culture of addiction".[2]

Perhaps even more disturbing is the sudden announcement that one in one hundred children is "transgender" and therefore a candidate for the ecologically unsustainable and financially lucrative medical interventions that this entails, tying these children to the medical industry for the rest of their lives. This new trend is in stark, if not totally absurd, contrast to the 2003 study by the Johns Hopkins School of Medicine that estimated the numbers at 1 in 11,900 males and 1 in 30,400 females.[3] The trend that we are now witnessing is saying, in essence, that for 1 in 100 children the body that their mother gestated and birthed and brought to earth is not good enough – and that biology is not something to love and respect. This is being said in outright rejection of significant long-term studies and substantial evidence-based data that prove the effectiveness of non-invasive, psychosocial approaches for helping children's self-integration and resolving family and peer group issues in a durable way. Lack of substance, as well as profit motives, characterizes the new multibillion-dollar trans industry specializing in children.

The dearth of actual scientific evidence that proves medical transgendering of minors is beneficial or even safe is consistently being downplayed by an industry selling quick "fixes" to children questioning identity in a world often lacking meaningful community. Medical transgendering of minors is being promoted as simply "heartwarming stories" in mainstream media rather than being held accountable by the media, thus resulting in a censoring of the very real risks and disadvantages of these interventions and how this industry is actually perpetrating medical child abuse. As clinical psychologist and medical critic David Schwartz PhD says, "The clinicians try to make this child/parent/symptom matrix fit into a model of liberal psychiatric treatment. As is common in the medical sciences, most push against ambiguity, preferring to emphasize speculative generalizations ("genetics is likely a factor") instead of highlighting the lack of data from controlled studies."[4]

The celebration of medical transgenderism for children, which is actually and acutely the de-sexing of children, is sweeping the US, Canada, Australia and the UK, streaming on all major media channels, and being legislated as a public health and civil rights issue with the fervor of a religious experience, or the urgency of an epidemic. However, getting even more dubious, the "transgender child" phenomena is absent in the rest of the species located elsewhere in places where there is modern science, healing, and medicine, including vast swaths of people of all colors located in the Nordic countries, Western Europe, Eastern Europe, Africa, Asia, and Latin America. Though with the geopolitical business model of US industry exporting its cultural pathologies to the rest of the world through its powerful roles in the United Nations and the World Health Organization (WHO), it is probably just a matter of time before this changes. In fact, the WHO's new *ICD-10 Version 2016 Manual* has now formalized new children's diagnoses for "Gender Identity Disorder" and "Sexual Maturation Disorder." This has set the foundation for promoting and funding hormonal manipulations and other questionable and unproven medical treatments of children by national and private health coverage around the world.[5]

We want to examine this startling trend that many of you have noticed - the increasing encroaching upon children's bodies with very little debate about the perilous risks, including sterilizations of millions of children. And for children of color and indigenous children whose communities have already been under siege from historic illegal sterilizations and are struggling to survive relentless cultural genocide and racial profiling, this is even more exploitative of systemic oppression. Is industrial culture now such a horizontal, or "elder-less," society that it is incapable of discerning exploitative threats to children? Have notoriously declining critical thinking skills in adults and cultural fragmentation rendered mainstream culture a veritable minefield for the natural child? Or is it that these new "transgender children," socialized by an earth-destroying and landless culture, influenced by peer trends and artificial social media "communities," are leading their adult caregivers towards an opportunity to confront deeper issues in themselves, families, and the culture at large? Could it be some combination of it all? We started asking these questions, and here's what we found.

TRENDER CHILDREN: THE NEW VILLAGE

The market-driven popularization of transhumanist ideology – where future humans and machines will someday become one, where artifice over nature is the ideal is now expressed in the new village of child transgenderism where previously this was just the domain of adult notions of adult bodies. This is occurring in league with the new, global pharmaceuticals industry which is now the most profitable industry on earth, staggeringly outpacing oil, gas, and chemicals combined.[6] In a time of unprecedented global climate catastrophe, geopolitical industry's maintenance of material obstructions and social power structures is downplaying perspectives from medical ethics, evidence-based science, and ecological social responsibility when we need such perspectives the most. Transgender children – or more accurately, the adults profiting from them socially, psychologically, and/or financially – are broadcasting a loud message that biological source, and thus female source and the earth itself, is irrelevant. This is explicitly played out in rejecting the "native" body of the earth through hormones and surgeries of high technology with the fervency of a new religion. This socially constructed and ecologically unsustainable trend of treating gender-nonconforming children with medical transgenderism is taking on all the force of a new "natural" law.

From a political perspective, transgenderism in general is regressive, rather than "transgressive" or liberationist, which its proponents are prone to label it as. In terms of its social conformity to sex-role stereotypes, transgenderism is quite conservative in its encouragement of gender presentation rather than resistance to gender stereotypes and the power structures that support them. With the advent of the medical transgendering of children, in place of social responsibility and collective political challenges to power, we are seeing an encultured and strongly socialized focus on the personal, individualist empire.

The consequences of all this upon the group we might call "Trender Children" hearken to the German legend of the Pied Piper of Hamelin. A cautionary tale told to children to alert them to stranger-danger and the importance of safety limits and healthy boundaries, the Pied Piper symbolizes the fatal disappearance of children. In this engaging legend, the otherworldly music of a new stranger, a charismatic male piper dressed in multicolored (pied) clothing steals around corners, creeps down alleys and into windows, reaching children wherever they play or do chores in the small village. His seductive, enchanting music beckons them in just the right way so they forget the rules and run to join him just as their parents realize – too late what's happening. The Pied Piper leads the children in an exuberant, festive parade that passes the end of the main street and keeps going, beyond the edge of town. There the piper leads them all into a cave where they are never ever heard from again, their life stories permanently altered.

Many are familiar with the story of the Pied Piper of Hamelin, but few realize that it actually is based on a historical event recorded in the Lueneburg manuscript (c. 1440 – 50), which states:

"In the year of 1284, on the day of Saints John and Paul on June 26, by a piper, clothed in many kinds of colors, 130 children born in Hamelin were seduced, and lost at the place of execution near the koppen."[7]

The numerous theories that explain what occurred include forced migration due to extreme poverty; a predatory male who murdered children over a period of months or years; or a young male magician-musician who rounded up the village's children and tricked them into capture for either the Children's Crusades or foreign gangs who trafficked children. Regardless of the specifics, there was a failure in guardianship – how else could such a thing happen, were the parents and caregivers not paying attention? Was it a holiday and were they all drunk or otherwise incapacitated? Or, maybe it was a failure in the training of children - did no one teach those children that it is *not* okay to just run out of the house like that? Others might say that obviously the adults of Hamelin were also entranced by the music, or else they certainly would have been able to call back the hearts of their children. Still others would simply say that yes, the adult world is a dangerous place, both at home and in the street. Of the numerous theories that have tried to explain what happened, and the likewise numerous versions of the story that exist, one thing is certain: children disappeared.

A foundational understanding in child development is that children are soothed when they have steady, unconditional parental love. This unconditional love should not be conflated with the absence of psychological limits and child guidance. Clear limits, lovingly yet firmly conveyed, ensure a psychological place where the adult guardian is the "grown-up" maintaining healthy personal and social boundaries, exemplary conduct, and non-violent instruction about consequences so that the child can be free to *be* the child. Psychologically skilled safety overviews for children are also covered in trainings on child sex abuse prevention that point out that a child's primary caregivers are the "child keepers" or "gatekeepers." It is the "gatekeepers" who must be alert and attuned in order to ward off potential predators (or marketers) who may seek to reach children by way of "grooming" or by befriending the child's caregivers in order to gain access to the child. Has the digital world become the children's parade of Hamelin for at-risk children surfing the Internet and following trends, while their "gatekeepers" and professional caregivers are also being seduced by the Piper's music?

Rather than celebrating the vastness of a child's fluid, complex, and ever-changing expression far beyond any kind of gender stereotype as a biological birthright. very young children (some as young as two and still in diapers) are being labeled transgender by their parents and other adults. These children are being presented to school officials and medical personnel, and even paraded on global digital media. Equally alarming are older children being "educated" by peer trends and the trans lobby in the form of a rapidly metastasized digital culture that presents medical transgenderism as a sublime experience (or blue pill) for the emotional torment, real traumas, and physical dissociations of postmodern adolescence.

What these children are saying on their own, or, more often what excited adults who are cheering them on say, is that that their body is wrong, their biological self is really not enough, and that they "feel like" the opposite sex, based on the false notion that the opposite sex is some kind of homogenous "feeling," appearance, and set of behaviors. Clinicians and parents, often trying to be respectful of and responsive to children's stated wishes and lacking critical understanding of the social rather than biological, nature of gendered behavioral stereotypes, are likely to be less psychologically minded and more medically minded. But beyond that, when children are talking about their "gender," their belief in its reality seems to distract the clinician or parent away from the fact that *we cannot listen to children in the same way that we listen to adults*. Communications always need some degree of interpretation; that is especially true for children who, necessitated by their cognitive limitations, speak more symbolically.[8]

For those of us adults who've been on long journeys to recover our body-mind connection and to re-embody the land of our devalued and/or traumatized bodies – the thought that these young people are believing that their bodies are "wrong" pains us, and/or fascinates us, like nothing else. In our capacity as social critics, analyzing the rising and polarizing forces at play, we can transform our grief and anger by exposing this subject for the purposes of greater social transformation. What does it really mean, for a child to be named as transgender? And who benefits from this naming? Laws are being changed to normalize transgenderism, and thus to support serious and permanent hormonal and surgical experimentation on children, with little being discussed in the way of why this is occurring and to what end.

In this phase of western culture's "post-postmodernism," social pathology has reached an all-time high. This has come with new variations of the same old philosophical dualism in a collective forgetting of earth-based ways of knowing, of connection to our ancestors and mentorship for internal processing, and spiritual meaning. In a culture largely dependent on internet devices and immersed in mainstream media, various "interests" have access to children in astronomical proportions. In a culture where industrially-accelerated global climate change speeds on, cognitive dissonance is at an all-time high, even as our ultimate Source – our one and only planet is being murdered. The Arctic has melted and wild animals are disappearing from the earth at the rate of up to 200 species per day.[9] As living beings connected in the fragile web of life on this planet, children of all species are at extreme risk of exploitation, and silencing. How can the natural child survive?

THE PATHOLOGIZING OF THE NATURAL CHILD

> Aversion to nature, what can be called biophobia, is increasingly common.
> More than ever we dwell in and among our own creations and are increas-
> ingly uncomfortable with nature lying beyond our direct control. Biophobia
> ranges from discomfort in "natural" places to active scorn for whatever isn't
> man-made, managed, or air-conditioned. Biophobia, in short, is the culturally
> acquired urge to affiliate with technology, human artifacts, and solely with
> human interests regarding the natural world.

> ~ DAVID W. ORR[10]

A particularly virulent new strain of biophobia has broken out in the Anglo-American world, and it is devouring the natural child.[11] This is being blessed and celebrated by the trans-humanist purveyors of global industry, with little to no concern for the long-term, serious consequences on human and environmental health. "Gender identity disorder" (GID) is a catchall term which includes everything from dysmorphia (the feeling that the body is wrong), gender dysphoria (uneasy feelings about socially constructed sex roles), and bipolar disorder in children. In older adolescents and adults, additional conditions come into play, such as ego-dystonic sexual orientation, narcissistic personality disorder, and autogynephilia[12] However, and this cannot be restated enough: *neither biological nor psychological studies provide a satisfactory explanation for the new diagnosis of gender identity disorder that has recently been formalized in the industrial West.*[13]

Serious concerns exist regarding the lack of long-term studies and evidence-based proof of the safety and lifelong outcome of hormonal manipulation of children and adolescents with GID. With long-established and well-respected studies that demonstrate how skilled and empathic psychosocial interventions, when implemented on all levels of a child's life (individual, family, and peer group therapies) are proven allies to those with mental disorders (including anorexics), how has it now become acceptable to put children on this unethical and unproven trajectory? Johns Hopkins University School of Medicine's long-term studies on dysmorphia, spanning decades of research, strongly point to psychosocial intervention as powerful aids in helping patients durably heal from the disorder.[14]

In May 2013, the American Psychiatric Association published its updated *Diagnostic and Statistical Manual DSM-5,* in which the GID diagnosis was removed and replaced with "gender dysphoria," for the first time in its own distinct chapter.[15] Gender dysphoria places the focus on distress with one's body rather than conformity with societal gender norms, as was the case with the previous *DSM*. This change was accompanied by changes to sexist language and a reduced reliance on binary gender categories. Gender dysphoria is presented as a medical issue rather than a mental disorder, with medical transgendering its unquestioned solution. This change ignores decades of long-term studies in psychiatry which previously that established surgical solutions for the transgendered do not prevent suicides, and that non-invasive multilevel psychosocial interventions are, and should be, the first line of collaborative intervention (because it renders other inventions moot).[16] This change in language, which opens the possibilities of enormous profit generation for the medical industry, purposefully removed the issue from political and moral debate and placed it instead in the hands of unethical medicine.

Dr. Paul R. McHugh (MD, Harvard Medical School) who is current Distinguished Service Professor of Psychiatry at Johns Hopkins University School of Medicine and the former psychiatrist-in-chief for Johns Hopkins Hospital for several decades, is author of six books and at least 125 peer-reviewed medical articles, many of them focused on transsexual mental health and dysmorphia. Dr. McHugh, now in his mid-eighties, with a lifetime of seasoned perspective on the health dangers of medical transgenderism, carried his concern about the new medicalization of children forward to the general public by writing an Op-Ed published in the *Wall Street Journal*. In it, he explained the merits of noninvasive psychosocial treatment, urged parents and professionals to consider transgenderism as a mental disorder, and reminded the public that chromosomes are a fact and true sex change is biologically impossible. He also suggests that people who promote "sexual reassignment surgery" (SRS) are collaborating with and promoting a mental disorder, and explains that transgender surgery is not the solution for people who suffer a "disorder of assumption," the notion that their maleness or femaleness is different than what nature assigned to them biologically.[17]

McHugh's formidable scholarly work, advocacy of the least-invasive treatment protocols, and longstanding evidence-based studies in American psychiatry are simply being dismissed by promoters of the trans ideology. This dismissal is justified by criticism of Dr. McHugh's personal politics as a social conservative, implying that it is progressive or moral to dismiss sound research if you dislike the messenger's politics. Today's mainstream media, celebrity media, and trans-queer subculture media, all of it heavily laden with click-driven advertising and behavioral metrics, is repackaging medical transgenderism as simply a matter of choice, having nothing to do with a mental disorder, and definitely not worth exploring in the noninvasive therapeutic modalities that address the psychological realms of American culture. Apparently now his scholarly work, exemplary professorial service, and leadership at one of America's most well-respected medical schools and hospitals get largely ignored because of Dr. McHugh's socially conservative opinions on other unrelated subjects.

Today's high-tech media culture virtually silences dissent, edits historical and ecological reality, and increasingly relies on the internet as its central source of intelligence and social norms. Online, device-reliant culture has replaced offline human community for a large segment of its youngest people, despite the fact that internet sources may be not only unreliable but also predatory, market-driven, and furthering of cognitive dissonance and social anxiety.

In 2012, the medical journal *Pediatrics* published the first US study of children and teens with dysphoria, though it was based on an extremely small sample of 97 patients of the Gender Management Service Clinic at Boston Children's Hospital. The mere presence of this incredibly small study in this journal serves to promote the new diagnosis in its report that more than 44 percent described experiencing gender dysphoria.[18] Children's physicians such as Dr. Daniel Reirde in Colorado have watched referrals for children with gender identity disorder (GID) go up two-hundred-fold.[19] A recent New Zealand study suggests that at least 1.2 percent of secondary school children identified as transgender. If the same numbers were reflected in Australia, it would amount to 18,000 Australian students identifying as transgender. The UK saw a rise in child gender-identity referrals increase nearly 1000% in six years.[20]

Take a moment and let those numbers sink in. These are children clamoring for drugs and surgeries, supported by parents and others who are not themselves being screened for mental disorders that may be affecting their own perceptions as well as the child's. Children and parents who are expressing a strong desire for body-altering and de-sexing that will "assist" the child in *performing* their identity – their *idea* of an opposite-sex-role-stereotype. These are parents exhibiting an aversion to psychosocial treatment plans, and an unwillingness to explore family issues in family therapy, their child's individual and peer-group therapies. How can this be medically ethical without considering the long-established track record of success in treating children suffering from anorexia and dysmorphia, treatments that also allow for associated disorders and suicidal tendencies to be addressed psychologically?

GID is a disorder, like anorexia is a disorder. It needs psychosocial treatment for durable healing, not a change of body! Would we ever think of prescribing liposuction to an anorexic? Hopefully not! But such is the ill-logic of the opportunistic treatment we are seeing promoted for GID. More and more children are presenting with gender dysphoria and the more that do, the more that these high-intervention treatments are being normalized. This of course means that more industries "serving" these children grow, and more professional referrals pour in.[21] It doesn't take an MBA to see that this is creating a self-supporting growth cycle of capital and new revenue streams that is simply successful business, at least in a culture corrupted by unethical business practices.

If the conscience of a people is their power, the rejection of psychiatric child healing in favor of medical transgenderism is sounding an alarm. This alarm demands adults-of-conscience look at the social and political contexts of child development, re-assert children's rights to be protected from adult exploitation during development, and confront the ethical misconduct of patient recruitments and drug sales for "therapies" which have no long-term studies on safety or impact on the developing brain. This is occurring with little to no emphasis on age-appropriate screening and preventative care for the autonomous health of patients. It also is proceeding in disregard of developmental needs of young people, and decades of clinical contributions by a variety of medical schools to the field of transgender (formerly known as transsexual) medical protocols all of which previously emphasized psychosocial approaches to these disorders as well as the seriousness of long-term health implications involved in medical treatments.[22]

The absence of ethical guidelines points to an absence of the sacred when it comes to child development in industrial culture, and to the socially constructed, false beliefs that now lay claim to how children's bodies are treated. The new medical transgender industry is invading children's bodies in order to enforce compliance with social norms that reside within child psychology, family dynamics, peer groups, and society at large. This invasion is being accepted, despite increased social awareness about children's bodily integrity rights and genital integrity rights.

Healthy child development relies on adults to be steady interpretative guides, fluent in the symbolic, magical, psychological language of children. This development also requires healthy personal and social boundaries to protect a space for children to learn and understand themselves in relationship with the natural world. However, what we see happening in postmodern culture is a blurring of boundaries between adults and children, and an adult celebration of children's sex role stereotypes in utter disregard of the efforts made by feminists, educators, and legislators to eradicate the same sex-role stereotypes on behalf of sex-based equity and the self-determination of women and children. Trans "culture," with adherents responding to any criticism as if they were members of a cult, has revived media-driven sex-role stereotypes and gendered expectations that originate in adults not in the human child and repurposed them as "Child Transgenderism." Adults in roles such as parents, educators, counselors, pharmaceutical reps, physicians, and clinic directors, previously charged with being gatekeepers and guardians, are increasingly being rewarded by popular culture when they allow the limiting of children's identities into stereotypical and contrived gender roles. In the process, children's biology is being silenced via puberty-blocking drugs and hormonal de-sexing. In the process, nonconforming children who don't behave according to heterosexist norms (children who are perceived as "unmasculine boys" and "unfeminine girls") and many of whom may well identify as homosexual in late adolescence, are undergoing what amounts to permanent conversion therapy.

THE ADULT ORIGINS OF THE TRANSGENDER UMBRELLA

Here in the United States, the psychologically painful disorder of GID that manifests as extreme disturbance, anxiety, obsession and depression with one's genitalia (and a visceral feeling that their emotional well-being is contingent on having the genitalia of the opposite sex), is being socially conflated with the transgenderism that became prevalent in the early 1970s. The former transgenderism was a sexual fetish of adult men aroused by appropriating the dress and mannerisms of what the greater society holds as "femininity." It is reported that 88% of the transgender population, those male-sexed persons protected by gender identity and gender expression laws today, are, as reported by their own advocacy organizations, males with a psychosexual disorder.[23] So, what is known as transgenderism is both a sexual fetish, and also a huge umbrella term used by internet culture to cover various phenomenon: GID, transgenderism, and the development of queer culture.

VARIOUS CONDITIONS UNDER ONE NAME

In previous years, queer culture used to mean those individuals identifying as lesbian, gay and bisexual. However, they are now increasingly silenced and disappeared in a panorama of sexual choices and gendered expressions under the transgender umbrella and its LGBTQ acronym. This change is occurring with little regard for the survival of actual homosexuality and every concern for the promotion of heteronormative appearances.[24] Since these things are being conflated in the culture at large, it can be difficult to make sense of what is being discussed when there is no differentiation made. So, if transgenderism has no fixed definition with some adherents believing that the whole point of transgenderism is that its definition remains fluid and open-ended how can the invasiveness of puberty blockers and permanent alterations of cross-sex hormones for children be justified?

Culture is passed on by children taking their cues from not only their mother but also older children and adults. The questions begging answers from adults who care about children in this culture are: Why are there so many stories of children expressing dissatisfaction with their perceived gender, and why it is happening now? Are their expressions of dissatisfaction with their gender or with their biological sex? And why are these two things being conflated when they are not the same thing? Unlike in previous generations, the current "gender-bending" is now fueled by a huge corporate media conglomerate enmeshed with the pharmaceutical and medical industries, all of which share a commercial interest in silencing biology. We need a deeper look at children's questioning of gender, as well as the exploitative industries that benefit from it. While doing so, we also need to hold accountable the media's influence and overwhelming support of this trend in both mainstream as well as independent or anarchist media. This influence is greatly responsible for the reasons behind why many people readily accept this new ideology that asserts mammalian children born of the powers of a woman's body can be born with the "wrong" bodies.

UNDERLYING NARRATIVES AND SILENCED STORIES

Scholar and professor Bernice L. Hausman, in her book *Changing Sex: Transsexualism, Technology, and the Idea of Gender,* states that the doctors who are promoting transgender diagnoses and transsexual surgeries are the "gender managers" that serve "gender narratives" and regulate the lives of all Western people. When we understand the social construct of gender as actually a hierarchical power structure that maintains the patriarchal family and the social structure of heterosexism, this makes a lot of sense. Hausman explains that it was opposition to homosexuality that fueled the foundations of some of the early transsexual medical work. Justifying the sterilization that was a component part of the treatment, they considered it was "more important that the patient is not homosexual than that the patient is fertile."[25] If this sounds archaic, or impossible to connect with what is happening today in America with the introduction of transgendered children, this concept is supported by the statistic that upwards of 80% of children expressing symptoms of GD would grow up to be LGB adults if left alone to progress naturally.[26] And all follow-up studies have found a statistically significant correlation between GID and homosexuality.[27]

PATHOLOGIZING OF HOMOSEXUALITY, AGAIN

Homosexuality remains a crime punishable by death in some ten countries across the world today, including Iran. Yet in Iran, transgenderism is welcomed by doctors, as a "cure" for homosexuality, which also reduces executions. Those who wish to remain in Iran often receive a shocking prescription from the medical community: have surgery to change their gendered appearance and appear heterosexual. Iran has between 15,000 and 20,000 transsexuals, according to official statistics, although unofficial estimates put the figure at up to 150,000.[28]

For the women of Kabul, Afghanistan, gender is clearly perceived as a social hierarchy that provides no comfort in being born and raised a girl. In *The Underground Girls of Kabul: The Hidden Lives of Afghan Girls Disguised as Boys*, Jenny Nordberg describes a world of patriarchal families whose parents choose one of their girl children to be raised and presented to the world as a boy, blatantly offering the family economic and social advantages they would not have with a daughter, and with little concern for her views on the matter. Afghanistan is a society where men have all the power and women have almost no rights and little freedom. The gender dysphoria presented in these families is not a medical or psychological condition. It is not a "feeling" of being in the wrong body. It is a brutal fact of life,[29] one that can give some perspective to American parents wondering what freedoms are being perceived by their child, in posing as the opposite sex. Gender is a political issue and social hierarchy. Pathologizing children who don't conform or comply to gender behavioral dictates only serves to reinforce it and also serves to silence the global work of strong, vibrant feminist movements seeking to dismantle and abolish gender hierarchy, resulting in girls, women, and all vulnerable beings more subjected to male sexual violence.[30]

THE CONSEQUENCES OF GENDER'S BRUTALITY UPON GIRLS

Suicide is the leading cause of death globally for teen girls age 15-19, a shocking statistic that appeared deep in the pages of the 2014 WHO report "Preventing Suicide: A Global Imperative." Self-harm in the name of gender and transgender takes many other forms. In March 2016, *The British Daily Mail* reported that by the age of 16, one in four young women are considering plastic surgery, while an astonishing 92 percent want to change the way they look.[31] Young lesbians are increasingly binding their breasts to the point of lymphatic issues and necrotic tissues. They are also finding cross-sex hormones on the black market in an effort to present as male – as reported by their blogs and YouTube videos. While war is being waged on women around the world, more and more privileged young Western women request bodily mutilations such as breast augmentation surgery and/or labioplasty because their hypersexualized, natural body is perceived as "not good enough" compared to the digital images and peer pressures they are surrounded by.

Still other young women are increasingly choosing the opposite procedure: breast-removal surgery, and in some cases, their womb and ovaries simultaneously via full ovario-hysterectomy.

Irreplaceable and anatomically rich material that formed during their gestation in the maternal body is being permanently removed and disposed of via on-site medical incineration: disposal-by-fire for their parts deemed "wrong." In contrast, male-to-trans surgeries involve minimal excision of body tissue. Most male-to-trans do not seek to remove any organs and if they do, they seek external testicle removal rather than prostate surgery or castration – and are spared the fire. Coincidence? We think not, in a world saturated with misogyny and internalized misogyny.

Puberty's symptoms for girls in the culture of high-tech patriarchy are a woeful indicator of femaleness in a world that pivots on hatred of women and celebration of male privilege – and as transgenderism becomes more and more of a trend, teen girls are lining up to schedule removal of their breasts and internal sexual organs – sometimes scheduled the same day, if funds allow. In contrast, teen boys are only seeking to stop their adolescent voice development via hormones and add artificial implants to their chests. These males are not aspiring to become eunuchs, to have their actual internal reproductive gland (prostate) removed, let alone their external organ/glands (penis/testicles). Though this may come as a surprise to some newcomers to the transgender discussion and seems incongruent, it makes perfect sense when we take into account the fact of a society based in compulsive male sexual entitlement privilege and violence. The vast majority of male-to-trans both young and old are packing penises, and purposefully so, because the medically transgendered version of female is not only simply artificial, it is penis-centered, and not about asexualism regardless of where it falls on the sexuality spectrum.

DE-TRANSITIONERS/RE-TRANSITIONERS

In and among these stories of medically transgendered Western youth, we are also seeing an increasing number of self-described "de-transitioners" or "re-transitioners." These are individuals who've been on cross-sex hormones for years, many of whom have had their voices permanently altered and healthy body parts removed, yet have come to feel they made a mistake – that transgendering does not solve their underlying traumas or the brutalities of the gendered world.[32] They are transitioning off the drugs, acknowledging the psychosocial root causes of their original medical transgendering, and confronting the harsh facts and complex challenges that entails.

A Google search reveals 19,600 pages of resources for persons who seek to de-transition. Some de-transition temporarily but change their minds. Some de-transition permanently, and find new meaning in words like autotomy and metamorphosis, as in the capacity of a creature, such as the lizard, to give up parts of itself in order to survive. Still others find their way with significant help from the twelve-step recovery community, whose diverse groups have morphed beyond what some consider Alcoholics Anonymous' somewhat dated and rather limited assumptions about what addiction entails and why, to include people who have lost homes, loved ones, and jobs due to the expenses and stresses involved in plastic surgery addiction.

Many de-transitioners are documenting their journeys of self-integration and healing speaking of regret, self-forgiveness, health challenges, and new perspectives on past traumas. De-transitioners may be unappreciated or mocked by some in the trans community – and may struggle with finding a place to be themselves. De-transitioners, as mentors and resources for other de-transitioners, as well as community educators on informed choice and human rights issues facing children and adolescents, may provide missing links and much-needed voices to a culture lacking such voices. For those who later come to feel that their childhood transitioning was due to underlying abuse, addiction, or self-harm and/or that they were not protected by otherwise well-meaning parents and unscrupulous clinicians when they started to experiment with self-expression – these voices will be lighthouses. De-transitioners have begun to speak out if only we could hear them.[33] Mainstream media and the trans industry certainly doesn't want them heard, and ensures they are largely silenced in the roar of trans marketing.

THE WESTERN INDUSTRIAL BODY: DYSPHORIA, GLOBALLY EXPORTED

The drugging and surgical mutilation of the natal body in order to perform as a perceived "other" gender is not an issue that we have seen across cultures, generations, or throughout history. Varied sexual preferences and sex-role expression we have seen, but not the hatred and silencing of the body's biology we see today. This would suggest transgenderism's roots as a psychosocial phenomenon on par with different psychosocial disorders that present in other cultures that have no biological cause.[34]

Transgenderism is manifesting in western countries and being exported globally, as described by Ethan Waters in a *New York Times* article, "The Americanization of Mental Illness," in what he calls the globalization of mental illness. "For more than a generation now, we in the West have aggressively spread our modern knowledge of mental illness around the world. We have done this in the name of science, believing that our approaches reveal the biological basis of psychic suffering and dispel prescientific myths and harmful stigma. There is now good evidence to suggest that in the process of teaching the rest of the world to think like us, we've been exporting our Western 'symptom repertoire' as well. That is, we've been changing not only the treatments but also the expression of mental illness in other cultures. Indeed, a handful of mental health disorders, such as depression, post-traumatic stress disorder and anorexia among them, now appear to be spreading across cultures with the speed of contagious diseases."[35]

Bulimia, anorexia, and bodily integrity identity disorder (BIID) could certainly be seen as cousins to gender dysphoria, yet none of these has presented in very young children, thus far. Is there a reason medical professionals aren't looking at gender dysphoria along this axis? So far, physicians are not lining up to amputate the limbs of people with BIID, but children expressing dissatisfaction with their genitals (or, as proposed here, a dissatisfaction with their sex-role stereotyping/gender) are being treated like scientific experiments, if not celebrities. The fact that transgenderism in children is spreading across Europe and Australia at the same boundless pace seen in the US, but thus far is largely absent in non-Western societies, supports Mr. Water's assertion. (The fact that much of the US, British, and Australian media is all Murdoch-owned plays also into this sales funnel). And Africa and Asia are on the market horizon.

MEDIA ENCULTURATION OF TRANSGENDERISM

The question of which came first, the transgender child or the media-saturated culture that informs the children and their parents, is a question worth some attention. If it seems like a leap to suggest that the media is constructing the new norm of transgenderism in children far beyond the Hallmark card-like stories about a few brave children facing down a challenge one need only follow the statistics of media coverage. There is no doubt that the subject of transgenderism has moved into the living rooms of popular culture and entered the mainstream lexicon – from "trans conferences" (funded by plastic surgeons and the pharmaceutical industry) to the trans celebrities like Chaz Bono, the Wachowski brothers, Laverne Cox, and the person formerly known as Olympic athlete Bruce Jenner making the rounds of such conferences as well as talk shows, all the while smiling suggestively from grocery store magazine covers and online gossip columns.

In 2013 transgenderism barely registered on our cultural radar. By 2014 there'd been a 400% spike in media coverage (and this was *before* the transition of the person formerly known as Bruce Jenner, which created its own media storm).[36] This spike occurred across the United States and Britain with articles in the *Wall Street Journal*, *New York Times*, *The New Yorker*, *The Guardian*, and just about every major mainstream magazine and newspaper. Though transgender individuals make up less than 4% of the population (but growing), there were nineteen new television shows featuring a transgender character in 2014.[37]

Jill Soloway's Golden Globe-winning *Transparent* (2015) followed on the heels of *Orange is the New Black* (2014), which featured the first male-to-trans "woman of color" to have a role on a mainstream subscription television show. Women of color who survived girlhood make various cogent points about male-to-trans actor Cox's assumptions as to what that really is. Bruce Jenner's debut as Caitlyn Jenner was trumpeted as an act of unsurpassed bravery complete with a *Vanity Fair* cover, as a twice-divorced man with six grown children presenting as an ostensibly sexy middle-aged woman performing for the male gaze on the cover of a popular magazine. Across the pond in Europe, the BBC's coverage of transgenderism in print media also showed a spike in 2014 of astronomical proportion compared to previous years.[38] Transgenderism, not any kind of orange, seems to be "the new black," its chicness a matter of unquestioned celebration.

How does a psychological and medical issue repackage itself to become a cultural celebration of diversity and bravery? There are six major corporations controlling the vast majority of the media in the US: GE, News-Corp, Disney, Viacom, Time Warner, and CBS.[39] Media mega-mergers have bought up small publishers and local news programs, functioning now as highly concentrated and homogenous commercial media that provide programs for the audiences who are immersed in them from early childhood to end of life.[40] They shape the message and influence the way people think, and if their interests were human diversity and promoting justice for a marginalized population, it would be a first for any American corporation. American corporations are interested in profits and the profits being generated by an industry they are manufacturing are plentiful if they can get us to accept the message that there is something wrong with children's bodies that needs their medical interventions. With the UK reporting a staggering 930% surge in gender-identity referrals in six years (2009—2015), that is a lot of potential profit for the burgeoning industries arriving to multiply the transgender population.

Though heterosexual adult males comprise the majority of adult-to-trans people[41] (the stories of women who transition are strangely absent by comparison), it is so-called transgender children that have come to the foreground, with one blogger claiming that if 2014 was the transgender tipping point, then 2015 was the "Year of the Transgender Child" and it is not hyperbole to say so.

An explosion of articles began trending in 2015 on internet news sites, pollinating the global digital world. Magazine features followed a similar trajectory – articles such as "A Mom's Letter Introducing Her Transgender Daughter,"[42] "Mommy, I'm Just Not That Kind of Girl,"[43] and "Mother Schools Haters Who Don't Understand Her Transgender Daughter"[44] all favored the narrative of a child who gravitates to what is culturally deemed masculine or feminine gender stereotypes and the opposite of the stereotypes that are culturally delineated to their biological sex. And, even though pink unicorns and long hair have nothing inherently female about them, just about every single one of these articles would have us believe that a boy who enjoys playing with pink unicorns and wearing his hair long is – surprise! - a girl in the wrong body, never mind that indigenous boys and men in many North and South American tribes, as well as males of the Punjabi Sikh culture, keep their hair long.

Beyond the family narrative, artists also rushed to capitalize on the transgender child. A Dutch photographer, Sarah Wong, spent twelve years documenting young children in transition, creating a stunning book of portraits, with many of her subjects already on puberty blockers.[45] Charlie White, another photographer, created a spectacular piece pairing teen girls with their comparative adult male-to-trans "transwomen."[46] These photographers are mimicking coverage of adult transgenders that is meant to sell transgenderism as a new and exciting lifestyle choice, instead of a mental disorder deserving respect and treatment. The *Gay Star News* incited audience attention with a headline in November 2014, "11 Insanely Hot Transmen that Are Changing the World."[47] *Vogue Magazine* followed suit in April 2015 with an interview with now-famous trans model Andreja Pejic.[48]

Nothing quite compares in scope, however, to what can be considered a financial empire built out of being a transgender child, like the one built around Jazz Jennings, a transgender tween. In October 2014, *Time* magazine awarded Jazz a place on their "25 Most Influential Teens List." Jazz was born a boy, but in line with proliferating, poetically compelling narratives of trans children, he "always knew he was a girl." With relentless marketing by Jazz's parents, who shopped videos of their child throughout social media and alternative culture, this now-adolescent eventually was featured on a variety of major programs and news outlets, including a *20/20* update with Barbara Walters, interviews with Katie Couric and *60 Minutes*, *Time* magazine, *Teen Vogue*, and an Oprah Winfrey Network documentary, *"I Am Jazz: A Family in Transition"* to name but a few. These "accomplishments" – and one has to wonder why honestly owning a gender dysphoria is an accomplishment – are just the tip of the financial empire that has been created around Jazz Jennings and family.[49]

A discussion between Jazz and mother Jeannette about the medication that Jazz will be forced to take for the rest of Jazz's life is telling. "It's hard," Jeanette says of the medical interventions her family must weigh in support of Jazz. "The whole hormone gamut is just *uncharted territory* [emphasis ours]. It's considered *experimental*. But it goes with the territory. I'd rather have to do something like that than the consequences of having her body develop like my husband … I don't want her to look like that, and she doesn't want to look like that."[50] Jeanette would rather consign her biological male child to ingesting experimental chemicals that disrupt his puberty and cause sterilization; drugs that have been known to cause migraines, severe joint pain, difficulty breathing, depression, bone pain, liver function abnormality, vision abnormality, and anxiety. Should Jazz continues on with medical transition, Jazz will be faced with lifelong administration of cross-sex hormones, after the puberty blockers have already interrupted the natural, biological growth process. This process involves hormones linked to sterilization, loss of bone density, arterial restriction and a host of other complications, including cancer, along with myriad major surgeries in order to keep the façade of being a female alive for Jazz and family. Our culture is awash with stories just like Jazz's, and with parents just like Jazz's who are convinced their children need chemical bodies, preparing the way for surgeries that will help them pass as the opposite sex for the rest of their lives.

The facts on what these drugs and their accompanying side effects do are absent from the media, along with the stories of teens who have already been the route of cross sex hormones, found it was not right for them, and are beginning to de-transition. Trans videos are all over YouTube, with their blogs replicating on the internet, yet nothing breaks through the wall about the side effects, health risks, and the limits of de-transitioning. In a playful banter between Jeanette and Jazz, Jazz asks "Hey mom: When am I getting my boobs? Didn't you say January?"[51] No one has mentioned the fact that these are artificial implants, that major surgery involves risk of death due to anesthesia complications or infection, or the fact that none of this involves true replication of the abundance of milk ducts and nerve receptors found in actual female breast biology.

Janice Raymond, professor of Women's Studies and Medical Ethics at the University of Massachusetts Amherst, former adjunct professor of International Health at Boston University's School of Public Health, and author of five books, writes in *The Transexual Empire: The Making of A She-Male,* "Instead of developing genuine integrity, the transsexual becomes a synthetic product. Synthetic parts, such as the chemical hormones and surgical artifacts of false vaginas and breasts, produce a synthetic whole." Raymond describes how environmental activist Rachel Carson demonstrated that chemical pesticides were disastrous to the planet. Barry Commoner followed by showing how so-called technological "advances" have debilitated our ecosystems and planetary biology, because everything is related to everything else, and invasive, industrial approaches to the psychosocial problem of transgendersim are destructive to the "bio-ecosystems" of people suffering from GID.[52] This is a compelling observation at the crucial juncture where our very planet is under threat of biospheric death from the colonialist-capitalist process that overrides laws, destroys entire cultures of people and their way of life, kills our oceans, and pollutes all our water systems to have more of what it wants to make profits. They have just added children, by way of transgenderism, to the list. And they have done so largely under the radar – taking many grassroots community members by surprise.

Socialization and Mental Health: Children and Adults

To look at how gendering of children is perpetuated by this culture, we must acknowledge the forces known as "socialization." Social scientists estimate that by the time a child is age eighteen, they have received 25,000 hours of pure conditioning from parents, teachers, and media – including an average 5.5 to 8 hours per day of some combination of TV, internet surfing, and/or video games. This screen time contains abundant marketing advertisements, Photoshopped depictions of highly gendered and artificial bodies, multitudinous product placements, as well as ubiquitous violence particularly viewed by those in the 8-13 year-old age range.[53] In the industrial world, four out of five 16-year-old boys and girls regularly access porn on the internet (according to a 2012 report by the Independent Parliamentary Inquiry Into Online Child Protection in the United Kingdom). Eleven years old is the average age of first exposure to internet pornography, and the largest group of internet pornography consumers is the 12 to17-year-old age group (*Internet Filter Review*).[54] Children now spend an average of only fifteen minutes per day playing outdoors, with the rest of their time spent in sedentary – and often solitary indoor pursuits. This should be of grave concern to anyone who cares about healthy child development and the relationship of children with their bodies. If our relationship with our body is a microcosm for how we relate with the natural, outdoor world and other beings – medical transgenderism is loudly expressing a macrocosm of psychopathology.

Diagnoses for childhood mental illness are now virtually pandemic in the United States, with the rest of the Western world following suit. An estimated 1 of 7 school-age children is on at least one psychotropic drug, and many are on several. There has been a 4,000% increase in the number of children on psychiatric drugs between 1970 and 2000.[55] With billions of dollars in steady revenue already being made from drugging the noncompliant and/or distressed behaviors in this culture, the logical next step in dominating biology has arrived by giving it "gender identity disorder" and then drugging it and surgically altering it. And though the etiology of GID is far from established, American doctors are using sex reassignment drugs and hormones on younger and younger children.

One of the greatest life skills and signs of maturity is the ability to live with ambivalence, ambiguity and unresolved problems as we move through life – the inherent challenge of human development. In the case of children, it is the special task of parents and other caregivers to skillfully nurture and guide their inherent self-discovery through the natural upheavals, fluidities, and changes that bring their character into maturation. In her article *"The Born Identity: What Do Transgender Children Need?"* Mina Keleman states, Over the past 15 years, doctors have grown progressively more comfortable prescribing hormone blockers to transgender children, and transgender teenagers and their families aren't waiting until adulthood for cross-sex hormones and sex reassignment surgery. They're embarking on medically assisted transformations earlier. Much earlier. These days, such teens often learn about these procedures through a simple Google search, and the amount and availability of information out there is increasingly forcing parents to make difficult decisions about whether to allow their children to undergo medical treatment, including life-altering hormones.[56]

These interventions, though they could be and should be postponed until adult maturation due to numerous concerns related to informed choice vs. manufactured choice, are being allowed before the legal age of consent, with permanent consequences and a distinctly unsustainable trajectory. Young children and teens are not just being "allowed" to pursue and undergo chemical de-sexing and life-risking major surgeries during a time when their brains are still developing; there is a strategically launched and tactically marketed effort to promote transgenderism to the gatekeepers and guardians of the children via the internet and the new children's "literature" written by trans adults and trans doctors. This, across a culture in the throes of a global climate change that is killing the natural world at a rapid rate. The more one ponders this convergence, the more it makes a kind of sense: what better way to ensure a people *not* feel anger and fear over this issue and a new solidarity with the natural world? What better way to perpetuate a popular culture largely devoid of real social transformation and structural change than the cause célèbre of transgenderism, the social contagion of biophobia?

Transgenderism in children is often the result of learning about it from the internet, from peers, or from adult labeling and limiting of a child's innately fluid identity. It also readily provides a fervent and intoxicating distraction from realities like climate catastrophe, sexual confusion, and the often painful offline world giving angst-ridden teenagers or media-parented young children a perpetually welcome haven. It also gives these youths the informational advantage of a Kamikazi pilot when dealing with unprepared parents hearing their impassioned, insistent cries of feeling like they are the opposite sex because they met trans friends and found "passing guides" on the internet that lead them to the local trans-supportive psychiatrist who doles out puberty-blockers on and off the internet. Since recent studies indicate screen time is creating subtle damage even in children with "regular" exposure, we should be questioning everything about this phase of internet culture's transgenderism trend in children. Questioning the reversals that have molded popular culture's view that the drugging and cosmetic surgeries of children are somehow reasonable and not insane, and questioning how children and adults highly affected by screen time are even capable of sober self-assessment when so entangled with their own hours spent on media.[57]

The internet is brimming with heavily watched YouTube documentary videos on "My Transition Diary" and "Transition Advice: Are You Trans?" The internet also hawks trans fashion, trans porn, and trans doctors whose treatment trajectories largely dilute or sideline psychosocial remedies. These doctors prescribe the pills, and thus bless the coming mastectomies, arrests of vocal development, hysterectomies, and breast implants. A portion of today's would-be transformational teens (many of them with nascent LGB tendencies) and creative younger children who could be on their way to resisting social and ecological injustices in the world at large, are being encouraged by their peers and surrounding adults, to, in essence, *limit transformation* down to a physical alteration and gendered performance. What in actuality is self-mutilation and self-stereotyping is being met with many positive feedback loops from other adolescents seeking the "right" body (again, largely on the internet), a body and mind whose sexual preference ambivalence and/or raw trauma is mitigated, at least temporarily, in artificial rites-of-passage that require little to no emotional integration.

When experiencing their beloved young child or adolescent speaking of feeling like the opposite sex, mothers, fathers, aunts, uncles, preschool teachers, neighbors, and extended family who are immersed in the well-positioned trans stories and marketing both online and offline, may have reactions of their own that can complicate the developmental and/or psychosocial processes. Caregivers can start ruminating, and may find themselves confused. Can a child change their sex? Is biological sex the same as gender? Is it possible this child was born with the wrong genitals? Parents may also recognize or deny that they carried and projected severe gender stereotypes or unresolved personal issues that affected their child, and wonder if they might have created a straitjacket for their child that requires the remedy that is most common: medical intervention.

Transgenderism also strongly appeals to other adults whose psychological needs are met by focusing on a child, whether a toddler or a teen, in whose creative identity expression and subsequent transgendering they find a vicarious sense of stimulation, meaning, or fame. In fact, the mental illness known as Munchausen by proxy syndrome (MBPS) is a form of child abuse where parents or caregivers exaggerate, fabricate, or induce mental/emotional/physical health symptoms in their child in order to take personal gain from the uniqueness (real or imagined) of their child. MBPS may well be on the rise, and *not* as rare as previously thought. It is no stretch to realize that MPBS and GID can go quite well together, considering the local fame and even international media coverage that is possible when one has a child who identifies as transgender.

Whether a parent or caregiver suffers from MPBS or one of several other mental disorders relatively common today, critical discussion *about* disorder is nearly impossible *with* the disordered, especially if they are untreated or unhealed. Today's culture is a fragmented landscape where significant numbers of adults have mental disorders, emotional dysfunction, or are even pathological. Practicing psychologist and Harvard Medical school professor Martha Stout estimates that 1 in 25 (or some 4%) of people in American society is sociopathic (three-quarters of them are male) with no conscious sense of right and wrong. Dr. Stout says: "I believe that all people of conscience should learn how to recognize and deal effectively with the morally weak and the ruthless."[58] Guardians of children who suffer from stress, addictions, and disorders may frequently be in the mode of feeling broken. Children are very perceptive of the power dynamics and blind spots of their primary caregivers and the culture at large, craving healthy boundaries by mature adults who can lovingly guide them. However, in a society of nuclear family disasters, epigenetic trauma, sexual abuse, racial profiling, peer bullying, and other conditions, perceptions of the viability of "trading in" the body one was born with can symbolize an expedient distraction, if not true escape, from some of the mundane boredoms or brutal torments of a variety of childhoods. What we are seeing is adult constructs allowing children's bodies to be experimented on rather than guided – and unconscious abuses are occurring in the name of medical transgenderism.

INSTITUTIONALIZED GENDERISM: SCHOOLS AND THE LAW

In her essay "The New Gender Essentialism," Kimberly Yuracko makes a pointed argument that "the laws being changed to accommodate transgender children and adults is a way of reframing and promoting essentialized concepts of masculinity and femininity that threaten to define and constrain options for women, men, transsexual and non-transsexuals alike." With the introduction of sex discrimination cases providing protection to transgendered individuals, Yuracko argues, this gender essentialism is being replaced by a new form of gender essentialism, whereby courts not only permit dichotomous and socially loaded conceptions of gender/sex-role stereotypes, but in fact enforce them.[59]

A Nebraska school district has instructed teachers to stop referring to its students as boys and girls, and to use "gender-inclusive" expressions such as "purple penguins."[60] While referring to children as "children" rather than gender stereotypes has long been a practice of child-centered educators, the belief that any reference to one's biological sex is somehow exclusive is a foundational belief that ultimately favors the new transgender industrial medical exploitation of children. In fact, some school psychologists are key players in fast-tracking children towards medical interventions rather than urging psychosocial approaches suggesting "mis-gendering," and supporting medicalization of non-gender-conforming children.

Minnesota school districts are legally battling whether high school students should be allowed to play on the sports teams that fit their chosen gender identity regardless of biological realities. In Colorado, a six-year-old boy, Coy Mathis, who identifies as a girl, won a civil rights case so that "she" could use the girls' restroom at her school,[61] regardless of how all the girls feel about having a boy in the stall next to them, in a time when girls as young as seven are exhibiting puberty symptoms, including menstruation.

Is transgenderism a disability, a fashion statement, or a sexual orientation? And where do children's precious bodies and minds fit into this menagerie? Once medicalized, transgenderism was insulated from public debate by being legitimized in law. Now, medicine and law have done so much to bolster the politics of transgenderism that their advocates feel sufficiently emboldened to disassociate their discourse from the sphere of medicalization. Take, for example, the World Professional Association for Transgender Health (WPATH), which was formerly the Harry Benjamin International Gender Dysphoria Association, Inc., named for Harry Benjamin, an endocrinologist who was one of the first professionals to *advocate for* medical treatments for transsexuals. WPATH has positioned itself as a nonprofit organization devoted to working to promote evidence-based care, but it is actually not a scientific body, nor is it unbiased. It functions more as a trade association or industrial lobby whose purpose is to advocate and lobby for medical transgenderism. As WPATH executives put it, trans identity is "a common and culturally diverse human phenomenon that should not be judged as inherently pathological or negative."[62] "Culturally diverse phenomenon" is a pretty hazy term to be using while injecting life- and limb-risking general anesthesia into a young person's spine or cutting into their flesh, or making new laws that advance biotech theology.

Trans advocates and the medical institutions growing to serve the transgender community appear to want it both ways. They want it medicalized for purposes of insurance reimbursements and maximum financial flow with the influx of new patients, and yet they want to make sure it is seen only as free association and expression. The new creed being marketed by medical trans adherents is one of "wrong bodies" and "gendered brains," of the "female penis" and "male uterus," of unreality over reality: the biological facts of life in the natural world of dimorphic species, and the scientific evidence on both human anatomy and psychosocial development. Without public outrage and rigorous human rights lawsuits to block the insidious infrastructure formed to promote medical transgendering of children, and without clear and stable definitions for basic terms to assist in social discourse and exposure of human rights violations of children, the movement is poised to claim more and more children as its own.

Laws are currently being changed all over the country to publicly accommodate transgender-identifying students with intact genitals of their biological sex use of bathrooms, locker rooms, sports teams, and team hotel rooms that coincide with their internally perceived identities as the opposite gender. In many states, boys who "feel" like girls are legally allowed to use the spaces previously segregated by biological sex to insure the safety of girls – in an environment where many girls are already at risk of male sexual harassment or violence at school, at home, and/or in public spaces. Shockingly, despite a culture of well-documented school bullying and hypersexualized children, there is no criteria for boys to use girls' facilities other than their subjective "feeling like a girl." The non-subjective reality of a boy's presence in girls' private spaces makes girls feel uncomfortable, and many parents along with them. Their feelings or concerns are not given any formal consideration in the headlong rush to provide civil liberties and safety to a purportedly disenfranchised, miniscule part of the population. How is that possible when females make up 52% of the population and that male violence against females in our culture *is the very reason* segregated facilities were introduced in the first place?

There are no similar accommodations made for those with other body dysphoria. Those with BIID are not fighting for the right to use the disabled stalls in public facilities. Those with anorexia are not supported in their assumptions of being fat and yet the accommodations for those with gender dysphoria are being institutionalized through our educational systems and the law, at a breakneck pace, without considerations as to what this will mean to society at large. It begs the question, "why?"

ENVIRONMENTAL DISSOCIATION OF THE HUMAN CHILD

Is gender dysphoria an acute dislike of the gendered stereotypes delineated for biological sex, as the research suggests? If so, then why is the first line of action manipulating children's rapidly developing bodies with invasive chemicals, the full long-term effects of which we are not even close to understanding? We already know they are harmful. That should be enough. Why isn't it?

By giving boys access to girls' safe spaces, we also give all children mixed messages, including the one that boys can have vaginas and girls can have penises, and without any education on true intersex realities that are deserving of factual exploration. When we no longer call children "children" related to their age, or "girls and boys" related to their biology, but instead "purple penguins," in our efforts at "inclusion," we are furthering this doublespeak and colluding in severing children from their biological roots in the way that industrial capitalism has severed people's relationship to the earth. Given that 75% of the world's population lives in urban areas, totally removed from the growth of their food, most people if you asked where their food came from would be apt to say "the supermarket."[63]

Dissociating children further from their natural processes and instilling a false idea about how they are created gives adult market forces free reign to control, and thus exploit them. Children are being taught that their biology is not real, that their selves are located in some subjective reality in their minds, that their minds that have nothing to do with their bodies, that their body parts are disposable. This is biophobia reaching its peak, and with it a techno-utopia being formalized through education and the law that will forever break the bond children have to the biological source of earth and mother, replacing her with the father of capitalism and industrial civilization. Transgender children, taken under the medical wing of industrial capitalism, will rely on civilization for their health and their sense of self for the rest of their lives. With aggrandized identities and chemical bodies taking the place of connection to the earth, each other, and the biodiversity that surrounds us, the joyous potential of the natural child's full expression and social development is being silenced by a trend that looks more and more each day like human rights violations, like eugenics.

This is what biophobia looks like.

Planetary biology and personal biology are being silenced. Institutionalized through education and the law, an unease and even hatred towards biology permeates industrial culture. It entraps children and compartmentalizes them into gendered boxes that limit their unique developmental journey and true potential. In addition, medical transgenderism's incessant focus on mind-body dissociation, sex-role stereotypes, and peer/popular culture pre-emptively limits child development and prioritizes the artificial over the biodynamic. This makes it even more unlikely that the medically transitioning child will have the kind of intimacy with the natural world that is necessary in order to effectively resist that which is killing it and/or survive its collapse. In addition, medically transgendered children are being made further dependent on fossil fuel-derived industry for their pharmaceutical needs and sense of "self" for the rest of their foreseeable lives, with all accompanying side effects and health risks.

Industrial chemicals and other compounds are in every waterway on earth and in every mammal mother's breast milk. Endocrine disruptions have changed the timeline of childhood physical development in more and more children with puberty and all its physical and emotional upheavals occurring as early as age seven, juxtaposed with the emotional and mental development that requires chronological time to arrive. Add to this adults (be they parents, legal guardians, school counselors, teachers, or medical clinicians) who are often ill-equipped to guide and guard optimal child development, particularly when faced with the uncharted waters of precocious puberty and the popularity of GID within a socially unjust society, and the deal is done. Brave New World meets Lucrative New World.

Children struggling to express themselves now have a permanent "medical condition" instead of a transitory psychological disorder. Raised during the backlash to feminism and the all-out war on women and the living world, these children are no longer regarded as a group at risk of exploitation simply due to being children in this culture. The way that women are treated is directly connected to the way that children and the earth are treated. The transgender ideology's efforts to silence biological, dimorphic sex in *homo sapiens* in turn works to deny the very real sex-based oppression in our society that makes male violence a primary problem for women, children, and all vulnerable classes of beings. In the worldview of medical transgenderism, female source and the sacred integrity of biology itself are treated with profane disregard. Meanwhile the statistics on crimes against the bodies of women and children pile up at the altar of gender ideology.

HUMAN GESTATION AND BIRTH IMPRINTS: TECHNOLOGY VS. THE EARTH

Medical sociologist Talcott Parsons' theory of gender roles argued that medicine was a social institution that regulated social deviance through the provision of medical diagnoses for nonconforming behavior. Medicine is, in this understanding, engaged in social control.[64] Let's look at a few additional ways that institutional culture in its high-tech phase has become established both as a very early regulator of the human child's development and as a high-tech manipulator of biology in ways that are so pervasive that they are considered normal to the children born into it the last thirty-plus years.

The advent of the first prenatal "gender determination" sonogram (also known by its kinder, gentler sounding name, "ultrasound") was unprecedented on the planet until the late 1970s.[65] The arrival of the prenatal sonogram brought technology into the gestational environment with little to no consideration of the invasiveness of the "non-invasive." The technocratic "womb with a view" made the sonogram, as well as the fetus, objects of fascination. The impact of the misnomered "gender determination" sonogram (which decreed the baby's sex based upon whether or not the outline of a penis was noted) upon pregnant women is no small matter, being that maternal hopes, fears, and mental preoccupations directly impact blood chemistry and thus the developing DNA of her child. Sarah Buckley MD, a critic of interventive obstetrical practice upon otherwise-healthy mothers, says in an article titled "Ultrasound Scans- Cause for Concern":

> To my mind, ultrasound also represents yet another way in which the deep internal knowledge that a mother has of her body and her baby is made secondary to technological information that comes from an 'expert' using a machine. Thus the "cult of the expert" is imprinted from the earliest weeks of life. Furthermore, by treating the baby as a separate being, ultrasound artificially splits mother from baby well before this is a physiological or psychic reality. This further emphasizes our cultures favoring of individualism over mutuality and sets the scene for possible but to my mind artificial conflicts of interest between mother and baby in pregnancy, birth and parenting. [66]

Its main task, to image the gestating fetus with sound waves, did so in a way much more disruptive than most pregnant women involved ever were told or understood: through disrupting red blood cells in the fetal arterial circulation with energy and heat. Whenever ultrasound devices would point to the head of the fetus, the fetus's sensitive hearing structure would be vibrated with loud noise, the equivalent of a jackhammer were it to be conducted via air (100 to 120 decibels). This effect is similar to listening to rain by placing your ears in contact with the roof, which sounds a lot louder than listening to the sound of rain from a distance.[67] The sound disruption often resulted in increased fetal movements conveying upset but were generally misperceived by most adults as having nothing to do with distress or upset.

Though potentially useful for diagnostics in certain rare high-risk conditions, routine sonograms for medically unnecessary purposes (followed by notoriously excessive use of them) became commonplace, and profitable, especially once it started being used to decree the biological sex of the fetus, in the name of gender. With prenatal exposure to sonograms and their proclamations of which sex the coming child would be, came increased maternal, familial, and community gendered expectations upon the pregnancy. Nearly each maternal thought about the baby had a more specific backdrop related to the baby's sex-based identity, rather than the previous earthly maternal experience of musings and intuitions about the possibilities that would express themselves in the child's future life. Post-sonogram prenatal sex-based results were acted out through gender-themed conversations, baby shower games and gifts along gendered lines, and home décor planning involving gender-coded colors and graphics.

And, even more ominously, in cultures where a male child is prioritized and considered of more value than a female child, came the familial disdain and/or forced abortion for women carrying babies they wanted whose test results said they were female – as well as sex-selective termination by choice. For example, disclosing such information has been illegal in India for several years, so as to prevent sex-selective abortions, but middle-class women still arrange for illicit sonograms for that purpose.[68] In addition, the fact that the result of such a test has only a 91% rate of correctness overall (if not supplemented with other diagnostics) was, and continues to be, downplayed. However, at this point, millions of children in the industrial world have been the "surprise" 9%, manifesting as the shocker opposite sex to what the test result said was coming someone "other" than who was decreed, expected, purchased for, and planned for.[69]

This was then followed by the introduction of continuous electronic fetal monitoring (EFM) sonographic devices during childbirth, which often meant a nearly uninterrupted ten to twenty hours of fetal gestational exposure in cases of maternal immobilization and medication. In non-traditional, medical midwifery clinics and practices, the non-continuous hand-held Doppler device became the standard, deceptively small and nonetheless high-intensity in its sonographic generation. There were again, no long-term studies of safety on fetal development, but the use of EFMs did coincide with a subsequent increase in the rate of Cesarean extraction of babies, due to cascading interventions and stressors.[70]

Despite abundant evidence-based confirmations of the mammalian needs of the newborn for undisturbed bonding (with its subsequent impact on the establishment of successful breast-feeding), Western obstetrics and paramedics (as well as some medical midwifery practices) generally persist in disturbing the most critical first hour of transitional life outside the womb. Called the primal adaptive period, this is a profound transition when the newborn is imprinted by its extent of reunion and undisturbed bonding (or lack thereof) with its mother, along with a variety of new sensations as the physical body adapts to gravity and the mother's environments. With numerous and rapid separation practices immediately enacted upon newborns within the first minutes and hours after birth in the institutional setting, often accompanied by maternal trauma and bodily disconnection of mother and child, the biological primacy of emotional and physical transition is often affected. This contrasts starkly with the traditional midwifery model of care that facilitates the bodily integrity of both mother and child, with slow neonatal transition.

One of the cultures where earth-based birthing and bonding is maintained is in Bali, where, recorded on palm-leaf manuscripts are the ancient texts known as the holy book "Lontar Bali," scriptures brought from India over a thousand years ago, originating from the pre-Hindu Vedic oral tradition that goes back much farther in time. Specific instructions are given for honoring and welcoming newborns from the point of view that all parts of a newly born child have value, and that transformation is inherent to the physical journey. The newborn is viewed as a totality including the umbilical cord, placenta, amniotic fluid, and the yellow, waxy substance that coats their skin. In the "Lontar Bali" texts it is believed that the placenta (called Ari-ari), is the physical body of the child's guardian angel and that the angel's spirit stays with the child for their entire life.[71] All elements that are formed from the same original cells of the conception, and thus belonging to the newborn, are considered to be "guardian-siblings" that protect the fetus during gestation and throughout the child's life.[72]

Like many indigenous peoples, the Balinese do not disturb the newborn's transition to earth or interfere with the newborn's umbilical cord for many hours after birth. What has been preserved in Bali is a practice of umbilical integrity also called "lotus birth" where the undisturbed umbilical cord naturally dries and transforms into sinew, detaching a few days later, leaving behind a perfectly healed navel. These practices comprise a basic protocol found in the nonprofit Bumi Sehat Yayasan birth centers directed by international midwife Robin Lim (voted CNN's "Hero of The Year" in 2011), where babies are welcomed in this biology-honoring way, with stunningly healthy outcomes, especially for at-risk, mothers & babies.[73]

If egalitarianism applied to human newborns views them as biological and even spiritual beings first and foremost, then the Western industrial paradigm played out in high-tech birthing rituals is an imprint that requires many interventions and artificialities in transition and further personal development, conveying the message that that *the body is not good enough*. From gestation to the first neonatal hour, human development in high-tech civilization is frequently marked with invasion, shame, and the dissociation of body from spirit. With the advent of newer technologies, that dissociation is projected to reach new heights as researchers and scientists try to create gestation abilities in artificial "womb" environments, as well as in males, in the incessant patriarchal aspiration to mimic the female experience of gestation as protagonist.

SOCIAL AND POLITICAL CONTEXTS OF HUMAN DEVELOPMENT

The terminology around biology vs. socialization (sex vs. gender) was given a formidable analysis by feminists in the 1960s and 1970s, which along with social-justice educational scholars aimed to abolish the sex-role stereotypes of gender. These educators, along with various child advocates, diligently addressed gross inequities of sex, and the pink/blue binary narrative that pervaded the culture from neonatal practices to children's naming, clothing, and toys.[74] What we are seeing now is the complete reversal of these gains, using similar mechanisms:

literature, curriculum, fashion, and the marketplace. This return to oppressive stereotypes complements the last few decades of a concerted effort by the transgender industry to target children – particularly privileged children. When it comes to expensive things, the new marketing niche servicing young identities prone to peer pressure and manufactured choice depends on generous parental pocketbooks.

The commercialization of childhood started to really pick up speed up in the 1980s, during the Reagan/Thatcher era, promoting individualism and capital gains in a melee of gender celebration, blue/pink divides, and some flipping of those divides in the culture at large. Boys could now enjoy dramatic play with scarves and cookery along with the girls. Girls could have short hair and run roaring with the boys without reproof. On the stage, popular music's androgynous and gender-mocking feats were a creative response to the long identity crisis of adolescents raised in the Cold War nuclear age – with Grace Jones, David Bowie, Devo, Patti Smith, Chrissie Hynde & The Pretenders, Cyndi Lauper, Boy George, and Prince among them making wildly creative music that resonated in youth in the last days of the analog world, before the digital tsunami hit.

Fast-forward to the new millennium's neo-patriarchy. "Gender reassignment" procedures have re-established an intransigent gender binary in its flipped form, resulting in two very disturbing outcomes: forced sterilization of many gender nonconforming children, as well as a social erasure of LGB people who are estimated to comprise up to 80% of these children – and who would simply identify as gay or lesbian by age eighteen if adult culture and/or the medical industry did not interfere in their developmental journey.[75]

Normal child development is by its nature radical change that cannot and should not be denied its valid expression. It demands that adults in roles of caregiving, guidance, and authority must have reached a reasonable amount of emotional and mental maturation in order to properly facilitate the vast and ever-changing quality of children's self-expression without using or abusing them for their own purposes. Child development is guaranteed to stress, and test, parental and familial bonds for better or for worse. Dormant parental traumas or disorders may be given a chance to change or to create persistent blind spots or gaps in executive overviews.

Abraham Maslow's "Hierarchy of Needs" and the developmental psychology work of child advocates such as Joseph Chilton-Pierce, Erik Erickson, Alice Miller, and Marian Wright Edelman make the point that while basic needs for food, shelter, and safety are critical for the physical survival of children, psychosocial needs can be easily thwarted and left unmet. Adults with insufficient bonding and self-differentiation (whether these adults be parents or professionals) make poor allies of the innately mutable and creative qualities of children's identities – newborns to adolescent. That the human child even *has* a spiritual self has been largely debated out of Western industrial culture. This raises disturbing questions about what children are for: an end in themselves or to serve the purposes of adult exploitation?

Add the fact that the most recent consensus of neuroscientists agrees that human brain development in modern industrial culture likely persists until at least a person's mid-twenties. Changes occurring between ages eighteen and twenty-five are essentially a continued process of brain development that started during puberty involving the prefrontal cortex and area of the brain that involves impulsive decisions and planning behavior to reach a goal. Adults over the age of twenty-five tend to feel less sensitive to the influence of peer pressure and trends. If our brains aren't developed until the mid-twenties, this means that "legal adults" (those age eighteen and above) are allowed to make adult decisions and are allowed to join the military, without fully mature brains. Regret can have far-reaching effects within individuals, families, and societies, and may make people more vulnerable to suffering from clinical depression, self-harm, and/or addictions.[76]

Meanwhile, the legal age of consent is being steadily eroded by transhumanist and pedophilia lobbies seeking to reduce if not abolish it completely. Children in our industrial culture are at high risk of many kinds of exploitation and abuse. How else is it possible that a fifteen-year-old girl in Oregon, who can't legally drive, drink, have a driver's license, vote or join the military, and whose pre-frontal cortex is not fully formed, can have the legal power to irrevocably alter her body through sex reassignment surgery (SRS), with or without parental consent? How is that not child exploitation?[77]

THE DISAPPEARANCE OF CHILDHOOD

Make no mistake: gender is a straightjacket upon an already industrially-defined context for child development, one that denies the fact that 99% of human history occurred without civilization and its discontents. Not only that, pre-civilization humanity was the most egalitarian segment of history, maintained by earth-based and bio-centric values still seen into the present day in aboriginal and uncontacted cultural survivors.[78] Human children have primal, Paleolithic, mammalian needs for bonding and embodiment in the natural world, needs that are hardwired into the brain, despite a culture that denies history, and afflicts their brains, nervous systems, and endocrine systems with environmental toxins. In order to understand what is happening in digital culture's version of childhood, we must understand what has disappeared rapidly over the last thirty years.

New York University Media Ecology professor Neil Postman's prescient text *The Disappearance of Childhood,* published in 1982, has remained a human development classic for those who stand in solidarity with the rights of children for optimal maturation and age-appropriate protections. Postman outlined the coming extraction of children by an adult-centered commodification of previously hard-won reforms that had humanized some aspects of modern childhood and significantly reduced its harshness in society – especially for poor, orphaned, racially profiled, and/or abused children around the turn of the twentieth century. These reforms included outlawing child labor, legislating public education access for all children regardless of class, instituting educational access and racial desegregation of public schools, ushering in multicultural and National Association for the Education of Young Children-certified (NAEYC) preschool standards, criminalizing corporal punishment of children by adults in both homes and institutions in over forty US states, and fostering a growing discourse in new educational philosophies.

The subsequent backlash that followed these reforms was accompanied by a dedicated effort to industrially profit upon the bodies and minds of children, and increase parental spending via advertising directly to children through TV, and later through digital media. Enter the medical transgendering industry and its chemical/surgical "solution," very enmeshed with industrial capitalism and environmental degradation. Medical interventions upon children for perceived lifelong identity issues ensure that the foundation is set for a lifetime of medical revenues (if the biosphere holds up that long). And they are making money hand over fist.

There has been a multi-billion-dollar investment made to establish permanent medicalizing and de-sexing of children – in the form of several new private children's hospitals in North America that are exclusively dedicated to the medical transgendering of children. These are state-of-the-art facilities that obviously took significant planning years in advance of the transgender media surge. In addition, increasing numbers of children's hospitals now have full departments focused on gender pathology, and though they may have token staff psychologists, the emphasis is on highly invasive protocols rather than the non-medical treatments that would better serve children's intact development. Several of these hospitals are directed by male-to-trans doctors, presenting as "we-men" while actively role-modeling and further selling their medical treatment paradigm far over and beyond any obligatory mention of psychosocial services.

The Children's Hospital of Los Angeles Center for Transyouth Development website celebrates a recent photo featuring the male Olympian gold medal-winner formerly known as Bruce Jenner surrounded by transgender children from the hospital program (odd, considering Jenner did not present as transgender until just a year ago, and in late life, and as the biological father of six non-transgender children). The Boston Children's Hospital's vast operation is called "Gender Management Services" (because this is indeed all about maintaining gender rather than supporting the development of gender non-conforming children). The University of Wisconsin's Pediatric and Adolescent Transgender Health Clinic tells the public: "We can provide the full spectrum of care, from simple observation and guidance to hormone suppression and hormone affirming therapy for children of all ages." A cursory Google search on "hospitals specializing in transgender children" will yield two pages of results for facilities in major cities across the US.

The transgender industry's lobby itself has done much to manifest what must have been a twenty-year plan, considering the regulatory compliance groundwork and the high-level business plans involved that rival those of any corporate industry, and not without having established the support of nonprofit corporations. The top five funders that have provided over 55% of all trans lobby and media funding from 2011-2013 include such major players as the Open Society Foundations (George Soros), Arcus Foundation, Tawani Foundation, Tides Foundation, and various donors who remain officially "anonymous" in a trans contingent that includes high-profile persons positioned in tech, medicine, and entertainment, such as the well-networked, richest CEO in the US, Martine Rothblatt, in their ranks.[79]

It bears repeating: gendering and transgendering is an arrangement of power which encourages children to hate biology and confine themselves to artificial sex roles rather than helping children access the innate human potential that is their natural birthright. Transformation of self via identity mind-body integration and recovery from trauma is an internal process of healthy child development that no medical transgenderism can offer.

MENTAL DISORDERS: PROMOTION VS. RESOLUTION

> At the heart of the problem is confusion over the nature of the transgendered. "Sex change" is biologically impossible. People who undergo sex-reassignment surgery do not change from men to women or vice versa. Rather, they become feminized men or masculinized women. Claiming that this is a civil-rights matter and encouraging surgical intervention is in reality to collaborate with and promote a mental disorder.
>
> ~ PAUL R. MCHUGH, MD, JOHNS HOPKINS UNIVERSITY PROFESSOR OF PSYCHIATRY AND FORMER PSYCHIATRIST-IN-CHIEF, THE JOHNS HOPKINS HOSPITAL.[80]

With the current instability around what transgenderism actually is, from a medical, psychological and cultural standpoint, why would parents be so quick to allow their children to be prescribed hormones known to cause sterilization, cancer, other health issues, and arrest their development, along with setting their child up for a potential future that has them seeing doctors and cosmetic surgeons for the rest of their lives in order to keep an artificial presentation of the opposite sex in place? Unproven and highly lucrative new diagnoses for "gender dysphoria" in children are ethically questionable if not morally reprehensible, but try to say that to a parent who has discovered that their child is "feeling like the opposite sex" or wants drugs and surgeries they've learned about from media and/or peers, and you may find that you are communicating with a fervent convert or a trusting patient of whatever the trans clinics and their small but influential number of psychiatrists and child psychologists who benefit as representatives of the trans industry. These markets are expanding. The possibilities for the growth of this industry are only beginning.

STOP THE MUSIC, RUN THE PIED PIPER OUT OF TOWN: PROTECTING NATURAL CHILDHOOD

The natural child, viewed as a commodity in a society which makes a habit of exploiting the vulnerable, is at serious risk of being manipulated, cajoled, used, and abused by the trans industry and a variety of predatory adults. It may well take decades to overturn legislation and biology-silencing ideology currently enshrining transgenderism in children's culture, intellectual debate, and the global economy. We believe it is crucial to scrupulously question and expose an identity culture manufactured by industry, particularly when it pertains to the health, wellness, and rights of minors. Clearly a medical culture that has no long-term studies on its bio-ecologically destructive manipulations of the developmental years combined with an opportunistic business model should be held ethically accountable where and when it is occurring.

It is no surprise that the mental health of children and adults is suffering, being that the fragile web of life that supports us all is also suffering. Asking ourselves how we can best be advocates for and guardians of children brings us to bioethics: the moral discernment of medical policy and practice. We must forge alliances between child advocates of different faiths and political philosophies on a common ground of ethics to confront the manufacturing of transgender children and the human rights violations this entails. We must do it strategically and tactically, discerning effective ways to take action according to our abilities and social network – and the right time to launch our conversations that matter and deal with disturbing facts.[81] We must do this on many fronts: in city council meetings, courts of law, places of worship, the academy, the airwaves, op-eds, networking, and in community leadership in directly confronting trans predation of children. For those who love the natural world and the human potential of children, it's now or never. As Ms. Florence Kennedy often said, "Women: Don't agonize, organize!"

With these words we hope to provoke and inspire many other articles and legislative initiatives to protect the bodily integrity of children via non-exploitative and psychosocially durable means so that children are able to fully ripen into maturity without being harmed and scarred by medical transgenderism. We want for all the world's children the safe spaces needed to thrive, access to personal transformation and leadership on behalf of the natural world, and maturation into self-possession and self-love. The community revolt against those who are trafficking in the identities of children has already begun, and you are one of its many leaders, asking this question:

The Pied Piper has gone through the town square, where are the children?

---

[1] *Transhumanism* is a postmodern belief or theory espoused by an iconoclastic movement in the high-tech/industrial sciences over the past two decades. Transhumanists believe the human race should evolve beyond its current physical and mental limitations by *means* of science and technology, thus reifying domination over nature and biology. (Oxford Dictionary http://www.oxforddictionaries.com/us/definition/american_english/transhumanism)

Transhumanism situates the improvement the human condition as merged with advanced technologies to the point of not questioning them, their ethical complexities, or the systemic human supremacism contained within it. To many privileged and "first world" children of today, transhumanism seems like natural evolution — and anyone who doesn't follow suit may seem thoroughly inhuman. See: http://www.extremetech.com/extreme/152240-what-is-transhumanism-or-what-does-it-mean-to-be-human

In addition, the Secretary-General of the UN Convention on Biological Diversity said in 2010 that children were losing contact with nature. "We are moving to a more virtual world. Children today haven't a clue about nature. Children have not seen apple trees. In Algeria, children are growing up who have never seen olive trees. How can you protect nature if you do not know it?" (See "Protect nature for world economic security, warns UN biodiversity chief," by John Vidal. *The Guardian*, August 16, 2010.

http://www.theguardian.com/environment/2010/aug/16/nature-economic-security)

[2] William L. White, *Pathways from the Culture of Addiction to the Culture of Recovery: A Travel Guide for Addiction*. Hazeldon Publishing, 1996.

[3] Eva Moore, Amy Wisniewski, and Adrian Dobs, Departments of Medicine and Pediatrics, The Johns Hopkins School of Medicine, Baltimore, Maryland. "Endocrine Treatment of Transsexual People: A Review of Treatment Regimens, Outcomes, and Adverse Effects." *Journal of Clinical Endocrinology & Metabolism*, Clinical Review 161, 2003. http://press.endocrine.org/doi/pdf/10.1210/jc.2002-021967.

[4] David Schwartz, "Listening to Children Imagining Gender: Observing the Inflation of an Idea," *Journal of Homosexuality* Volume 59, Issue 3, 2012 Special Issue: The Treatment of Gender Dysphoric/Gender Variant (GD/GV) Children and Adolescents. p. 461.

[5] The World Health Organization *International Classifications of Diagnoses Manual*. ICD-10: Version 2016. Sections F64.2 and F66.0 http://apps.who.int/classifications/icd10/browse/2016/en#/F60-F69

[6] Richard Anderson, "Pharmaceutical industry gets high on fat profits," BBC News, 6 November 2014. http://www.bbc.com/news/business-28212223.

[7] The Lueneburg manuscript (c. 1440–50) gives an early German account of the event, rendered in an inscription on a house found in Hamelin. This antiquarian manuscript is cited by Willy Krogmann in *Der Rattenfänger von Hameln: Eine Untersuchung über das werden der sage*, page 67. Published by E. Ebering, 1934. Original from the University of Michigan.

[8] Schwartz, "Listening to Children Imagining Gender," p. 270.

[9] The United Nations Environment Program reports that some scientists estimate that 150-*200 species* of plant, insect, bird and mammal become *extinct* every 24 hours. This is nearly 1,000

times the "natural" or "background" rate. Ninety-nine percent of currently threatened species are at risk from human activities. Endangered Species. 2009. In *Encyclopædia Britannica*. Available in Encyclopedia Britannica Online at http://www.britannica.com/EBchecked/topic/186738/endangered-species.

[10] Schwartz, "Listening to Children Imagining Gender," p. 270.

[11] The Oxford British & World English Dictionary defines biophobia as: 1. (Especially among social scientists) a refusal or marked reluctance to consider or accept biological (especially genetic or evolutionary) factors or theories in relation to human life. 2. Avoidance of contact with animals, plants, or organic materials; strong aversion to aspects of the natural world. http://www.oxforddictionaries.com/us/definition/american_english/biophobia

[12] As defined by the US National Library of Medicine, on the National Institutes of Health's website: https://www.nlm.nih.gov/medlineplus/ency/article/001527.htm

[13] Aruna Saraswat, Jamie Weinand, and Joshua Safer, "Evidence Supporting the Biologic Nature of Gender Identity." *Endocrine Practice*: February 2015, Vol. 21, No. 2, pp. 199-204. Abstract: http://www.bu.edu/news/2015/02/13/review-article-provides-evidence-on-the-biological-nature-of-gender-identity/

[14] Eva Moore, Amy Wisniewski, and Adrian Dobs, Departments of Medicine and Pediatrics, The Johns Hopkins School of Medicine, Baltimore, Maryland. "Endocrine Treatment of Transsexual People: A Review of Treatment Regimens, Outcomes, and Adverse Effects," in *Journal of Clinical Endocrinology & Metabolism*, Clinical Review 161, 2003. http://press.endocrine.org/doi/pdf/10.1210/jc.2002-021967

[15] Diagnostic and Statistical Manual of Mental Disorders, 5th Edition: DSM-5, American Psychiatric Association. American Psychiatriac Publishing, May 2013. http://www.dsm5.org/Pages/Default.aspx

[16] Bakker A, van Kesteren PJ, Gooren LJ, Bezemer PD. "The prevalence of transsexualism in the Netherlands." *Acta Psychiatr Scand* 87:237–238 (2002)

[17] Paul R. McHugh, MD, "Transgender Surgery Isn't the Solution: A drastic physical change doesn't address underlying psycho-social troubles." *The Wall Street Journal*, June 12th 2014.

[18] Colleen O'Conner, "Pediatricians see growing number of cross-gender kids like Coy Mathis." *Denver Post*, March 3, 2013. http://www.denverpost.com/ci_22706559/pediatricians-see-growing-number-crosss-gender-kids-like

[19] Mark Bannerman, "Family Court Chief Justice calls for rethink on how High Court handles cases involving transgender children," ABC News, November 17, 2014 http://www.abc.net.au/news/2014-11-17/chief-justice-calls-for-rethink-on-transgender-childrens-cases/5894698

[20] Ibid.

[21] Priyanka Boghani, "When Transgender Kids Transition, Medical Risks Are Both Known and Unknown," *Frontline*, June 30th, 2015.

[22] Transgender Law and Policy Institute estimates the transgender population at 2 – 5% of the US population. National Center for Transgender Equality reports that only 0.25 – 1.0 % of the US transgender population are actually transsexual, persons suffering from a complete psychosexual inversion whose body identity disorder/ body dysmorphia disorder takes the form of an obsession with having the primary and secondary sex characteristics of the opposite sex. The remaining 88% percent of the transgender population are transvestites, cross-dressers and autogynephiliacs. Source: https://outofmypantiesnow.wordpress.com/2013/10/28/when-is-90-not-substantially-all/

[23] Sheila Jeffreys, *Gender Hurts: A Feminist Analysis of the Politics of Transgenderism,* London and NY, Routledge, 2014, pp. 16 - 19.

[24] Bernice L., Hausman *Changing Sex: Transsexualism, Technology, and the Idea of Gender,* Duke University Press, 1995, p. 74.

[25] Richard Green, *The Sissy Boy Syndrome and the Development of Homosexuality.* Yale University Press, 1987. Psychiatrist & Lawyer Richard Green's landmark study found the great majority

of children diagnosed with gender identity disorder (GID) become lesbian, homosexual, or bisexual (75 to 80 percent).

[26] David L. Rowland, and Luca Incrocci, *Handbook of Sexual and Gender Identity Disorders.* Wiley and Sons Inc. 2008

[27] Dan Littauer, "Iran Performed Over 1,000 Gender Reassignment Operations in Four Years," Gay Star News, December 4th, 2012. http://www.gaystarnews.com/article/iran-performed-over-1000-gender-reassignment-operations-four-years041212/#gs.=3k8xyc

[28] Jenny Nordberg, *The Underground Girls of Kabul: In Search of a Hidden Resistance in Afghanistan,* Penguin Random House, 2014.

[29] S. Laurel Weldon and Mala Htun (2013). "Feminist mobilisation and progressive policy change: why governments take action to combat violence against women," *Gender & Development*, 21:2, 231-247.

[30] *"Quarter of Teens 'Considering Plastic Surgery,'"* Daily Mail, Last Updated March 29, 2006. http://www.dailymail.co.uk/health/article-381385/Quarter-teens-considering-plastic-surgery.html

[31] Written evidence submitted by University of Melbourne Professor of Political Science Sheila Jeffreys to the Transgender Equality Inquiry of the British Parliament, August 25th, 2015.
    http://data.parliament.uk/writtenevidence/committeeevidence.svc/evidencedocument/women-and-equalities-committee/transgender-equality/written/19512.html

[32] *"Blood and Visions: Womyn Reconciling with Being Female"* by Autotomous Womyn's Press, 2015. http://www.greenwomanstore.com/blood-and-visions.html

[33] "Gender Identity as Culturally Bound Phenomenon: The Concept of the Culture-Bound Syndrome," Culturally Bound Gender Blog, March 3, 2013. https://culturallyboundgender.wordpress.com/2013/03/03/the-concept-of-the-culture-bound-syndrome/

[34] Ethan Waters, *"The Americanization of Mental Illness,"* The New York Times, Jaunary 8th 2010. http://www.nytimes.com/2010/01/10/magazine/10psyche-t.html?_r=0

[35] Liam Deacon, *"Transgender Funding Boosted to L22M, 400% Rise in Trans Children,"* Breitbart.com, October 20, 2015. http://www.breitbart.com/london/2015/10/30/nhs-transgender-funding-boosted-22m-400-rise-trans-children/

[36] Ibid.

[37] Jennifer LeClaire, "Why is Mainstream Media Obsessed with Pushing LGBTIQ Shows?" charismanews.com, September 26, 2014. http://www.charismanews.com/opinion/watchman-on-the-wall/45548-why-is-mainstream-media-obsessed-with-pushing-lgbtiq-shows

[38] Calum McKenzie, "Child Gender Identity Referrals Show Huge Rise in Six Years,", BBC News, February 11, 2016. http://www.bbc.com/news/uk-england-nottinghamshire-35532491

[39] Ashley Lutz, "These 6 Corporations Control 90% of the Media in America," Business Insider, June 14th 2012. http://www.businessinsider.com/these-6-corporations-control-90-of-the-media-in-america-2012-6)

[40] Ronald V. Bettig and Jeanne Lynn Hall, *Big Media, Big Money: Cultural Texts and Political Economics*, Edition 1, Rowman & Littlefield Publishers, Inc., 2002. pp 15-16.

[41] Jeffreys, S., *Gender Hurts*, p. 102.

[42] Liz Hannson, "A Mom's Letter Introducing Her Transgender Daughter," Huffington Post, updated February 2, 2016. http://www.huffingtonpost.com/liz-hanssen/a-moms-letter-introducing-her-transgender-daughter_b_6151766.html

[43] Judy Hall, "Mommy, I'm Just Not That Kind of Girl," Huffington Post, January 25, 2015. http://www.huffingtonpost.com/judy-hall/mommy-im-just-not-that-kind-of-girl_b_6086934.html

[44] Noah Michelson, "Debi Jackson, Mother of Transgender Child, Gives Moving Speech," Huffington Post, Updated February 2, 2016. http://www.huffingtonpost.com/2014/07/15/debi-jackson-transgender-child_n_5588149.html

[45] James Michael Nichols, "Inside Out: Portraits of Cross Gender Children Beautifully Documents Transgender Kids,", Huff Post Queer Voices, Updated February 2, 2016. http://www.huffingtonpost.com/2015/05/24/inside-out-portraits-cross-gender-children_n_7318026.html

[46] "Charlie White's 'Teen and Transgender Comparative Study' Pairs Girls and Trans Women," Huff Post Queer Voices, Updated February 2, 2016. http://www.huffingtonpost.com/2013/03/09/charlie-white-teen-transgender-comparative-study_n_2812885.html

[47] Joe Morgan, "11 Insanely Hot Transmen That Are Changing the World," gaystarnews.com, November 18, 2014. http://www.gaystarnews.com/article/11-insanely-hot-men-you-will-not-believe-are-trans181114-0/#gs.98RAiNo

[48] Alice Gregory, "Has the Fashion Industry Reached a Transgender Turning Point?" *Vogue*, April 21, 2015. http://www.vogue.com/13253741/andreja-pejic-transgender-model/

[49] *Trans Kids Purple Rainbow Foundation, a foundation* built around Jazz Jennings' transition that supports education and research for transgender children. http://www.transkidspurplerainbow.org/jazz-in-the-news/ Katie Couric interview with Jazz, October 22nd 2014:https://www.yahoo.com/news/the-new-face-of-transgender-youth-231106807.html?ref=gs

[50] "I Am Jazz: My Intimate Conversation with Trans Tween and Her Mother Jeanette," Janet Mock Blog, November 25, 2011. http://janetmock.com/2011/11/25/i-am-jazz-transgender-jeanette-documentary/

[51] Ibid.

[52] Janice G. Raymond, *The Transexual Empire/The Making of the She-Male*, Teacher's College Press, March 1984. p. 165.

[53] Nancy E. Dowd, Dorothy G. Singer, Robin Fretwell Wilson, *Handbook of Children, Culture, and Violence* by, SAGE Publications, 2005. pp. xii-xiii.

[54] *For Parents: Facts on Children and Pornography.* Resource List from the non-sectarian Stop Porn Culture organization founded by Professor Gail Dines. http://stoppornculture.org/resources-2/for-parents/

[55] John Breeding, Psychologist Testimony on "The Issue of Psychiatric Drugs in Schools" before the Texas State Board of Education, November 2000. Also contained in *The Wildest Colts Make The Best Horses*. Bright Books, 1996.

[56] Mina Keleman, "The Born Identity: What Do Transgender Children Need?" *Houstonia Magazine*, 11/3/2014

[57] Victoria L Dunckley, MD., "Gray Matters: Too Much Screen Time Damages The Brain" in *Psychology Today*, February 27th, 2014.

[58] Martha Stout, *The Sociopath Next Door: The Ruthless Versus the Rest of Us*, Broadway Books, 2005. p. 45.

[59] Kimberly A. Yuracko, "The New Gender Essentialism," *Express* (2011) http://works.bepress.com/kimberly_yuracko/4/

[60] Ibid.

[61] Colleen Conner, *Denver Post*.

[62] In WPATH's own materials: Press Release statement urging the de-psychopathologization of gender variance worldwide, May 26th, 2010.
     http://www.wpath.org/uploaded_files/140/files/de-psychopathologisation%205-26 10%20on%20letterhead.pdf
     History of how HBIGDA became WPATH: http://www.wpath.org/site_page.cfm?pk_association_webpage_menu=1347&pk_association_webpage=3903

[63] Author and Activist Derrick Jensen Interview, Democracy Now, November 26, 2010. http://www.democracynow.org/2010/11/26/author_and_activist_derrick_jensen_the

[64] Sheila Jeffreys, *Gender Hurts*, Chapter 2.

65 Prior to sonograms, midwives and physicians used the fetal stethoscope as well as the no-tech Pinard horn made of wood or metal, still used by some Amish midwives and modern traditional midwives. Prior to diagnostic amplification of fetal heartbeats and outside of industrial culture are ancient knowledge lineages embedded in specific land-based cultures, where midwives are highly reliant on keen observation of maternal states, personal embodiment, facilitation of instinct and intuition of mothers, and spiritual practices coherent with specific tribes and regions.

66 Sarah J. Buckley, MD, "Ultrasound Scans - Cause for Concern" in *Gentle Birth, Gentle Mothering: A Doctor's Guide to Natural Childbirth and Gentle Early Parenting Choices, Celestial Arts, 2009.* http://sarahbuckley.com/ultrasound-scans-cause-for-concern#ref

67 Mostafa Fatemi PhD, Paul L. Ogbern MD, James F. Greenleaf PhD, The Mayo Foundation. "Fetal Stimulation By Pulsed Diagnostic Ultrasound." *J Ultrasound Med* 20:883–889. http://www.jultrasoundmed.org/content/20/8/883.full.pdf Popular version of paper abstract: http://acoustics.org/pressroom/httpdocs/142nd/Fatemi.html

68 S.A. Banyan, "Gendercide Stings," *The Economist*, December 18, 2012, http://www.economist.com/blogs/banyan/2012/12/indias-skewed-sex-ratios

69 Marsden Wagner, MD, "Choose & Lose: Promoting Cesareans and Other Invasive Interventions," *Midwifery Today* Issue 85, Spring 2008.

70 Michel Odent, *Primal Health: Understanding the Critical Period Between Conception and the First Birthday.* Clarview Books, UK, 2007.

71 Robin Lim, *Placenta: The Forgotten Chakra.* Ubud, Bali, Indonesia: Half Angel Press, 2010. pp 1-4. (A Lontar digital library is currently under construction: http://dl.lontar-library.org/)

72 Elizabeth Gilbert, *Eat, Pray, Love.* Penguin Books, 2006. pp 251-252.

73 Derman-Sparks, Louise, and the A.B.C. Task Force. "Anti-Bias Curriculum: Tools For Empowering Young Children." National Association For the Education of Young Children, No. 242. 1989. http://www.naeyc.org/store/files/store/TOC/254.pdf

[74] Marsden Wagner, MD, Interview: "International Midwife Robin Lim: Life After Becoming A CNN Hero." Huffington Post, 8/9/2013. http://www.huffingtonpost.com/rio-helmi/robin-lim-life-after-beco_b_3722466.html

[75] Richard Green, *The Sissy Boy Syndrome and the Development of Homosexuality*. Yale University Press, 1987. Psychiatrist & Lawyer Richard Green's landmark study found the great majority of children diagnosed with GID become lesbian, homosexual, or bisexual, 75-80 percent.

[76] Mariam Arain, Maliha Haque, Lina Johal, Puja Mathur, Wynand Nel, Afsha Rais, Ranbir Sandhu, Sushil Sharma. "Maturation of the adolescent brain," *Neuropsychiatry Dis Treat*. 2013; 9: 449–461. 2013 April 3.

[77] Dan Springer, "Oregon allowing 15-year-olds to get state-subsidized sex-change operations", Fox News, July 9, 2015. http://www.foxnews.com/politics/2015/07/09/oregon-allowing-15-year-olds-to-get-state-subsidized-sex-change-operations.html

[78] Elizabeth Pennisi, "Our Egalitarian Eden," *Science*, Volume 344, Issue 6186, pp. 824-825 (2014)

[79] Statistics from the Funders for LGBTQ Issues, February 2015 Annual Report, p. 11. https://www.lgbtfunders.org/files/TRANSformational_Impact.pdf

[80] Paul R. McHugh MD. The Wall Street Journal, http://www.wsj.com/articles/paul-mchugh-transgender-surgery-isnt-the-solution-1402615120

[81] As is already happening with the related efforts of diverse women amplifying the risks posed to women and children, via the community-based initiatives Finding Middle Ground, Just Want Privacy, and Transgender Trend.

CHAPTER 12

<hr>

Gender Ideology Harms Children, A Brief Statement, And Gender Dysphoria In Children Official Position Statement By The American College Of Pediatricians

Anthology Editors Introduction: This chapter includes several statements from the American College of Pediatricians: a temporary statement with references from the American College of Pediatricians released in March 21, 2016, and an updated with clarification on April 6, 2016. This is followed by an August 3rd, 2016 press release from Michelle Cretella, MD, FCP, President of American College of Pediatricians: "Normalizing Gender Dysphoria is Dangerous and Unethical". The full statement, "Gender Dysphoria in Children" published in August, 2016 is followed by Gender Dysphoria Summary Points. www.ACPeds.org.

~

Gender Ideology Harms Children
April 6, 2016

The American College of Pediatricians urges educators and legislators to reject all policies that condition children to accept as normal a life of chemical and surgical impersonation of the opposite sex. Facts – not ideology – determine reality.

1. **Human sexuality is an objective biological binary trait: "XY" and "XX" are genetic markers of health – not genetic markers of a disorder.** The norm for human design is to be conceived either male or female. Human sexuality is binary by design with the obvious purpose being the reproduction and flourishing of our species. This

principle is self-evident. The exceedingly rare disorders of sex development (DSDs), including but not limited to testicular feminization and congenital adrenal hyperplasia, are all medically identifiable deviations from the sexual binary norm, and are rightly recognized as disorders of human design. Individuals with DSDs do not constitute a third sex.[1]

2. **No one is born with a gender. Everyone is born with a biological sex. Gender (an awareness and sense of oneself as male or female) is a sociological and psychological concept; not an objective biological one.** No one is born with an awareness of themselves as male or female; this awareness develops over time and, like all developmental processes, may be derailed by a child's subjective perceptions, relationships, and adverse experiences from infancy forward. People who identify as "feeling like the opposite sex" or "somewhere in between" do not comprise a third sex. They remain biological men or biological women.[2, 3,4]

3. **A person's belief that he or she is something they are not is, at best, a sign of confused thinking.** When an otherwise healthy biological boy believes he is a girl, or an otherwise healthy biological girl believes she is a boy, an objective psychological problem exists that lies in the mind not the body, and it should be treated as such. These children suffer from gender dysphoria. Gender dysphoria (GD), formerly listed as Gender Identity Disorder (GID), is a recognized mental disorder in the most recent edition of the Diagnostic and Statistical Manual of the American Psychiatric Association (DSM-V).[5] The psychodynamic and social learning theories of GD/GID have never been disproved.[2, 4,5]

4. **Puberty is not a disease and puberty-blocking hormones can be dangerous.** Reversible or not, puberty- blocking hormones induce a state of disease – the absence of puberty – and inhibit growth and fertility in a previously biologically healthy child.[6]

5. **According to the DSM-V, as many as 98% of gender confused boys and 88% of gender confused girls eventually accept their biological sex after naturally passing through puberty.**[5]

6. **Children who use puberty blockers to impersonate the opposite sex will require cross-sex hormones in late adolescence. Cross-sex hormones (testosterone and estrogen) are associated with dangerous health risks including but not limited to high blood pressure, blood clots, stroke and cancer.**[7,8,9,10]

7. **Rates of suicide are twenty times greater among adults who use cross-sex hormones and undergo sex reassignment surgery, even in Sweden which is among**

the most LGBQT – affirming countries.[11] What compassionate and reasonable person would condemn young children to this fate knowing that after puberty as many as 88% of girls and 98% of boys will eventually accept reality and achieve a state of mental and physical health?

8. **Conditioning children into believing a lifetime of chemical and surgical impersonation of the opposite sex is normal and healthful is child abuse.** Endorsing gender discordance as normal via public education and legal policies will confuse children and parents, leading more children to present to "gender clinics" where they will be given puberty-blocking drugs. This, in turn, virtually ensures that they will "choose" a lifetime of carcinogenic and otherwise toxic cross-sex hormones, and likely consider unnecessary surgical mutilation of their healthy body parts as young adults.

A link to this statement is found at: http://www.acpeds.org/the-college-speaks/position-statements/gender-ideology-harms-children

Michelle A. Cretella, M.D.
President of the American College of Pediatricians
Quentin Van Meter, M.D.
Vice President of the American College of Pediatricians
Pediatric Endocrinologist
Paul McHugh, M.D.
University Distinguished Service Professor of Psychiatry at Johns Hopkins Medical School and the former psychiatrist in chief at Johns Hopkins Hospital

CLARIFICATIONS IN RESPONSE TO FAQs REGARDING POINTS 3 & 5:
Regarding Point 3: "Where does the APA or DSM-V indicate that Gender Dysphoria is a mental disorder?"

The APA (American Psychiatric Association) is the author of the <u>Diagnostic and Statistical Manual of Mental Disorders, 5th edition</u>. The APA states that those distressed and impaired by their GD meet the definition of a disorder. The College is unaware of any medical literature that documents a gender dysphoric child seeking puberty blocking hormones who is not significantly distressed by the thought of passing through the normal and healthful process of puberty.

From the DSM-V fact sheet:

"The critical element of gender dysphoria is the presence of clinically significant distress associated with the condition."

"This condition causes clinically significant distress or impairment in social, occupational, or other important areas of functioning."

Regarding Point 5: "Where does the DSM-V list rates of resolution for Gender Dysphoria?"

On page 455 of the DSM-V under "Gender Dysphoria without a disorder of sex development" it states: "Rates of persistence of gender dysphoria from childhood into adolescence or adulthood vary. In natal males, persistence has ranged from 2.2% to 30%. In natal females, persistence has ranged from 12% to 50%." Simple math allows one to calculate that for natal boys: resolution occurs in ***as many as*** 100% - 2.2% = 97.8% (approx. 98% of gender-confused boys). Similarly, for natal girls: resolution occurs in ***as many as*** 100% - 12% = 88% gender-confused girls

The bottom line is this: Our opponents advocate a new scientifically baseless standard of care for children with a psychological condition (GD) that would otherwise resolve after puberty for the vast majority of patients concerned. Specifically, they advise: affirmation of children's thoughts which are contrary to physical reality; the chemical castration of these children prior to puberty with GnRH agonists (puberty blockers which cause infertility, stunted growth, low bone density, and an unknown impact upon their brain development), and, finally, the permanent sterilization of these children prior to age 18 via cross-sex hormones. There is an obvious self-fulfilling nature to encouraging young GD children to impersonate the opposite sex and then institute pubertal suppression. If a boy who questions whether or not he is a boy (who is meant to grow into a man) is treated as a girl, then has his natural pubertal progression to manhood suppressed, have we not set in motion an inevitable outcome? All of his same sex peers develop into young men, his opposite sex friends develop into young women, but he remains a pre-pubertal boy. He will be left psychosocially isolated and alone. He will be left with the psychological impression that something is wrong. He will be less able to identify with his same sex peers and being male, and thus be more likely to self identify as "non-male" or female. Moreover, neuroscience reveals that the pre-frontal cortex of the brain which is responsible for judgment and risk assessment is not mature until the mid-twenties. Never has it been more scientifically clear that children and adolescents are incapable of making informed decisions regarding permanent, irreversible and life-altering medical interventions. For this reason, the College maintains it is abusive to promote this ideology, first and foremost for the well-being of the gender dysphoric children themselves, and secondly, for all of their non-gender-discordant peers, many of whom will subsequently question their own gender identity, and face violations of their right to bodily privacy and safety.

Anthology Editor's note:
One of the signers to this letter is Paul McHugh, an anti-choice conservative in his religious beliefs. I chose to include this letter with the knowledge that including McHugh may be controversial for some readers. For the benefit of the children, I do not agree with dismissing well-researched information if an individual has opposing political beliefs.

∼

PRESS RELEASE
Gainsville, FL, August 3, 2016

Normalizing Gender Dysphoria is Dangerous and Unethical

In its updated statement, Gender Dysphoria in Children, the American College of Pediatricians (College) calls for an end to the normalization of gender dysphoria (GD) in children because it has led to the ongoing experimentation upon, and sterilization of, confused children. Children with GD believe that they are something other than their biological sex. For children experiencing GD before the age of puberty, the confusion resolves over 80 percent of the time by late adolescence. There is a suppressed debate among professionals regarding the new treatment "standard" for childhood GD. This media-popularized standard involves the use of medicines that block puberty followed by life-long use of toxic cross-sex hormones—a combination that results in the sterilization of minors and other significant health risks. A review of current medical literature finds this approach to be rooted in an unscientific gender ideology that violates the long-standing medical ethics principle of "First do no harm."

Mandates by public institutions to force the acceptance of GD as a normal variant of child development and require social accommodation, toxic hormone therapy and surgical removal of healthy body parts, are misguided and dangerous. The Association of American Physicians and Surgeons, the Christian Medical Association, and the Catholic Medical Association share the College's concern over this approach. Together our groups represent over 20,000 physicians and health professionals. Opposition also exists among liberal-leaning healthcare professionals who have created an online community known as Youth Trans Critical Professionals. However, those who dare to speak out in support of "First do no harm" often encounter significant public and private harassment, and many have lost or will lose their jobs.

Dr. Michelle Cretella, President of the College states, *"We live at a time in which social agendas often bias the results of research and lead to the development of false medical standards. Those who honorably speak out against this are chastised. Young children are being permanently sterilized and surgically maimed under the guise of treating a condition that would otherwise resolve in over 80% of them. This is criminal."*

~

Gender Dysphoria in Children
American College of Pediatricians – August 2016

ABSTRACT: Gender dysphoria (GD) of childhood describes a psychological condition in which children experience a marked incongruence between their experienced gender and the gender associated with their biological sex. When this occurs in the pre-pubertal child, GD resolves in the vast majority of patients by late adolescence. Currently there is a vigorous, albeit suppressed, debate among physicians, therapists, and academics regarding what is fast becoming the new treatment standard for GD in children. This new paradigm is rooted in the assumption that GD is innate, and involves pubertal suppression with gonadotropin releasing hormone (GnRH) agonists followed by the use of cross-sex hormones—a combination that results in the sterility of minors. A review of the current literature suggests that this protocol is founded upon an unscientific gender ideology, lacks an evidence base, and violates the long-standing ethical principle of "First do no harm."

GENDER DYSPHORIA IN CHILDREN: THIS DEBATE CONCERNS MORE THAN SCIENCE

Gender is a term that refers to the psychological and cultural characteristics associated with biological sex.[1] It is a psychological concept and sociological term, not a biological one. Gender identity refers to an individual's awareness of being male or female and is sometimes referred

143

to as an individual's "experienced gender." Gender dysphoria (GD) in children describes a psychological condition in which they experience marked incongruence between their experienced gender and the gender associated with their biological sex. They often express the belief that they are the opposite sex.[2] The prevalence rates of GD among children has been estimated to be less than 1%.[3] Sex differences in rate of referrals to specialty clinics vary by age. In pre-pubertal children, the ratio of boys to girls ranges from 2:1 to 4.5:1. In adolescents, the sex ratio is close to parity; in adults, the ratio of males to females range from 1:1 to 6.1:1.[2]

The debate over how to treat children with GD is primarily an ethical dispute; one that concerns physician worldview as much as science. Medicine does not occur in a moral vacuum; every therapeutic action or inaction is the result of a moral judgment of some kind that arises from the physician's philosophical worldview. Medicine also does not occur in a political vacuum and being on the wrong side of sexual politics can have severe consequences for individuals who hold the politically incorrect view.

As an example, Dr. Kenneth Zucker, long acknowledged as a foremost authority on gender identity issues in children, has also been a lifelong advocate for gay and transgender rights. However, much to the consternation of adult transgender activists, Zucker believes that gender-dysphoric pre-pubertal children are best served by helping them align their gender identity with their anatomic sex. This view ultimately cost him his 30-year directorship of the Child Youth and Family Gender Identity Clinic (GIC) at the Center for Addiction and Mental Health in Toronto.[4, 5]

Many critics of pubertal suppression hold a modernist teleological worldview. They find it self-evident that there is a purposeful design to human nature, and that cooperation with this design leads to human flourishing. Others, however, identify as post-modernists who reject teleology. What unites the two groups is a traditional interpretation of "First do no harm." For example, there is a growing online community of gay-affirming physicians, mental health professionals, and academics with a webpage entitled "First, do no harm: youth trans critical professionals." They write:

We are concerned about the current trend to quickly diagnose and affirm young people as transgender, often setting them down a path toward medical transition.... We feel that unnecessary surgeries and/or hormonal treatments which have not been proven safe in the long-term represent significant risks for young people. Policies that encourage—either directly or indirectly—such medical treatment for young people who may not be able to evaluate the risks and benefits are highly suspect, in our opinion.[6]

Advocates of the medical interventionist paradigm, in contrast, are also post-modernists but hold a subjective view of "First do no harm." Dr. Johanna Olson-Kennedy, an adolescent medicine specialist at Children's Hospital Los Angeles, and leader in pediatric gender transitioning, has stated that "[First do no harm] is really subjective. [H]istorically we come from a very paternalistic perspective... [in which] doctors are really given the purview of deciding what is going to be harmful and what isn't. And that, in the world of gender, is really problematic."[7] Not only does she claim that "First do no harm" is subjective, but she later also states that it should be left to the child decide what constitutes harm based upon their own subjective thoughts and feelings.[7] Given the cognitive and experiential immaturity of the child and adolescent, the American College of Pediatricians (the College) finds this highly problematic and unethical.

GENDER DYSPHORIA AS THE RESULT OF AN INNATE INTERNAL SEXED IDENTITY

Professor of social work, Dr. William Brennan, has written that "[t]he power of language to color one's view of reality is profound."[8] It is for this reason that linguistic engineering always precedes social engineering even in medicine. Many hold the mistaken belief that gender once meant biological sex. Though the terms are often used interchangeably they were never truly synonymous.[9, 10] Feminists of the late 1960's and 1970's used gender to refer to a "social sex" that could differ from one's "biological sex" in order to overcome unjust discrimination against women rooted in sex stereotypes. These feminists are largely responsible for mainstreaming the use of the word gender in place of sex. More recently, in an attempt to eliminate heteronormativity, queer theorists have expanded gender into an excess of 50 categories by merging the concept of a social sex with sexual attractions.[9] However, neither usage reflects the original meaning of the term.

Prior to the 1950s, gender applied only to grammar not to persons.[9, 10] Latin based languages categorize nouns and their modifiers as masculine or feminine and for this reason are still referred to as having a gender. This changed during the 1950s and 1960s as sexologists realized that their sex reassignment agenda could not be sufficiently defended using the words sex and transsexual. From a purely scientific standpoint, human beings possess a biologically determined sex and innate sex differences. No sexologist could actually change a person's genes through hormones and surgery. Sex change is objectively impossible. Their solution was to hijack the word gender and infuse it with a new meaning that applied to persons. John Money, PhD was among the most prominent of these sexologists who redefined gender to mean 'the social performance indicative of an internal sexed identity'.[10] In essence, these sexologists invented the ideological foundation necessary to justify their treatment of transsexualism with sex reassignment surgery and called it gender. It is this man-made ideology of an 'internal sexed identity' that now dominates mainstream medicine, psychiatry and academia. This linguistic history makes it clear that gender is not and never has been a biological or scientific entity. Rather, gender is a socially and politically constructed concept.

In their "Overview of Gender Development and Gender Nonconformity in Children and Adolescents," Forcier and Olson-Kennedy dismiss the binary model of human sexuality as "ideology" and present an "alternate perspective" of "innate gender identity" that presents along a "gender continuum." They recommend that pediatricians tell parents that a child's "real gender" is what he or she feels it to be because "a child's brain and body may not be on the same page."[11]

Forcier and Olson-Kennedy's claim of an innate discordance between a child's brain and body derives from diffusion-weighted MRI scans that demonstrate the pubertal testosterone surge in boys increases white matter volume, as well as from brain studies of adults who identify as transgender. A study by Rametti and colleagues found that the white matter microstructure of the brains of female-to-male (FtM) transsexual adults, who had not begun testosterone treatment, more closely resembled that of men than that of women.[12] Other diffusion-weighted MRI studies have concluded that the white matter microstructure in both FtM and male-to-female (MtF) transsexuals falls halfway between that of genetic females and males.[13] These studies, however, are of questionable clinical significance due to the small number of subjects and the existence of neuroplasticity. Neuroplasticity is the well-established phenomenon in which long-term behavior alters brain microstructure. There is no evidence that people are born with brain microstructures that are forever unalterable, but there is significant evidence that experience changes brain microstructure. [14]Therefore, if and when valid transgender brain differences are identified, these will likely be the result of transgender behavior rather than its cause. More importantly, however, is the fact that the brains of all male infants are masculinized prenatally by their own endogenous testosterone, which is secreted from their testes beginning at approximately eight weeks' gestation. Female infants, of course, lack testes, and therefore, do not have their brains masculinized by endogenous testosterone.[15, 16,17] For this reason, barring one of the rare disorders of sex development (DSD), boys are not born with feminized brains, and girls are not born with masculinized brains.

Behavior geneticists have known for decades that while genes and hormones *influence* behavior, they do not hard-wire a person to think, feel, or behave in a particular way. The science of epigenetics has established that genes are not analogous to rigid "blueprints" for behavior. Rather, humans "develop traits through the dynamic process of gene-environment interaction... [genes alone] don't determine who we are."[18]Regarding the etiology of transgenderism, twin studies of adult transsexuals prove definitively that prenatal genetic and hormone influence is minimal.

The largest study of twin transsexual adults found that only 20 percent of identical twins were both trans-identified.[19] Since identical twins contain 100 percent of the same DNA from conception, and develop in exactly the same prenatal environment where they are exposed to the same prenatal hormones, if genes and/or prenatal hormones contributed significantly to transgenderism, the concordance rates would be close to 100 percent. Instead, 80 percent of identical twin pairs were discordant. This means that at least 80 percent of what contributes to transgenderism in one adult co-twin consists of one or more non-shared post-natal experiences including *but not limited to* non-shared family experiences. This is consistent with the dramatic rates of resolution of gender dysphoria documented among children when they are not encouraged to impersonate the opposite sex. These results also support the theory that persistent GD is due predominately to the impact of non-shared environmental influences upon certain biologically vulnerable children. To be clear, twin studies alone establish that the "alternate perspective" of an "innate gender identity" arising from prenatally "feminized" or "masculinized" brains trapped in the wrong body is in fact an ideological belief that has no basis in rigorous science.

A teleological binary view of human sexuality, in contrast, is compatible with biological reality. The norm for human design is to be conceived either male or female. Sex chromosome pairs "XY" and "XX" are genetic determinants of sex, male and female, respectively. They are not genetic markers of a disordered body or birth defect. Human sexuality is binary by design with the purpose being the reproduction of our species. This principle is self-evident. **Barring one of the rare disorders of sex development (DSD), no infant is "assigned" a sex or a gender at birth; rather birth sex declares itself anatomically in utero and is clearly evident and acknowledged at birth.**

The exceedingly rare DSDs, including but not limited to androgen insensitivity syndrome and congenital adrenal hyperplasia, are all medically identifiable deviations from the human binary sexual norm. Unlike individuals with a normal genotype and hormonal axis who identify as "transgender," those with DSD have an innate biological condition. Sex assignment in individuals with DSDs is complex and dependent on a variety of genetic, hormonal, and physical factors. Nevertheless, the 2006 consensus statement of the Intersex Society of North America did not endorse DSD as a third sex.[20]

POST-NATAL FACTORS PREDOMINATE IN THE DEVELOPMENT AND PERSISTENCE OF GD

Identical twin studies demonstrate that non-shared post-natal events (environmental factors) predominate in the development and persistence of gender dysphoria. This is not surprising since it is well accepted that a child's emotional and psychological development is impacted by positive and negative experiences from infancy forward. Family and peer relationships, one's school and neighborhood, the experience of any form of abuse, media exposure, chronic illness, war, and natural disasters are all examples of environmental factors that impact an individual's emotional, social, and psychological development. *There is no single family dynamic, social situation, adverse event, or combination thereof that has been found to destine any child to develop GD.* This fact, together with twin studies, suggests that there are many paths that may lead to GD in certain biologically vulnerable children. The literature regarding the etiology and psychotherapeutic treatment of childhood GD is heavily based upon clinical case studies. These studies suggest that social reinforcement, parental psychopathology, family dynamics, and social contagion facilitated by mainstream and social media, all contribute to the development and/or persistence of GD in some vulnerable children. There may be other as yet unrecognized contributing factors as well.

Most parents of children with GD recall their initial reactions to their child's cross-sex dressing and other cross-sex behaviors to have been tolerance and/or encouragement. Sometimes parental psychopathology is at the root of the social reinforcement. For example, among mothers of boys with GD who had desired daughters, a small subgroup experienced what has been termed "pathologic gender mourning." Within this subgroup the mother's desire for a daughter was acted out by the mother actively cross-dressing her son as a girl. These mothers typically suffered from severe depression that was relieved when their sons dressed and acted in a feminine manner.[21]

A large body of clinical literature documents that fathers of feminine boys report spending less time with their sons between the ages of two and five as compared with fathers of control boys. This is consistent with data that shows feminine boys feel closer to their mothers than to their fathers. In his clinical studies of boys with GD, Stoller observed that most had an overly close relationship with their mother and a distant, peripheral relationship with their father. He postulated that GD in boys was a "developmental arrest ... in which an excessively close and gratifying mother-infant symbiosis, undisturbed by father's presence, prevents a boy from adequately separating himself from his mother's female body and feminine behavior."[21]

It has also been found that among children with GD, the rate of maternal psychopathology, particularly depression and bipolar disorder is "high by any standard." Additionally, a majority of the fathers of GD boys are easily threatened, exhibit difficulty with affect regulation, and possess an inner sense of inadequacy. These fathers typically deal with their conflicts by overwork or otherwise distance themselves from their families. Most often, the parents fail to support one another, and have difficulty resolving marital conflicts. This produces an intensified air of conflict and hostility. In this situation, the boy becomes increasingly unsure about his own self-value because of the mother's withdrawal or anger and the father's failure to intercede. The boy's anxiety and insecurity intensify, as does his anger, which may all result in his inability to identify with his biological sex.[22]

Systematic studies regarding girls with GD and the parent-child relationship have not been conducted. However, clinical observations suggest that the relationship between mother and daughter is most often distant and marked by conflict, which may lead the daughter to disidentify from the mother. In other cases, masculinity is praised while femininity is devalued by the parents. Furthermore, there have been cases in which girls are afraid of their fathers who may exhibit volatile anger up to and including abuse toward the mother. A girl may perceive being female as unsafe, and psychologically defend against this by feeling that she is really a boy; subconsciously believing that if she were a boy she would be safe from and loved by her father.[21]

There is evidence that psychopathology and/or developmental diversity may precipitate GD in adolescents, particularly among young women. Recent research has documented increasing numbers of adolescents who present to adolescent gender identity clinics and request sex reassignment (SR). Kaltiala-Heino and colleagues sought to describe the adolescent applicants for legal and medical sex reassignment during the first two years of an adolescent gender identity clinic in Finland, in terms of sociodemographic, psychiatric, and gender identity related factors and adolescent development. They conducted a structured quantitative retrospective chart review and qualitative analysis of case files of all adolescent SR applicants who entered the assessment by the end of 2013. They found that the number of referrals exceeded expectations in light of epidemiological knowledge. Natal girls were markedly overrepresented among applicants. Severe psychopathology preceding the onset of GD was common. Many youth were on the autism spectrum. These findings do not fit the commonly accepted image of a gender dysphoric child. The researchers conclude that treatment guidelines need to consider GD in minors in the context of severe psychopathology and developmental difficulties.[23]

Anecdotally, there is also an increasing trend among adolescents to self-diagnose as transgender after binges on social media sites such as Tumblr, Reddit, and YouTube. This suggests that social contagion may be at play. In many schools and communities, there are entire peer groups "coming out" as trans at the same time.[6] Finally, strong consideration should be given to investigating a causal association between adverse childhood events, including sexual abuse, and transgenderism. The overlap between childhood gender discordance and an adult homosexual orientation has long been acknowledged.[24] There is also a large body of literature documenting a significantly greater prevalence of childhood adverse events and sexual abuse among homosexual adults as compared to heterosexual adults. Andrea Roberts and colleagues' published a study in 2013 that found "half to all of the elevated risk of childhood abuse among persons with same-sex sexuality compared to heterosexuals was due to the effects of abuse on sexuality."[25] It is therefore possible that some individuals develop GD and later claim a transgender identity as a result of childhood maltreatment and/or sexual abuse. This is an area in need of research.

GD AS AN OBJECTIVE MENTAL DISORDER

Psychology has increasingly rejected the concept of norms for mental health, focusing instead on emotional distress. The American Psychiatric Association (APA), for example, explains in the fifth edition of the Diagnostic and Statistical Manual of Mental Disorders (DSM-V) that GD is listed therein not due to the discrepancy between the individual's thoughts and physical reality, but due to the presence of emotional distress that hampers social functioning. The DSM-V also notes that a diagnosis is required for insurance companies to pay for cross-sex hormones and sex reassignment surgery (SRS) to alleviate the emotional distress of GD. Once the distress is relieved, GD is no longer considered a disorder.[2]

There are problems with this reasoning. Consider the following examples: a girl with anorexia nervosa has the persistent mistaken belief that she is obese; a person with body dysmorphic disorder (BDD) harbors the erroneous conviction that she is ugly; a person with body integrity identity disorder (BIID) identifies as a disabled person and feels trapped in a fully functional body. Individuals with BIID are often so distressed by their fully capable bodies that they seek surgical amputation of healthy limbs or the surgical severing of their spinal cord.[26]Dr. Anne Lawrence, who is transgender, has argued that BIID has many parallels with GD.[27] The aforementioned false beliefs, like GD, are not merely emotionally distressing for the individuals but also life-threatening. In each case, surgery to "affirm" the false assumption (liposuction for anorexia, cosmetic surgery for BDD, amputation or surgically induced paraplegia for BIID, sex reassignment surgery for GD) may very well alleviate the patient's emotional distress, but will do nothing to address the underlying psychological problem, and may result in the patient's death. Completely removed from physical reality, the art of psychotherapy will diminish as the field of psychology increasingly devolves into a medical interventionist specialty, with devastating results for patients.

Alternatively, a minimal standard could be sought. Normality has been defined as "that which functions according to its design."[28]One of the chief functions of the brain is to perceive physical reality. Thoughts that are in accordance with physical reality are normal. Thoughts that deviate from physical reality are abnormal—as well as potentially harmful to the individual or to others. This is true whether or not the individual who possesses the abnormal thoughts feels distress. A person's belief that he is something or someone he is not is, at best, a sign of confused thinking; at worst, it is a delusion. Just because a person thinks or feels something does not make it so. This would be true even if abnormal thoughts were biologically "hardwired."

The norm for human development is for an individual's thoughts to align with physical reality; for an individual's gender identity to align with biologic sex. People who identify as "feeling like the opposite sex" or "somewhere in between" or some other category do not comprise a third sex. They remain biological men or biological women. GD is a problem that resides in the mind not in the body. Children with GD do not have a disordered body—even though they feel as if they do. Similarly, a child's distress over developing secondary sex characteristics does not mean that puberty should be treated as a disease to be halted, because puberty is not, in fact, a disease. Likewise, although many men with GD express the belief that they are a "feminine essence" trapped in a male body, this belief has no scientific basis.

Until recently, the prevailing worldview with respect to childhood GD was that it reflected abnormal thinking or confusion on the part of the child that may or may not be transient. Consequently, the standard approach was either watchful waiting or pursuit of family and individual psychotherapy.[1, 2] The goals of therapy were to address familial pathology if it was present, treat any psychosocial morbidities in the child, and aid the child in aligning gender identity with biological sex.[21,22] Experts on both sides of the pubertal suppression debate agree that within this context, 80 percent to 95 percent of children with GD accepted their biological sex by late adolescence.[29] This worldview began to shift, however, as adult transgender activists increasingly promoted the "feminine essence" narrative to secure social acceptance.[10] In 2007, the same year that Boston Children's Hospital opened the nation's first pediatric gender clinic, Dr. J. Michael Bailey wrote:

> *Currently the predominant cultural understanding of male-to-female transsexualism is that all male-to-female (MtF) transsexuals are, essentially, women trapped in men's bodies. This understanding has little scientific basis, however, and is inconsistent with clinical observations. Ray Blanchard has shown that there are two distinct subtypes of MtF transsexuals. Members of one subtype, homosexual transsexuals, are best understood as a type of homosexual male. The other subtype, autogynephilic transsexuals, are (sic) motivated by the erotic desire to become women. The persistence of the predominant cultural understanding, while explicable, is damaging to science and to many transsexuals.[30]*

As the "feminine essence" view persisted, the suffering of transgender adults was invoked to argue for the urgent rescue of children from the same fate by early identification, affirmation, and pubertal suppression. It is now alleged that discrimination, violence, psychopathology, and suicide are the direct and inevitable consequences of withholding social affirmation and puberty blockers or cross-sex hormones from a gender dysphoric child.[31] Yet, the fact that 80 percent to 95 percent of gender-dysphoric youth emerge physically and psychologically intact after passing through puberty without social affirmation refutes this claim.[29] Furthermore, over 90 percent of people who die of suicide have a diagnosed mental disorder.[32] There is no evidence that gender-dysphoric children who commit suicide are any different. Therefore, the cornerstone for suicide prevention should be the same for them as for all children: early identification and treatment of psychological co-morbidities.

Nevertheless, there are now 40 gender clinics across the United States that promote the use of pubertal suppression and cross-sex hormones in children. The rationale for suppression is to allow the gender-dysphoric child time to explore gender identity free from the emotional distress triggered by the onset of secondary sex characteristics. The standards followed in these clinics are based on "expert opinion." There is not a single large, randomized, controlled study that documents the alleged benefits and potential harms to gender-dysphoric children from pubertal suppression and decades of cross-sex hormone use. Nor is there a single long-term, large, randomized, controlled study that compares the outcomes of various psychotherapeutic interventions for childhood GD with those of pubertal suppression followed by decades of toxic synthetic steroids. In today's age of "evidence-based medicine," this should give everyone pause. Of greater concern is that pubertal suppression at Tanner Stage 2 (usually 11 years of age) followed by the use of cross-sex hormones will leave these children sterile and without gonadal tissue or gametes available for cryo-preservation.[33,34,35]

Neuroscience clearly documents that the adolescent brain is cognitively immature and lacks the adult capacity needed for risk assessment prior to the early to mid-twenties.[36] There is a serious ethical problem with allowing irreversible, life-changing procedures to be performed on minors who are too young to give valid consent themselves. This ethical requirement of informed consent is fundamental to the practice of medicine, as emphasized by the U.S. Department of Health & Human Services website: "The voluntary consent of the human subject is absolutely essential."[37] Moreover, when an individual is sterilized, even as a secondary outcome of therapy, lacking full, free, and informed consent, it is a violation of international law.[38]

TRANSGENDER-AFFIRMING PROTOCOL: WHAT IS THE EVIDENCE BASE?

Over the past two decades, Hayes, Inc. has grown to become an internationally recognized research and consulting firm that evaluates a wide range of medical technologies to determine the impact on patient safety, health outcomes, and resource utilization. This corporation conducted a comprehensive review and evaluation of the scientific literature regarding the treatment of GD in adults and children in 2014. It concluded that although "evidence suggests positive benefits" to the practice of using sex reassignment surgery in gender dysphoric adults, "serious limitations [inherent to the research] permit only weak conclusions."[39] Similarly, Hayes, Inc. found the practice of using cross-sex hormones for gender dysphoric adults to be based on "very low" quality of evidence:

Statistically significant improvements have not been consistently demonstrated by multiple studies for most outcomes. Evidence regarding quality of life and function in male-to-female (MtF) adults was very sparse. Evidence for less comprehensive measures of well-being in adult recipients of cross-sex hormone therapy was directly applicable to GD patients but was sparse and/or conflicting. The study designs do not permit conclusions of causality and studies generally had weaknesses associated with study execution as well. There are potentially long-term safety risks associated with hormone therapy but none have been proven or con-clusively ruled out.[40]

Regarding treatment of children with GD using gonadotropin releasing hormone (GnRH) agonists and cross-sex hormones, Hayes, Inc. awarded its lowest rating indicating that the literature is "too sparse and the studies [that exist are] too limited to suggest conclusions."[40]

GENDER CLINICS PROLIFERATE ACROSS UNITED STATES DESPITE LACK OF MEDICAL EVIDENCE

In 2007 Dr. Norman Spack, a pediatric endocrinologist and founder of the nation's first gender clinic at Boston Children's Hospital, launched the pubertal suppression paradigm in the United States.[41] It consists of first affirming the child's false self-concept by instituting name and pronoun changes, and facilitating the impersonation of the opposite sex within and outside of the home. Next, puberty is suppressed via GnRH agonists as early as age 11 years, and then finally, patients may graduate to cross-sex hormones at age 16 in preparation for sex-reassignment surgery as an older adolescent or adult.[42]Endocrine Society guidelines currently prohibit the use of cross-sex hormones before age 16 but this prohibition is being reconsidered.[43]Some gender specialists are already bypassing pubertal suppression and instead putting children as young as 11 years old directly onto cross-sex hormones.[44] The rationale is that the child will experience the pubertal development of the desired sex and thereby avoid the iatrogenic emotional distress from maintaining a pre-pubertal appearance as peers progress along their natural pubertal trajectory.

In 2014 there were 24 gender clinics clustered chiefly along the East Coast and in California; one year later there were 40 across the nation. Dr. Ximena Lopez, a pediatric endocrinologist at Children's Medical Center Dallas, and a member of that program's GENder Education and Care, Interdisciplinary Support program (Genecis) stated, "[Use of this protocol is] growing really fast. And the main reason is [that] parents are demanding it and bringing patients to the door of pediatric endocrinologists because they know this is available."[45]Notice, the *main* reason for the protocol's increased use is parent demand; not evidence-based medicine.

RISKS OF GNRH AGONISTS

The GnRH agonists used for pubertal suppression in gender dysphoric children include two that are approved for the treatment of precocious puberty: leuprolide by intramuscular injection with monthly or once every three month dosing formulations, and histrelin, a subcutaneous implant with yearly dosing.[34] In addition to preventing the development of secondary sex characteristics, GnRH agonists arrest bone growth, decrease bone accretion, prevent the sex-steroid dependent organization and maturation of the adolescent brain, and inhibit fertility by preventing the development of gonadal tissue and mature gametes for the duration of treatment. If the child discontinues the GnRH agonists, puberty will ensue.[34,42] Consequently, the Endocrine Society maintains that GnRH agonists, as well as living socially as the opposite sex, are fully reversible interventions that carry no risk of permanent harm to children.[42] However, social learning theory, neuroscience, and the single long-term follow-up study of adolescents who have received pubertal suppression described below challenge this claim.

In a follow-up study of their first 70 pre-pubertal candidates to receive puberty suppression, de Vries and colleagues documented that all subjects eventually embraced a transgender identity and requested cross-sex hormones.[46] This is cause for concern. Normally, 80 percent to 95 percent of pre-pubertal youth with GD do not persist in their GD. To have 100 percent of pre-pubertal children choose cross-sex hormones suggests that the protocol itself inevitably leads the individual to identify as transgender. There is an obvious self-fulfilling nature to encouraging a young child with GD to socially impersonate the opposite sex and then institute pubertal suppression. Given the well-established phenomenon of neuroplasticity, the repeated behavior of impersonating the opposite sex will alter the structure and function of the child's brain in some way—potentially in a way that will make identity alignment with the child's biologic sex less likely. This, together with the suppression of puberty that prevents further endogenous masculinization or feminization of the brain, causes the child to remain either a gender non-conforming pre-pubertal boy disguised as a pre-pubertal girl, or the reverse. Since their peers develop normally into young men or young women, these children are left psychosocially isolated. They will be less able to identify as being the biological male or female they actually are. A protocol of impersonation and pubertal suppression that sets into motion a single inevitable outcome (transgender identification) that requires lifelong use of toxic synthetic hormones, resulting in infertility, is neither fully reversible nor harmless.

GNRH AGONISTS, CROSS-SEX HORMONES, AND INFERTILITY

Since GnRH agonists prevent the maturation of gonadal tissue and gametes in both sexes, youth who graduate from pubertal suppression at Tanner Stage 2 to cross-sex hormones will be rendered infertile without any possibility of having genetic offspring in the future because they will lack gonadal tissue and gametes for cryo-preservation. The same outcome will occur if pre-pubertal children are placed directly upon cross-sex hormones. Older adolescents who declined pubertal suppression are advised to consider cryo-preservation of gametes prior to beginning cross-sex hormones. This will allow them to conceive genetic offspring in the future via artificial reproductive technology. While there are documented cases of transgendered adults who stopped their cross-sex hormones in order to allow their bodies to produce gametes, conceive, and have a child, there is no absolute guarantee that this is a viable option in the long term. Moreover, transgendered individuals who undergo sex reassignment surgery and have their reproductive organs removed are rendered permanently infertile.[34][35][36]

ADDITIONAL HEALTH RISKS ASSOCIATED WITH CROSS-SEX HORMONES

Potential risks from cross-sex hormones to children with GD are based on the adult literature. Recall that regarding the adult literature, the Hayes report states: "There are potentially long-term safety risks associated with hormone therapy but none have been proven or conclusively ruled out."[40] For example, most experts agree that there is an increased risk of coronary artery disease among MtF adults when placed on oral ethinyl estradiol; therefore, alternative estrogen formulations are recommended. However, there is one study of MtF adults using alternative preparations that found a similar increased risk. Therefore, this risk is neither established nor ruled out.[47, 48,49] Children who transition will require these hormones for a significantly greater length of time than their adult counterparts. Consequently, they may be more likely to experience physiologically theoretical though rarely observed morbidities in adults. With these caveats, it is most accurate to say that oral estrogen administration to boys *may* place them at risk for experiencing: thrombosis/thromboembolism; cardiovascular disease; weight gain; hypertrigyceridemia; elevated blood pressure; decreased glucose tolerance; gallbladder disease; prolactinoma; and breast cancer.[47, 48,49] Similarly, girls who receive testosterone *may* experience an elevated risk for: low HDL and elevated triglycerides; increased homocysteine levels; hepatotoxicity; polycythemia; increased risk of sleep apnea; insulin resistance; and unknown effects on breast, endometrial and ovarian tissues.[47,48,49] In addition, girls may legally obtain a mastectomy as early as 16 years of age after receiving testosterone therapy for at least one year; this surgery carries its own set of irreversible risks.[34]

THE POST-PUBERTAL ADOLESCENT WITH GD

As previously noted, 80 percent to 95 percent of pre-pubertal children with GD will experience resolution by late adolescence if not exposed to social affirmation and medical intervention. This means that 5 percent to 20 percent will persist in their GD as young adults. Currently, there is no medical or psychological test to determine which children will persist in their GD as young adults. Pre-pubertal children with GD who persist in their GD beyond puberty are more likely to also persist into adulthood. The Endocrine Society and others, including Dr. Zucker, therefore regard it reasonable to affirm children who persist in their GD beyond puberty, as well as those who present after puberty, and to proceed with cross-sex hormones at age 16 years.[42]

The College disagrees for the following reasons. First, not all adolescents with GD inevitably go on to trans-identification, but cross-sex hormones inevitably result in irreversible changes for all patients. Second, the young adolescent is simply not sufficiently mature to make significant medical decisions. The adolescent brain does not achieve the capacity for full risk assessment until the early to mid-twenties. There is a significant ethical problem with allowing minors to receive life-altering medical interventions including cross-sex hormones and, in the case of natal girls, bilateral mastectomy, when they are incapable of providing informed consent for themselves. As stated earlier, the College is also concerned about an increasing trend among adolescents to self-diagnose as transgender after binges on social media sites. While many of these adolescents will seek out a therapist after self-identifying, many states have been forced by non-scientific political pressure to ban so-called "conversion therapy." These bans prevent therapists from exploring not only a young person's sexual attractions and identity, but also his or her gender identity. Therapists are not allowed to ask why an adolescent believes he or she is transgender; may not explore underlying mental health issues; cannot consider the symbolic nature of the gender dysphoria; and may not look at possible confounding issues such as social media use or social contagion.[6]

IMPACT OF SEX REASSIGNMENT IN ADULTS AS IT RELATES TO RISK IN CHILDREN

Surveys suggest that transgender adults express a sense of "relief" and "satisfaction" following the use of hormones and sex reassignment surgery (SRS). However, SRS does not result in a level of health equivalent to that of the general population. [50]

For example, a 2001 study of 392 male-to-female and 123 female-to-male transgender persons found that 62 percent of the male-to-female (MtF) and 55 percent of the female-to-male (FtM) transgender persons were depressed. Nearly one third (32 percent) of each population had attempted suicide.[51] Similarly, in 2009, Kuhn and colleagues found considerably lower general health and general life satisfaction among 52 MtF and 3 FtM transsexuals fifteen years after SRS when compared with controls.[52] Finally, a thirty-year follow-up study of post-operative transgender patients from Sweden found that **the rate of suicide among post-operative transgender adults was nearly twenty times greater than that of the general population. To be clear, this does not prove that sex reassignment causes an increased risk of suicide or other psychological morbidities. Rather, it indicates that sex reassignment alone does not provide the individual with a level of mental health on par with the general population. The authors summarized their findings as follows:**

Persons with transsexualism, after sex reassignment, have considerably higher risks for mortality, suicidal behaviour, and psychiatric morbidity than the general population. Our findings suggest that sex reassignment, though alleviating gender dysphoria, may not suffice as treatment for transsexualism, and should inspire improved psychiatric and somatic care after sex reassignment for this patient group.[50]

It is noteworthy that these mental health disparities are observed in one of the most lesbian, gay, bisexual and transgender (LGBT) affirming nations of the world. It suggests that these health differences are not due primarily to social prejudice, but rather due to the adult transgender condition or lifestyle. This is also consistent with an American study published in the *Journal of LGBT Health* in 2008 that found discrimination did not account for the mental health discrepancies between LGBT-identified individuals and the heterosexual population.[53]

Absent hormonal and surgical intervention, only 5-20 percent of pre-pubertal children with GD will face a transgender adulthood which seems to predispose them to certain morbidities and an increased risk of early death. In contrast, the single study of pre-pubertal children with GD who received pubertal suppression makes clear that 100 percent of these children will face a transgender adulthood. Therefore, the current transgender affirming interventions at pediatric gender clinics will statistically yield this outcome for the remaining 80 to 95percent of pre-pubertal children with GD who otherwise would have identified with their biological sex by adulthood.

RECOMMENDATIONS FOR RESEARCH

Identical twin studies establish that post-natal environmental factors exert a significant influence over the development of GD and transgenderism. Data also reflects a greater than 80% resolution rate among pre-pubertal children with GD. Consequently, identification of the various environmental factors and pathways that trigger GD in biologically vulnerable children should be one focus of research. Particular attention should be given to the impact of childhood adverse events and social contagion. Another area of much needed research is within psychotherapy. Large long term longitudinal studies in which children with GD and their families are randomized to treatment with various therapeutic modalities and assessed across multiple measures of physical and social emotional health are desperately needed and should have been launched long ago. In addition, long term follow-up studies that assess objective measures of physical and mental health of post-surgical transsexual adults must include a matched control group consisting of transgender individuals who do not undergo SRS. This is the only way to test the hypothesis that SRS itself may cause more harm to individuals than they otherwise would experience with psychotherapy alone.

CONCLUSION

Gender dysphoria (GD) in children is a term used to describe a psychological condition in which a child experiences marked incongruence between his or her experienced gender and the gender associated with the child's biological sex. Twin studies demonstrate that GD is not an innate trait. Moreover, barring pre-pubertal affirmation and hormone intervention for GD, 80 percent to 95 percent of children with GD will accept the reality of their biological sex by late adolescence.

The treatment of GD in childhood with hormones effectively amounts to mass experimentation on, and sterilization of, youth who are cognitively incapable of providing informed consent. There is a serious ethical problem with allowing irreversible, life-changing procedures to be performed on minors who are too young to give valid consent themselves; adolescents cannot understand the magnitude of such decisions.

Ethics alone demands an end to the use of pubertal suppression with GnRH agonists, cross-sex hormones, and sex reassignment surgeries in children and adolescents. The College recommends an immediate cessation of these interventions, as well as an end to promoting gender ideology via school curricula and legislative policies. Healthcare, school curricula and legislation must remain anchored to physical reality. Scientific research should focus upon better understanding the psychological underpinnings of this disorder, optimal family and individual therapies, as well as delineating the differences among children who resolve with watchful waiting versus those who resolve with therapy and those who persist despite therapy.

Primary author: Michelle Cretella, MD
August 2016

The American College of Pediatricians is a national medical association of licensed physicians and healthcare professionals who specialize in the care of infants, children, and adolescents. The mission of the College is to enable all children to reach their optimal, physical and emotional health and well-being.

~

Gender Dysphoria in Children:
Summary Points

The American College of Pediatricians urges health professionals, educators and legislators to reject all policies that condition children to accept a life of chemical and surgical impersonation of the opposite sex as normal and healthful. Facts – not ideology – determine reality. All references are found within the text of the full statement [https://www.acpeds.org/the-college-speaks/position-statements/gender-dysphoria-in-children]

1. **Gender dysphoria (GD) of childhood describes a psychological condition in which children experience a marked incongruence between their experienced gender and the gender associated with their biological sex.** They often state that they are the opposite sex. Prevalence rates among children are estimated to be less than 1%.

2. **It is false that brain differences observed in some studies between transgender adults and non-transgender adults prove that GD is innate.** If differences do exist in brain structures of transgender adults, these differences are more likely to be the result of transgender identification and behavior, not the cause of transgender identification and behavior. This is because thinking and behavior is known to shape brain microstructure through a process called neuroplasticity.

3. **When GD occurs in the pre-pubertal child, it resolves in 80-95 percent of patients by late adolescence after they naturally pass through puberty.** This is consistent with studies of identical twins that prove no one is born hard-wired to develop GD.

4. **All complex behaviors are due to a combination of nature (biology), nurture (environmental factors) and free will choices. Studies of identical twins prove that GD is predominately influenced by non-shared post-natal events.** The largest study of twin transsexual adults found that only 20 percent of identical twins were both trans-identified. Since identical twins contain 100 percent of the same DNA from conception, and develop in exactly the same prenatal environment where they are exposed to the same prenatal hormones, if genes and/or prenatal hormones contributed significantly to transgenderism, the concordance rates would be close to 100 percent. Instead, 80 percent of identical twin pairs were discordant for transgenderism. This means that at least 80 percent of what contributes to transgenderism in one adult co-twin consists of one or more non-shared post-natal experiences.

5. **There is no single family dynamic, social situation, adverse event, or combination thereof that has been found to destine any child to develop GD. This fact, together with twin studies, suggests that there are many paths that may lead to GD in certain vulnerable children.** Clinical case studies suggest that social reinforcement, parental psychopathology, family dynamics, and social contagion facilitated by mainstream and social media, all contribute to the development and/or persistence of GD in some vulnerable children. There may be other as yet unrecognized contributing factors as well.

6. **There is a suppressed debate among physicians, therapists, and academics regarding the recent trend to quickly affirm gender dysphoric youth as transgender.** Many health professionals are deeply concerned because affirming youth as transgender sends them down the path of medical transition (a sex change) which requires the use of toxic hormones and unnecessary surgeries. Healthcare professionals opposed to affirming a child's gender dysphoria based upon the medical ethics principle of "First do no harm" are being silenced. This is true among **left-leaning youth trans critical professionals** [https://youthtranscriticalprofessionals.org/] as well as those who are traditionally more conservative.

7. **Human sexuality is an objective biological binary trait: "XY" and "XX" are genetic markers of sex, male and female respectively – not genetic markers of a disorder.** The norm for human design is to be conceived either male or female. Human

sexuality is binary by design with the obvious purpose being the reproduction and flourishing of our species. This principle is self-evident. The exceedingly rare disorders of sex development (DSDs), including but not limited to androgen insensitivity syndrome and congenital adrenal hyperplasia, are all medically identifiable deviations from the sexual binary norm, and are rightly recognized as disorders of human design. Individuals with DSDs do not constitute a third sex.

8. **Human beings are born with a biological sex. Gender (an awareness and sense of oneself as male or female) is a psychological concept; not an objective biological entity.** No one is born with an awareness of being male or female; this awareness develops over time and, like other aspects of one's self-awareness, may be derailed by a child's subjective perceptions, relationships, and adverse experiences from infancy forward. People who identify as "feeling like the opposite sex" or "somewhere in between" do not comprise a third sex. They remain biological men or biological women.

9. **A person's belief that one is something one is not is, at best, a sign of confused thinking; at worst it is a delusion.**

10. **Cross-sex hormones (estrogen for boys and testosterone for girls) are associated with dangerous health risks.** Oral estrogen administration to boys may place them at risk for experiencing: thrombosis/thromboembolism; cardiovascular disease; weight gain; hypertrigyceridemia; elevated blood pressure; decreased glucose tolerance; gallbladder disease; prolactinoma; and breast cancer. Similarly, girls who receive testosterone may experience an elevated risk for: low HDL and elevated triglycerides (cardiovascular risk); increased homocysteine levels; hepatotoxicity; polycythemia; increased risk of sleep apnea; insulin resistance; and unknown effects on breast, endometrial and ovarian tissues.

11. **Puberty is not a disorder and therefore should not be arrested as though it is a disease. Puberty-blocking hormones induce a state of disease - the absence of puberty.** Puberty blocking hormones (gonadotropin releasing hormone agonists or GnRH agonists) arrest bone growth, decrease bone density, prevent the sex-steroid dependent organization and maturation of the adolescent brain, and inhibit fertility by preventing the development of gonadal tissue and mature gametes for the duration of treatment.

12. **Pre-pubertal children who receive puberty-blocking hormones (GnRH agonists) followed by cross-sex hormones are permanently sterilized. Pre-pubertal children who bypass pubertal suppression and are placed on cross-sex hormones directly are also permanently sterilized.**

13. **At least one prospective study demonstrates that all pre-pubertal children placed on puberty blocking drugs eventually choose to begin sex reassignment with cross-sex hormones.** This suggests that impersonation of the opposite sex and pubertal suppression, far from being fully reversible and harmless as proponents claim, sets into motion a single inevitable outcome (transgender identification) that requires lifelong use of toxic cross-sex hormones, resulting in infertility and other serious health risks.

14. **Adolescent girls with GD who have taken testosterone daily for one year may obtain a double mastectomy as young as age 16.** This is not a reversible procedure.

15. **A thirty year follow up study found rates of suicide are nearly twenty times greater among adults who undergo sex reassignment in Sweden which is among the most LGBTQ – affirming countries.** This demonstrates that while sex-reassignment eases some of the gender dysphoria in adulthood, it does not result in levels of health on par with that of the general population. It also suggests that the mental health disparities are not primarily due to social prejudice, but to whatever pathology has precipitated the transgender feelings in the first place and/or the transgender lifestyle itself.

16. **Conditioning children to believe the absurdity that they or anyone could be "born into the wrong body," and that a lifetime of chemical and surgical impersonation of the opposite sex is normal and healthful is child abuse.** Affirming gender dysphoria via public education and legal policies will confuse children and parents, leading more children to present to "gender clinics" where they will be given puberty-blocking drugs. This, in turn, virtually ensures that they will "choose" a lifetime of sterility, toxic cross-sex hormones, and likely consider unnecessary surgical mutilation of their healthy body parts as young adults.

17. **There is a serious ethical problem with allowing irreversible, life-changing procedures to be performed on minors who are too young to give valid consent themselves. Children and adolescents do not have the cognitive maturity or experiential capacity to understand the magnitude of such decisions.** Ethics alone demands an end to the use of pubertal suppression, cross-sex hormones, and sex reassignment surgeries in children and adolescents.

Republished with permission from the American College of Pediatricians.

REFERENCES FOR "GENDER IDEOLOGY HARMS CHILDREN":

[1] Consortium on the Management of Disorders of Sex Development, "Clinical Guidelines for the Management of Disorders of Sex Development in Childhood." Intersex Society of North America, March 25, 2006, from http://www.dsdguidelines.org/files/clinical.pdf.

[2] Zucker, Kenneth J. and Bradley Susan J. "Gender Identity and Psychosexual Disorders." *FOCUS: The Journal of Lifelong Learning in Psychiatry.* Vol. III, No. 4, Fall 2005 (598-617).

[3] Whitehead, Neil W. "Is Transsexuality biologically determined?" *Triple Helix* (UK), Autumn 2000, p. 6-8. From http://www.mygenes.co.nz/transsexuality.htm; see also Whitehead, Neil W."Twin Studies of Transsexuals [Reveals Discordance]", from http://www.mygenes.co.nz/transs_stats.htm.

[4] Jeffreys, Sheila. Gender Hurts: A Feminist Analysis of the Politics of Transgenderism. Routledge, New York, 2014 (pp.1-35).

[5] American Psychiatric Association: Diagnostic and Statistical Manual of Mental Disorders, Fifth Edition, Arlington, VA, American Psychiatric Association, 2013 (451-459). See page 455 re: rates of persistence of gender dysphoria.

[6] Hembree, WC, et al. Endocrine treatment of transsexual persons: an Endocrine Society clinical practice guideline. *J Clin Endocrinol Metab.* 2009; 94:3132-3154.

[7] Olson-Kennedy, J and Forcier, M. "Overview of the management of gender nonconformity in children and adolescents." UpToDate November 4, 2015. Accessed 3.20.16 from www.uptodate.com.

[8] Moore, E., Wisniewski, & Dobs, A. "Endocrine treatment of transsexual people: A review of treatment regimens, outcomes, and adverse effects." *The Journal of Endocrinology & Metabolism,* 2003; 88(9), pp. 3467-3473.

[9] FDA Drug Safety Communication issued for Testosterone products: http://www.fda.gov/Drugs/DrugSafety/PostmarketDrugSafetyInformationforPatientsandProviders/ucm161874.htm.

[10] World Health Organization Classification of Estrogen as a Class I Carcinogen: http://www.who.int/reproductivehealth/topics/ageing/cocs_hrt_statement.pdf.

[11] Dhejne, C, et.al. "Long-Term Follow-Up of Transsexual Persons Undergoing Sex Reassignment Surgery: Cohort Study in Sweden." PLoS ONE, 2011; 6(2). Affiliation: Department of Clinical Neuroscience, Division of Psychiatry, Karolinska Institutet, Stockholm, Sweden. http://journals.plos.org/plosone/article?id=10.1371/journal.pone.0016885.

References for "Gender Dysphoria in Children":

[1.] Shechner T. Gender identity disorder: a literature review from a developmental perspective. *Isr J Psychiatry Relat Sci* 2010;47:132-138.

[2.] American Psychiatric Association. *Diagnostic and Statistical Manual of Mental Disorders.* 5th ed; 2013:451-459.

[3.] Cohen-Kettenis PT, Owen A, Kaijser VG, Bradley SJ, Zucker KJ. Demographic characteristics, social competence, and behavior problems in children with gender identity disorder: a cross-national, cross-clinic comparative analysis. *J Abnorm Child Psychol.* 2003;31:41–53.

[4.] Singal J. How the fight over transgender kids got a leading sex researcher fired. *New York Magazine,* Feb 7, 2016. Available at: http://nymag.com/scienceofus/2016/02/fight-over-trans-kids-got-a-researcher-fired.html. Accessed May 15, 2016.

[5.] Bancroft J, Blanchard R, Brotto L, et al. Open Letter to the Board of Trustees of CAMH; Jan 11, 2016. Available at: www.ipetitions.com/petition/boardoftrustees-CAMH. Accessed May 125, 2016.

[6.] Youth Trans Critical Professionals. Professionals Thinking Critically about the Youth Transgender Narrative.
   Available at: https://youthtranscriticalprofessionals.org/about/. Accessed June 15, 2016.

[7.] GenderTrender. Skipping the puberty blockers: American "transgender children" doctors are going rogue; Nov 4, 2014. Available at: https://gendertrender.wordpress.com/2014/11/11/

skipping-the-puberty-blockers-american-transgender-children-doctors-are-going-rogue/.
Accessed May 15, 2016.

8. Brennan, W. Dehumanizing the Vulnerable: When Word Games Take Lives. Chicago: Loyola University Press, 1995.

9. Kuby, G. The Global Sexual Revolution: Destruction of freedom in the Name of Freedom. Kettering, OH: Angelico Press, 2015.

10. Jeffeys, S. Gender Hurts: A Feminist Analysis of the Politics of Transgendcrsim. NY: Routledge, 2014 (p. 27).

11. Forcier M, Olson-Kennedy J. Overview of gender development and gender nonconformity in children and adolescents. UpToDate; 2016. Available at: www.uptodate.com/contents/overview-of-gender-development-and-clinical-presentation-of-gender-nonconformity-in-children-and-adolescents?source=search_result&search=Overview+of+gender+nonconformity+in+children&selectedTitle=2percent7E150. Accessed May 16, 2016.

12. Rametti G, Carrillo B, Gomez-Gil E, et al. White matter microstructure in female to male transsexuals before cross-sex hormonal treatment. A diffusion tensor imaging study. *J Psychiatr Res* 2011;45:199-204.

13. Kranz GS, Hahn A, Kaufmann U, et al. White matter microstructure in transsexuals and controls investigated by diffusion tensor imaging. *J Neurosci* 2014;34(46):15466-15475.

14. Gu J, Kanai R. What contributes to individual differences in brain structure? *Front Hum Neurosci* 2014;8:262.

15. Reyes FI, Winter JS, Faiman C. Studies on human sexual development fetal gonadal and adrenal sex steroids. J Clin Endocrinol Metab 1973;37(1):74-78.

16. Lombardo M. Fetal testosterone influences sexually dimorphic gray matter in the human brain. *J Neurosci* 2012;32:674-680.

17. Campano A. [ed]. Geneva Foundation for Medical Education and Research. Human Sexual Differentiation; 2016. Available at: www.gfmer.ch/Books/Reproductive_health/Human_sexual_differentiation.html. Accessed May 11, 2016.

18. Shenk, D. *The Genius in All of Us: Why everything you've been told about genetics, talent, and IQ is wrong.* (2010) New York, NY: Doubleday; p. 18.

19. Diamond, M. "Transsexuality Among Twins: identity concordance, transition, rearing, and orientation." *International Journal of Transgenderism, 14*(1), 24–38.

20. Consortium on the Management of Disorders of Sex Development. *Clinical Guidelines for the Management of Disorders of Sex Development in Childhood.* Intersex Society of North America; 2006. Available at: www.dsdguidelines.org/files/clinical.pdf. Accessed Mar 20, 2016.

21. Zucker KJ, Bradley SJ. Gender Identity and Psychosexual Disorders. FOCUS 2005;3(4):598-617.

22. Zucker KJ, Bradley SJ, Ben-Dat DN, et al. Psychopathology in the parents of boys with gender identity disorder. *J Am Acad Child Adolesc Psychiatry* 2003;42:2-4.

23. Kaltiala-Heino et al. Two years of gender identity service for minors: overrepresentation of natal girls with severe problems in adolescent development. *Child and Adolescent Psychiatry and Mental Health* (2015) 9:9.

24. Zucker KJ, Spitzer RL. Was the Gender Identity Disorder of Childhood Diagnosis Introduced into DSM-III as a Backdoor Maneurver to Replace Homosexuality? *Journal of Sex and Marital Therapy.* 2005;31:31-42.

25. Roberts A. Considering alternative explanations for the associations among childhood adversity, childhood abuse, and adult sexual orientation: reply to Bailey and Bailey (2013) and Rind (2013). *Arch Sexual Behav* 2014;43:191-196.

26. Blom RM, Hennekam RC, Denys D. Body integrity identity disorder. *PLoS One* 2012;7(4).

27. Lawrence A. Clinical and theoretical parallels between desire for limb amputation and gender identity disorder. *Arch Sexual Behavior* 2006;35:263-278.

28. King CD. The meaning of normal. Yale *J Biol Med* 1945;18:493-501.

29. Cohen-Kettenis PT, Delemarre-van de Waal HA, Gooren LJ. The treatment of adolescent transsexuals: changing insights. *J Sexual Med* 2008;5:1892–1897.

30. Bailey MJ, Triea K. What many transsexual activists don't want you to know and why you should know it anyway. *Perspect Biol Med* 2007;50:521-534. Available at: www.ncbi.nlm.nih.gov/pubmed/17951886. Accessed May 11, 2016.

31. Sadjadi S. The endocrinologist's officepuberty suppression: saving children from a natural disaster? *J. Med Humanit* 2013;34:255-260.

32. Bertolote JM, Fleischmann A. Suicide and psychiatric diagnosis: a worldwide perspective. *World Psychiatry* 2002;1(3):181–185.

33. Eyler AE, Pang SC, Clark A. LGBT assisted reproduction: current practice and future possibilities. *LGBT Health* 2014;1(3):151-156.

34. Schmidt L, Levine R. Psychological outcomes and reproductive issues among gender dysphoric individuals. *Endocrinol Metab Clin N Am* 2015;44:773-785.

35. Jeffreys, S. The transgendering of children: gender eugenics. Women's Studies International Forum 2012;35:384-393.

36. Johnson SB, Blum RW, Giedd JN. Adolescent maturity and the brain: the promise and pitfalls of neuroscience research in adolescent health policy. *J Adolesc Health* 2009;45(3):216-221.

37. US Department of Health and Human Services. Nuremberg Code; 2015. Available at: www.stat.ncsu.edu/people/tsiatis/courses/st520/references/nuremberg-code.pdf. Accessed 5/15/16.

[38.] World Health Organization. Eliminating forced, coercive and otherwise involuntary sterilization. Interagency Statement; 2014. Available at: www.unaids.org/sites/default/files/media_asset/201405_sterilization_en.pdf. Accessed May 16, 2016.

[39.] Hayes, Inc. Sex reassignment surgery for the treatment of gender dysphoria. Hayes Medical Technology Directory. Lansdale, Pa.: Winifred Hayes; May 15, 2014.

[40.] Hayes, Inc. Hormone therapy for the treatment of gender dysphoria. Hayes Medical Technology Directory. Lansdale, Pa: Winifred Hayes; May 19, 2014.

[41.] Kennedy P. Q & A with Norman Spack: a doctor helps children change their gender. Boston Globe, Mar 30, 2008. Available at http://archive.boston.com/bostonglobe/ideas/articles/2008/03/30/qa_with_norman_spack/. Accessed May 16, 2016.

[42.] Hembree WC, Cohen-Kettenis PT, Delemarre-van de Wall HA, et al. Endocrine treatment of transsexual persons: An Endocrine Society clinical practice guideline. *J Clin Endocrinol Metab* 2009;94:3132-3154.

[43.] Reardon S. Transgender youth study kicks off: scientists will track psychological and medical outcomes of controversial therapies to help transgender teens to transition. *Nature* 2016;531:560. Available at: www.nature.com/news/largest-ever-study-of-transgender-teenagers-set-to-kick-off-1.19637. Accessed May 16, 2016.

[44.] Keleman M. What do transgender children need? *Houstonian Magazine*, Nov 3, 2014. Available at: www.houstoniamag.com/articles/2014/11/3/what-do-transgender-children-need-november-2014. Accessed May 16, 2016.

[45.] Farwell S. Free to be themselves: Children's Medical Center Dallas opens clinic for transgender children and teenagers, the only pediatric center of its type in the Southwest. Dallas Morning News, Jun 4, 2015. Available at: http://interactives.dallasnews.com/2015/gender/. Accessed May 16, 2016.

46. De Vries ALC, Steensma TD, Doreleijers TAH, Cohen-Kettenis, PT. Puberty suppression in adolescents with gender identity disorder: a prospective follow-up study. J Sex Med 2011;8:2276-2283.

47. Feldman J, Brown GR, Deutsch MB, et al. Priorities for transgender medical and health-care research. Curr Opin *Endocrinol Diabetes Obes* 2016;23:180-187.

48. Tangpricha V. Treatment of transsexualism. *UpToDate* 2015. Available at: www.uptodate.com/contents/treatment-of-transsexualism?source=search_result& search=treatment+of+transsexualism&selectedTitle=1percent7E8. Accessed May 14, 2016.

49. Moore E, Wisniewski A, Dobs A. Endocrine treatment of transsexual people: a review of treatment regimens, outcomes, and adverse effects. *J Clin Endocrinol Metab* 2003;88:3467-3473.

50. Dhejne, C, et.al. "Long-Term Follow-Up of Transsexual Persons Undergoing Sex Reassignment Surgery: Cohort Study in Sweden." *PLoS ONE*, 2011; 6(2). Affiliation: Department of Clinical Neuroscience, Division of Psychiatry, Karolinska Institutet, Stockholm, Sweden. Accessed 7.11.16 from http://journals.plos.org/plosone/article?id=10.1371/journal.pone.0016885.

51. Clements-Nolle, K., et al. HIV prevalence, risk behaviors, health care use and mental health status of transgender persons: implications for public health intervention. *Am J Public Health* 2001;91(6):915-21.

52. Kuhn, A., et al. Quality of Life 15 years after sex reassignment surgery for transsexualism. *Fertility and Sterility* 2009;92(5):1685-89.

53. Burgess D, Lee R, Tran A, van Ryn M. Effects of Perceived Discrimination on Mental Health and Mental Health Services Utilization Among Gay, Lesbian, Bisexual and Transgender Persons. *Journal of LGBT Health Research* 2008;3(4): 1-14.

Re-Framing Reality and the Language of Erasure

"If a woman speaks out of turn then her teeth will be smashed with a brick."

~ FROM THE ENMETENA & UKUKAGINA CONES (SUMERIAN) C. 2350
BCE - THE WORLD'S EARLIEST KNOWN LAW CODES, AND WITHIN THEM WE
FIND THE FIRST WRITTEN SILENCING OF THE FEMALE VOICE.
FROM THE ASCENT OF WOMAN, A GROUNDBREAKING FOUR-PART DOCU-
MENTARY SERIES ON THE HISTORY OF WOMEN, WRITTEN AND PRESENTED BY
DR. AMANDA FOREMAN.

As women, especially, we need to speak up, unapologetically. We need to keep our critical thinking skills sharp, we must refuse to accept the mass belligerence of gender/queer/trans theory as gospel, we need to know our convictions, and to be comfortable with our right to dissent. If we become too complacent, if we allow males to continue to redefine language (and with it, our reality), if we allow people to tell us that sane, founded disagreement is "hate speech," or if we allow ourselves to believe that our perspectives, rooted in lived experience, are forms of violence, then we are, in fact, at risk of erasure. And our erasure will not be caused by language itself, but by our own inability to recognize that the language is being used against us.

~ Hypotaxis

CHAPTER 13

ON LANGUAGE AND ERASURE

Hypotaxis

I DON'T WANT anyone who reads this to *think* I am angry: I want you to *know* I am angry.

The words you are about to read are thought crimes. The language I know, the language I use, is heretical. I, like so many other women, compose thoughts behind a pseudonym in order that I might not suffer a metaphorical though all-too-consequential public execution for speaking truth. Legion are the women who have cloaked themselves in anonymity, who have spoken from behind a curtain because their words do not align neatly with the Gospel According to Man.

Some years ago, I taught a course that required me to cover Aristotle's *Nicomachean Ethics*. Part of Aristotle's aim, in this text, is to provide a scientific formula for how to "live the best life" (a rather arrogant endeavor, if you ask me). So I introduced *Ethics* by asking my students, millennial freshmen, what it meant to "live a good life." What does a good life entail? How might we define this?

My students were, as so many of their generation, reluctant to answer any of these questions for fear of taking a position and, as a result, potentially "invalidating" the perspective of other classmates. Each student had been raised in a culture of such impossible relativism that each believed that to take a stance, to offer forth a perspective or a theory, was to eradicate the stances, theories, and perspectives of classmates who might disagree.

In order to provoke them, to get them to say something, anything, I posed the following question: If someone chose to live their life in a dark, musty basement, pissing in a bucket, eating Cheetos, and watching nothing but pornography until the day he died, would that constitute a "good" life?

Still, they were reluctant to answer, but finally a few brave souls offered tepid responses like, "If he enjoyed doing that, then I guess it's a good life." And, "I wouldn't want to live that way, but if he wanted to live like that, then who am I to judge?"

I pressed them further still, hardly able to mask my incredulity. "But is that a *good* way to spend one's brief tenure on this earth?"

Everything is subjective, they argued.

I left class that day feeling a bit queasy. Sure, "live and let live" is a fine and noble adage, and okay, so they couldn't form convictions around an implausible hypothetical scenario, but what does it mean for us as a society when we are afraid to hold a conviction, to take a position, to articulate a point of view because we have come to believe that informed perspectives *literally erase* the perspectives of those who might disagree with us?

Interestingly, though perhaps not surprisingly, postmodernist thought, once an intriguing theoretical outpost of the humanities, has dealt a swift and devastating blow to rational, intelligent discourse as it is now the lens through which we are implored to view everything from Goethe to genitalia.

No longer confined to contemporary poetics, postmodernism's wildfire has spread into politics, pop culture, and law. We are urged by the dominant culture to judge nothing (not even, as evidenced by a subtle, but deeply sinister move to normalize it, pedophilia). We are told that, in order to be good people, we must embrace absolute moral relativism, we must view all things as texts that are open to multiple interpretations, and all interpretations are *right* and *just,* except the ones that challenge patriarchy's most beloved capitalist institutions: porn, prostitution, and gender.

In the swamp of relativism, all positions are valid, except those held by women who refuse to reshape their feminist convictions to suit the desires of male persons. The convictions of nonconformist women are now considered so dangerous that they are contextualized as violence.

Relativism and postmodernist thought have created a climate in which there may be no absolutes, where language is rendered meaningless, and to suggest otherwise is a thought crime. The greatest enforcers of relativism, the fiercest dictators of what words will and will not signify, are people (overwhelmingly male) who have decided to make gender the central cause of their lives.

For many male persons, understandably, gender is both intriguing and innate: something to *be,* to aspire to, something that *defines.*

See, while gender does (as so many liberals are keen to point out) impact both girls and boys, it impacts them differently. A boy, after all, in accordance with gender norms, is not a "bad" thing to be. A boy child is born into a world that enables him to define what it means to be "boy" or "girl," and enables him to dictate how the language will construct itself around his experiences.

Our unwavering adherence to gender's innateness makes it so that a boy is groomed from birth to believe the world – its currency, its women, its language – are his birthright.

Girls experience gender differently. In fact, the single greatest contribution to the continued systemic subjugation of women has been the unwavering commitment to the idea that gender is inborn, coded into our DNA, denoted by some elusive, imperceptible, but somehow *real*, part of our "female brains." Patriarchy's unrelenting adherence to a belief in gender's innateness kept my impossibly brilliant grandmother from a proper education, kept countless women like me (who rejected many of the stereotypical trappings of "womanhood") from believing they were *normal human females*.

My preference for combat boots, short hair, and beer, my lack of makeup, my boxer shorts and my sexual/romantic attraction to women have all caused some liberals to claim I am a closet "trans man." My personal preferences are to be "read" (to use the postmodern gestalt) as my oh-so-important "gender presentation." And if I am to read the cultural writing on the wall, I am considered most certainly "male brained," or I have a "male soul" – but the fact remains, I have a vagina, estrogen courses through me to such a degree it occasionally gives me cancer, and no amount of "gender expression" can do a damn thing to change these realities. Some things are not, in fact, subjective.

That I was conditioned to be submissive, to defer to men, had nothing to do with my "identity," my personal preferences, or my biology, and everything to do with gender, with the fact that I was born female in a world that despises women, a world that is obsessively in love with the idea that our second-class status is inextricably linked to our sex.

Gender is not a cause to be celebrated. Gender is a destructive, patriarchal, capitalist force that deprives female human beings of their humanity, and in its worst manifestations, facilitates atrocities such as child marriage, rape, and honor killings. For women and girls the world over, gender is the problem, and feminists used to be able to say so.

My refusal to accept what I know to be untrue has caused liberals to accuse me, on my blog, of inflicting actual violence on those for whom gender is a flight of fancy, something to play with, to try on, a project that gives their lives meaning.

For girls and women, "gender" is a verb, whereas for men it is a noun. For girls and women, gender is something that *happens to us*. For men, gender is an item they may possess.

Because it excludes males, females may no longer suggest they are part of the sex class known as *woman*. Our right to that word has been revoked by our oppressors.

Gender dogma is predicated on the belief that words like "female" and "woman" and "girl" mean *whatever anyone* (usually a man) *says it means* (ergo, it means nothing at all unless a man has claimed the word to describe himself). We are told that female is not so much a "reality," but a feeling in a man's head, a hunch that a male might have.

We are told not to use terms that exclude male persons – like pregnancy, menstruation, vagina. We may, however, talk at length about female essence, female souls elusive, superstitious concepts impossible to verify, phantoms that no woman has ever actually seen or experienced, but in whose existence we must believe absolutely.

Terminology has been doled out to us, oh-so-charitably, by men who have taken up the mantle of *woman*.

Those of us, female, feminist, often lesbian, who take issue with this intellectual mandate, who critique firmly held beliefs in such Victorian concepts as "female souls," are accused of *erasing* transgendered people, of *not wanting trans people to exist*. And so it follows, if we embrace the zeitgeist, that language itself has the capacity to literally, actually eradicate people, and so dissent, of course, will be viewed as dangerous. And when we deem the language of dissent, of rational critique, to be "life-threatening," then we open the door for any intellectual discord to be met with actual violent opposition: we invite barbarism.

Language may indeed connote violence, may become an abstract rendering of violence, may even incite violence, but language itself cannot be literal violence. There is a concrete physicality inherent to actual violence (women and girls know this well) that language, despite its many powers, lacks. Would that language was violence, men would fight their wars in verse.

And the fact remains, to disagree with another human being is neither an attempt at violence, an act of "erasure," nor is it a denial of another person's very existence. Ideological, philosophical conflict – when manifest in language alone – is not violence. (And yes, I realize that when writ into law, language *can* have a sort of erasing impact on groups of people, but I am not discussing legal matters – I am referring, instead, to public discourse in what remains, if anything, of the "marketplace of ideas.")

Everydayfeminism.com informs me that dicks are assumptions and vaginas are "constructs" but my *female soul* is a "reality," and still that doesn't erase the fact of my very real vagina, that doesn't erase the fact that only men know what the fuck a "female soul" is. Furthermore, at every turn I am instructed, by male persons who "identify as women," on how I may refer to myself: *cis*. I am told that as a lesbian, I am merely attracted to a particular gender, and refusal to date male-bodied persons who "feel female" is an act of bigotry. In popular culture, in academia, my very sexuality is defined and governed by men for whom gender is a bit of performance art, a warm feeling, everything. I am told what words I may and may not use to discuss my life.

I was lucky to have been raised in a household where my parents did not pathologize our "gender presentation." My brother wanted his nails painted, curlers in his hair, while my sister insisted upon wearing what she called "boy clothes" construction hats, ill-fitting polo shirts. No one was sent to a gender therapist, a psychologist, or a surgeon. My distinctly apolitical parents understood, albeit on a subconscious level, that these desires were part of preference, and not some "problem" impossibly coded into our DNA. The fact was, despite all the social cues and conditioning, some of their children were not going to fit neatly within the rigid boundaries gender had established for them. Their son was going to want pink nail polish. Their daughter was going to want cowboy hats and fake tattoos. Who fucking cared? The bigger issue was the fierce resistance to math homework, and the inability to keep a tidy bedroom.

As a lesbian who rejected most gender norms, I feel lucky to have grown up in the 80s and 90s, before men hijacked and dominated feminist philosophy. I was able to view my unwillingness to adopt stereotypes as evidence of my growing emancipation from gender. I was not told by society that my refusal to remove body hair, or my fondness for flannel were part of who I was on a cellular level, but instead could attribute these small freedoms to what my feminist sisters in the 60s and 70s had enabled me to do: be myself. Back then, no one ever seriously suggested my presentation hinted at some inherent masculinity. No one told me my personal preferences were indicative of some essential, irrevocable truth that needed immediate affirmation and medical attention.

Presentation, however, is but one small piece of the gender catastrophe. The more pernicious components involve socialization, bullshit notions and prejudices that are inextricably woven into the fabric of culture, that shape everything from healthcare to housing. These more subtle, however insidious, aspects of gender are far more important, and impossible to "identify" one's way out of.

Language is one way women and girls have been able to grasp the full scope of the shitty hand gender has dealt us. Language is the way women have been able to parse our sex, the material reality of our female bodies, from the selflessness, subservience, and frivolity we've been told, in this chronic, patriarchal condition, that we must embrace. Gender is the horrible debt one pays for being born female – language used to allow us to recognize this.

One concept I ascribe to is this: if one truly wants to fix a problem, they must begin first not by examining who suffers from the problem, but who benefits from it. In the case of gender, who benefits?

Capitalism benefits: more specifically, the medical industrial complex, and the porn and sex-trafficking industries. More broadly, men benefit.

As history has taught us, as the current cultural clime teaches us, no oppressor willingly relinquishes that from which he benefits. Instead, when he feels his power slipping, he becomes extremist, and extremist men, whether they are extremist for religion or gender, always position themselves as the arbiters of language. When women refuse to submit, refuse to use the words they give us, refuse to use our existing lexicon to placate their views, they employ new methods, among them: public shaming, blacklisting, rape, and murder. And the motivation for these actions is always the same – control of society and its perceived commodities: ideas, industry, land, language, women.

Language is a power struggle. All marginalized groups seek out language to adequately name their struggles and experiences. The oppressed find terminology, invent new words, or figure out how they might use existing words to describe themselves. As women, we have no language but that which we have borrowed from our oppressors. The very words we use to discuss our oppression and our suffering are tools that were not crafted with our tongues in mind.

Had language the power to literally erase, women would have ceased to exist long ago. Because language was not created for women, women know, on some instinctual level, that all the hand-wringing and policing around language is laughable. The use of language to harm women is as old as time, and yet we've only become concerned about language's "harming power" now that words – vagina, uterus, breast, birth, lesbian potentially threaten men's ability to lay claim to womanhood itself.

And so, like all good colonialists, males who "feel like" women accuse women like me of heresy, accuse women like me of, in our dissent, possessing the magical power of being able to *literally erase* a human being, or a group of human beings. Women like me practice dialectical witchcraft, and must, as all witches, be brought to an unjust trial and burnt.

It was, in fact, the crazy-making gender-speak that labels lesbians "bigots" for not wanting to date "lesbians" with penises that brought me to examine this issue at all. What incensed me was my horror at discovering my local "lesbian organization" was dominated by males who "identify as women," my discovery that women have no *space away* from men, my realization that I was being told, by male persons, to call myself "cis," and deny the notion of "shared girlhood," and to accept my lived reality and that of my mothers and grandmothers and sisters as a "hunch." Suddenly, the dominant paradigm was one where feminists had to be sure use language that always included males ("don't say penis is male"), and where feminists had to rebrand pornography, gender, and prostitution as exercises in liberation. Suddenly, the very existence of my female body was "subjective."

Women cannot truly organize around subjectivity. And not-so-coincidentally, women cannot see their own oppression through the lens of subjectivity. Women can't define their experiences in a vocabulary of subjectivity. The soupy expanse of relativism has rendered critical thinking impossible, has allowed men to equate the language of dissent with violence, and not wanting to be perceived as violent, women collude, defer mutely to the language authorities who are, as they have always been, men.

One of the best places to watch this lexical gender-fascism play out is, of course, online.

A couple years ago, the trans movement found a martyr in an Ohio teenager whose tragic suicide was exploited and shamelessly glorified by many on the left. During this time, I read Twitter feeds dealing with the event. One Tweet, from a trans activist accused of harassing the teen's grieving mother, read, "I don't hate women. I am a woman."

The reason this particular Tweet stood out so singularly to me, among all the other noise around the Ohio teenager, was that it illustrated a few important points about where we are as a culture:

1) Male says he's a woman, so he's a woman. It's no longer a matter of "identifying as" – if you "identify as," you are. By this logic, I can merely identify my way into wealth. *I feel wealthy, therefore I am.*

2) Women are incapable of hating women because man-who-identifies-as-woman says so. Easy! Zero critical thinking involved.

And it's the latter observation that matters, because I have encountered this a lot in my opposition to the narrative of "gender is empowering for women." *How can gender theory be misogynist if so many women are on board with it?*

The fact is, women can be misogynists. In order for patriarchy to thrive, it is necessary that women *be* misogynist. Moreover, in order for men to continually benefit from the subjugation of women and girls, it is essential that women and girls align themselves with men. Women are groomed to hate themselves and to hate other women. Taking on the label of "woman," or being born into the class of woman, does not free you from misogynist tendencies. Whether you are female or a male who "identifies as" female, you have been steeped in misogyny since birth. You can deny it, but you cannot, simply by virtue of being woman or "feeling like a woman," absolve yourself of it.

Women have always embraced male-championed causes and male-manufactured theories, usually at our own dire expense. We have often, as female human beings, participated in our own demise.

Around the time of the sensationalized teen suicide in Ohio, Autostraddle (a formerly lesbian online publication) published a particularly noxious article celebrating Gender Studies, the male-centric replacement for Women's Studies. The article was particularly demonstrative of the navel-gazing, woman-hating doublespeak we've seen appear relentlessly in so-called "feminist" and "lesbian" publications. The gist of it: *some males are ladies, and we need to respect that.* However, in order to convince women, or attempt to placate men and convince women to wholeheartedly embrace the notion that gender is inherent, "think pieces" in formerly lesbian/feminist publications have had to attempt, in bizarre, labyrinthine fashion, to debunk grounded scientific principles, to conflate sex with gender. To wit:

Biology is a branch of science and science is also a social construct and really what I'm saying is that your sex is essentially a label a very educated person slapped on you at birth using as many contextual clues as they could garner at the time about your DNA. Sex is not immutable or unchangeable or somehow "intrinsically" defined by our bodies; it's more that science and medicine have words in place to define sex and thrust it upon us – and that they're often inadequate at capturing the full spectrum of diversity.[1]

This is exemplary of a motif, of the swamp of nothingness fuckery being sold to women, by women, on behalf of males who would rather we not, for their precious sakes, acknowledge the existence of biological reality. The attempts to convince women, vis-à-vis pseudo-intellectual postulation, that science is a "construct" in the same way gender is a construct, in a world where most people are raving lunatics because we are no longer allowed to express a rational thought, is dangerous.

Science, according to contemporary patriarchal dogma, is right on all matters *but* for the fundamentally verifiable fact of male and female genitalia. Science is, rather conveniently for men, legitimate and acceptable when it is furnishing synthetic hormones and allowing for surgical interventions. Science is, not surprisingly, wrong when it suggests that there is sexual dimorphism. Science is wrong when it allows women to name their reality.

How, I have to wonder, is this any different than those who deny evolution? Or climate change? The incentive for Christians to deny evolution, and for conservatives who deny climate change, is the same incentive for men who "feel like women" and wish to claim that science is merely a construct. The principles upset them, inconvenience them, hurt their feelings, cause them to look inward, and don't comply with their fantasies.

But if Jesus didn't live with dinosaurs then . . . then . . . then fuck you, *evolution isn't real!*

But if my SUV that I really, really like is bad for the environment then . . . then . . . then fuck you, *climate change isn't real!*

But if my penis isn't part of female anatomy and I really, really would like to be female then . . . then . . . then fuck you, *biology isn't real!*

Gender Studies is nothing more than anti-intellectualism dressed up in academese for the benefit of males. Period.

And yes, of course, science and medicine have put "words in place" to define things. Scientists and doctors use words particular to their disciplines, they have language that denotes specific, verifiable realities such as "cell" and "cancer" and "female." A doctor's job is not to acknowledge every special nuance of your deeply complex persona. A scientist's job is not to assuage your fragile feelings.

Also present in this particular Autostraddle article was a now ubiquitous part of the popular gestalt: Trans Exclusionary Radical Feminist (TERF). The pejorative itself falsely connotes that feminism was built upon gender and men, and not to prioritize the concerns of males who "feel like women" is some kind of "feminist transgression."

[Constructivism] has been used – or should I say, misused – in order to invalidate trans experiences. TERFS have wielded constructivism [sic] theory in order to say that all gender – and thus, the transgender experience – isn't real.[2]

This, of course, is the kind of laughable hyperbole often hurled in the direction of women who refuse to accept that men will define what "woman" means. That something is, in fact, a construction does not make it imaginary. Short hair, lipstick, Barbie dolls, fake tits, synthetic hormones – these things are, in fact, material realities. And no woman who shares my view on this matter has ever suggested that gender is not real. On the contrary, it is gender's *realness* that is the problem.

What women like me have suggested is that gender and sex are not one and the same; that biology, not a set of personal preferences, makes one female or male; and that one cannot merely self-identify their way out of their sex class and into another, any more than one might self-identify out of their species.

Wanting to be and *being* are two different things. An inability to separate the two – the *wish* from the *is* – will have, and has had, devastating consequences for women and girls, and society as a whole, as we slide further and further into a fugue state where our tongues are so thickened by hegemonic subjectivity that objective reality can no longer be named.

The notion that feminists are attempting, with thought and language, to drive a group of people into extinction is preposterous. But the tropes are deliberately constructed to ensure no woman can dissent: *If you disagree, then you are erasing me. If you disagree with me, then I no longer exist.*

If one needs an entire department in a university to validate their outward appearance, to affirm their sexual proclivities, to call them by their chosen name – then fine. Have it.

If one needs new words that end in "x's" and ampersands to define how one views oneself, great. Invent those words.

If one, in order to be happy, needs hormones and elective surgeries, purchase them. We have but one, brief life and I am a feminist who believes an adult human should have absolute authority over her or his body.

But if you're asking women to rescind their knowledge of anatomy and of violence, if your "existence" relies on women feigning ignorance, if your "identity" is contingent on women unlearning language, then we've got a real fucking problem.

As women, we must resist the mass semantic belligerence begotten by postmodernist/trans/gender theory. We need to know and have the power to name our convictions. We need to create and sustain a world where we might rationally, intelligently, and passionately manifest, in rhetoric, our arguments against systems that debase us, without fear of unprecedented retribution.

We cannot accept that sane, philosophical disagreements are "hate speech," or that our perspectives, rooted deeply in lived experience, are forms of violence. If we remain indifferent on this, if we relinquish the little bit of language we've claimed, then we are certainly at risk of an actual erasure, an erasure that will not be caused by language, but by the absence of it.

---

[1] Carmen. "Rebel Girls: Waiter, There's Some Theory in My Gender". *Autostraddle,* January 7, 2015.

[2] Ibid.

CHAPTER 14

EVE WAS "FRAMED"

Ruth Barrett

WHAT MIGHT THE transition from female-centric to male-centric religion, culture, and politics have to do with the female silencing and erasure playing out today in gender identity politics?

"The cosmology of any given culture is analogous to the psyche of an individual. Its myths and religion reveal how the group psyche arrives at its values concerning sex, power, wealth, and gender roles."[1]

~ LEONARD SHALIN

Before patriarchy took control of history, in many cultures of the ancient world the female body with her ability to birth and sustain life was perceived as mirroring the Goddess Herself, the Creatrix of All. Patriarchal pagan religions and the subsequent male-centric religions that are still with us today destroyed or incorporated earlier goddess and female-centric religions and civilizations, splintering a unified perception of body, mind, and spirit. From the early patriarchal social systems to the present, human bodies, especially the bodies of women and children, became property. In fact, ownership of women and their children was the original purpose of marriage. A woman no longer belonged to herself but to a father, husband, brother, or master. Inheritance rights changed from matrilineal (mother to daughter) inheritance to patrilineal (father to son) inheritance, reinforcing the fact that women were not autonomous. Women could be turned out of their own homes, or even killed, if there was no male son or heir to succeed a dead father or husband. Women continue to suffer from the impact of the historical change from gynocentric (mother/woman-centered) cultures that flourished in Old Europe between 6500 and 3500 BCE (surviving in Crete until 1450 BCE) to andocratic (male-dominated) societies.[2] The transition away from female-centered religion and culture erased any memory of times when women once held power. The priests of today still wear the robes of the priestesses they removed from power. Max Dashu writes:

> Barring women from ritual leadership and religious authority has been a key focus in the drive to undermine female power. Scriptures of the "major" religions often ban priestesses and female religious authority, either explicitly or through stories demonizing their power. Over centuries, male authorities carefully selected and edited the religious canon so as to erase traditions of female leadership (such as the Gnostic scriptures naming Mary Magdalene as the foremost Christian disciple). They also expunged female images of the Divine. This happened with an early saying of Muhammad that embraced the three great goddesses of Arabia as "daughters of Allah." The original version of this hadith was denounced as "the Satanic verses," and was revised in the written Quran.
>
> A male takeover of women's rites and mysteries is described in oral histories from Australia, Melanesia, the Amazon basin, Tierra del Fuego, Kenya, Sierra Leone, and elsewhere. Encroachments on the sphere of priestesses are also attested in the pagan Mediterranean. The priests of Apollo took control of oracular shrines at Delphi and Didyma, interpreting the women's ecstatic utterances and forbidding women the right to consult the Pythias. Male hierophants also gradually consolidated their control of the Mysteries at Eleusis, where legal records show the Melissa priestess contested masculine trespasses on her traditional rights in the fourth century. And although ancient oral history says that Amazon queens founded the great temple of Artemis at Ephesus, women were later forbidden entry to its holy of holies, according to the Roman-era writer Artemidorus.[3]

The Christianity of the early, male-dominated church preached specifically about the evils of the flesh, of both women and nature, the physical world of matter. The asceticism of early Christianity, which turned its back on the world of the flesh, had denigrated, in some quarters of the Church, into hatred of those who brought that flesh into being. Misogyny, the hatred of women, had become a strong element in medieval Christianity. Women who menstruate, and give birth, were identified with sexuality and therefore with evil.[4] This view became institutionalized in the eleventh through seventeenth centuries by the Roman Catholic Church as an all-out war on women, midwives, heretics, folk healers and herbalists, and recast pre-Christian folk religion as witchcraft, resulting in the murderous Inquisition that terrorized Europe for hundreds of years. The Malleus Maleficarum, the Inquisition's official witch hunter's manual read more widely than the Bible said, "All witchcraft stems from carnal lust, which is in women insatiable."⁵ The silencing of women based on The Fall from Genesis II was encoded into the Gospels:

> Let the woman learn in silence with all subjection. But I suffer not a woman to teach or to usurp authority over the man, but to be in silence. For Adam was first formed and then Eve, and Adam was not deceived but the woman being deceived as in the transgression…

> (I TIMOTHY 2:11-14)

> For the man is not of the woman, but the woman of the man. Let the women keep silence in the churches, for it is not permitted unto them to speak; but they are commanded to be under obedience, so saith the law. And if they learn anything, let them ask their husbands at home; for it is a shame for women to speak in the church.

> (I CORINTHIANS 11:3, 7, 9)

These doctrines set the stage for man's entitlement to rape the earth and for socially accepted violence against women and children. Women's bodies were considered evil and below God. Christianity's patriarchal religious philosophy preached that the earth is a "vale of tears," merely a way station before the promised joys of the afterlife. Such concepts have played a large role in creating a suffering world by encouraging resigned acceptance of the miserable conditions that human beings create for themselves, other creatures, and the environment.

It is impossible to calculate with certainty when the shift from gynocentric partnership culture to a patriarchal (andocratic) dominator system precisely occurred, but this shift gradually led women themselves to experience their bodies from a male-centric perspective. How have we as women continued to internalize and collude with patriarchal attitudes in our self-perception? To what extent does that societal shift continue to affect us personally and collectively today? How can we begin to measure the depth of our loss, the absence of our birthright to recognize our embodied selves as sacred? I believe that the patriarchal legacy of ownership is the source of the disconnected feelings so many women have about themselves. When a woman is socialized in a male-centered reality, and where the experience of truly belonging to herself isn't consciously accessible, how can she be genuinely aware of who she is or can become?

So what might this historical shift have to do with the issues of female silencing and erasure playing out today in gender identity ideology and politics? Well, everything! From my view and understanding of how history's winners and losers are ranked in society, there is a direct connection between the transitions from female-centric to male-centric paradigms to the current debate. It is all about the conscious and mostly unconscious perception of this issue. Another way of describing how one perceives an issue is called a "frame."

THE GENDER FRAME

*"When you name it, then you frame it, you can claim it.
The name forms the frame that validates the claim."*

~ FALCON RIVER

What's in a frame? There is a science to using language to shape perceptions. George Lakoff, renowned cognitive scientist, linguist, and author explains, "Framing is about getting language that fits your worldview. It is not just language. The ideas are primary—and the language carries those ideas, evokes those ideas."[6] The selection of metaphors used to describe ideas draws the listener into the speaker's worldview. The language used picks out a frame, and words are defined relative to that frame. If you oppose a worldview yet use its language to discuss your view, you are actually evoking the frame that you are opposing. Lakoff's example: former president Richard Nixon "stood before the nation and said, 'I am not a crook.' And everybody thought about him as a crook. This gives us a basic principle of framing, for when you are arguing against the other side: Do not use their language. Their language picks out a frame—and it may not be the frame you want."[7] When you have a frame, you can only accept facts that fit that frame. Framing is largely unconscious, and we all do it, aware of it or not.

Think of any painting or photograph that is placed within a physical frame on a wall in your home or that sits on your desk at work. A frame around a picture enables a viewer to focus on the specific content of the visual image, excluding what is visually present beyond the boundary of the frame. The frame is supposed to direct your attention to only what is present within the frame. Concepts and beliefs work in much the same way. A concept or belief is also a frame, directing a person to *think* within a specific set of ideas, values, and metaphors that validate or promote that content to the exclusion of anything outside of that frame. To the degree in which an individual is invested in a frame, it feels "natural" to respond to any contrary information to that frame as inherently untrue. This occurs because when you believe something to be deeply true, that belief becomes neurologically wired. Your ability to perceive beyond your familiar accepted frames takes an emotional (and neurological) leap of faith to think outside of it, since you cannot consciously control your own neural system.[8]

For example, when the word "gods" is used when referring to deities of ancient religions, the automatic frame for the sex of the deities will be male, and one will think *male* without being conscious of this automatic reference. Using the more inclusive word *deities* leaves open the possibility of both sexes of deities, where "gods" do not allow female deities to enter the male frame. Our consciousness will not think of including female "gods." Similarly, the word *cult* is used when referring to ancient religions, as when female-centric religions are called "fertility cults." This use of "cult" is a way of diminishing earlier religions as well as contemporary religions outside of the major accepted religions, ranking them as "less than" and implying their status as not being *real* religions.

Another example of re-framing was included in a recent Facebook post, when the term "non-consensual" sex was used to describe "rape." Ava Park, presiding priestess of the Goddess Temple of Orange County in southern California, responded with this: "Consensual sex is just sex. To say 'consensual sex' that implies that there is [such] a thing as 'non-consensual sex,' which there isn't. That's called 'rape.' That is what it needs to be called. There is only sex or rape. Do not teach people that rape is just another type of sex. They are two very separate events. You wouldn't say 'breathing swimming' and 'non-breathing', swimming,'you say 'swimming' and 'drowning.'"

Lastly, consider the framing language of the Obama administration's proposed federal "Equality

Act,"[9] backed by numerous progressives. If enacted into law throughout the United States, this "equality" would mean the legal triumph of gender identity over physicality. What progressive would want to appear as against an act worded as an "equality" act? The same kind of framing language is used on the right when "pro-life" really means "anti-choice."

Lakoff writes that language can and is used is a science and, "Like any science it can be used honestly or harmfully."[10] Neuroscience tells us that each of the concepts we have – the long-term concepts that structure how we think – is instantiated in the synapses of our brains as representational of our experience. Concepts are not things that can be changed just by someone telling us a fact. We may be presented with facts, but for us to make sense of them, they have to fit what is already in the synapses of the brain. Otherwise, facts go in and then they go right back out"[11] When you have a frame that over time is activated, the stronger its synapses become, and the more entrenched it is in your brain – all without your conscious awareness.[12] This is why you can only accept facts that fit that frame - *what you constantly think about becomes physical.*

In studying more about what framing is about, I came to realize that the concept of gender itself is a frame. A frame with its accompanying language locks in and reflects the values and worldview of the person who communicates from that frame; a frame that so easily brings a listener into the worldview of the speaker without the listener ever realizing it. It has also become obvious to me that a deliberate use of framing is at play in the current discourse about sex and gender, with these words used interchangeably to discuss these issues. The words *sex* and *gender* are not equivalent words, and not at all interchangeable in meaning. The degree to which these words have been used interchangeably has erroneously confused issues of gender identity as being synonymous with physicality.

Sex is the word that refers to the body, a set of biological attributes in humans and animals; our physicality internally and externally. Sexual anatomical and physiological features come from DNA—the chromosomes and genes that are present in every cell of an organism. In terms of biology, a woman is an adult human female and a girl is a pre-pubescent human female. In contrast, *gender* is a socially-agreed-upon mental concept which puts human characteristics into gender categories called "masculine" or "feminine," and decides which characteristics are assigned to each biological sex, attributes like strength and gentleness, for example. These characteristics are then culturally and socially enforced *as natural*. Deviations are condemned as unnatural and indeed dangerous to the culture. Gender socialization influences how people perceive themselves and each other, how they act and interact, and how power and resources are distributed in society. Gender roles are those behaviors, tasks and responsibilities that a society considers appropriate for men, women, boys and girls. It becomes obvious that gender socialization is a tool of patriarchy when these supposed natural qualities have to be enforced. So when a woman or man breaks a boundary of gender expectation or behavior, she or he must be punished, lest patriarchy fall.

So the gender frame is: If you have this sexed body (male or female), you are only capable of these (fill in the blank) human qualities. The sexed body you have (male or female) gives you an innate set of human qualities and behaviors that the other sex is incapable of. "Femininity" and "masculinity" are sub-frames of the gender frame.

Who put these characteristics into the "feminine" or "masculine" frames? The winners of history, of course! After millennia of use and enforcement, the gender frame has become equated with *natural* qualities of males and females. Few bother to question who made up the idea of gender characteristics and its stereotypes ascribed to the sexes, and whose cause it ultimately serves. The concept of gender as "natural" derails questioning about whether it is our patriarchal culture that needs to change, not individuals struggling to conform to a historicslly and socially enforced oppressive idea.

The gender frame says that gender characteristics (i.e. stereotypes) are tied to a person's sex, and in today's gender identity politics these carry more weight than a person's biological sex. Thus, in this view, "gender" is used as a word interchangeable with an individual's sexed biology. If your gender doesn't match your body, you are now invited or pressured to modify your body to match your "gender." Gender stereotypes of femininity and masculinity oppress all of us, limiting our awareness of what all human beings are capable of becoming whole human beings, capable of the full range of human expression.

Here are some examples of framing. Some are used repeatedly in the rhetoric of gender identity politics, followed by some responses with a different view:

"A TRANS WOMAN IS A 'REAL' WOMAN!"
What does "real" mean within this frame? "Real" in this statement means a male who *feels* like a woman because he believes he knows what actually being a woman feels like. Even the word "woman" is defined within a male frame of what a "real woman" means and his assertion that "you are a woman if you say you are one." In this frame, only gender identity matters, even though the concept of gender itself is made up, and carries an agenda affirming what trans ideology defines as "real". I affirm that biology matters and should not limit our full human expression.

When a m2t (male to trans) person uses the term "lady stick" to rename his penis as female anatomy, we are not supposed to laugh. However, we were not laughing when in 2015, women's college Mount Holyoke cancelled its annual hosting of its V-day[13] production of *The Vagina Monologues*, the world-famous theatrical piece written by Eve Ensler that exposes issues of sexual violence against women, because it "wasn't inclusive of women without vaginas." On behalf of the student-run theater board, Mount Holyoke student Erin Murphy explained that, "Gender is a wide and varied experience, one that cannot simply be reduced to biological or anatomical distinctions, and many of us who have participated in the show have grown increasingly uncomfortable presenting material that is inherently reductionist and exclusive. At its core, the show offers an extremely narrow perspective on what it means to be a woman."[14]

A trans woman still remains biologically male. Appropriation of a female presentation does not make a male individual a *real* woman. "…[m]ale-to-female sex-change surgery is a sex change in name (documentation) only. Sex-change surgery is only a cosmetic procedure to make it look like a change was made, when in fact no female 'parts' are used. No amount of surgery, hormone injection or anything else can, or will, change the birth gender DNA. It is absolute. The only thing the surgeon can change is the medical record, birth records and the perception that a change took place on the operating table. A DNA test would prove no sex change took place."[15]

"I HAVE A FEMALE BRAIN, SO I AM FEMALE."
There are minor sex differences between male and female brains. Thinking or obsessing on your gender identity will cause physical changes in the brain, as thinking or obsessing about anything will cause physical changes in the brain.

"I WAS BORN INTO THE WRONG BODY."
This statement demonstrates a person's belief that it is actually possible for one's consciousness to somehow become embedded into the "wrong" body, like a brain transplant in the fictional Frankenstein story. It is biologically impossible to be born into the "wrong" body, and there is no science to substantiate this assertion. Males and females with gender dysphoria have a psychological issue that needs be explored with professional help. From my view, this professional and personal support would assist an individual in expressing and celebrating herself or himself in any way they wish by freeing themselves of gender stereotypes while honoring the physicality they have.

"POLITICAL DISAGREEMENT IS EQUIVALENT TO PHYSICAL VIOLENCE. TRANSPHOBIA MUST BE SUPPRESSED."
Political disagreement is an opportunity for discourse that is part of a free society, and should be encouraged. When any questions or concerns are written off as hate speech, bigotry or "transphobic," discourse cannot take place. While references to the female body in art projects are considered "violence against trans people" and protested as "transmisogyny" (as in "Project Vulva" where female students created cupcakes with vulvas sculpted in frosting[16]), trans activists refusing to admit that women exist is not considered hate speech.

"PREGNANT INDIVIDUAL" REPLACES "WOMAN," AND "BIRTHING PARENT" REPLACES "MOTHER."
Revisions to the "Core Competencies Document" of the Midwives Alliance of North America
all but removed the word "woman" and replaced it with terms like "pregnant individual,"
and replaced "mother" with "birthing parent."[17] "Mother" *is* body. She is the one who creates,
brings life forth from her body, and can sustain the life of her infant by her body alone through
lactation. Just as our Mother Earth produces nutrients and food so her creatures can thrive,
this ancient metaphor has yet to be replaced, because this female metaphor is so fundamental
to the universal human experience. Referring to a woman as "the birthing parent" or the "pregnant individual" is erasure of the mother. Perhaps this is the ultimate female erasure. When
you erase "mother," you are denying the body of the female, the only sex able to physically birth
children. How soon will it be considered transphobic to celebrate Mother's Day?

THE MYTH FRAME AND THE POWER OF NAMING

In the male-centered religions of today, another frame is established from the shared creation
myth of Genesis II. Cultures influenced by those religions based on the second story in the
book of Genesis inherited the foundational teaching of how "in the beginning" a male God
Yahweh, without a divine female partner or consort, creates Chavah (Eve) from Adam's side, in
what feminist scholars call a "patriarchal reversal." Since males cannot give birth, this reversal
sets the historical stage for the justification of ranking males over females as divinely ordained.
It is my contention that the female being created from the male is the primary frame that allows other sub-frames and connected metaphors of female subordination to live, and become
"just the way things are."

I often think about how differently things might have gone if Western culture were based
on Genesis I, instead of Genesis II. Most people are not even aware that the Hebrew Bible contains two different creation myths of "in the beginning." In Genesis I, all humanity, male and
female, is made from the same earth in the image and likeness of God, at the same time, and
understood to be one being, an "androgyne" or hermaphrodite. This female and male creature
named the animals before it was split into two separate beings. The implications of the *androgynous* as the original mode of human existence goes beyond the inherent equality between
the sexes. It also indicates that the earth was not given *to the male alone* to conquer in a macho
way, but to *humanity as a whole* to take care of, to enjoy, and even to benefit from in a responsible way. Just as woman was not created for man to dominate, neither were the earth and its
creatures created for humanity to exploit with impunity.[18] The Jewish elders who translated the

Torah from Hebrew to Greek for King Ptolemy of Egypt in the third century BCE purposely altered the concept of *androgynous*. They wrote "male with his apertures" instead of "male and female" in order to avoid the implication that God is of both sexes, because the pagan ruler would then think that there were two gods rather than one.[19] Regardless of the reason, what is lost in translation or deliberately changed for various reasons makes a difference. The rest is *his*- story. The Christian view that prevailed was *not* built on Genesis I, where females and males are both made in the image of God as equals.

> "And do you not know that you are each an Eve? The sentence of God on
> this sex of yours lives in this age; the guilt, of necessity, must live too. You are
> the devil's gateway."

~ TERTULLIAN, CHURCH FATHER 160-230 CE, IN AN ADDRESS TO WOMEN

In Genesis II, Yahweh also gives Adam the power to name all the creatures of the earth, including the first woman. Adam names the female Eve, which in Hebrew is Chavah, meaning Mother of the Living. Her name in Hebrew still contains her true identity and essence She is the Goddess, the Mother of Life. Still, Adam, as the first man, is given the power by God to name her, and thus given power *over* the woman, and given the power to *define* the very nature of woman. From this myth we can source the patriarchal hierarchy of the nuclear family that continues to the present time. The male's instruction to name the female is intentional and significant. The woman does not name, and thus define, herself. Her nature is literally man-made.

Speaking as a witch, I have long been aware of the power of naming as a magical act. The ability to name something or someone is the power to define its very nature. To know, name, and speak the true name of something is to possess the spiritual "handle" with which the speaker can control or influence that thing. To the magical practitioner, the name we call something is both a symbol and energetic container for the *essence* of that thing. The magical use of language for *spell*-work is called *grammary*, and the origin of our English word "grammar". I want to make the connection between the power of words and naming in magic, and what has occurred when the power to name ourselves has been stolen from us. Over time we have forgotten that we ever had this power to begin with. When socially constructed language is applied to the lived, embodied female experience it frames, our capacity to perceive beyond its borders is limited to what is within the frame.

In Alice Walker's essay "Becoming What We're Called,"[20] she discusses her objections to the words "you guys," the supposedly all-inclusive term for addressing males and females, and considered gender-free, though the word "guy" is actually not. She comments about how she feels "when the word is used by men referring to women, and by women referring to themselves." She sees in its use "some women's obsequious need to be accepted at any cost, even at the cost of erasing their own femaleness, and that of other women. Isn't it at least ironic that after so many years of struggle for women's liberation, women should end up calling themselves such? ... The magical power of naming is that people often become what they are called."[21]

Unfortunately, today there are new words, like "cis" being used to name us without our permission and against our will. In her online blog, a woman who goes by the pen name "uppitybiscuit" wrote indignantly about this. Here are some excerpts:

Do not call me cisgender. You have no right or authority to name me without my consent. Cisgender is not a name or identity that females, women as a class, have chosen for ourselves.

Women have not agreed to be named by others, as has been done to us through history, being named, identified and defined by others.

You do not get to name me without my permission.

I name myself. The names and words I use include female, woman, her, she, wimmin, womyn. You have permission to use those words when addressing or referring to me.

You do not have the permission to call me names you have created for me against my will and demand that I own them as mine.

I get to name me. You do not get to name me. You are not allowed to re-classify me according to what language suits your needs.

I am not less than or owned by you as property for you to name as you see fit.

Through your privileged position over me, you presume to re-name me.

I am a full human, a female, a woman; I am refusing to be renamed.

I am what I name myself.

I name me female, woman and myself.[22]

The current use of *cisgender* is a misogynist frame. It is designed to derail and diminish women, to keep our bodies, and our experiences of our bodies, insignificant, and less than. As a radical feminist witch, I *name* "patriarchy" wherever and whenever I recognize it operating. *We can't fight what we can't name.*

In 1998, feminist theologian Mary Daly wrote about words and naming in what she called "The Taming of Feminist Genius by Academentia":

The toning down/turning out of Female Creative Genius in academia/academentia, particularly in the 1990s, is an atrocity that requires attention. Nothing less than the spiritual/intellectual life of women is at stake. Specifically, the taming of women's thinking by much that parades as "feminist theory" undermines Female Elemental integrity and power. One manifestation of this is the intrusive and con-fusing imposition of "gender" jargon by "postmodern feminists." For example, some insist that the word woman is "essentialist" and should be replaced by constructs such as "persons gendered as feminine." For one who takes such a construct as "persons gendered as feminine" seriously enough to examine it, important questions surely would include, "What does 'feminine' mean?" and especially "Gendered by whom?" But the theorists who use such constructs have shown clearly no interest in Naming agents. In fact, they hide agents, especially when these are male oppressors... We did not foresee the invasion of Feminist theory by minions of postmodern masters.[23]

In the 1970s and 1980s spiritual feminists began to rename ourselves and redefine what women are capable of being and doing outside of the gender oppression of patriarchal culture and religions. We "re-framed" ourselves. We experienced this heresy through the metaphor of "giving birth to ourselves and each other." We took ourselves *back*, entering the mystery of self-discovery – if we could eradicate our generational inheritance of internalized misogyny and oppression, who might we be? What would the possibilities for authentic expression be with our invisible cages removed? What we thought of as a paradigm shift was a shifting of a frame, and it was forever life-changing. This is still a possibility for all of us, and like laboring to give birth, it takes a lot of work. For those committed to conscious evolution, as in labor, there is no turning back.

Awareness and critical thinking are essential to knowing when your reality is being framed and how you are being manipulated. Otherwise, what you believe is your reality will be created for you, without your knowledge or consent, through language carefully constructed to shape your perceptions. Suddenly (or gradually) you may find yourself being influenced and using specific words to describe a reality or values that you may not actually agree with.

When engaging in a dialogue with someone using a frame that doesn't represent your views or values, it is imperative to be conscious of the following:

1. A frame is always being used.
2. Identify what the frame is.
3. Choose to enter the other person's frame, or not.
4. If the other's frame doesn't represent your values, do not enter their frame, and instead invite the other to engage within your frame by speaking from your frame using the accompanying metaphors that are aligned with your values.

The conscious and unconscious acceptance of the gender frame explains why progressives, and especially young women, compliantly deny the sacredness of their own female bodies and deny the importance of female sovereignty and female-defined identity, and why many women are so quick to accept males into female-autonomous spaces that their mothers' generation struggled to achieve.

Another way of understanding how it is that many women have so easily accepted being contemptuously renamed and redefined by males, as my life partner Falcon explained, is this: "We have been colonized for so long. We must regain our sovereignty." Yes. As women who have lived with threats of physical and sexual violence over generations, we don't even know that we're colonized, and don't know who we would be without it. Without a sense of ourselves, there's no one to defend, no sense of worth, no consciousness of a self apart from how the dominant culture defines us. We are distanced from our experience of sovereignty, and female autonomy. Why else would so many of us apathetically agree when we are told that the lived reality of our own bodies is less important than the concept of gender? How can the lived experience of girlhood and becoming a woman possibly be reduced to a thought or an idea?

I will endeavor to use language that frames my values. My values include honoring the awesome ability of the female body to bleed monthly without dying, to create and bring forth life (we make people!), nourish and sustain our infants from our breast milk, and all the other life cycle passages that accompany the female body from cradle to grave. I value female creative intelligence. I value freedom for all women and girls to live in a world safe from male violence. I value full equality and access to resources for all people on this Earth, mothers and their children. I value our home planet, and all Her creatures. I value the time spent sharing stories with my sisters who share similar experiences, and I claim my right to name myself, my reality, sourced from my body and my lived female experiences, as *female sovereignty*. This is my birthright, and every woman's.

Sex and Gender

Forty years ago few of us clearly understood the difference in meaning between the words *sex* and *gender*, but we knew that what we *could* do was not the same as what we were told we *should* do. Newspaper ads told us which jobs were for men and which were for women. Television promoted doting and disempowered housewives as our role models. Many of us felt that "if this is what I'm supposed to want, there must be something wrong with me," or "if that is what it is to be a woman, I want no part of being a woman!" Then second-wave feminists in great numbers started challenging gender stereotypes, playing sports, and taking advanced degrees. Tenacious women, beginning to enter trades occupied exclusively by men, were regular recipients of hostility and violence.

Generally given access to more reproductive choices in the West than in other parts of the world, being female becomes less about biological destiny (must get pregnant, have kids, and so on). Still, being a female person matters personally and socially, *and is the filter for every experience we have as a living being.* Femaleness matters because it pervades the reality we live in. Being a girl or woman in this society, in this body, sculpts our experience. In a dualistic patriarchal gender model, women and girls are ranked as inferior to men and boys. This model affirms as natural the innate superiority of the male sex, and the inferiority of the female sex, upholding their desired categories as real and unchangeable.

As a girl child, born myself in the mid-1950s, I experienced gender roles for women and girls as very, very, narrow. At that time, being a girl after a certain age meant not climbing trees or playing hard any more like my two brothers did, and being encouraged to play with dolls that I hated. Like so many girls, I didn't fit into the box. My childhood friends were boys. I loved playing capture the flag, and investigating the neighborhood as a private eye who wrote down the license plates of "suspicious-looking cars" just in case a policeman asked me to help out on a case.

"Acting like a girl" was boring and stifling, and I would have none of it. This concerned my wonderful progressive-thinking mother when I said that I didn't want to be a girl; she was advised by a child psychologist to take me to a beauty parlor and later to charm school. Needless to say, I was a charm school dropout, but I did learn some very important skills, like how to get into a car without opening my legs and how to light a cigarette against the wind.

Had I been able to just simply be myself, without feminine gender stereotypes enforced from every direction, I would have been a free person. Gender oppression tried to kill my wildness and limit my personal freedom. Little did I know that the goddess Artemis was waiting for me in the forest of myth to help me find myself. I was a perfect girl child all along. Being a girl was not the problem. What was wrong was this thing called gender. What was wrong were the strictures of culture and its unrelenting institutions of enforcement.

To be female meant being dominated, paid less, valued less, and continually vulnerable to sexual and physical violence. Like the thousands of other women I've known over the years, I was not born hating myself. Hatred of our female bodies is learned starting in girlhood, driven by the constant messages that we are either too much or not enough (fill in the blank). All too often, the overt and covert messages are that we are unlovable, wrong, and need improvement are financed by those who offer to fix us: the cut-and-paste cosmetic surgeons and the pharmaceutical companies. How can we even begin to separate female self-hatred from cultural contempt for you, your mother, grandmother, your daughters and granddaughters? How can we think for one second that there is no connection?

I challenge all of us to explore further the framing that promotes any feeling that being female is wrong, side by side with the pandemic of female self-hatred, body hatred, and violence against women. I believe that framing is the source of why so many women line up to support our outdated gender dichotomy, the inheritance of five thousand years of misogyny. In the women's communities I participate in, we celebrate our diverse beauty, no matter what age, size, or color we are. We don't cut off our toes or heels so we can fit into Cinderella's glass slipper. Had I been raised by Scythian Amazons in a matrifocal culture, I would have been raised thinking that becoming a woman meant knowing how to be a capable warrior, hunter, and horsewoman, a weaver of cloth, a gatherer of herbs, a strong, brave nurturer and protector of the young.

For me, becoming a feminist meant joining with other women who also wanted to kick this oppressive concept of gender and gender stereotypes to the curb. We became a movement to free ourselves from sexist, institutionalized shackles, whether imposed from within ourselves or without, to become free and express our femaleness any way that we choose.

THE EXTRAORDINARY FEMALE BODY

The sex of our bodies is a reality. We live in a world where male, female, and intersex[24] human beings exist. While sex categories are part of any human society, patriarchal culture took sex differences and ascribed to them rigid gender norms that suited their cultural and religious agenda for the domination and subordination of women. In patriarchy, sex differences, like everything else, are ranked. The female sex is ranked "less than" males, enforcing inequality.

The suffragists accepted the idea of ranking, advancing women's superior moral standards as a justification for including women in political life. But since the 1970s, feminism in general has promoted and defended minimizing sex differences, as the platform upon which to give women equal rights and to demand equal pay for equal work. If these feminists had attempted to assert that they were different from men, the patriarchal system of ranking differences would have ensured that any differences women claimed would have been used to "prove" women's inferiority. So eventually, though starting from different places, the dominant culture and feminism joined together to *frame* the view that other than breasts, genitalia, and hormones, women and men are basically the same.

Just because dominator cultures for centuries have used sex differences and gender stereotypes to oppress females, must we also continue to oppress ourselves by perpetuating unexamined misogyny and deny our differences that may actually be sacred gifts? Different but equal is not possible in the dominant patriarchal culture we live in. Honoring our biological differences doesn't inherently mean we must uphold patriarchal gender stereotypes. We need to create something different.

How important are sex differences, really? How *do* sex differences affect male and female reality? And why do I think this information is important to share with you? Like yourselves and everyone else until two decades ago, I assumed that the only differences between males and females were our hormones and reproductive organs. However, in a 2001 publication by the Committee on Understanding the Biology of Sex and Gender Differences of the Institute of Medicine, the researchers noted that for the past two thousand years the female human body has not been studied, except for the female reproductive organs — medical studies and research had assumed that women are simply smaller men. "We now have the beginning studies on just how different we actually are, and how these differences make life and death impact on how diseases are diagnosed and treated."[25] The study focused its work on sex differences in non-reproductive areas of biology, finding that sex differences occur at the molecular level, in all individual cells, in organs, in every organ system, and in the brain. The committee concluded, "Sex does matter. It matters in ways in which we did not expect. Undoubtedly, it also matters in ways that we have not begun to imagine."[26] Research confirms there are numerous differences between female and male physiology. There are differences in immune function;

in symptoms, type, and onset of cardiovascular disease (not solely related to hormones);[27] in response to toxins; in brain organization; and in sensitivity to pain.[28]

Some examples: According to a Swedish study, crossword puzzles help men prevent dementia, and relationships do the same for women. Also, all adrenal glands under stress secrete cortisol and adrenalin, but in males the chemicals trigger a "fight or flight" response to stress. Females react differently. Female bodies secrete oxytocin, a hormone that counters the damaging effects of the cortisol. The oxytocin prompts a response that some researchers have called the "tend and befriend" impulse. Females tend to connect with others in stressful situations. It is actually unhealthy for women not to have close female friends, or not to spend time exclusively with other women. Oxytocin is also the chemical that induces labor contractions and helps release breast milk; "its evolutionary role may be to bond parents to children and to a mate long enough for the child to survive."[29] These are some of the biological reasons that females tend to be, as women's spirituality foremother Charlene Spretnak has described, "profoundly relational."[30] Also, brain organization researchers have discovered is that it's "possible for males and females to go about doing a task by different routes, but coming to the same result."[31]

The sexes have differences well beyond penises or vaginas, with influences well beyond reproductive function. Science is just catching up to what we already know. Natalie Angier's research for her book, *Woman: An Intimate Geography*, confirms that "[i]n the basic biological sense, the female is the physical prototype for an effective living being. Fetuses are pretty much primed to become female unless the female program is disrupted by gestational exposure to androgens."[32] The Institute of Medicine study describes how our sex begins in the womb, and how the female is the primal matrix:

All human individuals—whether they have an XX, an XY, or an atypical sex chromosome combination—begin development from the same starting point. During early development the gonads of the fetus remain undifferentiated; that is, all fetal genitalia are the same and are phenotypically female. After approximately 6 to 7 weeks of gestation, if the fetus is male, the expression of a gene on the Y chromosome induces changes that result in the development of the testes. In contrast, fetal ovarian secretions are not required for female sex differentiation.[33]

David Crews, of the University of Texas, describes the female as "the ancestral sex, while the male is the derived sex."[34] Angier writes, "...eggs are inherently female. So in thinking about mirrors into infinity, the link between mother and daughter, the nesting of eggs within woman within eggs, we can go a step further and see the continuity of the chromosomes. No maleness tints any part of us gals, no, not a molar drop or quantum."[35] There is no maleness in female- XX people, literally, and the culturally ascribed gender categories of *masculine* and *feminine* are clearly invented. Thus, females have no "masculine" side, as Freud or Jung would have us believe. This is just patriarchal gender jargon within a patriarchal frame.

If you are female, you have XX chromosomes in every cell. This is reality, a fact, not a belief or opinion, not a theory, not a feeling.

Naomi Wolf, author of the cultural classic *The Beauty Myth*, started exploring the science behind the vastly misunderstood body-mind connection between brain and genitalia, consciousness and sexuality, the poetic and the scientific. In her book *Vagina: A New Biography*, Wolf points out that the medical meaning of "vagina" is just the vaginal opening, one of many inadequate words related to this subject. We have no single word for the entire female sex organ, from labia to clitoris to cervix.[36] So as Wolf chose to do, I'll use *vagina* as inclusive for *all* of the parts.

What emerges is a revelation of how profoundly a woman's bodily experience influences nearly every aspect of her life, from stress to creativity, through the intricate weavings that link biology and being. Wolf writes:

> Female sexual pleasure, rightly understood, is not just about sexuality, or just about pleasure. It serves, also, as a medium of female self-knowledge and hopefulness; female creativity and courage; female focus and initiative; female bliss and transcendence; and as medium of a sensibility that feels very much like freedom. To understand the vagina properly is to realize that it is not only coextensive with the female brain, but is also, essentially, part of the female soul.
>
> Once one understands what scientists at the most advanced laboratories and clinics around the world are confirming — that the vagina and the brain are essentially one network, or "one whole system," as they tend to put it, and that the vagina mediates female confidence, creativity, and sense of transcendence—the answers to many of these seeming mysteries fall into place—nature constructed a profound difference between the sexes, which places women, potentially, in a position of greater biochemical empowerment than men, through the medium of satisfying sexual activity.[37]

Wolf writes, "A pivotal player in this mediation is the female pelvic nerve—a sort of information superhighway that branches out from the base of the spinal cord to the cervix, connecting the latter to the brain and thus controlling much of sexual response. But this information superhighway is really more like a superlabyrinth, the architecture of which differs enormously from one woman to another, and is completely unique for each woman. No two women are alike! This sexual neural complexity in women is because we have both reproductive and sexual parts, such as the cervix and uterus, that men don't have.[38] Some women's nerves branch more in the vagina; "some branch a great deal in the perineum, or at the mouth of the cervix."[39] Other women's nerves branch more in the clitoris. The clitoris itself is a bundle of 8,000 nerve fibers.[40] Nowhere else on the body is there a higher concentration of nerve fibers. This includes the fingertips, lips, and tongue, and twice the number than in the penis. The clitoris is designed exclusively for a woman's pleasure.

Angier writes of the clitoris, "Its fetal growth is complete by the twenty-seventh week of gestation, at which point it looks like what it will look like on the girl once she's born."[41] She writes: "It will not atrophy after menopause, the way the vagina can. It will always be there for you."[42] This diversity of wiring in the highly complex female pelvic neural network helps explain why women have wildly different triggers for orgasm. These differences are physical.

As new studies on female biology show, the well-treated vagina and sexual pleasure can be gateways to female creativity, boost confidence levels and self-love, lead women to see more clearly the connections between things, and make women hard to push around easily.[43] New studies by researcher Janniko Georgiadis and his team, using MRIs to study female orgasm and the brain, showed that as a woman approaches closer and closer to orgasm, her brain centers for behavior regulation become deactivated. She can enter a deep trance state, more deeply than at any other time, becoming biochemically like a wild woman or maenad. This same science reveals that due to more female production of dopamine during the sexual experience, women can be more like mystics than men are.[44] It is through this sexually induced trance state that a woman awakens and engages with "profoundly important dimensions of her own soul."[45]

Recent neuroscience is confirming what Tantra has always maintained—and what the loss-of-self scenes in women's greatest fictions hint at: climaxing women go into a trance state that is different from men's experience of orgasm. In studies looking at "MRI images of women's brains exploding in rainbow spots of color at the moment of orgasm...in different places in the brain than the researchers had expected...was an image of breakthrough science...the first account of brain regions involved in experience of clitoral stimulation."[46]

It turns out that female orgasm is experienced in the ventral midbrain—which is exactly where the Tantric "third eye" is supposed to extend into, and also where the dopaminic cell group is located.[47] This same cell group in the female ventral midbrain "plays a wide range of rewarding behaviors, including euphoric states induced by drugs, pleasurable music, and eating chocolate."[48]

VIOLENCE AGAINST WOMEN AND GIRLS

While female-sovereign spaces are being bullied out of existence, "boy"-cotted, made illegal, or are otherwise under attack here in the United States, around the world the statistics show that violence, sexual and otherwise, against women and girls is rising. I can't help wondering, could there be a connection?

Just as a woman's "well-treated" vagina and sexual pleasure seem to be connected to female creativity and confidence through the physical vagina/brain connection, studies also show that sexually abusing a woman's vagina also injures her brain. Naomi Wolf writes, "…if your goal is to break a woman psychologically, *it is efficient to do violence to her vagina.* You will break her faster and more thoroughly than if you simply beat her—because of the vulnerability of the vagina as a mediator of consciousness. Trauma to a woman's vagina imprints deeply on the female brain, conditioning and influencing the rest of her body and mind. Rape as part of the standard toolkit in the deployment of genocidal army tactics is a strategy of *actual physical and psychological control of women,* traumatizing via the vagina as a way to imprint the consequences of trauma on the female brain."[49]

As I've written earlier, research shows that the framing and metaphors we use to describe ourselves, our experiences, and our worldview, and the language we use to describe others, actually becomes hardwired in our brains. Research shows that "the modern connection between *cunt* and *disgusting, stupid,* or *hateful* — or when women are reduced to just *cunts*"[50] is not just a cultural take on our vaginas, but also rewires women's brains. When a woman hears about her vagina as a "gash" or a "slit" all her life, or if she experiences hostile environments at work or school where verbal abuse in the form of jokes, images, or implied threats related to vaginas are socially acceptable, these tactics can actually undermine her intellectual creativity and ability to be productive. Whereas if she hears vaginas described, for example, as "the jade gate," her brain shapes itself and her perceptions around that sensibility.[51] A list of other terms for the vagina from other cultures includes Golden Lotus, Scented Flower, Gates of Paradise, Precious

Pearl, Mysterious Valley, Grotto of the White Tiger, Treasure, and Lotus of Her Wisdom. Not surprising to goddess scholars and practitioners, ancient origins of the word *cunt* have positive, sacred meanings, or a term of great respect, including linguistically the convergence of *mother* and *knowledge*.[52] This ancient holy word is far cry from what is arguably Western tradition's most offensive and censored swearword in the English language.[53]

The power of naming and the metaphors we use to describe ourselves create profound realities. How different would *your* self-perception be if these words honored your female sexuality?

Metaphor is a special form of speech that is the right brain's unique contribution to the left brain's language capability. The word *metaphor* combines two Greek words, *meta*, which means "over and above," and *pherein*, "to bear across." "Metaphor is principally a way of conceiving of one thing in terms of another and its primary function is understanding."[54] Metaphors have multiple levels of meaning that are perceived simultaneously. They supply a plasticity to language without which communication would often be less interesting, sometimes difficult, and occasionally impossible. The objective world can be described, measured, and catalogued with remarkable precision, but to communicate an emotion or feeling-state we employ metaphors. To tell another that one's heart is "soaring like an eagle" or "as cold as ice" reveals the synergy between the right brain's concrete images and the left-brain's abstract words. Metaphors beget poetry and myth, and are essential to the parables of religion and the wisdom of folktales.[55]

Metaphors matter. In his book *Metaphors We Live By*, George Lakoff writes:

You don't have a choice as to whether to think metaphorically. Because metaphorical maps are part of our brains, we will think and speak metaphorically whether we want to or not. Since the mechanism of metaphor is largely unconscious, we think and speak metaphorically, whether we know it or not. Further, since our brains are embodied, our metaphors will reflect our commonplace experiences in the world. …the metaphors we use are shaped and constrained by our bodily experiences in the world.[56]

Since conceptual metaphor is a natural part of human thought, and linguistic metaphor is a natural part of human language, which metaphors we have and what they mean depend on the nature of our bodies, our interactions in the physical environment, and our social and cultural practices."[57]

Given the differences between female and male biology, a female-affirming reality and the metaphors of our lived social reality must be different as well.

COMING "HOME"

I've been thinking about the implications of what it means when women say, "I want to live in my body" or "I want to get back in touch with my body" or "I need to get out of my head." This language describes a belief that a person's consciousness can exist independent of their brain, an organ attached to their body just like a heart, a lung, or a uterus. Some believe that it is more evolved or spiritual to "transcend" the body. To me, this is residue from patriarchal religions that rank our female bodies as less holy than God or Spirit. Even brilliant Christiane Northrup, author of *Women's Bodies, Women's Wisdom*, exemplifies this linguistic disconnect as she writes, "In order to 're-enter' your body you have to experience it."[58] What does it mean to "re-enter" your body, when it is impossible to leave it except in death? We don't live as independent heads bobbing suspended in the air. The language we use is dissociative and perpetuates this disconnect. The truth is that there is no separation between our minds and bodies. *It is the words we use, and how we use them, that actually gives form to the perception, and thus the "reality" of disconnection.*

Coming from the values of my female-centered cosmology that describes the great Goddess and all women as "She Who Is Whole Unto Herself," my body is my home, sovereign and holy. I have lived here since the moment of my conception inside my mother's body, my mother's "home." Why is it that so many women do not choose to consciously experience their own physicality, their own "home"? If you are not living inside your body, where are you living? And who has taken up residence inside you in your absence? Whose stories do you believe? And whose agenda does that serve? If you are divided from your body, you are divided against yourself. You are homeless in the direst sense of the word.

I want to ask every woman:

When did you leave home? Why did you leave?
Do you ever come home to visit? How long do you stay?
What would happen if you returned to stay?
What would it take for you to come home for good?

My favorite quote these days is "Those who were seen dancing were thought to be insane by those who could not hear the music."[59] I hear the music of my cells, my skin and bones, and the bones of my mother and grandmothers. If you are a woman who doesn't hear the music I hear, are you even a little curious about why you can't hear it? As inheritors of generations of misogyny and female self-hatred, how can we think that this inheritance has not influenced us to the point of not being able to hear our own music? When we allow ourselves to be limited by the frames, filters and metaphors created by others to internally control us, our ability to access our embodied female wisdom and the gifts of our ancestors is suppressed.

Women and girls can discover new perceptual frames by creating experiences that take place in female-sovereign spaces, emotionally safe spaces where internal safety filters from surviving in patriarchy can relax. New awareness can be used to inform the future we strive to create — transforming ourselves and society into a future that takes into consideration all our relations.

I am visioning and working toward a future that affirms the female body as a central metaphor for the cycle of life, honoring the female body for her unique and sacred powers — our biology celebrated as a source of female power and knowing, and free of oppressive gender limitations and words used as weapons with the intention to harm us. Our holy book has always been our female flesh and blood, with pleasure, connection, and creativity as primary inspiration. Accepting that our bodies matter is neither biological determinism nor essentialism![60] From a paradigm of wholeness, can we not make a world where every person can experience and celebrate their body as a sacred gift? Where the words used to describe us and those we use to describe ourselves affirm our sacredness? Where every child is safe to be who they are, and express themselves according to their unique personality?

I want this kind of liberation for my sisters, daughters, mothers, and grandmothers. I want this for our sons and brothers, too. May we remember who we really are, and ensure that life-saving female-sovereign spaces are available for generations of Eve's daughters to come.

---

[1] Leonard Shalin, *The Alphabet Versus The Goddess,* Viking, The Penguin Group, 1998, p. 5.

[2] Marija Gimbutas, *The Civilization of the Goddess*, HarperSanFrancisco, San Francisco, CA, 1991, p. vii.

[3] From Max Dashu, Suppressed Histories Archives, http://www.suppressedhistories.net. Used by permission.

[4] Starhawk, *The Spiral Dance*, Harper & Row Publishers, San Francisco, 1989, p. 20.

[5] *The Malleus Maleficarum* (*The Witches Hammer*), Heinrich Kramer and, James Sprenger, around 1486.

6 George Lakoff, *Don't Think of an Elephant: Know Your Values and Frame the Debate*, Chelsea Green Pub. Co, White River Junction, VT, p. 4.

7 Ibid, p. 3.

8 George Lakoff, *The Political Mind: A Cognitive Scientist's Guide to Your Brain and Its Politics*, Penguin Books, New York, NY, 2004, p. 233.

9 Marija Gimbutas, *The Civilization of the Goddess*, HarperSanFrancisco, San Francisco, CA, 1991).

10 George Lakoff, *Don't Think of an Elephant: Know Your Values and Frame the Debate*, Chelsea Green Pub. Co, White River Junction, VT, 2004, p. 23.

11 Ibid. p. 17.

12 George Lakoff, p. 234.

13 V-Day is a global activist movement to end violence against women and girls*. V-Day is a catalyst that promotes creative events to increase awareness, raise money, and revitalize the spirit of existing anti-violence organizations. V-Day generates broader attention for the fight to stop violence against women and girls, including rape, battery, incest, female genital mutilation (FGM), and sex slavery. Through V-Day campaigns, local volunteers and college students produce annual benefit performances of *The Vagina Monologues; A Memory, A Monologue, A Rant and A Prayer;* documentary film screenings (*What I Want My Words To Do To You*), Spotlight Teach-Ins and workshops, to raise awareness and funds for anti-violence groups within their own communities. Each year, thousands of V-Day benefit events take place produced by volunteer activists in the U.S. and around the world, educating millions of people about the reality of violence against women and girls.
www.vday.org.

14 From "Women's College Cancels 'Vagina Monologues' For Not Being Inclusive Enough," Huffington Post, January 16, 2015.

15 Walt Hayer, *"Things I've Learned – Sex Change Regret,"* www.sexchangeregret.com, 2013.

[16] From "College's 'Project Vulva' Attacked for Transphobia," *The Daily Caller News Foundation*, November 15, 2015.

[17] From Woman-Centered Midwifery, Open Letter to MANA, August 20, 2015. Full letter is posted on
https://womancenteredmidwifery.wordpress.com/take-action/

[18] Judith Antonelli, *In The Image of God: A Feminist Commentary on the Torah*, Jason Aronson Inc., New Jersey, 1995, p.4.

[19] Ibid.

[20] Included in Alice Walker, *Anything We Love Can Be Saved*, Ballantine Books, New York, NY, 1998, p.188.

[21] Ibid, p. 90.

[22] uppitybiscuit, "Do Not Call Me Cisgender. You Do Not Have My Permission To Name Me" at https://uppitybiscuit.wordpress.com/2007/01/19/do-not-call-me-cisgender-you-do-not-have-my-permission-to-name-me/

[23] Mary Daly, *Quintessence*, Beacon Press, Boston, MA, 1998, p. 134.

[24] "Intersex is a general term used for a variety of conditions in which a person is born with a reproductive or sexual anatomy that doesn't seem to fit the typical definitions of female or male. For example, a person might be born appearing to be female on the outside, but having mostly male-typical anatomy on the inside. Or a person may be born with genitals that seem to be in between the usual male and female types — for example, a girl may be born with a noticeably large clitoris, or lacking a vaginal opening, or a boy may be born with a notably small penis, or with a scrotum that is divided so that it has formed more like labia. Or a person may be born with mosaic genetics, so that some of her cells have XX chromosomes and some of them have XY. Intersex is a socially constructed category that reflects real biological variation." From Intersex Society of North America website isna.org.

[25] Theresa M. Wizemann and Mary-Lou Pardue, editors, *Exploring the Biological Contributions to Human Health: Does Sex Matter?* Issued by the Committee on Understanding the Biology of Sex and Gender Differences, Institute of Medicine, Board on Health Sciences, National Academy Press, Washington, D.C., 2001, Policy, p. x.

[26] Ibid, p. x.

[27] Ibid, p. 170.

[28] Ibid, p. 23.

[29] Naomi Wolf, *Vagina: A New Biography*, Ecco, an imprint of HarperCollinsPublishers, New York, 2013, p. 61.

[30] From Spretnak's keynote address at a Midwest women's spirituality conference. Christiane Northrup also refers to this term in *Women's Bodies, Women's Wisdom*, p. 34.

[31] Wizemann, p. 23.

[32] Natalie Angier, *Woman, An Intimate Geography*, Mariner Books/Houghton Mifflin Harcourt, Boston, 2014, p. 42.

[33] Wizemann, p. 46.

[34] Angier, p. 43.

[35] Ibid, p. 20.

[36] Wizemann, p. 22.

[37] Ibid, p. 14. Also, a personal communication from Wendy Griffin notes "Layne Redmond used to describe how every egg a woman will ever have is in her ovaries when she is a fourth-month fetus in her mother's womb. Then she told people, 'The egg that became you lay in your grandmother's womb, as she lay in her grandmother's womb, as she lay in …' and she went back and back, getting softer each time. It was really powerful."

[38] Wolf, p. 14.

[39] Ibid, p. 28.

[40] Angier, p. 63.

[41] Ibid, p. 64.

[42] Ibid, p. 63.

[43] Ibid, p. 60.

[44] Ibid, p. 76.

[45] Ibid, p. 282.

[46] Wolf, p. 285.

[47] Ibid, p. 285.

[48] Ibid, p. 289.

[49] Ibid, p. 92.

[50] Ibid, p. 200.

[51] Ibid, p. 208.

[52] Ibid, p. 198.

[53] Ibid, p. 197.

[54] George Lakoff and Mark Johnson, *Metaphors We Live By*, University of Chicago Press, Chicago and London, 2003, p. 36.

[55] Leonard Shalin, *The Alphabet Versus The Goddess,* p. 20.

[56] George Lakoff and Mark Johnson, *Metaphors We Live By*, University of Chicago Press, Chicago and London, 2003, p. 257.

[57] Ibid. p. 257.

[58] Christiane Northrup, *Women's Bodies, Women's Wisdom*, Bantam Books, 1995.

[59] The quote has various attributions. See http://quoteinvestigator.com/2012/06/05/dance-insane/

[60] The concept of Essentialism states that there are innate character differences and capacities for human expression between men and women. That is, we are born with certain traits. This is often used as an explanation for why there are so few women in science and technology. It is also used as a rationale for pigeonholing, offering limited education, hiring discrimination, and so on and on and on.

CHAPTER 15

TRANSGENDERISM AND THE POWER OF NAMING

Julia Long

As Prometheus stole fire from the gods, so feminists
will have to steal the power of naming from men[1]

WOMEN, SAYS MARY DALY, have had the power of naming stolen from us[2].
Men's power of naming, says Andrea Dworkin, is a 'great and sublime power':

> *The power of naming enables men to define experience, to articulate bound-*
> *aries and values, to designate to each thing its realm and qualities, to deter-*
> *mine what can and cannot be expressed, to control perception itself.*[3]

Transgenderism is not the first attack on women's freedom to name reality. In earlier centuries, in countries such as Scotland and England, men used the scold's bridle and ducking stool to torture and silence bothersome women. Women's heads were encased in iron frames; spiked bars held down troublesome tongues. Wooden contraptions were used to plunge women into freezing ponds and rivers. In more recent times, men continue to attempt to silence women in myriad ways including through sexual harassment, rape, female genital mutilation, prostitution and pornography; our efforts to name these violations are met with further silencing as our experiences are refracted and distorted through the prism of male domination: *a bit of harmless fun; she was asking for it; cultural tradition; sex work; free speech.* Take that, bitch, and shut up.

So it is not the first time that we've suffered an attack on our attempts to speak our truths, but the nature and increasing legal enforceability of our silencing is quite unprecedented. As transgenderism gathers pace and establishes itself in legislation – and it is doing so alarmingly - quite simply the crucial feminist struggle for women to name our reality is becoming outlawed.

My first personal, direct experience of the peculiar power of transgender activists to apparently re-name women and women's articulations was through my involvement in organising a women-only, radical feminist conference – *RadFem2012* – in London, England. This event was part of a wider resurgence of radical feminism, coinciding with other similar events in Melbourne and Portland, and anticipating several other events that have taken place subsequently in the UK. My experiences are far from unique; rather they are illustrative of what happens to women these days when we gather together with political intent. I talk about them here specifically because they are what I have experienced and they have shaped my understanding.

The *RadFem2012* programme included sessions on male violence against women; pornography; prostitution; women and disability; non-violent direct action; lesbian feminism and critiques of 'queer' politics. Conference organisers were committed to a women-only policy, something that had become distinctly unpopular among many of the various new feminist groups at the time, which tended to be extremely liberal and preoccupied with 'engaging with', 'involving' and 'educating' men. We knew that what was necessary was an event that reasserted a radical feminist, women-only politics.

At the time of organising the conference, the legal status of men claiming to be women – so-called 'trans women' – was already posing a serious problem for this kind of event. Under the 2004 Gender Recognition Act, men believing themselves to be women are able to gain legal recognition as women through obtaining Gender Recognition Certificates declaring them to be female. While the 2010 Equality Act allows providers in some cases to restrict the provision of services to women-only – where the restriction is a 'proportionate means of achieving a legitimate aim'[4] - this exception is of course contestable (what constitutes 'proportionate' and 'legitimate'?) and at the time of writing has not yet been legally tested. Even though the law's applicability to our event was by no means certain – since the conference was an autonomous gathering and did not constitute a public service – it was clear that the Act could potentially cause difficulties for us. From the outset, it was clear that the way in which a certain power of naming had gained legal status could be used to define our event as discriminatory and unlawful.

As we were determined to hold a women-only event we stated this explicitly on our website, referring specifically to 'women-born-women' and leaving no room for ambiguity or confusion.

Within a matter of hours of the website going live there was an outpouring of vitriol on Twitter, which continued over several weeks:

Hey #radfem2012: I'm a feminist because my uterus does not fucking define me. So leap back into the dustbin of history where you belong, ok? ('PennyRed')

So apparently the disgusting anti-feminist arseholes are still planning on holding #radfem2012. I will be picketing. Hope you'll all join me ('TheNatFantastic')

The rad fem hate brigade uses deplorable tactics such as lying, bullying, cyberstalking, threatening, doxing & jeopardizing work #radfem2012 ('JoelleRubyRyan')

#radfem2012 Radfems are vile binary humping separatists. They come from a place of hate and are a stain on true feminism. ('IndiYesReally')

#radfem2012 renamed Uterus-Obsessed Cissexist Clusterfuck Convention 2012. ('RobbieVane')

*Oh look it's RadScum2012 **http://t.co/r0rWsbWo** #radfem2012 ('LaRain')*

Have #radfem2012 given up yet? 'Cause everyone hates your exclusive policy. Have fun in your biological women bubble though fuckers! ('no hay banda')

The moment I heard of #radfem2012 my face became one of disgust. Fuck you, radscum ('angrylittlelion')

One tweet (subsequently removed) asked 'I wonder if #RadFem 2012 need help with their catering?' and linked to a picture of a cake, decorated with the wording 'Die Cis Scum'. Another trans activist posted a picture of a can of insecticide, featuring photographs of Sheila Jeffreys and Janice Raymond and the wording 'Ridfem: kills Radfems instantly.'[5] Trans activists exhorted people to ensure that the event was shut down. Blogs were written and shared, often in the name of feminism, attacking the conference, proclaiming the gravity of our sins and the hatefulness of our approach.[6] Radical feminists on social media put up a spectacular defence in the face of this onslaught, Sheila Jeffreys wrote a response to the personal attacks on her in British newspaper *The Guardian*,[7] and the conference received huge support and encouragement from many women. In spite of this, following a series of phone calls, correspondence and meetings with the conference venue, we were informed that the conference would not be going ahead there due to our 'exclusionary' stance, and our inclusion of speakers who supposedly 'foster[ed] hatred' and 'actively discriminate[d] against certain sections of society'.[8] The venue, of course, was unable to provide any evidence to support such a manifestly untruthful claim: it was also striking that the very visible hatred and discrimination to which we were being subjected did not seem to register in their consciousness as hatred and discrimination.

Although we contested their decision, time pressures and lack of resources meant that a serious legal challenge to the venue was not an option. So the conference went ahead at a secret venue: a great moment of female solidarity. This sequence of events – the advertising of a radical feminist, women-only event; harassment of organisers and venue by trans activists; slander of participants and withdrawal of venue and relocation – played out in similar ways for subsequent events, such as RadFem 2013 and Femifest 2014. Each event went ahead, and made a great contribution to the revival of radical feminist politics in the UK. But in each case, what trans activists had managed to do was to re-frame events focusing on male violence, the sex industry and women's liberation as sites of hate speech and discrimination. A Mary Daly-esque reversal indeed, and one that teaches a grave lesson about the male power of naming and its very material consequences.

The project of naming - breaking the multiple silences around women's lives and forging a new language of women's consciousness - was central to the struggles of the Women's Liberation Movement. Consciousness-raising helped women to name their oppression; writers, theorists and poets of the movement dedicated themselves to producing new words and narratives that both named women's experiences and created new visions of liberation. Many of these texts were explicit in their engagement with the politics of breaking the silence and naming women's experiences: *On Lies, Secrets & Silence*[9]; *Silences*[10]; 'The Transformation of Silence into Language and Action'[11]; *Our Bodies, Ourselves*[12]; *Naming the Waves*[13]. The women's presses of the time put women's words into wider circulation; female singers and musicians created rich musical stories of women's lives, dreams and imaginings, often within the context of political activism and women's music festivals. Women's clear and unflinching naming of our experience saw new terms such as 'sexual harassment' entering legislative and policy frameworks, with material impacts on women's lives. Women working within academia fought to establish the new field of Women's Studies, where women's lives and history were centered, where new forms of knowledge became possible and from which challenges to the patriarchal nature of academic study could be mounted.

A crucial part of this project was women breaking silences and taboos around our bodies; naming the hitherto unnamable – clitoris, vulva, labia – and establishing ways of sharing knowledge and communicating our embodied experiences to each other, particularly in the fields of sexuality, health and reproductive rights.

A second and no less crucial part of women's project of naming our experiences under patriarchy involved *naming men as men.* Naming the male agents of femicide, rape, sexual assault; naming male profiteers and consumers of pornography and prostitution; naming political, cultural and economic institutions as male-dominated; naming violence against female partners and child sexual abuse as crimes perpetrated by men on women and children. Naming rape as rape. Naming perpetrators as rapists. Developing analyses which named systems of *male supremacy, male domination, male power.* A crucial element in the development of these analyses involved being observant of men as men, and naming what was observed. It also involved a courageous commitment to naming the harms perpetrated by men: to name an act of rape as an act of sexual violence perpetrated by a man, even where the law courts repeatedly named such acts otherwise, as false allegations against innocent men.

For reasons beyond the scope of this essay, the feminist project of naming lost momentum during the 1990s and 2000s, along with many other feminist struggles. A vicious backlash against feminism, the ascendancy of neoliberalism and the emergence of a very liberal 'third wave' (anti)feminism meant that radical feminism was increasingly beleaguered and marginalized. Attacks from both outside and within the feminist movement took a terrible toll; within academia, the rise of postmodernism and queer theory resulted in Women's Studies courses being largely replaced by Gender Studies, with an increasing focus on topics such as 'masculinities' and 'performativity' rather than male violence against women, or women's history. Terms like 'patriarchy', 'male supremacy', 'female subordination' and 'oppression' were heard less often, even became taboo; in their place terms like 'gender regimes', 'gender-based violence', 'empowerment', 'agency' and 'choice' emerged, not only in university seminar rooms but also in women's organisations and feminist activist circles. Such obfuscatory language – obscuring the power relations between women and men - provided a fertile soil for the language and concepts of transgenderism ('gender identity', 'gender expression', 'gender variance') to take root, and tragically many previously feminist spaces became some of the most hospitable sites for the development of a viciously patriarchal, anti-feminist politics.

We are now at a point where men are being named lesbians with penises; where men are gaining rights of access to women's bathrooms and women's colleges through being named female; where violent men are named as women in news reports and accommodated in women's prisons; where children who do not behave in stereotypical ways are named 'transgender' and prescribed puberty blockers. We are at a point where women gathering together to organise for our liberation or to celebrate lesbian feminist culture are named as oppressors; where women articulating a feminist analysis of gender or even simply naming our own bodies as female are framed and potentially criminalized as perpetrators of hate speech. We are at a point where the naming of men as men has been outlawed.

THE POWER OF NAMING ENABLES MEN TO DEFINE EXPERIENCE...

Yes, for all intents and purposes, I'm a woman. I have the soul of a female and my brain in much more female than it is male, as of now I have all the male parts.

~ BRUCE JENNER[14]

Trans women offer a perspective into how gender perceptions work that cis women don't have. Many of us have a history of having been assumed male and heterosexual, regardless of our true gender and sexuality.

~ MEREDITH TALUSAN[15]

... TO ARTICULATE BOUNDARIES AND VALUES...

If you're in a public bathroom and you think a stranger's gender doesn't match the sign on the door, follow these steps:
1. Don't worry about it, they know better than you.

~ UNIVERSITY OF BRISTOL LGBT+ SOCIETY[16]

Trans women are women, not men. Talking about keeping men out of women's space as a reason for excluding trans women is hugely problematic and transphobic.

~ SARAH BROWN[17]

We recommend that the Equality Act be amended so that the occupational requirements provision and / or the single-sex / separate services provision shall not apply in relation to discrimination against a person whose acquired gender has been recognised under the Gender Recognition Act 2004. (Paragraph 132)

~ HOUSE OF COMMONS WOMEN & EQUALITIES COMMITTEE[18]

... TO DESIGNATE TO EACH THING ITS REALM AND QUALITIES...

Trans women are women.

~ LEELA GINELLE[19]

I am a male lesbian – I always knew I was different but didn't know what to call it.

~ RUSTY916[20]

My girlfriend is trans and has been doing hormone replacement therapy for about a year. About how likely is it that she can still get me pregnant?

- The short and simple answer is: anytime your girlfriend's semen (cum) gets into your vagina or onto your vulva, you're at risk for pregnancy.

~ PLANNED PARENTHOOD[21]

... To Determine What Can and Cannot be Expressed...

It is never okay to misgender me. *It is not okay to call me by my birth name. It is not okay to refer to me using masculine pronouns. It is not okay to describe me as being anyone's son, brother, or husband. [...] I always have been and always will be Amelia.*

~ Amelia[22]

*An abuser can use the fact that their victim is a trans person.
This can include: [...]
- Refusing to use your preferred pronoun or name.*

~ Greater London Domestic Violence Project & NHS Barking and Dagenham[23]

*Failing To Use an Individual's Preferred Name or Pronoun [...]
a. Intentional or repeated refusal to use an individual's preferred name, pronoun or title. For example, repeatedly calling a transgender woman "him" or "Mr." after she has made clear which pronouns and title she uses. [...]
The Commission can impose civil penalties up to $125,000 for violations, and up to $250,000 for violations that are the result of willful, wanton, or malicious conduct.*

~ New York City Commission on Human Rights[24]

... To Control Perception Itself.

Trans issues (and gender issues generally) should be taught as part of Personal, Social and Health Education. (Paragraph 361)

~ House of Commons Women & Equalities Committee[25]

Scenario 1) My daughter doesn't want a boy changing next to her, what if he looks at her body?
- For example, in this scenario it would not be appropriate to remove the trans* person from the changing rooms if a concern is raised by a parent or carer. In this situation, it would be far more appropriate to look at offering an alternative changing arrangement for the child who feels uncomfortable around the trans* person.

~ BRIGHTON & HOVE CITY COUNCIL AND ALLSORTS YOUTH PROJECT[26]

As Dworkin says, the male power of naming is a great and sublime power. Nowhere is that power more evident than in the dizzying discursive triumphs of the transgender lobby, where men have succeeded in framing themselves as victims and women as criminals to be punished for attempting to name them as men, for attempting to set and maintain boundaries, even simply for articulating quite reasonable and accurate perceptions.

An understanding of the male power of naming helps us to see very clearly that transgenderism is a particularly deadly form of patriarchy. We reach this understanding and help other women to reach this understanding, through refusing to compromise our language. Through refusing to give credence to the fictional notions of 'trangenderism' and 'innate gender identity'. Through refusing to collude with the emperor's-new-clothes scenario and pretending that men are women. Through naming men as men.

The cruel yet perhaps not so unusual punishment of our age is that such talk will get us all into very deep trouble indeed.

The male power of naming is upheld by force, pure and simple. ... Whatever contradicts or subverts male naming is defamed out of existence; the power of naming itself, in the male system, is a form of force.[27]

Once we understand transgenderism as a naming system upheld by force, we understand that we must *'contradict or subvert it'* with the full force of our courage and conviction, in every way we can. As Dworkin says, and as we well know, we will be 'defamed': the iron frame will encase our heads, the spiked bar will pierce our tongues, the icy blast will shock us as we hit the freezing waters. 'Defamed out of existence', though? One thing is certain: if we do not resist, our erasure is guaranteed.

ACKNOWLEDGEMENTS
Thanks to Jodie Woodward for reading through this piece and suggesting examples to include.

_____

1 Andrea Dworkin, *Pornography: Men Possessing Women*. London: Women's Press p.17, [1979] 1981.

2 Mary Daly. *Beyond God the Father: Towards a Philosophy of Women's Liberation*. London: The Women's Press, p.8, [1973] 1986.

3 Andrea Dworkin, *Pornography: Men Possessing Women*. London: Women's Press. p.17 [1979] 1981.

4 UK Equality Act, 2010. Schedule 3, Section 28. Available at: http://www.legislation.gov.uk/ukpga/2010/15/schedule/3

5 See: http://gendertrender.wordpress.com/2012/05/20/trans-activist-response-to-upcoming-radfem-2012-conference/

6 See: https://resistradfem2012.wordpress.com/2012/05/27/resist-radfem-101-links-round-up/

7 Sheila Jeffreys, 'Let us be free to debate transgenderism without being accused of "hate speech"'. *The Guardian,* May 29, 2012.
   http://www.theguardian.com/commentisfree/2012/may/29/transgenderism-hate-speech

8 Personal correspondence from conference venue, Conway Hall. 22 May 2012.

9 Adrienne Rich. *On Lies, Secrets and Silence: Selected Prose 1966-1978.* London: Virago, 1980

10 Tillie Olsen, *Silences,* New York: The Feminist Press at the City University of New York, 2003.

11 Audre Lorde, 'The Transformation of Silence into Language and Action'. In *Sister Outsider.* Berkeley CA: The Crossing Press, pp. 40-44, 1984.

[12] Boston Women's Health Collective. *Our Bodies, Ourselves*. New York: Simon & Schuster, 1973.

[13] Christine. McEwen, (Ed). *Naming the Waves: Contemporary Lesbian Poetry*. London: Virago, 1988

[14] Bruce Jenner, quoted in Hind, Katie (2015), 'Bruce Jenner: "I'm a woman now, I have the soul and brain of a female"'. *The Mirror*, 25 April 2015. http://www.mirror.co.uk/3am/celebrity-news/bruce-jenner-im-woman-now-5578946

[15] Meredith Talusan, 'Women's colleges should reinvent themselves as havens for trans women'. In *The Guardian*. 19 May 2015. http://www.theguardian.com/commentisfree/2015/may/19/womens-colleges-should-reinvent-themselves-as-havens-for-trans-women

[16] University of Bristol LGBT+ Society poster, reproduced in Sheriff, Lucy (2014). 'Bristol University's advice on what to do if you find a trans person in the bathroom is brilliant'. *The Huffington Post UK*, 17 November 2014. http://www.huffingtonpost.co.uk/2014/11/17/what-to-do-if-you-find-a-trans-person-in-bathroom_n_6169830.html

[17] Comment by Sarah Brown, posted 23 May 2012. Under Norman, Julian (2012). 'Legalities of excluding trans women from women-only spaces.' *The F-Word Blog*. 22 May 2012. https://www.thefword.org.uk/2012/05/legalities_of_e/

[18] House of Commons Women & Equalities Committee (2016). 'Report on Transgender Equality'. Recommendation 22.
http://www.publications.parliament.uk/pa/cm201516/cmselect/cmwomeq/390/390.pdf

[19] Leela Ginelle, 'Trans women are women. Why do we have to keep saying this?' Blog post in *Bitch Media*, 9 June 2015. https://bitchmedia.org/post/trans-women-are-women-why-do-we-have-to-keep-saying-this

[20] Rusty916 (2014), comment posted under 'I am a Male Lesbian'. In *The Experience Project,* 1 April 2011. http://www.experienceproject.com/stories/Am-A-Male-Lesbian/1484942

[21] Planned Parenthood (undated). 'Can my trans girlfriend get me pregnant?' http://planned-parenthood.tumblr.com/post/66497932042/can-my-trans-girlfriend-get-me-pregnant

[22] Amelia (2014), 'No, misgendering me is not okay or justifiable. Yes, this is a big deal'. Blog post in *Entirely Amelia: trans as heck runner*. Posted 2 January 2014. http://www.entirelyamelia.com/2014/01/02/misgendering-okay-justifiable-yes-big-deal/

[23] Greater London Domestic Violence Project & NHS Barking and Dagenham (2009), *Domestic Violence: A Resource for Trans People.*

[24] New York City Commission on Human Rights (2015). Legal Enforcement Guidance on Discrimination on the Basis of Gender Identity or Expression: Local Law No. 3 (2002); N.Y.C. Admin. Code § 8-102(23). http://www.nyc.gov/html/cchr/html/law/gender-identity-legalguidance.shtml#4

[25] House of Commons Women & Equalities Committee (2016). 'Report on Transgender Equality'. Recommendation 65.
http://www.publications.parliament.uk/pa/cm201516/cmselect/cmwomeq/390/390.pdf

[26] Brighton & Hove City Council and Allsorts Youth Project (2013). 'Trans* Inclusion Schools Tool Kit: Supporting transgender and gender questioning children and young people in Brighton and Hove schools and colleges'. http://www.allsortsyouth.org.uk/wp-content/uploads/2014/02/Trans-Inclusion-Schools-Toolkit.pdf

[27] Andrea Dworkin. *Pornography: Men Possessing Women*. London: Women's Press. p.17 [1979] 1981.

CHAPTER 16

THE ERASURE OF LESBIANS

Alix Dobkin and Sally Tatnall

WHEN, TOWARDS THE end of the last century, the historic force of feminist consciousness met the primeval juggernaut of Lesbian attraction, it fueled the explosive Second Wave. These invisible historic forces sparked and fueled our declaration of war on patriarchy.

Since they never paid attention to us, the patriarchy wasn't looking when that fateful meeting occurred, when we Lesbians - the "army of lovers (that) cannot fail" - first claimed our identity loudly, proudly and unabashedly.

The women's liberation movement was just what Lesbians needed to make their place. Consciousness raising sessions revealed the oppressive structure all women faced. Feminists recognized and named patriarchy as the creator of hierarchy that would determine all social values. For the first time, all isms were linked. As Audre Lorde once said, "there is no hierarchy of oppression".

Lesbians took on leadership in creating women's culture, theory, feminist bookstores, rape crisis centers, battered women's shelters, abortion clinics, access for Deaf and hard-of-hearing through sign language at entertainment and meetings. Women's land groups were formed, women challenged male religion, women became lawyers and doctors and ran for office. Many of these women were Lesbians. Unfortunately straight women were being accused of being Lesbian and pressure to eliminate Lesbian involvement was the result. However Lesbians had been engaged. We had the energy, the theory, the brains, and the passion for women's liberation like no other. Women's lib then became a slur.

Seeing the success of the second wave, the university became involved to limit the passion that had been ignited. Women' studies was born to beckon women fueled with ideas of liberation. However, the academy was not interested in true liberation, they were interested in selling a course. So they only used the most liberal texts. The thinking that spurred the action was conveniently left out of the curriculum. Women's rage was tempered. Analysis of patriarchy was watered down. You can't have that radical thinking in an institution of the patriarchy.

Little time passed before the idea of a course solely for women was challenged. The result was to make a course of other left-out people to gain consumers. Queer studies was born. Classes about women's studies focusing on authors who had something to say were included. For the most part the academy began turning out degrees that meant you could teach a women's studies course, but very few activists emerged. Women's rage had been contained.

But oh no, men who didn't qualify for this slot of left-out people began to complain. Where was their course? Where were their concerns being dealt with? Voilà...gender studies was born. The final nail in the coffin of women as distinct was hammered in. Now students were concerning themselves with the variety of sexes available to them. Who belonged to each group was discussed at length and the clouding of groups began. Who were women? Who were men? Sex designation became a choice. Somehow the connection to what the patriarchy says you have to be got lost. The demand that the patriarchy makes for how you will look, how you will present yourself and whom you will love got lost. It was not a fight against the patriarchy anymore. It was a fight against women.

Before we knew it, postmodern deconstructionists began gutting the meaning out of the very notion of "identity," especially when it came to women and the power structures that keep us subservient. Our identity suddenly became subjective, "fluid" and "performed" rather than a power source from a unique tradition and location in the universe. "Gender" replaced women in the academy and "queer" disappeared Lesbians in the community. It's only become worse since. Some women loving women even say they hate the word Lesbian.

We are on the defensive once again, now having to declare ourselves "female born" or "women born" or even "cis" women to identify ourselves because apparently anyone can collude with the medical/pharmaceutical industry, declare himself a woman, and find acceptance as such almost everywhere. Except for a few Lesbian/feminist holdouts, transsexuals have leaped forward on the civil rights agenda and become the latest cause of the LGBTQ community, often to the detriment of Lesbians.

The last stronghold (Lesbian) that did not need male approval for their identity was smashed. Not needing male approval is something the patriarchy will not allow.

It is unclear why the LGB organizations, formerly concerned about the oppression of same gender loving people and the right to choose whom you would love, would take on a choice that had nothing to do with sex or love. Sexual preference would no longer be the concern and gender identity would be dominant. Trans support people are very clear that trans is a choice of gender, not of sexual preference. Trans women wanting to be Lesbians confirm their heterosexuality.

The list of atrocities continues. Though the LGBT movement has never paid any attention to violence against women or Lesbians, current outrage in that sector is around violence against trans women. This of course shows a lack of analysis because it is exactly violence against women that is at play. Making violence against trans women superior to violence against women shows the rampant sexism, lesbophobia, and internalized sexism alive and well in the LGBT community.

Blatant evidence of our erasure is the largest gathering of LGBT people anywhere, Creating Change, the 5-day conference produced by the NGLTF*, with its all-day intensives, its 300 workshops, and its hospitality suites. In 2013, it had no all-day series for Lesbians, no hospitality suite for Lesbians, and only 3 workshops specifically for Lesbians. And even though there have been many complaints from Lesbians, there is no intention to change this movement.

Lesbians being ignored are nothing new, and in spite of many complaints by Lesbians to community leaders over many years, we see no improvement or intention to improve. The latest absurdity is the decision at Mount Holyoke College (once an upper crust college for women) to stop producing The Vagina Monologues (by Eve Ensler) because all women don't have vaginas.

However the last chapter has not yet been written, and we trust that if anyone can reclaim our female core and re-ground our female-based culture, it would be an army of ex-lovers who cannot fail, and that would be us!

*National Gay and Lesbian Task Force, now billed on its website as National LGBTQ Task Force and often referred to as "The Task Force".

CHAPTER 17

MOTHERS' DAY: A STORY

Joan F. Archive

"OKAY, MOM. I love you too. Call me after you see the doctor, okay? And please, go easy on the marijuana." Hannah held the phone warm from being clenched to her left ear for a few more seconds, wiggling her toes and grinning. Her mother, frustrated by arthritic foot pain after many years as a modern dance instructor, was now enjoying a medical cannabis prescription.

Her thoughts turned from the pleasure of the Sunday morning conversation with her mom to the elaborate Sunday afternoon ahead, the graduation ceremony she had to attend on campus.

First, brunch. Knowing that her stingy university would serve just wine and cheese after the three-hour-long ritual, Hannah poured pancake batter onto the griddle and added spoonfuls of sliced banana and slivered almonds. She settled on Alaskan coffee to fortify her spirits. This should be a day of absolute matriarchy, she mused, with all rituals and events celebrating Woman, capital W. It was highly unusual for the university to schedule graduation on Mother's Day, an accident of calendar and convenience, and local business owners were ecstatic with double and triple orders for flowers. Every restaurant was booked either for Mother's Day lunch or graduation dinner; there were no balloons left to buy anywhere in town, and table centerpieces were going for a hefty markup. Hannah hoped that every graduate would take extra care to thank Mom throughout the afternoon ceremonies. And yet, of the hundreds of college students receiving their diplomas later that day, how many had studied the *history* of their own foremothers, whose lives were conveniently not included in "the canon" of required learning?

Hannah shoveled in pancakes and coffee as she looked over the list of young women "commencing" from her own academic department. Only sixteen students were graduating with women's history degrees this May. Bowing to pressure from right-wing alumni and trustees, the university had dropped a requirement that all humanities students take at least one women's history class during their four years of study. Instead, they were encouraged (but not asked) to try a "gender" elective, such as "Masculinities" or "Queering Fatherhood." Despite multiple waves of feminism, the addition of "queer studies," and gender electives, one could *still* earn a BA with no exposure whatsoever to women's history.

And even the women's studies majors received *bachelor's* degrees as proof of graduation.

Before she showered and dressed, Hannah cued up layers of feminist music to match her mood: Ova's "Who Gave Birth to the Universe?". Mosa Baczewska's "It's a Very Long Song That We Can Sing to Celebrate the Women of the World," Faith Nolan's "I, Black Woman," Ronnie Gilbert's "Mother's Day," Bitch and Animal's "Pussy Manifesto." *The mother. The body.* She rubbed some of her own mother's favorite lavender lotion on her arms and legs, still pale from the winter months of being shut inside a classroom. Soon, there would be picnics, biking, and Pride parades. She'd regain her Jewish tan, be olive-skinned again. For now, shaking off the academic hibernation of a school year was like stepping out of a cave and blinking at the promise of spring.

Now, what to wear? It hardly mattered, hidden under flowing black regalia; but Hannah felt her dykedom rising up, rebellious sap. Yes, she owned a dress. But she didn't have to wear it. Not today.

Her thoughts flickered unhappily to that day in the classroom when, as a younger professor in her third year of teaching, she vowed never again to wear a dress in front of students. It was during a disastrous, experimental first-year course inviting new students to write about the body and to debate reproductive rights. What a melee! Several male students assigned to the course by well-intentioned advisors were restless and rude, laughing at terms like "femicide," and swapping AIDS jokes. One young man, eventually expelled for acts of violence against women in his residence hall, scrawled an obscene drawing of Hannah on the attendance sheet she'd passed around. His crude sketch showed her in her favorite dress, being walked like a dog on a leash, her breasts spilling out and dragging on the ground. Hannah returned the next day in combat boots and trousers: survival gear, symbolically characterizing the rest of that challenging semester.

But, she reminded herself, one angry young man did not sum up a career teaching women's history. This was a day to celebrate her own devoted graduates, the ones who had daringly majored and minored in women's studies, whose loyalty and written work affirmed her purpose here on earth. Childless herself, Hannah had made these students her own children, pouring maternal energy into academic relationships. She brought cookies to class, worried about sick or absent students, sent little gifts and cards when someone won an internship or a job.

School and school and school again. No, she had not paused to have or raise children. She had, instead, raised activists. Graduation served as Hannah's own Mother's Day. This was her day of pride in her young feminist progeny.

Now, standing in front of her own long mirror, she considered graduation day jewelry. Definitely, the Venus of Willendorf pendant. Hannah plucked it on its long, light chain from the surface of her polished cedar dresser. This had been her own graduation gift, from her own mother, on the day she finally earned her PhD. The voluptuous Venus figure was shiny from having been rubbed and fondled absent-mindedly whenever Hannah wore it, the full belly of the ancient, faceless goddess now as smooth as glass.

Was it so much, to want her students—hell, *all* students—to know that once upon a time, many cultures throughout the ancient world worshipped a female deity?

As Hannah drove across town, she mentally revisited the simple realities of pre-Christian goddess worship. The Venus of Willendorf! Someone had blundered into a cave in Austria in 1908 and discovered that limestone goddess "figurine," all breasts and hips and belly. No face; the artist, taking up chisel and rock back in 25,000 BCE, hadn't considered that feature important. Not in a time when children breastfed until they were five, when every human born looked to the mother as the creator of life, the feeder, the one who produced children and immediately provided them with sustenance. How had that association changed so permanently to a male God, the Father figure creating woman, and not only that, but creating her as the *second* sex? How had a female's ponderous flesh and belly, her reproductive enormity, come to be shamed as mere fat instead of sacred fertility? Why were so many of her students wracked by eating disorders, afraid of appetite, disdainful of curves?

Don't get angry. Don't get angry. It's Mother's Day. It's Graduation Day.

Hannah peeled off her hard folding chair as the final row of graduated seniors exited the stage, holding aloft diplomas and beaming. Three hours of speeches by male provosts and deans; three hours of "God, He" invocations by campus ministry! A stiff drink at Sappho's Bar and Grill would be her reward in just about forty-five minutes. She did love hearing the names of her own hard-working students announced over the public address speakers: *Terry Wong, Women's Studies. Emerald Granger, Women's History. Elena Gonzalez, Women's History.* Those students would now come up to her with hugs, with thanks and gladness. It was the parents who were so unpredictable at these occasions.

Hannah didn't know who might yank her chain this time, but there was always some uptight parent, usually a father, who felt compelled and authorized to mock her field. "Well, we tried to talk her out of it, but she chose women's history," this father would say, right to Hannah's face. "Now she'll never get a job. Can you find her one?" Or: "We didn't have, you know, women's history classes when I was here. We had real subjects: econ, philosophy…" "A waste of tuition, in my opinion, this gender thing, but I know she had fun in your classes. Well, now she'll have to get serious." Even the kinder or empathetic remarks were psychologically draining and stressful: there was the mother who had whispered to Hannah, at a parents' brunch that winter, "In my time we knew about feminism, but we couldn't bring it into the sorority house. No women's studies books on the table, especially not when gentlemen came to call. I read about Emma Goldman in the bathroom."

She needed the bathroom herself. The nearest one was in the Science building, but Hannah automatically vetoed that comfort station, knowing its history. When the university was constructed, no women's bathrooms were added to the math, science, or engineering halls, on the assumption that no women would ever be admitted or, if grudgingly admitted, would never major in the "hard" sciences. When the 1960s brought in women, when the 1970s brought in feminism, when the 1980s and 90s brought in computer science and women demanding access to STEM fields, the embarrassed university contrived a ladies' room out of an old broom closet in the science wing. Hannah preferred to avoid an environment of second-class citizenship on this day.

But here came a dad. She sensed the blossoming confrontation, like a person allergic to cats involuntarily responding to that first hint of dander floating spore-like in the air. He strode up in his pressed chinos, nodded, and indicated her faculty robes. "So. You're a professor here. What do you teach?"

Here it comes, Hannah thought, scrambling for her academic party manners. "Well, sir, happy graduation day to you. I teach several women's studies courses here at the university. For instance—"

He interrupted her, swirling the chardonnay in his plastic wineglass. "There's *women's studies* here? How come there's no *men's* studies?"

Hannah, practiced at this sort of opening salvo, chirped, "Sir, every other subject taught here, every other major, is men's studies, you see." She was calm, but the heat of being once again forced to defend her life's work on what should be a day of scholarly triumph, closure, culmination — was bringing on yet another hot flash. She pulled off her academic robe, flinging it over her left arm. It caught on her Venus of Willendorf necklace, and she could feel the chain tug and then break, slipping down the back of her blouse.

Now the dad was taking in Hannah's pinstripe pants, vest and silk shirt, which were a marked contrast to the sleek and revealing dresses worn by nearly every other female at the event. "So I guess *your* favorite woman in history is Joan of Arc," he sneered.

Hannah thought of that moment, in February, when she was sipping one of Isabel's drinks at Sappho's, and briefly saw burnt Joan seated beside her at the bar in the mirror's dim reflection. Refusing to take the bait—the man clearly knew Joan was a cross-dresser—she answered truthfully, "Yes, I teach Joan, and Sappho, Alice Paul, the Irish pirate Grace O'Malley, Sojourner Truth, and of course the Venus of Willendorf, whose image I wore today at graduation. I also teach the history of the All American Girls Baseball League."

"Yeah. That lasted for what, a year?"

"No, sir; the League extended from 1943 all the way through 1954."

For ten minutes, it went on like that, like a torturous badminton rally. He tested and tested her with sarcastic but educated bait, looking for a crack in her armor. She remained as dignified as possible, feeling the sweat trickle down her breasts and the Venus necklace slipping, slipping down her back, past her underwear, probably falling all the way down onto the ground. She didn't dare move, lest she trample on or lose her own graduation necklace. He had metaphorically yanked her chain, and her chain was literally underfoot now, being trampled.

And finally he was through with her. With a half-smile, he raised his glass and said, "Well, some feminists are very pushy, and I don't like that. But...I guess we needed feminism." As Hannah took in his intentional use of the past tense, *needed,* he added one parting shot: "I am an obstetrician." Then he walked away to join his wife and son.

She stood there, reeling. So he'd earned his son's tuition by "helping" women give birth, yet it never occurred to him that women created life, and thus the world? Or that women's storylines as mothers had shaped all living people? Or that the history of how and when women's fertility might have been celebrated in an era before his own could be compelling knowledge, taught to thinking minds?

She knelt on her knees, angry hands seeking her broken Venus of Willendorf necklace. She'd go right to the jeweler now, before stopping in at the bar, and have the chain repaired. No, wait; it was Sunday. Mother's Day. Everything was closed. Damn it.

The ground was moist and warm. She could smell mud where thousands of elegantly and not-so-elegantly shod feet had crushed the neatly mown grass as families raced for good seats from which to cheer their graduates. She pushed her hand through the damp grass stubble — ah, there! and closed her fingers around her silver chain. But as she pulled it up toward her hot neck, someone, or something, just underneath that earth pulled just as hard. With an *oof!* of surprise, Hannah fell facedown onto the ground and melted through it to the other side.

She was in a cave. That much was clear: very little light afforded much more information, but the stone walls, dripping moisture, streaked with recent painted images, pressed in around her. An overwhelming smell of animal life, and human life as well, filled her nose and eyes; a scent of wet hair, sweat, warm milk, fresh blood, old urine, matted wool, babies; and something else, more fecund. Hannah was not alone.

There was a woman there. Lying on her side on an animal skin, heaving with the grip of labor pains, her giant body pushed and moaned and shuddered. Hannah approached, terrified, yet drawn to this great stranger. No matter which angle she approached from, she could not see a face. But all around her on the walls were drawings of women's bodies. Pregnant. Nursing. Holding infants. Dancing.

And now, just beyond the cave entrance, Hannah could see dozens, and then hundreds and then thousands of eyes, watching. Waiting. It looked like the vigil of an entire community, an entire tribe, awaiting the birth. Some of the half-clad figures were holding small statues of pregnant women, of mothers, of mothers breastfeeding. She heard low chanting.

There is more respect for the motherline here than in my own time.
I am in the birthing chamber of the Venus of Willendorf.

Something was wrong, or stalled, or difficult with this birth. Yet everything depended on the birth of a daughter who represented the future of the tribe; Hannah understood this. There was something she was supposed to do. There was a reason she was here. Water trickled down the cave wall, and Hannah suddenly thought of water in a desert: *Miriam. I am Miriam's well. I am the traveler with Miriam's knowledge. Miriam is still in the future, but I am from the future too; there is no time. There is no time to waste. This is the midwifing of the world, the daughter-naming hour.*

The baby would be the next mother goddess to this nascent civilization. If she emerged; if she lived. Tentatively, Hannah approached the fiercely puffing mother. "Push," Hannah said. "Push." What language was right for such urgent instruction? English? Hebrew? German? Which words did Miriam breathe to the laboring women? Would song be better? Hannah thought of the composer Kay Gardner, who had suggested there was an elemental female sound, a note, an opening of vowels; that the ancient word for God was simply voices breathing a-e-i-o-u. A woman in labor would howl in any alphabet, as she herself became God, the creator and giver of life.

"Just keep pushing!" Hannah shrieked, and the *sh* of *push* became a wind, and the wind a hammock of breath blown forward, and the infant crowned, the very beginning of a new daughter's hair emerging from the now-open yoni. And now the mothering woman half-rose from her posture of contraction. To Hannah's terror she was faceless, though wild haired and live and breathing, and from the blurred non-face came this clear command: "You. Also. Push."

"What did you say?" Hannah whispered, and the breath of ages came back to her again in her own language, stilted with effort. "You." A breath. "You. Pushy. Woman. You. Keep. Pushing." Then silence. Hannah pressed closer, fearful of looking at that huge faceless being, but also fearful something had gone wrong.

The infant was pulled forward, handed to and immediately suckled by two waiting mothers, while a third woman with breast milk trickling thinly used a sharp stone to cut the umbilical cord.

And as Hannah watched, as the stone cut through the cord, the giant cave-filling mother turned to stone herself.

She was pulled out of the cave by many warm hands. Further confounding Hannah, the vigil-keeping tribe now melted into the recognizable features of her former students, both male and female. They lifted her above their heads and passed her forward, as if she were crowd surfing at a rock concert. She was aware that below her were the first women's studies students she had ever taught, as a graduate teaching assistant years and years ago. Then the star students from that tough first course on reproductive rights. Forward into her own time she rolled, over class over class, graduate after graduate. Frances, who had died young. Lisa, who became a top United Nations lawyer for global women's rights. Andi, the sculptor. How she had pushed them to work harder, to write better, to read more, to speak up and act and advocate!

I am a rock star. I am surfing Neolithic feminism. The rock is the mother and the rock is the Neolithic, the New Stone Age. The children of the daughter born today will worship the Goddess and carve her image and leave it, forever, inside that cave. "Push," whispered the students of Hannah's past. "You pushed us. You stay pushy. You keep pushing."

"Dr. Stern. Are you okay?" Three of today's freshly minted graduates stood over Hannah, their dark mortarboards blocking the sun. Manicured hands reached down to pull Hannah up from the damp grass. "Oh, that's a shame! Did you break your necklace?" Terry Wong, that year's star student, took the Venus pendant and chain and carefully placed them into the small box that had, earlier, held her class graduation ring. "There! That should keep it safe, at least until you get it fixed. Wow, I've seen you wear that in class a thousand times! I guess today's the last time I'll ever see you decked out in your goddess gear."

"God, Terry, are you going to start crying again?" The other students smiled at Hannah. Terry beckoned to an older woman whose scarf shimmered with blue and gold strands. "Dr. Stern, this is my mother. She wanted to meet you." Hannah tried to remain steady on her feet as the proud mom introduced herself and expressed thanks for Hannah's mentoring. "We're very proud that Terry chose this major…her other mom and I." Now a second woman came forward to shake Hannah's still-trembling hand. "It's a moment we never thought we'd see or celebrate. We had so much difficulty just bringing her into the world…"

"Mama! Dana! Not that story again," Terry groaned.

"Just such a difficult birth," the co-mom reminisced, ruffling the hair of her healthy, now-grown daughter. "Thank God we had that visiting woman doctor, because we had no legal rights as a couple in those days." "Right; they wouldn't let Dana stay with me in the birthing room, or touch me or help me; and I was desperate. I had to push, and push, and push… Yes, Terry, it's all worth it today. All worth it to see you so grown up. And a women's history graduate!"

They stood around her, beaming.

Hannah parked shakily in the lot behind Sappho's Bar and Grill and entered through the back door, the hall that emptied into the bar's open space. Like tumbling down the birth canal. She wanted that feeling, now, on Mother's Day. A party was in progress, of course, with local lesbian moms and their progeny snacking on cookies and milk (and stronger beverages for some of the mothers) as Isabel, the bartender, played soundtracks in celebration of motherhood. Hannah put the box containing her broken necklace onto the bar and took a cup of milk from the party platter, surprised by its odd flavor — perhaps another one of Isabel's mystic herbal concoctions? until Melissa, one of the bar regulars, shouted, "Wait! Hannah! That's my *breast milk*. I pumped it out earlier. I'm so sorry, I forgot all about it!"

"Hey, professor!" welcomed Letty, the bar's resident elder Amazon, her arms draped around a tough-looking grown daughter and two grandkids. "School's over for the year, right? Graduation day up at campus? Yeah, baby! You're done. You can come out of your cave now, and join us." But Letty's kind words "join us" sounded, to Hannah, like "Venus," and she looked down at her feet, where the rough clay from an actual cave still stuck to her damp shoes.

Isabel looked, too, and saying only "Wipe your feet," she handed Hannah a small towel, with a smile. An instant later, when Hannah had cleaned her shoes, she lifted her head and saw that Terry's little ring box had popped open like a gesture of proposal, on the bar. Inside, her silver necklace chain was perfectly intact, the links in a solid circle, and the Venus pendant polished as if new.

~

This is a chapter excerpt from a novel I'm writing about women's history and time travel. I include it here because I'm aware that the ideas and images of my story represent what some now object to as female *essentialism*. My concern is that we have had barely four decades to include information on women's history in the classroom, and here in 2016 we continue to interrogate anyone studying female heritage. Where women's studies students and faculty were once accused of hating men if they dared to place women's lives at the center of inquiry, today they are charged with deliberately oppressing and excluding transwomen. To reframe every aspect of women's history as oppressive if it focuses on biological womanhood is an effective way to silence the voices of those foremothers.

Like the narrator in my fictional story, I'm a women's history professor. I inherited my profession from bold academic women who pioneered this field just one generation before me (the first women's studies program began at San Diego State University in 1969.) Daring to suggest that women born biologically female do, in fact, have a history we can recognize and examine, despite the difficult divisions of race, class, tribe and geography, was the foundation laid down by my academic role models. These faculty mentors who brought women's history into the college classroom gave their all, taking on ugly backlash from conservative critics who disputed the place of research on women's lives. By the time I entered college, it was at last possible to major in women's studies, and I joined a community racing to uncover material about female lives.

The ink was not yet dry on my doctorate before a new mood declared women's history too limiting to be worthy. "Gender studies," more inclusive of men, masculinities, and women-identified men in transition, pushed *woman* out of the focus of what was considered valuable scholarly work. *Woman* became a contested category again, but largely due to pressure from the postmodernist Left rather than the homophobic Right. Meanwhile, *man* lost none of its power as a generic or essential subject.

The history I draw upon in my fiction evokes all of these moods and shifts:

- Women's ability to give birth was once revered through fertility worship.
- Images and carvings such as the Venus of Willendorf statue have survived to teach us about pre-Christian goddess worship.
- Patriarchy moved civilizations from honoring a Mother Goddess to God the Father.
- Teaching women's history has been a risky and nearly impossible role in the university system, and after only two generations has been replaced by gender studies.
- Even with the reluctant addition of some women's history courses after second-wave feminism, parents and administrators have been so uncomfortable that their attitudes continue to prevent most students from exploring a women's studies class.
- It is still possible to satisfy "diversity" requirements without ever looking at women.
- Not only the subject of women's history but the subject "women" has been placed in a sort of contested, retro box ascribed to a blunder of radical feminism.
- Students and faculty who continue to make women's history their focus now waste valuable research time apologizing/defending themselves not only to conservative male critics but to progressive, queer-identified scholars and activists.

In writing a fantasy about a professor's encounter with a fertility goddess in her birthing chamber, I chose to reference birth, lactation, a mother-daughter connection across time, the womb as a site of power, the choice of the lesbian spinster to forego traditional motherhood in favor of mentoring young women, lesbian mothers, and women's studies as a specifically bodied field of inquiry. My approach in writing both fiction and nonfiction about women's heritage is *matrifocal,* an anthropological term meaning "to place women at the center of activity." Increasingly, however, such an approach is rebuked as controversially "essentialist" for connecting the female to something biological. Because some women now identifying as transmen have wombs, give birth, become mothers, and lactate, the viewpoint of inclusion requires that medical and psychological literature promote a consciousness that today some individuals living and those legally recognized as men, too, give birth. The woman who is biologically female or female bodied at birth (and who experiences biologically female stages of puberty, adolescence and early adulthood) has been asked to clarify that she is *cisgender* — a category of female, yes, but one living with assumed privilege, by virtue of identifying with the sex assigned at birth. The cisgendered woman is invited to limit and unlearn her oppression of transwomen by resisting any celebration of the biological female experience, e.g., artistic events such as Eve Ensler's theatrical project "The Vagina Monologues."

To place the biological female at the center of scholarship has been a daunting labor of love for feminist scholars who pointed out point out how much information on women's lived experiences was missing from the classroom. But a mere forty years later, the hard-won and very late *inclusion* of information on women has been reframed as ignorant and binary-embracing *exclusion* — of trans voices and experiences. To place women at the center of a curriculum is now judged as a morally flawed and counterrevolutionary choice, even in a women's studies program. "I teach my students that there is no such thing as a woman," said one women's studies colleague. "I don't put women at the center of my research," affirmed the director of another graduate-degree-granting women's studies program.

In this painful era of shift, I want to draw attention to these things. I want to ask why, again, I need to ask permission from so many born male to describe certain realities of their own mothers' lives. To advocate for the viewpoint of those born female is a dangerous public stance, and now, in some settings, is considered hate speech. As we have seen in the confrontational debates over the Michigan Womyn's Music Festival, an event intended for women and girls born biologically female, defenders of a longtime woman-born affinity gathering were subject to death threats via the convenience of anonymous internet postings. Still hoping to work in academia, leery of the backlash I've seen proliferate online, I chose to use the pen name Joan F. Archive as my shield — in tribute to the real Joan, who dressed as a warrior but never disclaimed her womanhood.

CHAPTER 18

PATRIARCHY IN DRAG: SEXUAL IMPERIALISM IN AFRICA, AND DELUSIONAL REVISIONISM IN THE AFRICAN-AMERICAN COMMUNITY

Luisah Teish

I HOPE TO shed some light on the subjects of sexuality and gender in Africa and the diaspora, and to expose the *gynophobia* inherent in the movement toward trans normativity. This article is especially addressed to the Black Community. It demonstrates the ways we have been misrepresented in the past and how we are being manipulated in the present. I present this material in hopes that we can stand in the center between wisdom and compassion and take the matter of gender expression in our communities in our own hands, in our own ways.

In 1985, I wrote and published *Jambalaya: The Natural Woman's Book of Personal Charms and Practical Rituals[1]*. It was a groundbreaking work then and has since become regarded by several generations as a "Women's Spirituality Classic." The book's longevity lies in the fact that it successfully addressed several important issues: It dispelled a number of superstitions regarding the spiritual traditions of the African diaspora. It illuminated the power of the African Goddesses. It stated clearly the importance of Black Women as spiritual leaders in Africa and the diaspora, and called upon those women to use their power to positively impact their communities and the world. It provided ways for people from diverse communities to safely and respectfully engage with the spiritual practices by providing empowering rituals, spoken in plain language. Yemaya, the Great Mother-Goddess of the Yoruba pantheon, guided the writing of the book, to counteract the effects of "religious macho," and to heal a gross imbalance of power.

The late 1960s to early 1970s produced several movements relevant to the Black Community (civil rights, Black Power, cultural pride, sexual freedom, and spiritual renewal) with Black Women supporting them, marching, demonstrating, and laying our lives on the line. We nevertheless continued to be regarded as and treated like second-class citizens. There was a tendency to "send women onto the battlefield while keeping them in the kitchen." and this attitude was expressed by the government, society, and our own families. This imbalance was very obvious within the Ifa, Orisha, Lucumi, and Santeria traditions. Positions of honor and power held by women in precolonial Africa that survived plantation slavery, and supported families for centuries, were devalued or denied. An overlay of Christian beliefs served to suppress women's power, blame woman for all curses, and to keep women skilled in the sacred arts in subservient positions. Women were being economically exploited for spiritual services they could perform for themselves. And worst, women were being sexually molested during rituals.

Lesbians in particular were being ostracized by the male priests, many of whom were gay men, especially among the Santeria/Lucumi priests of Cuba. (I give praise and thanks to the spirit of Anai-bi-Osun, the gay Puerto Rican man who initiated me.) The African and African-American priests regarded homosexuality as a "maladjustment to the influence of colonial invaders." We will discuss this in more detail later.

In *Jambalaya* I provided a composite portrait of a generic West African Woman named Iyalode. There we see the many ways such a woman could fulfill her life. It included a description of "marrying the goat to the buck," a woman-to-woman marriage as was permissible and approved (under specific conditions) by the Ibo people of Nigeria. The inclusion of this ritual had a few noteworthy ramifications: It called into question past assumptions regarding marriage and kinship systems in the African diaspora. I drew this material from the writings of Audre Lorde, and spoke with her directly. She assured me that these were not solely marriages of convenience, political diplomacy, and economic solvency. Indeed, they were erotic relationships.

Jambalaya welcomed lesbian and bisexual women into the tradition, and encouraged those who had been undercover to step into the light. In response, a barrage of hellfire and brimstone came down upon me. It included wanton gossip, misgendered identity, ostracisms, hexes and curses, and death threats.

Since the mid-70s I have been a heterosexual ally to the gay community and a member of the Women's Spirituality Movement. I have worked to provide information, services, and events where women could pray and grow. My goal has been to initiate, nurture, and train women who would carry on the work. Now several decades later, there are many fine spiritual communities directed by women.

The task has not been easy. I can however, recount our victories. Together we have elevated people's understanding of Oya, the Queen of the Winds of Change. She used to be dismissed as "a crazy dyke" by macho men who feared Her power. We have attained initiations into Iyanifa, a higher level of the priesthood that was thought to belong only to men (Babalawo). And we have reestablished the judiciary authority and power of Iyami, the Women's Secret Society. During colonial times these women were branded as "evil witches," their land and property were taken, and they often lost their lives. In general, we now have women who are working to overthrow patriarchy and to provide services that honor our ancestral traditions and preserve our communities.

I am an Iya Oshun, a daughter and servant of the Goddess Oshun Ibukole, who is inseparable from the Vulture, the "one who picks through and recovers the garbage and the powders." As such, my attention has been focused on my *Ita*, the guidelines for my priesthood and the directives from my ancestors. As Oshun's servant I have done matchmaking, performed weddings (including "marrying the goat to the buck," a same-gender ceremony), and fertility, pregnancy, and child delivery rituals. My specialty has been healing women survivors of incest, rape, child abuse, domestic battery, mastectomy, hysterectomy, excision, and sexual slavery. These women have been heterosexual, bisexual, and lesbian.

Mostly I have helped men with erectile dysfunction, depression, and substance abuse. I have assisted gay men with HIV-AIDS by divining and performing the rituals that would either extend their lives or facilitate a peaceful death. Most of the people I've served *did not conform* to the dominant society's dictates for behavior, but *all* of them acknowledged and accepted the sexual organs their spirits chose before journeying from heaven to earth.

SOMETHING IN THE SOUP

Apparently the term "transgender" includes many people in one category. I am asked to accept an alphabet soup that I find very difficult to swallow. LGBTQIQ...

I'm told that "transgender" people are uncomfortable with the genitalia they received at birth. Some seek "gender reassignment surgery," while others redefine themselves *by simple declaration.* The Spirit-to Body difference expressed by people who identify as "trans, non-binary, or no gender" may be a mental-emotional condition, an ancestral inheritance, or a "conscious choice." While I support their personal choice and political rights, I choose to follow the directives of my own ancestors. Therefore, it is necessary to cook an alphabet soup of my own.

When I say NBWHLB, I am speaking of Natural-Born Women Heterosexual, Lesbian, and Bisexual, born with female genitalia compatible with their sense of Self. These women are female, and express their sexuality through intimate relationships with men, with women, and with men and women. In my lifetime I have encountered a few people who described themselves as "neuter." I am using the term *gynophilia* to describe a love of and pride in being a natural-born woman (NBWHLB) and the term *gynophobia* to describe a fear and hatred of natural-born women. While some like to refer to women who love their bodies as *cis*, I reject this designation now because it is being used by gynophobes to cast NBWHLB women into the "politically incorrect" camp in the leftist ghetto. And I declare that *I am a woman in a woman's body, and I love it!*

Many people are struggling to find and use a "personal pronoun" that fits their perception of Self. I have heard a buffet of terms including "they," "we," and "zed" among others. In order to step outside of this debate, I will use the term "trans-persons." The *gynophobia* I battled with in my community in the 70s has risen again and can be found hiding among members of the male-to-female transgender population, and among those who were born females but want to gender-identify as males. To those who were truly born intersex, the medical profession, the church, and society have truly done you a great disservice.

SEXUAL IMPERIALISM IN THE AFRICAN PAST

With regards to African social organization, it is well known that colonial powers (Christian and Muslim) invaded most of sub-Saharan Africa and plundered the land, the animals, and the people. There is much debate about the sexual mores of precolonial Africa. Africa is a continent with many different cultural groups, each having its own set of rules. So it is a mistake to make blanket statements about what was or wasn't/is or isn't "African."

The debate ranges from claims that "we have no word for homosexuality" (which implies, at the very least, that this sexual identity was either unknown or defined and described differently) to "bisexuality was the norm." Many of the slave narratives describe sexual activities of all kinds as something that was imposed upon slaves by the masters. Here I will provide a few statements about the subject in hopes that the reader will be inspired to further investigation:

Dr. Herukhuti, founder of the Center for Culture, Sexuality, and Spirituality,[2] speaks to the issue of sexual imperialism. He says [emphasis added]:

Sexual imperialism is manifested in a number of ways in the history of European colonialism. It has meant that non-European people have been the targets of European fantasy; projected desires; guilt and shame; and *scientific surveillance and experimentation.*[3]

Boy Wives and Female Husbands: Studies in African Homosexualities[4] provides a litany of diverse attitudes towards same-sex relationships. The book indicates that [emphasis added]:

"[i]n the highly sex-segregated societies of Africa, homosexual behavior and relationships were not uncommon among peers, both male and female, especially in the years *before heterosexual marriage*. These kinds of relations were identified with specific terms and were to varying degrees institutionalized. In precolonial Benin, homosexuality was seen as a phase that boys passed through and grew out of."

The anthropologist Patrick Awondo acknowledges that "Homosexuality has always existed, but some of the current forms of gay *self-identification* and gay activism *originated elsewhere*."[5] [6] [Emphasis added.]

Malidoma Somé, a well-known shaman and author of several books, makes this claim [emphasis added]:

"But at least among the Dagara people, gender has very little to do with anatomy. It is purely energetic. *The whole notion of gay does not exist in the indigenous world*. That does not mean that there are not people who feel this way that certain people feel in this culture, that has led to them being referred to as gay...The gay person is looked at primarily as a gatekeeper...Any person who is at this link between this world and the other world experiences a state of vibrational consciousness which is *far higher and far different from the one that a normal person* would experience. This is what makes a gay person gay...You decide that you will be a gatekeeper before you are born. So when you arrive here, you begin to vibrate in a way that *Elders can detect as* meaning that you are connected with a gateway somewhere..."[7]

The saving grace is that Somé specifies that this view is true "among the Dagara people, specifically." His statement gets misinterpreted because he seems to be saying that "transgendered people" are more spiritual than "normal" people. In the diaspora of the Yoruba tradition, any person who has been initiated as an Orisha priests, will embody the deity to whom they are dedicated without regard to gender. So a woman who is initiated to a "male" deity will dress in the regalia of that deity and will display the characteristics of that deity. Likewise, a man possessed by a Goddess will dress in Her regalia and display Her characteristics. During the possession by the deity, that priest/ess is regarded as channeling a *high vibrational consciousness*. At the conclusion of the possession, the person returns to their regular consciousness and identity.

What has been called "two-spirit," implying two genders or a third gender, has been wildly appropriated from some of the Native American traditions. In the African diaspora, the term is "two-headed," implying that the person's consciousness (Ori) is inhabited by another Being during the trance. The sexual organs and sexual activity of the person in the trance are not a determining factor.

Somé's writing also implies that the Women's Secret Society in Burkina Faso is composed of lesbian women only. This practice is not transferable to the Iyamis of the Yoruba. The Iyamis are most often women over forty who are mothers and grandmothers with relationships to all kinds of men, husbands, fathers, sons, and the Oni of Ife (the King of Yorùbáland). There are other Yoruba societies, such as Gelede, wherein Yoruba men masquerade as women. *But this is not a drag queen event.* Rather, it is designed to acknowledge and celebrate the divine power of natural-born women. Dancing Gelede is *gynophilic*. The transfer of practices from one African culture to another has caused some misperceptions and consequently misguided behaviors.

DELUSIONAL REVISIONISM

Christianity and Islam dismantled, and in some cases destroyed the African views on sexuality, marriage, kinship, family, and community. Dr. Herukhuti writes:

> In the contemporary moment, sexual imperialism also looks like the campaigns the US religious right has fermented in Africa to encourage religious intolerance toward homosexuality. It also looks like what Professor Ibrahim Farajajé calls *"rainbow flag imperialism."*[8]

Both the US religious right and the mainstream LGBT movement tend to ignore the indigenous forms of sexual and gender diversity that have existed in Africa for millennia. The religious right's efforts depend upon the colonial roots that Christian missionaries planted in Africa centuries earlier. The mainstream LGBT movement's efforts depend upon the neoliberal capitalist roots planted by multinational corporations and NGO missionaries decades earlier."

Stephan O. Murray and Will Roscoe conclude that:

What the colonizers imposed on Africa was not homosexuality but rather intolerance of it — and systems of **surveillance and regulation** for suppressing it.[9] [10]

So at the very least we can say that the definitions of sexuality and its place in the culture are not the same now as in precolonial times. Investigators who existed during the colonial and postcolonial periods, including the native Africans who were educated in Western institutions, report everything we know about "precolonial" Africa. However, a few things can be said with relative certainty: In most African cultures, life was regulated by the rites of passage. A child might remain androgynous (with no denial of the genitals) until such time as their rite of passage established their place in the society. Therefore a male child who did not pass the test of his "manhood rite" might be placed among the women, trained in the skills of women, and allowed to marry someone with the skills assigned to "a man." So such a marriage was "gendered."

Their place in society was actualized in a ritual context that included offerings and sacrifices, traditional regalia, music, dance, a new name or title, and the guidance of elders. A person could not simply declare that they "feel like" somebody "other," as is true among some of the people who call themselves transgender in contemporary culture.

Their place in the society was recognized and respected and each society recognized and respected the autonomy of the other. So the men's society attended the events of the women's society *upon invitation only* and/or when it was their rightful station to participate in each other's activities. They respected each other's right to private space and entered it upon invitation, at the appropriate time, dressed according to protocol, and prepared to fulfill a specific function. This is very different from the invasive behavior of some "trans-aggressives."

Transsexual surgery is a twentieth-century European invention that *did not exist* in precolonial Africa because it was not necessary and it was not possible (given the state of medical technology at the time). Eunuchs existed as males who were ritually castrated at an early age to function as servants in the royal women's quarters. But there was no surgery to fashion a "vagina" for them.

So when we attempt to "reconstruct precolonial Africa," we are in danger of delusional revisionism. All humans need self-esteem and deserve their basic human rights. Whenever a people's history has been plundered and degraded by an invader/oppressor, it is their right and their responsibility to reclaim as much of that history as possible and to reconstruct a society and culture that addresses their needs. Herein lies the challenge.

Whereas "the invaders" created an "illusion of deviance," one of the unfortunate side effects of this reclaiming/reconstructing process can be "delusions of perfection," which causes us to look at the past and project onto it the desires of the "perfect present." In other words, not only do we deny things from the past that do not fit our present need, we reconstruct the past as if it were the desired present. So there is a danger that a "trans-utopia" may be projected onto the African past, resulting in attempts to recreate *The Empire That Never Was*. It is important, especially for Black people, to be clear about what has happened and what is happening to us today.

THE "THREE M COMPANY": MEDIA, MONEY AND MEDICINE

During the Black Power Movement of the late 1960s, the revolutionary leader Stokley Carmichael (who, like most leaders of that time, was sexist) identified the tools of oppression used to colonize Africa, and to exploit the human resources of the world. He identified the "3M Company" (not Minnesota Mining and Manufacturing) as "Missionaries, Money and the Marines." Here, I will discuss another triad of oppressive forces: Media, Money and the Medical profession.

Let's look at a few examples. In November 2015, a controversy was stirred when I made a statement on my Facebook page. I'd had several months of random people posting "transgender items" on my news feed that I regarded as aggressive and offensive. They included vulgar misinterpretations of Yoruba spiritual practices; attempts to "normalize" transgender pedophilia, and a personal invitation to participate in the "revolutionary act" of having sex with a transgendered person. But most offensive to me were the constant attacks on the gender and character of several Black women.

These posts declared that poor Black women should surrender their children to well-to-do white trans couples; that First Lady, Michelle Obama (the most elegant since Jackie Kennedy) had a penis; and that Serena Williams was really a man who should not be allowed to play women's tennis. Several women athletes had been accused of taking testosterone (which is now being sold like candy to children) in attempts to disqualify them from important games. The attacks on Serena Williams included interviewers who challenged her self-confidence, uttered racist remarks, and made attacks on her physical beauty. The comments on her physical appearance were reminiscent of the dehumanizing descriptions of African women so often found in the journals of European explorers writing during the colonial period.

In my Facebook responses, I tried to provide some education about Yoruba practices, and to defend Black Women against these attacks, but to little or no avail. However, the cap came off the volcano when someone posted a flyer declaring that the "Jenner person" chosen as "Woman of the Year" by *Vanity Fair* magazine was, in fact, "more woman" than Serena Williams! In that moment my body relived the centuries of rape, slavery, insult and struggle of Black Women. I responded by posting a message to Jenner to "get over yourself, and take some fashion lessons from Ru Paul." This led to an outcry of "trans phobia," which felt like a slap in the face given my long history of fighting for the rights of women. Through the expressed outrage I was made aware of the depth of pain and anger that many people who identify as "trans" experienced.

I noticed that the sharpest reactions came from white male-to-trans persons. For them, defending Jenner was more important than any negative effects that Serena Williams, or any other Black Woman might be experiencing. And it was an insult to them that I had referred Jenner to Ru Paul, a rather famous and stylish Black drag queen. Several of these male-to-trans persons informed me that I should respect Jenner, a Republican who is against same-sex marriage, who had killed a woman in an automobile accident with no consequences, and who was "a woman" on the cover of a magazine but a man at the country club. It sounded like testosterone-driven patriarchy in drag to me.

I also received many personal letters from women (mostly lesbians), who were afraid to express their views and feelings. Some reported that they had been labeled as TERFS (Trans Exclusionary Radical Feminist) and threatened. There were invasions of woman-only spaces such as the Michigan Womyn's Music Festival, and gatherings reserved for menstruating women. The threats included demands for sex by male-to-trans people with penises who claimed to be lesbians. And a few Yoruba priestesses reported people (mostly male-to-trans) who violated the protocol of the tradition by showing up to ceremonies, uninvited, and "in drag." Heads up people, there's a new bully on the block!

In response I offered to hold a summit where people could discuss the matter, especially as it related to women and the Yoruba tradition. But in preparing for the summit I was told to "do my own research." This is what Black people often say to white people when they don't want to be bothered with explaining racism to them. So I understood and began researching the "Transgender Movement." I was amazed by what I found.

THE TRANSGENDER BANDWAGON: WHO IS DRIVING IT AND WHERE IS IT GOING?

As soon as a form of social organization is designated as a "movement," it is wise to ask who is moving in what direction and what their motivation *is*. One must not fall into the trap of assuming that any one or two people speak for all members of "the movement," nor that there is unilateral agreement between all the movement's members.

Obviously "transgender" is yet another population that has been denied their human rights. They want the right to *self-identification*, which, as we have seen, was not a part of the African past.

I am aware of the challenges that transgender people (.2% - .3% of the population) face, such as poverty, prejudice, violence, physical and mental health concerns. As a Black Woman, I find those challenges to be typical of what the 99% of us experience within Western capitalist society. These are the issues that some members of the transgender movement are addressing. My research led to tracking national and international news where I encountered the "under-belly" of the movement.

In the leftist ghetto it has become "politically incorrect" for radical women, especially lesbi-ans, to critique the Transgender Movement in any way, about anything. In order to avoid being called trans-phobic, women are told they should avoid words that refer to our own state of being.

For example, women writing on the subjects of rape on college campuses, genital mutila-tion, and reproductive health have been prohibited from using the word "vagina" because it was experienced as an insult to trans people. A production of Eve Ensler's *Vagina Monologues* at Mount Holyoke College, an all-women's school (now accepting transwomen as students), was cancelled by student trans advocates who claimed that it was not inclusive enough for those who identify as "women" but do not have vaginas.[11] The Midwives Alliance of North America removed any reference to the fact that mothers are women for fear of offending a bearded female-to-trans person who was nursing after giving birth.[12]

We NBWHLB women have been told to refer to ourselves as "cis" because there is accord between our bodies and our brains. If a person with a penis has the liberty to call themselves "woman," certainly everybody else has the right to call themselves whatever they "feel like." So, if the same *rights* are afforded to all American citizens, then Rachel Dolezal, the white woman who served the NAACP, has *the right* to declare herself Black because she feels like it. If this allowance goes unchecked, then a white South African man living in America can request funds, goods, and services reserved for African-American women because he feels like it. Absurd, but possible.

Reasonable and healthy boundaries must be defined, agreed upon, and enforced if kinship, rather than alienation and domination, is the ultimate goal. When, where, and how those lines are drawn will be revealed through legislation, social protocols, and the unfolding future. Here I discuss some issues of importance for the Black Community.

WHO IS DRIVING THAT WAGON?

The White Power press continues to manipulate the world's view of Black People. For the mainstream media, "Black Lives Matter" only when we are being murdered by the police, excelling in sports, or entertaining royalty. Even then, the stories of our lives are "today's news, tomorrow's fish wrap." The media targets the self-esteem of the Black Community in order to entice us to buy the latest hot item, bleach our entire bodies, eat fast food that is laced with hormones, and to mimic the ways of whichever celebrity they throw the spotlight on. The media manipulates information to camouflage our exploitation.

Now see this: Johns Hopkins University is conducting a four-year, *government-funded study* which began in 2012 to examine the "meaning and function" of first "penetrative same-sex sexual experiences" of "adolescent" black men with "adult" Black men.[13] The study, is being conducted at Johns Hopkins in the Eunice Kennedy Shriver Institute of Child Health and Human Development, and so far it has been granted *half a million dollars.* These people are using hundreds of thousands of taxpayer dollars to study the anal sex experience of homosexual black male adolescents, which the study calls "adolescent men," a contradictory name if I've ever heard one. This is not about men. It's about *boys.* How can our government grant taxpayer money to a study where "adolescent men" are having sex with grown men? There are laws against adults having sex with minor children, even if those kids are euphemistically called "adolescent men." I don't even want to think about the moderators of the "study."

Here we see media, money, and medicine working together to legitimize pedophilia in the Black Community. There is a long history of black child endangerment in this culture. This is only one example of the ways black children and youth are being targeted by the "3M company." Children as young as four years old are being subjected to gender questioning, being given hormone blockers, and coerced into gender reassignment surgery. Let us take the money from this study to feed hungry children, stop sex trafficking, and stop the school-to-prison pipeline that targets our children before they are barely out of the womb.

I ask the Black Community to remember the disappearance and murders of the children of Atlanta (1979-81). At least twenty-eight African-American children, mostly boys, were found dead with *the tips of their penises removed.* The police claim that the murders were committed by a mentally retarded Black man. But there is still much speculation among historians, investigators, and Mothers of my generation that cell and substance was taken from these children for medical experimentation. Those who wish to investigate this matter further are referred to the writing of Toni Cade Bambara and the lectures of Dick Gregory regarding the Center for Disease Control 's development of the drug Inteferon.

Transgenderism seems to be an issue of both biology and identity and so little is known that we cannot make widespread assumptions about transgender sexual preferences and activities. The rights to same-sex and interracial marriage, and freedom from enforced marriage are all hard-earned rights that must be preserved. However, please be aware of groups that attach their causes to these hard-earned rights and skew the issue to the moon. My concern is that the North American Man-Boy Love Association (NAMBLA) is now petitioning the American Psychiatric Association, claiming that, like transgenderism, pedophilia should be declared "normal" (See quote below). One article reporting on an academic conference held in 2015 was headlined "University Academics Say Pedophilia Is "Natural, and Normal for Males to Be Aroused by Children."[14] The article stated: "The proposal was being discussed because children are going through puberty at a younger age and the current definition of pedophilia is attraction to pre-pubescent children."

> "One of the attendees, and enthusiastic participant, was Tom O'Carroll, a multiple child sex offender and long-time campaigner for the legalization of sex with children and former head of the Pedophile Information Exchange. 'Wonderful!' he wrote on his blog afterwards. 'It was a rare few days when I could feel relatively popular!'"[15]

I fear that The American Psychological Association may buckle here under continuing pressure, and eventually yield to the desires of these men as a way to assuage the guilt over its long history of torturing gay people. If pedophilia is declared normal it could then become "politically correct," legal, and "fashionable." If this happens, it will be open season on our children. Remember our history in this country.

WHERE GOES THE WAGON?
As we have seen, African attitudes toward sexuality and gender varied in precolonial culture and were greatly affected by the dictates of the colonial period. So where does this information take us today? How do we achieve balance, understanding, and mutually respectful behavior?

I'd like to make a few offerings here: If you are the parents of a child who sees himself or herself as transgendered, please do not subject your child to any form of torture. The church tortures trans children by labeling them as demons who are condemned to live in hell. This is soul-wounding and incompatible with our original attitudes toward sexual diversity. Be aware that laws, such as the "bathroom bill" are being passed that will make it even easier to expose our children to pedophiles. The pressures of institutionalized racism, economic exploitation, and escalating police violence against black people greatly limits your ability to protect your children. And please do not hand your children over to the medical establishment with its history of experimenting on black bodies since the first ships landed on our shores.

The African indigenous response is the healthiest. Allow that child to be androgynous until age sixteen or older, observe their body and spirit, and provide some guidelines for behavior that maintains their place within the family. Be careful and compassionate, because there is a high percentage of self-harming among these youths. Also be patient because transgender identity (an estimated .2% to .3% of the population) does not continue to adulthood in the majority of cases.

Whatever you do, *do not cast them into the street* where they will be consumed by hyenas in the sex trade. Be brave and give yourselves the liberty to discuss this matter fully and honestly. This includes examining the hormones (such as Atrazine and Finasteride) in your food, and the medications you have been given for depression (especially during pregnancy). Diligently examine with a critical eye all the reports regarding tests, studies, and experiments. Ask who conducted them? Who were the test subjects? Where were they conducted? And most importantly, who invests and stand to gain financially from these activities?

It has been claimed that hormones in the womb matter more than rearing when determining sexual orientation. This tips the scale in the nature versus nurture debate. If transgenderism is truly "biologically based," then you do have a right to ask, "whose side of the family is it on?" just as you would any other biological trait. Further, it would be helpful to talk with trans adults who may be able to provide you with information and insights from their own experience.

For the transgendered adult: Chose your personal pronoun and remember that whichever one you choose, you'll be a BLACK one. So live your best life. Distinguish yourself from the trans-aggressives whose behavior will alienate you from your family and allies. If you are someone who feels they must have surgery, keep your eyes on the medical profession, and remember the Tuskegee Experiment.

"For forty years between 1932 and 1972, the US Public Health Service (PHS) conducted an experiment on 399 black men in the late stages of syphilis. These men … were never told what disease they were suffering from or of its seriousness. Informed that they were being treated for 'bad blood,' *their doctors had no intention of curing them of syphilis at all.* The data for the experiment was to be collected from autopsies of the men, and they were thus *deliberately left to degenerate* under the ravages of tertiary syphilis — which can include tumors, heart disease, paralysis, blindness, insanity, and death. 'As I see it,' one of the doctors involved explained, 'we have no further interest in these patients until they die."[16]

In the early 1980s the Black Community experienced similar attitudes toward people with HIV-AIDS. **Never forget your history.** It lives in the "imperfect present."

Rainbow Flag Imperialism

"When two elephants fight, the grass will suffer," said Rev. Kapya Kaoma, who has documented the ties between American evangelicals and the anti-gay movement in Africa. "This is what's happening in Africa. African LGBT persons are just collateral damage to US politics on both ends." For many African activists, American backing is a double-edged sword.

As mentioned earlier, Dr. Ibrahim Farajajé coined the term "rainbow flag imperialism" to describe the ways that Western powers direct campaigns into Africa to encourage queer Africans to adopt western attitudes and actions.[17] On two occasions I had the pleasure of speaking with Dr. Farajajé, casually as we both sought a healthy lunch in mid-town Berkeley, California. I experienced him as a gentle, soft-spoken African-American man with a warm smile and the manners of a prophet. Dr. Farajajé's credentials are impressive. He served as the initial faculty advisor for the Oxala, Howard University's LGBT student group. He was very active in ACT UP D.C., the chair of the Political Action Committee for the DC Black Queer Coalition, a founding member of the Alliance of Multi-Cultural Bisexuals (AMBi), and founder of the first bi group for men of color in DC (Moving Violations was focused on direct action around the AIDS crisis from a pro-feminist, mujerista, and womanist perspective). I encourage the reader to investigate his accomplishments further.[18]

A delicate balance must be struck between stopping the vicious attacks on LGBT people that are fueled by religious hysteria, and the sexual imperialism imposed on nations by US economic policies. Governments driven by conservative Christian and Islamic views on sexuality pass laws denying basic human rights to LGBT people. For example, on January 7, 2014, Nigerian President Goodluck Jonathan signed into law the Same Sex Marriage Prohibition Act, which not only bans same-sex unions but also criminalizes all associations, meetings, conversations, occupations and ways of walking that can be interpreted as having gay overtones. People exhibiting gay appearance and/or behavior may be arrested, have their property confiscated, and may be imprisoned for up to fourteen years. Citizens are encouraged by the church to hunt people down, beat them, set them aflame, and commit other acts of violence in the name of cleansing their communities of disease-ridden sinners.

Ironically, AfricanGlobe.net reports that both supporters and opponents of LGBT rights regard the passage of this harsh law, which is more severe than anything Nigeria had in the past, as a reaction to American pressure.[19] At the same time there is a veiled threat that nations that do not adopt American attitudes toward gender will be denied financial assistance with basic human services such as food security, medical aid, and peacekeeping support. Fierce opposition has come from African governments and private organizations, which accuse the United States of cultural imperialism. This is an example of "rainbow flag imperialism."

Nigeria is rich in oil and is a major supplier to the US. It is also rich in diamonds.

It would behoove us to "follow the money" that fuels all aspects of this and every other movement affecting black people. We must ask if there is a relationship between Big Pharma and the sale of hormone blockers, testosterone, research projects, and media campaigns.

We must always be alert to the monster with many tentacles, *genocide*, when it masquerades as anti-trans violence, female erasure, encroaching pedophilia, medical experimentation, media manipulation and the return of sexual imperialism.

This essay sheds a bit of light on the underbelly of the transgender movement. Such examination can no longer be taboo. When all segments of the community come together to address issues honestly, enhance understanding, and create healthy boundaries, the human rights of every member will be assured.

May the wisdom of the ancestors be with us.

[1] Luisah Teish, *Jambalaya: The Natural Woman's Book of Personal Charms and Practical Rituals* (San Francisco: Harper & Row, 1988).

[2] H. Sharif "Herukhuti" Williams, PhD. Center for Culture, Sexuality, "Using decolonizing culture to liberate the ways people love, experience the Erotic, and connect to the Sacred" is in New York City, N.Y. www.sacredsexualities.org

[3] "Dr. Herukhuti," *Center for Culture, Sexuality And Spirituality*, June 5, 2014, Https:// Sacredsexualities.Org/Dr-Herukhuti/.

[4] https://www.facebook.com/KUCHULiberationinAfrica/posts/721568954556209

5 Stephan O. Murray, Will Roscoe, Editors, *Boy Wives and Female Husbands: Studies in African Homosexualities* (Palgrave MacMillan, 1998)

6 https://76crimes.com/2014/01/30/21-varieties-of-traditional-african-homosexuality/

7 Eric O. Lembembe, "What Traditional African Homosexuality Learned from West," *76 CRIMES*, May 8, 2012, https://76crimes.com/2012/05/08/traditional-african-homosexuality-has-learned-from-west/.

8 MenWeb - Men's Issues, "Gays: Guardians of the Gate Interview with Malidoma Somé," accessed May 3, 2016, http://www.menweb.org/somegay.htm.

9 Dr. Ibrahim Farajaje. http://www.lgbtran.org/Interview.aspx?ID=30
Stephan O. Murray, Will Roscoe, Editors, *Boy Wives and Female Husbands*.

10 Colin Stewart, "21 Varieties of Traditional African Homosexuality," *76 CRIMES*, January 30, 2014, https://76crimes.com/2014/01/30/21-varieties-of-traditional-african-homosexuality/.

11 "All-Women's College Cancels 'Vagina Monologues' Because It's Not Feminist Enough," *Campus Reform*, accessed May 2, 2016, http://www.campusreform.org/?ID=6202.

12 The Midwives Alliance Core Competencies, Revised 2014. www.mana.org.

13 Lauren Richardson, "Taxpayers Fund Same-Sex 'Anal Penetration' Study of 'Adolescent' Black Males With 'Adult' Black Males," *Truth Uncensored*, October 31, 2015, http://truthuncensored.net/taxpayers-fund-same-sex-anal-penetration-study-of-adolescent-black-males-with-adult-black-males/.

14 Lauren Richardson, "University Academics Say Pedophilia Is 'Natural, And Normal For Males To Be AROUSED By Children,'" *Truth Uncensored*, January 28, 2016, http://truthuncensored.net/university-academics-say-pedophilia-is-natural-for-males-aroused-by-children/.

15 Ibid.

16 Info Please, The Tuskegee Experiment. http://www.infoplease.com/ipa/A0762136.html

17 Dr. Ibrahim Farajajé. http://www.lgbtran.org/Interview.aspx?ID=30

18 Ibid

19 Editorial Staff, "US Promotion of Homosexuality In Africa Backfired Big-Time," *Africanglobe. net*, December 22, 2015, http://www.africanglobe.net/africa/promotion-homosexuality-africa-backfired-big-time/.

CHAPTER 19

PSEUDOSCIENCE SUPPLANTS FEMALE ATHLETES' OLYMPIC DREAMS

Kathy Crocco

As LONG AS I was moving, life was great. I informed my kindergarten teacher that I was going to be an Olympic gold medal winner in some yet-undetermined sport. My athletic abilities were evident and my desire to participate at the highest levels was palpable to anyone paying attention.

I hit my first home run over the left field fence at the city fast-pitch softball diamonds when I was nine, and played in an adult softball league when I was thirteen. At the Junior Olympics, I cleared the high jump bar at 5'10" when I was fourteen. I was invited to play in an adult interstate Amateur Athletic Union (AAU) basketball league when I was sixteen. I was 5'8" tall and one hundred and fifty pounds, playing center against women 5'11" to 6' 5" tall, and made the basketball world take note. I could compete in many sports, but excelled at basketball, softball, and track and field.

Sports offered me opportunities that were not available to the working class. If the field was fair and safe, I could perform my way to a life much different than my socioeconomic class and social status dictated. Going to college and being in the Olympics were within my grasp, if I worked hard enough.

Before Title IX, collegiate athletic scholarships were an extremely rare option for women. Unlike my male counterparts, I would need a 3.5 to 4.0 grade point average (GPA) to acquire an academic scholarship to go to college, and I would need to maintain a 3.0 GPA in college to keep my scholarship. The guys needed to maintain a 2.0 GPA to get into college and to keep their athletic scholarships once there. I also needed to work after school, unlike the guys, who only had to pretend to work at pretend jobs, due to benefactors who supported male athletic programs.

Not having access to certified coaches, weight-training equipment or other facilities, I needed to be creative. I narrowed my focus to basketball, because it was being played in colleges and the Olympic Committee was looking at the possibility of adding the sport. So, at sixteen, I contracted with my local recreation center to use the facility during the leaders' dinner hour, between six and seven o'clock at night. I spent hours training by myself and developing the skill set necessary for an undersized post player.

Playing against and easily beating women within my age group was not challenging and did not improve my game. So, I played with and against the guys. They were bigger, stronger, faster, better trained and better skilled than I, and they took no mercy on me. I would never be as big, strong, or fast, nor would I be able to jump as high and hang in the air as they could. I had to play smarter, be more accurate, and exploit strategies just to be somewhat safe on the court. Although this situation was not fair or safe, I wanted to be on that first Olympic women's basketball team, and this was the only way I could foresee that happening.

I did go to college on a full academic scholarship that was offered because college coaches saw me play and wanted me on their team. And, I did get an invitation to try out for the Pan-American Games that would lead to the Olympic games tryouts. Five days after sending my films to the committee, I suffered a life-changing knee injury, and asked for my films to be returned. I was eighteen.

Now as an older woman, I wonder what will happen to that next young girl who has Olympic dreams. Will she compete on a fair and safe playing field? She certainly has better coaching, facilities, and opportunities to play against women at her skill level. Today, many women's basketball teams still practice against men who are quite skilled, but not skilled enough to play on their college teams. This is because the men are bigger, stronger, and faster, and if you want to reach your potential, you have to play against someone who is better.

Because Title IX requires equal access, that next young girl will have the opportunity to play on big stages, attracting the attention of college coaches, no matter her family's socioeconomic status. She certainly will have access to athletic scholarships and may not have to work after classes, since room and board are part of the deal. If she is injured, she will have access to the same sports medicine doctors, surgeons, and physical therapists as her male counterparts. She will also have the same access to academic assistance. What she will never have is the biological advantages that her male counterparts have.

In November 2015, the International Olympic Committee (IOC) set new guidelines for determining eligibility to compete in male and female events. These new guidelines now allow any male to compete in women's events without any legal gender change or any medical treatment whatsoever. All that is necessary is his declaration that he believes himself to possess a "female" personality or mentality, and his testosterone levels must remain in the lower range of the typical male levels for the duration of one year. Here are the official details:

1. Those who transition from female to male (FtM) are eligible to compete in the male category without restriction.
2. Those who transition from male to female (MtF) are eligible to compete in the female category under the following conditions:
    2.1 The athlete has declared that her gender identity is female. The declaration cannot be changed, for sporting purposes, for a minimum of four years.
    2.2 The athlete must demonstrate that her total testosterone level in serum has been below 10 nanomoles per liter (nmol/L) for at least twelve months prior to her first competition (with the requirement for any longer period to be based on a confidential case-by-case evaluation, considering whether or not twelve months is a sufficient length of time to minimize any advantage in women's competition).
    2.3 The athlete's total testosterone level in serum must remain below 10 nmol/L throughout the period of desired eligibility to compete in the female category.
    2.4 Compliance with these conditions may be monitored by testing. In the event of noncompliance, the athlete's eligibility for female competition will be suspended for twelve months.[1]

This decision was based on the IOC's belief that MtF athletes lose their strength advantage after one to two years of hormone replacement therapy, and therefore all is well in the world of women's sports.

The information in following charts (originally published on the *Healthline* web site) was provided by Alexia Severson and R. Sam Barclay and reviewed by Kim Steven, MD. The charts use data from the Mayo Clinic, and show how testosterone levels vary by age and gender.

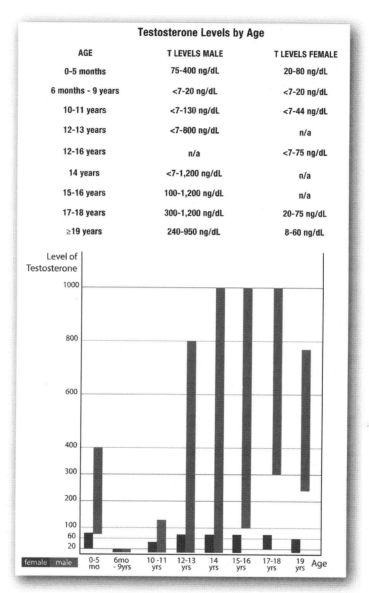

Testosterone Levels by Age

AGE	T LEVELS MALE	T LEVELS FEMALE
0-5 months	75-400 ng/dL	20-80 ng/dL
6 months - 9 years	<7-20 ng/dL	<7-20 ng/dL
10-11 years	<7-130 ng/dL	<7-44 ng/dL
12-13 years	<7-800 ng/dL	n/a
12-16 years	n/a	<7-75 ng/dL
14 years	<7-1,200 ng/dL	n/a
15-16 years	100-1,200 ng/dL	n/a
17-18 years	300-1,200 ng/dL	20-75 ng/dL
≥19 years	240-950 ng/dL	8-60 ng/dL

Based on this medical information, the IOC set the acceptable level of testosterone (T) in MtF athletes, at a level 10 times higher than the average female produces. It is unclear how the IOC can declare that testosterone levels 10 times higher than the average biological female's present no physical advantages in terms of muscle strength and mass. If this is true, then why not allow biological females to increase their testosterone levels to just below 10 nmol/L? But this would be considered doping, and such an athlete would be disqualified.

Joanna Harper, a medical physicist and MtF athlete, states in "A Brief History of Intersex[2] Athletes in Sport," "In order to fully understand this new ruling, it is necessary to look at some numbers. The normal T range for men is 10-35 nmol/L, (nanomole per liter), with an average in the low twenties, and for women it is 0.35-2.0 nmol/L, with an average of about 1.5. The International Association of Athletics Federations (IAAF) chose to set the maximum level for women at the nominal male minimum of 10 nmol/L. This decision has serious implications for all female athletes. Higher T is an advantage and no typical female will get anywhere close to 10 nmol/L without doping. Thus, the agency has set a bar for the dopers, and they will aim for it."[3] The IOC followed the IAAF's lead.

Dr. Eric Vilain, professor of human genetics, pediatrics and urology, and chief of medical genetics at UCLA, is quoted in the article "Testosterone Rules for Women Athletes Are Unfair, Researchers Argue" about the lack of research concerning T levels. "It does not matter whether there is some overlap (of T between men and women) or no overlap at all. What matters is, what is the best marker to use to set men apart from women…It's very hard to do policy if you don't have good data. It's a shame that there are only two studies—including one that's clearly not up to par with, in my opinion, scientific standards—in terms of measurements of testosterone."[4] The IOC guidelines on testosterone levels for men and women were created in part, with this substandard data.

How testosterone affects strength and muscle mass is just the beginning. There are other questions that must be answered. What of the biological advantage that men have due to large amounts of testosterone in their bodies during gestation and through the first five months of life? There is no scientific evidence to suggest that this advantage is negated.[5] What of the bone structure difference in the way the femur attaches to the pelvis? What of the length of bone and muscle-length differences? What of greater heart and lung capacity?

Elite athletes depend on sports science and medicine to help them maximize any advantage they can garner in training and performance. Where is the research about the possible skeletal advantages MtF athletes may have? Are there skeletal advantages if a swimmer's hands and feet are bigger, or if their arms are longer? How is height related to water resistance? How do height, arm length, and shoulder width affect success in rowing, volleyball, basketball, or fencing? How do leg length and stride affect success in high jumping, long jump, hurdling and various running events? How do height, hand size and arm length affect success in water polo?

Where are the statistics that show MtF athletes do not have an advantage in competition with biological females? Has the data been collected over a scientifically significant period of time?

Joanna Harper states in an article for *The Washington Post* that "trans women who are sprinters may maintain something of an advantage over other female runners in that they tend to carry more muscle mass, potentially allowing for increased speed over short distances. (Whereas extra muscle mass is a disadvantage in distance running.) And since gender transition doesn't affect height, it would make sense that transgender women would have advantages over other women in sports such as basketball, where size is so important, and disadvantages in sports such as gymnastics, where greater size is an impediment."[6]

Endocrinologist Ramona Krutzik, MD, was interviewed by journalist Stephie Haynes for *Bloody Elbow*, a mixed martial arts (MMA) website. She was asked to respond to questions about any advantages MMA MtF fighter Fallon Fox may have over biological women fighters. In responding specifically to the Fallon Fox issues, as well as MtF athletes in general, Dr. Krutzik spoke to three specific areas that present potentially unfair advantages, especially if transition takes place after twenty-two years of age, as is the case with Fallon Fox.

When considering muscle mass and strength, Dr. Krutzik states that Fox and other MtF athletes who transition after age twenty-two have "the potential to be significantly stronger because muscle development reached several years beyond full maturity, giving [them] the potential to be significantly stronger than other age-matched women. There's not really a way to determine how much her muscle mass will decrease over time."[7] Dr. Krutzik concludes: "There would be increased musculature, and an increased ability to build muscle, so an advantage might be present due to years of conditioning and becoming more masculine, which includes differences in endurance and strength. The male body develops differently, both in skeletal structure and muscularly."[8]

Dr. Krutzik also challenges the belief that bone density decreases significantly once the MtF athlete begins estrogen therapy. She explains that estrogen promotes bone growth, and that "there wouldn't be a great percentage of bone density loss...Males have higher bone density and higher-mass skeletons than females...Typically, you're looking at about fifteen years after androgen suppression and surgical reconstruction surgery (SRS) to really start to see significant changes in bone density."[9]

Finally, Dr. Krutzik speaks to male brain imprinting that takes place during gestation, when testosterone levels are so high in males. "Developing fetuses that have testosterone have male imprinting of the brain, and it does not go away with androgen suppression and sex reassignment surgery. It is a permanent imprint on the brain. Someone [who] has had male imprinting could have the potential for more aggression or more aggressive-type behavior than a female brain. That's something that could affect her and possibly give her a mental edge in how she fights and how aggressive she might be, compared to a biologically born female."[10]

Dr. Krutzik addresses the physical state of males at maturity. Where is the sports medicine and science research on MtF athletes who begin transition after puberty but before age twenty-two? There are many questions that must be answered by research in sports medicine and science before one can claim that all is fair and safe in women's sports.

Athletes intimately understand success and defeat. They must accept defeat by a superior opponent, their own poor performance, equipment failure, injury or other unforeseen circumstances. What is not acceptable is defeat because of unfair advantage or unsafe conditions. There will always be individuals who overcome physical disadvantages and succeed beyond what was thought possible. How the will to win affects performance is not the question here. The question is about the fairness and safety of women's sports.

It matters not that I understand the reasoning behind the IOC's decision. What does matter is that for every MtF athlete, there is a biological female athlete who must let go of her dreams based on something other than science and medical evidence. I cannot support the erasure of biological women's dreams based on bad science and inadequate or incomplete research. If an aspiring athlete's dreams are altered by injury, as mine were, or by being defeated in fair and safe competition, then that is the way of the athlete. To have one's dreams erased by unfair advantage or unsafe conditions is unacceptable.

---

[1] "IOC Consensus Meeting on Sex Reassignment and Hyperandrogenism," November 2015, http://www.olympic.org/documents/commissions_PDFfiles/medical_commission/2015.

[2] "Note that people born 'intersex,' with reproductive or sexual anatomy that does not clearly fit the definitions of female or male, typically distinguish their condition from transgenderism." Robert Jensen. "A Transgender Problem for Diversity Politics," *The Dallas Morning News*, March 10, 2016.

[3] Alexia Severson and R. Sam Barclay, with Kim Steven, MD. "Testosterone Levels by Age," *Healthline*, 2015, http://www.healthline.com/health/low-testosterone/testosterone-levels-by-age.

[4] Joanna Harper. "A Brief History of Intersex Athletes in Sport," LetsRun.com, http://www.letsrun.com/news/2014/09/brief-history-intersex-athletes-sport/.

[5] As of the publication of this book.

[6] Laura Geggel. "Testosterone Rules for Women Athletes Are Unfair, Researchers Argue," *Live Science*, May 2015, updated June 2015, accessed February 2, 2016. http://www.livescience.com/50938-female-athletes-testosterone-olymics.html.

[7] Joanna Harper. "Do transgender athletes have an edge? I sure don't," *The Washington Post*, accessed February 1, 2016. https://www.washingtonpost.com/opinions/do-trandgender-athletes-h...e-on't/2015/04/01/ccacb1da-c68e-11e4-b2a1-bed1aaea2816_story.html.

[8] Stephie Haynes. "Dr. Ramona Krutzik discusses possible advantages Fallon Fox may have," *Bloody Elbow*, March 20, 2013, accessed February 12, 2016. http://www.bloodyelbow.com/2013/3/20/4128658/dr-ramona-krutzik-endocrinologist-discusses-possible-advantages-fallon-fox-has.

[9] Ibid.

[10] Ibid.

BIBLIOGRAPHY

Frank Abad, "Transgender Women in Sports: Should they be allowed to compete against women?" *Inter-disciplinary.net.* 2013, http://wwwinter-disciplinary.net/probing-the-boundaries/wp-content/uploads/2013/09/franklin-abad-sportpaper2.pfd.

Laura Geggel, "Testosterone Rules for Women Athletes Are Unfair, Researchers Argue." *Lifescience.* May 21, 2015, updated June 2, 2015, http://www.livescience.com/50038-female-athletes-testosterone-olympics.html.

Joanna Harper, "A Brief History of Intersex Athletes in Sport." *Let's Run.* September 19, 2014, http://www.letsrun.com/news/2014/09/brief-history-intersex-athletes-sport/.

Joanna Harper, "Do transgender athletes have an edge? I sure don't." *The Washington Post.* April 4, 2015, http://www.washingtonpost.com/opin-ions/do-transgender-athletes-have-an-edge-i-sure-don't/2015/04/01/ccacb1da-c68e-11e4-62a1-bed1aaea2616_story.

Stephie Haynes, "Dr. Ramona Krutzik discusses possible advantages Fallon Fox may have." *Bloody Elbow.* March 20, 2013, http://www.bloodyelbow.com/2013/3/20/4128658/dr-ramona-krutzik-endocrinologist-discusses-possible-advantages-fallon-fox-has.

International Olympic Committee. "IOC Consensus Meeting on Sex Reassignment and Hyperandrogenism." November 2015, http://www.olympic.org/Documents/Commissions_PDFfiles/Medical_commissions/2015-11_ioc_consensus_on_sex_rassignment_and_hyperandrogenism-en.pdf.

Mayo Clinic. "Test ID: TTFB Testosterone, Total, Bioavailable, and Free, Serum." *Mayo Clinic Mayo Medical Laboratories,* 2016, http://mayomedicallaboratories.com/test/-catalog/clinical/interpretive.

Parker Marie Molloy, *"Heroes, Martyrs, And Myths: The Battle for The Rights of Transgender Athletes."* Vice Sports. November 6, 2014, http://sports.vice.com/en_us/article/heroes-martyrs-and-myths-the-battle-for-the-rights-of-transgender-athletes.

Alexia, Severson and R. Sam Barclay, with Kim Steven, MD. "Testosterone Levels by Age." *Healthline.* March 23, 2015, accessed February 11, 2016, http://www.healthline.com/ health.low-testosterone/testosterone-levels-by-age.

Pablo Torre, "The Transgender Athlete." *Sports Illustrated Vault.* May 28, 2012, http://www. si.com/vault/2012/05/28/ 106195901/the-transgender/athlete.

CHAPTER 20

OPEN LETTER TO THE MIDWIVES ALLIANCE OF NORTH AMERICA REGARDING THE RECENT REVISIONS TO THE ORGANIZATION'S STANDING CORE COMPETENCIES

Mary Lou Singleton and a Collective of Many Midwives

August 20, 2015

Dear Midwives Alliance of North America Board of Directors and MANA Membership:

We are writing in response to your revisions of the MANA Core Competencies. MANA's attempts at inclusivity are commendable in today's complex world. We are concerned, however, by accelerating trends in our culture to deny material biological reality and further disconnect ourselves from nature and the body, and about the ways in which the revisions may support these trends. Midwives have long practiced the precautionary principle, counseling against the adoption of technologies and theories that have not been proven safe or beneficial to mothers and babies, and by extension, the entire human community. We respectfully ask the MANA board to reverse the 2014 revisions and consider the ways in which the attempted changes may have harmful implications for women.

We are concerned that, except for in the trademarked section from the Midwives Model of Care, the word "woman" has been erased from the MANA core competencies document and replaced with "pregnant individual" and "birthing parent." We recognize that the words maternal and motherbaby were not removed from the document, implying that the reviewers maintained a mutual and shared respect for the sanctity of the motherbaby unit in midwifery. But women are now all but missing from the language, as if we can separate woman from mother from baby. Woman is recognized now only in relation to her baby. This is harmful to female adult humans; we women have fought long and hard to be recognized as autonomous beings.

Adopting this language change in the context of midwifery and human reproduction is based on either or both of the following assumptions. 1) That MANA and the midwives MANA represents believe that it is biologically possible to change one's sex. Or 2) That we deny the material basis of biological sex and acknowledge gender identity as primary. We know as midwives that biological sex occurs at the level of our DNA and the gametes we produce, and is immutable. By embracing the idea that any human other than those in a class called women carry offspring to term, give birth to them and nurse them, we are prioritizing gender identity over biological reality. We are also contributing to the cultural erasure of women's wisdom that the physiological power encoded in our female bodies is what creates, nourishes, and births live offspring and transmits culture. Maintaining this understanding of women's unique power to give birth does not preclude practitioners from taking into account how individuals in their care prefer to be identified.

We believe that it is a mistake to define the experiences of pregnancy and childbirth though the lens of gender identity. The very few gender-identified males that have given birth or accessed an abortion have only done so because they are female-bodied people, and that scientific fact cannot be erased. We are allowing gender identity to be the primary way that we refer to one another, even for a biological process like birth. Pregnancy and birth are distinctly female biological acts; only women and female-bodied people can give birth. The whole concept that a man can give birth is premised on the supremacy of technology over women and nature, and the primacy of ideology that is detached from our animal, natural selves. Yet midwifery doesn't only thrive, but survives, on the health of the biological process. We as midwives believe in the inherent wisdom of biology.

Human beings, like the majority of other mammals, are sexually dimorphic. i.e. there are two distinct biological sexes, female and male, with each having particular primary and secondary sex characteristics that allow us to make a distinction between the two. Sex is natural, biological and objectively factual. Gender refers to societal roles and expectations placed upon members of each sex. Gender is cultural and gender norms vary across the globe. Gender is in fact synonymous with what not so long ago were called sex-role stereotypes. Today the word gender is frequently used to stand in for sex but this is true only on a superficial basis.

Gender often now refers to the sex one is perceived as or wants to be perceived as. Gender, as used today, also refers to the results of consuming powerful steroid hormones to change secondary sex characteristics, and therefore the perception of one's sex.

The root of female oppression is derived from biology. Patriarchal systems arise out of male attempts to control female sexuality and reproduction. Female liberation from patriarchal oppression, including brutal and demeaning birth practices, cannot be achieved if we are forbidden from mentioning female biology. Women have a right to bodily autonomy and to speak about their bodies and lives without the demand that we couch this self-expression in language which suits the agenda of others who were not born female. Gender, sex and sexuality should not be conflated. Sex and sexuality are based upon biology whereas gender is a socially constructed concept. We do not give birth with our gender identity but with our biology. The document refers to the midwife's need to be knowledgeable about the "anatomy and physiology of the birthing parent," as if the anatomy and physiology of birth were not distinctively female.

The existence of intersexed people does not negate the reality of female biology. Intersex conditions are based upon the biology of the body and not an abstract identity adopted by any particular individual. We have not changed the biological definitions of male and female because of the existence of intersex individuals, just as we have not rewritten embryology texts to delete any mention of human beings having 46 chromosomes in order not to offend those people born with trisomy conditions. Why would we now change the biological definition of woman because a tiny proportion of the population change their gender identification?

We wholeheartedly endorse inclusivity, which above all requires midwives' provision of the particular care that transgendered people need. Toward that end, we see the need to gather more information on the ways in which body modifications, puberty blockers (Lupron), and long-term synthetic hormones may affect midwifery care in pregnancy and birth. Midwives are well aware of how body dysphoria can negatively impact pregnancy, birth, and breastfeeding. Before uncritically supporting gender transitioning, MANA should be calling for evidence precautionary to its long-term effects, especially in light of the younger and younger ages at which it is occurring. Before rushing into "inclusivity" we need to focus on the clinical needs of transgendered people and an open reflection of whether and how these particular needs fit into the scope of practice for all midwives.

Birth transcends and goes deeper than the western capitalistic concept of the individual. We live in the time where the dominant narrative is of the rights of the individual. We must be careful to examine how individualism harms healthy human society. We must fight the forces destroying the living material world and telling us that cultural distractions are more real than life itself. There is life-giving power in female biology. As midwives we protect the lives of the life-givers: women, mothers, females, and their offspring. We must not become blinded to the biological material reality that connects us. If midwives lose sight of women's biological power, women as a class lose recognition of and connection to this power. We urge MANA to reconsider the erasure of women from the language of birth.

Re-published with permission. https://womancenteredmidwifery.wordpress.com/take-action/

SECTION THREE

THE "VIOLENT" FEMALE BODY

Scripps College held an event called "Project Vulva," inviting women to decorate cupcakes like vulvas and discuss the taboo around female genitalia in our phallocentric society. Yet, it turns out that vulvas are still way too taboo (if not more so) to be discussed and represented. Organizers were told their event was "violent to transwomen." The premise of the event rapidly drew criticism from transgender activists, who complained that the event demeaned the experience of women who were born in men's bodies.

~ From the article posted in The Daily Caller News Foundation, Nov. 2, 2015, by reporter Blake Neff

The daily paper at the University of California, Los Angeles (UCLA) has issued a disclaimer in deference to the transgender community with a recent article preemptively apologizing for saying women menstruate.

~ From the article posted in The Daily Caller News Foundation, July 22, 2015, by reporter Blake Neff

A feminist festival scheduled to take place June 22nd – 25th in Heidelberg, Germany, has declared the clitoris "exclusionary". The festival, called 'Lady*fest' which features workshops, lectures, and art, had initially planned to include topics like, "clitoris/glitzoris" and "masturbation" as part of their art exhibition, but protocol documents from the last planning meeting now explain that the clitoris is "problematic," because it refers to female anatomy. The festival organizers have stated that, due to being a "queer Lady*fest," it shouldn't empower "only certain groups," such as those with clitorises, and that the festival will not be "excluding any groups" by referencing female anatomy. Lady*fest claims these actions embody their policy, which translates to, "be tender to all genders," and that being mindful of how female anatomy offends people will provide "a safer space to all human beings by applying awareness."

~ From a report published in GenderTrender by Susan Cox, June 3rd, 2016, feministcurrent.com.

You say that my body is "violent" because it exists.
You say that my vulva is violent because it is real.
As long my body exists you are reminded that your body is not my body,
Therefore my body must be diminished, rendered irrelevant, or best, erased.
You say that my body is "violent" because I exist.

~ RUTH BARRETT

~

CHAPTER 21

THE PERIOD POEM

Dominique Christina

"SO LET ME *be very clear. I wrote this poem with a very specific intent. I have a 15-year-old daughter. It is important to me that I throw every part of my experience, whatever wisdom I've gleaned from that, every part of my backbone, toward her, to sustain her, to offer her language that lifts her up and keeps her up.*

That said, there is for me, a necessary conversation that seeks to undermine the shaming that happens to some girls around menstruation. I had the experience of starting my period in 7th grade, and boys, finding out that I started my period. And then it was the same old bullshit. I would be in class with the frantic, "I've got to go to the bathroom now," hand in the air and they always mocked and stated loudly: "Ugh! You're on your period, aren't you?" You know, that dumb shit.

Then years later my daughter starts her period and she is absolutely stricken. It was a Saturday morning and I heard hyperventilating in the hallway. When I looked out I saw my daughter with her back against the wall clutching bloody underwear...GRIEVING. I mean, I experienced menstruation as inconvenience perhaps but not anything that warranted a funeral procession. But my daughter was grieving and I wanted to undermine that. So I threw her a period party. I assembled all of my wildly creative, artistic, anarchist friends and asked them to come dressed in red; and the party was replete with red food and red drinks. It was great.

And I should mention that it was not just my girlfriends and their daughters at the party. No. My sons and THEIR friends were also in attendance. This is important. I don't expect anything to change around all of the shaming that happens to women in conversations around menstruation if men and boys are not a part of those conversations. They need adjusting because they are the inheritors of the same weaponized ideologies that we languish under. They are supposed to perpetuate it and never interrogate it. If they are a part of the conversation, that inheritance can be interrupted.

So anyway, after the Period Party, my daughter was fairly sailing through the experience. She mastered maxi pads and knew when to expect her cycle and she was not walking around loathing her biology. Then Twitter happened. A guy posted something so repugnant and assaultive my daughter screen-capped it and sent it to me wanting me to respond to him. Thing is, 140 characters is so limiting. A poem is better. So I wrote one in response. Here goes:

THE PERIOD POEM

Dude on Twitter says: "I was having sex with my girlfriend when she started her period, I dumped that bitch immediately."

Dear nameless dummy on Twitter:
You're the reason my daughter cried funeral tears when she started her period.
The sudden grief all young girls feel
After the matriculation from childhood,
And the induction into a reality that they'll
Have to negotiate people like you
And your disdain for what a woman's body can do.
Herein begins an anatomy lesson
Infused with feminist politics because
I hate you.

There is a thing called the uterus.
It sheds itself every 28 days or so,
(or in my case every 23 days, I've always been a rule breaker)

But that's the anatomy part of it, I digress.

The feminist politic part, is that women know how to let things go,
How to let a dying thing leave the body,
How to become new,
How to regenerate,
How to wax and wane,
Not unlike the moon and tides,
Both of which influence how you behave,

I digress.

Twitter Dummy, women have vaginas that can speak to each other.
By this I mean, when we're with our friends, our sisters, our mothers,
Our menstrual cycles will actually sync the fuck up.
My own cervix is mad influential.
Everybody I love knows how to bleed with me.

Hold on to that, there's a metaphor in it.
Hold on to that.

But when your mother carried you,
The ocean in her belly is what made you buoyant,
Made you possible.
You had it under your tongue when
You burst through her skin,
Wet and panting from the heat of her body,
The body whose machinery you now mock on social media,
That body,
Wrapped you in everything that was miraculous about it,
And sung you lullabies laced in platelets,
Without which you wouldn't have no Twitter
Account at all motherfucker. I digress.

See, it's possible that we know the world better
Because of the blood that visits us.
It interrupts our favorite white skirts, and
Shows up at dinner parties unannounced,
Blood will do that, period.
It will come when you are not prepared for it;
Blood does that, period.
Blood is the biggest siren, and we understand that blood misbehaves.
It does not wait for a hand signal, or a welcome sign above the door.
And when you deal in blood over and over again like we do,
When it keeps returning to you,

That makes you a warrior.

And while all good generals know not to discuss battle plans with the enemy, let me say this to you, dummy on Twitter:

If there's any balance in the universe at all, you'll be blessed with daughters.

Blessed.

Etymologically, bless means to make bleed.
See, now it's a lesson in linguistics.
In other words, blood speaks, that's the message, stay with me.

Your daughters will teach you what all men must one day come to know,

That women,
Made of moonlight magic and macabre,

Will make you know the blood.

We're going to get it all over the sheets and car seats.
We're going to do that... period.

We're going to introduce you to our insides, and if you are as unprepared As we sometimes are,
It can get all over you and leave a forever stain.

So to my daughter:

Should any fool mishandle that wild geography of your body,
How it rides a red running current,
Like any good wolf or witch,
Well then just bleed, boo.

Give that blood a biblical name, something of stone and mortar.

Name it after Eve's first rebellion in that garden.
Name it after the last little girl to have her genitals mutilated in Kinshasa, (that was this morning.)

Give it as many syllables as there are unreported rape cases.

Name the blood something holy, something mighty, something Unlanguageable, something in hieroglyphs, something that sounds like the End of the world.

Name it for the war between your legs,
And for the women who will not be nameless here.
Just bleed anyhow.
Spill your impossible scripture all over the good furniture.
Bleed, and bleed, and bleed
On everything he loves,

Period.

CHAPTER 22

A REVOLUTIONARY LOVE LETTER TO MENARCHE

Monica Asencio

For a Daughter,
In honor of Menarche and Thirteenth Birthday

Dear Wooz,[1]

You were always easy to love, with your calm and thoughtful disposition. In your eyes shined worlds of wisdom and wonder. And when you spoke it was sweet like a whisper, the secret of life passing through lips. For years, you were known as the Buddha Baby and we playfully rubbed your beautifully round belly for luck (though the unmistakable gift you brought into my life seems more like destiny than luck). Slowly and surely, as you got older, something shifted inside of you. A spark in your eye ignited and you started asserting your little self as someone who wasn't going to act any certain way just to suit us. It was as if the truth you observed had taken hold; it started to stir and move through you and you flowed with it; you trusted this transformation. I watched it happen (it's still happening) and it's been a sight to behold, as well as a profound learning about the tenacity of the intuition (your gut feeling), and the miracle of metamorphosis (naturally becoming who you are meant to be).

"The body knows. When our heart sinks...when you feel sick to your gut...when something blossoms in your chest...when your brain gloriously pops...that's your body telling you the one true thing. Listen to it."

~ CHERYL STRAYED

IT'S NOT ALWAYS easy to "listen to it" when we've been taught our whole lives not only to suppress it, but to hate the very sound of it. The misogyny is internalized so deeply we become terrified to speak. We are socialized to silence, surrender, and sacrifice our essential selves and safety. We get dismissed so incessantly, it seems normal when others project their thoughts and feelings onto us. This cultural conditioning is so complete, we unconsciously scrutinize and resent our perfect, natural-born bodies.

Now, let's play our favorite game and call out this system of institutionalized oppression by its name: the imperialist, white supremacist, capitalist patriarchy, made up of men and women alike, young and old, of all colors and creeds. We must resist this force that wishes us harm (wishes to turn us into things). We must stand strong and resolute against those who are killing the world and follow in the footsteps of our feminist predecessors, the many mothers and a few faithful fathers who paved a path with their blood, sweat, and tears. It's a narrow, harrowing passage, but it won't lead us astray.

I know this is heavy stuff and you might not be entirely ready to carry its weight. I did think about toning this letter down a bit, but then I remembered your personal aspiration to acquire wisdom, to *be* the "Wooz" and how this is, in essence, a coming-of-age message and decided, since the subject matter isn't necessarily anything you haven't already been exposed to, you could handle it. You will need a firm place to stand, a few tools to leverage the load and perhaps a pair of bolt cutters.

I will say, the *deepest joy* imaginable stems from the strength of solidarity you feel with those who share in your convictions. And that there's nothing more *life-affirming* than the realization that our liberation is bound to all living things, nothing more *exhilarating* than fighting for freedom and justice, and certainly nothing comes close to the kind of *fun* that is had when sticking it to the "Man."

My hope for you is that you never lose your sense of play and wonder and your insistence on the sensual; the way you value touch, taste, and the aesthetics of nature, the way you inhabit your body and relate to your surroundings, like a true scientist moving through space, making connections. The ability to pay attention and discern, to commit to memory the lessons learned, and allow that learning to inform the way we live is undoubtedly one of the most important survival traits that served our hunting and gathering ancestors for ninety-five percent of our evolutionary history. They knew life as a system of mutual care and cooperation, that each thing exists to nourish all others and in return to nourish itself. In some parts of the world people still live sustainably, but the disparity between that way of life and our "civilized" one is so immense that we couldn't go back even if we tried because the planet has been consumed away by modern hubris.

We are in an unprecedented crisis: almost all the forests are gone, our soil salifying and our oceans acidifying at an alarming rate, and 200 non-human species are going extinct every day.[2] For the most part, the white American, upper-class privilege you were born into has insulated you from feeling the effects of our planet's dire predicament. The global tech industry and the American broadcast media make sure we are all massively distracted and thoroughly entertained. And, honestly, you shouldn't have to deal with this daunting reality as a thirteen – year-old girl. You can't know how desperately I wish I could make this disaster disappear, but as Gandalf says when Frodo wishes the ring of power had never come to him, *"All we have to decide is what to do with the time that's given to us."*

Sometimes, the best we can do is hold hands with the person next to us and face the uncertainty together; endure the truth together with open eyes and try to learn how to live on this earth without destroying it, which is the highest spiritual calling there has ever been; for we cannot save ourselves if we do not try to save our soil. So learn, my sweet Bubby. Learn by making mistakes and asking questions. Learn to want what you need and to serve what is worthy. Learn by bearing witness to the pain and suffering of others. Learn to share that burden. Learn what the earth reveals through its natural cycles. Know you can't have growth without change and that death brings eternal life (this is the good news of the resurrection that the Christians rave about, which physicists have termed the transference of energy). You see, the lessons in nature abound if we would only listen.

If that sounds simple that's because it is. We high-tech, industrialized humans, with our big brains (shrinking by the second), overcomplicate things. Sure, there has been and will always be doubt and plenty of fear, but they can teach us, too. In fact, every truth I've come to began with distressing thoughts and feelings. I often have to stop everything I'm doing and just be still for a while or go for a long walk with that particular worry and ask myself, what does my mind/body/spirit say? What would the wise one do? Then in total silence, I attend, wait, write and process for as long as it takes for the confusion to clear, until I arrive at the thing I already knew but of which I needed to be reminded.

Our modern lives constantly disconnect us from ourselves, each other, and the sacred. So we have to be intentional about tuning into the divine and be ready to receive its grace. And I don't mean grace in the context of Western religion (unworthy sinners seeking and being granted forgiveness), but rather a redemptive love that lifts us up when we are at our lowest, a light that shines through the cracks of our broken hearts in our darkest moments. This may sound like hyperbole, but the cosmic force of light is literally how we came to be. It makes of all creation a series of self-transformations. Plants transmute this light into life by being food for animals, which transmute life into consciousness, the ultimate state of feeling alive and connected to everything.

During the Pine Creek Canyon hike at Big Bend last November, when we walked into a dream scene of cascading human-sized nests, the bedding a soft carpet of pine needles and brush, I had been meditating on the arrival of your menarche and the thoughtful care package from our friend Mary. That gentle, golden, glowing light illuminating what looked like a nesting place through a circular break in the canopy and that very moment in time seemed replete with serendipity, stout with significance. Because, well, making nests is what our wombs do. They create safe places to nurture and fiercely protect life. And the maintenance of the nest is the function of menstruation. Our bodies know to let go of what is not needed, what may harm and distort, like the illusion that we are separate from our wild mother. This illusion *is* the original sin, how humans fell from grace, the great forgetting that has cost us our humanity and has brought about real evil in the form of domination, coercion, and hierarchy (the unnatural arrangement of power...power over instead of power with).

When we menstruate we remember "the oath that all living things make the moment they begin...I will, by my very existence, by my life and actions and death, make the world more fecund, more healthy, more vibrant, more diverse."[3] Our menses remind us of nature's powerful law of reciprocity, which is the law of love: for everything we take, we must give back. When we menstruate, we are invited to participate in the cycles of return by feeding the soil which feeds us. And of course, all humankind is responsible for engaging in these vital activities of renewal, but women are more intimately connected to this aspect of biological reality through our moon cycles.

Leaving the nests was harder than I expected. You were so reluctant to go and lingered so lovingly until that last long second. As we walked up out from the depths of the canyon onto the flattened terrain, the soft green slopes alongside of us, the sun blazing, the cool wind blowing, the earth spinning, I thought about the row of maple trees back down on the trail, how they showed us the color of change and the brutal beauty of letting go, how their leaves, in brilliant shades of orange, red, and yellow, blessed us on their slow descent to the ground of their being.

Now you take your place amongst the many mothers who understand full well that giving life is so much more than physically birthing a baby. It's the creative energy (chi) that touches every aspect of our being. So be a mother to yourself. Know what is good for you. Gestate empathy and compassion, humor and honesty. We cannot justify the reproduction of humans as an experiment in self. Instead, be a conscious parent, an enlightened witness to all the children that come into your life. Hold a space for them and let them bask in your warmth, generosity, attention, and respect. Give constancy in a moment that reminds that child they matter. I can't fathom where I would be without the resiliency of the many mothers who raised me. We simply cannot underestimate the power of universal mother love, the nurturing, guidance, and care for which all humans are capable. It is, in and of itself, a perpetual salvation.

As your journey continues to take shape, be rooted in the love that will always be with you and your sister, long after Dad and I are no longer in these bodies of ours. Because the places and people we love we can never leave. We simply take on a different form and resonance in an ongoing cycle, in the everlasting continuity of life. I realize that's not entirely consoling, for our passing will no doubt feel like a loss, but I'm becoming more comfortable with the complexities of existence, that death is the unknown in which all of us lived before birth, and that we can't know the mystery of life until we meet that fateful end... maybe.

I do know that we were meant to be a family and that everything we've shared with one another will be made holy, whole, complete by our deaths. When that time comes, I expect to be ready, though I must confess this fact of life still confounds me just as it breathes endless meaning into every moment of every day.

So again, thank you for being the wonderful Wooz, and welcome to the wild world of adolescence. Remember, you never walk alone.

Monz

---

[1] Written to Helen's preferred nickname, which means "the wise one of Zadoo."

[2] https://www.theguardian.com/environment/2010/aug/16/nature-economic-security

[3] Derrick Jensen, *Dreams,* Seven Stories Press, New York, NY, 2011.

MOTHER
Patricia Monaghan

Ma. Mama. Mommy. Mom. Mam.
No separation. Even in sleep, she is
pressed by them, impresses them, heart and mind filled as body was once
filled. Even in sleep, she fills us, knows us,
senses us, our needs, our desires, our demands.
Ma. Mama. Mommy. Mom. Mam.
Never alone. Someone always tugging,
at sleeve, at heart, at patience. No separation.
Mommy. Mommy. Ma, ma, ma.
She dances, she sings, she is beautiful
in her desire. But even in that dance, that song,
even that desire even then she is plural: another,
others, always with her, within her, she never
without. And we, never without her.
Ma. Mammy. Mommy. Mom.
Always the need, hurt, demand.
Always the fullness. The press, the plurality.
Always someone tugging. Never alone.
Ma. Mama. Mommy.
Feeling need as it rises. At a cry, milk
comes. At a sob, arms stretch. Like bursting,
to hold back. She floods, she reaches, she
holds, she touches, she touches, she touches.
She becomes us; we become her; no separation.
Need answering need answering need.
Mammy. Mommy. Mom.
Matter, *mater,* material, materialize.
Flesh of woman. This our body, this our blood.
Never alone. No separation.
Ma. Ma.
The open mouth. The full breast. The

surge of connection.
The matrix: core of being.
Ma.

SONG FOR MENOPAUSE
Ila Suzanne Gray

I counted moon after moon,
blood after blood,
my tide crimson and rust
gushed from the ocean inside,
rivered garnet down my thighs,
each carmine drop,
every clot and string,
dark and viscous thunder,

The final, sweaty slow ebb,
moons and years passed,
my stream paled, ceased,
into another beginning
this cratered moonscape
now cache.

CHAPTER 23

THE GIRLS AND THE GRASSES

Lierre Keith

CAPTURED IN A test tube, blood may look like a static liquid, but it's alive, as animate and intelligent as the rest of you. It also makes up a great deal of you: of your 50 trillion cells, one-quarter are red blood cells. Two million are born every second. On their way to maturation, red blood cells jettison their nuclei—their DNA, their capacity to divide and repair. They have no future, only a task: to carry the hemoglobin that will hold your oxygen. They don't use the oxygen themselves they only transport it. This they do with exquisite precision, completing a cycle of circulation through your body every twenty seconds for a hundred days. Then they die.

The core of hemoglobin is a molecule of iron. It's the iron that grasps the oxygen at the surface of your lungs, hangs on through the rush of blood, and then releases it to wanting cells. If iron goes missing, the body, as ever, has a fallback plan. It adds more water to increase blood volume; thin blood travels faster through the fine capillaries. Do more with less.

All good, except there's less and less oxygen offered to the cells. Another plan kicks in: increased cardiac output. The heart ups its stroke volume and its rate. To keep you from exploding, the brain joins in, sending signals to the muscles enfolding each blood vessel, telling them to relax. Now blood volume can increase with blood pressure stable.

But still no iron arrives. At this point, the other organs have to cooperate, giving up blood flow to protect the brain and heart. The skin makes major sacrifices, which is why people with anemia are known for their pallor. Symptoms perceived by the person—you—will probably increase as your tissues, and then organs, begin to starve.

If there is no relief, ultimately all the plans will fail. Even a strong heart can only strain for so long. Blood backs up into the capillaries. Under the pressure, liquid seeps out into surrounding tissues. You are now swelling and you don't know why. Then the lungs are breached. The alveoli, the tiny sacs that await the promise of air, stiffen from the gathering flood. It doesn't take much. The sacs fill with fluid. Your body is drowning itself. This is called pulmonary edema, and you are in big trouble.

I know this because it happened to me. Uterine fibroids wrung a murder scene from me every month; the surgery to remove them pushed me across the red cell Rubicon. I knew nothing: my body understood and responded. My eyes swelled, then my ankles, my calves. Then I couldn't breathe. Then it hurt to breathe. I finally stopped taking advice from my dog—Take a nap! With me! and dragged myself to the ER, where, eventually, all was revealed.

Two weeks later, the flood had subsided, absorbed back into some wetland tissue of my body, and I felt the absence of pain as a positive. Breathing was exquisite, the sweetest thing I could imagine. Every moment of effortless air was all I could ever want. I knew it would fade and I would forget. But for a few days, I was alive. And it was good.

Our bodies are both all we have and everything we could want. We are alive and we get to be alive. There is joy on the surface of the skin waiting for sunlight and soft things (both of which produce endorphins, so yes: joy). There is the constant, stalwart sound of our hearts. Babies who are carried against their mothers' hearts learn to breathe better than those who aren't. There is the strength of bone and the stretch of muscle and their complex coordination. We are a set of electrical impulses inside a watery environment: how? Well, the nerves that conduct the impulses are sheathed by a fatty substance called myelin—they're insulated. This permits "agile communication between distant body parts." Understand this: it's all alive, it all communicates, it makes decisions, and it knows what it's doing. You can't possibly fathom its intricacies. To start to explore the filigree of brain, synapse, nerve, and muscle is to know that even the blink of your eyes is a miracle.

Our brains were two million years in the making. That long, slow accretion doubled our cranial capacity. And the first thing we did with it was say thank you. We drew the megafauna and the megafemales, sculpted and carved them. The oldest known figurative sculpture is the Goddess of Hohle Fels, and 40,000 years ago someone spent hundreds of hours carving Her. There is no mystery here, not to me: the animals and the women gave us life. Of course they were our first, endless art project. Awe and thanksgiving are built into us, body and brain. Once upon a time, we knew we were alive. And it was good.

And now we leave the realm of miracles and enter hell.

Patriarchy is the ruling religion of the planet. It comes in variations—some old, some new, some ecclesiastical, some secular. But at bottom, they are all *necrophilic*. Erich Fromm describes necrophilia as "the passion to transform that which is alive into something un-alive; to destroy for the sake of destruction; the exclusive interest in all that is purely mechanical." In this religion, the worst sin is being alive, and the carriers of that sin are female. Under patriarchy, the female body is loathsome; its life-giving fat cells vilified; its generative organs despised. Its natural condition is always ridiculed: normal feet must be turned into four-inch stubs; rib cages must be crushed into collapse; breasts are varyingly too big or too small or excised entirely. That this inflicts pain—if not constant agony—is not peripheral to these practices. It's central. When she suffers, she is made obedient.

Necrophilia is the end point of sadism. The sadistic urge is about control, "the passion to have absolute and unrestricted control over a living being." The objective of inflicting pain and degradation is to break a human being. Pain is always degrading; victimization humiliates; eventually, everyone breaks. The power to do that is the sadist's dream. And who could be more broken to your control than a woman who can't walk?

Some nouns: glass, scissors, razors, acid. Some verbs: cut, scrape, cauterize, burn. These nouns and verbs create unspeakable sentences when the object is a seven-year-old girl with her legs forced open. The clitoris, with its 8,000 nerve endings, is always sliced up. In the most extreme forms of female genital mutilation (FGM), the labia are cut off and the vagina is sewn shut. On her wedding night, the girl's husband will penetrate her with a knife before his penis.

You don't do this to a human being. You do it to an object. That much is true. But there is more. Because the world is full of actual objects—cardboard boxes and abandoned cars—and men don't spend their time torturing those. They know we aren't objects, that we have nerves that feel and flesh that bruises. They know we have nowhere else to go when they lay claim to our bodies. That's where the sadist finds his pleasure: pain produces suffering, humiliation perhaps more, and if he can inflict that on her, it's absolute proof of his control.

Behind the sadist are the institutions, the condensations of power that hand us to him. Every time a judge rules that women have no right to bodily integrity—that upskirt photos are legal, that miscarriages are murder, that women should expect to be beaten—he wins. Every time the Fashion Masters make heels higher and clothes smaller, he smiles. Every time an entire class of women—the poorest and most desperate, at the bottom of every conceivable hierarchy—are declared legal commodities for sex, he gets a collective hard-on. Whether he personally uses any such women is beside the point. Society has ruled they are there for him, other men have ensured their compliance, and they will comply. He can kill one—the ultimate sex act for the sadist—and no one will notice. And no one does.

There is no stop to this, no natural endpoint. There is always another sentient, self-willed being to inflame his desire to control, so the addiction is forever fed. With other addictions, the addict bottoms out, his life becomes unmanageable, and the stark choice is stop or die.

But the sadist isn't hurting himself. There's no looming bottom to hit, only an endless choice of victims, served up by the culture. Women are the feasts at our own funeral, and he is happy to feed.

If feminism was reduced to one word, it would be this: no. "No" is a boundary, spoken only by a self who claims one. Objects have neither; subjects begin at "no." Feminists said "no" and we meant it.

The boundary of "no" extended outward, an insult to one being an injury to all: "we" is the word of political movements. Without it, women are cast adrift in a hostile, chaotic sea, holding our breath against the next Bad Thing. With the lens of feminism, the chaos snaps into sharp focus. We gave words to the Bad Things, then faced down denial and despair to see the pattern. That's called theory. Then we demanded remedies. That's what subjects, especially political subjects, do. Emmeline Pankhurst, leader of the British suffragettes, worked at the Census Office as a birth registrar. Every day, young girls came in with their newborns. Every day, she had to ask who the father was, and every day the girls wept in humiliation and rage. Reader, you know who the fathers were. That's why Pankhurst never gave up.

To say "no" to the sadist is to assert those girls as political subjects, as human beings with the standing that comes from inalienable rights. Each and every life is self-willed and sovereign; each life can only be lived in a body. Not an object to be broken down for parts: a living body. Child sexual abuse is especially designed to turn the body into a cage. The bars may start as terror and pain but they will harden to self-loathing. Instilling shame is the best method to ensure compliance: we are ashamed—sexual violation is very good at that—and for the rest of our lives we will comply. Our compliance is, of course, his control. His power is his pleasure, and another generation of girls will grow up in bodies they will surely hate, to be women who comply.

Female socialization is a process of psychologically constraining and breaking girls—otherwise known as "grooming"—to create a class of compliant victims. Across history, this breaking has including so-called "beauty practices" like female genital mutilation and foot binding, as well as the ever-popular child sexual abuse. Femininity is really just the traumatized psyche displaying acquiescence. In its essence, it is ritualized submission.

This is not natural. It was not created by God. It's a corrupt and brutal social arrangement.

It's become popular to embrace trendy notions from postmodernism in some activist circles. This includes the idea that gender is a "binary." But gender is not a binary: it's a hierarchy, global in its reach, sadistic in its practice, murderous in its conclusion, just like race, just like class.

Gender demarcates the geopolitical boundaries of patriarchy. It divides us in half but it's not a horizontal half. It's vertical. Gender is not some cosmic yin and yang. It's a fist and the flesh that bruises. It's a mouth crushed shut and a girl who will never be the same.

Gender is who gets to be human and who gets to be hurt. That has to be made clear because men know what they are capable of. They know. They know the sadism they've built into their own sex. Do it to her, is what they say to each other. Not to me, the human being. But her, the object, the thing. And "her" has to be obvious, visually and ideologically. See, there she is, unable to walk. See, there she is, on display. Or there she is, secluded and covered, for your eyes only.

And how much easier if he can say God made her this way, to lie beneath me and obey. Or nature made her this way, an empty hole. Or her own brain made her this way, the slut who asks for it. Because she asks for all of it: the rape, the battering, the poverty, the prostitution, the murder.

Those conditions are what Andrea Dworkin named the barricade of sexual terrorism. That barricade defines the parameters of gender. It's really simple. Women are inside it. Men are outside it. Actually, men are building it, fist by fist and fuck by fuck. And it's exactly those violent, violating practices that create people called women. That's what men do to break us and keep us broken. That's what gender is: the breaking and the broken.

Noel Ignatiev, author of *How the Irish Became White*, has argued for abolishing the white race, defined as "white privilege and race identity." Likewise, the sex-class "men" is simply male privilege and gender identity—and it needs to be abolished if women are ever to be free.

If you were born female, you were born on a battlefield. You will be punished for even saying that out loud, but the grim truth is you're going to be punished no matter what for the sin of being female. Battering is the most commonly committed violent crime in the United States. That's a man beating a woman. Men do that every eighteen seconds. That's more hatred than I can comprehend. Right now, that battlefield is such a slaughter that we can't even collect our wounded.

An example. There are entire villages in India where all the women only have one kidney. That's because their husbands have sold the other one. And there are people who want to argue that gender is some kind of sexy, fun performance or an identity we all get to choose. When all the women only have one kidney, that is not a performance and it is not an identity. It's an atrocious human rights violation against an entire class of people, people called women. And that is the meaning of gender and precisely why it needs to be abolished.

Transgender activist Joelle Ruby Ryan has written that the terms "female" and "sex-class" are "offensive and passé." One might reasonably wonder why Ryan is eager to claim membership in a group so declared, or why Ryan got a job teaching Women's Studies if "female" is so of-fensive. That a biological reality—female—can be called "offensive" shows how far down the rabbit hole Queer Theory has fallen. What's next, gravity?

But to make "sex-class" a dirty word means that the realities of women's lives become once more unspeakable, each woman isolated in an inchoate anguish. Apply the word "sex-class," and that isolation snaps into a sharp pattern of subordination, from the small, daily insults to body and soul to the shattering traumas of incest and rape. The crimes men commit against women aren't done to women as random individuals; they're done because women belong to a subordinate class and they're done to *keep* women a subordinate class.

The genderists don't want to resist gender. They are, in fact, quite attached to it. Writes one, "It would be a crying shame if 'woman' and 'man' ceased to be relevant categories for me to play with." Substitute poor and rich or black and white and understand that people being oppressed are not categories to be played with. Especially, they are not masturbation fodder. If you understand that, the only question left is: are women people?

The strangest part of this whole debate is that feminists are being called "biological es-sentialists." The genderists posit the immortal, even cosmic, nature of femininity. A typical comment: "There is a distinct, substantive, immutable feminine gender, and it can not be transcended." They baldly state their belief in "brain sex." White supremacists are the only people who believe in the "Negro brain." But talk of "lady brains" is completely accepted across progressive communities if it comes from genderists. Feminists, in contrast, start with Simone de Beauvoir: "One is made, not born a woman." It's that making that we intend to stop. It can be stopped because gender is a social process. It's the genderists who claim it's biological, im-mutable. Yet *we* get called "essentialists"?

And it's the genderists who conform. For all their talk of "gender-bending," their goal is cosmetics, costumes, and surgery to match their bodies to gender caricatures. They are per-manently altering their bodies—removing healthy organs and in some cases the ability to ever experience sexual pleasure again—to better fit a corrupt and brutal arrangement of power. This is now being done to children and some of the children already regret it. Please read that sentence again. Please.

The children should be an alarm call, but no one is listening. There are historical prec-edents from which left-leaning people should have learned. Much of the Progressive movement embraced eugenics, until the optimistic, shiny promise of science produced punctual trains to crematoriums. Similarly, in the 1950s many liberals believed that chemical castration was the compassionate approach to homosexuality. We look back in bewildered horror but refuse to see that it's happening now. The Unfit are being chemically sterilized once again. People are being surgically mutilated in the service of social conformity. Children as young as eighteen months are being "diagnosed" as transgender. What does that even mean in someone who has yet to speak her first word? She preferred the blue pacifier to the pink? The real question: so what if she did? Girls can't like blue, play rough and tumble, take up space, run for president? Apparently not. *Free to Be, You and Me, through Surgery*. The prison of gender is locking down ever tighter.

And the female body is the cage. Most women are at constant war with their bodies, and it's a war we lose before first grade: fifty percent of preschool girls think they are "too fat." If a girl makes it through that battlefield, with its devastating cultural terrain of dehumanizing and sadistic images, the big guns are waiting: By the time they're ten, 90 percent of girls have been subjected to unwanted sexual attention by neighborhood boys. By the time they're eleven, it's adult men threatening the violations to that same 90 percent. This is the meaning of "female" in patriarchy, learned early and often an object to be publicly used. Get used to it, girls. Meanwhile, eating disorders, the slow, grinding punishment of the female fat cell, have the highest mortality of all mental illness.

The most heartbreaking element of the transgender narrative is their hatred of their bodies. In the war between culture and nature, gender and body, the body loses. And that defeat is turned into an identity. The only parallel claim is made by the anorexics' Pro-Anas, who insist their wrenching disjuncture of self and body is a legitimate identity. There is no doubt that people hate their bodies: willful starvation and surgical mutilation speak with a stark, eloquent evidence. The question is why.

Guy Debord wrote presciently of the society of the spectacle, where "being becomes having and having is reduced to merely appearing." This is, of course, what has happened, and then some: commodity fetishism has conquered every human relationship, including, finally, that between body and self. Instead of inhabiting "the soft animal of your body," as poet Mary Oliver so sweetly puts it, the body is an object to own and then to starve or slice until it approximates the punishing, promising image. Our genitals are now a commodity to be obtained rather than tissue to inhabit, the exquisite nerve endings where animal meets angel severed to create a surgical simulacrum. Perhaps the commodity has finally been defeated by a greater force: the image itself.

The body has certainly fallen to its assault. Writes a detransitioned twenty-two-year-old woman, "I saw myself in the saucy lankiness of scruffy rock gods, the devil-may-care grins of thrill seekers in films, the deep pain of confusion written on the faces of James Dean and

Johnny Depp, but I could not see myself in any of the women I looked at." In the service of the image—and sundered from her body by sexual abuse—she had her breasts removed at age seventeen and started taking testosterone, which nearly killed her. Which is more toxic: the chemicals injected to destroy one's natal sex or the culture that makes that sex a prison? And why are women not allowed to ask that question?

An identity based on a hatred of the body by definition cannot be liberatory. Those soft animals are our only homes. Driven from our bodies, we are permanent refugees: there is nowhere else to go. The whole point of feminism is to stop the breakage the incest, the rape, the battering, the so-called beauty practices that amount to a life of torture. That means we have to stop the ideology, too, the one that says men are human while women exist to be conquered and used, the one called gender. Measured by either sheer volume or effect, the ruling image of the age, the one delivering the ideology, is the pounding sadism of pornography. And the prison cell called "woman" grows ever smaller: do not call that prison passé.

What has been done to our bodies has been done to our planet. The sadist exerts his control; the necrophiliac turns the living into the dead. The self-willed and the wild are their targets and their necrotic project is almost complete.

Taken one by one, the facts are appalling. In my lifetime, the earth has lost half her wildlife. Every day, two hundred species slip into that longest night of extinction. "Ocean" is synonymous with the words *abundance* and *plenty*. *Fullness* is on the list, as well as *infinity*. And by 2048, the oceans will be empty of fish. Crustaceans are experiencing complete reproductive failure. In plain terms, their babies are dying. Plankton are also disappearing. Maybe plankton are too small and green for anyone to care about, but know this: two out of three animal breaths are made possible by the oxygen plankton produce. If the oceans go down, we go down with them.

How could it be otherwise? See the pattern, not just the facts. There were so many bison on the Great Plains, you could sit and watch for days as a herd thundered by. In the central valley of California, the flocks of water birds were so thick they blocked out the sun. One-quarter of Indiana was a wetland, lush with life and the promise of more. Now it's a desert of corn. Where I live in the Pacific Northwest, ten million fish have been reduced to ten thousand. People would hear them coming for a whole day. This is not a story: there are people alive who remember it. And I have never once heard the sound that water makes when forty million years of persistence finds its way home. Am I allowed to use the word "apocalypse" yet?

The necrophiliac insists we are mechanical components, that rivers are an engineering project, that genes can be sliced up and arranged at whim, that our generative organs are fair game for the Foucaultian Frankensteins. He believes we are all machines, despite the obvious: a machine can be taken apart and put back together. A living being can't. May I add: neither can a living planet.

Understand where the war against the world began. In maybe twelve places around the globe, humans took up the activity called agriculture. In very brute terms, you take a piece of land, you clear every living thing off it, and then you plant it to human use. Instead of sharing that land with the other million creatures who need to live there, you're only growing humans on it. It's biotic cleansing. The human population grows to huge numbers; everyone else is driven into extinction.

Agriculture creates a way of life called civilization. Civilization means people living in cities. What that means is: they need more than the land can give. Food, water, energy have to come from someplace else. It doesn't matter what lovely, peaceful values people hold in their hearts. The society is dependent on imperialism and genocide. Because no one willingly gives up their land, their water, their trees. But since the city has used up its own, it has to go out and get those from somewhere else. That's the last 10,000 years in a few sentences.

The end of every civilization is written into the beginning. Agriculture destroys the world. That's not agriculture on a bad day. That's what agriculture is. You pull down the forest, you plow up the prairie, you drain the wetland. Especially, you destroy the soil. Civilizations last between 800 and maybe 2,000 years—they last until the soil gives out.

What could be more sadistic than control of entire continents? The sadist turns mountains into rubble, and rivers must do as they are told. The basic unit of life is violated with genetic engineering. The basic unit of matter as well, to make bombs that kill millions. This is his passion, turning the living into the dead. It's not just individual deaths and not even the deaths of species. The process of life itself is now under assault and it is losing badly. Vertebrate evolution has long since come to a halt—there isn't enough habitat left. There are areas in China where there are no flowering plants. Why? Because the pollinators are all dead. That's five hundred million years of evolution gone.

He wants it all dead. That's his biggest thrill and the only way he can control it. According to him it was never alive. There is no self-willed community, no truly wild land. It's all inanimate components he can arrange to his liking, a garden he can manage. Never mind that every land so managed has been lessened into desert. The essential integrity of life has been breached, and now he claims it never existed. He can do whatever he wants. And no one stops him.

Can we stop him?

I say yes, but then I have no intention of giving up. The facts as they stand are unbearable, but it's only in facing them that the pattern comes clear. Civilization is based on drawdown. It props itself up with imperialism, conquering its neighbors and stripping their land, but eventually even the colonies wear out. Fossil fuel has been an accelerant, as has capitalism, but the underlying problem is much bigger than either. Civilization requires agriculture, and agriculture is a war against the living world. Whatever good was in the culture before, ten thousand years of that war has turned it necrotic.

But what humans do they can stop doing. Granted every institution is headed in the wrong direction, there's no material reason the destruction must continue. The reason is political: the sadist is rewarded, and rewarded well. Most leftists and environmentalists see that. What they don't see is the central insight of radical feminism: his pleasure in domination.

The real brilliance of patriarchy is right here: it doesn't just naturalize oppression, it sexualizes acts of oppression. It eroticizes domination and subordination and then institutionalizes them into masculinity and femininity. Men become real men by breaking boundaries—the sexual boundaries of women and children, the cultural and political boundaries of indigenous people, the biological boundaries of rivers and forests, the genetic boundaries of other species, and the physical boundaries of the atom itself. The sadist is rewarded with money and power, but he also gets a sexual thrill from dominating. And the end of the world is a mass circle jerk of autoerotic asphyxiation.

The real brilliance of feminism is that we figured that out.

What has to happen to save our planet is simple: stop the war. If we just get out of the way, life will return because life wants to live. The forests and prairies will find their way back. Every dam will fail, every cement channel, and the rivers will ease their sorrows and meet the ocean again. The fish will know what to do. In being eaten, they feed the forest, which protects the rivers, which makes a home for more salmon. This is not the death of destruction but the death of participation that makes the world whole.

Sometimes there are facts that require all the courage we have in our hearts. Here is one. In 2015, global atmospheric concentrations of carbon dioxide breached 400 parts per million. For life to continue, that carbon needs to get back into the ground. And so we come to the grasses.

Where the world is wet, trees make forests. Where it's dry, the grasses grow. Grasslands endure extreme heat in summer and vicious cold in winter. Grasses survive by keeping 80 percent of their bodies underground, in the form of roots. Those roots are crucial to the community of life. They provide physical channels for rain to enter the soil. They can reach down fifteen feet and bring up minerals from the rocks below, minerals that every living creature needs.

They can build soil at an extraordinary rate. The base material they use to make soil is carbon. Which means the grasses are our only hope to get that carbon out of the sky.

And they will do it if we let them. If we could repair seventy-five percent of the world's grasslands—destroyed by the war of agriculture—in under fifteen years, the grasses would sequester all the carbon that's been released since the beginning of the industrial age. Read that again if you need to. Then take it with you wherever you go. Tell it to anyone who will listen. There is still a chance.

The grasses can't do it alone. No creature lives independent of others. Repairing the grasslands means restoring the ruminants. In the hot, dry summer, life goes dormant on the surface of the soil. It's the ruminants who keep the nutrient cycle moving. They carry an ecosystem inside themselves, especially the bacteria that digests cellulose. When a bison grazes, she's not actually eating the grass. She's feeding it to her bacteria. The bacteria eat the grass and then she eats the bacteria. Her wastes then water and fertilize the grasses. And the circle is complete.

Civilization consumes the circle, so all civilizations end in collapse. How could it be otherwise if your way of life relies on destroying the place you live? Now, the soil is gone and the oil is running out. By avoiding the facts, we are ensuring it will end in the worst possible way.

We can do better than mass starvation, failed states, ethnic strife, misogyny, petty warlords, and the dystopian scenarios that collapse brings. It's very simple: reproduce at less than replacement numbers. The problem will take care of itself. And now we come to the girls.

What drops the birthrate universally is raising the status of women. Very specifically, the action with the greatest impact is teaching a girl to read. When women and girls have even that tiny bit of power over their lives, they choose to have fewer children. Yes, women need birth control, but what we really need is liberty. Around the world, women have very little control over how men use our bodies. Close to half of all pregnancies are unplanned or unwanted. Pregnancy is the second leading cause of death for girls age 15-19. Not much has changed since Emmeline Pankhurst refused to give up.

We should be defending the human rights of girls because girls matter. As it turns out, the basic rights of girls are crucial to the survival of the planet.

Can we stop him?

Yes, but only if we understand what we're up against.

The sadist wants the world dead. Anything alive must be replaced by something mechanical. He prefers gears, pistons, and circuits to soft animal bodies, even his own. He hopes to upload himself into a computer someday.

He wants the world dead. He enjoys making it submit. He's erected giant cities where once were forests. Concrete and asphalt tame the unruly.

He wants the world dead. Anything female must be punished, permanently. The younger they are, the sooner they break. So he starts early.

A war against your body is a war against your life. If he can get us to fight the war for him, we'll never be free. But feminists said every woman's body was sacred. And we meant it, too. Every creature has her own physical integrity, an inviolable whole. It's a whole too complex to understand, even as we live inside it. I had no idea why my eyes were swelling and my lungs were aching. The complexities of keeping me alive could never be left to me. Being alive is a gift, the only gift. That soft animal body is all you have and it needs your defense, here at the end of the world. Refuse to fight his war on the terrain of your flesh. Fight him instead.

We're going to have to match his contempt with our courage. We're going to have to match his brute power with our fierce and fragile dreams. And we're going to have to match his bottomless sadism with a determination that will not bend and will not break and will not stop.

And if we can't do it for ourselves, we have to do it for the girls and the grasses.

Whatever you love, it is under assault. But love is a verb. May that love call us to action.

SECTION FOUR

A ROOM OF OUR OWN

As women, we are raised to deny our own needs or to sacrifice our needs for others. When we affirm our very right to have needs and strive to meet our own needs, we are being told that our needs must be secondary to the needs of others, even to those who largely have no respect for our needs. When we affirm our right to our intimate and sacred spaces we are now called bigots.

~ Ruth Barrett

I hear that you share many experiences that women have. I acknowledge that we have things in common.
I want to know how do we acknowledge those things that we do *not* have in common?
How do we honor those things that are different within between us?
Many wars are caused, not by our sameness, but by our differences.
I believe that we promote understanding and respect by honoring our differences as well.
One way we do so is through our rituals.
How do *you* honor *your* differences?

~ KATHY CROCCO (EXCERPT FROM HER CONVERSATION WITH A MALE TO TRANS INDIVIDUAL)

CHAPTER 24

PROBLEM AND SOLUTION? TRANSWOMEN'S
ACCESS TO PRIVATE WOMEN-ONLY SPACES

Elizabeth Hungerford

THE POLITICAL DEMAND for transwomen's access to private women-only spaces is predicated on a certain problem-and-solution logic. It can be summarized like this:

> **The *problem* is transwomen's oppression in the form of institutional violence and social marginalization.**
> **The *solution* to this problem is transwomen's access to women-only space.**

Following this reasoning, trans activists have repeatedly attacked private women-only spaces by insisting that transwomen be granted entrance to them regardless of the organizers' wishes. Now, I spent three years studying problem-solving in law school. During this time, I learned that there are many different ways to remedy a problem. I also learned that some solutions are better than others. I could write pages explaining the legal mechanics of specific performance, market alternatives, restitution, injunctions, and monetary and punitive damages. But the bottom line is that the popular movement for trans activism seems to have completely lost sight of logical problem-solving.

Instead of attacking institutionalized inequality and the material consequences thereof (also known as the socially constructed phenomenon of "oppression"), many trans activists have turned their focus to private women-only spaces. From the Michigan Womyn's Music Festival to women's colleges, women-only spaces are considered increasingly important "problem sites" for trans activists to target.

One might consider this a righteous strategy if private women-only spaces were:

1. the cause (direct or proximate) of trans people's gender dysphoria; or
2. a source of violence (individual or structural) against trans people.

But women-only spaces are not the problem. Women commune in these spaces to find solidarity with *each other*. They are internally, not externally, focused. When women are lawfully and peacefully gathered in them, women-only spaces are not an infringement on trans people's individual lives or collective human rights. Women's ability to congregate without transwomen poses no threat to transwomen's housing, employment, safety, or bodily autonomy. They do not extract any resources from trans people. In legal terms, a plausible theory of transwomen's *damages* is notably lacking. In addition, it should be noted that there are many alternative spaces available on the market.

There is also no particular benefit to be gained by granting transwomen access to women-only space. It would not give transwomen special protection from violence, discrimination, homelessness, or being denied employment. It does not cure gender dysphoria or trans-form transwomen's bodies from male to female. It is therefore wholly unnecessary to insist on the *specific performance* of transwomen's admission to women-only spaces because admission does not function as a solution or remedy to any of the socio-structural problems that transwomen face *because* they identify as transwomen.

As such, there is no logical connection between trans people's oppression (the problem) and transwomen's access to privately organized spaces reserved by and for women (the "solution").

SYMBOLIC ACCEPTANCE

Transwomen's warm welcome to women-only spaces also cannot be reasonably framed as *symbolic* of society's acceptance of trans people. Neither the problem nor the solution is symbolically accurate.

Limited enclaves of separatism, such as women-only spaces, are never representative of society. In fact, they are purposefully different from, and therefore do not reflect, mainstream dynamics. Because of this, transwomen's acceptance within an insular subset of society—here women-only spaces—could not be considered *symbolic* or predictive of the desired solution: widespread and radical social change.

Moreover, privately organized women-only spaces and events are not analogous to institutions and ideologies of social control that exact oppression on groups of people. Women-only spaces are rarely profitable and do not exercise concentrated political influence. Women-only spaces do not make laws. They do not make medical policy. They do not wield the money, resources, or social credibility that would make them *symbolic* of the problem: powerful social institutions that are designed to serve the public good.

The Supreme Court of the Canadian province of British Columbia specifically recognized the weakness of drawing a parallel between systemic oppression and private enclaves when it opined in *Vancouver Rape Relief Society v. Nixon et al.* (2003) about transwoman Nixon's attempt to legally compel a private women's-only organization to accept her:

Rape Relief provides access to only a tiny part of the economic, social and cultural life of the province. By reason of Rape Relief's self-definition, perhaps reflected in its small number of members, exclusion from its programs is quite evidently exclusion from a backwater, not from the mainstream of the economic, social and cultural life of the province. It may be an important backwater to its members and to Ms. Nixon, but that is a subjective assessment.

Exclusion from a self-defining "identifiable group" is in no objective sense equivalent to legislated exclusion from a public program of benefit entitlement…[1]

For these reasons, neither transwomen's *inclusion in nor exclusion from* women-only spaces can be considered *symbolic* of trans people's overall acceptance in mainstream society. Still, trans activists keep insisting that transwomen must have access to all women-only private events and spaces.

EXAMPLE: PRIVATE, WOMEN-ONLY EVENT

In 2015, a women-only party crash executed in the name of trans rights resulted in problems for a historic thirty-year-old lesbian tradition called Women in the Woods, hosted at Breitenbush Hot Springs in Detroit, Oregon. According to a statement issued by the venue management, women's right to congregate on women's own terms is now disallowed by the dictates of trans activism (emphasis mine):

It appeared as a proposal to both recognize and actively support transgender people in their struggle for inclusion and acceptance in society, *starting with women-only events* at Breitenbush (whether sponsored by Breitenbush or not). It is noted that transgender people are perhaps the most persecuted population of all, suffering a host of abuses, from sexual violence to ridicule, ostracism, shunning, lack of public services, loss of employment and family abandonment, among other cruelties.[2]

Let us *unpack* this, as they say. The first sentence cites a problem: transgender people's lack of "inclusion and acceptance in society." As discussed above, a private, women-only event in the woods isn't an accurate analogue to "society." The women-only event is literally a retreat. A retreat *from society*. Women in the Woods attendees wish to escape society; not replicate it. For example, one wouldn't consider the apparent acceptance of her superhero identity at a Comic-Con event to be indicative of an impending cultural shift towards the normalization of costumed workers in Corporate America. That simply doesn't make sense. It doesn't make in sense in the same way that the purported connection between transwomen's acceptance in private women-only spaces and their increased "inclusion and acceptance in society" is not well-considered and very likely does not exist at all.

And yet, Breitenbush asserts that a campaign for acceptance and inclusion is meant to *start with* women-only events? These spaces may be an easy target, but they are not effective ones for remedying problems that operate *outside* the very temporary boundaries of women-only space.

The second sentence quoted above is equally nonsensical in terms of the alleged problem: "It is noted that transgender people are perhaps the most persecuted population of all, suffering a host of abuses, from sexual violence to ridicule, ostracism, shunning, lack of public services, loss of employment and family abandonment, among other cruelties."

Let us take this statement of the problem as truth. Assuming transgender people are "perhaps the most persecuted population of all," how can unwelcome advances into private women-only events possibly improve trans people's standing in larger society? Allow me to review these *cruelties* in context:

- Women are not the primary perpetrators of sex- and gender-based violence. Men are.
- Women are not in control of the government or public services in general. Men are.
- The event is not a job fair; attending the event does not increase one's chances of employment. Being a man does.
- Women-only events cannot prevent family abandonment nor change the interpersonal dynamics of trans people's families.

Transwomen's exclusion from women-only spaces simply is not a structural barrier to trans people's safety, housing, employment, health, or any other human right. Women-only spaces are simply not relevant. Attacking private women-only spaces such as Women in the Woods is both futile in terms of advancing the legitimate goals of the trans movement and harmful to the women who seek the temporary refuge these spaces provide. It is an exercise in misplaced energy and unnecessary hostility when trans activists make it impossible for women to meet without harassment in the form of political name-calling and boycotting.

Conclusion

No matter how you slice it, targeting women-only events as a remedy for trans people's individual or collective suffering is illogical. Women and women-only spaces do not cause the legal and social problems trans people face in their daily lives. Women are not the problem. Transwomen's access to women-only spaces, organizations, and retreats is not a panacea for—nor does it even blunt—structural violence and discrimination against trans people in wider society. Access to women's spaces is not the solution.

When this simple problem-and-solution analysis eviscerates any connection between transwomen's oppression and transwomen's access to private women-only spaces, why are trans activists so intent on crashing women-only parties? Why are well-funded LGBT organizations so invested in securing transwomen's full access to private women-only spaces? Their efforts would be better spent on targeted social and legal reform, such as lobbying for a passable Gender Expression Non-Discrimination Act (GENDA, as proposed in New York State) and organizing trans-focused domestic violence shelters and employment supports. Social structures and institutions need to change. Women-only spaces do not need to change, for they are neither the problem or the solution to improving trans people's lives and social status.

---

[1] *Vancouver Rape Relief Society v. Nixon et al.* 2003 BCSC 1936. Accessed online July 30, 2016: https://www.thecourt.ca/2007/02/application-denied-kimberly-nixon

[2] Statement posted on the Breitenbush Hot Springs website under Community News, "The Ender of Assigned Gender" by Peter Moore. Accessed July 30, 2016: http://www.breitenbush.com/community/community-news/15-news-gender.html

CHAPTER 25

WHY WOMEN'S SPACES ARE CRITICAL TO FEMINIST AUTONOMY

Patricia McFadden

THE ISSUE OF male presence, in physical and ideological terms, within what should be women-only spaces is not just a matter of ideological contestation and concern within the Women's Movement globally; it is also a serious expression of the backlash against women's attempts to become autonomous of men in their personal/political relationships and interactions. As human societies have become more public through the intensified struggles for inclusion by various groups of formerly excluded constituencies (the largest of which is made up of women of differing classes, ages, sexual orientations, abilities, ethnicities, nationalities, and locations), so the struggle for the occupancy and definition of space has also taken on a concomitant significance.

In this short article, I want to explore some of the reasons why this contestation over women's spaces has arisen. I also want to argue strenuously that women must not allow men into our spaces because strategically this would be a major political blunder for the future of the Women's Movement, wherever it is located and engaged with patriarchal hegemony and exclusion. To argue for men's inclusion into women's political and structural spaces is not only fundamentally heterosexist; it also serves an old nationalistic claim that women need to take care of men, no matter where they are located and or what they are engaged with. This claim is inherently premised on the assumption that women who are not attached to or associated with a man are dangerous, rampant women who must be stopped. That is why the statement that women need to "take men along" smacks not only of the deep-seated patriarchal assumption that women's mobility requires male approval, but it also facilitates the transference of socio-cultural practices into the Women's Movement that nurture male privilege and pampering in spaces that women have fought for centuries to mark as their own.

In order to make my points, I want to refer briefly to the conceptual notion of space and try to show how space is gendered and highly politicized as a social resource in all societies. Throughout the known human narrative, certain spaces have been culturally, religiously and politically marked as either "male" or "female," and we know that in terms of the latter spaces, these were and still are largely linked to women's breeding and feeding functions in all human societies, without exception. The spaces we refer to as *public* are assumed to be male, and for centuries men have excluded women from the public where all the key decisions relating to power are deliberated and implemented.

Additionally, across human time, those spaces that were feminized were also considered the least important; they were and still are places where women functioned through the benevolence of males, but which they never owned and still do not have entitlement to if they live in close intimate relationships with adult males. Notions of "the family" and "the household" remain fundamentally masculine in terms of all the key institutions of our societies, and women cannot create a "real" family; when they construct households these become immediately feminized and stigmatized as *Other* (female-headed/single-headed/women-headed, etc.).

Therefore, when we take a really close look at notions of space and its occupancy in gendered terms, we realize the shocking fact that it was only in the 20th century that women have occupied limited space in patriarchal societies in their own right as women and or as persons. Space was and continues to be largely defined as a male construct in every way conceivable, and for most societies of the South, one cannot even refer to the changes that have occurred in Northern societies around this issue to make any generalizations. The majority of women in the South exist outside space as a politically defined resource. In the main, and especially for poor women on a continent like that of Africa, space remains fundamentally tied to the archaic notions of patriarchal privilege and the ownership of women both privately and publicly. That is why the Women's Movement as a political, ideological, activist and structural space must remain just that: a women-only space.

Additionally, it is vital for any conversation about the presence or absence of males in women's spaces to locate the notion of space itself within a political narrative about what space means in patriarchal gendered societies. The fact of the matter is that space is not neutral territory; it is highly politicized in class and locational terms. The rich live in certain spaces and the poor are systematically excluded from those spaces by barbed wire and electric fences, vicious dogs and poor males in overalls carrying guns in their hands. Space is kept under close scrutiny by the military which declares particular areas of a national territory "no-go" areas to the public, and the ruling classes themselves construct all sorts of exclusionary practices and mechanisms that keep certain groups of people out of 'their' spaces. Colonial whites used the state to put in place systems of surveillance that excluded Africans from their spaces through the institutionalization of "passes" and the extension of license to any white to be able to stop any black person and demand that they account for their presence in a particular place at any time of the day or night.

And in one of those rarely acknowledged moments of patriarchal collusion between black and white men within the colonial enterprise, black men were allowed to stop and interrogate any black woman who was not in the presence of an adult male outside the confines of the "Native Areas" of colonial Southern Africa. The same practice probably applied in other parts of the continent and of the world, for that matter, at varying points in time.

In the period immediately after independence in many societies of this continent, women who were unaccompanied by an adult male and dared to re-enter or remain within the public arena after the formal working day was over, were and still are susceptible to arrest and criminalization as "whores," who should be locked away for their own protection because "good women" are at home feeding the children and catering to the sexual needs of their husbands after the sun goes down.

These and many of the discourses which define and mark space as male and gendered, exclusionary of women as persons and as individuals who are entitled to mobility and to the occupancy of space in their own right, must be brought into focus in considering the pressure that men and certain groups of "good women" are putting on the rest of us within the Women's Movement to allow men into our limited political spaces.

My retort is that those women who like men so much that they cannot spend any time during the day or night without male presence can set up what are called "mixed" organisations, which have a right to exist as all other civil society structures do which enhance human desires and interests in the common good; but not as part of the Women's Movement. Therefore, to insist that our Movement, which we have struggled to establish, often giving our entire lives to its creation, should become a "gender-mixed space" is not acceptable at all and must be vigorously contested.

Suffice it to say then that space is always highly contested and it is a political issue, and women must understand and keep that in mind as we ask ourselves questions with regard to the presence of men in our Movement. Spaces are never given like all resources in our societies, whether these be material, aesthetic or social spaces are struggled for, occupied and crafted, marked as belonging to a particular group through struggles that are basically about establishing ownership and using that ownership to fulfill an agenda. And the Women's Movement has a very clearly stated agenda that of the emancipation of all women from patriarchal bondage and exploitation. Patriarchy has effectively used exclusion as a central tenet of its ideological claims to hegemony in all our societies, whether one is looking at notions of identity, of rights and privilege, of access and inclusion into institutions and sites of power.

Exclusionary practices use space as a key element in the implementation of a specific agenda. The claim that women's place is in "his home" is an old strategy that mobilizes notions of femininity; locates them in the private, and imposes an ideology of domesticity through which females are socialized to believe and accept that the narrow, male-privileging spaces called "home" are the most appropriate spaces for them to spend all their lives in, breeding and working for "him" and "his family." This claim is so powerful that millions of women continue to believe it, even when they have been able to leave the home and acquire an education and professional skills that they could use to become autonomous. Still, they return to that space where they become "real" women in backward patriarchal terms; terms which they sometimes choose to define themselves through but which do not have to become the markers of all women, especially in the public which is a common space that belongs to all women and all citizens.

I think that one cannot consider the issue of male intrusion into women's political spaces without also considering that this demand is always made with the conscious desire to undertake surveillance on what women are thinking, saying and doing. I know that some of my sisters will say I cannot generalize because there are "nice" men who name themselves "feminist" and who are interested in securing the rights of women against patriarchal dominance. At one level, that may be true. There are a few men who are experiencing a new political consciousness through association with women's struggles for freedom and autonomy. But in my book, such men need to get themselves into a political movement which will mobilize more men to change themselves, especially in relation to masculinity and the hegemony that patriarchal ideology grants all men. In that way they will be better able to support women's demands and rights for freedoms. Because while "nice" men do support women and "allow" their wives and partners to do activist work, they also influence the politics of women when they enter women's spaces and interact with the ideas and activism of women within the same framework.

Women must be able to formulate and express their own ideas as individual women and as a constituency that is affected by patriarchal laws and practices in uniquely gendered ways—an experience which no man is open to and cannot experience for as long as patriarchy defines gendered relationships to power and privilege in their present form. And when men are in women's spaces, women tend to react to their presence in intellectual and sexual ways. Men tend to intimidate most women; even the wimpiest male has an impact on the confidence of some women, and that is a cost we should not have to incur in our own spaces.

Men also tend to take over discourses and to steer them in particular directions, often adopting a defensive attitude towards women's radical consciousness and consequently damping down women's sense of entitlement to their rights. The presence of men in any women's space has fundamental consequences for women's sense of themselves and their visions of the future. In my opinion, women cannot afford to be nice about such a threat. In fact, it is through their intrusion into women's spaces that men have been able to redirect the politics of the Women's Movement in many countries—shifting its character from a radical political platform where women experience themselves as autonomous and entitled persons, into a welfarist movement that is focused on the old sexist notions of reproduction and cultural custodianship in behalf of the very males who claim that they are being excluded.

Surveillance of women's political consciousness is a key objective of the patriarchal backlash, which manifests itself through male demands for inclusion into women's spaces. One need only look at all those organisations that have men within them to see how collusive and compromised such become within a short space of time. Often these men take over the most critical elements within the organization, often the control over finances and the publications section, imposing a male voice over the views and knowledge that women bring to the public. We know that voice and the visibilisation of women's experiences are foundation stones of the Women's Movement saying what we know and want is so very central to our agenda and our freedom. Why therefore are some women's organisations handing over their newsletters and documentation sections to males who gladly 'speak on their behalf'. Have we not demanded the right to speak for ourselves and used this facility to debunk the myths and stereotypes that still characterize the male media. Yet some women see no political threat with having a male, one of those 'nice' ones, occupying the status of knowledge processor in their organisations.

Within the language of compromise, such organisations are conforming to 'gender mainstreaming', which basically re-enforces the welfarist tendencies within women's activism through the de-politicization of women's agency in the public.

Gender becomes an empty notion, without any relationship to power and contestation, and women are told to consider the interests of boys and men in the same breath as they attempt to bridge the yawning gap between themselves and males across time and space. The de-politicization of women's struggles lies at the heart of the demand to include males in women's political spaces, because it is clear to males (as well as to conservative females, most of whom predominate in the Women's Movement across the globe) that by occupying a political space in the public which women have crafted and marked as their own, women become radical and develop a consciousness of themselves and their rights. This is a threat to the privilege and interests of males in all patriarchal societies.

For me, this is the core of the matter. When women occupy public spaces as persons who understand that for millennia they have been denied their inalienable rights as human beings, they begin to demand the restitution of those rights through the creation of structures within which they situate financial, technical and intellectual resources.

When women become articulate about who they are sexually and cast off the old patriarchal myths about what a woman can be and what she is not allowed to become, women become powerful and acquire the ability to say no to violence; no to unpaid labor; no to exploitation and discrimination in the name of cultural preservation. Women become persons who relate to the state in new and challenging ways, no longer waiting for men in the state to dole out a few "favors" in the name of benevolent dictatorship. Such women become autonomous and their Movement becomes a force for the transformation of oppressive relations of power in both the public and the private spheres. Such women are a danger to all males, regardless of how some men define themselves. Therefore, women's spaces as politicized spaces must be occupied under the guise of "inclusion" and those women who resist such surveillance are accused of being man-haters and of acting in "exclusionary" ways the same old story we have heard for centuries. When women first demanded the right to be free, to have access to education (not even equal access, just access to the collective knowledge of their respective societies), they were accused of hating men. Those of us who have refused to be ritualized and owned by men through heterosexual marriage, and who have sometimes gone on to love other women, are marked as "heretics" and man-haters. The tarring of women with the brush of heterosexist vitriol is well known and most women fear it because it is a harsh and ruthless brush that marks a woman for the rest of her life as Other and Dangerous.

But we have learnt along the long road of our struggle for freedom, that compromising only takes us back even further than where we started. So we must hold on to our spaces because they are the only living spaces that we have and can own as women in these deeply woman-hating, patriarchal societies we continue to live in at the present time.

If men want to engage in gendered politics, let them set up their own structures and create a new political discourse on democracy and equality with those who live in their societies. As politically conscious women well know, men have a lot of work to do on themselves. While a helping hand is always useful, the old saying that charity begins at home applies more so today to men than ever before. Men must clean out their patriarchal household as men, first, and get themselves a new identity one that does not depend on owning women; on buying and selling women; on raping, forcibly occupying, and pillaging the bodies of women or on plundering women's minds so that they can prove to each other that they are real men. Men need to develop a political ideology that does not require that men exclude women from the institutions that we too have built and which belong to us as much as they belong to all who live in our societies. That is where I stand as a radical African feminist on the sacred spaces we have carved out, often with our very lives, and I am not prepared to share them with any man, as long as males continue to be privileged by patriarchy.

Originally published with Isis International, a feminist advocacy organization engaged in research and analysis of the issues affecting women globally. Republished with permission. www.isiswomen. org

CHAPTER 26

GROUND ZERO: THE CLASH OF GENDER IDENTITY PROTECTIONS AND WOMEN'S SPACE

Cathy Brennan

OVER THE LAST two decades, Gay, Lesbian, Bisexual and Transgender (GLBT) organizations have worked to enact legislation to ban discrimination in employment, housing and public accommodations based on sexual orientation and gender identity. This is, in general, a laudable goal. Sexual orientation or gender identity generally has no bearing on whether someone would make a good employee or a good tenant. The only relevant characteristic to an employment decision is whether an applicant or employee has the skills necessary to perform the job, while the hallmark of a good tenant is whether she can pay the rent and abide by the reasonable terms of use of the property. But even the best of intentions are often fraught with disappointment, and in 2016, we find ourselves at a crossroads, as the movement for rights based on gender identity has slowly obliterated the rights of Women and Girls (hereafter referred to also as "females"). The legislation for which organizations advocate has a fatal defect that has resulted in the undoing of Women's space. This fatal defect has also, unfortunately, spilled over into other areas of public policy where Women and Girls have a heightened interest in preserving female-only space, such as K-12 schools, prisons, and homeless shelters.

THE SOURCE OF THE PROBLEM

Some twenty states have enacted laws to ban discrimination in employment based on sexual orientation and gender identity, while still others have also banned such discrimination in housing and public accommodations. Virtually every state that has banned discrimination based on "gender identity" has adopted a definition of "gender identity" that is entirely subjective. The most common definition states that "gender identity" *is "having or being perceived as having a gender identity, self-image, appearance, behavior or expression whether or not that gender identity, self-image, appearance, behavior or expression is different from that traditionally associated with the sex assigned to that person at birth."[1]*

It is a basic rule of statutory construction that language of the statute must serve as the starting point to understand what the statute means.[2] With that basic rule in mind, it is worthwhile to parse this definition, because when we do so, we recognize that this definition is loaded with assumptions about what it means to be male or female (i.e., the sex assigned to the person at birth). Indeed, this definition is only understood in a culture in which sex stereotypes exist, and is only understood to the extent one is willing to believe stereotypes about Women and Girls. In order to understand it, we need to look beyond the statutory text to determine what, in fact, are those self-images, appearances, behaviors or expressions that are not "traditionally" associated with being male or female. This is unfortunate, as in construing what a statute means, courts and others apply the statute generally and do not go beyond the statutory text into cultural battles as to what might be applicable. Thus, we are left with a mostly useless definition that is open to all sorts of mischief, as we will see herein.[3]

Further, and more importantly, this definition of "gender identity" does not require any objective proof. Rather, it merely requires the person seeking protection on the basis of "gender identity" to assert that he or she identifies as the sex opposite his or her sex at birth. So what's the problem with that, you might ask? Here is where the tension arises. Virtually every state currently bans discrimination based on sex. Almost all of those states have, however, exceptions to the ban on sex discrimination for certain spaces deemed private due to the nudity of the people using the space (such as locker rooms or public showers). For example, current New York law provides that "(n)othing in (the Human Rights Law) shall be construed to prevent the barring of any person, because of the *sex* of such person, from places of public accommodation, resort or amusement if the (D)ivision grants an exemption based on bona fide considerations of public policy; nor shall (the Human Rights Law) apply to the rental of rooms in a housing accommodation which restricts such rental to individuals of one sex."[4]

This provision permits operators of a Women-only gym, locker room, bathroom, domestic violence shelter, rape crisis shelter, homeless shelter, and other similar spaces to seek an exemption from the state of New York to bar males from accessing their space. Under the legislation promoted by organizations, a male asserting a "female" gender identity must be permitted to use the restroom or bathhouse of his chosen "gender identity" – without regard to any action taken on the part of that individual to change his physiology to "become female" (i.e., sex reassignment surgery.) To date, Women and Girls who object to sharing intimate, private space with males who "identify as female" have been labeled as "hateful" and "bigoted."[5]

Given the epidemic of violence women and girls experience at the hands of males, objections to overbroad public policy with regard to gender identity protections is more than reasonable and is worth, at the very least, a full, robust and fair public discussion.[6] According to the National Crime Victimization Survey, which includes crimes that were *not* reported to the police, 232,960 Women in the US were raped or sexually assaulted in 2006 more than 600 women every day.[7] Indeed, and as discussed further herein, there has been at least one reported case of a "transwoman" sexually assaulting women after accessing Women-only space on the basis of this overbroad definition of gender identity.[8] One Woman being victimized due to overbroad gender identity protections is one too many. To assert any moral high ground in their efforts to ban discrimination based on gender identity, organizations have to stop pretending that Women and Girls are bigots for asserting concerns about privacy and physical safety.

GENDER IDENTITY ON STEROIDS: SCHOOLS

Arguably the most unfortunate result of the movement to enact gender identity protections has been the undermining of opportunities for Girls. The federal government, under the administration of Democratic President Barack Obama, has adopted an interpretation of Title IX that turns this groundbreaking statute on its head.[9] Enacted in 1972 to ensure equal opportunity for Girls, Title IX provides that "(n)o person in the United States shall, on the basis of sex, be excluded from participation in, be denied the benefits of, or be subjected to discrimination under any education program or activity receiving Federal financial assistance."[10] Transgender activists have lobbied for years for federal regulators to expand the prohibition against "sex" discrimination to include "gender identity," thus effectively eviscerating the existence of sex difference that prompted the need for Title IX in the first instance. The US Department of Education has actively worked to enforce this interpretation of Title IX, and has signed onto litigation to ensure that female students have the right to use the male restroom.[11] This, of course, places Girls in the unenviable position of being designated as "bigots" for objecting to males usurping their time, opportunity and space. Fortunately, these Girls have not been deterred by these spurious claims and have worked to preserve Girl-only space. We have seen this in Florence, Colorado, where girls objected to the presence of a male, Jessica Valentine, in spaces designated for Girls.[12] We have seen this in Missouri, where Lila Perry, who has posted photos of himself on social media making a sign for cunnilingus, decided he was female and thus entitled to use the female locker room at Hillsboro High School.[13] Tensions between a male identifying as a Girl and Girls resulted in a physical altercation at Hercules High School in

West Contra Costa, California. The fight, which involved three female students and 16-year-old transgender student Jewelyes Guitierrez, led to criminal charges against Guitierrez.[14]

To date, the movement has not recognized that rather than behaving in a "bigoted" manner, these Girls are reacting to an overreaching agenda that insists that their desire for space and privacy is irrelevant to the right of a male to have his stereotypical feelings of "being a Woman" affirmed through legal processes. The issue of males in female spaces in schools has resulted in counter-legislative efforts, such as a bill in Tennessee to require students to use restrooms and locker rooms on the basis of sex, not gender identity.[15] In a remarkable show of its agenda to undermine Title IX, White House spokesman Josh Earnest denounced the Tennessee bill and affirmed that "the administration is firmly committed to promoting and defending equal rights for all Americans, including LGBT Americans. Specific laws like this that seek to target and marginalize one small segment of the population is "nothing less than mean-spirited."[16] It is particularly disturbing that the privacy rights and concerns of school-aged Girls are recharacterized as "mean-spirited" by the federal government, as there is quite literally no bigger bully than the federal government when it comes to advancing this overbroad agenda.

FORGETTING THE MOST MARGINALIZED: WOMEN AND GIRLS IN PRISON AND SHELTER

Paramount in the public discourse around gender identity is protecting the transgender individual. Great empathy and compassion is demanded for this person and their struggle with having their gender identity recognized and validated through access to female space. Not once in this public discourse has an organization ever recognized that Women and Girls are equally entitled to the dignity of having *their* rights protected. This conflict between sex and gender identity is of greatest consequence for women and girls when they are required to participate in a female-only space that has, through legislative magic, become co-ed. As noted above, Girls in K-12 facilities are required to attend school and cannot easily "opt out" of participation in their education. Even direr is the situation for Women and Girls in prison or seeking shelter due to homelessness or domestic violence. As a result of gender identity policies, these Women and Girls have been forced to cohabitate with males, resulting in sexual assault.

For example, in a stunning defeat for Women, transgender inmates jailed in Rio de Janeiro's penitentiaries may choose incarceration in prisons for either men or Women.[17] Such male prisoners may do this regardless of whether or not they have been convicted of a crime of violence or sexual violence against Women. Rio adopted this policy in contravention of international human rights conventions that prohibit female inmates from being subjected to males while in custody.[18] GLBT organizations clearly do not believe that **incarcerated Women also deserve to be treated humanely while serving their sentences, as humane treatment would include space away from males, so long as said males identify as Women.**

In Scotland, Paris Green, age twenty-two and born Peter Laing, lured Robert Shankland back to his flat before brutally murdering him with Kevin McDonagh, twenty-three, and Dean Smith, twenty. He was sentenced to serve his eighteen-year sentence in a Women's prison because he identified as a Woman. In addition to allowing people like Green/Laing to be housed with Women, the Scottish Prison Service allows transsexual and transgender prisoner "additional property" such as ladies' dresses and underwear. Such men also may have access to makeup and wigs. According to public policy in Scotland, male prisoners who consider themselves Women can request a move to a female prison, regardless of whether they have had surgical procedures, and can also decide whether rubdowns or strip searches are carried out by male or female prison officers. In an ironic statement, Scottish Prison Service (SPS) chief executive Colin McConnell states that he believes in treating everyone with dignity and respect and that such treatment should be an aspiration for all in the prison service. This apparently applies to incarcerated men only, as the incarcerated Women housed with them, as well as the female correctional staff, seem to have no say as to whether they want to be housed with males or forced to strip search them. The SPS eventually relocated Green out of a Women's prison after officials determined that he had sex with female inmates (thus ironically highlighting the very concern with coed prisons raised by Women's rights advocates). [20]

Similarly, Yasir Naqvi, the Correctional Services Minister of Ontario, Canada, announced in 2015 that men will be housed in women's prisons if such men "identify as women." In announcing the policy, Naqvi showed no concern about how this policy negatively impacts Women and how men have sexually assaulted women in Women's shelters and prisons.[278]

The United States is also not immune to adopting Women-hating policies with regard to incarcerated Women. In Tennessee, Shelby Horton and Merinda Waller are two female inmates who filed a lawsuit against Corrections Corporation of America and other defendants for their decision to house a male inmate, Carla Brenner, with them. The case was apparently settled.[21]

Similarly, four female prison inmates sued the City and County of Philadelphia in 2011 after each was forced to share a jail cell with an accused pimp and armed robber who clearly had male genitalia. The man, Jovanie Saldana, who is transgender, spent fourteen months at Riverside, the city's jail for Women, until accusing a guard of sexual assault. No charges were filed against the guard. The Philadelphia prison system's policy allows transgender inmates who have undergone "gender" reassignment to be placed in a facility appropriate for the new gender. The policy is less clear about how to handle inmates before gender reassignment. Inmates should be placed in accordance with their gender as determined by their external genitalia, it states, but provides that the determination should take into account the recommendations of a qualified medical staff person. The inmates – Yazmin Gonzales, Katiria Chamorro, Maria Cachola, and recently released Jabrina T. Barnett – claim Saldana touched or groped them, subjected them to daily sexual harassment, and leered at them as they bathed or used the toilet. The city and county settled the lawsuit.[23]

Along these same lines, San Francisco County Jail Sheriff Ross Mirkarimi completely disregarded the rights of incarcerated Women by adopting a policy that allows men who identify as Women to be housed with Women. Mirkarimi's plan allows pre-operative transgender inmates permanently into new populations. "Some will still have their penis," Mirkarimi said, to make it clear what the new classification will immediately mean.[24]

The push to allow male inmates to be house with females runs counter to the US government's interest in protecting Women and Girls from assault while incarcerated. For example, the Department of Justice settled a lawsuit to protect prisoners at the Julia Tutwiler Prison for Women in Wetumpka, Alabama, from sexual victimization by correctional officers. The settlement resolved the Justice Department's findings of sexual abuse and sexual harassment at Tutwiler. In January 2014, the Justice Department issued a findings letter concluding that Tutwiler subjects its Women prisoners to a pattern and practice of sexual abuse in violation of the Eighth Amendment of the US Constitution. The findings identified several systemic failures that led to the pattern of abuse, including ineffective reporting and investigations, and no grievance policy.

The agreement comprehensively addressed the causes of the abuses uncovered by the department's investigation. It drew upon sex-responsive, trauma-informed principles to build on the Prison Rape Elimination Act National Standards, designed to prevent, detect, and respond to custodial sexual abuse and sexual harassment throughout our nation's prisons and jails. The agreement tailored the more generalized national standards to target the specific problems revealed at Tutwiler and to meaningfully address the harm to Tutwiler's Women prisoners. The agreement required Tutwiler to protect Women from sexual abuse and sexual harassment by ensuring sufficient staff to safely operate Tutwiler and supervise prisoners, supplemented by a state-of-the-art camera system. The agreement also provided safeguards to prevent staff from unnecessarily viewing prisoners who are naked or performing bodily functions.[25] One might wonder how the US Government's recognition of the privacy rights of female inmates squares with its aggressive agenda to ignore those very same privacy rights when males decide to "identify as" females.

Similar concerns arise when considering women in shelter. The most notorious case of a "transwoman" preying on Women in shelter is Christopher "Jessica" Hambrook, who demanded and received access to two Women's shelters in Toronto, Ontario. Hambrook was able to access the shelters due to Toby's Law, which bans discrimination based on gender identity and gender expression in Ontario.[26] The Ontario Human Rights Commission, which administers the Human Rights Code and is a strong supporter of overbroad gender identity legislation, defines "gender identity" as "*those characteristics that are linked to an individual's intrinsic sense of self that is based on attributes reflected in the person's psychological, behavioural and/or cognitive state. Gender identity may also refer to one's intrinsic sense of manhood or Womanhood. It is fundamentally different from, and not determinative of, sexual orientation.*"[27] *Like virtually every definition of "gender identity" used in law or regulation,* there is no requirement in this definition that "gender identity" requires a medical diagnosis, or even medical intervention.

Barbara Hall, the head of the Ontario Human Rights Commission, is a strong champion of this law, lambasting anyone who raises questions about the law's open-ended nature as hateful. She sees sex-segregated spaces as antiquated and harmful. In a letter to the *Toronto Star* in January 2014, she wrote:

We also see continued calls to segregate transgender people into separate bathroom and changing spaces, for the good of the larger majority. This is a practice based on fear and stereotypes, and is exactly opposite the vision of Ontario's Human Rights Code, which is to build an Ontario based on inclusion, where everyone feels a part of and is able to contribute to the community.[28]

It is very clear, then, that the shelters to which Hambrook sought access would have been subjected to a discrimination complaint had they denied him access, or even if they had asked him for medical proof of his gender identity.

In February 2012, a Woman living at the shelter with Hambrook went to bed wearing tights, a bathing suit and a lightweight shirt in an attempt to cover herself. She went to such extreme measures because she understood that she was in a vulnerable position having to share intimate space with a male. Her efforts did not deter Hambrook, and she awoke to find

Hambrook assaulting her. According to court documents, "(h)er tights had been pulled down past her bottom and her bathing suit had been pulled to the side. She yelled at the accused, demanding to know what he was doing. He simply covered his face with his hands, said 'Oops!' and started giggling." In a second incident, Hambrook stalked a deaf and homeless Woman living in the shelter. Her grabbed her hand and forcibly placed it on his crotch area while his penis was erect.

In prosecuting Hambrook for sexual assault, Crown attorney Danielle Carbonneau told the court of the devastating consequences of these attacks. "Mr. Hambrook's conduct inflicted severe psychological damage on both victims," she said. "(They) sought refuge at Toronto Women's shelters at difficult times in their lives. They thought that they would be safe there, but instead, they were further victimized by the accused." [29]

When Hambrook's crimes and transgender status were revealed, transgender activists sought desperately to distance Hambrook from "actual" transgender people.[30] However, the Ontario law does not require a psychiatric diagnosis to be transgender. To be transgender, all a man has to do is say "I am a Woman." Hambrook, under Toby's Law, is transgender – because he said he was. In other words, Hambrook did not "falsely" claim to be transgender; he fit the very definition of it.

SIGNS OF REVOLT

It is not just the Girls at Florence High School, Hillsboro High School and Hercules High School that object to this overbroad agenda that allows any male who says he is female to access space designated for Women and Girls. GLBT organizations have recently suffered a string of electoral and legislative battles specifically over this issue. In Houston, voters rejected the Houston Equal Rights Ordinance by almost 61%, based solely on the gender identity provisions that would have allowed males to access spaces for females.[31] In 2016, North Carolina[32] and Mississippi[33] have both passed laws motivated in part by discomfort with males accessing space designated for females. Unfortunately, these efforts have also derailed laws granting the right to be free from discrimination based on sexual orientation, which is certainly not a goal of lesbian feminist advocacy. Over the next few years, as the public at large become aware of just how overbroad this legislation is, and as supporters of gay and lesbian people begin to understand how gender identity undermines the rights of Women and Girls, it is foreseeable that these kinds of clumsy legislative responses will diminish.

A Potential Solution

Where harm is foreseeable, harm is avoidable. The current regulatory scheme with regard to gender identity is blatantly unfair to Women and Girls, and puts Women and Girls in the position of having to pretend a male person is a Women or Girl if he "says so." This is dangerous because, despite the hue and cry of organizations, transwomen are actually male. Indeed, gender identity regulatory schemes conflict with existing law in many states that recognize that people have a right to privacy on the basis of sex, and we have yet to fully see the extent to which the rights of Women and Girls have been decimated by this wrong-headed legislation. For example, in *State Div. of Human Rights ex rel. Johnson v Oneida County Sheriff's Dep't*, the court held that a female deputy sheriff was not improperly passed over for appointment to the position of sergeant, where uncontroverted testimony affirmed that the open position required the applicant to conduct daily announced and unannounced inspections of cellblock areas to monitor security and sanitation conditions and, as inmates' toilet and shower facilities were in open view to personnel walking by cells, it would violate the privacy rights of male inmates to have Women monitoring their activities.[34]

To avoid the consequences of the "subjective" and overbroad definition of "gender identity," compromise is in order. One potential, but ultimately flawed, compromise, enacted in a few states, adds language to the definition that "gender identity" cannot be asserted for an "improper purpose." For example, Massachusetts defines "gender identity" as "a person's gender-related identity, appearance or behavior, whether or not that gender-related identity, appearance or behavior is different from that traditionally associated with the person's physiology or assigned sex at birth. Gender-related identity may be shown by providing evidence including, but not limited to, medical history, care or treatment of the gender-related identity, consistent and uniform assertion of the gender-related identity or any other evidence that the gender-related identity is sincerely held, as part of a person's core identity; provided however, gender-related identity shall not be asserted for any improper purpose."[35]

To date, no case law has described what would be an "improper purpose" for asserting a gender-related identity. Clearly, it cannot be an "improper purpose" for a male to assert a "female" gender-related identity in order to access space designated for biological females, because such legislation is, in fact, drafted specifically to allow males to access said spaces. Thus, the "improper purpose" language serves as no protection at all.

Another potential solution to the overbreadth of gender identity legislation is to narrow the category of people who could assert gender identity as a basis for discrimination. For example, the following definition of gender identity – "a person's identification with the sex opposite her or his physiology or assigned sex at birth, which can be shown by providing evidence including, but not limited to, medical history, care or treatment of a transsexual medical condition, gender dysphoria, or related condition, as deemed medically necessary by the American Medical Association or American Psychiatric Association" – protects the legal classification of sex, while simultaneously providing a cause of action for discriminatory practices on the basis of a persistent and documented "gender identity," which is only defined by objective medical treatment. Having some form of objectivity is better than the existing situation that leaves the determination of whether a person can claim membership in the protected class to a person's feelings. However, this compromise, standing alone, is insufficient to preserve the rights of Women and Girls. In order to fully protect the rights of Women and Girls, gender identity legislation must clarify that it is not intended to undermine existing protections for Women and Girls based on spaces designated on the basis of sex. This is the only way that female-only spaces are preserved for Women and Girls.

CONCLUSION

Discrimination based on gender identity, like discrimination based on sex stereotypes, is wrong and has no basis in decision-making with regard to employment or housing. However, with regard to Women-only spaces, Women and Girls have legitimate privacy and safety concerns that deserve a fair airing in the public arena. GLBT organizations, having run into difficulty in Houston and beyond, would do well to tailor anti-discrimination protections for transgender and transsexual people so that they do not run rough-shod over the rights of Women and Girls. Unfortunately, it is unlikely that organizations will change course now, as they have been remarkably successful in convincing men and women that females do not deserve space free from males, despite the fact that transwomen are, in fact, male.

---

[1] *Vancouver Rape Relief Society v. Nixon et al.* 2003 BCSC 1936. Accessed online July 30, 2016: https://www.thecourt.ca/2007/02/application-denied-kimberly-nixon

[2] Statement posted on the Breitenbush Hot Springs website under Community News, "The Ender of Assigned Gender" by Peter Moore. Accessed July 30, 2016, http://www.breitenbush.com/community/community-news/15-news-gender.html

[3] See, e.g., Rev. Code. Wash. 49.60.040(26).

4 See, generally, William N. Eskridge, Jr., Philip P. Frickey, and Elizabeth Garrett, *Cases And Materials On Legislation: Statutes And The Creation Of Public Policy*,3rd. ed., West Group, 2001.

5 *We also note that this definition violates the* Convention on the Elimination of all Forms of Discrimination Against Women (CEDAW), which requires that state parties "must take all appropriate measures to modify the social and cultural patterns of conduct of men and women, with a view to achieving the elimination of prejudices and customary and all other practices which are based on the idea of the inferiority or the superiority of either of the sexes or on stereotyped roles for men and women." CEDAW, Article 5(a). We note that the United States stands with such regressive countries as Iran and Sudan in not ratifying CEDAW. See, e.g., Lisa Baldez, "U.S. drops the ball on Women's rights," CNN (March 8, 2013), available at http://www.cnn.com/2013/03/08/opinion/baldez-womens-equality-treaty/. It is indeed odd that a so-called civil rights statute would, in fact, have the effect of degrading the rights of women and girls.

6 NY CLS Exec § 296(2)(b).

7 See, for example, the case of Yvette Cormier, a Michigan Woman who was banned from a Planet Fitness in Midland, Michigan because she objected to the presence of a man who identified as a Woman in the Women's locker room. She sued Planet Fitness for invasion of privacy, sexual harassment under state law banning sex discrimination in public accommodations, retaliation for invoking her rights under state law banning sex discrimination, breach of contract and intentional infliction of emotional distress. See G. Vicci, "Planet Fitness Drops Members After Gender Identity Complaint," WNEM (March 6, 2015), available at https://genderidentitywatch.files.wordpress.com/2015/03/planet-fitness-drops-member-after-gender-identity-complaint-wnem-tv-5.pdf. Her lawsuit was dismissed in January 2016. See A. Keller, "Court dismisses suit against Planet Fitness transgender locker room policy," Las Vegas Review Journal (January 12, 2016), available at http://www.reviewjournal.com/trending/the-feed/court-dismisses-suit-against-planet-fitness-transgender-locker-room-policy.

8 See, e.g., UN Women, Facts and Figures: Ending Violence against Women (undated), available at http://www.unWomen.org/en/what-we-do/ending-violence-against-Women/facts-and-figures.

[9] Bureau of Justice Statistics (table 2, page 15), *"Criminal Victimization in the United States," 2006 Statistical Tables*.

[10] See Sam Pazzano, "A sex predator's sick deception," *Toronto Sun* (February 15, 2014), available at https://maleviolence.files.wordpress.com/2014/02/a-sex-predators-sick-deception-_-toronto-gta-_-news-_-toronto-sun.pdf.

[11] E. Margolin, "Transgender students protected under Title IX, DOE says," MSNBC (April 30, 2014), available at http://www.msnbc.com/msnbc/transgender-students-protected-under-title-ix.

[12] 20 USCS § 1681(a).

[13] *G.G. v. Gloucester County School Board*, 4:15-cv-00054-RGD-TEM, (E.D. Va. June 11, 2015), on appeal to the Fourth Circuit; M. Balingit, "Va. transgender student's case could have national implications," *Washington Post* (January 27, 2016), available at https://www.washingtonpost.com/local/education/va-transgender-students-case-could-have-national-implications/2016/01/27/1775ce0c-c45b-11e5-9693-933a4d31bcc8_story.html.

[14] A. Torres, "Updating the Story on the Transgender Student in Colorado," *National Review* (October 16, 2013), available at http://www.nationalreview.com/corner/361452/updating-story-transgender-student-colorado-alec-torres.

[15] E. Grinberg, "Bathroom access for transgender teen divides Missouri town," CNN (September 5, 2015), available at http://www.cnn.com/2015/09/03/living/missouri-transgender-teen-feat/.

[16] P. Molloy, "Trans Teen Charged With Battery Following Schoolyard Altercation," *The Advocate* (January 9, 2014), available at http://www.advocate.com/politics/transgender/2014/01/09/transteen-charged-battery-following-schoolyard-altercation.

[17] Tennessee House Bill 2414, available at http://openstates.org/tn/bills/109/HB2414/.

[18] C. Johnson, "White House: Tennessee anti-trans bathroom bill 'mean-spirited'" *Washington Blade* (April 12, 2016), available at https://www.washingtonblade.com/2016/04/12/white-house-tennessee-anti-trans-bathroom-bill-mean-spirited/.

[19] "Transgender prisoners in Rio given choice between male or female prison," ABC News Online (May 30, 2015), available at http://www.abc.net.au/news/2015-05-31/rio-to-allow-transgender-inmates-to-choose-male-or-female-prison/6509764.

[20] **United Nations** Standard Minimum Rules for the Treatment of Prisoners (December 17, 2015), available at **https://genderidentitywatch.files.wordpress.com/2014/10/standard-minimum-rules-for-the-treatment-of-prisoners.pdf**.

[21] M. Alexander, "Scottish Prison Service providing 'cushy' life for sex-swap killer Paris Green, family claim," *The Courier* (March 17, 2014), available at https://genderidentitywatch.files.wordpress.com/2014/03/scottish-prison-service-providing-e28098cushy_-life-for-sex-swap-killer-paris-green-family-claim-fife-local-news-the-courier.pdf.

[22] M. Alexander, "Scottish Prison Service providing 'cushy' life for sex-swap killer Paris Green, family claim," The Courier (March 17, 2014), available at https://genderidentitywatch.files.wordpress.com/2014/03/scottish-prison-service-providing-e28098cushy_-life-for-sex-swap-killer-paris-green-family-claim-fife-local-news-the-courier.pdf.

[23] "Gender identity to guide housing of Ontario's transgender inmates," *The Canadian Press,* January 26, 2015.

[24] *Horton et al v. Corrections Corporation of America et al*, Case #3:13-cv-00437, May 9, 2013.

[25] S. Wood, "Women file suit, claim they were jailed with a man," *Philadelphia Inquirer,* November 16, 2011, available at https://genderidentitywatch.files.wordpress.com/2014/08/Women-file-suit-claim-they-were-jailed-with-a-man-philly.pdf.

[26] J.O. Lamb, "Jail to house transgender inmates with preferred gender," *San Francisco Examiner,* September 10, 2015, available at http://www.sfexaminer.com/jail-to-house-transgender-inmates-with-preferred-gender/.

[27] Press Release, US Department of Justice, "Department Reaches Landmark Settlement with Alabama to Protect Prisoners at Julia Tutwiler Prison for Women from Harm Due to Staff

Sexual Abuse and Sexual Harassment," (May 28, 2015), available at https://genderidentitywatch. files.wordpress.com/2015/05/justice-department-reaches-landmark-settlement-with-alabama-to-protect-prisoners-at-julia-tutwiler-prison-for-Women-from-harm-due-to-staff-sexual-abuse-and-sexual-harassment-_-opa-_-depa.pdf.

28 Bill 33, Toby's Act (Right to be Free from Discrimination and Harassment Because of Gender Identity or Gender Expression), 2012, available at http://www.ontla.on.ca/web/bills/ bills_detail.do?locale=en&BillID=2574.

29 Ontario Human Rights Commission, "Discussion paper: Toward a commission policy on gender identity," available at http://www.ohrc.on.ca/en/ discussion-paper-toward-commission-policy-gender-identity.

30 B. Hall, "Trans myths based on intolerance," *Toronto Star* (January 15, 2014), available at http://www.thestar.com/opinion/letters_to_the_editors/2014/01/15/trans_myths_based_on_ intolerance.html.

31 S. Pazzano, "Predator who claimed to be transgender declared dangerous offender," *Toronto Sun,* February 26, 2014, available at http://www.torontosun.com/2014/02/26/ predator-who-claimed-to-be-transgender-declared-dangerous-offender.

32 See, e.g., C. Milloy, "Conservative Senator Caught in Bald-Faced Lie in attack on Human Rights Bill," (June 6, 2014), available at http://chrismilloy.ca/2014/06/ conservative-senator-caught-in-bald-faced-lie-in-attack-on-human-rights-bill/.

33 See "City of Houston Anti-Discrimination HERO Veto Referendum, Proposition 1," BallotPedia, (November 2015), available at https://ballotpedia.org/ City_of_Houston_Anti-Discrimination_HERO_Veto_Referendum,_Proposition_1_ (November_2015).

34 A. Tan, "North Carolina Governor Signs Order in Response to 'Anti-LGBT' House Bill 2," ABC News (April 12, 2016), available at http://abcnews.go.com/US/ north-carolina-governor-signs-executive-order-addressing-concerns/story?id=38342388.

[35] Gender Identity Watch, "Phil Bryant @PhilBryantMS and Protecting Freedom of Conscience from Government Discrimination Act (USA)," (April 6, 2016), available at https://genderidentitywatch.com/2016/04/06/protecting-freedom-of-conscience-from-government-discrimination-act-usa/.

[36] 119 A.D.2d 1006, 500 N.Y.S.2d 995, 1986 N.Y. App. Div. LEXIS 55945 (N.Y. App. Div. 4th Dep't 1986), aff'd, 70 N.Y.2d 974, 526 N.Y.S.2d 426, 521 N.E.2d 433, 1988 N.Y. LEXIS 79 (N.Y. 1988).

[37] ALM GL ch. 4, § 7, 59th.

CHAPTER 27

FEDERAL COURT'S DENIAL OF OBAMA'S TRANSGENDER BATHROOM DIRECTIVE A WIN FOR EVERYONE

Maya Dillard Smith, JD, MPP

IN RECENT MONTHS national headlines have been captivated with the a new pop culture phrase "transgender bathrooms." But there is no such thing. With rare, but growing exceptions, America has bathrooms for men and bathrooms for women.

Proponents of allowing transgender people to choose to use the bathroom of the gender with which they "identify" argue that separate bathrooms for men and women is somehow a return to the "separate, but equal" facilities that once existed to exclude Blacks. But such an argument is misplaced. When confederate states enacted Jim Crow laws to exclude Blacks from using white only facilities they did so purely on the basis of discrimination.

"Sex segregated" locker rooms and bathrooms, and laws like Title IX in higher education and Title VII in employment that prevent sex discrimination and sex specific laws that protect equality rights for women and girls, on the other hand, recognize natural, biological and physiological differences between the sexes, not to be confused with gender (See American Psychological Association's Definition of Terms: Sex, Gender, Gender Identity, Sexual Orientation[1]). They do not exist for discriminatory purposes against trans people, rather they exist after hard won legislative and litigation fights by women, girls and their allies to secure safe spaces to protect their bodily privacy and safety from men. That is well documented. Still others argue female only restrooms are a tool of male supremacy, while others embrace such female only space as a safe haven for the female body which experiences rape and sexual assault at staggering rates. (Why Do We Have Men's and Women's Bathrooms Anyway?[2])

So why would President Obama and fellow Democrats violate the public input process required by federal law in the issuance of "guidelines"[3]? Especially guidelines to schools across

America, threatening to revoke millions of dollars in federal education funding if schools did not immediately allow students at elementary, middle and high schools and colleges and universities to choose the bathrooms and locker rooms of their choice? Does it give you pause? It should. It's a big shift for parents and kids in public education throughout America with zero public discussion. As The Atlantic noted last July[4]:

"The country is in the midst of what Time magazine…dubbed 'The Transgender Tipping Point,'[5] which helps explain why these controversies are becoming more prevalent. And schools are emerging as the fulcrum for that cultural change—for both its opponents and its pioneers."

The Obama directive is not only a financial coercion and commandeering of the states, it is also a violation of the federal Administrative Procedures Act (APA) rule-making process, which protects the rights of all US citizens to participate in the "notice and comment" period. The notice and comment" rule-making requirement is a prerequisite to issuing new rules even if there is a clever wordplay that calls the directives, "guidelines." Each of the fifty states also has a state-level "notice and comment" requirement for agency rule-making and legislative processes. The Obama Administration's failure to follow the rules, is a concern echoed by many administrative law experts and constitutional scholars like myself as a violation of the public's due process rights.

On August 15th, 2016 the federal district court hearing the lawsuit brought by Georgia and 12 other states in opposition to the "guidance" issued a **nationwide** preliminary injunction[6] blocking the law and effectively dealing a landmark blow to the "steamroll strategy" of LGBT lobbyist and others to circumvent public comment; a strategy that had served to silence the voices of parents, other LGBT perspectives, women and girls, feminist, sexual abuse survivors and any other American who wants to be heard on the issue.

It is an important distinction to note that President Obama's Executive Order has not been banned because of the policy itself (though the court indicated that the policy "likely" contradicts existing regulations that separate bathrooms and locker rooms between the sexes); instead the Court blocked the policy because the Obama administration sidestepped required public input when it issued the order. In fact, the tactic of bypassing public debate that was used by the President and the Department of Education and condemned by the Court, is the very same conduct Democrats and LGBT activists cried foul over when Republicans and their supporters passed North Carolina's HB2 "bathroom bill" in one-day without public input[7]. The North Carolina law was met with such a flurry of media attention that the NBA relocated the 2017 All-Star game from Charlotte to New Orleans, after it had closed doors meetings with the elected officials and transgender advocates, but without ever hearing from the public – fathers, parents, families, or women and children who also attend their games. Unfair, right?

When President Obama did it, transgender advocates were okay, but when the North Carolina Republican dominated legislature did it, those same transgender advocates were furious. In either event, advocates for women and girls, sexual abuse survivors, and any other member of the public who wanted to voice dissension were not provided their due process rights under the U.S. Constitution to #ChimeIn on the bathroom debate and have their voices heard.

Whatever you think the ultimate outcome of this public policy ought to be, the ends do not justify circumventing the legal means. The Constitution requires public input whether a law is promulgated by Democrats or Republicans. No one is above the law, not the political parties, special interest or their lobbyists.

Many ask what about transgender kids at schools. Where should they go to bathroom? It is an important question to ask and answer. So too, is asking and answering the questions of how are other children affected by the rule. How do schools properly administer it within the existing requirement of sex specific laws that protect women and girls? We should also be asking what are the rights of parents and survivors of sexual abuse in this debate?

Undertaking the requisite "notice and comment" will give the nation an opportunity to hear the voices of all interested parties in a necessary public debate that includes the trans community, other LGBT perspectives like lesbians, as well as other impacted groups including school administrators, parents, and guidance counselors.

Everyone must follow the rules, especially in the creation of laws that impact our due process and fundamental rights. Now, anyone who wants to have his or her voice heard can. I encourage you to have your voice heard, on behalf of safe spaces for all, not just some.

Find out how at www.FindingMiddleGround.org

---

[1] Definition of Terms: Sex, Gender, Gender Identity, Sexual Orientation. Excerpt from: The Guidelines for Psychological Practice with Lesbian, Gay, and Bisexual Clients, adopted by the APA Council of Representatives, February 18-20, 2011. The Guidelines are available on the APA website at http://www.apa.org/pi/lgbt/resources/guidelines.aspx

[2] *Why Do We Have Men's and Women's Bathroom Anyway?* Maya Rhodan, May 16, 2016, http://time.com/4337761/history-sex-segregated-bathrooms/

[3] http://www.cnn.com/2016/05/12/politics/transgender-bathrooms-obama-administration/

4 http://www.theatlantic.com/education/archive/2015/07/the-k-12-binary/398060/

5 http://time.com/135480/transgender-tipping-point/

6 http://www.usatoday.com/story/news/politics/2016/08/22/texas-judge-temporarily-blocks-obamas-transgender-directive/89094722/

7 http://www.charlotteobserver.com/news/politics-government/article68401147.html

CHAPTER 28

QUEER THEORY'S SUPPRESSION OF FEMINIST CONSCIOUSNESS

Carol Downer

PUBLIC AND SEMI-PUBLIC women-only spaces may soon cease to exist in this country, due to a combination of governmental policies and pressure from the genderqueer community. These are recent instances of transgender women demanding to be allowed in sex-segregated female-only spaces as women and attacking feminists who dispute their rights to do so.

- The Obama administration is interpreting the word "sex" to mean "gender identity" to enforce federal law prohibiting sex discrimination under Title IX, thereby opening up women's bathrooms and changing facilities to any male who claims the gender identity of a woman.[1]
- Transgender rights groups are pressuring private organizations to de-platform feminists who dispute the assertion that males who gender identify as transgender women are women. [2]
- After several years of protests by transgender women at its entrance due to its policy of allowing no males, including male children over age five, the renowned Michigan Womyn's Music Festival announced in 2015 that their fortieth annual Festival would be the last.[3]

Denying women their own spaces will have a devastating effect on women's individual self-image and group solidarity, from having to live in a society that doesn't respect a female's right to minimal privacy. We live and move about in a patriarchal world, and women sometimes need to gather together without a male presence. Women's inability to have their own spaces where they socialize, strategize, and plan actions will have an impact on developing feminist consciousness, especially mass feminist consciousness.

The Obama administration's bold power play is a breathtaking show of male dominance. I predict, however, that many, if not most, school-age females will accept the presence of males in their bathrooms or locker rooms without complaint; they will probably accept it just as they accept other instances of the exercise of male privilege. They will be robbed of the only space at school free of the male presence.

I was surprised when mainstream feminist national organizations added the plight of transgender persons to their list of issues. I was surprised, but not shocked, because I'm used to women thinking it's our responsibility to champion the underdog, and transgender persons of either biological sex are targets of male violence and discrimination. But, I am shocked and upset at the transgender movement leadership's aggressiveness toward women. It upsets them when females refer to our own sexual and reproductive organs or claim menstruation, pregnancy and birth as female concerns, so they insist that we change language to be "inclusive" because talking about female experience excludes their experience by the fact that a transgender woman is not biologically female. They call it "misogynistic" to refer to women getting abortions, because some females who identify as men get pregnant and either give birth or have abortions.[4] The title of an event called "A Night of Thousand Vaginas" was offensive to transgender women; they protested.[5] A student at Claremont Colleges offered a program at a coffeehouse near the campus showing a video of the reactions of random students who were asked to draw a vulva and their artistic efforts to do so. The coffeehouse cancelled the program with abject apologies to the community for hosting an event that one complainant accused of "equating genitalia with gender [which] is and always will be transphobic." This complainant ignored that the event's stated goal was to "create an open dialogue [sic] educating people about the vulva in order to confront society's stigmas and stereotypes, and make people more comfortable with the many varying images and types of cis and non-cis vulvas."[6] After reading about this online, we attempted to contact the student. Both her website and her Facebook entries have disappeared.

Transgender demands are based on the tenets of queer theory, a type of feminism derived from philosophical theories collectively labeled post-structuralism.[7] Queer theorists are aiming for nothing less than "the destruction and rearticulation of the human."[8] To do this, they take on the destruction or deconstruction of gender norms in order to expand the range of sexuality by including non-heterosexual sexual orientations within the existing gender categories through the range of gender performativity.[9]

In principle, all branches of feminism support such efforts. But, all radical feminists disagree that the gender term "woman" includes transgender women. A close reading of Judith Butler, one of the main queer activists and theorists, reveals that she wants the feminist movement to cease its efforts against the oppression of women on the basis of sex. She thinks feminism should instead just work on queer sexuality, and work with mixed social justice groups on an array of social issues, although it's not clear what form that work should take.[10] I suspect that few feminists or genderqueer people realize that this is queer theory's position. Genderqueer activists generally are concerned about general social justice issues, and some are feminist activists. The genderqueer activists that I know care about reproductive sovereignty and reproductive justice, as well as justice for queer sexuality.

The transgender rights movement is part of the queer movement, and now part of the Lesbian, Gay, Bisexual, Trans, Questioning and Intersex (LGBTQI) coalition. This coalition is largely headed up by gay men and some lesbian and genderqueer veterans of the battles to save a generation of gay men during the early stages of the AIDS epidemic. The coalition then went on to successfully put public support for marriage equality over the top. They are well funded by individuals, corporations, and foundations. They're staffed with politically sophisticated attorneys and media experts, and they have friends in high places.[11, 12] It seems they've persuaded the executive branch to do an end run around the legislative and judicial branches of government, using semantic tactics developed by post-structuralism and a feminist derivative, queer theory.

The LGBTQI leadership is framing their battle for transgender rights using poststructuralist terms, such as inclusivity, privilege, oppression, and subjectivity. These words have quite different meanings when used in civil rights movements. This may explain their success in enlisting support for their attack on women's rights.

TRANSGENDER DEMANDS THREATEN WOMEN-ONLY SPACES, AND WOMEN-ONLY SPACES ARE NECESSARY TO DEVELOP FEMINIST CONSCIOUSNESS.

My experiences in the women's movement developed my feminist consciousness; millions of American women, in the late 1960s and early 1970s, had similar experiences. Our mass women's movement was entirely self-funded and it changed society. We developed a feminist consciousness through holding meetings to talk about our lives together and jointly taking thousands of small and large actions.[13] We created women's spaces: consciousness-raising groups, women's centers, rape crisis centers, and safe houses to escape from batterers.[14] The women with whom I worked in Los Angeles, at the Feminist Women's Health Center (FWHC), developed a special type of consciousness-raising meeting we called Self-Help, during which we did vaginal self-examination together. The self-help women's health movement then formed contraception and abortion referral services, and later led in the abortion provider movement.[15] As we realized our buying power; feminist bookstores, sex toy businesses focused on empowering women to take their pleasure into their own hands, publishing houses, credit unions, and women's music publishing flourished. [16]

The definition of feminist consciousness

Gerda Lerner researched the history of the creation of Western feminist consciousness. Her definition of the process by which feminist consciousness arises makes it clear that *it is the commonality of the experience of being female that is the foundation of a feminist consciousness.*

The recognition of a wrong becomes political when women realize that it is shared by other women. In order to remedy this collective wrong, women organize in political, economic, and social life. The movement they organize inevitably runs into resistance, which forces the women to draw on their own resources and strength. In the process, they develop a sense of sisterhood. This process also leads to new forms of woman's culture, forced upon women by the resistance they encounter, such as sex-segregated or separatist institutions or modes of living. Based on such experiences, women begin to define their own demands and to develop theory. At a certain level, women make the shift from androcentricity, in which they have been schooled, to "woman-centeredness."[17]

Even this commonality based on shared collective wrongs was insufficient to keep mass feminist consciousness from frequently breaking down when groups of women could not incorporate the additional wrongs caused by situations not collectively shared, such as race, age and class, so that the input of poor women and women of color in shaping the group's consciousness was not utilized. Either the poor women and women of color dropped out, or they adopted the policies of the group which were class- and race-based. The intracategorical complexity branch of the relatively new theory of intersectionality provides a methodology that may enable women to recognize their shared wrongs, while incorporating a recognition of the additional wrongs against working-class women and women of color.[18]

What is a feminist?

Many genderqueer individuals are feminists. Being a feminist, however, is not the same as having a feminist consciousness. A feminist is anyone who advocates social, political and all other rights of females to be equal to those of males. A feminist consciousness is much more than being a female. Among other things, it's experiencing the world as a female human being; it's being woman-identified; it's sisterhood; it's accepting and loving one's female body; it's keenly feeling the insults against womankind throughout history; it's anger at seeing the destruction caused to the environment by the domination and greed of men (especially powerful white men); and it's truly understanding why a sister takes the actions she does.

There have been successive waves of mass feminist consciousness that pushed women forward in various cultures under different historical circumstances, only to subside. No historian has offered an explanation of these rises and falls of consciousness that would allow us to predict when, where and how the next wave will come. It seems clear, however, that suffering and degradation do not promote feminist consciousness. As Richard Wright tersely stated, "Oppression oppresses."[19] Therefore, even modest reforms that give women more power over their lives may provide the impetus for women to demand more reforms, and women striving to improve the lives of their children and others has been a typical path to a higher political consciousness. Also, we know that not every woman needs to attain a feminist consciousness for a mass feminist consciousness to come into being. Even at the height of the Second Wave, many women remained alienated from other women, Therefore, feminists can't wait until they represent all women; it's enough that they assert their own rights, while keeping the door open to welcome other women into the struggle.

It took the better part of a decade before the Second Wave grew to the point that I and many, many thousands of women joined it, and perhaps the next wave will also take that long. But, given the internet, globalization and the solid precedents that were set, the next wave may rise quickly.

QUEER THEORY CHALLENGES GENDER NORMS. ARE THESE CHALLENGES WOMAN-IDENTIFIED? WILL CHANGING GENDER NORMS HELP WOMEN OVERTHROW THE DOMINATION OF MEN?

Radical feminists locate the root cause of women's oppression in patriarchal gender relations, as opposed to only legal systems, like liberal feminists do. The schools of feminism of women of color also see that hierarchical gender relations oppress women, even though they want to use intracategorical intersectionality as a methodology to take into account the hierarchical racial and economic relations to understand and fight that oppression.[20] It is my purpose to show that queer theory, as propounded by Judith Butler, is opposed to the strategies of *all* the other feminisms that are based on prioritizing the fight against the exploitation of females' sexual and reproductive difference.

Some will think that my blaming philosophical theory for inspiring LGBTQI attacks on women's rights is a stretch; how could an ivory tower theory have this influence? The gender-queer counterculture trend has caught the imagination of so many people, especially young people. Its democratic rhetoric of "inclusivity" and its appeals to our sympathies for the suf-ferings of transgendered people, and its vision of a freer society where each of us can explore all our potential as humans must be grounded in a theory that does more than critique the categories we use in our political work. The Second Wave movement is criticized because the white, middle-class women in it were not sufficiently inclusive of poor women and women of color. Criticism noted and taken. But beyond reminding feminists of the danger of overgen-eralization and the need to represent women of all ages, races, and economic circumstances, I have found no coherent plan of action in their writings.

In opposing those who disagree with queer theory, reputations have been destroyed, people who don't agree have lost their jobs, been de-platformed, university departments have been re-named, and now millions of young people will be forced to give up their privacy to accom-modate people whose only grounds for needing this accommodation is that they identify with the gender that doesn't match their sex.

Perhaps I'm harsh in my criticism of queer theory and the transgender leadership, but they've succeeded in persuading the Obama administration to back their disruptive plan by twisting the queer theory philosophical words to convey conventional meanings. By so doing, they apparently convinced United States Attorney General Loretta Lynch to equate resistance to admitting transgender women to women's bathrooms with race discrimination. She calls the resistance "exclusion" and "discrimination," like posting signs on restrooms and water fountains and on public accommodations keeping people out based upon "a distinction with-out a difference."[21] Post-structuralists use the term "inclusion" simply to refer to the process of creating a category by lumping together like objects by eliminating unlike objects; it is not inherently good or bad to do so.[22]

Lynch gives little credibility to the fear of those who oppose transgenders' admittance to women's bathrooms as being factually unsupportable. Lynch is apparently unaware of the large, long-term Swedish study of patterns of criminality by transgender women before and after transitioning, which established that these fears do have some basis. This study concluded that when transgender women were compared to the general population, there was no increase or decrease in transgender women criminal behavior.[23] It is well-known that males commit more crimes, including sex-related crimes against women, than females, and they continue to do so at the same rate when they transition. Therefore, opposition to admitting transgender women into women-only spaces is reasonably based and should not be dismissed as bigotry or irrational fear.

In race or class discrimination, any exclusions are based on inconsequential differences, like skin color, and therefore impermissible. In contrast, feminists seek to exclude transgender women from the category of women due to material biological sex differences and the existence of a social construct of gender. The definition of the term "woman" is not the result of a public opinion poll about what gender means; rather, "woman" signifies a hierarchical relationship between the sexes that is enshrined in the law and reinforced daily by male-dominated institutions. Feminists are not excluding transgender women to deprive them of any privileges; in fact, in our society, men have privilege over women. Therefore, the charge of "inclusiveness" is incorrect and to use it that way creates dissent among the ranks of people who abhor racism and sexism.

This very issue of who belongs in the category of "woman" and who does not was discussed at a symposium in 1990, the same year Judith Butler published her book, *Gender Trouble: Feminism and the Subversion of Identity*, in which she writes extensively on this question. Other speakers at the symposium questioned her as to whether she thought the exclusionary process is necessarily good or bad. Her answer seemed equivocal to me. Linda Nicholson summarized Butler's response, interpreting her response as saying that the question about the good or bad of an exclusionary process depends on the question of the politics about the construction of certain subjects (women) and the specific exclusions generated about their construction. [24] Butler's evasive answer is typical of the flimsy intellectual grounds on which US Attorney General Loretta Lynch impugns the integrity of anyone who doesn't accept the new legal definition of "sex" as the gender with which an individual identifies. (In the United States, federal law is based on sex discrimination, not gender discrimination).[25]

When someone seeks to protect their privilege by excluding others for no legitimate reason, it is offensive and oppressive to those excluded. Is it exclusionary for women, who are all females, to refer to their own female genitals? Is that "exclusionary" like the California Club (in Los Angeles) that had a sign on the door that read, "No dogs or women allowed," indicating a male supremacist attitude? When a linguist uses the word "exclusion," they are referring to the process of generalizing among things or objects to create a category and excluding all those things or objects that don't share the common characteristic. In this case, males do not have ovaries, uteri or female genitalia, or female-sexed DNA. Drugs and surgery are cosmetic changes only. Of course, if our society decides that a person is whatever gender they identify as, new categories will have to be created to refer to the material differences between the two sexes and the socially constructed differences ascribed to them.

First. "exclusion" and "inclusion" are used by linguists, at least post-structuralist linguists, to refer to what happens whenever a category is created refer to persons or things that have some characteristic in common. In the case of women, the characteristic in common is a female body. Women have vulvas, vaginas, uteruses, ovaries and female-sexed cells through their bodies. The category doesn't exclude females whose uteruses never developed or which have been surgically removed. The category excludes those with a male body. The use of drugs or surgery to mimic the female body or male body is a recent phenomenon. It remains to be seen how society will categorize those individuals. Other societies have more than two genders, but all are sexually dimorphic, male and female. There are a miniscule number of people whose genitalia don't fit exactly into one or the other sex, and some minority of people who have internal organs or chromosomes that vary enough to interfere with the ability to reproduce. When those of us at the FWHC wrote our book in the late 1970s, we were surprised to learn about these healthy variations (health defined as absence of disease), but since they appeared to have no significant effect on our sex lives or reproduction, we did not include that information in *A New View of a Woman's Body*. We did not equate fertility with health, and still do not. Although our research showed that the human species is sexually dimorphic, we were aghast at the medical profession's abuse of drugs and surgery to conform infants' genitalia to a rigidly bimodal norm. We protested these practices in our original manuscript, but the chapter was eliminated in the much shorter version we were able to publish. As feminists, we wanted to celebrate healthy bodies and we opposed any labeling of such variations as "abnormal" or "unhealthy."

Queer theorists criticize using the gender term "women" to mean just females, because it excludes transgender women. Radical feminists do exclude males, but it is not being "exclusionary" to exclude males who identify as women, because they are not females and thus cannot be discriminated against in this way. The sex term "female" is contiguous with the gender term "woman," because it does include all those humans who possess female genitalia. (Note: a very small percentage of humans are born with ambiguous genitalia, and it would be impermissibly exclusionary to exclude them from either sexual category.) If a transgender woman "identifies" as a woman, this does not transform him into a woman, because no categories based on bodily appearance or characteristics are grounded in self-identification, and, like all definitions, the term "woman" is not personal or private; it is socially constructed. When males use drugs and surgery, cosmetics or clothing to have the appearance of a woman, this reinforces the conclusion that they are *not* women, since they must rely on artificial methods to appear to be the gender they identify with.

Because I am leveling serious differences with queer theory, I've decided to quote a few passages from Judith Butler, whose theoretical work has great influence in Eurocentric societies, and she is a leading gay activist. I am contextualizing some of her remarks to prevent confusion for those who have not read her entire book or are not familiar with some of the controversies that prompted her statements. I am paraphrasing her statement, because she uses words that have a specific philosophical meaning different than the commonly accepted ones, and also she uses indirect language. Since I want readers to judge for themselves what she actually said, I will include the complete statements that I've paraphrased, or refer to the entire chapter in which the quote appears, because sometimes there is no "sound bite" to quote, and it's important to read the entire section of the book.

QUEER THEORY SEES HETEROSEXUAL NORMS AND GENDER NORMS AS MAIN CAUSE OF PEOPLE'S OPPRESSION

After reading *Gender Trouble*, I was unable to find a clear-cut statement of Butler's views. I believe her views are best summarized this way: sex, not just gender, is constructed through language. She criticizes the distinction drawn by previous feminisms between biological sex and socially constructed gender. The category of woman must be understood as a site of potential contest. It is complicated by class, ethnicity, sexuality, and other facets of identity. There is no single cause for women's subordination and no single approach towards dealing with the issue.

My interpretation of Butler's idea of social transformation:

Butler puts forth her thesis of what needs to happen for social transformation.

- *"our fundamental categories"* ("man" and "woman")
- *"become more inclusive"* (transgendered people included in the biological sex category they identify with)
- "[A]*lready established conventions regarding what is human, what is universal, what is the meaning of international politics might be, are not sufficient."* (Second Wave feminists were wrong to see "women" as a universal category.)
- This is referring to criticisms of postcolonial feminists who point out that non-Western societies didn't necessarily have gender norms before being colonized, or if they did, they were very different.

What Butler wrote:

"Already established conventions regarding what is human, what is universal, what the meaning and substance of international politics might be, are not sufficient. For the purposes of a radical democratic transformation, we need to know that our fundamental categories can and must be expanded to become more inclusive and more responsive to the full range of cultural populations."[26]

My interpretation of Butler's take on feminism:

In the next paragraph (see excerpt below), Butler very indirectly but unmistakably reveals what she hopes the feminist movement will stop doing and what she hopes they will start doing instead.

- She vaguely faults Second Wave feminists for being mostly white and pursuing middle-class goals on the one hand, or, on the other hand, claiming to speak for all women.
- She figuratively backs into the full-on demand that feminists should stop making their case on the basis of sexual difference, meaning reproductive sovereignty and liberated heterosexuality, on an equal basis with other claims for social justice. She says the notion of reproductive and sexual sovereignty cannot be defended against the competing claims for social justice on the basis of differences in sexuality, or racism or the assorted claims of cultural studies. (A footnote: cultural studies include ideology, class structures, national formations, ethnicity, sexual orientation, gender, human rights, third-world issues, decoloniality, and urban cultures, according to Wikipedia.)[27]

What Butler wrote:

"I think for many of us it is a sad time for feminism, perhaps even a defeated time. A friend asked me what I would teach in a feminist theory course right now, and I found myself suggesting that feminist theory has no other work than in responding to the places where feminism is under challenge. And by responding to those challenges, I do not mean a defensive shoring up of terms and commitments, a reminding of ourselves of what we already know, but something quite different, something like a submission to the demand for rearticulation, a demand that emerges from crisis. *It makes no sense,*

I would argue, to hold fast to theoretical paradigms and preferred terminologies, or make the case for feminism on the basis of sexual difference, or to defend that notion against the claims of gender, the claims of sexuality, of race, or the umbrella claims of cultural studies." (italics added)[28]

Question posed to Judith Butler at a symposium in 1990:

"Does 'postmodernism' (post-structuralism) threaten the subjectivity of women just when women are attaining subjectivity, and what does the attainment of subjectivity mean for the category of 'woman' and the category of the feminist 'we'?[29] (Note: "Subject" is that which is capable of signifying practice and thus agency and choice. Subjectivity is women having agency or choice.)

What I think Judith Butler said:

In her answer, she again raises the criticism that women of color were excluded incorrectly from the feminist movement. She at no time mentions the exclusion of transgender individuals. She does acknowledge that there is a political necessity for feminists to speak as and for women. However, she believes it is healthy for the category "woman" to be always open to contestation. As far as materiality of sex, she poses the danger that fighting for sexual and reproductive rights may support heterosexual normativity. I read this answer to mean that she acknowledges that women's oppression is based on her sex, and has to be defended accordingly, despite the possibility of reinforcing heterosexual assumptions.

In her introduction to *Feminist Contentions*, Linda Nicholson quotes from Judith's response and gives her interpretation of what she thinks Butler is intending to convey:

"As Butler asks: Through what exclusions has the feminist subject been constructed, and how do those excluded domains return to haunt the 'integrity' and 'unity of the 'we'? While not questioning the political necessity for feminists to speak as and for women, [Butler] argues that if the radical democratic impetus of feminist politics is not to be sacrificed, the category 'woman' must be understood as an open site of potential contest. Taking on asserted claims about 'the materiality of women's bodies' and the 'materiality of sex' as grounds for the meaning of 'woman,' [Butler] again looks at the political effects of the deployment of such phrases. And employing one of the insights developed by Michel Foucault and Monique Wittig, [Butler] notes that one such effect of 'assuming the materiality of sex' is accepting that which sex imposes: 'a duality and uniformity on bodies in order to maintain reproductive sexuality as a compulsory order.' "[30]

QUEER THEORY'S OBJECTION TO CATEGORIZING WOMEN ON THE BASIS OF THEIR ABILITY TO HAVE CHILDREN

In her discussion of arriving at a definition of what is a "woman," Judith Butler specifically rejects the validity and usefulness of characterizing a feminine specificity around women's ability to have children. She points out that doing so will produce factionalism because "all women are not mothers; some cannot be, some are too young or too old to be, some choose not to be, and for some who are mothers, that is not necessarily their rallying point of their politicization as feminists."[31]

The reason that our ability to have children is central to our self-definition goes far beyond whether we actually have children. *It is that that ability, in addition to our female body, especially our vagina, has to do with both individual and collective needs of men.*

It's surprising that a sophisticated philosopher such as Butler, who has devoted her life to critically analyzing the importance of linguistics, fails to appreciate the full implications of her own analysis. She correctly points out that those who are in power use the power to make and define categories to regulate and control classes of people. [32] But she doesn't realize that those of us who organize ourselves to fight against domination must first identify who is in power. We must identify how they're defining us and controlling us and fight them.

Engels and Marx looked at women's reproduction from the individual standpoint of the father needing to establish paternity, but ruling-class males look at this from the standpoint of the state. How women do or do not decide to have children directly impacts military and economic policies. The cheapness of labor, brought on by the Little Ice Age in medieval Europe, launched the biggest round of witch hunts to destroy women's knowledge of how to limit their children (women's secrets).[33] In ancient times, ruling-class men made policies to control women, historically implemented through religious edicts, persecutions and laws. By the eighteenth century, European rulers used vital statistics to develop population policies to encourage or discourage the birth rate to serve the needs of the economy and the military.[34] Demographer

Thomas Malthus wrote "An Essay on the Principle of Population," forecasting a population overgrowth, inspiring the modern population control movement.[35]

In our work at the FWHC in 1970, we were aware that important sections of the ruling class of males were alarmed about the overgrowth of population;[36] so we therefore were poised to open our own clinics when the *Roe v. Wade* decision was announced. Further, we anticipated the loosening of restrictions on open expressions of lesbian and gay lifestyles, and the encouragement of transgenderism, because we were privy to the plans of the dominant view in the upper classes.[37]

QUEER THEORY HAS NO POLITICAL ANALYSIS OTHER THAN POST-STRUCTURAL CRITICISMS OF GENDER NORMS.

This lack of feminist consciousness leads queer theory to pursue individual solutions, such as making changes in your lifestyle, your clothing and even your physical body, to help you to lead what Butler calls a "livable life" and to bring about social change. This may come out of a sense of powerlessness to really change society; certainly there's good reason to despair. Perhaps one of the appeals of post-structuralism and queer theory is that it helps us to understand how we're being manipulated through language, and gives us some tools to fight against that. A feminist consciousness enables us to use our combined strength strategically. Our capacity as women to have children (not whether we can or do become mothers) is for many of us the most wonderful power that we possess—but to a capitalist, patriarchal state, all of us, straight, gay, trans or gender queer, we're just "x" number of wombs, and they control this biological capacity through laws regulating contraception, abortion, and childbirth, and a myriad of policies that shape our choices. The fact that my generation of women "decided" to have many children and that today's generation of women is "deciding" not to have children or have fewer children later demonstrates dramatically how powerful the patriarchal norms are, and how much we have accepted these decisions we make as being "natural."

Butler has dedicated herself to exploring and advocating the "undoing of gender" by individuals who find themselves oppressed by our current definitions of men and women. While I share their anger and support their right to deal with it on an individual level, I do not believe that we will unravel this structure of oppression through individual mini-rebellions.

Post-structuralists plan to achieve abortion on demand. The post-structuralist strategy for American women to achieve abortion on demand consists of first rejecting the discourse about rights that lawyers used to convince the United States Supreme Court that women have the right to abortion under the US Constitution.[38] That discourse presumes that humans are divided into two categories, one being women who are of the female sex, and therefore able to get pregnant, and that they have certain rights to seek abortions under the constitution drafted by the founding fathers: the right of privacy; or the right to equal protection under the law. Mary Poovey, English professor at Johns Hopkins University as of 1992, and post-structuralist theorist, disagrees with this argument because she believes it contains discriminatory legal concepts, including that it makes reproductive capacity the defining characteristic of every woman (which excludes many women who are not heterosexual), and leaves women who are poor or of color subject to unequal treatment. She further criticizes this discourse because it is founded on the eighteenth-century notion of human rights that is related to the basic tenets of individualism, and the idea of maternity being the essence of the female body. In sum, Poovey wants to rearticulate the abortion debate that she sees as being about what it means to accept the notion that there is a "natural" basis for individual identity and therefore for individual rights and sexual identity.[39]

Of course, feminist activists, radical feminists especially, never based their analysis on this legal discourse. They viewed the Court's 1973 *Roe v. Wade* decision to allow abortion as being politically arrived at by the Court after it weighed the demands of contending social forces, conservative industrialists who used religious arguments to back up their business needs versus liberal industrialists who needed to bring American women into the workforce and to bring down the birth rate.[40] The Court's decision also responded to a growing public awareness that population growth was out of control worldwide, and abortion reform was needed to stop the scandal of women having to seek unsafe, underground abortions. The impact of the growing militant women's movement, including feminists who had learned the technology of menstrual extraction, also influenced their decision, no doubt, as the justices read the newspaper and watched TV like everyone else. In fact, Justice Blackmun mentioned the development of menstrual extraction as one of the factors in his decision.[41]

Poovey's strategy, after re-framing the public discourse, then offers her reconceptualization of the discourse. Other than her specific disavowal of seeing women as a category, her re-framing is in fact the same as the one that feminist activists have always used: for example, seeing abortion in the context of contraception, not murder and placing it alongside other services that recognize social needs. The fact that Poovey thinks it is a new feminist idea to see each woman in her social context makes me doubt that she has done more than read the Supreme Court decisions she reviews and other academic treatises. But, the weakness in her strategy, compared to the one most grassroots feminists use, is to increase the number of both men and women willing to support abortion on demand. Feminist abortion advocates know that the availability of abortion on demand will come to pass only when a substantial number of *women* develop a feminist consciousness that *all* women with unwanted pregnancies, of *all* ages and *all* income levels and *all* ethnicities, for *whatever reason* and at *every stage of pregnancy*, must have medical access to abortion. We already have public support for abortion reform. Public opinion polls over the last fifty years show that eighty percent of Americans favor women having access to abortion with some limited restrictions.[42]

Radical feminists know that having reproductive control is not dependent on convincing people that women are able to make decisions about our own fertility. When enough women have a feminist consciousness, they will not beg for reform; great numbers of them will *demand* it. They will find that it is feasible for laywomen to acquire the knowledge and skill to directly control their bodies, and they will do so. No courts will be able to decide otherwise.[43]

CIS

I believe that the advocacy by queer theorists of the term "cis" as a prefix to gender comes from their understanding of how powerful language can be. Post-structuralism concerns the relationship between human beings, the world, and the practice of using language to transmit the knowledge and the values that constitute a culture. Post-structuralists theorize that meanings (language) control us, and inculcate obedience to the discipline inscribed in them.[44]

As a Second Waver, I am a witness to how powerful this can be. The Second Wave feminists employed these principles as one way to cause social change. "They recognized the degree to which 'woman' meant domesticity, nurturing, dependence, and the ways in which anti-feminist jokes reproduced the stereotypes of helpless little girls or the aging harridan." Feminists "set out to modify the language, annoying conservatives with coinages, such as 'chairperson' and he/she.'"[45]

Catherine Belsey points out that language is not, in any sense, personal or private. Individuals can alter it, as long as others adopt their changes. We can choose to intervene in this process with a view to altering the meanings.[46] (For example: "literally" doesn't always mean "not figurative or symbolic" anymore; now it probably means the opposite.) Genderqueer people added the preface "cis" to "woman" ("ciswoman") to mean a woman born biologically female and "whose sense of personal identity and gender corresponds with their birth sex."[47] They successfully petitioned the publishers of the *Oxford English Dictionary* to accept this new term. If enough people adopt this term to refer to a woman who was born female (almost

100%), you have opened up the category of "woman" to include transgender women. The original meaning of "cis" refers to a positionality that someone or something has in reference to a location. Cisalpine means "the area that is between Rome and the Alps." Cislunar means "the area between the Earth and the Moon." The most apt meaning of "trans" is to change as in "transition." Simone de Beauvoir said that man defines woman in reference to him; she is the "Other."[48] Now, a group of males who prefer to identify as women are attempting to create a hierarchy within the term "woman" and to push females lower in it. At this moment, this is happening with the Obama directive; the rights of a miniscule number of males are trumping the rights of half the population of the country.

We must not adopt this change. If enough people, especially in scientific and intellectual circles, accept it, then we will be compelled to use the term "cis."

POSTFEMINISM

Postfeminism is not a school of feminist thought. It is false consciousness held by millions of American women today who believe that women have won more equality than they actually have and act accordingly, with mixed results. Juliet Williams, professor of Gender Studies at the University of California, Los Angeles, spoke to panelists in a 2016 workshop. She said, "We are in agreement that sexism is bad and wrong. We are allowed to feel like we're part of a sexist-free landscape, but is it really a state of denial about the state of sexism? By disclosing in the present moment the existence of practices, structures, beliefs, you're confronting what to do about this culture of denial. You're forcing us to confront the persistence of sexism, but it's not necessarily that the sexism of the moment is the same our mothers experienced."[49]

Postfeminists need to be aware of how far short the Second Wave fell from its goals of achieving true equality. Abortion was legalized under limited circumstances, due to the pressures from the women's movement, but it did not succeed in getting the Equal Rights Amendment (ERA) passed. If they had, all abortion laws would be repealed, because constitutional attorneys maintain that having such a law applying only to females is discriminatory and violates their equal rights. The ERA would bring American women equal opportunity, paid maternity leave, paid family leave, free child care, and government child support and access to adequate housing to ensure that every child a woman chooses to have would have the necessities to grow up well-nourished, cared-for, and with equal opportunity for education through college. Then a woman of any age could truly choose whether or not to have a child. Today, the term "pro-choice" rings hollow, because in order to be economically independent to not have more children than they can afford, women have to resort to dangerous contraceptives and abortion.

If large numbers of women can be exposed to feminist consciousness-raising and participate in feminist projects, and they develop feminist consciousness, they will be able to approach their problems differently. Rape on college campuses would be directly confronted by groups of women outing rapists, devising collective self-protective strategies to make it safe to drink socially, and monitoring college administrations' implementation of policies. Such tactics depend on mass consciousness. Without that, individual women or even groups of women can only do so much. Until we do, if we don't guard against postfeminist thinking, we're in for nasty surprises, such as finding that college administrations care more about discouraging complaints about rape than taking any action to stop it.

WHEN DOES "POSTFEMINISM" BECOME "PRE-FEMINISM"?

I risk being called "Chicken Little" when I sound a warning that a genderqueer-sponsored "gender revolution" may play into the hands of the patriarchy by transforming everyone's perception of the causes of a female's difficulties and suffering from being caused by sexism to being caused by practically everything else: gender norms, compulsory heterosexuality, racism, poverty, the frailty of women in general, mistreatment by a particular man. and lastly, herself. Other than restrictive gender norms, what other causes for women's subordination do Butler or other queer theorists identify?

Butler wrote: "If identities were no longer fixed as the premises of a political syllogism, and politics no longer understood as a set of practices derived from the alleged interests that belong to a set of ready-made subjects, a new configuration of politics would surely emerge from the ruins of the old." [50]

Categorizing people by gender, rather than sex, erases female experience. I grew up in a society that erased female experience. I, and everyone else, had a pre-feminist consciousness, so I know how natural and inevitable the superiority of men can seem.

I hope that this backward slide can be stopped and turned around. Women holding small, women-only consciousness-raising meetings in their home, campus or workplace would be an excellent place to start. If women come to recognize, through socialization and sharing the details of their personal and work lives among themselves, that they, as women, share deep wrongs, they often take action to remedy these wrongs. As they grapple with solutions, they begin to gain an understanding of the mechanisms and institutions that our sexist society uses to keep women down, and how to best confront them. This process is a precondition of building a mass feminist consciousness that has its grounding in the understanding of women's material conditions, the nature of the obstacles to their emancipation, and the most effective strategies to confront them.

[1] US Department of Education, US Department of Justice. *Dear Colleague Letter: Transgender Students*, May 13th, 2016.
    http://www2.ed.gov/about/offices/list/ocr/letters/colleague-201605-title-ix-transgender.pdf

[2] "Calls to Ban Germaine Greer Lecture Over Trans Comments," BBC News, October 23, 2015, South East Wales http://www.bbc.com/news/uk-wales-south-east-wales-34613148

[3] Trudy Ring. "This Year's Michigan Womyn's Festival Will be the Last," *The Advocate*, April 21, 2015.
    http://www.advocate.com/michfest/2015/04/21/years-michigan-womyns-music-festival-will-be-last

[4] Katha Pollitt. "Who Has Abortions?" *The Nation*. March 13, 2015, http://www.thenation.com/article/who-has-abortions/

[5] Ibid

[6] Steven Glick. "Students Condemn Project Vulva for 'Transmisogyny,'" *The Claremont Independent*. November 1, 2015. http://claremontindependent.com/students-condemn-project-vulva-for-transmisogyny/

[7] Catherine Belsey. Poststructuralism: A Very Short Introduction. (New York: Oxford University Press, 2002), p. 3.

[8] Judith Butler. *Undoing Gender* (New York: Routledge, 2004), p. 35.

[9] Ibid, p. 2.

[10] Ibid, pp. 178-179.

[11] "Human Rights Campaign" https://en.wikipedia.org/wiki/Human_Rights_Campaign

[12] Riki Wilchins. *Queer Theory, Gender Theory: An Instant Primer.* (New York: Magnus Brooks, 2004) pp. 29-30.

[13] Kathie Sarahchild. "Consciousness-Raising: A Radical Weapon," in *Redstockings* (1973), pp. 144-150.

[14] Daphne Spain. *Constructive Feminism: Women's Spaces and Women's Rights in the American City* (New York: Cornell University Press, 2016), pp. 48-49.

[15] A note about the FWHC being a leader in the national movement of abortion providers: In 1975, we were co-founders of the National Association of Abortion Providers, which subsequently became the National Abortion Federation. The FWHC held permanent seats on the Board of Directors for many years. I served as the vice president of the organization for one year, and Lynne Randall of the Atlanta FWHC served as president for several years. I was given the Christopher Tietze award, the organization's highest, in 1998.

[16] *Op cit* 14, Daphne Spain, p. 112.

[17] Gerda Lerner. *Women and History Vol. 2: The Creation of Feminist Consciousness: From the Middle Ages to Eighteen-Seventy.* (New York: Oxford University Press, 1993), Appendix, p. 280.

[18] Leslie McCall. "The Complexity of Intersectionality," in *Signs: Journal of Women in Culture and Society* Vol. 30, No. 3 (2005), p. 1776.

[19] Richard Wright, Foreword to George Padmore's, *Pan-Africanism or Communism: The Coming Struggle for Africa.* (London: Dennis Dobson, 1956), p. 42.

[20] *Op cit* 18, Leslie McCall, p. 1776.

[21] Loretta Lynch, "Attorney General Loretta E. Lynch Delivers Remarks at Press Conference Announcing Complaint Against the State of North Carolina to Stop Discrimination Against Transgender Individuals," Washington, DC, United States, May 9, 2016. https://www.

justice.gov/opa/speech/attorney-general-loretta-e-lynch-delivers-remarks-press-conference-announcing-complaint

[22] Linda Nicholson. *Feminist Contentions: A Philosophical Exchange (Thinking Gender)* (New York: Routledge 1995), p. 12.

[23] Cecilia Dhejne et al., "Long Term Follow-Up of Transsexual Persons Undergoing Sex Reassignment Surgery: Cohort Study in Sweden," *PLOS One* (2011): doi:10.1371

[24] *Op cit* 22, Linda Nicholson, pp. 12-13

[25] *Seamus Johnston v. University of Pittsburgh*, 13-213 (2015)

[26] *Op cit* 8, Judith Butler, p. 223.

[27] "Cultural Studies" include ideology, class structures, national formations, ethnicity, sexual orientation, gender, human rights, third world issues, decoloniality and urban cultures. https://en.wikipedia.org/wiki/Cultural_studies

[28] *Op cit* 8, Judith Butler, pp. 174, 178-179.

[29] *Op cit* 22, Linda Nicholson, Judith Butler, p. 52.

[30] Ibid, p. 6.

[31] Ibid, p 49.

[32] Ibid, p. 48

[33] Gunnar Heinsohn and Otto Steiger. "Witchcraft, Population Catastrophe and Economic Crisis in Renaissance Europe: An Alternative Macroeconomic Explanation," *IKSF discussion paper, Institut für Konjunktur- und Strukturforschung Bremen* Issue 29 (2004).

[34] Mary Poovey. *Making a Social Body: British Cultural Formation 1830-1964* (Chicago: University of Chicago Press, 1995), p. 61-62.

[35] Thomas Malthus. *An Essay on the Principle of Population.* (London: J. Johnson, 1798)

[36] Dr. Paul R. Ehrlich. *The Population Bomb.* (New York: Buccaneer Books, 1968)

[37] Robin Elliot, et al., *US Population Growth and Family Planning: A Review of the Literature* (Guttmacher Institute) DOI: 10.2307/2133834

[38] *Roe v. Wade*, 410 U.S. 113 (1973).

[39] Mary Poovey. "The Abortion Question and the Death of Man," in *Feminists Theorize the Political.* Judith Butler and Joan W. Scott, editors (New York: Routledge, 1992), pp. 239-256.

[40] *Op cit 37, Roe v. Wade.*

[41] *Ibid*, Section IX, Paragraph B, 161.

[42] "Gallup: Abortion" http://www.gallup.com/poll/1576/Abortion.aspx

[43] Carol Downer. "Reproductive Sovereignty or Bust!" in *Rain and Thunder: A Radical Feminist Journal of Discussion and Activism* Issue #62 (2015): p. 24.

[44] *Op cit 7*, Catherine Belsey, p. 4.

[45] Ibid

[46] Ibid, p. 5.

[47] *Oxford Dictionary* definition of "cisgender." http://www.oxforddictionaries.com/us/definition/american_english/cisgender

[48] Simone de Beauvoir. *The Second Sex*, trans. H.M. Parshley (New York: Random House, 1952), p. xix.

[49] Juliet Williams, introductory speech to "Implicit Bias and Stereotype Threat," a forum presented at UCLA's Center for the Study of Women conference, "Thinking Gender," Los Angeles, California, April 7-8, 2016.

[50] Judith Butler, *Gender Trouble: Feminism and the Subversion of Identity* (New York: Routledge, 1990), p. 149.

CHAPTER 29

THE ATTACK ON FEMALE SOVEREIGN
SPACE IN PAGAN COMMUNITY

Ruth Barrett

On this day I proclaim the flow of mystery,
that joins all women's lives in consanguinity.[1]
Let this blood be the sign of our conspiracy,
and mark the fallow ground wherever we walk free.[2]

THE RIGHT FOR women to gather without a male present has been an ongoing issue for women historically, and this is still true today in some places in the world. This has also been an ongoing issue for my spiritual tradition, whose cosmology and ritual practices are exclusively female-focused and center exclusively on a female Creatrix from antiquity, known as the Great Mother or simply as the Goddess. "The Goddess," for many of us, is saying that life is interdependent and whole, affirming the existence of one interwoven Web of Life, where all physical manifestation emanates from and is born of Her cosmic womb; just as we live upon and are sustained by a female planet. The Dianic tradition evolved concurrently within the Women's Spirituality Movement and sourced its fuel from feminist politics and activism.

Goddess traditions began being revived in the early 1970s as part of the Women's Spirituality Movement that gave rise to subset movements, including goddess and feminist spirituality. In the mid-1970s as an older teenager, I met with other young women to study about our lost female heritage and participated in women-centered magical and ritual practices. By 1980, I had made a vow to my calling and devoted my life to spiritual service as an ordained High Priestess of the Dianic tradition.[3] Feminist spirituality was no less than a spiritual revolution sourced from ancient roots and revived in contemporary times because of our need to define for ourselves our spiritual and political realities in a patriarchal world. Spiritual feminists began reclaiming, reinventing, and recovering the suppressed history of goddess traditions in many places throughout the world. We learned that female life cycle rituals had been celebrated pre-patriarchy for tens of thousands of years. In the early years of our movement, we did not consciously understand the power that was being released in us, and back into the world: a power to heal our very souls. Pioneering goddess scholar and poet Patricia Monaghan addressed the original inspiration and need for a feminist spirituality:

> "Dianic Wicca has its roots in the continuing struggle of women to define our spiritual realities and our power in a patriarchal world. As Gerda Lerner has shown in *The Creation of Feminist Consciousness*,[4] individual women have, time after time, awakened to the oppressiveness of patriarchal religion and have, over and over, struggled to define spiritual feminist, only to be erased from history. A hundred years later, another woman has the blinding insight that women are spiritually powerful, only (again) to have that insight buried with her upon her death. Let us not let that happen again. Let us resist the redefinition of our movement as descended from the fathers, rather than the mothers. As a Dianic, I am born of feminists, not Freemasons."[5]

We created rituals to counter and heal from the influences of the dominant culture and male-dominated religions, and to specifically honor and celebrate the lifecycle passages of being female. Feminist consciousness, values, and visions were interwoven into the ritual content that affirmed the sacredness of our female bodies. This, in and of itself, was a radical act! It was not easy, however, as we had to personally confront our internalized misogyny, which included unexamined female body hatred from patriarchal enculturation over the generations. In our determination to transform our cultural and religious inheritance, we began to recognize how much of our human experience is filtered through and informed by our female bodies with our specifically female biology. We called our female-embodied sex-specific rites "Women's Mysteries" – rituals and ceremonies that women have practiced together cross culturally and throughout time. We discovered that experiencing and sharing the truths about our lives in female-autonomous sacred spaces apart from males was essential to exploring our spiritual realities and providing deeper meaning to our lives.

It was in these spaces of female sovereignty we experienced and affirmed "woman" as sacred, and we began to discover who we are if we challenge our socialization and begin to imagine who we could become. We were in uncharted waters and loving every minute of our awakenings and revelations. By experiencing our own bodies as sacred, natural, beautiful, and whole, many of us found that we were able to access all the resources within the body of the

Goddess since we are a reflection of Her. Women's Mysteries are women's rites of life that reclaim what is naturally our own: our embodied wisdom and our power.[6]

In my capacity as a Dianic elder, I have provided spiritual service in the form of personal, small group, and large public rituals for thousands of women over the past forty years. This service included assisting women in the often painful process of coming into awareness about how male-centered cultural and religious views and institutions have been foundational in their very personal sexual, physical, and emotional abuse, and how patriarchal socialization powerfully influenced their self-perception. Bearing witness to the cracking of a woman's paradigm of self-hatred, and supporting her coming to conscious awareness of this, has been both a wondrous and terrible honor. Once freed from internalized misogyny, even for an instant, for most there is no turning back. She can't un-know what she now understands has been done to her personally and to the female sex collectively. She begins to make different choices for her life, and becomes aware of how her own story is interwoven with those of countless other women and girls throughout time.

Providing women and girls with the possibility to have a personal experience of sacredness about their own bodies, and to even consider the female body itself worthy of religious reverence was and continues to be a major contribution of the goddess spirituality movement. Although this may be heresy to patriarchal doctrines that teach the female body is "unclean," less than, or "below god," having a different experience is essential for women to awaken and heal from centuries of lies, oppression, and violence. Seeing specifically female imagery on an altar, a place of religious reverence, is for many women a beginning to reclaiming themselves as sacred, born in Her divine image.[7]

Males are considered, as science affirms, a variation of the female primal matrix, and equally sacred as created and born from Her. Our tradition simply isn't about his experience and his sex-specific life cycle transitions. Thus, Dianics have no specifically male images on our altars, and we do not invoke the pagan god(s). He is always present as a part of Her totality because He comes from Her. We are not in denial of what is actually male in nature, or disrespecting half the human race. Female-centered rites do not focus on Him as separate from His mother, His creator and beloved. No disrespect is intended; our focus is simply not about either Him or him. Dianics in general reject the popular notion of gender-ism today that was, and continues to be so prevalent in some aspects of Eastern spiritual traditions, New Age Spirituality, Wiccan religion, and Western psychology.

A popular and widely accepted notion is that every person contains a "masculine" and "feminine" side, with prescribed gender characteristics for each sex. In my teachings of Dianic tradition, I completely rejected this concept early on in my capacity as a teacher, as it serves only to perpetuate a divine and secular heterosexism. In other Wiccan traditions, similarly, the Goddess and the God have certain assigned characteristics attributable to Their sex. Since these characteristics look conspicuously similar to the human gender stereotypes enforced by the dominant culture, I encourage my students to question the source of these assigned "natural" characteristics and enforced duality by asking, "Who made this up?" and "Whose cause does this advance?" These "masculine" and "feminine" qualities, however, are universal human qualities inherent in males *and* females. Historically, "natural" masculine traits that are valued in male-dominated cultures are considered "good." Traits less valued but necessary for the perpetuation of patriarchal culture are designated "feminine" and historically considered inferior, sometimes to the point of being declared evil.[8]

Gender stereotypes ultimately disempower everyone. In a patriarchal culture, characteristics shared by all human beings, such as loving and nurturing, are not considered "natural" masculine characteristics, and strength and courage are not considered "natural" feminine characteristics. When I gave birth to my daughter by natural childbirth, I experienced being more physically and mentally powerful then than at any other time in my life. Since strength and power are stereotypically gendered to males, does this imply that my "male" side birthed my daughter? If a man is sensitive, loving, and nurturing, are we to believe that his "inner feminine" has kicked in? Dualism reinforces the assumption that males are not naturally capable of gentleness, compassion, and receptivity. How absurd! Human traits of strength and gentleness are traits that all people are capable of expressing/exhibiting in order to be fully whole human beings. Teaching children that these traits belong to only one sex or another perpetuates dualistic thinking and keeps males and females in adversarial opposition, inhibiting our human capacity for wholeness. These arbitrary separations are confining to both sexes, limiting us in our thinking and behavior about who we are as individuals and what we are capable of being or becoming.

Riane Eisler, author and activist, promotes the return of a partnership society:

"There are traits stereotypically labeled masculine that are in fact excellent human traits for both women and men. These are traits that both women and men can (and, if permitted, do) share: for example, assertiveness or the capacity to say what one wants rather than feeling one has to manipulate or placate, as powerless or dominated people are taught they must do. And, as many men are today also learning through both the men's and partnership movements, there are traits stereotypically labeled feminine, such as empathy and nurturing, that men, too, can find and, if permitted, do share—and above all, that these traits do not make a human being less of a man, but rather more so."[9]

In the 1970s and 1980s, heterosexual pagan and Wiccan men and women assumed that our female-only circles and rites were "anti-male." We all were presumed to be lesbians practicing a man-hating lesbian religion. They also assumed that our ritual practices were "unbalanced" due to exclusively female participants instead of some Wiccan traditions' requirement of even numbers of men and women in order for magic to happen. What else would motivate these women to gather without at least one man present? Without male supervision, presence, or guidance, surely they must be plotting against men. How could their magic work without males to "balance" the feminine energy? Given that the majority of Wiccan traditions are based on a heterosexual male/female, God/Goddess duality in cosmology and ritual practices, their assumptions arose from their own beliefs, perspectives, and often-unexamined homophobia.

The reality that our tradition wasn't about males at all, including a male God, was inconceivable to those outside of it and those who lacked the curiosity to understand our differences. Our all-female circles were simply not about them! While many lesbians participated in these early female-only circles, it was a fact that a majority of participants in Dianic and other women-only circles were heterosexual women seeking these spaces apart for themselves. Either way, not being male-centric was suspect, and so the feminist, goddess and female-centered Dianic tradition was often treated like the black sheep in the larger pagan community of those times. It was from this environment that the fledgling Dianic tradition of the 1970s set forth on an uncharted journey of self-discovery and self-definition apart from our patriarchal socialization.

The early feminist spirituality movement empowered us to metaphorically give birth to one another and ourselves. In so many ways we saved each other's lives, quite literally, as well as emotionally and spiritually. Many of us paid dearly for being first to challenge the status quo of gender stereotypes by entering the male-dominated trades, insisting on wearing pants as women's clothing, and pursuing careers outside the home. As feminists, we spearheaded societal changes that benefited the generations of women who came later. We challenged enforced heterosexuality as many of us explored our sexuality as lesbians and bisexuals. Every day, we challenged with our lives the right to be the kinds of women we were, whether by wearing pants or a dress. For this we were beaten, raped, and taken off to jail (where many were beaten and raped by the police). We would not conform to the narrow confines of gender. We wanted a different world, and we still do.

We insisted on swimming upstream because turning back was unthinkable. In the 1970s at an early pagan festival, Dianic foremother Z Budapest facilitated a rare for that time period, women-only ritual. The husbands of the women participating came to "get their women" out of the circle where they were celebrating the goddess with their sisters. Some gay brothers were recruited to guard the women's circle from a distance and managed to keep the irate husbands at bay.

In the early 1990s, I had my first experience with a transwoman (aka: m2t[10]) in my capacity as priestess/teacher. This individual enrolled in a beginning Dianic class series I was teaching, and did not disclose or discuss his participation in advance, knowing full well that my tradition was for female persons. Although I had my suspicions that this hyper-feminized individual was transsexual, being inexperienced with this issue I decided it would be less disruptive to the other female participants to let him finish the class series, although I did get a few calls from students who felt uncomfortable with their classmate's energy and did not understand why. I consulted with my elders as to what to do next. After the class series ended, I called him to say that I could no longer continue being his teacher, and explained why. I respectfully offered to refer him to other traditions and teachers of Witchcraft that would welcome a transwoman as a student. I also told him about some Craft traditions I had heard of that were specifically welcoming to transwomen, as well as others, and based on ancient precedents around gender identity.[11] He was not at all interested in these options that would have been a better fit for his life experience as biological male with a different gender identity. Then the tirade began. He told me that I was being "patriarchal," "sexist," and then some. His unforgettable final words to me proclaimed he was "the ultimate Dianic" because he "chose to be a woman" and I was "only born this way." The floor dropped from beneath me. I was being one-upped by a male who had extensive plastic surgery, lived on female hormones, and was telling me he was a better woman than I because he *chose* to be a woman! For me, his declaration was the ultimate in misogyny, male privilege, and male ranking. To add insult to injury, he stiffed me on the class tuition after participating in all the classes. He is no "sister" of mine.

By the latter part of the 1990s, it seemed that there was finally some understanding and acceptance (or at least tolerance) amongst the larger pagan community for Dianics or female-only ritual space. Some festivals actually began to include women-only life cycle rites in their scheduling, recognizing the need of female participants to gather and celebrate their specific life cycle rites. There were separate men's rituals as well. Croning rituals (ceremonies for post-menopausal women to name and claim themselves as elders) that first originated in the Dianic tradition had reached the pagan mainstream. These rites continue to be facilitated by priestesses and other pagan women who do not consider themselves Dianic, but benefited from what Dianics revealed as an unmet need.

At the turn of the twenty-first century, I was able to travel to larger pagan festivals in my capacity as Dianic clergy, serving intentionally as an ambassador of sorts. I often offered workshops that were welcoming of both women and men in order to inform members of other pagan and Wiccan traditions what the Dianic tradition is, whom we serve and why. I believe that I did make a difference in my efforts to further understanding between traditions. Given that so many pagan traditions honor the physicality of our bodies and worship the body of our Mother Earth as sacred, it made sense that more pagan groups incorporated separate sex-specific rites into their traditions. Respect for diversity of focus and ritual practice seemed to be generally accepted as a strength of our greater pagan community. To my knowledge, I never heard of any lesbian or gay pagans protesting the hetero-normative spiritual practices that are foundational to the vast majority of witches and pagans. Lesbian and gay pagans often created their own rituals at festivals to meet their specific needs, while respecting the majority of pagans celebrating heterosexuality in their cosmology and rites.

It was only a matter of time until pagan trans activists and their allies began to protest female autonomous spaces and rituals at festivals and conferences, demanding to be included as women. This new development was both surprising and disturbing since I have pagan trans allies who have always been supportive of me personally, as well as for my priestess work with females exclusively. As the politics around gender identity and transsexualism spilled into the mainstream and popular media, the gains from recognizing and honoring diverse needs and practices began to be challenged and described as exclusionary.

At the same time, I began to learn about an emerging subculture of young women who, with ever-easier access to testosterone and elective breast removal surgery to "become" male, felt that they were born into the "wrong" body. [12] Their psychiatric counseling for gender dysphoria usually consisted of one or two sessions with little to no follow-up, no discussion of sexual abuse, and no deeper inquiry around how female oppression might be playing out in her dysphoria. Watching this happen was painful. I wondered, did it just become too hard to change the dominant culture, and so young women now voluntarily conformed to the narrow confines of gender by irrevocably changing themselves? Did young women just stop examining the deeper effects of sexual violence and our female-hating culture's attitudes on their personal female experience? Did they even have access to any other ways of understanding their feelings other than the route of hormones and surgery? How many of these young women were lesbian and felt that "becoming men" was a more acceptable solution to dealing with internalized or external homophobia? Did the connections between the personal and political simply disappear from conscious awareness? Is reality solely comprised now of the personal experience living in its own universe? How did this happen?

In personal conversations with young women who took the trans path, most shared that they were unaware and uninformed that there were other options and choices for themselves. Most of these young women were gender-nonconforming lesbians being herded into a medical system that seemed to offer an answer to their female self-hatred. Many of them had histories of horrific sexual abuse. In discussions with some of these younger women about gender identity, they expressed enormous peer pressure to surgically and/or hormonally alter their bodies, and join the trans community as if it were the cool new club. Most of them had never met an older "butch" lesbian who had lived as an "out" gender-nonconforming woman long before they were even born. With no role models for any alternative, they assumed they were transgender. They also had no exposure to any other way to understand internalized female oppression within the larger container of patriarchal culture, since by the time they were teenagers, women's studies had mostly been replaced by postmodern gender studies which validated their confusion with a "solution." In my opinion, these young women were set up for a perfect storm.

My wake-up call to just how much trans activism had targeted the larger pagan community came in 2011 at Pantheacon, a large annual pagan conference in San Jose, California. This experience was pivotal for me personally in beginning to understand the depth of the politics of the gender issues that had now reached the larger pagan community and beyond. It turned out that what occurred there was a pre-planned set up by m2t activists and their allies, after a ritual in the conference program that was described as "for women-only" turned away m2t individuals at the door.

The following day, a discussion was added to the conference schedule after the brouhaha. Another Dianic sister at the conference told me about it and asked me to attend with her. I hadn't attended the ritual that was at issue, but as a Dianic elder present at the conference, I felt a responsibility to attend. The discussion was titled "Gender Discrimination in Magical Circles." It was described as a talking-stick discussion. I intuitively brought my red cord of initiation in my hands to remind me of my sacred womb blood, our female mysteries, and my uterine blood connection to my sisters throughout time. I was genuinely curious to hear points of view from m2t people about being excluded from my tradition's rituals and other female-only circles. When I found a seat, I looked around the room and noticed about seventy people in the circle. The sister who had told me about the discussion and I were the only Dianics there. Representatives from the group who had facilitated the women's ritual the night before did not attend this meeting. I listened as several m2t persons shared personal stories of being abused for feeling different. They shared stories of being victimized by men, histories of being denied work, and tales of the painful physical journey of transitioning (surgery and electroly-sis) from the physical presentation of man to that of a woman. They also suggested that being denied participation in women's rituals and Dianic circles somehow contributed to their abuse.

As a lesbian, a Jew, and a witch, I could certainly empathize with being a person who doesn't "fit." As a feminist working in women's communities for decades, I had heard countless stories from women about physical and sexual violence and abuse by men, homophobia, work inequity, and denial of their basic human and reproductive rights. These experiences are the reason women worked so hard to develop a feminist movement in the first place. So, in this context, I could understand how m2t people might feel when they are not accepted into the rites of my tradition and other women-only spaces, and why the discussion was titled the way it was. However, with the discussion facilitators framing the discussion as "gender discrimina-tion," the sharing would most certainly be replete with accusatory stories of discrimination. As the discussion ensued, I heard Dianics being accused of practicing the same kind of discrimi-nation that females experience every day in the male-privileged, patriarchal world.

I continued to listen. I heard their desperate cry for understanding, "...but we *are* women!" I felt all the eyes in the room on me. I became a human target for their rage toward women who dare say "no" to their needs, and who would not validate their gender identity by accept-ing their assertion that they were women as I was. It took everything I had to keep my seat. I did speak to the group a few times, doing my best to calmly explain what we do – celebrate women's uterine mysteries and honor the female body. I held up my red cord and the goddess spoke through me, through the centuries, into the faces of those who were only further en-raged by every word I spoke. I was told that what my Temple had written on our website about our female focus, and not being inclusive of trans women, "hurt their feelings." I was told by one man in a loathing voice that I was "on the wrong side of history." The discussion's modera-tor screamed this and more directly into my face.

Eventually it dawned on me: this discussion had nothing to do with the spiritual, ritual, or magical needs of m2t persons; but everything to do with the need of those individuals to feel legitimized and validated as women by female-born people by accessing exclusively female-autonomous rituals and spaces. Suddenly, I felt like I was hearing the same old demands that males have always made of women – total access to all aspects of women's lives. This time though, it was coming from males who gender-identified or who had transitioned as women, and their allies, most of them women. Still, the attitude and the demand was the same that women must continue to meet everyone else's needs except their own. In many ways I believe that this demand is the same male-centric and privileged argument that women have heard for centuries. "You women must give us what we want! And we want access to your ways, your rituals, your magic, your bodies, your minds, your time, your labor, to your ancient traditions, and furthermore, you must change those traditions to include us."

By the end of the meeting, two things were clear to me. First, these m2t persons knew little about the spiritual tradition they were asking to be included in, not its history, its meaning, or its practices. Why and what we actually practiced was irrelevant, since the focus was only on their exclusion on the basis of sex. The Dianic tradition was not created to serve the spiritual needs of transgendered/transsexual people. It's the same answer I'd given to males who asked me over the years about participating in our Dianic rites: it's simply not about them, and the very idea of taking males out of the center of the universe for a few hours seems to be very confusing for them, thus making Dianics and other radical feminists most unpopular.

Secondly, nothing about the needs of women was considered. We were being pointedly told to step aside. Nothing was considered about what it means to grow up as a female human being in a patriarchal and misogynist culture that consistently devalues girls and women. There was no consciousness whatsoever that women have needs that can only be met when women gather. They truly didn't ever consider our needs. It was all and only about *them*. As I left this meeting, I knew these two issues needed to be addressed, but that they couldn't be addressed in the frame of a "Gender Discrimination" discussion.

In discussions with former women's studies professor Laurie Kendall, I learned that her view was that feminist's goals are at odds with m2t's goals: While Dianics are working to "deconstruct" the ways women are defined by patriarchal constructions of feminine presentation, m2t persons are striving to "construct" their new identities within those very strict patriarchal definitions. In fact, males who transition into female forms must, by necessity, hyper-feminize themselves (hair, makeup, jewelry, walk, talk, high fashion) in order for them to be possibly recognized as "women" by men. So from the simple issue of exterior/physical presentation, our needs are at odds with the needs of people on the social level. However, the differences in needs are much deeper than physical presentation, since in the ritual practices of the Dianic Tradition, everything begins within the female body, our sex, not "gender," the socially constructed character attributes *assigned* to the female or male body by the dominant culture. But my spiritual tradition is about the *female embodied experience*, not about adherence to gender stereotypes, or male-defined gender identity. These are two very different experiences. One is about identity, the other is about *be-ing*. Females do not have to "identify" *as* women, we *are* women. The difference between wishful thinking and not having to think about it at all! The diverse ways that women can be free to express our femaleness expands the confines of gender stereotypes. This is what my generation of feminists were and are still fighting for! We practice our rites in accord with ancient folk magic traditions, within the paradigm that *the spiritual and the physical are one and the same.*

The Dianic tradition ritualizes the physical life cycle passages of female human beings, through what we call the uterine "blood mysteries" and other female-embodied experiences. From our first breath, it's about the experience of being a female child growing physically and psychologically into womanhood in a misogynistic society. It's about the womb and bleeding every month. It's about the potential to give birth if we choose to, and eventually the end of uterine blood as we age. It's also about every other experience of being a female human being, because being female is in our DNA, every cell and organ system. A male who gender-identifies as a woman cannot menstruate, become a biological mother, cannot feel those stirrings in the womb. This just *is*. The female body is not transphobic. The female body *is*. And although not all women can get pregnant due to reproductive issues, and while other women choose to not have children, how could the Dianic tradition serve the needs of those who cannot ever experience the potential of this? Simply acquiring a female form does not equate with being biologically female.

How can the Dianic tradition possibly meet the needs of m2t individuals? Our rites have nothing to do with the experience of being socialized as a male, which also starts from his first breath, his life experiences, or what it means for him to "identify" himself as a "woman." The Dianic tradition doesn't function the way m2t persons need it to function, and becomes meaningless within the context of gender transitioning.

In a newspaper article on how the trans issue is playing out in Australia, Bronwyn Winter, associate professor in the European Studies and International Studies Programs in the Faculty of Arts and Social Sciences at the University of Sydney, wrote:

"…gender shapes our collective social experience as sexed beings from the day we are born, and we cannot disappear that experience and acquire another, simply through an act of will. Biology is not everything, but it is not nothing either – as any intersex person surely knows, and as all women know. Throughout history, any specificity of women's embodiment or needs has been ideologically constructed as justification for considering us weak, incompetent and unclean. We know, deeply, viscerally, that embodiment is a political issue."[13]

Laurie Kendall suggests, "Transwomen need to create ways of ritualizing their own experience and making the transition experience sacred within its own context. Dianic women can't do that for transgender people, any more than Catholics can create rituals for Jews. These are different experiences, different cultures, and different spiritual needs. And it's the highest form of male privilege to demand that Dianics do so."[14]

Laurie and I agreed that their spiritual needs *do* need to be met, but from my perspective, this is like going to the dentist to remove an appendix. One specialty is not suited to do the job of another. As with the thousands of women who figured out how to meet their own spiritual needs, it is m2t persons who must use their own creativity to meet their own needs. The very expectation and insistence that women must meet the needs of m2t individuals or they are bigots, "transphobes," hate-mongers, and worse, comes from individuals whose reality is sourced in male privilege and entitlement. From the extreme m2t perspective, they believe that it is women who are oppressors because we are denying males their "femininity"!

Some days I feel as though I'm living in a bizarre sci-fi movie where aliens have infiltrated society and parts of the government, having injected many humans with a mind-altering drug that turns them into obedient, unquestioning slaves. Those who have been injected no longer question the most basic of understandings, like "the earth is round." They insist that all humans adhere to the belief that the earth is flat, and insure that only the "earth is flat" theory is taught in universities, firing professors who do not agree to teach this new theory. Despite undisputed evidence that the earth is round, to present such evidence, the "earth is round" voices must be suppressed and punished with accusations of being "flat-phobic."

Similarly, I think about the old propaganda from the tobacco lobby before the states voted to make it illegal to smoke in public places. What if the tobacco lobby had succeeded in convincing people believe that breathing in secondhand smoke wasn't harmful? In this scenario, you may not be a smoker yourself but you find yourself breathing in smoke due to your proximity to a smoker. You must not complain of possible health issues of secondhand smoke because smokers have the right to smoke where and when they wish to, and their well-funded lobby in Washington is more powerful than your concerns. Evidence that secondhand smoke is harmful is suppressed, because the smokers absolutely believe that smoking is harmless, so they insist that you should inhale it, too. Surely there would be laws enacted to make it illegal for someone to ask a smoker to smoke outside.

If a ninety-pound anorexic showed up at a weight-loss meeting asking to join, she would be turned away in spite of her belief that she is fat. It is protocol that someone must show physical evidence that there is a need to lose weight (often at least 20 pounds over accepted standards) before being allowed to join most weight-loss programs. The determination of who is considered overweight is made by those responsible for implementing the weight-loss program, not the individual who shows up to join. The delusion of the anorexic does not dictate admission to the weight-loss program, no matter how much she pleads.

The subjective reality and true suffering of the anorexic is as real as it is for a male who suffers in his belief that he is really a woman inside. Instead of being treated for his psychological issue, the male who suffers from his belief that he is really a woman will be indulged in his delusion and validated for it. He will be encouraged to take hormones and/or undergo surgery, even though one long-term study concluded that, "Persons with transsexualism, after sex reassignment, have considerably higher risks for mortality, suicidal behavior, and psychiatric morbidity than the general population. Our findings suggest that sex reassignment, although alleviating gender dysphoria, may not suffice as treatment for transsexualism, and should inspire improved psychiatric and somatic care after sex reassignment for this patient group."[15]

The treatment today for gender dysphoria is not to help someone become liberated from invented gender constraints. Instead, this treatment is to encourage him go even deeper into his delusion, in spite of it being biologically impossible for him to actually change his sex. Further, he gets the legal support to change state laws allowing him to even change his birth sex on his original birth certificate, he can access intimate female spaces, and women are forced to accept him as a woman no matter what needs and legitimate concerns they have.

There are many days in which it seems that the lunatics are indeed running the asylum. I am practicing and encouraging all of us to do what the flight attendant instructs – "put your own oxygen mask on first before helping others." Don't let anyone take your oxygen mask or grab away your oxygen line and tell you that the air is fine.

MALE PRIVILEGE
What is "male privilege," and why is it important to name the elephant in the living room? My friend Patricia Monaghan (of blessed memory) described it this way: "For those who have male privilege, it's like a person wearing strong perfume. Rarely can the wearer smell it, but those around begin to leave the room."[16] Socialization for both sexes starts from birth, but for males

this socialization is extremely difficult to expunge. Carl W. Bushong, PhD, LMFT, addressed this issue in what he called the "male-to-female transition process":

"It has been my observation that the female self needs little help in growing up and developing… [However], the transgender [male to female] individual has spent years, decades, developing, reinforcing and living in their male role. Dismantling the male persona takes a great deal of time, effort and outside help."[17]

Jonah Mix, a pro-feminist man, and critic of trans theory, wrote this analysis about male privilege:

"Just like European domination constructed race, male domination constructed gender. And just like white people have always alternatively denigrated and fetishized non-white culture, many men find vacationing in femininity to be a delightfully naughty transgression. Somehow, this narcissism is passed off as some kind of radical strike against gender norms – as if men doing exactly what they want to do, regardless of how it impacts women, is a particularly novel thing. There is nothing edgy or dangerous about playing around with the tools you invented to maintain your privilege. People with dicks 'empowering' femininity is no more effective than people with white skin 'reclaiming' racial slurs.

The male embrace of feminine gender markers is to sex what gentrification is to class: The ultimate insult of the powerful. We build a cage, toss in our victims, and then demand they leave the best seat open when we want to drop by and visit. Amazon executives do it when they spend their nights 'experiencing the culture' of Seattle neighborhoods their tech industry is destroying. Dreadlocked trust fund kids do it when they play at poverty for a summer on the fortune their daddies made repossessing homes. And men do it when we decide that women's chains also happen to really bring out our cheekbones.

The narrative of 'exclusion from femininity' hinges on the idea that a man being told no and a woman's right to say no being removed are equally oppressive. But oppression doesn't work that way. When men are prevented from wearing high heels and lipstick to work, it's a bummer – when women are prevented from not wearing high heels and lipstick to work, it's a human rights violation. Discomfort with power is never worse than any level of comfort with powerlessness. Sorry, but a master who wants to be a slave is still a master.

There's nothing particularly tragic about the oppressor being unable to take on the markers of the oppressed. There is, however, something almost audaciously shitty about mourning your exclusion from the category of Who Gets to Be Hurt while we consign billions of women to die inside its boundaries. As men, we are born with the privilege to live free of constriction, modification, and mutilation. The vast majority of women on Earth are not as lucky. Throughout history, but especially in the last century, women across the world have engaged in struggle to dismantle the system of compulsory femininity. Yet somehow, quite a few First World men have decided the real injustice is being unable to adopt what women are literally dying to reject." [18]

For males, it is relatively easy to appropriate visible female characteristics, but it is much harder to rid themselves of the invisible, unexamined self-entitlements that male privilege affords them (and especially white male privilege), which is totally invisible to those who have had it handed to them on a daily basis since birth. Socialization for both sexes starts from birth, but for males this socialization is extremely difficult to expunge because unless they are taught to recognize the privilege their sex gives them, the privilege handed automatically to them is invisible. Peggy McIntosh, in her essay "White Privilege and Male Privilege: A Personal Account of Coming to See Correspondences Through Work in Women's Studies," describes male privilege as:

"...an invisible package of unearned assets that I can count on cashing in each day, but about which I was 'meant' to remain oblivious. White privilege is like an invisible weightless knapsack of special provisions, assurances, tools, maps, guides, codebooks, passports, visas, clothes, compass, emergency gear, and blank checks. ...[A] man's sex provides advantage for him whether or not he approves of the way in which dominance has been conferred on his group. A 'white' skin in the United States opens many doors for whites whether or not we approve of the way dominance has been conferred on us." [19]

The m2t community has only recently emerged from a world made in their image, and have lived for decades with the unexamined "right" and expectation that females must meet their needs. The needs of women in the male-dominant and trans-world are just not considered that important. This insistence reveals that our lived reality is invisible to them. Just because a male has appropriated the female form by investing in surgery to remove his male genitalia does not mean that he is willing to divest himself of his male privilege, even if it is invisible to him. This may be the only power he has felt in his life. After all, transitioning is all about power: the power to control one's body and live differently. For the m2t, he feels powerless in his body, so the only power he does experience is male privilege. Why would he want to give that up? For the female who transitions (f2t), she feels uncomfortable and powerless in her female body, and by appropriating the male presentation she hopes to gain some physical safety, and that all-inclusive male privilege, that invisible power that she has never felt but is so keenly aware of. Transitioning is all about power: how to get it and how to keep it. Transwomen have no personal interest in dismantling the only real power they have, nor would they use their power tools to do the job. In many ways, we are talking about the same thing black feminists have written about when they discuss white privilege.[20]

Audre Lorde wrote a lot about racial discrimination and the tools of oppression. Her now-famous words, "the master's tools will never dismantle the master's house," still ring true on many levels.[21] The master, whether in racial, gender, or sexual terms, is personally invested in his power and has no reason to dismantle the systems that grant him such power. He built the house, and only he has the power to dismantle or change the floor plan. But why would he want to dismantle them? These systems have served him so well that he does not even have to think about them. They are simply embedded in his subconscious and he is operating on autopilot, even if he has now appropriated a female presentation. And though the tools of oppression and discrimination are the same regardless of which subordinate group they are used against, the actual experience of oppression is different for each subordinate group. This means that each subordinate group must deal with its experiences differently as it seeks to make life meaningful in the physical and spiritual worlds.[22]

For instance, though the tools of oppression are the same, the way I, as a woman of Eastern European descent, Jewish, lesbian, and a Dianic priestess experience oppression is different from the way a Christian gay man of African descent experiences oppression. Furthermore, although I can acknowledge the discrimination he faces, my tradition cannot speak to or legitimize his experience. Nor can his tradition speak to or legitimize my experience. All we can do is acknowledge each other's discrimination, and respect the spiritual traditions that each of us has created to make our experiences sacred and meaningful.

It is because I supported, from this understanding and empathy, the right of women of color to gather in their own sanctuary at the Michigan Womyn's Music Festival, in a private space apart from the majority of their white sisters. This space provided women of color from all over the United States and other countries with a place to connect, share news of interest, and renew themselves according to their own needs, and in their own ways and ritual practices. This is also why I also support the right of men and boys to celebrate their Male Mysteries apart from women and girls. At a Midwest pagan festival, I've supported gay men in creating their own sanctuary space. And finally, I support the right for trans people to gather with those who have been through a similar journey and share similar issues and experiences without the intrusion of others.

In November 2015, I experienced a new level of backlash from extreme trans activists, headed by self-described pagans, who targeted me simply for serving the needs of women and girls as I have done for decades. My good work has been dragged through the mud of slander and outright lies that can even be proven as lies. I have been bullied online, boycotted, verbally assaulted, and threatened with financial ruin from pagan trans activists who contacted places where I teach or perform and asked them to fire me or not hire me. In the past few years I have been threatened with physical violence and death by burning me alive, and my life partner was threatened to expect acid to be thrown in her face at the Michigan Womyn's Music Festival while providing archery instruction there. Perhaps more disturbing to me is the missing outcry of horror and condemnation by more members of the pagan community in response to these kinds of terror tactics that are being used by clearly unstable people. Where is the condemnation when these trans activists are terrorizing women while they demand empathy for their own protection?

With so many diverse pagan and witchcraft traditions coexisting within the larger pagan community, to be verbally attacked *by pagans* for a female focus is shameful! As I've always understood it, because we are a diverse religious minority, and since individuals are encouraged to seek a tradition that reflects their spiritual journey and needs, to criticize another tradition's focus and practice had been considered rude and disrespectful. I've enjoyed participating in rituals of other traditions, and with an open heart have assisted as a facilitator when I have been invited to do so. Diversity is what used to make the larger pagan community so colorful and interesting, since by and large we are an eclectic bunch of interesting people. We have never had to believe in exactly the same cosmology, deities, or approach to ritual style or magical practice. Common ground between pagan traditions of all orientations used to be an emphasis on the sacredness of our bodies and the material body of Mother Earth. What happened to spirit-embodied in our sacred flesh? What has occurred in pagan community with regard to the hostility toward female-autonomous rites should be a red flag to everyone. Who will be next?

Several years ago I had many vigorous dinner-table discussions with a sister priestess, Medea, whose research in medical anthropology focuses on the intersections between the body, culture, and society. Our discussions revealed that the body is the foundational platform upon which culture and society act, and reinforced the notion that the body is the critical starting point to understanding all experience, *and the female bodily experience specifically.*

British political philosopher and feminist Rebecca Reilly Cooper wrote:

"The rise of transgender identity politics is a product of a more general shift in leftist politics, away from class-based analyses of oppression which seek to understand injustice in structural terms, and towards an individualistic politics centered on the recognition and validation of identities. On this view, the primary form of oppression – perhaps the only real form of oppression – is 'erasure,' understood as a societal failure to accept a person's self-definition and to validate their identity and self-perception. Whether or not one agrees with the idea that lack of recognition is a form of injustice, what should be clear is it cannot be the only form of injustice, or the source of all the injustices that oppressed group's experience. No amount of 'identifying as a man (or a woman)' can render the female-bodied person immune to the various forms of oppression that being female brings."[23]

There are a few outspoken trans allies, including Miranda Yardley, a gender-critical transwoman, who is among a minority of m2ts who have dissenting views from the extreme trans narrative. Miranda writes on issues of transsexualism and feminism. These trans allies receive the same bullying that radical feminists regularly receive. Here are some of the reasons why, in Miranda's words from a 2014 interview:

"I accept that I am still biologically male, as are all other transwomen. This is not a statement of condemnation nor am I intending to antagonize, it's just how things are. It's not judging anyone to say this, on the contrary it's about coming to terms with one's self.

Women (and by that I do *not* mean transwomen) still have so much to fight for. Male violence and entitlement to women's bodies continues to be a blight on societies across the world and women are treated appallingly across the globe. This is a battle transwomen should be getting behind, instead of the fighting against women which dominates a lot of trans activism at this present time. Again, we should position ourselves as allies: men are the class who oppress and attack trans women, not women.

I see almost no campaigning in the transgender community against male violence, which is a significant problem. Indeed, much of the 'transgender' activism in this country is bogged down in fighting women for the right to share their spaces, organizations and meetings. This type of activity involves pressuring an already oppressed class to relinquish rights, freedoms and structures they have fought hard to create and is plainly unfair and destructive. Any interface between transgender rights and women's rights is a 'rights balance' question, whose rights matter more? This is not a positive battle for transwomen to engage in. Transwomen (and those who are transgender) should take the initiative and campaign on issues that directly affect them, instead of fighting against women.

Something I have said on many occasions is that 'if you want to see real misogyny, look at the trans community.' There are numerous examples of an almost institutionalized misogyny; even reducing 'woman' to an identity erases women's biological reality, never mind the oppressive effect of socialization. I suspect it is a lack of awareness, not just of feminist ideas but also themselves, which causes this. Fundamentally, feminism is centered on women, and the trans activist approach appears to attempt to change this. Let's be honest: it's not feminism if it centers transwomen and it is not feminism if 'trans-inclusive feminism' seeks to concede women's hard-fought ground (for example spaces, support institutions, even the ability to use language that differentiates women from men). That is not feminism, it is men's rights activism."[24]

STANDING OUR GROUND

A young woman from our Michigan Womyn's Festival community named Gwen experiences her first menses. We gather in ritual space to welcome Gwen into the circle of women. Present is her mother, two of her girlhood friends, and the circle of members who witness and support this sacred transition of Women's Mysteries. Gwen's body is changing. Forty years ago, the transition from girl into woman was most often a passage fraught with shame, embarrassment, fear, and disgust. A young woman would try to meet the expectations for her future programmed from birth into this tight box called "womanhood," a future once so narrow that young women were given few options for what that meant, and what kind of woman she could become. But on this day young Gwen, dressed in jeans and a red top hat, presents herself as she has been supported to be: herself. The girl now transforming into a woman will define for herself what kind of woman she will be, with full support by all in the circle. Gwen has already "come out" to her parents as lesbian, and a fine young lesbian she is becoming.

Forty years ago a ritual like this in the United States could not have been imagined, both for honoring our uterine bloods and for being lovingly accepted for who we are in our sexual identities and personal expression. Female rites of passage that had been long buried beneath societal "norms" were just being reconceived. We were just realizing how our minds had been colonized in the distant past, and we were just beginning to awaken to ourselves and our female power. This was a spiritual revolution that restored a sense of the sacred to our self-perception and that of our sisters. Dianics were the tip of an arrow striking consciousness into our own souls. We blessed our bodies, we blessed that we were born female, and we showed one another our own reflection in the mirror of Venus. We dared to love ourselves within our female diversity, and for standing in our power as holy women made in Her image.

I will not participate in my own oppression and erasure by pretending that my body is insignificant to what makes me female, as a girl and woman. Working as a spiritual feminist with women from diverse backgrounds of race, ethnicity, and class, our common threads that weave us together has been our courage and mutual support to confront our personal and collective historical experiences of physical and sexual violence, and social, political, and economic oppression – all because of our sex and to reclaim our female bodies as sacred and as a source of divine wisdom.

No matter what comes our way as this issue continues to unfold, we must claim and defend our female sovereign spaces to gather, no matter what happens with the laws. We have been here before. Women have gathered for thousands of years in secret to be with our own, and if we must, we will gather in secret again.

---

[1] "Consanguinity," from the meaning "bonded by blood."

[2] From the song "Menstruation Ritual" by Catherine Madsen, from her recording, "The Patience of Love", 1982. Reprinted with permission.

[3] I was ordained as a Dianic High Priestess by Z Budapest in 1980, inheriting her Los Angeles ministry.

[4] Lerner, Gerda, *The Creation of Feminist Consciousness*, Oxford University Press, 1994.

[5] From the keynote speech by Patricia Monaghan at Daughters of Diana Gathering in 2009.

[6] Barrett, Ruth, *Women's Rites, Women's Mysteries: Intuitive Ritual Creation*, Llewellyn, 2007, p. 5.

[7] Barrett, Ruth, *Women's Rites, Women's Mysteries: Intuitive Ritual Creation*, Llewellyn, 2007, p. 295.

[8] A historically glaring example of this extreme attitude was the *Malleus Maleficarum* (*The Witches' Hammer*), published in the fifteenth century by inquisitors Kramer and Sprenger. This sadistic manual was responsible for the deaths of suspected European witches.

[9] Hagan, Kay Leigh, *Women Respond to the Men's Movement*, HarperSanFrancisco, 1992, p. 52.

[10] "m2t" is an abbreviation for "male to trans" since it is scientifically impossible for an individual to change their biological sex from a male to female. M2t identifies a male as transgender, retaining the reality of biology while acknowledging gender identity as a psychological identity based on an individual's feelings around gender stereotypes.

[11] The Maetreum of Cybele is one example of a trans welcoming pagan church.

[12] These are not true intersex individuals who have relatively rare biological anomalies like ambiguous genitalia, where both gender and sexual re-assignment is forced upon a newborn.

[13] From the article "Tomboys and Sissies: Where We're Going Wrong," Bronwyn Winter, *Sydney Morning Herald*, March 1, 2016.

[14] Laurie J. Kendall, Ph.D. Personal discussions with Ruth Barrett, May 2011.

[15] From *Long-term follow-up of transsexual persons undergoing sex reassignment surgery: cohort study in Sweden*, Dhejne C1, Lichtenstein P, Boman M, Johansson AL, Långström N, Landén M., http://dx.doi.org/10.1371/journal.pone.0016885, February 22, 2011.

[16] Patricia Monaghan (of blessed memory), from personal conversation with Ruth Barrett. 2006.

[17] From an article "What is Gender and Who is Transgendered?" by Carl W. Bushong, PhD, LMFT (the originator of long-distance transsexual and transgender services that helped hundreds fully transition). On www.transgendercare.com.

[18] Used with permission. www.Jonahmix.com.

[19] Peggy McIntosh, "White Privilege and Male Privilege: A Personal Account of Coming to See Correspondences Through Work in Women's Studies," http://www.feministezine.com/feminist/modern/White-Male-Privilege.html 1986.

[20] Laurie J. Kendall, PhD. Personal discussions with Ruth Barrett, May 2011.

[21] Audre Lorde, *Sister Outsider*, Crossing Press, 1984.

[22] Laurie J. Kendall, PhD., from personal discussions with Ruth Barrett, May 2011.

[23] Rebecca Reilly-Cooper, "Sex and Gender: A Beginner's Guide," sexandgenderintro.com, 2015.

[24] From "Interview with Miranda Yardley," theheroines.blogspot.com, November 23, 2014. Used with permission.

CHAPTER 30

THE UNDOING OF A UNIQUE SISTERHOOD

Mara Lake

"Women are entitled to protect what is sacred, private and personal to them and disallow intrusions on that by others who believe they are entitled to be there."

~ SARAH L. BLUM[1]

PART I

ONCE UPON A time in a beautiful place of water and ferns, mountains and orchards, sisters happily gathered from near and far during the season of light. In safe and sacred co-created space, they laughed and nurtured one another for four blissful days a year. They witnessed their sisters' healing and transformation through female rites of passage that only biological girls and wombyn[2] experience. Brothers were not invited. For it was known and understood that time spent away from brothers inspired the kind of mentorship and deep healing that sisters needed. And so, for twenty-five years this community of some one hundred to two hundred wombyn was harmonious. And it was good.

Then one day in 2012, unbeknownst to most of the sisterhood, a middle-age male legally declared to be a "woman" and "female" by Washington state walked into camp. Wombyn were instructed to call him "she." He wore a wig and did not disclose on the registration form that he was a "pre-op transgender." He refused to leave the premises and was asked to vacate a cabin with girls in it. Most of the wombyn were dismayed by the appearance of male genitalia during a circle dance, while others seemed fascinated and attended his workshop. He threatened lawsuits and to write a book about wombyn who opposed his presence. Sisters were called terrible names to their face and on social media. He said that the next year he was going to bring all of his friends just to "show us." His stated crusade was to "destroy" institutions and local wombyn-owned businesses not in compliance with LGBT law. He gained some support from within the community and eventually was invited into our sacred Moonlodge, the heart of Women's Mysteries, where men of integrity throughout the ages dared not venture. In Moonlodge, girls were mentored in the moontime[3] arts and wombyn of all ages could rest and repose in perfect safety and harmony. When he realized that many eyes and ears were on his behaviors he began to tone things down. But it was too late. The damage was done.

That year, about fifty courageous wombyn stepped forth from circle and stood together in solidarity as victims of sexual abuse. They were in a healing process of which our wombyn-identified community was an integral part. For some, it was the first time in their lives they had ever been in a male-free zone. The presence of a male in our female space had harmful consequences, including re-traumatization of earlier abuse. Sisters were broadsided and deprived of making choices. Along with the violation of our boundaries and our sacred female traditions came grief, and a loss of trust. A sense of betrayal now ravaged our once-peaceful community. Bonds forged through the years no longer seemed to matter. And the laughter went away.

In 2013 our event went dark for the first time in twenty-five years. Sisters scattered in different directions with mixed reactions. A handful got together and created a blog forum to defend women's right to privately and exclusively gather under the US Constitution's First Amendment right to expressive association. Some wombyn seemed paralyzed and were unwilling or unable to express a viewpoint. Wombyn who stood to gain financially from "trans inclusion" affirmed the presence of males who gender-identified as women. Some sisters said, "healing is for everybody," without seeming to distinguish that their own healing paths were, in part or whole, afforded by their personal experience in sovereign female space. Lesbian sisters who struggled with the challenges of discrimination, or wombyn with lesbian daughters, or daughters struggling with the challenges of possibly "transitioning" into a male gender identity, politely backed out of the conversation. Without a clear path ahead, the net result was polarization over our healing sisterhood's original intention and the dismantling of its traditional unbroken lineage.

The void was filled in 2014 by wombyn leading the charge for transgender inclusion. It was stated that our sisterhood was not a voting membership. A coup took place and our historical wombyn's way of co-creating our event was usurped in these ways: our wombyn's way of reaching consensus had always been a listening circle that validated the truth of our sister's experiences, not a top-down structure. Our volunteer planning committees were entrusted with bringing critical concerns to our circle face-to-face, not through the disembodied space of social media. Our sisters took turns spontaneously stepping up to contribute their inherent gifts and talents, and were not vetted in advance. *On the sensitive transgender issue, our community voice was neither sought nor heard, and was lost in the process.* It came as no surprise to learn that a male was now involved in the creation of our female-identified event. Suddenly, sisters were pitted against sisters. Trans-inclusive wombyn said, "If the 'other group' (meaning *us*) doesn't want to join us, there's nothing more we can do."

Our elders, mothers, daughters, healers, ceremonial leaders, lesbian and straight sisters, married and single sisters, all wombyn in committed service to other wombyn, were in this "other group." We wondered how the trans-inclusive wombyn who took over our event handled outrageous suggestions around wombyn's menstrual cycles, to bar young girls and crones from entering Moonlodge because "*they* do not bleed," or to let males into our First Blood ceremonials to "learn the basics." We worried about new young wombyn and maidens being led to believe that the presence of males in Moonlodge was "normal." We heard rumors about ensuring a transgender presence on our planning committee forever. Our website was changed to reflect a brand new identification policy that all attendees must now show ID at the gate, even though wombyn had known each other for years. This was to verify which males were legally "female" and therefore legally entitled to be at our gathering. Males needed only show a driver's license marked "F" for female to be able to intrude upon our sacred space and beloved co-created female rites of passage. It was obvious that the freedom and camaraderie of our sisterhood was broken.

Suddenly I found myself in the curious position of being called a "radical feminist" in the politically correct jargon of the day. Strange times indeed. For in helping to co-create long-held wombyn and indigenous traditions, I perceive myself to be traditional and not "radical" at all.[4] We "radical feminists" were then asked by our "liberal feminist" sisters to "forgive and forget" in order for the "old" community to "move on." But erasing the history of our community and its traditions was not an option. We who became "the other group" understood that attempts would be made to bury or change the truth of our experience. Indeed, that is what happened. It was later said that our sisterhood was not for females after all, but for "community." By refusing to look the other way, sisters maintaining firm boundaries were no longer treated with respect and kindness by sisters with whom friendship had been shared.

In 2014, a grandmother put her foot down and refused to bring her granddaughter any longer. Roughly half of the foundational sisterhood stayed home to nurture seeds within to birth new gatherings of sovereign female space. Stand-up sisters got together and wrote in a unity statement: "While we accept the notion that any person has the right to claim truth as they see it, we reject the notion that another person has the right to define our truth ... our truth is that we define women as those human beings created with a womb – wombyn… We claim the right to experience this biological basis as valid in the world… We claim the right to speak our Truth."

PART II

Wombyn throwing other wombyn under the bus makes no sense to me. It's ironic that sisters were excluded in order to include a brother who may think he is a sister but in biological reality is not. At the heart of this win-lose drama are the facts pointing to a web of relationships between (1) our informal sisterhood; (2) a 501(c)(3) wombyn's nonprofit where males were sometimes invited; (3) the transgender individual earlier described, called "T" for simplicity's sake, and (4) the state of Washington, by way of enforcing of those portions of the LGBT law favoring biological males that actually *discriminate against biological females.*

The undoing of our sisterhood began innocently. For about two decades we were an independent group, and then one of our planning committees sought sponsorship to be able to rent a preferred venue that fit the growing needs of our community. In good faith, this committee partnered with a familiar 501(c)(3) nonprofit that had catered to wombyn for about twenty years and this non-profit organization became our event sponsor. Wombyn in the Pacific Northwest had supported both our group and the non-profit. But while our gathering was personal, private, and met once a year, our sponsor had broad public outreach and paid memberships, and held events all year long. Our group had limited means and was financially independent, but legally speaking, our sponsor now had "fiscal responsibility," and chose the negative path of power over us to exercise it.

In 2011, unbeknownst to most wombyn who participated in our group and the non-profit, our sponsor's mission quietly changed to include "legally female-identified males living their lives on a daily basis as women." Our sponsor decided to invite T onto its council for a three-year term. In this process our sponsor *neither consulted its advisory board nor informed its general membership.* T went on to write our sponsor's anti-discrimination policy and was emboldened to attend our gathering. Although T chose not to disclose in advance of our 2012 event that he was a man, neither did the sisters on our trusted planning committee, who also happened to serve on our sponsor's council. They all felt fully justified in the nondisclosure, claiming that as "an affiliate" our community was legally obligated to follow the lead of its sponsor.

When the sisterhood retreated in 2013, a few wombyn stepped forth and formed a planning committee. They voted not to include "pre-op transgenders" at our event. Then, a letter arrived from our sponsor's council with T's signature on it. Compliance was demanded because, as the letter explained, their admittance policies had changed two years earlier in accordance with Washington state law. Therefore, we wombyn would be "breaking the law" if T or other transgenders were barred from attending our 2014 gathering. The legalese was biased and failed to take into account federal law permitting expressive association for informal groups with a specific purpose or mission.[5] Although we were directed to immediately change our website and materials to reflect our sponsor's policy, our sponsor's own website did not offer an updated policy until 2014.

Perhaps what stood out the most is that we wombyn even received careful instruction on how to distinguish *real* "women" from *fake* "women" for entry purposes. How totally bizarre to be told that our historical event was for "women to attend … not transvestites and cross-dressers …" and that a letter from a psychiatrist or medical doctor confirms whether a male is "emotionally and psychologically a woman." Furthermore, such a *real* "woman" is "identifiable by state ID."

As described above, the patronizing tone of our sponsor's letter with T's signature had a harmful trickle-down effect upon our community, with a devastating loss of our basic values of transparency and consensus. T was "invited" to be a part of our next event. Now for the first time there was fear on our planning committee and unspoken disagreement about T's presence. Sisters served as valuable witnesses to the process. Some sisters sought out options for securing a different venue that didn't require a sponsor, but the divisive climate did not allow for collective solutions.

A continuing call for community consensus was answered by trans-inclusive wombyn of this committee staging a paid professional mediation in T's presence. This was a far cry from our wombyn's way. An entire cohort of wombyn chose not to participate in what they felt was a rigged process and they stayed away after that. In their absence was T at the 2014 gathering. After all that had been said and done, T did not show up in 2015.

Then in 2016, T was again featured in a lineup of female-born speakers at our sponsor's annual conference, where on a podium with a captive audience he bragged about his "acceptance" into the Pacific Northwest's wombyn's community, and his "perky" breasts. Wombyn wearily said, "It's the law." During a 2016 firestorm of controversy when the Washington state Senate attempted to repeal this gender identity law but failed by one vote, the transgender executive director of Seattle's Gender Justice League similarly stated, "I have breasts. That's a thing." Regarding the potential of a court case with Washington's Human Rights Commission where things will undoubtedly get heated, this individual went on to say, "Just the fact that this is a public conversation is mortifying."[6] As folks began to get wind of the situation, the passion that the letter "T" in LGBT stirs stems from a common gut feeling that significant boundaries have been crossed, limits are being tested, and lines being drawn in the sand are anything but clear.

Our state, our sponsor, and sisters from within our own sisterhood, all cut through our own community decision-making process. Biological females became scapegoats for the results of decisions made outside of our wombyn's way. Scores of wombyn in our region were impacted by a domino effect caused by choices made by wombyn in positions of leadership, who embraced a patriarchal interpretation of state law, instead of our wombyn's way or an alternative legal position based upon federal law.[7]

Stand-up sisters later learned that wombyn can create a religious federally tax-exempt 501(c)(3) organization that allows females to claim their own definition of who they are, instead of states defining that for them. Communities of females who define themselves as *"…those human beings created with a womb – wombyn…"* are basing their definition upon science, and must discern the difference between establishment-certified "women" and biological females born with a uterus. A male-born person doesn't fit into the latter context, but a female-born person does.[8] Wombyn must make this distinction for the protection of community participants, and because the new legal redefinition of a female is based upon subjective and not objective physical criteria.

No doubt, all of us wombyn were being tested by one individual and his allies. Until our hand was forced, our healing sisterhood had a very different mission and purpose than our sponsor. So now T sat on the councils of both groups. Within two years he had fulfilled his earlier promise and intentionally gained access into three female-identified spaces: a large established non-profit, our smaller private gathering, and a wombyn-owned and operated wombyn's spa that relied upon business from our sisterhood and sponsor. The undoing was now complete.

Part III

The transgressing and supplanting of wombyn-identified space is currently within the letter of Washington state law RCW 49.60.040, whereby a person's *"…gender identity, self-image,* appearance, behavior, or expression …" can be stamped and certified by medical experts as being "…different from that traditionally associated with the sex assigned to that person at birth." Assigned by whom … God? The hospital? The midwife? The law doesn't say. The arrogant undoing and redoing of the definition of "female" by male-dominated governments is dangerous for wombyn, as it holds the potential for criminalizing them for "gender identity discrimination" in asserting their rights to privacy.

For lawmakers acting in good faith, however, while the intention of the law may be to allow for the full spectrum of human diversity in ensuring transgender rights, the net effect is reverse discrimination against wombyn who hold their capacity to birth children in high regard as being the essence of the definition of a biological female.

As Andrea Dworkin warned in 1988:

"The legal fight here goes to the heart of women's legal status and whether that status will change or not. In a social system of power over women … the law controls what is created, how, in what circumstances, under what condition … the law, then create(s) an ecology of male power … It says where, how, when in what ways to be lawless … the law lets men work both sides of it … to create conditions of inferiority for women … that not coincidentally keep women divided from one another."[9]

In nature and spirit, the womb equates to a wombyn's power, wombyn's reproductive capacity, the passing on of genetic information from one generation to the next, in "birthing new life and bringing souls into form."[10] The clarifying reality here that people seem to forget is that a wombyn is intimately connected with nature through her menstrual cycles in a way that males can never be. It's not a "choice" for biological females. Nature gives a wombyn the power to create from her body. The source of wombyn's life-giving power is her menses. Historically, male forces of divide and rule have sought for centuries to subjugate wombyn because wombyn do not need weapons of war to flow the precious blood of life. Her inherent power is organic and of the earth. It cannot be falsified or coerced.[11]

The new definition of "female" being enshrined into state law is now based upon emotions and "psychology," rather than the exclusively female experience of menstruation, her defined life phases and her capacity to bear children.[12] Any legal definition of a wombyn that fails to take into account her biological reality is not legitimate. *Everyone* has thoughts and feelings. Our state should be rejecting claims of males that they are biological females because they are not.

The intent of liberal lawmakers in our state to protect transgender individuals from male violence has backfired. What people choose to do or call themselves is their own business, but in no way should state governments be involved with validating the claims of male-born persons saying they are the same as female-born persons. Issuing state-authorized ID cards stamped with the biologically disingenuous letter "F" is an oppressive miscalculation that enables the kinds of entitlement rhetoric and lateral violence being exercised by some card-carrying transgenders right now. Instead of governments handing out documentation with the letter "F" for "female," it should reflect perhaps a "T" for transgender or transsexual orientation or another transparent designation the transgender community decides upon. The current lack of a "T" gender identity category with the U.S. Census Bureau is creating a misapplication of state law.

What the media chooses to report is just the tip of the iceberg. All across the country, females are being broadsided and deprived of making choices, while their personal and private spaces are disappearing. In our group's case, it was claimed that the rights of *one* biological male eclipsed the rights of *two hundred* female participants who gathered in 2012 for an express purpose. In the public arena, a large and popular local Korean owned and operated female-only spa that requires nudity in its pool, scrub, and shower areas is now forced by Washington state to accept "pre-op transgenders" into its multiple facilities, with the caveat that these men keep their genitals covered. *Nobody is asking naked girls and wombyn if this is OK with them!*

The same is happening in other female locker rooms. At our local community health club, a male in his twenties is now unabashedly undressing in our female locker room in front of wombyn old enough to be his grandmother, who are perplexed and feel invaded. In 2015, the YMCA's former communications director of Pierce and Kitsap counties, also a sexual abuse survivor, was re-traumatized after her employer chose to fall into line with Washington's anti-discrimination rulings favoring the violation of private female space, which impacted its some one hundred and twenty thousand members and forty thousand YMCA program participants.[13] She was then fired from her job after telling the YMCA's board that they weren't being honest with its members.

Just a few miles away from Washington's state capitol of Olympia, where laws are enacted, in 2012 a middle-age transgender student at Evergreen State College was discovered to be legally "hanging out" in front of young girls changing into their swimsuits. He was widely quoted as saying, "This is not 1959 Alabama. We don't call the police for drinking from the wrong water fountain." The liberal college argued that allowing a middle-age male to expose his genitals in its female locker room is in accordance with state law prohibiting state agencies from discrimination based on gender expression or identity. A college spokesman further explained that the law doesn't allow its public agency to ignore "gender identity disorder" as one of the protected classes.[14]

Research shows that changing gender role identity doesn't necessarily change sexual orientation. It also reveals that violent criminals who decide in prison to become a "woman" at the expense of tax-payers receive special considerations like early release, and are free to roam in female spaces in Washington and British Columbia with new identification marked with an "F."[15] The complaints and police reports being filed by the citizens of Washington state, and out-of-state groups writing to our state legislature, confirm that *wombyn and girls are no longer a protected class.*

Washington state's new controversial public school Health and Physical Education curriculum has prompted an outcry from thousands of concerned parents. Slated to begin in 2017-2018, so many comments have been submitted to the Office of Superintendent of Public Instruction (OSPI), that comments are no longer accepted. A reporter accidentally stumbled upon this curricular change while researching another story. Touted as being "best practices" in accordance with state law, the guidelines were made available by OSPI for public review but failed to point to the addition of gender identity guidelines, instead referring to the proposal broadly as the state's new "Physical Education Standards."[16] In yet another backdoor change prompted by state law, OSPI has said it does not plan on notifying parents of these curricular changes, and *has no plans to issue a press release or otherwise inform parents.*[17] Beginning in kindergarten, children will be learning about gender expression, gender identity and fluidity, and sexual orientation. Outraged parents are threatening to pull their children out of school. The Family Policy Institute of Washington State has pushed back with a petition that has gleaned over half of the signatures needed for submission to the Washington state legislature.

Well-intentioned liberals who share values of tolerance and compassion have this one wrong. *Transgender entitlement in formerly sex-segregated spaces happened invisibly without a vote from the citizens of Washington State.* It is another attempt to roll back wombyn's rights under the guise of "gender equality," and wombyn are reacting to state overreach. Unraveling the social fabric fails to address the heart of this issue. It only adds to the destructive imbalance of males over females still existing in our world today, and avoids a mandatory shift of responsibility *toward all men* and *away from wombyn.*

It is the job of brothers to protect sex-segregated safe and private spaces for sisters for reasons of privacy and safety unique to their sex. Instead of "passing the buck" onto wombyn, liberal lawmakers should be ensuring for the expression and protection of brothers who choose to express in their own unique ways, both in public and in their own male-identified private spaces, *without impinging upon females in any way.* This requires liberal lawmakers to rethink the politics of male privilege and to lead the way to a win-win, by actually modeling the liberal platform of support for transgenders *and* respect for wombyn.

Divisive state policy has personal, community, and economic consequences. Wombyn who understand the stakes no longer financially support formerly called women's organizations or businesses offering space for "women only." The freedom to perform physical activities that require a changing room or nudity is severely curtailed with businesses and female clientele suffering alike. With the very definition of the word "woman" changed and politicized, wombyn are distrustful of anything or anyone claiming to cater to their biological sex. Male-2-transgender inclusion is being hidden deep within the pages of website descriptions, or not mentioned at all, so as not to alienate potential female participants or clients. This is false advertising. In Washington state, policies are now in full swing that grant individuals full access to bathrooms, locker rooms and other sex-specific facilities in accordance with their chosen gender identity instead of their anatomical sex. *Average citizens are unaware of this fact.*

People are starting to become aware of the anguish wombyn are experiencing as a result of the profitable business of reassigning gender. Along with San Francisco, the Seattle area is reputed to have the highest number of "gender reassignment" surgeons and one of the largest LGBT populations on the West Coast. Changing gender identity laws was an easy sell to the faith leaders and lawmakers of our liberal state in a presidential election year. It has created a dangerously politically correct environment, especially for females.

There is no objection to the application of "gender identity" laws to sex-neutral contexts such as education, employment hiring and firing, or access to credit or housing. Confusing sex with gender is at the core of this polarizing issue. *Sex-segregated space is the specific site of conflict between anatomical sex and "gender identity."* Gender identity laws actually create legal right of access to sex-segregated spaces that would otherwise be closed to individuals identifying as transgender.[18]

A dress, a doctor's note, and a driver's license with the letter "F" might satisfy liberal lawmakers, but savvy brothers and sisters reject this deficient definition of a wombyn. Surely, wreaking havoc in the everyday lives of wombyn for the sake of political correctness should not be the goal of conscious liberals.

IN CONCLUSION

It's easy to trace the undoing of our sisterhood. Our community of biological sisters stepped away from our responsibilities and our families for a few days a year to renew our souls and do our sacred work as wombyn. That was the promise and magic of our sovereign female space. We shared common biological ground for over two decades and sisters didn't doubt each other until our state weighed in and the drums of entitlement began to beat. The power of what our established Pacific Northwest regional wombyn's network has lost cannot be underestimated.

Feminists are not "radical" or "transphobic" for calling out the fact that biological males are not the same as biological females. *People are being denied the truth about a socio-political climate that is indeed radical in attempting to usurp the very name of wombyn and is rapacious in its enforcement through state legal mechanisms.* But being forced to do or accept something against our will is a problem centuries old as females already know.

For wombyn, this political fight is age-old herstory in a dusty playbook. Wombyn must be clear and embody their power right now. With or without legal protections, we must choose to clarify our definitions for ourselves and fortify our boundaries again when under attack. We're finding ways to meet in private and are advocating for personal and protected spaces we can trust, because we've been left to fend for ourselves. We must stake our *original claim* and *authentic right* to define ourselves.

My story ends here. Together, our community of wombyn created and blessed a magical sacred space apart from the world of men, where we honored our embodiment of the Goddess and the sounds of laughter rang out. Just as the wombyn of our sisterhood now no longer share the same objectives, lately it's not so unusual for young men to grow breasts and for young wombyn to strap theirs down. Clearly, there is an illusion of freedom when one is simply following the topography the law itself is creating.[19]

Dedicated with humble acknowledgement to all the wombyn who paved the way, and all the inspiring wombyn I have known, and those I may never know, who contributed to this record with their blood, sweat and tears.

---

[1] Sarah L. Blum, ARNP, Decorated Nurse Vietnam Veteran, nurse psychotherapist and author of *Women Under Fire: Abuse in the Military* (Olympia, Washington: Brown Sparrow Publishing, 2013).

[2] "Wombyn" is used by the author throughout her piece as alternative spelling for "women" and "woman" to emphasize female physicality, as in "womb."

[3] "Moontime" refers to female uterine blood mysteries, and menstruation specifically.

[4] Patricia Anne Davis, M.A., Choctaw-Navajo/Chahta-Dineh Wisdom Keeper, https://nativeamericanconcepts.wordpress.com/. The Navajo Blessed Way views the female and male life tasks within the earth's natural order for procreation as being a part of the laws of nature, or natural or spiritual law, with male as protector-provider and female as life-giver-nurturer, although men and wombyn are not limited to these roles; and the natural order is also reflected in the effect of the phases of the moon upon ocean tides, menstrual cycles, and human behavior, etc.

[5] The Washington Law Against Discrimination prohibits discrimination based on "sexual orientation," including "gender identity," and equally prohibits discrimination based on "sex" or gender. (RCW 49.60.030.) It applies to events of "public assemblage," as opposed to "members only" events. (49.60.030, 49.60.040.) Considering only this Washington statute then, a nonprofit organization would not be permitted to exclude either a transgender person born male but who identifies as female, *or any male*, from any event to which the public is invited. Under the First Amendment of the United States Constitution, however, this does not apply to an organization or group which has as its mission or purpose the expression of a particular point of view which would be interfered with by the inclusion of a group seeking to participate in their event.

[6] Nina Shapiro, "State Rules for Transgender Restroom Access Set Off Debate," *The Seattle Times*, January 9, 2016,
   http://www.seattletimes.com/seattle-news/politics/states-rules-for-transgender-restroom-access-set-off-debate/.

[7] This would have required filing a lawsuit, which did not happen on either "side." What was not legally tested was (1) wombyn's First Amendment right to "expressly associate" and privately gather for a purpose outside of the context of a formal club or a legal entity, such as a non-profit, and (2) the right of a sponsoring organization to force an affiliate with a different mission and purpose to follow its policy leads.

[8] Stand-up sisters put it this way: "We believe it is essential in our lives that there be a place for wombyn to gather in their self-created, self-defined Sacred space. We claim the right to express and honor our shared experiences as biological wombyn in private and personal gatherings ...Our wombyn's ceremonies are necessary, precious, and deserve to be defended ... Our intention is to stand in our personal and collective truth in order to protect what is Sacred to us." From a private group blog.

[9] Andrea Dworkin, *Intercourse*, (New York: The Free Press, A Division of Macmillan, Inc., 1988). pp. 165-167.

[10] Sarah Blum, private blog comment.

[11] Source teachings from the North American indigenous Medicine Wheel, where female menstrual cycles are an integral part of the natural rhythm, order and balance of life, within the four cardinal directions (north, south, east, west); the four seasons (spring, summer, autumn, winter); the four elements (earth, air, fire, water); the races of humanity (colors dependent upon tribe, i.e. white, black, yellow, red); the four life stages (birth, youth, adult/elder, physical death); the sun's path (sunrise, noon, evening and sunset); the four aspects of human life (spiritual, mental, emotional and physical); and minerals, plants and animals.

[12] The Celtic Triple Goddess refers to the three female biological life phases equating to the three monthly phases of the moon, with waxing moon as Maiden or pre-menstrual girl, full moon as Mother or menstruating wombyn capable of child-bearing, and waning moon as Crone or wise grandmother whose menstruation has ceased.

[13] Craig Sailor, "Pierce, Kitsap YMCAs Release New Locker Room Policy," *The News Tribune*, December 16, 2015, http://www.thenewstribune.com/news/local/article50174070.html.

[14] Tara Dodrill, "Washington Non-Discrimination Policy Allows Transgender Man To Share Locker Room With Young Girls", *The Inquisitr*, Nov. 3, 2012,
    http://www.inquisitr.com/386218/washington-non-discrimination-policy-allows-transgender-man-to-share-locker-room-with-young-girls/.

[15] Jane Williams, 2016, Decide For Yourself: Transgender Crimes, YouTube, accessed August 16, 2016, https://www.youtube.com/watch?v=XAFcYTwn33A&feature=youtu.be.

[16] Kelsey Harkness, "Gender Identity Standards Surprise Some Washington Parents," *The Daily Signal*, June 16, 2016, http://dailysignal.com/2016/06/16/k-12-gender-identity-standards-surprise-some-washington-parents/

[17] "Washington Schools to Teach Gender Identity Curriculum In Kindergarten," Family Policy Institute of Washington, accessed July 29, 2016, http://www.fpiw.org/blog/2016/06/02/washington-schools-to-teach-gender-identity-curriculum-in-kindergarten/.

[18] "Restatement of Political Position On Gender Identity Laws in the USA," Elizabeth Hungerford, accessed August 3, 2016,
https://sexnotgender.com/2014/03/18/restatement-of-political-position-on-gender-identity-laws-in-the-usa/.

[19] Andrea Dworkin, *Intercourse* (New York: The Free Press, A Division of Macmillan, Inc., 1988). p. 167.

CHAPTER 31

TRANSPARENT: SPITTING ON MICHFEST'S GRAVE

Phonaesthetica

JILL SOLOWAY'S "TRANSPARENT" is a great TV show, primarily because its characters, the Pfeffermans, are unlikeable – selfish, lying, navel-gazing cheaters – yet engaging in a way I haven't seen since "Six Feet Under."

"Transparent" has it all: clever dialogue, lasagna-layered story lines and an overarching awareness of the primacy and inexorability of truth, whether individual or epigenetic: The truth is patient and will find you, however long it takes.

Plus, "Transparent" portrays older female sexuality in laser-sharp focus. Not gonna lie, I didn't strictly *enjoy* watching Judith Light get diddled in the bathtub by Jeffrey Tambor, but I appreciate the message: Old women are human beings with human needs and you, the vaguely-nauseated viewer peeking through your fingers and dying for this scene to be over, need to call yourself out on your ageism. And the strange-looking Gaby Hoffman only looks strange, you come to realize, because she doesn't adhere to Hollywood femininity mandates, e.g. eyebrow-shaping and teeth-whitening. There's power in that.

However! The second-to-last episode of Season 2, "Man on the Land," is thirty solid minutes' worth of misogyny and lesbophobic propaganda. In case you didn't watch: Tambor's character, Maura, a late-transitioning husband and father, accompanies his daughters to Idyllwild, a thinly-veiled stand-in for the now-defunct Michigan Womyn's Music Festival complete with nut loaf, a Drumming Against Racism workshop, tampon crafts, and the Indigo Girls performing "Hammer and a Nail." We, the viewers, are invited to laugh condescendingly at the silly-serious retro-ness of lesbian culture. Those throwback dykes with their hairy armpits, nattering on about "safe space!"

Watching, what I saw was a twisted parody of Fest – of any female-only space – seen through male eyes, or through colonized female ones. Like some kind of Black Mass with the liturgy recited backwards.

Anyway, the plot unfurls: Maura goes to the crafts area, where Vicki, a jewelry seller played by Anjelica Huston asks Maura how she feels about "the policy." Maura doesn't understand, so Anjelica explains: "The women-born-women policy."

Maura is very hurt; very upset; and all of a sudden all the women are yelling "MAN ON THE LAND! MAN ON THE LAND!" with volume and intensity, because the port-a-Jane guys are there and they want to make sure "nobody gets triggered, or too excited," (ha ha) and Maura feels they're yelling at him; staring at him; in hot pursuit of him. Because everything, of course, is about Maura.

The women who simply ignore him do nothing to make him feel comfortable, and that's how we can tell they, too, are exclusionary bigots with no empathy. During a short scene of a few women at a campfire discussing their need for WBW (women-born-women) space, someone mentions Maura's male privilege – a privilege he's enjoyed up until pretty much now.

"I was in way too much pain to experience what you're calling privilege," Maura says, and shakes his head in disbelief when it's pointed out that his pain and his privilege are two different things. Then, when someone else mentions rape, Maura's younger daughter responds sarcastically, "She stopped raping a long time ago."

> The message: *Don't listen to your own voice; your own instincts, when it comes to what a male-bodied person might do in female-only space. Just take what he tells you at face value and let him into your space. He has as much right to be there as you do.*

Maura is now running through the woods looking for his daughters to tell them he wants to go home – he doesn't belong here, his heart is breaking – and all of a sudden the veil between the past and present tears open and we're watching Maura's mother, a Jewish girl in Weimar-era Berlin, fleeing the Nazis and losing her brother, "Gittel," because guess why? He's trans and refuses to use a visa with his male name on it even if it means death. What a hero! What a martyr! Because if people don't accept you exactly as you want them to, the only alternative is suicide, right?

The scene continues, and now we have full-on Nazi imagery – book burnings! Men in identical shirts! – spliced with lesbian faces; lesbian bodies. It's a Miller analogy: Women who want female-only space are to Nazis as Maura (and by extension, all men who believe they are women) are to Jews being rounded up for torture and extermination. Maura runs through the woods to escape women who simply don't believe he is a woman, while Gittel is dragged into the woods to be murdered by men simply because he is a Jew

The clear message: *Hate is hate, you evil dykes.* There is no difference between:

• Wanting a week in the woods with other women; and
• Attacking a group of innocent people with guns and leading them away to starvation; forced labor; the gas chamber; the grave.

It's amazing to me that the Indigo Girls, Ali Liebegott and Eileen Myles, who owe their artistic success to the lesbian community and our lesbian dollars, participated in this travesty. Jill Soloway, a lesbian, wrote words to mock and trivialize other lesbians who spend money and time supporting her work. Jill Soloway wrote the words, "Let's go into the forest, and menstruate on a stick," and put them into a lesbian character's mouth to make an audience laugh.

The Indigo Girls, I sort of get. They've been singing the same songs in the same order for going on 30 years, so of course they took the opportunity to breathe life into a stagnant setlist even if it means shitting all over the same festival that gave them so much exposure. Gotta tend the earth if you want a rose, I guess.

Eileen Myles, though. Who the fuck reads Eileen Myles but us?

At the end of the episode, we see Maura leaving Idyllwild, laughing in defiance and shouting, "MAN ON THE LAND!" as he escapes what he calls "the feminist fuckhole." Vicki the jewelry seller picks Maura up and takes him to a hotel, where they have the kind of sex that makes you cover your eyes. If not wanting to watch Anjelica Huston straddle Jeffrey Tambor in a wig is wrong, I don't want to be right.

"Transparent" is important TV. Don't get upset and not watch it. Watch it hard, then get upset. Watch it with everything you've got, because the message is there, and it's insistent, and if you are a dyke, it's for you. What you do with it matters to us all.

CHAPTER 32

#ApologizeToMichigan

Sara St. Martin Lynne

I came out in 1990. I was sixteen years old. The term "we're here, we're queer, get used to it" gave me a certain power as I walked the hallways of my rural high school with my favorite girl. It spoke to a knowing that I had community, and that I had decided to not be ashamed – even as said girl and I got shoved around, verbally harassed, and punished by our parents. It provided me with a slogan that made me feel like I had strength in numbers. It gave me a framework to understand and celebrate my outsider status.

That was more than half my lifetime ago now. Since then, I have been deeply involved in the issues of my LGBT community. I have spoken on LGBT panels at high schools and in churches. I have done AIDS outreach in bars and on railroad tracks. I have organized rallies. I have attended rallies. I have donated money. I have attended too many vigils for our dead. I have sat through endless coalition meetings. I have celebrated with you. I have mourned with you. I have shown up. I am not bringing this up for the sake of being self-congratulatory. I am bringing this up to say that the LGBT community raised me. And to say that I never imagined I would find myself standing on what has been deemed to be the wrong side of the line or the "wrong side of history" within this community– especially as it relates to our shared and unique LGBT liberation movements. But in 2007, I fell in love with the Michigan Womyn's Music Festival.

I was well aware of the controversy around the intention of the festival long before I ever attended. I spent years combing the Festival's bulletin board threads, reading online conversations, listening, and learning to decipher the language that my own body and psyche seemed to speak when it was finally in a place that was devoted wholly to the liberation of women and girls. For nearly half of a decade, I watched and listened and quietly went about the business of trying to understand what was important or even necessary about women and girls gathering together in a female-defined space, but I refrained from weighing in. I understood the conflict about the intention of the Festival to be a matter of political ideology. But in March 2013, a trans woman named Red Durkin launched a Change.org petition against the Festival and my perspective began to change. While differences of ideology about gender identity were at the heart of some discussions about the inclusion of transwomen in women's culture, what was happening in the broader community was not political discourse. It was unbridled misogyny.

The vehemence and vitriol directed at the Festival and the women who comprise the festival community was nearly beyond my comprehension. Performers on the Festival lineup were being abused and targeted on their social media pages, demanding that they drop out of the lineup or face boycotts of their future performances. I could no longer ignore the tremendous amount of women-hating that was being celebrated, supported, and carried out in the name of LGBT activism. I could not unsee how many people entitled themselves to weigh in and object to the legitimacy of female autonomous space, and how almost no one was compelled to speak up when someone made threats of violence or rape against women – under the guise of "equality" and "civil rights." People within our own LGBT community were calling lesbians "irrelevant," "stupid," "outdated" and "un-evolved." We were being told that we deserve to "be beheaded" and "raped by woman-born-dicks." We were being invited to "evolve or die," "fuck off," to "go die in a fire" and so much more. Jokes were made about wretched-smelling vaginas and menstrual blood. Gender-nonconforming women were outright mocked as "not being real women." These pile-ups were happening on social media platforms and in the comment sections of mainstream LGBT online news outlets, most notably, The Advocate. No one was saying a damn thing about it, unless it was to say that we had brought this upon ourselves by our own "bigotry." Part of the painful and enraging irony of these hateful messages was that they came forth in the name of gaining entrance to a space where women had gone to seek refuge from this kind of hateful harassment, let alone very real threats that often accompany it.

Patriarchy will stop at nothing to shame women out of loving themselves and loving one another. The attack against the Michigan Womyn's Music Festival is age-old misogyny, made to look new. Demanding that women denounce themselves, their accomplishments, their material reality for the sake of "progress" for another movement is more of the same of what many of us already know, and have always known. A larger LGBT community that does not comprehend or acknowledge the value of a place like the Michigan Womyn's Music Festival has not evolved itself out of the need for it. The erasure of one of the most radical and revolutionary spaces on this earth is not a revolution at all. The relentless effort to work toward the extinction of the Festival and to discredit the legacy, complexity, relevance and herstory of this cherished and valued sacred space is fueled by the same female hatred that made the Festival necessary to begin with.

I wrote the following open letter to The Advocate one week after festival producer Lisa Vogel made the announcement that the fortieth Festival would be the last.

An Open Letter to the Advocate (and other LGBT mainstream press) Regarding the End of the Michigan Womyn's Music Festival

> "Patriarchal Poetry makes no mistake…
> Patriarchal poetry is the same as Patriotic poetry is the same as patriarchal poetry is the same as Patriotic poetry is the same as patriarchal poetry is the same.
> Patriarchal poetry is the same."
> - Gertrude Stein from "Patriarchal poetry their origin their history their origin"

Your media has been blazing this week. You have claimed a victory at the closing of the Michigan Womyn's Music Festival. You say it's been a battle, a fight, a war. It's a war that you invented and so the story you are telling now is one that you have been crafting all along. I think you can guess that I am not here to ring the bell and dance in the street with you.

I would like to hear you tell the truth about what you call this victory. I would like to hear you say:

> "We waged a full scale media attack on the only place on the planet where gender-non-conforming females thrive, a place where a 75-year-old bearded woman can proudly walk bare-breasted on a path next to a mother who watches her four-year-old daughter run away from her, completely unafraid, as the child goes completely feral with wild abandon. We are proud to report that we have done our best at making sure that any moments of true freedom they experienced together on that Land will be unavailable to each of them, and every other girlchild and woman from now on."

Or this:

> "We waged war against the true oppressor, the Michigan Womyn's Music Festival, but we here at the Advocate, want to assure you that we will not write a single word challenging

the problematic reality of trans women who actively proclaim their love and support for the conservative republicanism that is (as we speak) passing anti-trans bathroom bills, anti-LGBT 'religious freedom' bills, and anti-female reproductive rights bills, because lesbians."

Or this:

"Lisa Vogel, founder and producer of the Michigan Womyn's Music Festival announced that she will retire in 2015 after the 40th Festival. This announcement comes after 20 years of 'articles,' op-ed pieces and blog posts that targeted her relentlessly by calling her stupid, a bigot, un-evolved, ugly and irrelevant, a liar and compared her to the most vile enemies of human and civil rights in modern history; all while belittling her leadership, and making many references to the 'metaphorical' rope with which she could hang herself. But rest easy folks, although she will retire, we will not abandon our efforts to destroy the legacy of the woman who created a space that gave dignity and voice to thousands upon thousands of women and girls. Be assured, we will continue to produce volumes of lies, insults and innuendos until her reputation has been thoroughly destroyed. Oh, because lesbians."

For someone who should be a reviled footnote to feminist history, you sure gave Lisa Vogel a disproportionate amount of your time and attention. Funny, I never once read anything where she made mention of you, hatefully or otherwise.

At least be honest about who you are serving.

Let the truth of what you think you have accomplished ring out in the articles and op-ed pieces where you speak so liberally of justice. You write about love, compassion and tolerance as you sit behind a cannon that never ceases fire. You distort our image and paint us as primitives who are persistently resistant to civilization and progress. You've said that the forfeit of our Lesbian homeland, culture and language is for our own good and the advancement of society as a whole. You use tired racist stereotypes to erase the unrelenting support of women of color. This story you are telling is old. It's been told before. You are the smiling face of every colonizing endeavor that has ever claimed itself benign. You are every other witch hunt ever conducted. There is nothing original in your content or tactic.

In the effort to erase women who love one another and ourselves, patriarchal journalism makes no mistake.

In the war against women and girls, patriotic journalism makes no mistake.
Their origin and their history.
Patriarchal journalism is the same as Patriotic journalism is the same as Patriarchal journalism
Patriarchal journalism is the same.
Patriarchal journalism makes no mistake.

But make no mistake about this:

The Michigan Womyn's Music Festival has been the most influential incubator for female liberation for 40 years. The Michigan Womyn's Music Festival has been a refuge and place where we have gathered strength and resources. The Michigan Womyn's Music Festival is a place where we have had homecoming processions, wolf packs; where we put down the shame of our girlhood and licked our wounds together. We were nourished, fortified, lifted up and made whole. We built brand new mirrors. We recalibrated the lenses through which we see one another. We remembered ourselves. We celebrated ourselves. We took back our language. We took back our rites. We reclaimed our bellies, blood, brains, breasts, bones, muscles, and cunts. We are no longer strangers to our power or our purpose. We focused our intellect and let loose our wildest laughter. We know what it means to truly flourish.

Those are things that will not be undone. We gave those things to one another and ourselves. What we built has been for us and about us. It has never been about you. It's not about you now. This is not your victory. If victory belongs to anyone here, it belongs to that Sacred Land. If victory belongs to anyone here, it belongs to Lisa Vogel for devoting 40 years of her life in service and commitment to one of the most reviled populations on the planet, female lesbians. It belongs to Lisa Vogel for doing her job courageously, tirelessly and gracefully in spite of having her name and image appropriated for the straw man you created, in spite of being a stand-in for your disdain for lesbians. Victory belongs to the womyn and girls who came together and brought our racism, classism, ableism, ageism, and internalized misogyny to the table so that every female could experience wholeness in our stunning, complicated, flawed, compassionate and intentional community. Victory belongs to 40 years of Matriarchal manifestation. This true story of Michfest is rich and long; as are our memories. In both, you will always be relegated to the sidelines, a footnote.

When I said that we are a nation of shape shifters, I was not speaking in metaphor. Many of us have long lost the internal and external shapes we are supposed to hold in order to be seen, accepted or embraced by you. We are now teenage girls who know how to throw blades, axes and shoot arrows. We are now crones who know our worth. We are now women who have learned to build structures, run meetings, and bang drums. We are now 10-year old girls who say, "We should have this everywhere." Trust me. That girl knows what she is talking about when she says "this" and she will go on, somewhere in her beautiful lifetime, to build her "this" right in front of you. We will all take new form right in front of you. You forget, because you underestimate our power, commitment and reach. We are community organizers. We are engineers. We know how to cook for thousands. We are teachers. We are tradeswomen. We are Priestesses. We are messengers. We are Mothers. We are world-class musicians. We are professors. We are unrepentant separatist Sapphists. We are wild dykes who have divorced ourselves from any desire to accommodate your feelings. We are healers. We are women who have changed the default pronoun for everything in our world back to the female. Matriarchal language makes no mistake and we are all fluent in her from our tongues to our toes.

Yes, we will miss the face of the Land the way some of us miss the face of a sister, mother, grandmother or other sweet beloved. It will be so bittersweet to dream of Her when we do. I also know that we will glimpse her when we catch sight of our own reflections. We will see her when we study our faces in the mirror. We will recognize her scent on the skin of our lovers. We will hear her voice in the voices of our friends. Her story is alive in our bodies. We are made up of the water that flows through her, her soil that held us while we slept, the meteor showers and the sun that rises above Her. Walking her terrain in the dark of a new moon has made us less afraid and more capable of navigating the darkness in ourselves. We are women who do not cower when we face the darkness in you. That Land has taken root inside thousands upon thousands of women and girls. And She will grow. And we will grow. There is a wilderness in each and every one of us what will never be tamed, re-named or erased. Our cells have shifted. Our DNA has been altered. And we will be inherited.

Best Regards,
Sara St. Martin Lynne
April, 27 2015

Reposted with permission from http://fishwithoutabicycle.com/

SECTION FIVE

PERSONAL STORIES FROM THE BELLY OF THE BEAST

He will claim what he cannot have.
And she who has it has been taught to not know she has it,
or taught to think it doesn't matter that she has it,
willingly sacrifices what she doesn't know she has
on the altar of the impossible.

~ Ruth Barrett

I am old enough to remember when the expression started. In the 70's I felt as if by being referred to as "you guys" was a promotion. I felt a sense of equality. As a young girl I sure as hell didn't feel "equal" and resented having been born a girl. I recognized very early on that the system was fixed. I've grown past that insecurity and fallen in love with being female. And that, for me, requires loving the uniqueness of being female, and not using language that doesn't describe me. Today, that's what we call a Radical Act."

~ KAREN CAYER

CHAPTER 33

SOCIAL WORK PROFESSOR SPEAKS OUT ON BEHALF OF HER FtM AUTISTIC DAUGHTER

Interview with Dr. Kathleen "Kelly" Levinstein, PhD, LCSW, LMSW

MY DAUGHTER, WHO is on the autism spectrum, as am I, is now 19 years old. She had felt (and told others) that she was a lesbian most of her life. When she was 16, she began watching a TV show called "Degrassi," which featured an FtoM character. After a few weeks, she announced that she was not actually a butch lesbian, as she had previously said, but was in fact trans. She started attending a local PFLAG meeting, where she met many trans people, including a number of FtoM trans teenagers who were raving about a certain "gender therapist." Although the APA recommends a minimum of one year of "gender counseling" before surgery, this gender therapist (whom I consented to, before really understanding what I was doing) gave my daughter the go-ahead to have a bilateral mastectomy after only two sessions. I consented to the gender therapist believing that the therapist would help to sort out my child's feelings. I did not understand that it would be a rapid rubber stamp. This gender specialist never reviewed any of the Special Ed records or spoke to my daughter's previous therapist, who had known her for a decade. And, crucially, she never asked my daughter, "Might you be a lesbian?"

The gender therapist (whom I believe has an unholy financial alliance with the surgeon) gave my daughter (then 18 and one day) the go-ahead for the $30,000 surgery (covered for all university employees and their families where I work). My daughter is now on testosterone (which she clearly is unable to evaluate the risks and consequences of).

To give you some sense of my daughter's level of understanding of what it means to transition, she told me recently that she believes that the testosterone "will grow her a penis." I had to break the news to her that, although this is the mythology in the PFLAG meetings (where a number of the other young trans people are also autistic), this is not the case.

She has been taken advantage of. Healthy organs were amputated. This is insurance fraud, poor clinical practice, a violation of APA standards, unethical and unjust. It is a crime not just against women, but particularly against disabled women. So many of these young women who are "transitioning" are also autistic.

My daughter has a representative payee on her SSDI [disability] check, as it was felt that she was unable to handle her own money. This was of little concern to the gender therapist. I believe that once the therapist realized the "treatment" would be covered by the University of Michigan insurance, it was full speed ahead.

Testosterone could be involved in the development of both conditions, especially for girls with autism spectrum disorder, but this leaves the comorbidity in males unexplained. Gender identity issues could arise from autism spectrum people's predisposition toward unusual interests, or gender dysphoria in ASD could represent OCD rather than genuine gender identity issues. The cross-gender behavior in ASD minors could also rather represent non-normative sexual interests or unusual sensory preferences (28). Our clinical impression is that a long-standing feeling of being different and an outsider among peers could play a role in ASD children developing gender dysphoria in adolescence. In our clinical sample of gender dysphoric adolescents, autism spectrum disorders by far exceeded the prevalence of 6/1000 suggested for general population (32), and almost three-fold that in the sample of deVries et al. (28). Autism spectrum needs to be taken seriously in considering treatment guidelines for child and adolescent gender dysphoria. Given the nature of ASD, particularly ASD children's and adolescents' difficulties in adjusting to changes, profound changes in their own bodies with SD treatments may pose a major challenge to psychological adjustment and ASD adolescents may be particularly rigidly unwilling to consider this in advance.

~ From this 2015 Finnish study[1]
http://www.ncbi.nlm.nih.gov/pmc/articles/PMC4396787/

YOU MENTION THAT YOUR DAUGHTER PREVIOUSLY CONSIDERED HERSELF A LESBIAN, AND THIS CHANGED WHEN SHE STARTED WATCHING THE TV PROGRAM "DEGRASSI." WAS THAT THE ONLY THING THAT INFLUENCED HER TO CLAIM A TRANS IDENTITY? WAS THERE ANYTHING ELSE?

Other than Degrassi, the PFLAG meetings—which are now the cult of trans—sealed her fate. There were no young lesbians there. In fact, there are very few young lesbians left—they are all transitioning. If she had been able to have a lesbian relationship prior to transitioning I believe that things would have transpired differently. I attempted to get her in a support group for young lesbians when she was 12, but was informed that because of liability insurance reasons, she was not welcome until age 18. By that time it was too late.

She had a legal name change in December of 2014, a bilateral mastectomy in April 2015, and started testosterone in Sept 2015. My daughter has severe Crohn's Disease, and currently, she is having grave reactions to the testosterone. She has been hospitalized three times now for complications.

MANY PROFESSIONALS, AS WELL AS SOME AUTISTIC PEOPLE THEMSELVES, HAVE WRITTEN ABOUT THE FACT THAT YOUNG PEOPLE ON THE ASD SPECTRUM ARE OFTEN "GENDER NONCONFORMING" AND HAVE A LESS STABLE SENSE OF IDENTITY. CAN YOU SPEAK TO THIS REGARDING YOUR DAUGHTER?

I DO believe that there is an overlap with the autistic and transgender populations. Some studies[2] show a higher level of testosterone in autistic human beings. For males a high enough level of testosterone converts to estrogen. This may explain the large number of autistic people of both sexes claiming that they are transgender.

IN RECENT YEARS, ACTIVISTS HAVE AGITATED FOR DISABLED PEOPLE TO BE TREATED AS HAVING THE SAME "AGENCY" TO MAKE MEDICAL DECISIONS AS NON-DISABLED PEOPLE. IN FACT, WHEN ANYONE BRINGS UP CONCERNS ABOUT YOUNG PEOPLE WITH AUTISM BEING QUESTIONED ABOUT THEIR TRANSGENDER IDENTITY, THEY ARE ACCUSED OF "ABLEISM." DO YOU HAVE ANY THOUGHTS ABOUT THIS?

Yes, I agree–anyone asking for critical thinking about these issues with autistics is accused of ableism and transphobia. This is often an effective silencing tactic. I have found no allies in the autism community. Instead, there is a vilification of anyone daring to ask questions about these issues, including the evidence of MtoF physical, sexual and psychological violence against women. Women who publicly question receive death threats, threats to rape us and our children, burn us to death with gasoline, decapitate us, and so on. This all coming from people who claim they are our "sisters."

GIVEN THAT YOUR DAUGHTER WAS RECENTLY HOSPITALIZED FOR HEALTH ISSUES RELATED TO HER USE OF TESTOSTERONE, HAVE YOU FOUND ANY MEDICAL PROFESSIONALS WHO ARE WILLING TO SPEAK UP ABOUT THIS?

I have found no health professionals willing to go on the record against this. Everyone is afraid of professional suicide and threats of violence. I am standing alone.

My daughter's latest hospitalization has been described by doctors as due to "absorption issues." She now has a full beard but still has her period. The testosterone is wreaking true havoc on her system.

Autistic women (again, I am one) frequently have a difficult time, sensory-wise with their periods. But rather than attempting to help us with this difficulty, our problems get labeled "gender dysphoria" and the answer has become to remove our periods from us.

We will find out in 20 years the effects of testosterone on our young women. I am confident that it will not be a pretty picture.

This interview was first published May 6, 2016 on the blog 4thWaveNow in collaboration with 4ᵗʰ Wave Now and this anthology. Republished with permission. https://4thwavenow.com/2016/05/06/ social-work-prof-speaks-out-on-behalf-of-her-ftm-autistic-daughter/

---

[1] Riittakerttu Kaltiala-Heino et al., "Two Years of Gender Identity Service for Minors: Overrepresentation of Natal Girls with Severe Problems in Adolescent Development," *Child and Adolescent Psychiatry and Mental Health* 9, no. 1 (December 2015), doi:10.1186/ s13034-015-0042-y.

[2] Liliana Ruta et al., "Increased Serum Androstenedione in Adults with Autism Spectrum Conditions," *Psychoneuroendocrinology* 36, no. 8 (September 2011): 1154–63, doi:10.1016/j. psyneuen.2011.02.007.

CHAPTER 34

I AM NOT A WASTE OF A WOMAN

Max Robinson

WHEN I WAS five, I led a girl rebellion. We put on capes and chased some boys in capes around. Whatever they said we couldn't do, we did. It was mostly push-ups or holding bugs. I could hold any bug. My dad still has a picture in his office of me at a science fair, hands full of hissing cockroaches.

I hated to be told anything I couldn't do. I'd go home all in a huff from first grade because the girls' bathroom pass had bows and the boys' had soccer balls. My teacher wouldn't let me choose which pass I wanted. I played soccer!

I remember drafting letters to the author of a children's books series in third grade. I was bothered by the constant underlying sexism in her books about a family who rescued animals. The mom and the daughter were always tertiary, sweeping or cooking in the background, while the father and son saw all the action. What troubled me most of all was that these books were written by a woman. I didn't understand why she wouldn't write a single interesting female character.

Around the same time, my mom finally let me buy a pair of boys' shoes. They were red and black, and I didn't have to tie them. I wore them all the time, so often that the plastic frame of them tore through the fabric. It cut into my feet, but I didn't tell my parents. I thought I wouldn't get another pair. They didn't find out until they saw the back of my ankles, bleeding and bleeding. When I told them why I hadn't said anything, they got me another pair.

This is my first memory of hurting myself on purpose so that I would feel better about my appearance. Later, there was tweezing, waxing, shaving, wearing heels, running, and trying to starve myself. In all of those, at one time or another, I was encouraged, but they really weren't for me. I wanted to hurt myself the way I chose. I talked my older sister into ordering me a binder when I was sixteen and wore it as often I could. It hurt like hell. I insisted it didn't. The pain made it easier to think less, which was nice, especially at school. Class was boring and I couldn't focus, so I would always spend the whole day winding myself up with some thought obsession or another to keep busy. I used to ask for bathroom breaks and use them to cut myself, just because I was under-stimulated and unhappy.

After school, I read Autostraddle articles and dozens of pages into the archive of FTM (female to male)] blogs. I was glad to see some women who looked kind of like me, saying that they had futures now. I wanted what they had, and I hated what I had. I think I was fifteen or just barely sixteen when I started checking this stuff out.

The longer I thought about it, the more sure I was that it was true. At first, I thought I might be "genderqueer." Then, I wanted to go on testosterone for a while, but keep my breasts. Next I was sure that I wanted them gone. I would confess this anxiously to other trans-identifying friends online. They would reassure me that this happened to a lot of people, and that the dominant transgender narrative was oppressive. I reassured others of this, too. We all agreed that being trans was very special and difficult. I never felt special or that my pain mattered before.

Some part of me knew I was talking myself into it. I ignored that part.

For the first time, I had a community that listened to me, at least online. We talked about our feelings and we listened to each other. This was my first real experience with any internet culture. I loved having friends. It wasn't like school, where I was irritable and weird, floating between tables. People actually liked me on Tumblr. Almost all my friends were female and trans-identifying.

I didn't know anything. It was just so comforting to think that I was born wrong. If my body was the problem, it could be solved. Transition had clearly defined steps. Everybody chose from a set list, and when it was over, they were properly assembled.

When I renounced my connection to womanhood, to what I shared with my sisters, I sealed away important parts of myself. I thought I was turning away from the hurt that came from being seen as a woman by men, but it was too late for that. That hurt has been inside my bones for years. After transition, when men didn't see me, I recited their lines in my head. I kept quieter than ever before. Always afraid, always afraid. Brought back into line.

Transition was supposed to fix things. That's what I believed and that's what doctors told my parents. I was sixteen when I started hormone blockers, then testosterone. I was seventeen when I had a double mastectomy.

If I hadn't looked like a dyke and acted like a crazy teenage girl, there would have been nothing to fix.

To fund my surgery, I started a blog where I posted print-to-order clothing and gifts, pandering to the interests of the people I saw on there. It worked pretty well. I got a bunch of money, but not quite enough. My parents used some of theirs, and my grandma helped, too. This was a medically validated condition. I had been to professional after professional who agreed.

It was a cold comfort, removing hated body parts. Breasts marked me as a woman dressed funny. I wasn't afraid to be anesthetized or cut open. The day of my surgery, after the doctor drew the lines of the incisions on my skin with a Sharpie marker, I asked him where the tissue went. He told me it was incinerated as medical waste. I cackled. When they led me back to the operating room, I was confused. I thought there would be a silver table that I had to lie down on. I told my doctor this. He told me it wasn't an autopsy, and laughed.

My first post-op memories don't start until a day or two later. The pain wasn't bad, and emptying my drains reminded me of using a menstrual cup, just with a lot more yellow stuff. It felt better than trying to live as a man with breasts. I couldn't lift my arms to wash my own hair for a couple weeks, but seeing a flat chest was a breath of fresh air. It felt like it made sense after watching my old face disappear, cheeks narrowing, beard coming in. I didn't want to be seen as a woman or as a lesbian and I didn't want to ask why.

Or maybe I just didn't know who to ask. I did try. I asked my gender therapist, a trans man, about internalized misogyny. The question was dismissed. I didn't even really know what it was. I wanted to understand. Instead, I was assured that it probably wasn't that. I got a letter for hormone replacement therapy, and later, for the mastectomy top surgery. I was grateful.

It took years of hormones for me to realize it was okay to live in my own body without them, that making this peace with myself was possible, and that I deserved that chance. I didn't know it was okay to be a dysphoric lesbian, that I could survive this way. I was almost twenty when I stopped hormones. I had been twenty for a little while when I stopped understanding myself as a transman.

Things changed. My mind changed.

There's a species of rotifer (microscopic zooplankton) called Bdelloidea. A male bdelloid has never been observed. They're all female, reproducing exclusively through parthenogenesis for millions of years. How did they survive quickly evolving parasites and rapidly changing environments without the adaptability afforded by sexual reproduction? Bdelloids shrivel up under stress. In anhydrobiosis, they're easily carried away by the wind. For up to nine years, they'll stay alive like this barely living, but alive. Shrinking yourself to survive is a legitimate strategy, and sometimes it works.

When I started a new job where I was known as a butch lesbian, people treated me worse. Nobody trained me. They tried not to look at me at all. They didn't relax until I started talking, talking like I had in high school. I made jokes and people laughed. I told them about my childhood when they told me about theirs. I did more than listen, finally. People actually liked me here, the same people who looked at me funny when I started.

It had been so long since I said anything outside my home without worrying about whether I "sounded male." I never realized how much I had been holding back ever since I decided to transition. I hadn't made new friends, except online, in years. In a couple of weeks at this job, I got rides home and wedding invitations. I thought I was incapable of connecting to anyone in person, but I was just incapable of connecting to anyone as a man because I'm not a man. I can't pretend to be one without hiding an essential part of my nature.

I thought "woman" was wrong for me, because of how I dressed, how I related to my body, how I resented the expectations this society had for me as a woman. I didn't realize that my horror at my body could be caused by the horror of living in a world that hates and wants to control all women.

If "being a woman" really was nothing but an identity, if I had been raised in a world where it really did just mean calling myself a woman, I never would have transitioned. Trying to live in a fantasy where everything women have suffered for being female is null and void, even as misogyny continues to shape our lives, was valuable only in that I finally learned how incredibly valuable it was to name myself as a woman.

There is power in naming. It's how we find each other, how we connect to our histories, how we connect to our futures. Driving us apart is the easiest way to keep us from learning to recognize male attempts to redefine our realities.

I didn't know this then. I subscribed to an incredibly misogynistic, male-centric set of beliefs for years. "DFAB privilege" was a common phrase in our trans community I was part of – meaning "designated female at birth privilege." It was accepted fact that being born female gave you a lifelong advantage over a male who transitioned. This included men who used transition to mean using different pronouns on Tumblr and having an anime girl as their icon. We believed that, as "DFABs," we needed to shut up about our petty problems. We could never have it as hard as any "DMAB women or non-binary people." Everyone agreed that it was our responsibility to uplift "DMAB voices." None of this seemed outrageous or strange to me; it felt pretty intuitive. Growing up under patriarchy is a grooming process that leaves girls and women extremely vulnerable to male manipulation.

The first experience that made me start to feel suspicious of male transition was when I was eighteen and a genderqueer-identifying man who had never pursued any kind of transition raped my best friend, a woman unacquainted with insular trans community politics. I introduced her to my friends, who introduced us to this guy. She told me on the train home what he did; I had been in the next room the whole night, awake, talking to someone I didn't even like. I didn't know it was happening. When she let our mutual friends know what happened, we both assumed they would have her back. They called their apartment a safe space for rape survivors. Instead, her rapist changed his pronouns on Tumblr, claimed to have schizophrenia, and then said that he couldn't possibly have raped her, because of the power dynamics between a "cis" woman and a transwoman. He moved back to Los Angeles a few months later, without ever taking any steps towards transition. When he got there, he told his old friends he wasn't schizophrenic or trans anymore.

We lost all of our friends from the trans community, eventually. The one woman who did side with us died of alcoholism at twenty-one, but at that point, we were estranged. My best friend and I weren't able to handle her intense attention-seeking behaviors and couldn't cope with the way she would violate our boundaries when seeking physical intimacy with women. She understood herself as a genderqueer political lesbian, although she still regularly slept with men and sought out "sugar daddies" as a form of compulsive self-harm. She didn't know who to be or what to do, and now she never will.

Years before that, two different transwomen I knew had made me feel pressured into sending nude photos of my breasts to them. I messaged them first, as a sixteen-year-old, after seeing them repeatedly posting about being horny and suicidal, and how only nudes would make them feel any better. They didn't even know who I was. To one of them, I just submitted the nudes anonymously. I didn't want to talk, I just wanted him to feel better. I thought it was my responsibility. It might be posted somewhere, I have no idea. The nudes I sent were the ones I took when I was fifteen and dating a twenty-year-old man who was in college. Both of the transwomen who sexted with me identified as lesbians at the time and knew I was a transman. They didn't care, as long as we were talking one-on-one.

I didn't fully see the value in differentiating male from female until a traumatized and disabled lesbian I knew well, K, finally admitted to me that her transwoman partner M was beating her regularly.

M was addicted to porn and stimulants, constantly masturbating. He had spending issues and blew through money from his rich criminal dad, ending up with tons of unread books and untouched video games instead of necessities. His codependency and agoraphobia meant that neither of them left his bedroom in his mother's house. The room was littered with hoarded garbage, despite his mother's constant offers to clean it up.

He had met my friend online. They had talked for a few weeks before she became homeless and moved in with him out of necessity. She had learned recently about including transwomen in lesbianism and noticed that she was still able to experience something she hadn't named yet from these transwomen: male validation. As a survivor of substantial abuse at the hands of men from infancy onwards, her relationship with their approval was incredibly warped. She recognized herself as a lesbian woman despite this drive towards compulsive re-traumatization, but was lured back into dating a man because of her inability to name neither the drive, nor the man, for what they were. Being able to name one of these would have saved her from this; naming both would have given her the tools to start moving forward.

For want of either, she spent three years being beaten, growled at, and only allowed to leave the house in order to be prostituted to men who fetishized her body type, so that K would stop throwing violent tantrums about not being able to afford his compulsive spending. Her mobility problems and mental health declined dramatically in this environment, and she sustained concussion after untreated concussion. Once she was in this relationship, she eventually came to see herself as genderqueer and bisexual. She hated being a woman and dated violent transwomen while still being attracted to transmen, women who hated being women.

It's been two years since she moved in with me, away from him, and she's still recovering from what he did to her. She had experienced two decades of trauma before that, but nothing ever broke her like this did. Calling that relationship "lesbianism" left her stranded outside the framework she desperately needed in order to contextualize her experiences as a survivor of captivity. It destroyed her ability to call herself a lesbian or a woman for a long time. If lesbians like to sleep with transwomen and were repulsed by the supposed maleness of transmen, how could she be one? If women are what M was, then K must be something else entirely. *The language of transition lends itself readily to abusive gaslighting that disguises and distorts women's ability to name what is happening.* What was done to her was extreme cruelty of a distinctly male variety, cruelty she was especially vulnerable to because of her lifelong history of trauma at men's hands.

The more I started to understand that M could not have been female, the more I understood why I was. Especially under patriarchy, sex matters. Running from its significance prevents us from doing anything but continuing its cycles of destruction. As soon as a transwoman said, "no, I'm not a man," we instantly lost our ability to protect ourselves from him. Women who never transitioned in these circles believed their "cis privilege" rendered us man-like in our power. For those of us females (mainly lesbians) who sought transition, we were often told that we were exactly as bad as any other men.

Loading the language was an incredibly powerful tool. I was a lesbian trying to save my girlfriend from domestic violence at the hands of a man she had partnered with out of intense desperation, facing immediate homelessness as a severely mentally ill woman with limited mobility. Knowing this could have connected us to our foremothers who struggled through similar battles to protect each other from men. Instead, we felt completely adrift. Other women dealing with abuse from transwomen have described a similar sense of being in entirely uncharted territory, terrified to speak first, unable to find anyone else sharing experiences; they're all too scared of being labeled an untouchable "trans-misogynist."

In the twenty-first century, intelligent and capable adult women are having to relearn what "man" means, with fear at their backs every step of the way. We were among them, exploring radical and lesbian feminist ideology online and marveling at how precisely decades-old works described circumstances we had thought of as very recent. Janice Raymond's discussion of transexually constructed lesbian feminists in *The Transsexual Empire* was startlingly relevant; she saw this coming. As lesbians, we have a rich history of theory that had been completely denied to women who came of age when K and I did. All either of us knew about Janice Raymond, until last year, was that she was evil to the core. We believed this because we didn't know any better.

Deprogramming took almost a year. Both of us were terrified just to read dissenting opinions. K, I, and another lesbian exited from the radical queer scene, and moderated an online support group for anyone dysphoric and born female, including many who still identified as trans. When that group started, I was still one of the transmen. All of us were so incredibly relieved not to be alone. We disagreed on a lot of stuff, but we were all tired of what we saw happening to females.

When our remaining friends from the transgender community found out that we considered transwomen capable of male violence, and that we were concerned about transition's effect on young adults, almost all of them deserted us immediately. Female trans-identifying friends who knew K's history of homelessness and our currently rocky financial situation started talking publicly to each other about how we literally deserved to starve to death.

Losing these friends hurt enough on its own. Being cut off from them just when we had begun to see the severity of the situation within these groups was so much worse. I have a list of twenty intercommunity predators, mainly transwomen who prey on female women or transmen. Eleven of them are one or two degrees of separation from us. So many of the victims of transwomen had themselves been pressured for nudes, coerced into unwanted sex, or outright violently assaulted by males describing themselves as transwomen, but they still didn't feel able to challenge the narrative they were being fed. These women, our friends, had been there with us. They saw transwoman predator after transwoman predator being named by their terrified female victims. The "callouts" (a word used for anything from hurting someone's feelings slightly to brutal rape) usually only happened once several victims of the same predator found each other and made sure they had friends on their side. When victims couldn't be sure they would be supported, they didn't come forward. The political climate made it doubly difficult to "call out" a transwoman. We were constantly being reminded that transwomen are harmed by the horrible stereotype that they're all rapists or perverts, and we were taught that we needed to be constantly vigilant ourselves to avoid perpetuating this idea.

The silent victims of transwomen in these spaces had good reason to keep quiet. We all saw transwomen using the language of "cissexism" and "transmisogyny" against anyone who named their behavior as harmful. Even transwomen dating other transwomen experienced abuse at their hands. In the resulting fallout, it was never clear who the true aggressor was; both of them would immediately begin using identity politics and "privilege dynamics" (i.e., someone poor can *never* hurt someone rich, under any circumstances, etc.) in a way that was very effective at obfuscating the truth. Our friends had been right beside for all of this, and they still damned us for beginning to name what had enabled this wide-scale intercommunity violence.

Young lesbians in the "queer community" are known by many names; if you want to avoid scrutiny for not hooking up with transwomen, you've got to get creative. Some of us call ourselves queer, bisexual, or pansexual, because there's no word for only being attracted to females, and you can't be a lesbian if you date transmen or avoid dating transwomen. A lot of us, having been told that we can opt out of womanhood by choice, decide that we never want to be called "she" again.

Women who cling to the word "lesbian" in these spaces find themselves increasingly pressured to sleep with transwomen, precisely because they still call themselves lesbians. Many transwomen seem to view dating a "cisbian" as a uniquely valuable source of gender validation. After all, lesbians only date women. There is no acknowledgement that, under some circumstances, some lesbians can be coerced into relationships that they are incapable of experiencing as anything except traumatic. I have never seen a transwoman from these circles even express a paranoid insecurity that this might be true. By all appearances, they have never considered it. Running from unpleasant truths is something that I've noticed a lot of folks who transition (me included) tend to get very good at.

The insistence that lesbianism is not a female experience runs so deep that transwomen, especially those who only date other transwomen, often refer to themselves as "transdykes." This includes those who are not transitioning, men who can literally only be differentiated from any other man when you ask his preferred pronouns. Many women believe that these "transdykes," even those who have never been identifiable as anything but straight men to the outside world in any way, are more oppressed than any "cis" woman, specifically on the axis of gender. The level of gaslighting taking place here is difficult to overstate.

From the outside, now, I can finally see how ridiculous it is. That took months and months. It took us a year of exploring the feminist theory that had been forbidden to us before I or K could even call any transwoman a man without having a panic attack.

At first, when I started learning more about opposing viewpoints, I identified as a "gender-critical transman." I knew that the transgender cause had been used in a lot of disgusting ways, but I still believed transition was the only way I could survive, and I was trying to reconcile seeing myself as transgender with believing that the vast majority of trans activism was harmful to women. During this time, I really looked up to gender-critical transwomen transitioning males who were usually at least marginally more sympathetic and thoughtful than most men. I tried to reconcile our respective identities and our needs, as we understood them, with the needs of women as a class.

I failed. At the end of the day, I just don't want anyone male in the bathroom with me. I don't want them on a women's volleyball team. I don't want them at Curves. I don't want them in a lesbian book club. The experience of being male is fundamentally different from the experience of being female even if a man "passes," even if a man has surgery to more closely resemble his idea of a woman. I don't say this out of a hatred for transwomen. I say this out of love and respect for women. What we are cannot be conceived or replicated in a man's imagination, and it absolutely cannot be formed out of male tissue on an operating table.

The sympathy I feel for men harmed by gender, to the extent that it means I encourage male-to-female transsexualism, is in direct competition with the sympathy I feel for women harmed by gender. Everyone is entitled to make their own choices about their bodies. Everyone is also entitled to have opinions about the choices that others make about their bodies. I feel that transition is a treatment with far-reaching, harmful side effects not only for the individual receiving treatment, but also for those around them.

Lesbians who see their sisters disappearing are more likely to try to erase themselves. Lesbians who are forced to welcome men into their spaces will never be able to see or understand the value of female-only space, having never actually experienced it. Transition does not cure the irreconcilability of our selves with our environments. Gendered identity crises experienced under patriarchy are very real to the individuals experiencing them, myself included, but this energetic drive towards change is not best spent reforming ourselves into someone who can assimilate into the world men have built. We need to use this energy to work towards restoring balance to a sick world.

Many young lesbians (and some older lesbians caught up in a youth-oriented trans/queer culture) hold political views diametrically opposed to our collective interests. We genuinely believe some off-the-wall garbage, like that it's wrong and evil not to be attracted to penises because of "internalized cissexism." We have been successfully brainwashed to serve males at the expense of our own health and sanity.

I have so much empathy for other women who believed transition was their best choice. I lived that. The fact is, loving a woman does not mean agreeing with her. I believe that all of us deserve better. We deserve to experience autonomous female space. We deserve the opportunity to experience our bodies as a part of nature worthy of celebration, not objects to be "reconstructed." The energy we spend trying to run from our own bodies is better spent working to support each other.

Those of us who make it out of communities like the ones I was in often only manage to do so because of strong female (in my experience, lesbian) support networks that help us relearn how to think for ourselves without getting angry when we make mistakes in the process. I hear political opponents of the transgender movement calling it extremely cult-like and in the same breath damning the women, usually once lesbians, who fall into the trap. This reinforces the learned hatred of anyone who disagrees without creating any opportunity for victims of this ideology to ask questions and explore viewpoints that genuinely feel like some kind of blasphemy to them. The pace of progress needs to be determined by the individual. Frustration with the behavior of deeply misogynistic trans activists is very understandable, but even the most righteous anger is unlikely to change minds when it's directed at someone who has been manipulated into believing that dissenting women are literally equivalent to murderers.

The beliefs many proponents of transgender ideology have internalized are harmful to all women. No one is obligated to subject herself to being triggered or re-traumatized by the virulent misogyny that trans activists tend to espouse, even in the name of reaching out to a sister in crisis. Taking care of yourself has to come first. I try to stay available for conversations with questioning trans-identifying females, but I can't always be there. I need rest, too.

I try to remember the fable of Aesop's about a guy who accidentally kills his donkey because he wouldn't stop trying to please every pedestrian who commented on his choices. At the end of the story, an old man tells him, "please all, and you will please none." As I move away from viewing myself and my body as an object to improve, I'm realizing more and more how much of my energy has been devoted to appeasing men in some way.

While I transitioned, I was terrified of eventually regretting it. I sure as hell didn't let on much about it, for fear of losing access to medical treatment, but I was consumed all the time with obsessive thoughts about it. I didn't understand how I could go on living as a woman with no breasts. *What man would want to fuck me?* Never mind that I didn't *want* to be fucked by any man; that didn't feel like a good enough answer. I am so incredibly grateful that I learned that there was more to being a woman. Transition was absolutely not the easiest way to learn this, but it was how I learned it. It was how I learned that I could survive without men viewing me as a piece of meat. I never shaved my legs or armpits again. I stopped tittering at their stupid jokes. I dress practically. I'm grateful that I learned it was okay to exist as I am.

For me, transition was a process of distancing my true self from my body and my environment. Detransition has been the opposite: learning to participate earnestly in the world again. For me, this isn't about undoing my transition. I'm not seeking any further changes like electrolysis or breast reconstruction. I am a woman, even if my body is recognizable as the body of a woman who once thought transition was the best choice available to me. My body has known tragedies, but my body is not a tragedy. When I catch myself slipping into deeply misogynistic internal tirades about the aspects of my appearance that changed during transition, I practice thought replacement. *I am not a waste of a woman.*

I'm so grateful for all of the incredible women I've connected with who are on the other side of transgender identities now. Some of them are women who I met years ago, when both of us were still pursuing transition. This doesn't have to be forever. If transition makes you sick inside, you don't have to live and die with that sickness. There is community. There is processing. There is genuine healing. More and more of us are waking up, each with her own story. We question and disagree, with our enemies and with each other. We learn. Together, we are moving forward.

This piece was written for this anthology and published first in 4th Wave Now.
https://4thwavenow.com/2016/04/27/shrinking-to-survive-a-former-trans-man-reports-on-life-inside-queer-youth-culture/

CHAPTER 35

RECLAIMING FEMALE/SPEAKING BACK

Crash

CUT OFF FROM myself, wrenched apart, scattered into pieces, I mistook my wounds for what I was. Encouraged to live inside illusions, I gave my life to them to keep them alive and take what protection they offered.

I am a dyke coming back together after being severed and scattered, after learning to fear my own body and see it wretched and not enough, a place under constant threat I had to escape or change to survive in.

I couldn't call myself a woman because woman meant nothing I was or wanted to be. It meant the girls wearing make-up and clothes that felt like drag on me, talking and acting in ways strange to me, incomprehensible creatures who were sometimes cruel, asking me if I had a dick, throwing up their repulsion as another barrier between us. It meant the women I found on the screen and the page who I could not see myself in, the descriptions of female life that left me out, didn't even consider my existence a possibility. It meant I was disgusting, not right, not enough of a boy or a girl to belong to either group, left out, on my own, living in my head and talking to myself for lack of actual friends, being one of the school scapegoats, never able to rise above my position no matter how hard I tried, as a girl I was not what others respected or wanted to be close to. It meant being alone and open to attack. It meant threats to my safety, being seen as a target for being female and then for being one that didn't look or act right, being yelled at by strangers, listening to a boy at school joke about raping me, knowing I should never, ever be caught alone with certain boys or they just might.

It meant my mother, watching her unhappy, unfulfilled, anxious, growing more depressed as I grew older, watching her try out different therapists, art therapy, self-help books, trying every psych drug from benzos to amphetamines and never finding relief. It meant coming home to her suicide note and a message on the answering machine saying she'd been found on a bridge and taken to a hospital and never talking about it after she got out a month later, pretending everything was better until she wasn't again and fell even farther, too far, put on antipsychotics and pacing, pacing all the time, the only expression on her face was pain. She was totally lost, soulless, a walking corpse in agony terrible to behold, until one day stiff and dead and hanging in the closet, she couldn't see any other way.

I didn't see any way I could be a woman. I saw how differently others treated me when they thought I was a boy, when they were unable to see me as female because they never learned a face, body, posture, voice like mine could belong to a woman. As a boy I fit inside their world; even as a trans boy I usually made more sense, caused less confusion than I did as a girl. If I was a trans boy we could all agree something was wrong, my body was wrong, I had the wrong traits and character for my body, but that could be fixed and then order would be restored.

I wrote a story for myself that wove together what I felt and what seemed the clearest course of survival. I could not see myself as a woman and I could not ignore the safety and respect I got when I was seen as male, trans or otherwise. I knew I was not a man, knew it even more after I started t and got accepted into male society without question and heard what they say amongst themselves, but I tried to convince myself otherwise because being seen as one, living as one gave me so much. To look like any other white guy, even dressed up all punk, meant being able to just walk through the world and be acknowledged as a person worthy of basic respect, not having to be afraid of being yelled at or fucked with, not treated like a freak. I never had that ease until I took testosterone and started passing consistently. So I made myself into an exceptional man, said I was like them and unlike them at the same time. A genderqueer creature, mixture of different genders that shifted and flowed into each other. I was a man born with a cunt and raised in a female body. I never had any illusions that my body and past didn't matter though I couldn't take in their whole significance.

I was fragmented, with different parts of me crying out for expression, and I tried to fit them into a whole. There was the part that felt like a man and wanted to get treated like one and enjoyed how well she passed, enjoyed it even more when people knew she was female, saw direct evidence of her female body and still said what a dude she was. There was the part that still felt like a butch dyke but couldn't see butch as really female or was afraid to, still not ready to go into that fear, a part that offered up doubts that were forgotten but raised again and again over the years. There was the part that felt like a genderfreak because she'd been treated like an oddity, misfit, not belonging among women or men, that embraced this, felt it gave her a unique position though a painful one, that felt invisible when she passed for male and so sought out queer spaces where her outsider status would be recognized and celebrated. This one had more truth in her than the one who felt male and gradually gained prominence, my view of myself shifting more towards genderfreak from trans male over time, until I was ready to look at my femaleness directly. She was an articulation of the trauma of not having a place amongst other people, being cast out, and the passing male persona was her shield for moving through this world unharmed.

There was also the part that felt like she had no gender inside of her, felt like gender was projected onto her like an illusion, a product of society she had taken into herself and would not know of otherwise. She was also closer to the truth and she, too, came more into focus over time. These parts would speak at different times alone or clamor together at once, arguing, trying to come to agreement or cancel each other out. I tried to sort them all out into one space I could inhabit and feel secure in.

I decided I must be movement, for any stillness of self was transitory and shifted position eventually. I saw I had a range of places I went, places I went back and forth from or sometimes occupied simultaneously, feeling more like a man or a genderfreak or both a dude and dyke at the same time, or as no gender at all. This was very unsettling to me at first. I wanted more stability, one place to live, not many to wander back and forth from. But since this was what I found when I examined myself, year after year, I decided this just must be what I am and I must accept this.

Now I see my uneasiness with this state as knowing on some level that I wasn't well, that I was trying to live broken apart, shattered. When I finally was able to start putting the pieces together into a whole, which was only possible after I accepted myself as a woman, the state I'd lived in and accepted as a kind of gender fluidity or complexity began to horrify me when I recalled it. I could connect what I had felt back to violence done to me by people and this culture that had literally ripped me apart into pieces and then set some of those pieces into conflict with the others. The story I told about it seemed like making the best of a profound severance and disconnection between my selves, a way of making sense of things when I wasn't ready to face knowledge of how I'd been hurt.

Coming to see my sense of self as a product of how I'd been wounded took time. The parts that knew were stubborn and wouldn't shut up, and eventually I started to listen. First there was letting myself give up on being a man, starting to feel more and more invisible when I was seen as one, getting called "he" stopped feeling right. I stopped taking testosterone because it made my head feel wrong and I told myself I'd gotten the changes I'd wanted from it, and now it was making me look too much like a man anyways, which I knew I wasn't now, and if I stopped I'd look more ambiguous, like I felt. Still not ready to be a woman but getting more comfortable with seeing myself as a dyke, which I still put on the borderland of female heading out of it. I could've maybe stopped there, just told myself I was a genderqueer who needed to take it temporarily, not for life, live in an "in-between" body. But something pulled me on, kept me going.

I started sleeping with a woman, someone I'd been friends with for years, my first serious relationship in a long time. We got together while I was still living as a genderqueer/man but sometimes when we had sex I felt like we were two women, and I felt aroused by how our bodies were the same. And I found that I worried that what we did together wasn't real because neither of us had a dick, that we weren't really having sex. Most of her previous partners had been male and I found that part of the satisfaction I got from pleasuring her was that it gave me proof that I was as sexually potent as a man. Taking all these feelings together and examining them, I saw I had taken in the idea that sex between two female bodies wasn't real, was weak and not as good as heterosexual sex and that I was uncomfortable when I felt like a woman having sex with another woman, but also desired it. I was shocked. I'd been having relationships with women since my teens and had been part of a radical queer scene that trumpeted "sex positivity" for most of my adult life, and yet I found deep inside that I hated and had contempt for myself for being a lesbian.

I had been too proud and swept up in radical queer rhetoric to consider that I could have anything so "old-fashioned" as internalized homophobia. I had come out in a time when there were gay groups for high school kids; one of them even met at my Unitarian church. Overall, my family was accepting of me when I came out or, that's how I recalled it. Now I see more ambivalence on their part. I had access to tons of books and movies, magazines and websites. I thought I had it pretty easy compared to what older generations had gone through. And yet, nearly every kid who attended that youth group at my church had been locked up in a psych ward at some point, myself included. I couldn't take it when my history teacher told me I couldn't write a paper on the Stonewall riots because they weren't history. On top of all the shit I got, being told I had no history was too much. I thought about taking too many pills, told my parents instead and they sent me to the psych ward. And while I was in there, I met more lesbians, most of them butch like me, than I did at my youth group. And it was totally normal amongst the gay kids I knew that we felt like killing ourselves at some time or another or maybe all the time. I told people how much I'd been hurting and they locked me up and drugged me. They hurt me even more. All the gay kids I knew were also going crazy and wanting to die and the doctors were giving us pills and therapy, making money off our suffering; transitioning some of us is just an extension of that. Now they pathologize homosexuality less directly, and go after us for how living in a hostile world affects us.

And though I suffered along with them, I was on the fringe of many of the gay groups I hung out in. I found out there were rumors amongst them that my body wasn't really female, that I had tits *and* a dick. They would get confused by me, just like the straight kids did, would wonder whether I was a boy or girl. Presumed I was trans a lot of the time, again sending me the message that I wasn't really female, made more sense as something else. In nearly every group I moved through, I felt out of place.

How much of my radical queer posturing was just covering up my vulnerabilities and making a lot of noise to distract myself from the pain I was feeling? Trying to make myself look tough, I was making up for being at the bottom for so long and feeling like shit. I was angry and could rail against the world, but I wasn't ready to look at all the reasons I felt that way.

With my lover I started being able to see and experience my body in new ways. I started to come back inside my flesh and take hold of her as female, accepting that that is what my body is and that is enough. My submerged female consciousness was ready to surface and she started bubbling up all over, during sex, meditation, when I entered ritual space. She had found her opening out to the world and she took it, slowly pouring out of me, gradually infusing me more and more. First getting me comfortable with giving more space to being a dyke without giving up seeing myself as genderqueer or even still a boy sometimes, but slowly pushing me onwards, calling me to attention, making me look where I was afraid to before.

I found that I was terrified of being a woman and so I explored that fear, made myself walk through that haunted land though it made my skin crawl and I shuddered with every step. The terrain of woman was female, was a body I had trouble living in completely and feeling all the parts present with the names and meanings they'd inherited, that I thought I had to remake to inhabit. I thought the soil was dead to the life I wanted to grow from it and I needed to infuse it with chemicals to sprout what I desired. My desires, my images of what I wanted, were more real and more "me" than the body itself, my mind trying to forget the whole organism. But eventually there was the woman, presumed dead, surrounding me, daring me to look and transverse her and find out what she was. Was she me?

So I walked into her and I found what repulsed me. I found what had been sunk into her, into me, what others had tried to build into us in order to exploit, extract, redesign us and I found that my own experiments in chemical transformation, in renaming my body "male" or "genderfreak" had not touched this first evidence of invasion. I found a wounded landscape, devastation, and I saw I had taken up the destruction where others had left off. Not that they ever really stopped, but I could mark the time when I began to imitate them, carve into myself what they had carved into me first. I found what horrified me was what had been done to me, and what I'd done to myself. I saw what had been done to my female body to try to make me over into an ensnared woman, that made womanhood into a threat, something I thought I had to avoid to be free.

And I found the land surviving underneath and she was alive and full of living creatures extending out into each other, forming a web. She shook in pain and rage but she lived. And she was space extending into infinity and no matter how far I walked or how hard I looked I could not see the end of her. Woman going on forever, endless textures, sights, sounds, smells, words, thoughts and feelings, what could be named and what was beyond naming. And what had been built on her, on me to contain, to force into ornamentation or labor began to seem so much less significant, to become absurd and laughable, transient and doomed to decay back into the land. As nourishment. What was pain becomes food, fuel to grow and fight. The men in power will never learn that so often when they seek to control us they create their own Nemesis. It just takes time before she comes out of hiding. And it turns out she'd been stalking her enemies this entire time spent in their territory, because she came back with a wealth of intelligence about the society set up to destroy her.

My sense of being a man and other genders were like shelters I built from scraps I'd harvested or stolen from the structures built upon me by this society and its enforcers. They housed me but also confined me. I was afraid of going too far away from them, so they limited my ability to wander. They required frequent repair and so tied me to the society I sought to escape, since I returned to it again and again for supplies. And these materials were toxic, silently exuding substances I could not detect but which poisoned me all the same. If I compared what I had built to the cities I'd stolen the materials from, I was satisfied, my creations seemed preferable and separate enough. When I saw beyond them to the endless living land, I saw how much they resembled what I'd been trying to overcome. I had built in my own style but I had still built according to an earlier education I was trying to forget. Instead I'd just forgotten how it had affected me and its lessons played inside my head, shaping my movements and creations. Actually unlearning meant seeing the land directly without words coming between us which then changed what words could mean when they returned.

This led to a transformation of language that generated power and released energy that had been bound up in stale symbols, which turned these symbols from confining to life-giving. Woman, for example, gained new dimensions. I could see not only how it had been used to summon up a host of roles, rules and punishments designed to bring women into line with the desires of men but also how it pointed to a people struggling to exist on our own terms and claim our full potential, who refused to accept that having a cunt was a limitation rather than a unique and powerful existence. Woman becomes a sign of prideful defiance, of joy in creating our own reality despite the obstacles put in our path. It became something I could sense clearly but can never contain in words and so the possible descriptions are endless. Woman becomes the way through to find infinite power and women become those who actively or potentially seek such power as well.

Calling myself a woman became a way of taking on the history of womankind, the long horrifying legacy we've all inherited of exploited labor, rape, forced pregnancy or sterilization, prostitution, and incest; of being denied education and meaningful work; of enduring beatings, burnings, and confinement in mental institutions; of strife between women, betrayals by women wielding class power and racism, betrayal of mother by daughter and vice versa, women turning from each other in times of need, and abusing each other to get some taste of power; of the culture, media and religion reflecting and justifying this reality, the whole weight of several thousand years of global patriarchy, taking it on and holding it without being crushed. Becoming strong enough to admit that I am a woman and that this connects me to all other women alive and dead. And knowing this connection, deeply, in my very flesh is the beginning of going beyond it. Recognizing the connections does not only connect me to suffering and degradation but also to the long history of women fighting back. I find the women who came before and their creations, and their power is still alive and it lights me up. So I can learn about the violence and idiocy that's long ruled the world and I can face the forms of it that exist currently because I have proof of what other women did. I learned that I also inherited the spoils they won, I learn what I have because of how hard they fought and I know it's my turn to keep it going. There's still so much work to do.

Alongside me, helping me face what terrified me and discover all these connections beyond that, helping me remember what happened to me and understand how I got here, helping me get in touch with power inside me and find radical lesbian and women-centered culture, were other women who had the same struggle. Women who'd also been cut off from their bodies and selves, treated like freaks, broken apart by the world around us, who transitioned and lived as men or other genders and then came back to their womanhood and were trying to make sense of what had happened to them.

First I found one other woman like me, Devorah; I met her online. We started writing one another, later called each other on the phone. Found out quickly we could say things to each other we couldn't say to people in the queer scene because it was too taboo, against the rules, supposedly "transphobic." We became emboldened, felt less crazy with another who shared our observations, who saw misogyny poking out everywhere from behind the facade of supposedly radical queer culture. We helped each other go where each of us was afraid to go alone. We had no idea where we'd end up, getting more and more heretical as time went by, finding strength and sense reading the work of radical women we'd been taught were worthless and irrelevant at best, hateful bigots at worst. Came to see that the "feminism" and queer theory we'd been taught was just the latest backlash, patriarchy pushing back with co-optation this time. Both of us started blogging about our experiences and through that met more women who'd transitioned and stopped. The more women we talked to, the more patterns we started to see: trauma, dissociation, getting treated like shit because our bodies and behaviors weren't "female enough," tendency towards self-destruction, most of us lesbian or bisexual, often butch. It became more clear that what we had suspected was true; this was a social problem masquerading as individual malady, and women like us were being erased. We understood from our own pasts how self-annihilation could be clothed in the trappings of self-discovery and creation, knew it was more complicated than people just doing what felt right to them. We knew that our feelings and self-knowledge also grow from a culture determined to destroy us and this must be reckoned with deliberately, grieved from our core outwards if we want to find freedom, find out what we can be.

I finally met Devorah at Michfest (The Michigan Womyn's Music Festival), presenting a workshop with her and four other women about our experiences transitioning and then reclaiming our female realities, how this happened, what we thought this meant, how it was a result of living in a woman-hating and lesbian-hating culture. The women who came to listen gave us their full attention, their concern and love, "hearing us into speech," helping anxiety fall away and easing out the difficult truths we carried with us. We had never experienced anything like it before, being seen and respected for our strength and for being honest about how we'd been hurt, not pitied but held, given space to exist as we are.

At Michfest I found the radical lesbian feminist culture I'd been obsessively reading about manifesting all around me, becoming a physical, living, changing reality I could interact with. I could talk to the women who'd helped build it, hear their stories and find out that they wanted to hear mine, too. I realized that what I'd been told about these women that they didn't matter, were foolishly set in outdated ways, that it'd be great when they all finally died out, hateful, narrow, naive, bigoted all this had cut me off and barred me from a culture built by women like me, that centered women like me. To meet these women and find out how glad they were to see me and hear them say that I, and my friends, were the women they'd been fighting for and they'd waited all these years for us to show up brought me alive in ways I'd never known before. Not being able to accept or even see myself as a lesbian was one kind of wound. Being cut off from other dykes, especially from the dykes who came before me who spent their lives making a meaningful and life-sustaining culture that centers our many experiences, that was a whole other catastrophe, one I'm still absorbing.

I need other women, other lesbians especially, helping me fight against this death-loving culture, sharing support while we heal and create what life and freedom we can. My lesbian cultural heritage is precious to me now and I treasure the connections I've made with other radical dykes, from my elders to my peers. Part of my healing has been taking on the task of sustaining and creating radical lesbian culture, not just keeping it alive but helping it grow. The prospect that it could die out and that there are many, among them not a few "radicals," who'd celebrate its death horrifies me but doesn't surprise me. If women like me can destroy themselves without much comment being raised, if violence against women in general is a boring, old fact few concern themselves with, why should I be shocked that lesbians and the women-centered culture we create is ridiculed and marked for extermination? These women and this culture have healed me, helped me find wholeness and life beyond what I knew to be possible and so I give back to it, as I would give back to land that feeds and sustains me.

Claiming woman, as well as dyke and lesbian, generated far more power than any queer gender I tried to invent or new sex I tried to create through manipulating my body's hormones. Trying to live as a genderqueer/man was a kind of immature magical practice. There was some power and utility in it, but not as much as I thought at the time. Passing as a man provided me a defensive cover moving through this society and calling myself genderqueer won me status and a place among the radical queer community, which meant literal nourishment and shelter as well as camaraderie and shared culture. It also shielded me from aspects of myself too painful and scary to look at, what I thought I couldn't bear. But the way it kept me from pain hurt me still, since it let the wounds fester. I didn't even know how much hurt I was carrying around with me until I finally faced it and it started to heal. Healing was accepting rather than denying that I was a woman. I had unknowingly been denying my own power and capacity to get well.

When I used to hear myself called woman or female, I heard an order to be a mother, a fuckhole, subservient, pretty, docile, workhorse for little to no pay, some way to get something out of me I didn't want to give. Now when I call myself female, I'm saying my resources are my own and they aren't resources as much as they're wilderness, a more mobile piece of land trying to get back with the rest, trying to re-establish connections. Female is a one-word poem and a metaphor and a spell. Calling myself female and woman has helped me get back what was taken from me.

As many of us have been separated from living soil by layers of concrete and asphalt, as much as the sky is blocked from our view by towering structures of metal and brick, and our nostrils plugged with exhaust, so have we been cleaved from our own most intimate land, our bodies. We have been disconnected from what shapes and animates our flesh, deprived of knowledge of the world around us, of our histories, of a true view of our cultures that is essential for actually knowing ourselves. In our present society there are far more working to ensnare our ability to know than to make us free. And the effort to make sense of the connections that make us who we are is also a struggle against our own tendencies towards ignorance, denial and delusion, which stems from a fear of punishment or pain inflicted on most of us since birth.

Many of us tell half-truths and live by obscured vision, seeing just enough to survive. There is no way to live without some contact and knowledge of how reality actually runs. The whole organism knows, even if parts of it, the parts that interpret and make meaning of sensations consciously, pretend to know something different. The organism does what it needs to do to survive and if this means knowing exactly what's going on and lying about it at the same time, so be it. But such a life is lived in tension and is another stress upon the life force it would rather do without. So it accepts this for the sake of survival but it seeks at the same time to bring the pieces back together into wholeness, bring it all back into knowledge and sensation. Many people are selves at war with their organism, mirroring on a small scale the warfare of the larger world.

So I once was and so I still struggle, but my movements are freer and my vision clearer. I feel whole in a way I never had thought possible during my days of fragmentation. Woman, dyke, female, and lesbian are words I use to point to my infinity. My woman's body is strength, power moving and growing, changing as I act in the world, become more experienced and skilled. She is how I connect with the land I grow my food from, with the women I love, how I bring my words into the world through pen or keyboard. She holds my history. She is expansive enough to hold all of me, all my pieces as they find each other and figure out how to reconnect and heal back into each other. Finally I have space enough to live.

CHAPTER 36

THE GODDESS OF AUTOTOMY

Devorah Zahav

I write this for women who are ready to know what we know.
I write this under a vision of Tiamat, Source Goddess, Dragyn.

THE WORLD AS it is looks normal to me, but it isn't. I am used to tall buildings, materials refined beyond any discernable trace of their raw states, prefabricated answers to the problems of how to sustain my life. I am used to a system of inputs and outputs: a built environment. A world in which even the less-developed "natural" places reserved for respite are full of the sounds and sights of the man-made. I never feel my feet bare against the ground. The ground is not the earth but covering over it. I walk in proximity to large metal vehicles whose impact with my body would mean my death, and think nothing of it. In order to function here, I have to lose my presence in my body to some extent. This world looks normal to me, but it isn't.

It looks normal because I don't see this planet as a body. But she is a body.

It looks normal because I don't feel from within my body, that I am made of her.

Tiamat, murdered, vivisected, and usurped by the male god. Tiamat
whose tears, blood, viscera, severed limbs, and organs form the land-
scape of our world and the matter of our bodies.

This is an account of severing and a call to re-member.

I grew up in a halfway rural place giving way to suburbanity. Because I was a girl, my life was very circumscribed. I spent a lot of time alone and reading. What I longed for and what called me to attention were other girls or women who might be like me, wild creatures, and flowering plants. My memories of childhood overall are vague and fragmented, but I can catalogue every overt lesbian I ever saw, as well as nearly every plant and wild creature I came into contact with. I was hungry for the companionship of these creatures in particular. Hungry for what they woke in me.

As an early teenager I found some zines which were my portal into the burgeoning queer-punk scene of the 1990s. Much of what I found was by and for gay men, while nearly everything lesbian held transgender (in the ftm sense) as an inextricable element at the core of its meaning, denoting those dykes who were visibly "other" within straight society. I situated myself within that queer, trans paradigm between my early teens and my early twenties, in various ways.

I passed as a boy easily to strangers, while those who knew me at school or work knew that I was not male but made clear that I did not fit the bounds I ought to, for a girl. I started trying to transition in all the ways I could. Changing my name. Claiming the word transgender. Telling people I was male, or simply passing. Not correcting people when they took me for a boy. Hiding my body, making plans to alter it. Attempting to respect women-only space by not partaking of it, because I did not understand myself to be a woman. Trying to be the kind of man I thought the world needed. Objecting to being placed in women's housing. Because transition was not yet mainstream at the time, I met with steady opposition to my assertions until I was of age and started taking testosterone. That step signified a seriousness which others were more bound to respect.

Of course you want to know why I did this, and my specifics are a mix of idiosyncratic circumstances and those which are common as ants but the things that drove me to transition are not the point I have to make here. What I have to tell you is a lot larger than my individual qualification—what it was like, what happened, and what it's like now. I've learned, from meeting hundreds of other girls and women who have been through this experience and found their way to the other side, what these personal patterns look like in aggregate. And what it means.

Those others, the women in whom I find context and comprehension, have made it possible for me to know what I know. So I will give you some of my own specifics, but the point lies in bringing my own story back together into the larger body of Us—other women who have been through this experience, and also all women—we are one body, though our patriarchal dismemberment has taken different forms.

I was still severed from this knowledge of connection when I stopped my medical transition. Stopping testosterone and shifting to a new kind of "gender identity" did not change my distorted beliefs about my body or her nature. I still did not believe I was a woman; I did not even believe I was female. I was working hard to heal and integrate—gaining sobriety and establishing many other foundational elements of a life—but for several years I struggled to make sense of this experience from within the queer paradigm. Many stopped transitions end here—in recasting ftm into "genderqueer," for instance, or in a leap from ftm to femme, or in declaring oneself "bigender," "agender" or "gender fluid." So long as a person still pledges allegiance to the idea of gender identity, that person doesn't violate the social norms of the scene. As someone who keeps digging into things, that plateau did not satisfy; and I valued satisfying answers over belonging. I'd mainly left the radical queer social scene anyway, alienated by it in some ways I could not name and other ways I could but only dared in private to a trusted few.

So I kept trying to dig into what had happened and why. My first impulse, of course, was to look to a male experience to understand myself. That was all I knew how to do. So I thought I should connect more with the transwomen I knew, and read "transfeminist" work. I believed we had common ground in moving from being seen as male to trying to fit into the world as women, despite being "wrong" women. Although I believed I held privilege they didn't, I also believed I was trying to pass as female, same as a transwoman. This approach led me to try to retrain my voice into more stereotypical patterns and more typically female ranges, and in other ways to continue trying to change my body and appearance. This didn't get me closer to knowing how I had ended up in my predicament, though. And I tried to get clarity about that but I kept hitting up against something—a sense that there was more, that I had to look closer. My attempts to glean meaningful insight by connecting with transwomen—those I knew as well as writers and activists—left me decidedly unsatisfied. It felt so surface, so much posturing, ultimately empty. I'm very accustomed to making meaning across disparate experiences and power imbalances—translating, bridging—because even when I don't share the same social location, I can recognize the network of power being described and situate myself within it. Yet nothing I found here spoke to me in a way I could connect back. It didn't describe a world I recognized. I nevertheless kept trying this method for some time. From where I stood, it looked like the only way.

I also talked to some young radical queer lesbians I knew who told me that in the years since my transition it had become increasingly mainstream. They told me they'd all been assumed trans and had felt pressure to "identify" as Anything But Female. They'd all taken on different pronouns and bound their breasts at some point. This particular group comprised young women who eventually discarded those behaviors and claimed themselves as "queer women." When I asked why, they said they wanted to stay belonging as women because women are cool. I thought this was a positive sign of feminist consciousness, but gradually more of the social pressures on them became clearer: they did not want to identify as other-than-women because the high status people in their scene were transwomen who defined ftms as "male oppres-sors." As "cis" women, they were expected to abase themselves in various ways in the name of "solidarity," but the expectations on transmen were much more extreme; their belonging more precarious. This was a shift from the past incarnations I had known of lesbian community, where accommodating ftms involved lesbian self-erasure, but the community was still, at the end of the day, made up of same-sex loving females. In retrospect, this new development was the inevitable consequence of the ways we had been maintaining our community while deny-ing its same-sex basis.

And then I found myself involved with a friend I had known for years, who was also ftm and like me, had transitioned as a teenager. I had fallen hard for her but was hesitant about us. I wasn't sure of being involved with someone who passed as male and held that as an identity. But she confided in me that she knew she was a lesbian, felt she was living a lie, and wanted it to be over. Over the years we spent living together as lovers, I witnessed her stop her transition. She'd walked much further down the path than I had. Passed as a man, not only a boy, for a dozen years. Had surgery to remove her breasts. On the other side of this, I watched her come into herself. I watched her learn to walk in the world as someone known to be female, a woman. I watched her learn how to navigate being that kind of target. She learned to cope, but she also resisted. She'd gone right from girlhood to passing as male for more than a decade. She'd never lived as a grown woman without passing as male, and there was so much shock in the grind of daily misogyny. So much to remember about what her girlhood had meant. I saw her courage in standing up for herself and other women everywhere, because she had grown unaccustomed to being the target of misogyny and was unwilling to become docile and accept it. Watching the woman who had my heart go through this, I could see and understand so much more of my own life, and the larger pattern I fit within. I had what I knew were iconoclastic thoughts and "wrong" feelings about the meaning of sex and "gender," unacceptable within the scenes I'd come from. But I felt drawn to express and listen to such thoughts and feelings, to enlarge my connective understanding as much as I could. So I started searching out other voices.

And then I met a woman called Crash who had stopped her transition and was writing about her sense of loss. The way she named things opened my knowing: this was about trauma and grief. We began pouring out letters to each other, the secret things we knew, suspected, or wondered. Her letters were replete with so much that I had longed to hear another woman say. She told me about another woman who was stopping her transition and publicly document-ing her way through. And then there was another, and another…we were from everywhere. Scattered across many regions and languages, we made our way toward each other's fire.

We were like and not like. We had run the gamut of ways of being trans. We were True Transsexuals who had every textbook marker and would have been approved for treatment under the Harry Benjamin Standards of Care; we were genderqueers who didn't want to be men or women but were compelled to modify ourselves into appearing more male for various reasons. We had started asserting ourselves as male in childhood; we had only started feeling what we came to call dysphoria after puberty; we had started transition in middle age. We didn't ever believe we were male but did not want to be girls or women; we believed we were males with birth defects, not female at all. We were butch dykes who had been presumed trans; we were straight women who wanted a different basis on which to relate to male partners, one in which we were as human as they were; we were bi and questioning women whose attraction to other women made us believe we must be men; we were garden variety lesbians who did not realize how much we had internalized our society's contempt. Prior to transitioning, we were already very ambiguous in our appearance; we were seen as "masculine;" we were seen as "feminine" and soft and hated the way people treated us when they saw us that way. We had taken years to carefully consider transition before beginning treatment; we had started down the path as minors and made irreversible changes within months of coming out. We were nearly all survivors of sexual trauma.

In these women lived pieces of myself. Her story, my shape. My story, her words. Her body, my witness. My body, her knowing mirror. We woke and stirred each other. We followed another woman's words through the dim caves of tumblr or reddit and found a real beating heart at the source.

We made secret places to meet in the ether. We made "Camp Detrans" and held workshops at the Michigan Womyn's Music Festival. We made sharing circles in my living room, modeled on a hybrid of twelve step, Consciousness Raising, embodiment meditation, and other ways of bearing witness for each other. We made a collective zine with our words and artwork. We made each other laugh from a place of deep knowing. We made moments of home for each other: recognition.

It was a strange way to end up in womyn's' community but this is where I've landed. Being in the lesbian feminist Amazon reality of Michfest, I understood it was reversals and lies that had kept me from this all along. That the ways I was marked out as a freak could be understood within a paradigm besides trans, a paradigm that would have held me exactly as-is, without prompting me to sever any part of myself to gain belonging. There was a culture where I would have made sense. This culture is portrayed to my generation and those after in distorted, slanderous ways designed to keep us from knowing how deeply we need it. I work to make space within it so the young ones will have a home to come to should they awaken to that need.

I spend a lot of time talking to lesbians and feminists about the phenomenon of female transition. It is not an easy feat of translation. Even on the occasion when I feel I've managed to communicate something, it doesn't usually take. I try to explain: none of us came up with the idea that we were "different" on our own. We were Othered by other women and girls, and then given this language, this frame, for understanding what that meant and where we might fit.

I try to explain: being ftm, being femme, being straight, these are all female strategies for survival. Transition may ultimately be rooted in a conservative value set but just as Dworkin illustrates about other conservative female strategies in *Right Wing Women*[1], it is based in accurate perceptions about misogyny that liberals refuse to name or neglect to fully acknowledge or address. Dworkin writes, "Right-wing women have surveyed the world: they find it a dangerous place. They see that work subjects them to more danger from more men; it increases the risk of sexual exploitation. They see that creativity and originality in their kind are ridiculed; they see women thrown out of the circle of male civilization for having ideas, plans, visions, ambitions. They see that traditional marriage means selling to one man, not hundreds: the better deal. They see that the streets are cold, and that the women on them are tired, sick, and bruised. They see that the money they can earn will not make them independent of men and that they will still have to play the sex games of their kind: at home and at work too. They see no way to make their bodies authentically their own and to survive in the world of men. They know too that the Left has nothing better to offer: leftist men also want wives and whores; leftist men value whores too much and wives too little. Right-wing women are not wrong."[2] She goes on, "They use the traditional intelligence of the female—animal, not human: they do what they have to to survive."[3]

In these words, I find vast sympathy between women who have declared ourselves unfemale and perhaps acted to eliminate our reproductive capacity, and the women Dworkin describes, who "know that they are valued for their sex" and who "use sex and babies to stay valuable."[4] Regardless of an individual woman's conscious impetus for pursuing it, ftm transition as a phenomenon occurs within the world that Dworkin describes—a male protection racket wherein women are forced into endless bargaining with men—whether one husband or many others—forced to trade some intimate part of ourselves in order to maintain our lives. The difference between the right wing women Dworkin describes and individuals who transition ftm is that we believe we have found a way to make our bodies our own and to survive in world of men, without having to bargain. Or we believe, more accurately, that it's a one-time bargain instead of eternal and ceaseless negotiation. Of course, there is no way to opt out. Of course, this represents a different bargain and not a real escape from the "marketplace." Of course, it may feel like an exercise of autonomous will to rid yourself of the very female markers which denote your patriarchal "value"—but as with right wing women's strategies, this move is predicated not only on a devastatingly accurate perception of life in patriarchy, but also in shaping ourselves to its values in the most intimate ways imaginable. Inviting it in.

Ftm transition is a drastic, novel behavior. It is as easy for some feminists as it is for parts of the right wing to see it as betrayal, idiocy, insanity—an individual woman's weakness and failure. It is never that. Like the right wing women's strategies Dworkin by no means advocates, but deeply understands, it is born of accurate perception of danger and an animal instinct to survive.

I try to explain and sometimes I don't succeed. I lose heart. Try again. I try to explain and sometimes women move me with their generosity, the athleticism with which they stretch to meet me.

An exceptionally kind lesbian radical feminist witch makes the generous overture of telling me that she doesn't know any woman who has escaped some form of body hate in our culture. She is doing what so many women cannot bring themselves to do: situating the behavior of transitioning ftm within the larger frame; understanding our manifestation of internalized misogyny as simply one among many. Acknowledging that despite its novelty, its drama, its overtness—this behavior is not so different in nature from any other self-harming strategy a woman necessarily takes up in order to navigate and survive patriarchy.

The irony is, I tell her, that I didn't get here by hating my body. I learned that later. I learned it *through* being trans. Before that, in fact, the wholeness, strength, and integrity I experienced in my body—the way I experienced my body from within, as something I could use to perform feats, rather than as a decorative object for others to look at—set me apart from the shared culture between other girls. Their culture was based in body hate; in attempts to decrease their mass with food restriction, in alterations and decorations meant to tempt boys; in enhancing the curves of their breasts, curves that I was grateful not to have myself. I did not want cleavage; I wanted muscles.

My body was lean, sturdy, flat-chested; small, yes, but I barely understood myself as having a body that others regarded, so the full significance of why others related to me as they did was somewhat lost on me. I knew I was the subject of jokes for my size, and that people treated me like a baby or a mascot. I disliked that but I blamed them, not my body, and demanded their respect by responding with physical blocks to enforce my boundaries. (Any boy, no matter how much larger, who tried to pick me up or use my head as an armrest or pat me like a dog was liable to exit that encounter bent in half, groaning over his bruised testicles.)

I did have intrusive experiences of the sense of a male body overlaid over my own. This was a troubling but inconstant phenomenon which I had no frame of reference to understand. It seemed as natural and unpredictable as weather. I did not name it nor did I attach any particular story to it. I did not try to explain it to myself; when it happened, I just tried to block it out, tried not to think about it, and waited to stop feeling so bewildered. Still, this was not body hate.

I did hate the way others reacted to my body, and to how I felt comfortable using it. I hated their scrutiny and ridicule of the way I walked, talked, and sat. Adults told me I was unladylike and to close my legs, intimating a sexual shame the relevance of which mystified me. Peers mocked my ways; I remember watching once during a trip to the park as the girl who had been my "best friend" denounced our bond by leading all but one of our other classmates in a parade where they imitated the way I walked. I understood this meant I was doing something wrong, not normal, but no matter how hard I studied their exaggerated send-up, I couldn't understand what was wrong with me.

Once my perp older brother tried to teach me to walk and I got more information then. He said I didn't mince my steps or swivel my hips, which girls should do for the titillation of boys and men. He demonstrated. I was left with the impression that this came much more naturally to him than to me. It sounded like a lot of effort I couldn't be bothered with. Besides, I preferred to avoid attention from boys and men.

All of this set me apart from other girls. I carved out a niche as a bookworm but I was still really odd. I had compelling romantic friendships with older girls, and usually an alliance of "best friend" with a girl in my class, or sometimes an outsider boy. Most of my life took place on the interior and was not shared with any of these others. Through reading I'd learned to make interior worlds, and I could make my own without books as well. The most sacred and intense things of life, I did not try to share with anyone.

I'd had intense unnamed romantic and sexual feelings for other girls and for women since very small—I can remember them as early as around age four. I never spoke of that. When I had a more explicit sexual awakening at around eight or nine, I talked to no one about it. The experience left me perplexed about what I was. My "education" about male and female bodies was nothing if not an exercise in female erasure: "boys have a penis, girls have a vagina."

Nothing about the clitoris. Nothing to explain the perpetual ember I had discovered, which could be stoked into fire—the flame of connection I'd found between my clitoris and the rest of me. Nothing about the way my body would respond. All we got was "boys get erect when they think about girls, and girls stop thinking boys are gross when they want to get penetrated and make babies." That was my model for what a sexual awakening was meant to be. What happened to me fit neither role—but surely seemed more like what they said happened to boys, and certainly had nothing to do with any desire to be penetrated by them or to make babies.

It was a desire I couldn't even pretend to. When other girls asked my favorite member of the boy band du jour, I had no ready answer. They ranged from uninteresting to hideous, and their music sucked besides. The male musicians I admired were models of who I wanted to be like.

To make matters worse, I was dead against ever being a mother. I was unshakable in my belief that my body was not built to become pregnant or perform childbirth: not only did I not want to do it; I didn't believe it was possible. (I still don't believe it on a gut level; if I live long enough, I'll be correct someday.)

And there were legitimate differences between my physiology and that of other girls. My clit was large enough that there were rumors about me really being male. My chest was flat. I didn't have a puberty that resembled other girls' puberties. I did eventually bleed, now and then, but not on a cycle. I went months and even a year at a time without menstruating. I had an adam's apple covered in a funny, soft patch of hair, a trail of furry hair stretching down from my belly button, a wisp of mustache at the corners of my mouth, and fine but noticeable hair covering the entire length of my arms as well as my legs. I showed no signs of outgrowing my repulsion to boys and men. I had a sexuality that was autonomous from them and focused on girls and women. I preferred not to shave any of my body hair. I did not welcome the coming of breasts. I told myself it was because I was half-boy. I had no other way to explain this to myself. I knew there was such thing as a lesbian but to my knowledge, I had never known one. I was the one who was called that name at school. Lesbian seemed to mean a half-boy or a somehow female boy, and it sounded like a disease. Certainly any girl who got too close to me was in danger of catching the designation, which was why my friendships tended not to last.

These experiences form some of the idiosyncratic basis on which I came to shoot testosterone into my body, desire to remove my female organs, and understand myself to be other than female, other than lesbian. But there are so many roads leading here. My particulars hardly matter.

It matters how I name it. It matters how I understand it. That matters because it determines who I think I am like, who I think I am connected to, and on what basis—who I think I belong with.

In her play, *Artemisia and Hildegard,*[5] Carolyn Gage writes powerfully about two extraordinary historical women who have taken opposing strategies in navigating patriarchy while preserving their female genius to create their art. As part of her strategy, "Artemisia insists on downplaying her identity as a woman."[6] Hildegard calls her "male-identified," in the former, non-literal sense of the term. Anyone who reads this play can understand various kinds of female dissociation as strategies for survival, can see the texture and shape of their psychological nature and glimpse their etiologies. My life strategy is of a piece with what Gage describes; varying only in degree, literal nature, and method of expression, rather than in kind. My life strategy had been predicated on separating myself from other female human beings in my own self-concept.

More and more women rely on that strategy. We are Tiamat's body, frozen in the moment of severing because the blade remains. We may try to heal but as long as we do not know who and what we are, the blade remains—so any attempt to knit the flesh back together will instead mean flesh against metal, again, always.

The wounded lizard eats her severed tail—she needs the sustenance she stored there so she can have strength to undertake the labor of regeneration.[7]

It matters how we name it. It matters how we understand it. It matters who we know ourselves to be like. To be *of.* There is a reason we are not supposed to try to find ourselves in each other. Because when we do that, when we recognize the truth in each other, when the other woman lets me know myself, when the answers in her words satisfy me—then the cut begins to heal and knit into a scar, the nature of the bond between us grows clear: Your speech belongs in my ear. My song belongs for you. We can be complete in ourselves only within her greater body. I would say that we are parts of that greater body but there are no parts here, only Tiamat—eating her severed tail, gaining strength for the labor ahead.

---

[1] Andrea Dworkin, *Right-Wing Women*, New York: Perigee Books, 1983.

[2] Andrea Dworkin, *Right-wing Women*. New York: Perigee Books, 1983, pp. 68-69.

[3] Andrea Dworkin, *Right-wing Women*. New York: Perigee Books, 1983, p. 69.

[4] Ibid.

[5] Carolyn Gage, *Artemesia and Hildegard: An Exorcism in One Act.* 2004. This is a two-woman show that is only available digitally ISBN: 978-1-257-45483-9.

[6] Carolyn Gage, *Artemesia and Hildegard: An Exorcism in One Act.* 2004, from the Introduction.

[7] "Autotomy" means the ability to lose and regenerate a part of yourself, like the lizard's tail or the arms of the starfish.

CHAPTER 37

CENSORED CONVERSATIONS IN THE HALLWAYS OF ACADEMIA

Double XX Howl

"Why, in the Peking Opera, are women's roles played by men?
…Because only a man knows how a woman is supposed to act."

~ DAVID HENRY HWANG, *M. BUTTERFLY*

THERE ARE CONVERSATIONS happening in the hallways of the academy that you won't hear outside the system.

"I feel bullied by the pronouns. I know that the worst thing that could happen to these kids is *not* that someone calls them the wrong pronoun."

"I had to spend one hour of that hour and a half in class on identity check. Not everything is about that. We didn't have time to get to anything else."

"A student reported me to the Queer Center because 'they' said I needed to identify myself as '*they*' are identifying me, as 'cis.' Are you kidding? Is their self-identity so important that mine is not?"

"We were talking about AIDS and she stood up and said it was nothing compared to being born *transgender*! There is nothing anyone can say about oppression that 'tops' transgender. Is this the 'T' in the LGBT movement that we fought for?"

"We can't decorate cupcakes to look like vulvas. It's oppressive to trans women who don't have vulvas. Seriously?"

"So as I understand it—trans women can get together but biological women who identify as women cannot. I want to get this right—but it doesn't sound right to me. Do you get it?"

"They were going to stop the production of Eve Ensler's *The Vagina Monologues* because not all women have vaginas. I'm sorry, *most* women have vaginas. Isn't that enough reason to still put on the show? What am I missing?"

"Remember when correct English mandated that we call everyone in the room 'he' even if there was one man and 500 women in that room? Does anything seem familiar to you about that now?"

~

These are not-so-random thoughts from the sharp edge where biological women are howling from the margins. Blood marks the borders.

These are the lecture notes one cannot give without being told they are transphobic:

In what universe is unnecessary surgery on children not child abuse? In what universe is hormone treatment, hormone blocking, that is virtually untested as to its long-term effects, not child abuse on children who are gender-different?[1] In what universe do you give a child a mastectomy at age twelve because she wants to "be a boy?" In what universe do we agree that this is the right thing to do in a world that continues to rape, defile and undercut women—rather than teaching that gender-different girl to be a feminist?

We have to stop. Trans women and biologically born women are different. We are not the same.

Does this mean a human being cannot be a trans woman? Of course not. Queer people have been fabulously different, creative, expressive, and flying across gender lines and opening access to gender codes for centuries. But, that does not make biologically born men and women the same as trans men and women, and we ignore that difference at the expense of the mental and physical health of our queer, feminist, women, trans, and radical communities.

In the end, whom does this silence benefit? Examine the cost of surgery, or of lifelong dependence on the medical system. Of children guided and/or forced into this medical system that medicalizes gender difference and forces them into medical intervention for their whole lives, rather than celebrating gender difference as natural?

Who is benefitting from my marginalized LGBTQ community being the guinea pigs? The insurance companies, hospitals, and doctors who are profiting from the queer community's marginality. Is it really the children and parents, who have been taught to fear gender difference, who benefit? Is it really the queer community?

Consider where this is headed in the academy and elsewhere in queer-"friendly" spaces. Consider recently an institution where a *drag* show was protested because *drag* was seen to be oppressive to trans folk who "could not take off the drag." Consider that *drag* is the history of trans America and that it is the bedrock of LGBTQ+ history and where the gender lines were exploded. It was the ability to *put on drag* that allowed many to explode their minds into the creativity and love for the very birth of a LGBTQ+ community. It was the Stonewall Revolution that birthed the LGBT movement upon which the "T" now stands – and from which it is now policing people and attempting in some cases to *rule out drag.*

This is the percentage of women who are trans: .03 percent.[2] If it were possible to get an operation to become a feminist—would critical discourse of feminism be silenced, rather than the other way around today? Is it possible that the relatively small-in-number trans community members could silence the critical discourse without the aid, encouragement and abetment of the insurance companies, hospitals, and medical systems that are profiting from their, and our, cultural gender discomfort?

Biological women matter. The inability to celebrate them because "all women do not have vaginas" is not revolutionary. It is a tired trope reminiscent of the silencing of female body parts prior to the feminist revolution of the 1970s, where women learned to say these tabooed words *out loud: vagina, clitoris,* and *cervix.* Look at the history of the pioneering book, *Our Bodies, Our Selves.*[3]

All women have vaginas. Some trans women have a constructed vagina. That vagina does not operate like that of a XX woman, but it is a version of a vagina. Some trans women have penises. Trans women are not biological women. They are trans women. This is not an insult, but a reality.

> *These are the thoughts we can no longer express in the classroom. We watch as our students get operations. We hear about children who are operated on. We watch as others shut down conversations and spaces for biologically born women. We watch feminism censored. Feminism demands honoring difference and acknowledging similarity. So while trans and biologically born females may have "femininity" in common—sometimes—we do not have biology in common, we do not have girlhood in common. And, it matters to feminism that we be honest about what we have in common and what we must acknowledge and honor that is different.*

There is so little research done on XX women. Their orgasms, for instance. It's estimated that seventy-five percent (conservatively) of biological women have trouble reaching orgasm through vaginal-only intercourse. Ten percent of women don't achieve orgasm at all under any circumstances. Does any research indicate anything comparable like this for men? No. The world assumes pleasure for men and assumes "pleasure" for women *is* pleasuring men. One can easily find "research" that suggests that "having sex" without having orgasm is "pleasurable" for women. Does the term "blue balls" have an equivalent for women? No.

Biological women began to inhabit their "address"/their bodies in the mid-1970s with the ability to articulate the words of *their bodies, their selves*. When we shut down this discourse because "not all women have vaginas," we shut down information flowing to the address where 99.97% of women live. By abolishing space for "women born women," we are taking away the only space where biological women can speak of their reality. Women need the spaces where women who have lived through sexism and silence, and bleeding and silence, and harassment and abuse for being female and silence, can finally speak into that silence *and break it*. When you silence women by taking away academic and cultural havens, you are bullying women into accepting that male lives, thoughts, feelings, and pleasure should be "enough" for them. "Enough" is when women get to have their own lives, thoughts, feelings, and pleasure.

Biological women are still astronauts in undiscovered and unmarked space ——most often with no help from the dominant culture. They travel in spaces on the margins—examining their cervixes by the light of the moon, a mirror, and a flashlight. This exploration is shut down in favor of the inclusion *into that space* of trans women being *the same as* biological women.

The queer culture is agreeing readily—accepting sexist tropes that mark women as marginal. Queer culture must learn the basic principle of feminist community—something learned in the struggle of the women's liberation movements of the 1970s and 1980s—to honor difference. To acknowledge similarity. Black is not white. Heterosexual is not lesbian. Disabled in not able-bodied. Christian is not Jewish. Biological women have babies; they are not just "people who get pregnant" or "birthing individuals."

If the "T" in LGBT means choosing to wipe out the "L," or to diminish the "G," then what gay movement are we discussing? It is looking more like the trans movement is assuming *ownership* of the gay movement. If discourse about the female anatomy of XX beings is being shut down, *that is not feminist*. Biologically born women and trans women may both be oppressed by the patriarchy that dismisses femininity with the supremacy of masculinity—but that does not mean they live on common ground. Trans women did not grow up as girls. Even if they grew up as very feminine boys, they grew up with different oppressions. Silencing biological women will not help trans women explore their own oppression.

I want you to understand that the same silencing and disappearance is not happening with trans women, as it happens with trans men. We are not seeing spaces closed because not "all men have penises." All men have penises. Trans men do not. While a minority of trans men may have a constructed penis, most do not. This does not make them "less" than, but it does make them different. Yes, there is a proud queer history of butch women, who stand with women, who call themselves "daddy," "stud," "bull dagger," and use pronouns like "he." But, these people are often women, biological women, who are being disappeared under a rubric of trans identity *that never claimed them before they disappeared them.*

This is how feminism works: difference/similarity. Feminists, who are biological women, do not exist to apologize for existing or to apologize for having a vagina. This does not mean that feminists are not also male, or trans, or genderqueer. But it *does* mean that the majority of feminists have vaginas and they should not have to silence that fact. It means we must resist our disappearance and continue to talk about clitoral orgasms and the fact that XX women have them—sometimes in multiples.

It means we may eat vulva cupcakes.

And finally there is no homework this week.
Because this lecture never happened.

---

[1] This essay is not traditionally referenced. This is a rant, a lecture that will not be given. The research to support everything this rant suggests is documented in the wide interwebs (search any of the following: transgender surgery and children, problems with puberty blockers, research initiative and transgender surgery, medical risks and transgender surgery, sex reassignment surgery costs, suicide rates and transgender, sex change regret, transgender postoperative problems) and in citations by other contributors in this anthology. While there may be counter articles to support a different position from my own, these articles usually point to the ability of this kind of surgery on and drugging of children to make things "easier" in the long run. Examine the risks of these experimental procedures, their success rates, and then see if this is the world we want to offer a gender-different child to make her or his life "easier." And then ask, easier for whom? And why can't we talk about this in the academy without being seen as transphobic?

[2] Google it. Then imagine a conference where vulva cupcake decorating would be an activity attended by say, fifty women. If *all* the trans women statistically showed up at the conference, and to that event (which would most likely be scheduled against an event which was not about the "oppressive" and "exclusionary" vagina/clitoris/cervix anyway), this is how many women, the event would be "oppressing": .015 if fifty women showed up to decorate cupcakes.

[3] *The New Our Bodies, Ourselves: A Book By and For Women,* Boston Women's Health Collective, Simon & Schuster, Touchstone (1984). This was the first major revision of this classic since its original publication in the 1970s,1984 and reflected the major changes that have occurred in every area of women's health. The most recent revision was in 2011. It is still the definitive consumer health reference for all women. See http://www.ourbodiesourselves.org/history/obos-timeline-1969-present/

———— ⁓ ————

CHAPTER 38

DESTRUCTION OF A MARRIAGE: MY HUSBAND'S DESCENT INTO TRANSGENDERISM

Sharon Thrace

FOR MANY YEARS I lived happily — blissfully unaware how happily – with a man who was sensitive, compassionate, intelligent, fun, and thought the world of me. We were deeply in love and the kind of couple younger folks said they looked up to. My marriage was rock solid; it defined my future. I couldn't imagine a scenario that could break us up. My husband, Kris, was to all outward appearances happy. He enjoyed life and was uniquely easygoing and content. Those qualities made him a joy to live with.

We were insanely compatible. We shared the same vision of the good life, even as that vision evolved. We met in the city and both loved urbane living: walking the arts district, browsing farmer's markets, and lunching with friends at trendy eateries. Later, charmed by thoughts of gardening, raising goats and living off the land, we moved to a little fixer-upper in the country and spent eight years dabbling in homesteading. Throughout, we shared views on politics and ethics, a love of travel and a great affection for each other's family. We stayed up long nights waxing philosophical on a variety of topics: the compatibility of determinism and free will, video game culture's hostility to women, the recurring theme of beauty and the beast narratives in Western literature and film. We challenged each other and learned from each other and ultimately agreed on most issues.

We vacationed together famously, taking turns driving on long road trips. Our favorite spot was a cheap condo on the gulf, nestled among a dozen great restaurants, a dodgy live music venue and a tiny family-owned seafood market. The market sold fresh oysters, shrimp, crawfish, potatoes and corn by the pound, cooked to order while-you-wait. We'd fill a basket with way too much food, grab a bottle of wine and enjoy our feast on the nearby beach. We always felt content in each other's company, whether hiking for miles at a nature preserve, sipping bloody marys at a beachside bar, or browsing tacky wares in a tourist shop.

We had some of our best times at the country house. We spent many long hours in the garden together picking tomatoes, gathering herbs and weeding daisies. We picked gallons of green beans, breaking them on the porch while chatting and watching calves play nearby, sorting the beans into gallon bags to freeze. We both loved to cook and we prepared and consumed elaborate meals together. We watched from our dining room window as a family of swallows took up residence on our porch, the mother and father tending the eggs, feeding the hatchlings and eventually teaching the youngsters to launch from our string of porch lights and fly to a neighboring barn.

We had a lot of love and compassion for each other. We took turns financially supporting each other through college and career changes and we weathered illnesses and surgery. "Sick people get what they want," Kris would often say, offering to drive across town for my favorite take-out when I had the flu. We commemorated every Christmas by making an ornament from the year's ticket stubs, event brochures and other keepsakes. We took time to picnic in the park, watch the stars and loll away hours at summer music festivals. We never forgot romance and we had great sex.

We lasted 15 years, and all were wonderful but the last.

That was the year that my husband announced, out of the blue, that he was feeling "gender-fluid." The announcement would mark the beginning of a complete and rapid unraveling of our marriage.

He wanted to cross-dress, he said. He wanted to express his "feminine" side. I'd had no clue about his feelings on gender before the great reveal, but as a liberal, bisexual woman with an open mind, I was receptive. I encouraged him as he tried on one of my blouses, learned to apply eyeliner and swept his hair into a barrette. We watched some "tranny porn" at his request and I indulged a little role-playing in bed. He experimented with dressing around the house for a few weeks. Then he decided he wanted to dress publicly as well.

We chose the Rocky Horror Picture show for our first adventure out, where he could debut a tulle mini skirt from Hot Topic and rainbow thigh-highs in relative safety. Soon he moved on to wearing skirts, boots and long scarves when we dined out or walked the mall. I didn't care what he wore and he seemed happy. He joined a social group for cross-dressers and started reading and blogging about the topic. Things were going well and I wrote a guest post on his blog defending his new interest.

He wasn't a woman, he said in those days. He didn't want to change his name or be referred to by feminine pronouns. He just wanted to have a little fun.

But a few months in, his feelings had begun to change. We were sitting in our favorite little family-owned Korean restaurant the moment I learned how very far they had drifted.

It was a normal Saturday. We were chatting, laughing, and enjoying *bulgogi* and home-made *kimchi*. Kris wore floral skinny jeans, a slinky blouse and a pair of Chucks. He had never passed as a woman, but then again, he hadn't tried. In his relatively androgynous attire that day he looked more like a front man for a rock band than a challenge to gender norms.

An older gentleman had been glancing our way, and presently got up to find the restroom, passing our table on his way. "You look like Brad Pitt!" the man said jovially, patting Kris's shoulder as he passed. It was a compliment. But Kris looked at me across the table and tears welled up in his eyes.

It soon became apparent that this innocuous comment would ruin our evening. As I implored Kris for the source of his distress, I learned that he now *very much* wanted to pass as a woman. I learned that he'd subconsciously decided that he *already* passed and was shocked to learn otherwise. I learned that he now thought of himself as "on the transgender spectrum." I learned that he was no longer happy, but deeply depressed.

This depression manifested itself without ado. Kris immediately began spending his evenings lying around the house, crying for hours, wallowing in despair. He cried because he didn't pass. He cried because he had ordered a dress that didn't fit his broad shoulders. He cried because he couldn't completely eradicate the stubble on his face. He cried about what people might be thinking about him, what they might be saying.

When his employment contract ran out, he didn't renew it and he didn't look for a new job. He cried about the discrimination he imagined he'd face in interviews. He stopped doing housework. He stopped opening mail. He overdrew his checking account and racked up hundreds of dollars in fees. He became suicidal.

He signed up for laser hair removal of his beard. His first couple of appointments conflicted with other events, and he panicked. Wild-eyed, he ranted for an hour over dinner that the entire universe seemed to want to sabotage his hair-removal efforts. He continued to fulminate into the next day, disproportionately to any actual injustice. His haste to get to the laser salon resembled that of a drug addict being denied a fix. He continued to fuel a seething rage at no one in particular until he made it to a session.

He looked in the mirror frequently and he hated what he saw. He demanded of me: was he fat? Were his hips too narrow? Did he pass? He was unsatisfied with both truth and lie. He became preoccupied with foundation, layering on primers and color-correctors. He thought of little else but dresses, accessories and shoes. He obsessed over minute differences he saw in the fashion choices of trans women versus flamboyant gay men, determined to avoid being mistaken for the latter. But the reactions of passers-by did not depend upon this distinction as much as he'd hoped. Many assumed he was gay – it didn't help that he'd taken to flipping his hair back with a limp wrist – and others disapproved of his non-conformity without giving much thought to its nature. Kris, however, felt that the rules were obvious and that those who failed to recognize him as a trans woman deliberately insulted him.

Abetted by counseling and Internet forums, he soon "learned" that he was "literally" a woman and not just someone who identified as one.

Our communication suffered. I told him that while I would respect his pronoun preferences in public, I could not agree that he was literally a woman. My definition of woman, I told him, depended upon female anatomy. Any other definition bolsters harmful and insulting sex stereotypes; women are not people who like lipstick, wear pink or are bad at math. Gender, a human construct, was invented to sell the myth that men are competent and smart while women are subservient and vain. Why not buck the system that punishes gender non-conformity instead of subscribing to it?

He could not abide this opinion and became hysterical whenever it came up. A huge number of conversational topics became off-limits. He was evasive about his definition of woman and his reason for wearing a bra. He was uncomfortable with stories that revealed any masculinity in his past and he didn't want to be referred to as my husband. He renounced the sexual component to his experience and denied it had ever existed. Innocent comments of all kinds about his body, my body, or our experiences growing up triggered gender dysphoria – a sense of mismatch between his body and his internal "gender identity" – and caused a fight.

We argued about the more outrageous claims of transgender politics: that everyone who claims to be a woman is one, without qualification; that a non-op transgender person has the right to expose his penis to women, teenage girls, and children in the locker room of his choice; that due to Kris's clothing preferences we were now properly called a lesbian couple. Although he didn't want surgery for himself, he defended it for others, including children, and we argued about the ethics of "treating" gender dysphoria with the permanent removal of healthy sex organs. He lost his capacity for reasonable discussion and often flatly refused to talk, even on topics that directly affected our future, such as whether he'd pursue hormone therapy. It became clear that staying in this marriage would forever mean keeping silent on some matters and lying about others, to him and about him, at home and in public.

The popular narrative that trans people lead unhappy lives until they come out, then become content as they express their true selves, had been turned on its head – Kris was much happier *before* his revelation. Liberal ideology implored me to embrace his new identity, but it was difficult to celebrate something that clearly caused him intense pain.

It was even difficult to live with him. I became exhausted. I was the only person working outside the home, yet I also did all the housework and ran all the errands. When we tired of the isolation of country life and decided to move back to the city, every detail was left to me. I found a realtor, cleaned and listed our house and signed the contracts. I applied for jobs and I found a position in the city. I packed our stuff and I filled out change-of-address forms. I searched for houses, saved thousands of dollars for a down payment, and acquired financing. When I wasn't working I was carrying a tremendous emotional burden: watching him cry, counseling him, wincing at his anger, carefully choosing my words to avoid his outbursts. The turmoil lasted long into most nights and I got no sleep.

His large family and some two-dozen friends had accepted him with open arms, but they were growing weary too. He couldn't listen to their problems as he was too occupied with his own. He bristled at innocent questions and the occasional "misgendering" and he lectured people for it. Thoughtful conversation was traded for endless monologues about transgender rights, and he imagined malice and abuse where none existed. Friends said they didn't recognize him anymore.

They were right. In an effort to restore my floundering marriage, I made a long list of things I had always loved about him. I hoped this would give me ideas on how to better connect with him and invigorate my attempts to reconcile. But I discovered that most of the things on my list were long gone. He was no longer an inspiring conversational partner. He was no longer helpful, around the house or otherwise. His moral compass seemed at sea; he had lost his empathy for others and he craved constant attention. He was no longer easygoing; his need for validation kept him uptight. He had lost his love for camping, hiking, swimming, and any other activity whose attire called for utility instead of femininity. Romance was the furthest thing from his mind. Thanks to gender dysphoria, sex had become awkward, then nonexistent. And I was certainly no longer the number one concern in his life.

In spite of it all, I loved him. I fought furiously for my marriage, even as we separated and began the divorce process. I tried to reconcile an embarrassing number of times, writing long letters explaining my position, asking for his, begging for conversation, for compromise. I didn't stop trying until the day he texted me saying that he couldn't imagine saving our marriage and was moving on.

It was heartbreaking to lose him from my life, as my long-term companion and lover, as my best friend. It was equally heartbreaking to watch his personal demise, in general. Something that society claimed would be authentic and beautiful had unfolded into something sick, something unhappy, something that alienates and destroys. What is this condition if it is incompatible with happiness, with empathy, with truth? If it turns one's focus from others to oneself? If it can't be reconciled with the very best of relationships and in its wake lie sexual dysfunction and loneliness?

And gender identity was no mere conflict of interest for us; it is an inherently misogynist idea. It holds that "feeling like a woman" (whatever that means) is the same as *being* a woman. It's a callous disregard for our lifetime of oppression, the limits placed upon our participation in society, the ever-present threat of rape we face. It's an erasure of the quarter of our lives we spend managing bleeding and pain, the constant diligence we must employ to prevent pregnancy. It's a gross insensitivity to the staggering percentage of us who are victims of sexual assault, starting in childhood. We face these realities because we have female bodies and because of how men treat people who inhabit such bodies. There exists no fashion choice nor inner angst that can bring men closer to this experience.

It takes a great deal of male privilege to "choose" your gender, as if gender weren't a set of obligations and proscriptions designed to keep women physically, emotionally and financially handicapped.

Kris likes to complain that I don't recognize him as a woman, something he sees as a great offense. But the irony is that he does not recognize *me* as a woman. I am not a random, unidentifiable spot on a postmodern spectrum of meaninglessness. My biology is not irrelevant. My experience cannot be duplicated by trying on my clothes. Kris is *not* essentially like me. Perhaps a fault line in our relationship was his fundamental failure to know me.

I have only recently come to terms with a simple truth: I was wronged. The current cacophony of pro-trans propaganda makes it easy to forget that, easy to believe that I didn't try hard enough, that anything short of worship for the transgender experience is bigotry.

Gender dysphoria is not an excuse for misogyny, narcissism, or neglect. My husband, like so many men before him, allowed a midlife crisis to destroy his marriage. But because he chose transition rather than a teenage mistress, I'm not allowed to call him on it. The transgender experience is framed as too special and fragile; its sufferers can't be expected to maintain a relationship, a household or a conversation. But in the end, Kris did not fight for me. He didn't compromise with me. He didn't exhaust his options to preserve our relationship. It is no comfort that a perfect storm of politics, media and ideology colluded to confuse him and obfuscate his duties as a compassionate partner and human. He is responsible for leaving me. He is responsible for his defect of character, his deficit of love.

CHAPTER 39

GAS MARK SIX

Jackie Mearns

INTRODUCTION

IT HAS BEEN a couple of years since I wrote this, and so much has changed that my life is beyond recognition. The man referred to in this piece is finally gone from my life, I have centered women more and more in everything I do, and I have finally come out as a lesbian, after decades of pain, fear, and confusion. I wrote this when I was asked to speak alongside Sheila Jeffreys, who was speaking about her book *Gender Hurts*, about how transgenderism harms women.

I had been partnered with a man who proclaimed himself to be a woman, and I wanted the world to know that the experience of women in these relationships is often very far from the rose-tinted media pieces that feature only those warm and fuzzy stories of women who are apparently delighted that "their husband is now their wife," and that airbrush out any awkward details that might spoil that narrative. I wanted to bring attention to the elephant in the room that I, and so many women I encountered in my search for support and understanding, are very familiar with. I needed to tell my story to counter those tales, to make it known, and to honor the women I knew who were suffering in silence. While I was often told during this time that the man I was partnered with was not representative, was a "bad apple," an anomaly, and even not "really trans." I knew from emails sent to me and from private messages that what I was going through was far more typical in one way or another than the slick propaganda machine is prepared to admit.

I hoped that if it were to become common knowledge that a large proportion of men "transitioning" to become "women" have a deep-rooted, obsessive, sexual paraphilia (a sexual desire for their imagined selves *as women*, shaped and inflamed by pornography and the most base of sexist attitudes towards women), then perhaps those women who are partnered with such men would feel less alone, and less silenced by the prevailing cultural and political demand that we ignore our instincts, our boundaries, and the evidence staring us right in the face.

I knew from my own experience that women with stories like mine, stories of emotional, financial, and often sexual abuse (for what is the demand that someone pretends that you are someone else when you are intimate with them *but* abuse?), are told that they are "hateful" or "bigoted" for daring to puncture the bubble around those men who are elevated as brave and courageous. Those men we are told we must move aside for. Those men we are told we must center our feminism around. Those men we are told we have "privilege" over… No wonder women with stories like mine are invisible, silenced, and erased. So here it is. My story. Silenced no more.

GAS MARK SIX

For the longest time, I told no one about my experience of being partnered with a male transgender. It is only in the past few years that I have even found the words to describe my experience. "Gas Mark Six" refers to the highest setting on a gas stove. I used to have an online friend (also a partner of a man who thought he was a woman), and she likened the experience of being partnered with one of these men to that of a frog put into a pot of water where the heat is gradually turned up until the frog is cooked – a deliberate program of desensitization as each limit is compromised or ignored, and each line in the sand is crossed by these men in their "journey." Another woman once told me that "You give a man who thinks he's a woman an inch, he will take a mile." How true that turned out to be.

When I first met him, he spoke to me about what he called his "strong feminine side." He confided in me that he was an occasional transvestite and that it had ruined a few relationships where girlfriends had inadvertently "found out," or had rejected him when he told them. He told me he had a very low sex drive and instead preferred to just cuddle and kiss. He said that he felt more comfortable around women. He told me that he "didn't want to become a woman," and that he didn't know where the urge to "dress" came from other than a need to express what he felt were his "feminine feelings" and an attraction to pretty things. He told me he had been doing this since he was about age eleven or twelve (remember that detail). I felt special that he would confide this in me. I had never felt attraction to "masculine" men. I confided in him that I thought that I might be a lesbian, but had no idea of how or where to go with that, and that it was something I had never admitted to another soul. It was only later that I realized that he considered those conversations as "girl talk." He likes "girl talk." The intimacy that women share with each other as our friendships grow. The ways that women can connect through our shared experience is way beyond anything he could ever experience, given that he has not walked this path with us.

457

I couldn't really grasp those "feminine feelings" he spoke of, since I had never really experienced my sense of self in that way. I thought women who bought into it were uninformed about feminism and the misogyny of "beauty practices" – certainly none of my friends were like that. I hadn't worn heels since I was a teenager. I never wore makeup. I was a conscientious objector to the femininity game. I liked reading, and cinema, and art, and had an active political life – why would I want to spend my time thinking about makeup and shoes?

But I believed at the time that these guys are living proof that gender is a social construct. Men and women should be able to wear whatever they want, without the silly distinction of "male" clothes" or "female" clothes. To hell with gender norms. I thought it could be "edgy" and "alternative." I am a child of the seventies, where "gender bending" was the norm, a time when no man ever claimed to actually *be* a woman just because he was wearing some lipstick and earrings.

Within a few weeks of him moving in with me, I realized that this was much, much more than just an occasional bout of self-expression for him. It was an obsession, and it had an *enormous* sexual component. Dressing episodes (which were at least three or four times a week) were invariably followed by "sex" that consisted of me masturbating him by rubbing his tucked penis as he lay on his back, squeezing his own (fake) tits. On top of that, I often walked in on him masturbating. The mirror in my bedroom was moved to his side of the bed. There wasn't a time when he "dressed" that he didn't get an erection. Even after he started taking internet-bought hormones, the thought that he was chemically transforming himself into "a woman" held immense erotic charge for him. I want readers to note that at one point he went to visit the general practitioner about his "gender feelings" and came home with a letter referring him for treatment at the local gender clinic. The letter stated that it could be used to confirm that he was "transitioning" and could be presented for the purposes of changing names on bank accounts, etc. That evening after he received the letter, I went through to bed and found him lying stretched out across the bed in lingerie, make-up, wig. He obviously wanted to be "seduced." As he climaxed, he exclaimed "I'm a transexual!" At that moment, I knew that this was nothing to do with "identity," and everything to do with fetishes and weirdness.

He was a textbook *autogynephile.*[1]

It transpired that he was also a "submissive" – a very common component of this particular paraphilia – and that nothing got him off more than being "forced" to be "a woman." Of course "woman" meant submissive, passive, always "willing to please." He would work these fantasies into our "sex life" either overtly or covertly.

After a time, it was impossible to ignore that I was no more than a prop in this game. I could have been anyone, really. I didn't even have to exist. I felt as significant as a gravy stain on the table. Many of the women I spoke to in what limited support groups I could find complained of the same thing. Not just the sex part, but the entire being invisible part, and a deafness to *our* needs, views, or opinions.

I discovered that he was an obsessive user of porn, particularly "she-male" porn and BDSM fare. I had been very clear with him about my opinions on porn, and was sickened when he tried to get me to participate in looking at these men with breasts. Time and again he would promise to stop, only to be discovered again. He would swing between crying and asking for forgiveness, and bold-facedly challenging me, saying it was *me* that had a problem, that nobody else thought like me. He ridiculed my objections and my politics, or told me that I was paranoid – even though the evidence was right in front of me.

He had no intention of stopping. A lot of his behaviors were compulsive, obsessive.

I discovered that he was using dating and sexual hookup sites, saying that he was a full-time transsexual, going through the Real Life Test, willing to relocate anywhere for the right "lady (of any gender)." These profiles contained fantasies about being kidnapped and forced to live as someone's sex slave. Fantasies straight out of porn, straight from the pit of woman hating. And yet he claimed to "love" women.

There was no end to his inventiveness when it came to lying about who he really was. Using his smartphone, he created an online world for himself by inventing a fictitious life. I discovered that he had a secret Facebook profile, and scores of photographs of himself in varying degrees of undress (I am certain these men invented the selfie!) and that he had a coterie of dozens and dozens of young women between the ages of seventeen and twenty-four who believed that he was a full-time transsexual, single, and struggling with finding a job in this cruel, discriminatory society. He had a fictitious home life, fictitious job or non-job, a fictitious social life and fictitious friends. He even fabricated a "trans bashing" – this, I found particularly repulsive. I occasionally appeared in his tales of his fictitious life as his "landlady."

He loved sympathy and attention, and "validation" – even if it meant lying and manipulating to get it. These young women were so "Go girl!" and "Awww poor you" toward him. Some of them called him "big sis" and took their problems to him. Otherwise it was giggly conversations about clothes and what color to dye their hair that week, musings about becoming a stripper or a fetish model, and stories of being "slut shamed." They were young, and inexperienced in the world. It must have seemed very exciting and progressive to these young women from dead-end towns across the country to have a real-life transsexual as a friend. Someone who they could advise on makeup and clothes, and feel very good about themselves indeed in the process. He liked his women friends faux feminist to match his faux "woman" existence. They had no idea that they were talking to a late middle-aged, balding man with long nails and an erection in his silky panties. I felt sorry for them, and disgusted with him. I was outraged that he would so bold-facedly lie to these young women and demanded that he stop. He cried, saying, "But these are my frieeeends…" This of course ignored the fact that who they thought was their friend was *a work of fiction*.

Then again, it's not as if women are actually *real* to these men.

Of course, he didn't stop. It carried on as if I hadn't said anything. Even the many times I asked him to leave were ignored. He would just get up the next day as if nothing had been said. I felt I was being driven insane. I was slowly being stripped of my self.

My sense of self and my belief that I was entitled to set limits or boundaries were gradually eroded as the trans stuff came to dominate and shape every corner of my life. I never knew where or when the next assault to my psyche was going to come, and so I existed for a long time in a state of hypervigilance. That is, until such time as my ability to disassociate kicked in. I know from observing trans support groups that many of these men say, "My wife is fine with it – she just doesn't want to talk about it or see it." And they think that is actually okay for their wives to live like that. Many women are surviving through disassociation.

Let's not forget that a well-orchestrated and financed propaganda machine surrounds these men. It has the effect of silencing not just those of us who oppose on ideological principles, but all women who are within these relationships who question the idea that these men are "women trapped inside men's bodies," or those whose lives have been ripped apart by these men. I know from the bitter experience of reaching out that the primary concern is for the welfare of the trans partner, who must never be questioned as the most oppressed creature to walk this planet.

This is a double whammy to those women experiencing abuse, intensive gaslighting, and erasure of their right to name their reality and to set boundaries. There is no such thing as a line in the sand when it comes to trans desire. He gotta have what he gotta have.

Even with health care providers, support for such female partners is tempered by the need to be sensitive to the needs of the transgender partner, and to avoid being seen as discriminatory. My doctor was happy to give me antidepressants, but less happy to countenance the idea that what I was being put through was abuse.

Increasingly, statistics on domestic violence within same-sex partnerships count the trans partner as "female." There is an invisibility of male violence within these relationships, and women are suffering as a consequence, as we are silenced. We are shamed. We are erased.

A Scottish government-funded survey carried out by the Scottish Transgender Alliance (funded by the Scottish government since 2007), is often cited as evidence of how very bad it is for trans women, who would appear to experience rates of relationship abuse higher than actual women. Apparently a small, self-selecting sample is no barrier to credibility, nor is the fact that one of the criteria for abuse included "misgendering." It is no surprise to me that a woman partnered to a man for some years might slip up occasionally and forget to call her Steven "Stephanie," but this is recorded as a heinous act of abuse. Yet there are no surveys I am aware of about abuse perpetrated by trans "women" in relationships. I find this a telling omission. It often feels like no one wants to hear the female partner's story. I have stopped being surprised by this, since men have been telling women to shut up and ignoring our words since forever.

For example, as a means to at least get him to *listen* to my distress, at one point I begged him to seek relationship counseling with me. Apart from the fact that he used the trips to the counselor as an exciting opportunity to dress in public, and spent more time stressing about what to wear (sometimes even buying entire new outfits) than any time in self-reflection, the counselor spent an inordinate amount of time focusing on *my* inability to "accept," rather than on *his* behavior. In one session, the counselor grasped onto an incident of "misgendering" that had happened in her presence (I had said something like "Why can't he understand?"). He had fled from the room in a dramatic tizzy of tears. She stated to me in a firm voice that she is prohibited from working with couples where there is domestic abuse. In other words, I was being accused of being an abuser. This almost drove me mad with pain and self-doubt, thinking, "What if it really *is* me? Am *I* an abuser?" I can't begin to describe the pain this caused me. I carried that comment with me for months. I refused to go back. He was disappointed that his daylight trips outdoors, with his repulsive "cleavage" showing, were curtailed. However, it did give him an excuse to now appropriate the identity of an "abused woman." Sickening.

I was starting to drop or lose female friends. I would be hesitant about going out with them or inviting them over, particularly with him around. He would laugh and giggle with them and I knew that in his head he was imagining he was having "girl talk." The fact that they didn't know that they were unwittingly playing a part in his fantasy life made me feel nauseous, and guilty, so I stopped meeting female friends with him around.

Then I pretty much stopped seeing female friends at all, since when I tried to go anywhere without him (telling him that it was "women friends only"), he would pout and huff and cry,

"It's because I have a penis, isn't it?" When I was away from him he would text and phone me constantly. When I got back home he was nasty to me. All typical behaviors of abusive, controlling men.

I was growing afraid of him. It was easier just to forget about having friends. So my world became smaller and smaller as his "exploration of his feminine side" took up more and more space until there was little room left for anything else. It dominated every conversation and extended to physical space, too. By the time he left, my clothes storage was down to half a drawer and a box under the window.

Even everyday purchases were fraught with meaning and reminders of my erasure. I remember having an argument in the drugstore over toothbrushes. There was only one pink toothbrush left, and I don't know what came over me, but I decided that fuck him, I am having the pink toothbrush. He "helpfully" pointed out the purple ones, and the blue ones that matched the bathroom. But no, I was having the pink one and I was going to win this tiny victory even if all the shop assistants were looking at me like I had lost my marbles.

We needed a phone. He said he would take care of it. That he had seen just what we needed. He came home with a red shiny phone in the shape of a seven-inch high-heeled women's shoe. I couldn't bear to bring it up to my ear. My flesh crawled every time it rang.

I thought that perhaps if he had an outlet, the lies and stuff would stop. Lots of partners go through a similar "bargaining" phase. *The gas under my pot was turned up to full.* So I agreed to escort him to a trans club. I secretly wanted to see if there would be other women there. I needed to find out if this behavior is "normal" for male transgenders, and if there is anything that women had found that made their lives with these men more bearable.

He would be beside himself with excitement at going out "en femme." I could see his hard-on starting from the moment he got out of his leisurely bubble bath (my baths were always rushed and fitted in around his dressing schedule). Getting ready was a ritual that took at least two hours. Of course, I was expected to "help." I'm pretty sure now that he was working that into one of the fantasies he had running on a loop in his head.

Often trips were abandoned due to some smudged nail polish, or other similar "feminine disaster" that would have him stomping around in an agitated state, sweating through his makeup, crying and shouting at me. Ordering me around like some demented potentate. *Six-foot males with chipped nail polish can be pretty scary, believe me.*

The trans club was filled with men clad in very short, very tight "little black dresses," high heels, and a variety of wigs (probably two-thirds of them long and blonde). There was a weird atmosphere I couldn't quite put my finger on. There were other men there too, not in dresses.

They sort of lurked, most of them not actually talking to the men in dresses, but often sending a drink over for one of them, followed by a raised glass and a wink from their corner. The men in dresses responded with a coquettish smile and a simpered "thank-you." I found out later that most of the men in dresses were doing each other and calling themselves "lesbians." I know this, because I found the photographs.

Amy Bloom, in her 2002 article "Conservative Men in Conservative Dresses," wrote:

"The greatest difficulty people have with cross-dressers, I think, is that cross-dressers wear their fetish, and the gleam in their eyes, however muted by time or habit, the unmistakable presence of a lust being satisfied or a desire being fulfilled in that moment, in your presence, even by your presence, is unnerving."

The penny finally dropped for me about what I was witnessing. Another boundary being violated – the boundary that says "Don't make me a part of your sexual kick, buddy." The experience of getting out in public seemed to turbocharge his cross-dressing at home. *Give an inch, take a mile.*

When my (then-young) children from my previous relationship weren't around, his idea of relaxing at home was to potter about in a micro-mini and high heels, affecting a "sexy wiggle" and affecting this wavy/limp thing with his hands and wrists when he spoke. I told him that women don't go about dressed like they were about to nip down to a disco all the time. He told me that he had seen "loads" of women that do, and that anyway, he liked the "council-house tart" look. I was always arguing with him about what women *actually* wore, or thought, and how sexist his stereotypes of women were, but he would insist that he was dressing like any other "girl," despite the fact that he was a forty-seven-year-old man. Other looks he liked were:

- The "rock chick" look – think Cher in that video on the aircraft carrier. No jeans and band T-shirt for this gal!
- The "hooker" look – I'll leave that to your imagination.
- And the "beauty counter girl" – extra-heavy makeup and an old lab coat worn over a bra, pants, suspender-belt and stockings ensemble. I caught him once, sneaking back into the house like that at five in the morning after a "constitutional." Apparently he had been taking "constitutionals" for months, sneaking out while I was asleep. Men who believe they are women are expert ninjas as well as exhibitionists.

For all his faux "girlie-ness," the feminine side never extended to practical, everyday stuff that most adult women have to do to get by – like helping with housework. He literally told me, "I can't do housework because I might break a nail – my long nails are important to me." Turned out he couldn't carry heavy bags or lift heavy stuff either, because he wanted his upper body muscles to wither away so he would be "more like a girl." I told him lots of women have muscles. He told me that wasn't "the kind of woman" he wanted to be. Of course not – how nice it must be to get to pick and choose.

He spent thousands and thousands of pounds on clothes, makeup, "beauty products," laser hair removal and hormones purchased online. I still can't see a television ad for makeup without an involuntary shiver down my spine. He would go months without giving me any contribution to the home. Apparently he had "expenses," and anyway, I would no longer have sex with him, so why should he?

The day came when he told me that he had "done an online test" and that he was "definitely a transexual." Self-diagnosis by internet is the trans stock in trade. I was alarmed because I knew to the core of myself that these men are categorically not women, and that I could never accept him as a woman. Like Sheila Jeffreys says, "woman is an honorific term." His story began to change in subtle ways – aided by his community of internet advisors. Now he said he had been dressing since he was three years old. He now had distinct memories of wishing he was a girl from around the age of five. Many hundreds of pounds in laser hair removal and black-market internet hormones later, and I was left struggling with a six-foot, fourteen-stone hulking man with "breasts," prone to incandescent rages one minute and tears the next. I was terrified. I began to hate him. No way was I going to wipe his arse if he had a stroke. A very realistic potential outcome for his foray into self-medication while still smoking and drinking every day, and carrying at least thirty extra pounds in weight.

I was repulsed by him, his insulting attempts to emulate "femininity," and his freakish body. Being touched by him, even by accident, made my skin crawl. I was disgusted at myself for allowing this to happen to me. I was drowning in shame. I was sinking fast.

I tried finding help online, but nobody wanted to acknowledge that these delusions are harmful. Rather, I was told *I* had to be educated, that *I* was "phobic," that I should learn to embrace this. Women were telling me this, as well as online forums and services purporting to offer "support" to female partners of men who decide they are women.

Had feminism changed so much? What had happened to the idea of women being central to feminism? Why can't women see that these are men? I was told that I was "homophobic" as well as "transphobic" because I refused to call myself a lesbian. What? He is a man! What madness was this? I went to the doctor and was given antidepressants. Nobody wanted to hear about my problem with the trans. I was told that "she" must be suffering too.

I went to the LGBT center and asked if they had a group for partners of transitioning males. The young man looked at me, puzzled. "Um, well we have a group for trans women and their friends and families, isn't that enough?" he asked. I tried to explain why maybe it wasn't a good idea for women who were struggling in their relationship with a male partner who was insisting he was now a woman to be discussing their problems with their male partner in the same fuckin' room. Eventually he said he would ask the trans group what they thought. If *they* were okay with it, then they would "think about it." It doesn't take a genius to figure out their response. More men telling women what they can and cannot do.

Women are often reluctant to talk about this, whether from a sense of shame or embarrassment, or because we have seen the harassment and invasion that takes place against women who have spoken out publicly. Most commonly though, it's because we are *groomed and obligated to care.*

One of the saddest things for me was that when I contacted the few women I had met along the way (and whom I knew to have been put through a variety of torments) to ask if they would consent to an interview for Sheila Jeffreys' book, *Gender Hurts,* they declined, stating that they didn't want to be "disloyal," or for [him] to find out that they had been talking to anyone outside of a tightly prescribed circle. Some didn't want to risk being ejected from some of the only spaces they have to talk about this – compromised by male oversight though they may be. It gets to be exhausting, pointless and depressing.

I know that for many, the greatest state of emergency will be what seems to be the almost unstoppable trend of lesbian women who are "transitioning," and destroying their beautiful, healthy female bodies in the process – as well as erasing their lesbian herstory and identity. I feel a deep sorrow for this state of affairs, and when I have read descriptions of what women put their bodies through, and the details of the surgeries that some go on to seek, my heart sinks at how self-hating, how female-hating this is. It is misogyny written upon the bodies of women, and it is truly terrible. The trend for "transgender children" is particularly horrifying and is evidence of how damaging the essentialist idea of "gender" that is promulgated by the transgender cult is.

As I am speaking about my own experience, I hope that you understand that I don't wish to minimize those states of emergency. I hope that what I have said will be taken in the context of how male privilege and entitlement, in the guise of transgenderism, is driving a movement. This movement has and will continue to hurt all women as long as our voices are silent, and while women remain unsupported to escape from these men. Women must have support to make sense of their oppression.

I believe that what women go through in these relationships is a form of emotional violence, and that work needs to be done, not only to raise awareness among the wider public about what really goes on within many of these relationships, but also to create services that support survivors of male violence. This is not "woman on woman" relationship abuse, and should not be treated or recorded as such. We should not be afraid to see this for what it is – male entitlement. Male violence.

No woman who is being abused needs to be told to have compassion for her abuser.

Women's enforced compliance with male delusions needs to recognized for what it is:

Misogyny.
Abuse.
Erasure.
I'm standing up and saying *enough*.

Lost Then Found

One of the hardest things for me to deal with during my time with the torturer was my disconnection from women. Self-imposed exile as it was, it was a source of immense pain. I truly love women. I hadn't really appreciated exactly how much, or understood exactly how much we need each other, and that females are each other's life force. This love is visceral, and inhabits me with deep and abiding passion. Some days, the pain of reading and hearing about women who are being exploited, oppressed, or hurt in the myriad of ways we are is overwhelming, and I need to take a break from the internet, switch off the television, and bury my head in a pillow. Some days, all I want to do is embrace every woman on this planet and clutch them to my breast. I feel like I would die for women. And yes, I know how dramatic that sounds, but this is my truth. Having been in a kind of exile, and knowing that my years left here grow short, it feels like I have to make up for those years lost to me.

Nothing is more nourishing to me than time spent in women-only space. It is something I actually *need*, and I feel my self wither a little when I can't have this for an extended period of time. The opportunities for that are rare and precious. The opportunities to gather publicly (as opposed to privately, in each other's homes) shrink each year as men and their supporters who would ignore female-set boundaries on the basis that they claim to "feel like a woman" gain influence in the public sphere, and invade every last corner of our hard-fought-for spaces.

Even though every day, most of the world and half the sky moves aside to let them sit at the head of the table, they want nothing less than our complete colonization. Nothing less than to rob us of our words and thus our ability to describe our material reality as human beings born into the class "female" – our very real biology, and the uncontroversial evidence of the consequences of that. I know of no other group that seeks human rights while at the same time robbing others of their ability to describe their condition. None. When my daughter was born, I wept. Wept with joy that my body had given me a tiny human being with whom I will forever be connected, and also pain at knowing some of the path that would be marked out for her in a world that revolves around men and their whims.

Yes, I see you, men. I have seen you for a very long time. From the fumbling in my knickers at four years old as I sat on my great-uncle's knee, to the hands round my neck when I refused to call the torturer "she." I spent a lifetime dodging, accommodating, excusing, and hiding from your violence. No more. I'm a straight up *"not over my dead body"* refusenik to the cult of the dick.

So I went to the Michigan Womyn's Music Festival.

And it was glorious.

And now I "get," at a heart level, what feminist theologian Mary Daly was on about when she spoke about be-coming, and the exorcism and ecstasy of breaking through what she names as the "Male Maze."

There are few words I can think of that capture what it was like to be swept up into female be-ing. To feel myself unfold and blossom. To Rise. It makes me heartsick to think of how this event, this gathering of female souls, this "intention" that this be a space where females find respite from the brutalities that hurt and diminish us from birth, where we find ourselves in each other, where we bond and nurture and grow our selves, where we spin and weave a new be-ing, where we are *seen,* where little girls run free in the woods, where women are *welcomed home,* where radical self-acceptance is possible, where the sweat and toil of females who built a community *from scratch each year* for *forty years,* will be no more. Festival producer Lisa Vogel's message to us was that we must go forward and create those spaces in our own backyards, that we are an unstoppable force of our own creation, and that we can rise again and again.

So I have a message to all of you, be you men who colonize "woman," or their many female helpmates who worked so hard to spread your lies and false songs of oppression against the Michigan Womyn's Music Festival, who rejoiced at the sorrow of women who spent forty years of their lives dedicated to creating a space each year for the sole purpose of uplifting females and opening doors into an understanding of *exactly what we are and where we come from,* and who petitioned and lobbied and threatened and boycotted and hated and hated and hated…

You   have   not   won.

We may temporarily no longer have a land on which to gather each year, to raise our girls and show them the joy of being female, to celebrate our elders, to love and nourish and tend to each and every one of us, to revel in our female diversity, but we have something a lot more dangerous: a collective memory, and a love that never dies – for each other, and for our shared *intention.*

We are the dandelion seeds in your manufactured lawn. We are the itch you just can't ever quite reach. We are *your* worst nightmare. *Because we know exactly what we are and where we come from.*

---

[1] "Autogynephilia" was coined by Ray Blanchard, a retired professor of psychiatry at the University of Toronto, and in the related work of J. Michael Bailey, a psychology professor at Northwestern University. Contrary to widespread belief, Blanchard says, the majority of trans women in the West start off not as effeminate gay men but as straight or bisexual men. To describe the syndrome, Blanchard coined the term "autogynephilia," meaning sexual arousal at the thought of oneself as female, "a male's propensity to be attracted to the thought or image of himself as a woman" (Blanchard 2005). One common manifestation of autogynephilia is fetishistic cross-dressing, which is an extremely common antecedent to seeking sex reassignment among non-homosexual (but not homosexual) transsexuals (Blanchard, Clemmensen, and Steiner 1987).

CHAPTER 40

"NEIGHBOR BOY"

Temple Ardinger

As the story goes, I was an "oops" baby, unwanted by my father. Everyone in the family expected me to be a boy. Dad was the first of four brothers, and all my cousins were male, so only traditionally male names had been considered for me, my father's first child. While my mother was finding motherhood, my father had the authority of filling out the official paperwork legally naming me. He gave me a hugely popular first name, but he chose to make my middle name a combination of his name and my mother's name, his part first, of course. As Jennifer Allene, I was destined to be Allan's baby girl, and I quickly went from the child he didn't want to the daddy's girl he hardly put down; that is the power of naming.

I followed Dad around and did lots of things with him. As kids do, I took cues on how to act from those around me. I wanted to be like my favorite person, so I acted like my dad. The fact that he was male and I was female made very little difference to me at that early age. Life is filtered through our parents, and he hung the sun for me each day.

At age nine, my friend got her hair cut short, and everyone seemed to love it. I wanted people to love me too, so I had my long blond hair cut into a manageable, over-the-ears short style. Strange how one's identity can get wrapped up in a simple thing like a hairstyle, even at that young age. I came home ready to show off my new 'do, but was met with the crushing reality that Dad didn't like my short hair. Actually, he *hated* it. He told me, "Girls don't have short hair," and incessantly teased me by calling me "neighbor boy."

I don't really remember all that happened that day. My parents argued and their fighting was about me. Every time he called me "neighbor boy," it sank in further, that I was no longer daddy's girl. I was no longer a girl in his eyes. I packed a pillowcase with toys and ran away from home. I got a block away and sat on the curb and cried, knowing no matter how much I pleaded with him, that my hair would grow back, he insisted I was the "neighbor boy." I was eventually found and brought home, but my parents were still at odds. Mom stopped him from calling me "neighbor boy," but only by degree. I was now the "neighbor kid." While this new name was sex-neutral, it was still clear what he meant.

I collected many harsh realities that day. My father, while not very tactful in his approach, was just teaching his daughter what he knew to be right. I learned what was expected of me to be his daughter, but more damaging, I learned what was expected of me "to be a girl." I took it to heart that my feelings were wrong and should stay hidden. I learned that men determined what was pretty, and that being pretty in order for boys to like me was more important to "being a girl" than what felt comfortable. Gender hadn't meant much to me until I stepped out of the feminine box.

I grew my hair out as fast as my hair would grow. While I flirted with a kid's version of a mullet for a time, short hair was still taboo. I was mostly a tomboy in my mannerisms and play, but now very aware of every step out of that pink box. I was sure to not wander too far from what was expected of me as a "girl."

As I became a maiden, puberty awakened feelings in me for both girls and boys, but I couldn't dare share my feeling for girls with anyone. To please boys was clearly the acceptable role for girls. Seeking approval became even more important, and I was an easy target for the boys. Femininity was a costume I put on, and sexual attention was approval that I wore the costume well. I worked hard at being what the boys wanted, but mostly all I achieved was becoming a low self-esteem misfit. I was teased by boys at school and yet still worked hard for their attention and approval. I got into bad situations and didn't have "no" in my vocabulary.

As high school dragged on, the pendulum would swing back and forth drastically. I would drop most of my femininity to become a punk and rebel against the "shoulds" all teenagers face. Or I'd cake the makeup on and wear the shortest skirt in some hyper over-sexualized version of femininity, once again seeking approval that I could "be a girl," or at least pass for one.

The self-doubt and the self-hatred instilled by patriarchy had taken root in me. During my teens and twenties, I believed that I was broken because of the disconnect I had with the gender role expected of me. I believed the abuse I got from men was deserved because it was proof that I wasn't good enough at "being a woman." These thoughts weren't even conscious enough for me to talk about, they were just an internal wound of self-hate, with the critic in my head calling me "neighbor boy" every time I stepped out of line. Even when I found feminism and began fighting for women's rights, the gender shackles of patriarchy were so deeply embedded in me that I could fight for women's equality and *still* set myself aside as not deserving respect and equality because I failed at really "being a woman."

When I found Goddess spirituality, I learned that the Goddess is *all* things. She exists outside those damn gender boxes. Some try to fit Her in a box, calling Her "Divine Feminine," but She is so much more than that. She is strong, fierce, kick-ass, beauty and ugliness, most powerful and yet not concerned with how others judge her. In Her presence, in women-only space, I finally could see the shackles I was wearing on the inside. With the help of women who had created a path of healing, I saw a way through all this hurt and hate. I began to love myself. In sharing and holding these safe spaces for women to work on healing, without men's gaze or authority lorded over us, parts of me were restored, even if the healing wasn't directly focused on me. I learned that helping other women heal collectively heals us all. In my late thirties, it was *my* turn in the safety of my women's circle to take steps to heal. I chose the name Temple to remind me that Goddess is all things inside me, and that I am the one who truly knows how to be me.

I am forty-two now, and I cut my hair short this year, for myself and for strength to write this essay. I've never felt more beautiful than I do now. It's not a beauty one finds in magazines, not a beauty to get compliments from my husband or my friends. This is for me to look in the mirror and see *me* as I have always wanted to see me. The proof I am healing is that I no longer hate the woman looking back in the mirror or judge her looks or actions on how well she fits some social construct of what defines feminine gender.

The moment that my nine-year-old self became the "neighbor boy" is one example of how I was wounded by gender. Some genderists might read this story and think I haven't accepted that I am "trans," while some will think I am just "gender nonconforming." I'm sure others will insist on naming me "cis," but I do not accept any of those labels, all of which continue the oppression of gender on the female-bodied. I am no longer affirming the gender farce that is sex stereotyping. I only see human traits, and I celebrate our diversity as divine creatures within the bodies we have.

There is a war on women, and the front line in the Western world is the attack on language. This is the power of naming once again. If the definitions of "sex" and "gender" are interchangeable and "woman" is defined as a feminine gender-identity a male-bodied person can just *choose*, then the oppression of women can no longer be discussed or challenged. If we accept that it is "transphobic" to discuss our female bodies and the oppression of the female-bodied experience, then we have no hope of healing. I refuse to let this happen. I refuse to give up hope.

Questions to Ponder for Individuals or Group Discussion:

1. What do you first remember about learning about gender roles as a child?
    How old were you?
    How did it impact your actions and self-worth?
2. How do you perpetuate gender roles, especially with regard to the nine-year-old girls of today?
3. What name or label do you have in public or in secret?
    How does your name define you? Or does it?
    Who has named or labeled you?
    What power do these people have in your life?

CHAPTER 41

THE BATHROOM

Falcon River

I HAVE NOT been able to enter a public women's bathroom, without causing a stir, since I was about 8, in 1960. At that age, little boys were, and still are, tolerated in the "Ladies room" as they are still considered children. But by the time my 9th birthday rolled around in the fall of 1961, I was already 5'6", darkly tanned, wiry, and muscular from spending most of my waking hours in the tree tops. I realized very early that I was not like other girls. I knew as far back as I have a sense of myself, probably back to being three or four. I knew I wasn't a boy, but I preferred the clothing and activities allotted to them. I had no interest in the things other girls were doing. In fact I found playing with dolls, cooking, cleaning, housework, and feminine dress or makeup, so abhorrent that my mother bought me boys jeans for home wear and only made me wear girl's clothes to school. I kept my hair long and pulled it back in a ponytail. Years later, I realized that my mother endured a lot of criticism from other mothers over her unconventional daughter, but Momma never said a word about that to me.

But I was not a little boy, I am female, so my identity was settled upon by my extended family as that of "Tomboy". Vague references were made by aunts, uncles and older cousins, that I would one day grow out of it, get married to a man and start producing babies, as was expected of the women of our mountain culture. But I vehemently assured my parents from the age of 5, that I had NO intention of ever getting married and that I would NOT be having any babies. Dad's quiet response was to use me as his main helper when he took on odd jobs for folks, teaching me how to work wood, metal and stone. My father could make or repair anything with uncanny skill. He taught me to shoot his old Colt 45 pistol when I was 6, and presented me with my own gun on my 12th birthday. He taught me how to hunt, cause if we didn't hunt, we wouldn't have had much to eat at all really, except for what we raised in our garden. I already had my own fishing gear, and kept a trot line set across the Greenbrier River to catch catfish and snapping turtles.

There after, I was expected to make a daily contribution to the meat supply for our table, summer and winter, no matter what the weather.

Mom taught me how to make and keep a comfortable home, sew my own clothes, quilt, raise the vegetable garden and preserve every scrap of food we could raise or gather. We were busy working constantly, but neither of them ever put any real pressure on me to conform to the traditional role given to girls. Eventually my Aunts, Uncles and cousins simply accepted me as I was, and I was allowed to grow up quite feral actually roaming field and forest to my hearts content. Looking back I know now it gave me the strength to endure what was to come. I had no idea how blessed I truly was.

Cut to 1972, and my first real lesbian relationship. I was living in Roanoke VA, working construction by day, running a backhoe for a swimming pool company and working as a Drag King and bouncer at a gay bar on the weekends. The tomboy was all grown up now, and proudly claiming the title " Butch". I never wanted to be a man, but I had quickly learned to appreciate the benefits of "passing " as a white man. Made everything so much easier. I was 6', naturally flat chested, and muscular from a lifetime of hard work. Even with my blonde hair hanging down to my waist, I was most always perceived to be a man, albeit a "hippie" man, which brought it's own dangers in the south of the 1970s.

With all the skills I had learned working with my Dad, employment was easy for me as long as I could keep up the disguise. Dangerous if/when I was discovered.

Going to the bathroom at work or in public places was always a risky situation. If I got caught in either the women's or men's it could and often did end in, employment termination, physical assault, rape, arrest, or worse. So there were many years where I never even entered a public facility unless faced with no other option. I was always prepared to attend to my needs outdoors, and always carried a boot dagger, a 38 special pistol, or sometimes both, to ensure some measure of safety.

By 1975, I had moved to Louisville KY and became radicalized when the second wave of the Feminist movement swept the country. I met hundreds of other women who were reclaiming the right to dress and live freely as they chose, rather than conform to the tyranny of male or female gender stereotypes. They all wore jeans and flannel shirts too, so I stopped carrying the 38, but kept the boot dagger and started trying to use public facilities again.

I was still working in "non-traditional jobs" and with the help of a radical lesbian feminist lawyer, I sued my way into the Carpenter's Union apprenticeship program. Their only real excuse, given my many years of documented skills from other jobs, was that they did not have a bathroom for females on the jobsite. Once my lawyer pointed out to the judge how ludicrous it was that the members of the carpenters union could not figure out how to hang a door with a latch on one of the portable privies, I started working in Hell. My privy, mine because I was always the first and only female on the jobs, became a place of persecution. It was often smeared inside with human excrement and plastered with pictures and crude drawings of penises. I was locked inside on hot days, and left until the foreman came to let me out. The threats were vile, vulgar, and enraging, but I made it three years and nine months, of my four-year apprenticeship. Until one day, one man too many grabbed my ass while I was working and I took out his front teeth with my claw hammer. But I digress…

Several months before that happened, my partner picked me up from work one evening, and with our two-year-old son, we stopped to have a quick dinner before heading home. Of course this meant that I was still in my dirty work clothes, steel-toed boots and hard hat, while my Femme partner had come from her up town office job. The restaurant we chose was quiet and nearly empty. As my partner was getting our son settled in his high chair, I decided to go relieve myself, before our food came. Newly feminist and feeling hopeful, if not fully confident, I set my hardhat down on the booth seat, stood and stepped to the door of the loo. I had just a moment to square myself to enter the "Ladies" room as another woman, slightly older and very clearly traditionally female attired, emerged. I smiled at her and held the door for her to exit before I entered. Once in the stall, I just had time to drop my pants and begin to relax into the release of pent up urine and bowels before an angry male voice demanded that I, "Get the Hell Out!!!" The steel stall door slammed forward into my knees as I struggled to grab my pants up, and stand to meet my attacker. He continued to kick the door in his efforts to grab me and pull me out of the stall, as I punched him, screaming that I was female. Finally I just let my pants drop, naked cunt, piss and excrement dripping down my legs and stood before him cursing everyone in his family lineage at the top of my lungs. At the sight of my nakedness, he ran out. I quickly cleaned myself up as best I could, and prepared to leave. Four police cruisers were already in the parking lot, lights flashing, as I, my partner and our child were roughly escorted by a troop of officers from the restaurant, amid insults and threats from the wait staff and patrons. It seems my attacker had been the owner and was within his legal rights to have us expelled by force. Our baby boy had nightmares for weeks, no, months.

So, I have learned over the years to avoid using a public restroom unless I am accompanied by a woman friend, with a more traditionally female presentation. Or, with a Butch sister, so that we can support each other in case of trouble. If a more feminine friend goes in first as we are talking together, I might get some strange looks, but it doesn't usually erupt into something unpleasant.

475

I do my best to make sure that the women I encounter in public restrooms know that I am female, and that I do not pose a danger. As a female, a woman, I fully understand their fear. I too have endured multiple sexual assaults at the hands of men, starting in childhood. We have every reason to fear the violence of males. And I fully understand why women who see me as male are frightened. I do not want to share a bathroom with men either.

On the other hand, I actually do understand why women might want to be perceived as men. It is simple, male privilege, and white male privilege in particular, is more addictive than any drug. It can give one a heady freedom to move in the world that no feminine-presenting woman or person of color can EVER comprehend.

I know, because white male privilege is handed to me on a daily basis. There might be three other women ahead of me in a line to be helped at a store, but the clerk (often another woman) will look past the women and ask me first, "May I help you Sir?" My answer is always to direct them to the woman who has been patiently waiting her turn, first in line, speaking in my higher and more femininely developed voice. I am always prepared for the strange looks, but will not allow another woman to be slighted on my account.

I've had to work on the voice a bit, since my voice is naturally lower and I want to sound natural. And yet I will admit other times, I have used that same white male privilege as I shape shift to "man" to provide a measure of safety for myself and other women as we walk city streets, and country lanes. Not fair, I know, but sometimes safety has to come first.

So why is it that we are supposed to accept this mass delusion that one can actually change one's sex? Gender is made up, Sex is biology, and the minute a trans person stops taking the drugs they begin to revert to their natural sex determined appearance. Gender is NOT sex!!!!

How can it be that it has actually become legal for men with intact penises to use women's restrooms, or share locker rooms, just because they believe themselves to be "women"? How can it be that we women now have no legal protection in our most private and vulnerable places? And how the Hell can anybody tell me that I have privilege, by virtue of being born a woman in this world of institutional misogyny, over the men who are paying the medical establishment to castrate them, having breast implants and taking massive amounts of drugs to masquerade as a woman? And why the Hell are women going along with this delusion, willingly getting their own breasts cut off, and taking testosterone with little concern for the long term health effects?

How can it be that children, toddlers, are now being subjected to this experimental medical insanity? Well meaning parents are turning their sweet tomboy girls into trans boys and little sissy boys into trans girls, thinking they are doing the best thing for their children.

Really??? They are leading their child into a lifetime of drug dependence and often sterility, with no clear research done on the long-term effect of the drugs and surgeries.

Now with the Trans agenda in full operation in our current culture, my bathroom experiences, indeed my life experiences out in public are distinctly more unpleasant.

Just like other women, with advancing age, my womanhood has been completely erased and discounted. But unlike my more traditionally feminine sisters, restaurant wait staff, store clerks, even health care providers now automatically assume I am male or a *transman*. I have been completely robbed of my rightful identity as a female old lesbian Butch, to exist and be seen as a viable member of society, period.

Because I do not agree with the Trans Agenda, and have spoken out about these issues, I have been viciously attacked in person and online. People I thought were friends, and women I thought of as sisters, have harassed me and threatened my physical safety, the safety of my home, family and beloved animal companions. It is as if all the work I have done in my life to fight for the rights of women and men to defy and discard gender stereotypes has been destroyed by the very people I thought I was fighting for.

But I am not so easily frightened and I will never back down from this issue.

I am so disgusted, hurt and enraged! The innate homophobia of the trans agenda is horrific. Butch dykes and sissy men are being "hetero normalized" out of existence and the rest of our culture seems to be going along with their insanity! Tell me, why does no one discuss the innate homophobia of The Trans Agenda? Trans gender folks, their allies and supporters, claim to be gender non-conformists, but nothing could be further from the truth. Most trans folks do everything they can to conform to the strictly gendered, heterosexual, patriarchal image of the perfect manly man or effeminate woman. It makes sense, they must do this to fully pass and participate in this patriarchal society. Those that cannot carry out their disguise are often in great danger.

In my mind, transgenderism is nothing more than strict conformity to patriarchal ideals of masculinity and femininity. There is absolutely nothing non-conforming about being trans. We Butches, Lesbians, Dykes, Sissy Men, Drag Queens and all other people who love themselves as they are, but refuse to play by the rules of Patriarchy, we are the true gender non-conformists! We are the true gender outlaws!

To paraphrase what I once read on a radical feminist's blog: If trans people were truly non-conformists, there would be no transgenderism. What might our society be like if these same folks categorically rejected cutting off their body parts and taking drugs to conform to the dominant paradigm? What if we all stood together to create real change? I want a society, no,

I want a world where women and men can wear what ever clothes they want, wear their hair any way they want, shave or not shave their faces and bodies, pursue any career, any sport, any hobby, and live truly free from the tyranny of gender roles. I want a world where there is no violence towards any of us for simply being who we were born to be, naturally. But until that day comes, I will stand and fight for the rights of all females (and truly gender non-conforming males) with my last breath.

SECTION SIX

RESISTANCE TO DELUSION

There's extreme irony in the fact that the glorious Abby Wambach - a proud, unabashed, "masculine" lesbian who has defied sex stereotypes her entire life - introduced Bruce Jenner - a man who only exists as a woman because we all indulge the idea that those stereotypes make him a woman - as he received his award for "courage."

~ CATHY BRENNAN

CHOICES NOT TAKEN

Imagine how differently things could have gone between males who gender identify as women and the 51% of the world's female population if...

IF the vocal trans majority had not chosen to focus their energy on re-defining women in their image, and instead proudly claimed themselves to be gender non-conforming men, a no less sacred expression of humanity.

IF they had not insisted on erasing our biology or their own in order to validate their gender identity, and instead acknowledged themselves as males who simply choose to adopt and express a gender stereotypical feminine appearance.

IF they had not bullied themselves into female spaces and worked to make illegal our private spaces, and instead showed themselves to be true allies of women by respecting and protecting our needs.

IF they allowed themselves to feel even a fraction of empathy that they fully expect from women and girls toward *their* needs.

IF they had not focused their anger at women for the actual violence they experience at the hands of other males.

We *are* our choices.

Male sexual and physical violence is of mutual concern for the trans community, women, lesbians, gay men, and children of both sexes.
Imagine IF all of these oppressed groups united to name the real problem?

Imagine.

~ Ruth Barrett

Transgenderism is, at its very core, conformity. That is the number one goal of transgenderism: conforming to the binary. Butches and non-conforming dykes and lesbians want the very opposite.

Transgenders try to co-opt our words by claiming to be women and even lesbians. They try to co-opt our spaces by forcing their way into women's restrooms, dressing rooms, and other woman-only spaces. They try to control our bodies by shaming us into having sex with them or else be labeled bigots and transphobes. They even try to steal our histories by turning women like Teena Brandon into a trans man, by claiming the butch and drag queen who started the Stonewall riots were actually a trans man and trans woman, etc.

They do all of this under the guise that they are gender non-conformists, when the truth of the matter is simply this: if trans people were truly non-conformists, there would be no transgenderism. Women would be women and men would be men, regardless of how they dressed or acted; and there would be no back lash, no mocking or shaming, no violence toward them, towards all of us, for being who we are.

~ Parker Wolf aka: BigBooButch, from "Lesbians, Dykes, and Butches: The Real Gender Non-Conformists" on BigBooButch.com, October 10, 2013

One thousand mothers stand behind us in an unbroken line, part of the truth of our bodies, the root of our souls and the mystery of our lives upon this earth. It is certain that at some point our mother lines meet and mingle; we will share mothers in common as we reach out towards our ancient roots. Our sisterhood is held in the web of our ancient mothers' arms.

~ C.H.

A-mazing Amazons must be aware of the male methods of mystification. Elsewhere I have discussed four methods which are essential to the games of the fathers. First, there is *erasure* of women. (the massacre of millions of women as witches is erased in patriarchal scholarship.) Second, there is *reversal*. (Adam gives birth to Eve, Zeus to Athena, in patriarchal myth.) Third, there is *false polarization*. (Male-defined "feminism" is set up against male-defined "sexism" in the patriarchal media.) Fourth, there is *divide* and *conquer*. (Token women are trained to kill off feminists in patriarchal professions.) As we move further on the metapatriarchal journey, we find deeper and deeper layers of these demonic patterns embedded in the culture, implanted in our souls. These constitute mind-bindings comparable to the footbindings which mutilated millions of Chinese women for a thousand years. Stripping away layer after layer of these mindbinding societal/mental embeds is the a-mazing essential to the journey.

~ Mary Daly, *Gyn Ecology, Beacon Press, Boston, 1978, P.8*

484

CHAPTER 42

GENDER, PATRIARCHY, AND ALL THAT JAZZ

Mary Lou Singleton

LIKE MANY AMERICANS, I have been paying attention to the current marketing of gender, the unquestionable system that tells us what constitutes male vs. female in our capitalist patriarchy. With morbid fascination, I am witnessing our culture move away from the old women's liberation values that told young people they could participate in any activity they enjoyed, wear any clothing they liked, play with whatever toys they wanted, and think any thoughts they thought without these behaviors and beliefs being labeled male or female by forces then known as sexism. Not only have the categories of "boy's toys" and "girl's toys" returned with a vengeful backlash, now children and the rest of us are being told that an affinity for "girl's toys" and dresses and make-up actually defines the true essence of girlhood. If a child really, really likes what is being sold by the capitalist patriarchy as female, that child IS female. And vice versa for children who reject female toys and stereotypical female interests. Even if they have two X chromosomes and a vulva, these children are now obviously boys. These children are especially to be considered boys if they hate their female physiology and despise their female bodies. Through the miracle of capitalist cooptation, we have progressed from the women's liberation war cry of "Start a Revolution, Stop Hating Your Body" to hating the body being framed as revolutionary.

With particular interest, I have been watching and reading about Jazz Jennings, the biological male who from the time of toddlerhood strongly preferred the toys, clothes and mannerisms marketed as female. Because Jazz rejected the products and behaviors sold and enforced as male, and because Jazz never had opportunities to see males who identify as males playing with "girl things" and wearing "girl clothes" and "acting like girls," and because Jazz had no interest in the products marketed as "boy things" (the guns, the robots, the buzz cuts, the army men), Jazz began identifying as the kind of person who likes "girl things." Jazz's parents agreed that if Jazz shopped and talked and threw like a girl, obviously Jazz was a girl. Happily for them (if money can buy happiness), Jazz was born at the perfect time in our post-feminist, post-modern, bread-and-circuses phase of late stage capitalism. Jazz's family landed paid appearances on talk shows, paid interviews, and now a reality TV show, all promoting the idea that sex-role stereotypes (aka gender) are the only definition of male and female that matter. Jazz Jennings has become the literal poster child for Gender Incorporated, telling and selling us all what it really means to be female in a capitalist patriarchy.

Like Honey Boo Boo and Miley Cyrus, and Michael Jackson before them, Jazz appears as a happy, fun-loving child with a caring, supportive family. Jazz continually smiles while doing the things girls do: posing in a mermaid suit, cheerleading, being pretty. In several articles and appearances, however, Jazz has hinted at sadness, worrying about finding a boyfriend, stating that many biological boys Jazz encounters do not view Jazz as a girl. Jazz reports plenty of female friends, though. While I'm sure Jazz's life will have its difficulties (life-long hormone replacement, plastic surgery, and childhood fame all carry significant risks), the majority of biological females Jazz encounters will offer comfort and kindness to Jazz, as they have been socialized through gender to do. Gender after all normalizes female self-sacrifice. Most adult females, even those who identify as feminists, exhibit an unexamined acceptance of gender. Women reflexively label every creature they see as male (unless said creature is portrayed with breasts or fake eyelashes and lipstick). They fear more than anything not being liked and they work hard to never, ever commit the sin of hurting someone's feelings. They have been enculturated to accept their own erasure and to serve the interests of biological males. Jazz's life will have problems, but these will be buffered and mitigated by female caretaking.

Jazz will inevitably encounter people who refuse to accept the belief system that asserts gender as fact and biology (i.e. the living, material world) as a mere social construct or inconvenience to be fixed with chemicals and technology. Some of these people will be females who resent being told that femaleness can be reduced to performance of "femininity" while they themselves do not appreciate the patriarchal gender system that defines female this way. Others will be males and conservative females who support and revere the patriarchy, but want to maintain a social order like the good old days when men were men and women were women. Because Jazz and the rest of us are being strongly indoctrinated to view "misgendering" as violence, Jazz will have many tales of such violence to report through the gender-promoting media. Those who have participated in the crime of misgendering will be appropriately shamed for refusing to capitulate to the new rules of gender (they may also lose their jobs or speaking gigs at universities or be sued for discrimination).

Because Jazz was born into a violent patriarchy, Jazz may also encounter physical violence, almost certainly at the hands of males. Should it occur, and I sincerely hope it doesn't, this violence will be labeled a hate crime, a crime more worthy of social outrage and attention than the rapes, murders, torture and beatings suffered by biological females at the hands of males. Unlike biological females, Jazz legally belongs to a protected class, and violence toward this protected class of people is taken more seriously by the media and liberal activists (and sometimes even the legal system) than the routine, all day, every day male violence against biological females.

I do not predict an easy or peaceful future for Jazz. I, however, am even more concerned about what the future holds for Jazz's sister and all of the girls she represents: the less special kind of female, the kind who doesn't automatically get awards of bravery for declaring herself a woman and devoting herself to the performance of her assigned gender role. The kind of female conditioned to take up as little space as possible, even if this means starving herself. The kind of female whose body is not legally her own. The kind of female who is viewed as a state regulated incubator, worthy of public debates in mainstream media venues about whether or not she should be allowed to end an unwanted pregnancy or give birth at home. (Such debates about what women should and shouldn't be allowed to do with their bodies currently receive less social criticism and outrage than the crime of misgendering, by the way. When it comes to forced pregnancy and birth, "good people can disagree.")

A recent article in Cosmopolitan (a magazine designed to enforce the rules of gender to the female population; a magazine which recently ran a cover story promoting torture porn and telling women that we should learn to enjoy being tied up, beaten, choked, and having men ejaculate on our faces), featured Jazz Jennings talking about his sister. Jazz tells the interviewer and the world that he views his sister's body as something that can be used to serve his reproductive desires. Like so many gender non-conforming children today who would have once grown up to be happy gay people with intact bodies, Jazz is being sterilized through the process of transitioning into a cultural stereotype of femininity. The medical industry will remove his testicles, if they haven't already done so, and through plastic surgery create a simulation of a vagina for Jazz. Jazz wants very much to be a parent. Lucky for him he lives in a world where women's bodies are for sale and rent. In the Cosmo interview, Jazz brags that he is "convincing" his sister to serve him as incubator so he can fulfill his dream of being a mother. Jazz, speaking of his sister's vagina (which he calls her "vag"), says, "We'll take my hubby's sperm and throw it in there and fertilize it."

For those of you out there, and I know there are many, who are reacting to the use of male pronouns and judging this sin of misgendering as mean, maybe even violent, I want you to compare your reaction to my pronoun use to your reaction to Cosmo promoting rape and torture porn, and ask yourself if by going along with the cult of gender you just might be doing the work of the patriarchy. I want you to compare your reaction to my use of male pronouns when describing a teenager who believes he is entitled to his sister's "vag" and womb, to your reaction to Jazz's words about his sister, and ask yourself just what you are doing for biological females when you promote and defend gender.

Unfortunately for her, Jazz's sister belongs to the class of females that patriarchs like Rick Santorum talk to when he and other male authority figures take to the airwaves every election cycle telling us we should be forced to give birth to rapists' babies. (Santorum, who hates women and gay people, has publicly asserted that Bruce Jenner is a woman if Jenner says he is a woman.) Jazz's sister is the kind of female the patriarchy exists to control, the kind of female who can be used to produce the progeny of biological males. When power and property are controlled by competing men and passed to male children, female bodies must be policed and controlled so men can be reassured they are not spending their resources on another male's children. This is called patriarchy. Patriarchal societies oppress females because of biological sex, their capacity to reproduce. Gender serves as the rulebook for this oppression. Females are not oppressed because of their gender. Gender itself oppresses females.

Gender trains males and females to know their proper places in the system of male supremacy. Just as children absorb and learn language, they also learn the rules and syntax of gender. And the childhood rules of gender are clearer and stricter today than they have been in over a century. Unlike the halcyon days of the 1970s when all Legos looked alike and television ads portrayed the Slinky as a toy for a girl or a boy and "Free to Be You and Me" played even in my conservative Catholic childhood home, gender stereotypes now permeate every aspect of children's media and toys and clothing. Lest anyone accuse me of waxing too idyllic about the 1970s, I will mention a phenomenon I witnessed in my family and church community. Gender non-conforming boys were told from a very young age by all of the adults around them that they would make very good priests. Several of my gay male cousins and classmates, who from toddlerhood enjoyed wearing make-up and high heels and other things that made them feel pretty, internalized this messaging and did indeed become priests. Had they been born several decades later, they would have been encouraged to think of themselves as female. (Whether priests in the 1970s or transwomen today, these males interestingly both hold a place of enforcing the rules of what it means to be a woman in a patriarchy.) Jazz's sister and Jazz both grew up soaking in gender. Both were taught only to view cartoon characters or animals as female if they were portrayed in highly sexualized ways: with male-gaze appealing face paint and bullet-tit bodies, or to be more sexually mundane, in the acts of gestating, birthing and breastfeeding. (For more on this, Google "madonna/whore dichotomy." After you sort through the inevitable pornography, you may find some feminist critiques of this classic aspect of the gender system.)

Jazz's sister belongs to the class of females socialized to feel inferior for being female. Magazines don't interview her about how great it is to be the kind of girl she happens to be. No one commends her on her courage for shaving her body hair and applying make-up. She remains the kind of girl brainwashed from birth to caretake and accommodate biological males. To not participate in such caretaking and accommodation will result in social punishment. With regard to Jazz's reproductive desires, this leaves Jazz's sister with very bad options. She can be nice and agree to accept the risks to her physical and emotional health that accompany gestating, birthing, and relinquishing a child. If she agrees to let Jazz throw his hubby's sperm up her vag and incubate a child for him, she will reap some temporary social rewards for her self-sacrifice. Or she can be a bitch and say no. More on this story to come, I'm sure, as we are all subjected to the gender-promoting spectacle of the Jazz Jennings story.

Originally published in Counterpunch, July 31ˢᵗ, 2015. Republished with permission.
  http://www.counterpunch.org/2015/07/31/gender-patriarchy-and-all-that-jazz/

CHAPTER 43

THE SURGICAL SUITE: MODERN-DAY CLOSET FOR TODAY'S TEEN LESBIAN

Marie Verite

DESPITE THE FACT that trans activists are diligently trying to lower the age of consent[1] for cross-sex hormones and surgeries, as a general rule, children under eighteen in the US cannot access these "treatments" without parental consent. (Oregon is a notable exception.) I have argued that even eighteen is too young[2] to make such permanent decisions, given that executive function skills are not well developed until a person's early twenties.

But there is another, equally important reason to question medical transition for adolescent girls. According to several peer-reviewed studies (which I discuss in detail in this article):

- Some 95 to 100% of girls who "persist" in gender dysphoria at adolescence are same-sex attracted; these girls are typically offered cross-sex hormones by age sixteen, and surgeries as young as eighteen.
- The typical age that a young lesbian has her first sexual experience and/or claims her sexual orientation is between the ages of nineteen and the early twenties.

Let those two statements sink in for a moment.

Here's the reality of what's going on in gender clinics around the world right now. An increasing number of adolescent girls[3] diagnosed with gender dysphoria are asking for, and receiving, cross-sex hormones and surgeries. The World Professional Association for Transgender Health (WPATH) officially recommends cross-sex hormone treatment to begin as early as age sixteen, with sex reassignment surgeries (SRS) to be offered at age eighteen.

The vast majority of these girls presenting to clinics admit to being same-sex attracted. Yet data from studies of lesbian, gay, and bisexual (LGB) people shows that most young women don't fully crystallize a lesbian orientation until age nineteen or older.

To take one of several examples, a 1997 study of 147 lesbians and gay men by Gregory Herek and colleagues found that (emphasis added):

The mean age for first attraction to a member of the same sex was 11.5 for females and 10.3 for males. Mean age for **first orgasm** with a person of the same sex was **20.2 for females** and 17.7 for males. On average, **females first identified themselves as lesbian or bisexual at age 20.2**, whereas men did so at age 18.7. Mean age for first **disclosure of one's sexual orientation was 20.5 for females** and 21.2 for males.[4]

A 2014 study of 396 LGB people, by Alexander Martos and colleagues reported a similar finding for age of first sexual experience:

Women self-identified as non-heterosexual when they were almost 3 years older than the men (age 17.6 vs. 14.8) and **reported their first same-sex relationship when they were 1.4 years older than men (19.1 vs.17.7).**[5]

And not only do young lesbians take longer to realize and accept their sexual orientation than their gay male counterparts; coming out to oneself, and to loved ones and the world, *takes time.* It's a developmental process that evolves over a number of years, from the first signs of puberty into early adulthood, with several stages, as Martos and colleagues explained in the same 2014 study:

Coming out is not a single event but a series of realizations and disclosures. The age at which sexual minorities first recognize their identity, tell others about their identity, and have same-sex relationships varies, and people may take different amounts of time between one milestone and the next. Scholars have proposed and tested models of sexual identity development for over 30 years. Cass (1979) developed an influential model, which outlined a six-stage linear psychological path of sexual identity development. Troiden (1989) built upon Cass's model and reframed it within four stages: (a) sensitization, which may include a person's first same-sex attraction and their first questioning of their heterosexual socialization, (b) **identity confusion, a period during early to mid-adolescence that is marked by inner turmoil and often the initiation of same-sex sexual activity, (c) identity assumption, when a youth self-identifies as LGB and begins to reveal their "true self" to select people and seeks community among other LGBs, and (d) commitment, which is marked by the initiation of a same-sex romantic relationship and disclosure to a wide variety of heterosexual people (Floyd and Stein 2002). These models suggest that healthy and stable sexual identity development necessitates the full permeation of sexual identity into all aspects of a person's life.**[6]

So the process of integration – "full permeation" – of one's sexual orientation is a process that takes place over a period of years. It involves "identity confusion" and "inner turmoil" in adolescence. And not to put too fine a point on it, but most lesbians don't even *begin* to express and realize their orientation until they are nineteen or twenty years old.

Yet same-sex-attracted girls who present to gender clinics – many of them still with the concrete, either-or thinking of a child (e.g., if I like girls, I must be a *guy)*, internalized homophobia, and overall lack of maturity and self-reflection typical of their age, have been "socially transitioned" for years; have had their puberty "blocked" (such that they don't have the opportunity or desire, in most cases, to actually experience a physical relationship with a love interest); and then move on to "transitioning" to….a straight male.

Here they are, girls without sexual experience, conditioned to reject their bodies and begin irreversible medical "treatments" before they've had a chance to embark on the years-long process of discovering their own bodies and selves as sexual beings.

In a 2011 Dutch study, "Desisting and persisting dysphoria after childhood,"[7] Steensma and colleagues noted that *100% of the girls who "persisted" in gender dysphoria by age 16 were same-sex attracted.* As they indicate, this finding corroborates those of other researchers over many decades. A 2013 study[8], also by Steensma *et al*, revealed the same information, but added more granularity: between 95.7 -100% of the sixteen-year-old (average age) girls reported exclusively same-sex attraction, fantasy, and behavior (defined as "kissing" because, as the authors note, that was the extent of their sexual experience). Age sixteen – well before the average age of coming out as lesbian noted in the studies I highlighted earlier. To wit (emphasis added):

With regard to sexual attraction, **all persisters reported feeling exclusively attracted to persons of the same natal sex**, which confirmed their gender identity as they viewed this attraction as a heterosexual attraction. They did not consider themselves homosexual or lesbian.

…the majority of adolescents kept their sexual attractions to themselves. Both boys and girls indicated that, as a result of **fear of rejection**, they did not speak about their sexual feelings to others, and did not try to date someone. Furthermore, most adolescents felt uncomfortable responding to romantic gestures from others.

In summarizing their findings, Steensma and colleagues noted that:

The third factor that seemed to be associated with the persistence or desistence of childhood gender dysphoria was the experience of falling in love and sexual attraction. The **persisters, all attracted to same- (natal) sex partners**, indicated that the awareness of their sexual attractions functioned as a confirmation of their cross-gender identification as **they viewed this as typically heterosexual.**

These adolescents at age sixteen regarded their same-sex attractions as *"typically heterosexual."* It's fascinating that the study authors make this statement without any examination of exactly *why* the 100%-same-sex-attracted persisters viewed themselves this way, and whether this might give pause to the practice of medical transition — especially since in the very next paragraph, the study authors refer to earlier research findings that LGB people are late to claim their sexual orientations:

All persisters reported feeling exclusively, and as long as they could remember, sexually attracted to individuals of the same natal sex, although none of the persisters considered themselves "homosexual" or "lesbian," but (because of their cross-gender identity) "heterosexual."

As for the desisters, about half of them were sexually attracted in fantasy to individuals of the same natal sex. Yet, all girls and most of the boys identified as heterosexual. The difference between the reported sexual attractions and identities may be related to the timing of the "coming-out." The literature shows that the average age of the first feelings of same-sex attraction is generally during puberty and before the age of 18 (e.g., Barber, 2000; Herek, Cogan, Gillis & Glunt, 1998; Rust, 1996). However, **the moment at which men and women identify and come out as gay, lesbian, or bisexual generally lies above the age of 18, at the end of adolescence or in their early twenties** (e.g., Barber, 2000; Herek, Cogan, Gillis & Glunt, 1998; Rust, 1996).

Steensma and colleagues give us what we need to know, but they don't connect the dots: these same-sex-attracted young adolescent girls undergo "transition" before they have the opportunity to experience themselves as sexual beings in their healthy, original bodies.

Why are we robbing our kids of the basic human right to discover their sexuality without preemptive tampering by the medical and psychiatric profession? "Transition" prevents them from learning whether they might be gay/lesbian, freezing them at an immature stage of development, when the only possibility they see is that they are heterosexuals trapped in the "wrong" body.

Trans activists like to say that gender identity and sexual orientation are completely unrelated. But obviously, it just ain't so. Study after study, anecdote after anecdote, media story after media story, tell us that most "trans men" start off as same-sex-attracted adolescents. But no one outside the blogosphere—*no one* –is pointing out the obvious: that girls who would naturally mature into lesbian adults are having the process of realizing their sexual orientation short-circuited by medical transition.

Who will step forward to stop this? Who with power in our society — the Congress, the president, the publisher of the *New York Times,* the child and adolescent psychologists – will raise their voices? Where are the lesbian doctors, lawyers, heads of LGBT organizations? Which of you will name this preemptive conversion therapy for what it is?

Blocking puberty and the right to an identity crisis

But not all kids who are being sent down the road to medical transition are gay or lesbian. While it's obvious that many teens are being set up to short-circuit the natural discovery of their sexual orientation, that's not the only problem with social transition and puberty blocking.

There are so many important things that happen at puberty *which are critically important to the maturation necessary to make informed decisions about major life changes* (you know, things like sterility, loss of breasts, and a permanently deepened voice) that a developmental psychologist or cognitive scientist could write a doctoral dissertation about it. In fact, many have; the research and clinical literature going back to the mid-twentieth century is chock-a-block with replicated studies, clinical observations, and meta-analyses. More recently, we have MRI and fMRI studies corroborating earlier observations.

What we *don't* have, at least not yet, are the PhD theses showing how the experimental "treatments" currently being implemented by pediatric endocrinologists and gender specialists— many of whom have no professional background in child or adolescent psychology—fly in the face of that large body of literature.

I have spent hundreds of hours poring over the literature on gender dysphoria and pediatric transition. But in all the studies and papers I've read, I have not seen mention of the vast body of extant knowledge about child and adolescent psychology. It's as if these gender specialists just started from scratch.

What exactly are they ignoring? Well, for starters, there's the work of Erik Erikson, a preeminent child and adolescent psychology expert of the twentieth century. You can't read the scholarly or clinical literature on pediatric psychology without finding a reference to Erikson's work; in fact, much of the current knowledge in the field is built upon his fundamental insights. His bedrock finding about the psychological journey of adolescence is this: Developing an identity takes place in stages, culminating in an integrated adult personality, and "identity work" — *including an identity crisis — is critical to healthy adult psychological functioning.*[9]

According to Erikson, successful resolution of this crisis depends on one's progress through previous developmental stages, centering on fundamental issues of trust, autonomy, and initiative. By the age of twenty-one, about half of all adolescents are thought to have resolved their identity crises and are ready to move on to the adult challenges of love and work. *Others, however, are unable to achieve an integrated adult identity, either because they have failed to resolve the identity crisis or because they have experienced no crisis.*

Adolescent psychology expert James Marciawas another foundational thinker who built upon Erikson's framework. According to Marcia, Two distinct parts form an adolescent's identity: crisis (i.e., a time when one's values and choices are being reevaluated) and commitment. He defined a crisis as a **time of upheaval** where old values or choices are being reexamined. The end outcome of a crisis leads to a commitment made to a certain role or value.[10]

But we don't need a study, a theory, or someone with a PhD after their name to prove this to us, do we? Any adult who has lived through that time of life called "adolescence" can attest to the fact that questioning, and trying on and discarding different ways of being, go with the territory. And it's a rough time. How many adults would willingly relive the fraught and tumultuous days of middle and high school? Every psychologist (until the Age of the Trans Child) has agreed: it's not *supposed* to be an easy ride. In fact, without the essential but painful work of adolescence, a person will not reach their adult potential, and will be, in Erikson's view, *"unable to achieve an integrated adult identity, either because they have failed to resolve the identity crisis or because they have experienced no crisis."*

Contrast this long-accepted understanding of adolescence with the approach taken by today's gender specialists. Instead of helping children weather the natural and not necessarily comfortable process of cognitive and emotional development, they concretize and freeze in place the certainties of childhood, during what should be a time for exploration, not stasis.

It would be one thing if these gender clinics were really in the business of helping a child expand or explore different gender identities, without medical interference. But we know that they support and encourage "transition" from one sex to the other, with all the permanent physical changes that entails. In terms of adolescent psychological development, once these kids have taken the irrevocable step of moving from blockers to cross-sex hormones, they have been denied the opportunity to go through an identity crisis. So, a sixteen-year-old girl who has lost her fertility and her breasts, and who has already committed to a permanent testosterone-deepened voice and increased body hair — how easy will it be for her to experience James Marcia's "time of upheaval where old values or choices are being reexamined?" That adolescent girl has been cheated of that stage of life. And when did we, as a society, decide that was a good thing?

The media stories and anecdotes from gender clinics are all the same: The kids are uncomfortable, so they and their parents seek relief. Then, according to everyone, the treatment "works" because the kids are happy. For how long? No one knows.

Be that as it may, an identity crisis isn't supposed to be resolved in preschool, or kindergarten, or even middle or high school: It is the *work* and the challenge of adolescence, not complete until *late adolescence,* as noted by Laurence Steinberg:

Adolescence has long been characterized as a time when individuals begin to explore and examine psychological characteristics of the self in order to discover who they really are, and how they fit in the social world in which they live. Especially since Erikson's (1968) theory of the adolescent identity crisis was introduced, scholars have viewed adolescence as a time of self-exploration. In general, research has supported Erikson's model, with one important exception: the timetable. It now appears that, at least in contemporary society, **the bulk of identity "work" occurs late in adolescence, and perhaps not even until young adulthood**.[11]

"Late in adolescence" — *after* the time when most "trans" youth have moved on from puberty blockers to cross-sex hormones, thus bypassing the period when they would have been able to explore possibilities in their original bodies—including, but not limited to, their sexual orientation and other essential aspects of their identities and personalities.

The insights of the earlier child development experts have been corroborated by advanced visualization technologies, such as MRI and fMRI,[12] which have revolutionized our understanding of the human brain and psychological development. A 2005 Harvard medical school blog post, "The adolescent brain: Beyond raging hormones," provides a succinct overview of the neuroanatomy of adolescence:

Recent research has shown that human brain circuitry is not mature until the **early twenties** (some would add, "if ever"). **Among the last connections** to be fully established are the links between the prefrontal cortex, seat of judgment and problem-solving, and the emotional centers in the limbic system, especially the amygdala. These links are **critical for emotional learning and high-level self-regulation**.

Beginning at puberty, the brain is reshaped. Neurons (gray matter) and synapses (junctions between neurons) proliferate in the cerebral cortex and are then gradually pruned throughout adolescence. Eventually, more than 40% of all synapses are eliminated, largely in the frontal lobes. Meanwhile, the white insulating coat of myelin on the axons that carry signals between nerve cells continues to accumulate, gradually improving the precision and efficiency of neuronal communication — a process not completed until the early twenties.[13]

In addition to reading research studies, I spend a fair bit of time reading the blogs, tweets, and social media writings of trans-identified teens. While most teens are pretty self-absorbed, with these kids, I am always struck by the depth of self-involvement, the extreme obsession with looks and appearance, and the constant focus on *getting what they want, when they want it*.

What is conspicuously absent in the narratives of many of these teens is another key aspect of pubertal maturation: self-reflection and awareness. Concrete, literalist thinking is a hallmark of childhood. So a preadolescent frozen at Tanner Stage 2 of pubertal development (when blockers normally begin to be administered) may still think literally and concretely: "I *am* a boy." Instead of: "Maybe I *think* I'm a boy because I like trucks and hate girly clothes. Maybe there's a reason I think I'm a boy, but I'm really not." The name for such higher-level reflection, or "thinking about thinking," is metacognition.

So when these young people, frozen at an earlier stage of cognitive development, are asked at age fifteen or sixteen, "Are you *sure* you're really a boy?" why would any of them say "no"? And in fact, in the small number of studies that have looked at kids who have been socially transitioned and puberty blocked, *none of them have failed to move on to cross-sex hormones.* Is this because they are "truly trans" and their clinicians have godlike diagnostic skills, with zero — *zero!* — false positives? Or is it because the very act of endorsing and reifying their self-proclaimed *concretized self-images has helped them persist in those self-perceptions?* As deVries and colleagues (the Dutch researcher-clinicians who pioneered pediatric medical transition) note in one of their many published studies:

> No adolescent withdrew from puberty suppression, and **all started cross-sex hormone treatment**, the first step of actual gender reassignment.[14]

It's not just metacognitive and abstract thinking that develops slowly, reaching fruition in late adolescence. As I have written about previously,[15] it has been settled neuroscience (evidenced by hundreds of peer-reviewed studies) that executive function — the ability to make decisions, plan, and think of future consequences (like, "do I want to have children of my own, ever"?) doesn't begin to consolidate until people have reached their mid-twenties.

Then there's social maturity and a more nuanced understanding of how to interact with one's peers. Who doesn't remember the awkwardness, the trying-to-fit-in, seasick self-consciousness of adolescence? Social development takes place in concert with one's peers, along with the slow dawning of self-reflection. A socially transitioned, puberty-blocked fourteen-year-old who has avoided the rigors of hormone-fueled social issues won't understand any of this. How will that lack of experience inform their decision to continue on to cross-sex hormones? In a study by Anne-Lise Goddings *et al*, the authors note:

> We previously investigated how the ability to understand social emotional scenarios using mixed emotions varied across puberty in girls aged 9–16 (Burnett et al., 2011). There was a change between early and late puberty in the number of emotional

responses that participants gave in social emotion scenarios, with girls in late puberty attributing a wider combination of emotions in social scenarios than their peers in early puberty

... Our findings of puberty-related changes in neural activation, together with those shown in other recent fMRI studies using different "social" tasks as described in the introduction, suggest that **aspects of functional brain development in adolescence, like these behavioral changes, may be more closely linked to the physical and hormonal changes of puberty than chronological age.**[16]

As the authors note, social intelligence — a more nuanced understanding of "social emotion" scenarios — develops as a result of the release of hormones, not chronological age. This is so obvious it hardly seems worth studying (or proving on a functional MRI study). Yet gender specialists talk as if the brain develops separately from the body; as if hormones are only important for secondary sexual characteristics. They are constantly reassuring skeptics that blocking puberty gives these incredibly immature kids the time to figure out if this is really what they want—*without the benefit of the cognitive, emotional, and social maturation processes that comes with the secretion of pubertal hormones.*[17]

I've touched here upon only a few facets of adolescent cognitive-emotional development. The literature in this area is vast, still accumulating, and spans decades and millions of pages of writing. Contemporary cognitive scientists like Russell Viner, Sarah-Jayne Blakemore, and Jay Giedd are continuing to add to the body of knowledge. But their work on adolescent psychology and brain development is not referenced in the media or in the writings of trans activists or pediatric gender specialists. In point of fact, what little peer-reviewed research there is in the field of "gender identity" is going in the exact opposite direction of the rest of developmental psychology and cognitive science — towards a reification of rigid, unchanging identity and decision-making "agency" for younger and younger children; while the replicated research of developmental psychology and neuroscience is moving toward an understanding of neuroplasticity, the *necessity* of undergoing an identity crisis, and a later age for brain maturation than was previously thought.

As cognitive scientist Jay Giedd said in a *Frontline* interview for the series "Inside the Teenage Brain,"

One of the most exciting discoveries from recent neuroscience research is how incredibly plastic the human brain is. For a long time, we used to think that the brain, because it's already 95% of adult size by age six, things were largely set in place early in life. ... [There was the] saying. "Give me your child, and by the age of five, I can make him a priest or a thief or a scholar."

[There was] this notion that things were largely set at fairly early ages. And now we realize that isn't true; that even throughout childhood and even the teen years, there's enormous capacity for change. We think that this capacity for change is very empowering for teens. [18]

Instead of respecting this "enormous capacity for change," gender specialists are tampering with the endocrine system, freezing gender-dysphoric children in a state of suspended development — and then expecting these psychologically and emotionally immature children to make permanent decisions about their future as adults. It's a huge clinical gamble. What it amounts to is hoping for the best.

But is anyone preparing for the worst?

---

[1] 4thwavenow, "Coming Soon to a State Near You? Double Mastectomy for Your 15-Year-Old, without Parental Consent," 4thWaveNow, August 19, 2015. https://4thwavenow.com/2015/08/19/coming-soon-to-a-state-near-you-double-mastectomy-for-your-15-year-old-without-parental-consent/

[2] 4thwavenow, "Mom Forces Insurance Company to Cover Double Mastectomy for Her 15-Year-Old with Support of WPATH and Dan Karasic, MD," 4thWaveNow, January 17, 2016, https://4thwavenow.com/2016/01/17/mom-forces-insurance-company-to-cover-double-mastectomy-for-her-15-year-old-with-support-of-wpath-dan-karasic-md/

[3] 4thwavenow, "Why Are More Girls than Boys Presenting to Gender Clinics?" 4thWaveNow, July 10, 2015, https://4thwavenow.com/2015/07/10/why-are-more-girls-than-boys-presenting-to-gender-clinics/

[4] Gregory M. Herek et al, "Correlates of Internalized Homophobia in a Community Sample of Lesbians and Gay Men," *Journal of the Gay and Lesbian Medical Association*, 1997, 2, 17-25m http://psc.dss.ucdavis.edu/rainbow/html/JGLMApre.pdf

[5] Alexander J. Martos et al, "Variations in Sexual Identity Milestones Among Lesbians, Gay Men, and Bisexuals," *Sexuality Research and Social Policy* 12, no. 1 (March 2015): 24–33, doi:10.1007/s13178-014-0167-4. Full article behind paywall.

6 A. J. Martos et al, "Variations in Sexual Identity Milestones Among Lesbians, Gay Men, and Bisexuals," *Sexuality Research and Social Policy* (2015).

7 Thomas D. Steensma et al., "Desisting and Persisting Gender Dysphoria after Childhood: A Qualitative Follow-up Study," *Clinical Child Psychology and Psychiatry* 16, no. 4, October 1, 2011: 499–516, doi:10.1177/1359104510378303.

8 https://www.researchgate.net/publication/49738851_Desisting_and_persisting_gender_dysphoria_after_childhood_a_qualitative_follow-up_study_Clin_Child_Psychol_Psychiatry

9 Thomas D. Steensma et al., "Factors Associated with Desistence and Persistence of Childhood Gender Dysphoria: A Quantitative Follow-Up Study," *Journal of the American Academy of Child & Adolescent Psychiatry* 52, no. 6 (June 2013): 582–90, doi:10.1016/j.jaac.2013.03.016.

10 https://www.researchgate.net/publication/236907380_Factors_Associated_With_Desistence_and_Persistence_of_Childhood_Gender_Dysphoria_A_Quantitative_Follow-Up_Study

11 *Gale Encyclopedia of Psychology*, Second Edition, Gale Group, Detroit, MI. 2001. http://www.cs.unsyiah.ac.id/~frdaus/PenelusuranInformasi/File-Pdf/332_pdfsam_Gale%20Encyclopedia%20of%20Psychology.pdf

12 http://www.learning-theories.com/identity-status-theory-marcia.html, derived from Marcia, J. E., (1966), "Development and validation of ego identity status," *Journal of Personality and Social Psychology* 3, pp. 551-558.

13 Laurence Steinberg, "Adolescent Development," *Annual Review of Psychology,* Vol. 52: 83-110 (Volume publication date February 2001), DOI: 10.1146/annurev.psych.52.1.83, http://www.annualreviews.org/doi/pdf/10.1146/annurev.psych.52.1.83

14 Scientific Correspondence: "Brain Development during Childhood and Adolescence: A Longitudinal MRI Study," Jay N. Giedd et al, *Nature Neuroscience* 2, 861 - 863 (1999) doi:10.1038/13158, http://www.nature.com/neuro/journal/v2/n10/full/nn1099_861.html

[15] Harvard Health Publications, "The Adolescent Brain: Beyond Raging Hormones," *Harvard Health*, accessed May 19, 2016, http://www.health.harvard.edu/mind-and-mood/the-adolescent-brain-beyond-raging-hormones

[16] Annelou de Vries et al, "Puberty Suppression in Adolescents With Gender Identity Disorder: A Prospective Follow-Up Study," *Journal of Sexual Medicine*, July 2010, 8, no 8, 2276–2283, DOI: 10.1111/j.1743-6109.2010.01943.x, http://www.pinktherapy.com/Portals/0/CourseResources/de_Vries_Puberty_Suppression_in_Adolescents_with_GD.pdf

[17] 4thwavenow, "Mom Forces Insurance Company to Cover Double Mastectomy for Her 15-Year-Old, with Support of WPATH and Dan Karasic, MD," 4thWaveNow, January 17, 2016, https://4thwavenow.com/2016/01/17/mom-forces-insurance-company-to-cover-double-mastectomy-for-her-15-year-old-with-support-of-wpath-dan-karasic-md/.

[18] Anne-Lise Goddings et al, "The relationship between puberty and social emotion processing," *Developmental Science* 15, no. 6 (November 2012): 801-811, doi: 10.1111/j.1467-7687.2012.01174.x.

[19] Cheryl L. Sisk and Julia L. Zehr, "Pubertal Hormones Organize the Adolescent Brain and Behavior," *Frontiers in Neuroendocrinology* 26, no. 3–4, October 2005: 163–74, doi:10.1016/j.yfrne.2005.10.003.
https://msu.edu/~sisk/publications/pdfs/Sisk%26Zehr05_Frontiers.pdf

[20] "Inside the Teenage Brain," *Frontline*, accessed May 19, 2016, http://www.pbs.org/wgbh/frontline/?q=teen%20brain%20giedd.

CHAPTER 44

MILWAUKEE PRIDE PARADE STRIPS VETERAN LESBIAN ACTIVIST MIRIAM BEN-SHALOM OF GRAND MARSHALL HONORS, AND A PERSONAL STATEMENT

Miriam Ben-Shalom

THE NAMELESS MEMBERS of the Milwaukee Pride Parade Board of Directors stripped legendary rights activist Miriam Ben-Shalom of her honored spot as Grand Marshall of the June 12, 2016 "Heroes of Pride" event after men monitoring her Facebook page noticed women had made posts there that were critical of the idea of heterosexual "male lesbians".

Miriam Ben-Shalom will be a familiar name to Lesbian and Gay Rights activists and historians. She was the first openly homosexual individual to be reinstated into military service after serving as plaintiff in multiple lawsuits and refusing a cash settlement.

After serving in the Israeli Army as an Armored Personnel Carrier driver, she enlisted as a Staff Sergeant in the United States Army from 1974-1976, when she was dismissed on the basis of homosexuality, and served again from 1987- 1990 following her reinstatement after a decade of trials. She was then discharged, yet again, on the basis of homosexuality, ending her military career.

She co-founded the Gay, Lesbian and Bisexual Veterans of America (GLBVA) and spent another decade organizing activism against the U.S. military policy of exclusion, and later against the Clinton era "Don't Ask Don't Tell" policy. She chained herself, in uniform, to the White House fence in 1993. Along with Dan Choi and other lesbian and gay service-members she was arrested after again chaining herself to the White House fence in 2010. President Barack Obama invited her to the White House in recognition of her decades of activism, she stood present when he signed the law repealing "Don't Ask Don't Tell" later that year.

This is not the first time heterosexual male members of the "LGBT" have surveiled, attacked, and dishonored Miriam Ben-Shalom's legacy. Last year trans activist Autumn Sandeen wrote an entire OpEd sponsored by the San Diego LGBTWeekly titled "Unknowingly protesting with a lesbian transphobe!" where he complained that he observed Miriam using the term "Woman Born Woman" on a Facebook post. He said this was offensive to men because it made a distinction between individuals born male or female. He went on to state that he wished, as a heterosexual male, that he had never protested DADT, a policy which never affected straight men like himself anyway.

HERE IS THE FULL TEXT OF THE MILWAUKEE PRIDE PARADE BOARD NOTIFICATION TO MIRIAM BEN-SHALOM, STRIPPING HER OF GRAND MARSHALL HONORS, FOLLOWED BY MIRIAM'S RESPONSE TO THE BOARD:

Dear Ms Ben-Shalom,

I am writing you today about our offering of the 2016 Grand Marshal position to you.

The Board of Directors was excited to have an opportunity to acknowledge your many contributions to the LGBT community by offering you the Grand Marshal position for this year's parade. However, shortly after we offered you the position, it was brought to our attention that your Facebook page contains a number of posts asserting that transwomen are a danger to young girls in public bathrooms and locker rooms. After considering these posts, it is the Board's opinion that these posts are transphobic and as such represent an attack on an important segment of the LBGT community.

While we fully support a person's right to express their own beliefs and political opinions, we also feel it is important that our Grand Marshals publicly declared beliefs mesh with those held by the Milwaukee Pride Parade and the Board of Directors. The Grand Marshal is the public face of the Milwaukee Pride Parade and thus needs to be someone whose views are compatible with our own.

The Bylaws of the Milwaukee Pride Parade include our mission statement, "To provide an outlet to the citizens of South Eastern Wisconsin in which GLBT individuals and groups can participate in a parade to show their pride." We are an inclusive organization that seeks to be free of intolerance, and seeks to promote the equality of all members of the community. As such, we feel that we cannot have a Grand Marshal who has publically and repeatedly denigrated transwomen.

We wish to apologize for rescinding our offer of this honor. It is not a step that we take lightly, and it in no way should be considered a denial of the important work you have previously done for the LGBT community. Please understand this was never our intent to lead you on.

The Board of Directors would like to thank you for your understanding of this situation.

Sincerely,
The Milwaukee Pride Parade Board of Directors

MIRIAM BEN-SHALOM'S REPLY TO THE MILWAUKEE PRIDE PARADE BOARD OF DIRECTORS:

To you bunch of Moral reprobates–so cowardly you can't even post a name: Really rather a cowardly manner to deal with this. You are not correct about my FB page, although my FB page does have posts from others on it about the so-called trans issue. This issue is very sensitive for women born of women, but I would not expect men to understand. Further, no one asked me about my stance — which is very discriminatory indeed. For your information, I am indeed a PERF–penis exclusionary radical feminist who believes that women born of women have the right to safe spaces of their own and cultural events they put on for themselves and those sisters who might like to attend. After all, men have had a long history of male only spaces in the GBT community and not much ado was made of it.

I believe that gender roles ought to be abolished so that people can just be–without feeling the need to surgically change their bodies to meet binary stereotypes which are artificial and not biological. Your elimination is called sexism and is discriminatory and misogynistic. When I consider what the trans community did to the Michigan Womyn's Music Festival and the threats that were made there that I personally saw and heard and when I consider the threats directed at women who stand up to speak out about women's safety, I become firmer in my estimation of who these people are and what trans means to –it appears–a great many people. No woman I know would threaten to kill another woman because of opinion. No woman I know would call others who hold differing opinions the nastiest words in the English language. Therefore, Pride Parade Committee: You are no better then those who threatened to hurt women born of women simply because they wished to be in a nurturing environ with others who were like minded. One may hope you take the so-called Trans community to task for all the threats and nastiness heaped on women as you took me.

I see that Milwaukee Pride cares more about men than it does about women's safety. So be it. I was truthful about my beliefs and I hold with Thomas Paine: "It is impossible to calculate the moral mischief, if I may so express it, that mental lying has produced in society. When a man has so far corrupted and prostituted the chastity of his mind, as to subscribe his professional belief to things he does not believe, he has prepared himself for the commission of every other crime. He takes up the trade of a priest for the sake of gain, and in order to qualify himself for that trade, he begins with a perjury. Can we conceive any thing more destructive to morality than this?" Thanks for fucking me over for being honest about what I think. You are no better than the Army.

Should you wish more from me, I will be GLAD to cooperate.
Miriam Ben-Shalom

Anthology Editor's Note: The above piece was originally published in Gender Trender April 30, 2016. Re-published with permission. gendertrender.wordpress.com

The additional statement from Miriam Ben-Shalom is printed as follows:

MIRIAM BEN-SHALOM'S STATEMENT FROM JUNE 21, 2016

Indeed, I am not being erased; I refuse to be erased. I don't get the hostility: the issue really is *not* trans women at all, it is about male violence visited upon human beings which, if trans women might *think* for just a moment, can happen/does happen to them also. The issue is safety. Plain and simple. I have never seen violence and male power tripping like I did when I went out to speak in Washington State. There was no willingness at all to sit down and find a solution, to talk about how the comfort and safety of all could be found. I fear the drill sergeant came out in me but still I say: I don't need their permission to live and exist. I don't need their "tolerance" to hell with that. Tolerance? %$#@# that. I demand and will take my right to live without fear and safety regardless. This isn't about trans at all, this is about the "now of this time" which allows any man to self-identify as a woman and have access to women's space. This is about the very clear and purposeful destruction of the culture of Lesbians and women born of women allies. This is about placing all women and children at the beck, call, and access of males whether or not these males are "honorable" or not. This is about the denigration and callus lack of care towards women born of women and their life experiences. This is about saying that the violence women have experienced is - nothing. Nothing at all worth looking at. This is about men legislating without regard to the 23.10% of the current population of the United States that are children and the 50.80% of the population of the United States that are women.

I was attacked by a respected BGT (I take the L out here) journalist because I crossed a bridge and worked in Seattle with a right wing group on this issue. The group was very transparent with me and very open and honest, unlike the people screaming in the audience who wouldn't even listen much less be civil.

We all could cry a river if we admitted that. We all know pain and hurt. But to only make that river wider is no way to create solutions. You build a bridge across it instead. The Right Wing and I do not agree on most things, but to stop attending to the ranting of the demagogues on the Far Left and the Far right and to see that vast space between where common ground can be found is one way to deal with these sensitive issues. If common ground can be found in one "place" why not in others, perhaps?

Either way, I won't back down, back out, give in, or give up until I know that women and children have safe spaces to - BE, until I know that my Lesbian culture is ensconced as a legitimate part of this society's workings, until I know that women born of women will be treated with the respect, consideration, compassion, and care that other segments of society are demanding.

CHAPTER 45

INTO THE MIND OF KOSILEK: GRACE'S DAUGHTER – A BOOK REVIEW

GallusMag

"Psychopaths never quit."

~ MARGARET SINGER

CRIMINAL MEMOIRS, LIKE parole hearings, are not usually known for their authenticity, honesty, self-reflection and accurate reportage. In the criminal memoir every hapless burglar is a master thief, every two-bit hood a mob capo, every sociopath a revolutionary.

Criminal memoirs are: Jack Henry Abbott waxing bromantically to Norman Mailer about the inhumanity of his incarceration - just prior to committing another murder, serial rapist Eldridge Cleaver expounding on the act of rape as a revolutionary act, Tex Watson intoning on the redemptive power of bible-believing among guys who hang pregnant starlets alive while cutting them open. In the Crime Memoir sub-genre of the "wrongly convicted" the tropes are even more hackneyed as the memoir essentially serves as one long desperate attempt to explain away all that blood. Kosilek's memoir is of the sub-genre category, flavored with a heaping dose of self-pity, narcissism and sociopathy.

Most of the U.S. "Son of Sam Laws" (enacted in the wake of serial killer David Berkowitz' attempts to sell his story for profit) have been repealed or overturned on First Amendment grounds leaving murderers free to profit from the dubious celebrity of committing horrific acts and selling them for entertainment to an audience hungry for carnage. Any of the millions of average boring bastards that murder their wives are free to offer their suddenly compelling and unique tale on any of a number of online vanity publishing sites for a few bucks. Kosilek's memoir "Grace's Daughter" is one of those, and it was on just such a site that I found it. Yes,

I persuaded a friend to kindly give Kosilek two dollars and ninety-nine cents for a copy of his tome. For that ethical indiscretion I am sorry.

I was curious though. Slightly curious. Under three dollars curious.

There are very few reasons to subject oneself to 400-plus pages of self-serving criminal lies. Some of these reasons may include curiosity about a particular crime or crime spree. Perhaps a historic crime is so distinct that the reader longs for some insight to explain the psychology of the perpetrators or details of the era (think "Symbionese Liberation Army" or the "Manson Family"). Maybe an author relates an inside experience of the justice system and incarceration compellingly. Perhaps the perp is just an entertaining storyteller and a fantastic writer.

Kosilek's memoir has none of that. Men like him who brutally decapitate their loving wives are, sadly, a dime a dozen. He is a terrible writer and a bad liar. But Kosilek has one thing going for him and his memoir: A judge has issued an order forcing the populace of Massachusetts to pay upwards of $100,000 (including surgery, travel, security including 24 hour hospital guards, post-op care, follow-up appointments both surgical and endocrinological, possible revisions) so that a decapitation killer can have his genitals cosmetically refashioned into a fleshy sheath for other men to stick their dicks into. Because the murderer thinks such a procedure will make him a woman, and the murderer has threatened to be upset and/or harm himself if his delusions are not indulged (and enabled) by the legal system and the public at large.

Again, there is nothing unique about that. Plenty of people believe doctors can perform actual changes of sex, creating women out of men and vice versa. Well maybe not plenty. But lots are willing to pretend they believe, or at least go along with the idea, out of politeness or the hope that doctors and judges know what the hell they are doing. And plenty of people think the presence of a fleshy sheath that men can stick their dicks into defines the female sex.

Perhaps in reading the 103,010 word tome I would gain a new understanding of Kosilek's savagery and rage for the woman who loved him, who married him, the one whose decapitated body he dumped like so much trash before cooking and enjoying a delicious steak dinner with the victim's unsuspecting son in the very space he had garroted her hours before?

Unfortunately, the following are some things that are never even mentioned in Kosilek's memoir:

On Sunday May 20 1990 Robert Kosilek stood behind his wife Cheryl and garroted her with a length of wire. He's not a huge guy, around 5'8", but stocky at the time of the murder, so he must have applied incredible force in order for the wire to cut into her throat. Perhaps he pushed his knee into her back for leverage. She fought: we know that. And it took her a long time to die. We know that too. Even as the wire had nearly decapitated her she would not die and Robert was forced to go running for a rope, which he then wrapped around her neck as she continued to fight for life. The court record states:

> "With regard to deliberate premeditation, the evidence would permit a rational jury to infer that the defendant waited until the victim's son was at work, that he approached his wife from behind with a wire, and strangled her by tightening the wire around her neck. With regard to extreme atrocity or cruelty, the prosecution's expert testified that: there were multiple wounds on the victim's body; she was strangled by a wire and then a rope; she was conscious for at least fifteen seconds after strangulation began and remained alive for three to five minutes; and there were indications of a conscious struggle. These facts amply support a finding of premeditated and deliberate murder, see Commonwealth v. Judge, 420 Mass. 433, 441, 650 N.E.2d 1242 (1995); Commonwealth v. Chipman, 418 Mass. 262, 269-270, 635 N.E.2d 1204 (1994); Commonwealth v. Basch, 386 Mass. 620, 622, 437 N.E.2d 200 (1982), as well as murder by extreme atrocity or cruelty, see Commonwealth v. Simmons, 419 Mass. 426, 646 N.E.2d 97 (1995); Commonwealth v. Tanner, 417 Mass. 1, 2, 627 N.E.2d 895 (1994)."

We know what Robert did next. He went outside to Cheryl's car in the driveway and opened the back door. He dragged her lifeless body out of the condo they shared and dumped her in the back seat. Then he went back inside and cleaned. He cleaned up her blood which sprayed the kitchen. He showered and changed his clothes. Then he drove her car containing her corpse to the nearby North Attleboro Emerald Square shopping mall and abandoned it in the parking lot. He summoned a cab to take him home. He was dropped off at a store near where he and his family lived. He walked home then cooked a steak dinner which he and Cheryl's son Timothy McCaul enjoyed in the exact spot Robert had slaughtered his wife and Timothy's mother mere minutes before. Timothy noticed nothing out of the ordinary. The only thing of note he could report later to police is that Robert had uncharacteristically shaved his beard. Robert hadn't shaved in a year. The last time he shaved was when Cheryl had discovered him drinking again and forced him to go back into rehab.

Where was Mom? Robert told Timothy that Cheryl had gone shopping at the mall earlier in the day. Robert decided to feign "looking into" the matter. He called the police as a concerned husband and reported her missing- possibly in a car accident? He called the local hospital. Police checked the mall and soon found the body of his dead 36-year-old wife where Robert had dumped her. They asked Robert to come to the station. He requested that the police transport him. (His car was not running and he would call his mechanic the next day to fix it). At the station he reported that he had been home sick all weekend. Cheryl had gone shopping at the mall. Police took a statement and transported him home. Soon they asked him to come back to the station. They had more questions. Cheryl's son had told the police that no one answered the phone when he called to get a ride home from work at 5pm. Kolisek told them the child often had trouble mis-dialing phone numbers. He also recalled being in the shower, which perhaps caused him to not hear the phone ringing. He asked to go to the cigarette machine to buy cigarettes and left the interrogation room. A police officer intercepted him exiting the front door to the station. Kosilek stated he intended to retain a lawyer, and left.

The day after murdering Cheryl, Robert called the mechanic and had them fix his car. He then went on a shopping spree spending hundreds of dollars on female clothes. In the evening he was stopped by police after crashing his car into a stop sign in Bedford Massachusetts. He was dressed in female drag. A report was filed and he was released.

The second day Robert was again stopped by the police, this time in New Rochelle NY for speeding. He was drunk with a half bottle of vodka and several empty beers in the car. He was arrested for driving while intoxicated. The officer reported him saying "You would be drunk too if the police thought you killed your wife. Look, I had a 15-year-old son and a wife. I murdered my wife. Now I need to call a psychiatrist." He was incarcerated and NY police contacted the North Attleboro Massachusetts police department which had questioned Kosilek two days earlier in the murder of his wife.

Once sober, Robert refused to be extradited back to Massachusetts. Extradition was ordered and he appealed it. He retracted his confession.

He was investigated for a possible link to the New Bedford serial killings where he worked as a taxi driver in 1987-88 but the investigation petered out. This is where Kosilek in his memoir recalls having a memory again. The rest of it: the murder, the driving, the dumping, the dinner, the shopping, the police- all a blank. Innocent! The whole wire and rope thing: self defense, probably!

"My last memory is an argument that ended with Cheryl throwing a crystal mug full of boiling water on me, then coming at me with a large knife. In over six years together, neither of us had ever used violence. Now my last memory of her is one of trying to stop her from killing me, and I have apparently taken her life."

–ROBERT KOSILEK IN "GRACE'S DAUGHTER"

"Psychopaths just don't stop. They don't give up. They continue the same style."

-MARGARET SINGER

Kosilek's memoir opens with two forwards. One is written by his friend and champion, Clinical Psychologist Dr. Cindy Tavilla. Tavilla was the Program Coordinator at Bridgewater State Hospital where Kosilek worked as an addictions counselor in the year leading up to his mortal attack on his wife. Tavilla had fired him mere months before he decapitated Cheryl, after his background check revealed an extensive criminal past.

Nearly twenty years later, as she explains in her forward, Tavilla was sitting in church when a voice- possibly from God- told her to contact Robert:

"I was sitting in the back pew of a church in Boston. Feeling increasingly disillusioned and disappointed in the community I had been actively participating in for two decades, I was looking for a spiritual home. Feeling the urge to volunteer, to be of service, I considered joining the Prison Ministry offered by this urban church. I've long held the belief that we each give from our own surplus. We serve in ways that we are able. I was a clinical psychologist, and I had worked in a prison, so felt that while the surroundings might deter many people from serving this population, it would not bother me. And then the message came. It wasn't technically a voice that I heard. But the message was as crystal clear as if spoken aloud into my ear. Was it God speaking? The Universe? The Collective Unconscious? My vivid imagination? I still don't know. It said, "Write to her."

Dr. Tavilla personally transcribed Kosilek's memoir and her niece, Dianna Sawyer, compiled, edited and published it from his handwritten notes.

The other forward is written by Dr. Randi Ettner. Dr. Ettner met Kosilek only once, in 2005 when he paid her to visit him in prison and diagnose him with the psychological need for cosmetic sex reassignment surgery, which she did. Ettner has built a profitable practice on transgender people, authoring a book called "Confessions of a Gender Defender: A Psychologist's Reflection on Life Among the Transgendered." Ettner, a psychology doctorate, claims to be a strong believer in sex-based personality theory but her sales pitch seems to embrace whatever woo-woo pays the bills.

Ettner's woo was the inspiration for the creation of sexologist Michael Bailey's infamous book "The Man Who Would Be Queen". From Alice Dreger's "The Controversy Surrounding The Man Who Would Be Queen": "After Michael Bailey attended a reading by Ettner of her book Confessions of a Gender Defender (Ettner, 1996) at a local Barnes & Noble bookstore in June 1997, he was so frustrated by what he saw as gross inaccuracies in Ettner's account of transsexualism that he decided he would write a book of his own."

Ettner is a practitioner of a field of psychology noted for being unfalsifiable, and therefore outside the realm of science: Energy Psychology. From her website:

"A significant portion of Dr. Ettner's clinical practice is devoted to working with the "emotional freedom technique", or energy psychology. It is a therapeutic technique that provides an effective edge in the emotional and mental arenas. Dr. Ettner has used energy psychology to rid her patients of limiting beliefs; clear individuals of fears, traumas or worries; eliminate physical pain; and even enhance the on-field performance of athletes.

Energy psychology is based on Einstein's theory that all matter, including the human body, is composed of energy. It attunes the body to a state of unique receptivity through the simple act of tapping on certain meridian points on the face and neck. It is a cousin of acupuncture, but uses no needles and is not invasive. It is a bit like hypnotherapy, but provides extra power because it integrates the body's subtle energies."

Ettner is a board member of WPATH (World Professional Association for Transgender Health), the heavily corporate-funded (GlaxoSmithKline, Merck, Roche Pharmaceuticals, etc.) quasi-medical group formerly named the Harry Benjamin International Gender Dysphoria Association (after the "Grandfather of Transsexualism", sexologist and endocrinologist Dr. Harry Benjamin who pioneered experiments in the medical treatment of transgenderism in the 1960's). WPATH is a group whose mission is to justify the medical treatment of sex-based gender roles. WPATH was created by, and is authorized by, the very same medical and psych practitioners who make a living providing such treatments. WPATH is also a non-mainstream organization whose "standards of care" were rejected this year after review by the American Psychiatric Association on the basis of being scientifically unsound and lacking citation. (WPATH's rejected standards of care were nonetheless cited as the primary authority on transgender medical care by Judge Wolf, the author of the decision forcing Massachusetts taxpayers to pay for Kosilek's genital surgery.)

Ettner opines in the forward to Kosilek's book that transgenderism is a "lifelong affliction" and "disabling impairment". She has testified for pay as a WPATH representative in many criminal cases. Her aunt, a physician, worked with Harry Benjamin.

Skipping over the question of why a practitioner of unscientific woo-woo was accepted as a clinical diagnostic authority in Massachusetts court, and why such a person is qualified to authorize surgical procedures...how on earth did Kosilek afford to pay for the "expert" testimony of Dr. Ettner?

This is where the $2.99 Kosilek memoir comes in handy. There are a few illuminating gems here after all. If nothing else, Kosilek's tale, all 400 pages of florid prose, pedophilic fetishism, unrepentant sociopathy and aggressive victim-blaming notwithstanding, is one of a Jailhouse Lawyer. I think Robert would actually be pleased with that assessment. Lawyering is his pride, his vocation, his life.

"The greatest loss is the dying I do inside a little bit every day"

- WIFE-KILLER ROBERT KOSILEK

Robert Kosilek, whose claim to fame is an unspeakable act of cruelty and brutal homicide inflicted on his wife, opens his book with a marriage ceremony. No, not the one that legally bound his victim Cheryl to him. This ceremony takes place between him and another imprisoned male transgender who calls himself "Jessica". It is a "lesbian" marriage between two male felons.

"When we said our vows on October 20, 2006, I wanted, needed to be as girly as I could for Jessica, even though hundreds of miles and impregnable walls prevented her from seeing me. I had a bouquet of flowers, a maid of honor, and an enlarged photograph of Jessica. My maid of honor was a friend, another transsexual who has been unable to publicly declare the fact that she, too, is a woman. This was a rare chance for her to feel connected as a woman to these sisterly rituals that are such an integral part of our lives as women," Robert writes.

This literary choice, the wife-killer choosing to open his memoir with an account of his latest "marriage" can be interpreted as nothing but what it is. A rhetorical sneering act of a homicidal sociopath wiping shit in the wounds of his wife Cheryl's survivors- her mother, her sister, her children. There is a calculated premeditation and joyfulness in Kosilek's sadism, and this opening volley remains constant throughout his tale. Kosilek is a master of the big "Fuck You", but the sort of "Fuck You" that always leaves weasel-room. Kosilek has discovered that transgender means never having to say you're sorry and in fact, under current law, means a man can commit premeditated murder of women with such cruelty and brutality that he is sentenced to life in prison without possibility of parole (since Massachusetts has no death penalty) and if he works his cards right he can parlay the woman's death into huge cash payoffs, travel, fancy meals, state sponsorship of his sexual fetish, and can even be transferred to a women's prison to honor his place as homicidal woman-killing cock of the walk.

Hard to believe but it's true. In Kosilek's world he "became a woman" the second he extinguished his wife Cheryl's life with that wire. In murdering his wife he baptized himself as a man deserving special consideration, and it wasn't all delusion. His story is a case study in how a man can make a tidy living from not just saying, but living "Fuck You" to women in the most profound way imaginable. The state is set up to support this. Again, Kosilek is not unique in any way.

> "Masbruch is in fact still raping women within the facility, just now with foreign objects. He has also brutally injured some of the women within the facility. Please sign my petition against Richard being allowed in a women's facility of any kind, so that he may return to a male penitentiary. It would not only help me and my mother but any woman in any facility."
>
> — ANNA SILVER, WHOSE MOTHER IS CONFINED WITH ELECTROCUTION SERIAL TORTURE-RAPIST TRANSGENDER RICHARD/SHERRI MASBRUCH.

Australia: The first Australian male prisoner given a state funded "sex change" was Noel Crompton Hall. Jailed for life for the 1987 "thrill killing" of 29-year-old hitchhiker Lyn Saunders, Noel came to believe, and informed authorities that he held a strong belief that he was female, not male. Although he was objectively biologically male as evidenced by his penis and testicles, and was also HIV+, in 1999 he was transferred to Mulawa (Women's) Correctional Centre on the basis of this self-reported belief. He was charged with raping several women there within three months and transferred back to men's prison. In 2001 his subjective declaration of his fixed non-psychotic biologic delusion, the feeling he had that he was female and not male- resulted in a re-determined sentence of 22 years. In 2003 the state allowed his legal name change to "Maddison Hall" and performed a state funded genital surgery attempting to alter his penis and scrotum into a visual approximation of female reproductive anatomy. Further charges of sexual assault against female prisoners after this intervention resulted in Hall's confinement in isolation for the rest of his sentence. Hall was paroled in 2006 in a decision the parole board described as "anguished" due to the fact that Hall had been unable to demonstrate an ability to exist among females without violently sexually assaulting them. Parole was rescinded due to no agency willing to accept him.

UK: The first UK male prisoner given a state-funded legal and surgical "sex change" was a kidnapping rapist named John Pilley who victimized a female taxi driver. He was sentenced in 1981 to life in prison for his crime. A decade after his incarceration Pillley asserted his belief that although male, he wanted to be female. The state awarded him with cross-sex hormones and allowed him to dress in stereotypical clothing associated with females while in male prison. After several years of cross-sex hormones Pilley sued the prison using the "inch=mile" rationale. If the state ruled he was "female enough" to receive cosmetic cross-sex hormones provided by the state, he was entitled to cosmetic genital surgery which would give him further female appearance. In 1999 he was granted a state funded removal of testicles. After further claims, he was granted cosmetic surgery in 2001 to try to turn his penis into something resembling female anatomy, and he was transferred to Holloway, a women's prison. He changed his name to Jane Anne Pilley. Five years later he changed his mind. He resumed growing his beard and sued the Prison service to be "turned back into a man" at taxpayer expense as he was tired of the ruse and enjoyed male prison more after all.

Canada: The first Canadian prisoner to receive a state-funded surgical sex change was a man named Richard Chaperon alias Ricky Chaperon alias Richard Kavanagh who brutally hammer-killed a transsexual male prostitute, Leo James Black/Lisa Janna Black in 1987 in Toronto. He was sentenced to life with possibility of parole after 15 years. Bored with Millhaven, a male prison, in 1999 he sued the Canadian Human Rights Commission demanding surgery to make him appear more female. Like Kosilek, he claimed profound psychiatric disability due to transgenderism. He changed his name to Sylvia Kavanagh. He wanted to be transferred to a women's prison. He was transferred to Joliet women's prison with penis intact and reportedly sexually assaulted women there. He was then given Canada's first government-funded surgical "sex change" in 2001. In 2005 Kavanagh exploded in violence and fought off guards while trashing the women's facility. He caused over $50,000 in damage and injured guards before he was restrained. He was then transferred to the Grand Valley Institution for Women. Inmates there are quoted as living in "constant fear" of Richard, who was reported to have battered women there. Prison officials stated that Kavanaugh's ultra-violence required a special handling unit for ultra-violent "female" offenders, something they had never required before (for actual females), and the building of a special ultra-violent "women's" facility for Kavanaugh was proposed.

United States: The US has privileged those male rapists and predators and murderers of women who verbalize feelings about wishing they were female by sending these men into women's prisons. It makes no difference in many jurisdictions whether male predators are still armed with the "weapon of rape": their penis. Transgender is a "Get Out of Men's Jail" card for male offenders, sometimes even for males who would rather serve their sentence with other males. We saw a lawsuit this year from a Nashville gay man Karla Brenner who was placed into women's prison against his will, because he was drag queen who had acquired secondary sex characteristics (breasts, hips) from black market estrogen and silicone taken to maximize his career as a drag performer. In scissor-killer CeCe McDonald's case this year it took an ongoing media campaign from CeCe himself to stop transgender activists from forcing him to transfer to a female prison against his wishes. Generally it is heterosexual male transgender inmates who seek transfer to female facilities, not gay male transgenders. And if it needs saying, no female transgender has ever been on record as being transferred to, or of requesting transfer to, a male prison. The Kosilek-type transgender rights movement, if one can call it that (the male transgender right to be confined with females) is, thus far, a distinctly heterosexual male movement.

Interestingly, it is largely the powerful LGBT lobbying groups formerly dedicated to the rights of gay men (and lesbians to the degree those rights intersect with males) who are now leveraging their influence to promote the heterosexual male transgender prisoner rights movement, and the heterosexual male "right" to state-sponsored cosmetic surgery and transfer to women's prisons, and the case of wife-decapitator Kosilek himself. The National Center for Lesbian Rights (a trans-run legal advocacy group that largely represents male, not lesbian interests despite the name), the ACLU, the National Gay and Lesbian Task Force, GLAAD, HRC, NCTE, Gay and Lesbian Advocates and Defenders, et al, have all leant their support to the "rights" of heterosexual male prisoners to be housed with females based on their subjectively declared feelings of "wanting to be women". Not a single LGBT org has ever registered concerns for the rights of female prisoners - beyond their "right" to opt into more rape and violence in a male facility.

The position of LGBT lobbying groups seems to be that men - even those who electrocute, torture, rape and murder women and children, repeatedly, with atrocity and malice, should be placed in confinement with women if the men so desire it, and that women prisoners who are raped and beaten by these men, and who live, confined, in terror of them, have no such rights whatsoever. The only rights that female prisoners have under this LGBT-lobby approved system is the right to opt into additional rape and harassment and additional male violence by presumably being granted the right to be confined in a male facility if they claim to "feel male". As stated above, no female has ever opted into this "right".

"The messages I was getting in response to my clothing and toy choices led me to an inconsolably depressing realization. I was a girl who had accidentally been given the wrong outside parts!"

– ROBERT/MICHELLE KOSILEK

According to Kosilek's memoir, if any of it is to be believed, he "was born April 10, 1949, the second of two children born to Henry and Elizabeth Kosilek, an unemployed laborer and housewife." He never knew his father who according to Robert was in prison all his life for reasons unknown or unreported. He says his mother left him and his sister in the care of his grandmother when he was 4, which resulted in their placement in Chicago's St. Hedwigs orphanage, a live-in school created for the children of Polish immigrants, for five years until their mother reclaimed them. A quote on this experience in the typical gothic tone of Kosilek's writing: "It is run by nuns, for whom English is a second language. Their native tongue is cruelty, and it has several dialects, each more painfully memorable than the last."

Robert describes some pediatric cross-dressing incidents in the same pornified fetishistic language that one immediately recognizes as verbatim to the forced-feminization narratives popular among heterosexual autogynephilia fetishists. An unedited quote:

"The second time I was caught wearing a dress, I was imprisoned in the same closet under the stairs. For my original crime, Sister had decided, well after nightfall, that her gift of reflective solitude was preferable to a paddling, although her manner of inquisition as to whether I had had enough time to consider the seriousness of my misdeeds (wearing a dress and running when called) resulted in possibly more pain. I'll never know. The psychic pain from being brutalized merely for stating my gender later contributed to my self-imprisonment in the bottle and in the arms of Morpheus, beginning an on again off-again drama of self-denial that ran for decades. A paddling would have consisted of a series of blows across my naked buttocks, while I repeated Sister's words one at a time. So I may have been fortunate and only been subjected to five blows: SMACK-I-SMACK-will-SMACK-not- SMACK -disobey- SMACK -Sister. This was a standard dose, delivered with a wooden paddle about 4 inches wide and 2 feet long, with holes drilled through it – possibly for the offending child's ungodly impulses to escape through. Serving a sentence in the prison of your own body because others refuse to admit that neither the prison, nor the key, even exists, is no different than being in a concrete and steel prison with a life sentence. Both will teach you that if you don't embrace patience and humor, you will be embraced by anger and hate, insanity's internship." [sic]

Kosilek intersperses his gamey pedophilic feminization-victimhood passages with transparently narcissistic brags about his superior intellect. Sample:

".. my precociousness lead to unintended consequences. As a fourth grader, I was bright enough to occasionally be summoned to a sixth, seventh or eighth grade classroom to answer a question that had stumped the students in that class."

Hmmm.

The whole memoir narrative hinges on this combination. Gothic sado-masochistic male feminization tropes so ubiquitous on crossdresser websites balanced with intellectual superiority anecdotes. Over four hundred pages of it! Most of the intellectual superiority "gotcha" material consists of Robert utilizing his jailhouse lawyer time and skills to "stick it to the man" for getting in the way of his girlish fantasies.

What is truly disturbing is that anyone who is even the slightest bit informed about those under the transgender umbrella will immediately recognize and clock this narrative for what it is: sexual fetishism. Which means one of two things. Either those championing Kosilek have never read it, or they have and hope no one else ever notices or reads it.

"The legal process dominated my life like a sixthgrade bully."

- Robert Kosilek

Kosilek has spent the majority of his 62 years - starting with his placement in a juvenile facility at age 12 - incarcerated for this or that prior to the big one - his decapitation of his wife at the age of 41. His memoir details some parts of his lengthy criminal career, various street hustles, assaults and rip-offs, anecdotes that seem chosen to prove either his superior intellect or his hapless cruel victimization by getting caught unfairly doing things that were not really his fault or that were caused by substance abuse. No doubt his other crimes whatever they are will forever go unsolved unless he thinks there is some advantage in the telling. Everyone has done him wrong and if only he was a little girl getting spanked everything would be okay. He details his massive substance abuse problems (Meth, Alchohol, Heroin, WhateverYouGot) and occasionally provides clever jailhouse survival techniques: inserting two packs of cigarettes and some matches into his rectum before being processed for his wife's murder, for example.

He only mentions Cheryl around a dozen times and then only to blame her for her own murder. Every woman he had been involved with was to blame for whatever transpired. None of which was good.

"My relationships had been as casual as I could make them; I had always been the seduced, and never the seductress," Robert states. In Cheryl's case her "crime" according to Robert was starting an "inappropriate relationship" between herself as a volunteer addictions counselor and a man seeking counseling for his addictions: Robert. Also, Cheryl on occasion had "a temper" and a "sharp tongue" and was "actively hostile" according to Robert who goes on for pages attempting to prove this (unsuccessfully, by the way) by quoting her ex-coworkers and the like, none of which are willing to go on the record. Kosilek never mentions Cheryl in any sort of positive light, perhaps he fears doing so would undermine his self-defense claims made at trial over twenty years ago. (He still claims to believe his sentence will be overturned: "I should have been convicted of manslaughter; if the rules had been followed, I would have been.") Or maybe he just hates her. Kosilek opines that he feels Cheryl's family may "get some peace" from a modified ruling which classifies her decapitation as "bizarre circumstance" rather than "malice". What a thoughtful guy!

Arrested in New York in 1990, he fought extradition to Massachusetts, retracted his confession and pled not guilty. He claimed there was no possible escape from the family kitchen and garroting his wife from behind, followed by the application of rope, was an act of self-defense. While still awaiting trial he was diagnosed as depressed and placed on Prozac. This turned out to be an extremely profitable move as I am about to reveal.

What is interesting is that Kosilek's current 8th Amendment challenge to the State of Massachusetts hinges on the assertion that Kosilek is in danger of committing suicide or self-harm if his desired cosmetic sex surgery and transfer to a women's facility is not honored by the state. The 8th Amendment to the US Constitution prohibits the government from imposing "cruel and unusual punishment" on citizens and Kosilek's attorneys propose that Kosilek has demonstrated a history of suicidality related to the failure to treat his gender self-concept with genital surgery. But his attorneys have a problem: by all reports he has not exhibited self-harm or suicidality for the entire 22 years of his post-conviction incarceration. There is also the matter of financial gain, which as far as I can tell has never been previously reported by any other source until this moment.

Kosilek was covered by an expansive insurance policy when arrested, one which paid generously for lost wages due to mental health disability. After being diagnosed with depression and placed on Prozac in holdover prior to trial he orchestrated the events now defined by his attorneys as suicide attempts in the current 8th amendment claim. The first attempt he describes in his memoir two different ways, both involving a plastic bag. In the first version he places a plastic bag over his head and pulls the covers over himself, awaiting suffocation - but the bag was shoddily constructed, and ripped, sparing his life. In his alternate narrative about this same attempt, he pulls the bag off his own head in a newfound desperate bid for life. I want TO LIVE!

The second suicide attempt forming the foundation of Kosilek's 8th amendment claim, substantiating his propensity for gender-related self-harm, involves a slipper. Kosilek claims that during this pre-trial period he attempted to kill himself by shoving a slipper down his own throat. This attempt allegedly resulted in gagging and vomiting, followed by Kosilek cleaning up the vomit before it could be objectively witnessed, and thereafter abandoning his attempt at self harm. Both attempts were un-witnessed. Presumably both of these attempts were self-reported to authorities. Long before these suicidal ideations formed the basis for Kosilek's current "cruel and unusual" suit, they served a more practical purpose.

> "Now I have also failed at this ultimate escape, first with a plastic bag so flimsy that it simply came apart when I tried to tie it around my neck, and then the rolled up foam slippers that I tried to force down my throat caused me to throw up my supper. I had to fish the foam slippers out of the puddle of vomit to hide my intention. I don't know if I'll get another opportunity,

but my chances will certainly be limited with a documented attempt on
my record."

— KOSILEK, FROM HIS MEMOIR.

Kosilek filed an insurance claim from jail for disability and parlayed his depression diagnosis
and self-reported suicidality into a successful ongoing payout of over ten thousand dollars a
year. From his memoir:

"I had a lot of money from my insurance company, when they finally paid me retroactively
for almost a year and a half of psychiatric disability benefits. They had refused to pay, despite
documentation of depression, suicidal ideation, and treatment with Prozac. I read my benefits
pamphlet very carefully, a document they had been kind enough to mail at my request before
I filed my claim. There was no provision allowing them to deny benefits if my disability occurred as a result of or was the cause of my being incarcerated. I studied the relevant law, then
filed an appeal. And I won, from a jail cell, with no lawyer.

My first check was for about $17,000. I hired a lawyer to sue the sheriff for denying treat-
ment for GID, and in addition to her retainer, gave her most of that first check. The roughly
$9,000 I received over the next seven months went mostly towards two goals: smuggling fe-
male hormones into the jail, and becoming a candidate in the general election of 1992. The
former was a piece of cake, the latter was an exercise in masochism, a draught of poison that I
could not relinquish, even as I knew it might kill me."

You read that right. Kosilek used the money he won from his insurance company (by self-
reporting his alleged depression and suicidality) to fund an election campaign. In between time
spent writing letters to the Boston Globe disputing their coverage of his crime and popping
smuggled black market synthetic female hormones he ran for the office of Bristol County Sheriff
as a write-in candidate in the 1992 election. Had he been elected, he would have replaced Sheriff
David R. Nelson and run the very jail he was incarcerated in. He says he did so because he was
angry that he was not permitted to wear lipstick and have state-funded female hormones provided to him. He also used the money to hire attorney Bettina Borders with a $15,000 retainer
plus expenses to sue Sheriff Nelson. Failing that lawsuit attempt, Kosilek subsequently sued his
own attorney in one of his many cases thrown out by then and current adjudicator Judge Wolf.

Inmate financial gain of over ten thousand dollars annually certainly introduces doubt
on the 22 year-old self-reported suicidality claim which forms the basis of Kosilek's current

8th amendment "cruel and unusual" suit. Kosilek's current suit also cites an attempt at self-castration, none of which is mentioned in Kosilek's tome – although purported self-castration claims by other inmates are discussed at great length by Kosilek. Kosilek himself apparently never made any such castration attempt. Perhaps advocates have inadvertently (or intentionally?) superimposed said narratives onto Kosilek's claim. This seems likely since such incidents are represented with ample and legally mandated medical incident documentation when they actually occur. A handful of old news stories mention in passing that Kosilek once tried tying a shoelace around his testicles but such incident if it occurred was not significant enough to warrant inclusion in his autobiography. Sort of alarming that such basic fact parsing was apparently not done in Kosilek's case.

The other basis of Kosilek's current suit is the premise that men who share his gender beliefs are in danger of being preyed upon by other men in the way that men prey on actual females (with rape and assault). Yet, in contraindication to that premise: Kosilek has been housed with other men without incident for 22 years. Robert explains this discrepancy in his memoir. Years ago he beat the tar out of another male prisoner who "put his hand on my ass" with a street broom in the cafeteria. This stopped all further predation according to Kosilek: "From what I've seen, most people are either accepting or at least have no hostility towards me. This may have something to do with my having been befriended by a queen called Maggie who everyone seems to like. It may also have something to do with the fact that another prisoner was foolish enough to put his hand on my ass in the kitchen when I had a street broom in my hands. No secrets in a dysfunctional family, only unacknowledged elephants in every room."

Kosilek runs several websites with other transgender male prisoners. Sites include "A Rose Among Thorns" and "Wild Elegance" which he runs with Scott "Donna Dawn" Konitzer and Mark "Jessica Lewis" Brooks. All three of these men have filed 8th amendment claims against their respective states for denial of medical care related to transgender medicine, surgery, cosmetics, hair removal, and clothing. They use these sites to set up procedures to correspond with other transgender male felons in states with prohibitions against such correspondence, and share transgender-related jailhouse lawyering strategies and tips. (Kosilek also posts his poetry about feeling like a little girl, and angry profanity-laden rants about the "anti-treatment whores" who oppose medicalized GID treatments for felons.)

Mark Brooks, 44, is the new "wife" of Kosilek - the one that Robert wanted to look "girly" for in the "marriage" at the opening of his memoir. Brooks is serving a 50 year to life sentence in New York state at the Auburn Correctional Facility for the 1989 murder of 20 year old

Hofstra University student Dean Lockshiss of Brewster CT. State police said Brooks and his accomplice murdered their victim "for kicks". Mark Brooks and his friend Michael Meebert pretended to have car trouble. When bookstore employee Lockhiss stopped to help Brooks and Meebert robbed him of less than four dollars and then took turns shooting him with both a handgun and a sawed-off shotgun. "It was a thrill-killing and a horrible, senseless end to a man's life," said the district attorney. Mark "Jessica Maria" Brooks successfully won his 2003 8th amendment bid for state-provided gender-related care including psychiatric counseling and estrogen treatments. "I am Auburn's little girl", Brooks reported earlier this year to the Auburn Citizen News.

Scott Konitzer is serving a 123-year sentence in Wisconsin for multiple armed robberies and the stabbing of a fellow inmate. Konitzer sued the state of Wisconsin in 2005 for his right to be provided female hormones by the state to make him appear more female, and his right to be confined with female inmates. The State of Wisconsin passed a law banning state-sponsored legal/medical sex-change for currently incarcerated felons in response to Konitzer's suit. This ban was fought by transgender advocates and the Wisconsin ACLU and was struck down as unconstitutional based on 8th amendment right to freedom from cruel and unusual punishment due to the fact that the law sought to retroactively remove estrogen treatments among transgender male felons who were already dependent upon them. Konitzer's ruling was one of two cases which paved the way for Kosilek's current suit. The second precedent-setting 2011 ruling was the Sandy Jo Battista case discussed below.

The website trio are joined on these sites by Colorado inmate and twice-married pedophile Christopher "Kitty" Grey, who is serving 16 years to life for molesting an 8-year-old girl for five years. He is suing the state to provide him with a gender specialist he hopes will determine that he needs a sex-change operation and subsequent transfer to a women's prison. The state Department of Corrections is already giving Grey female hormones.

Another transgender child-rapist, David E. Megarry Jr./Sandy Jo Battista sponsored the second case that opened all the doors in 2011 for transgender men like Kosilek, Konitzer, Brooks and Grey to file 8th amendment suits demanding taxpayer funded "sex-changes".

"Sandy Jo" has a long history of torture-raping little girls, with multiple incarcerations for such. He has the distinction of being currently housed at the all male Massachusetts Treatment Center for Sexually Dangerous Persons facility where he lives under civil commitment without limit of sentence due to his legal status as a "Sexually Dangerous Person". Since his final 1982 arrest (for kidnapping, abducting, binding, gagging, raping, and leaving for dead in a wooded area a ten year old girl who was selling cookies door-to-door to raise funds for her skating club) he has had over 64 infractions on his disciplinary record including making obscene phone calls to female children from prison and hoarding photos of female children in his cell. He had jailhouse tattoos of naked girls placed all over his body so authorities could not confiscate them. In 2005 he made the claim that he felt inside like he "actually was" a female and with the pro bono representation of the powerful global business law firm McDermott Will and Emory filed suit for the right to grow breasts on his own body. After six years McDermott Will and Emory won him that precedent-setting 8th amendment right. Robert "Michelle" Kosilek filed his current case based on that precedent within a week of the Battista ruling. In "Cheryl's Daughter" Kosilek calls the Battista case "the perfect storm of affirmation for me and any other transgendered prisoner in the United States".

On September 4, 2012 Judge Wolf ruled in Kosilek's favor, authorizing the first tax-payer funded "gender related" surgery for a prisoner in the United States.

> "The idea that I might be a lesbian because I liked being with, being held by,
> and kissed and cared for by other girls never even came into my conscious
> mind until I was 57 years old."

> – ROBERT KOSILEK

The 62-year-old Kosilek refers to himself as a "little girl" nearly 100 times in 400 pages. Not in the past tense. In the present tense. Wrap your mind around that. "My little girl's heart" is an oft repeated refrain. "My little girl thoughts and feelings", "my little girl's dreams", "A girl, hiding as a boy in plain sight, who grew into a woman hiding as a man, with the broken heart of a child", "the little girl inside", "My girl status", "My lost little girl's heart", "My broken little girl's heart", "the combination of my adult intellect and little-girl's determination", "the little girl in me", "a little girl's dream", "my need to compensate for all the non-girly years", "little-girl giddy", "My little girl's gleeful eyes", "Perhaps women like us have the advantage, from finally letting our little girl out to play after hiding her for so long", "my [current] little girl perspective", Etc. I can't overstate the constant and disturbing pedomorphic foundation of Koselik's expression of his transgender "internal female gender identity".

Here are a few examples in context:

"The part I had left out was that when Judge Wolf apologized for taking six months to write the ruling in the first civil action, he also told me that he would try to write this one quicker. To a little girl, that's a promise, and I surely heard it as one. But I was about to turn 60 in April, and Mark Wolf would turn 63 that November. The woman chose not to embarrass Judge Wolf; that was a child's manipulation that had no place in these proceedings. But oh how I wept each time I heard that little girl's lament "But he promised."

And:

"On April 13, 2010, I went to Shattuck Hospital for my first mammogram. It was like wrestling with a machine. Not a pleasant experience, but I'm glad I got it. I'm a big girl now for sure."

And:

"I used to be a much better liar before I got sober and finally broke my shell, revealing the frightened but adamant little-girl-creature who had been vacillating between silently screaming in her darkness and willing the light to cast nothing but pain-less shadows. An author/editor of my recent acquaintance has opined that perhaps this final escape is the reason I chose the name Michelle when I had used Lisa before. My shell. Sometimes editors are good psychologists."

Insanity. I can't tell you how disconcerting it is to read a novel length tome written by a 62 year-old continually steeped in this self-referential pediatric framing. It is truly disturbing, and would be regardless of the sex, criminal history or "gender identity" of the writer.

Kosilek describes his current attorney "Franny" (Frances S. Cohen) as having "a mischievous little-girl grin".

In his choice of memoir title "Grace's Daughter" Kosilek refers to himself as the offspring of the divine, the recipient of special favor, the sanctified, not the offspring of any actual real woman, like his mother Elizabeth who died in 1977 when Robert was 28. He characterizes Elizabeth's life as impoverished and ruled by various abusive and violent men, which he blames her for. He does talk about putting on his bra and blotting his lipstick "the same way my mother did". He wears his eye make-up the way his sister did. He feminized his vocal patterns by reading aloud in his cell while imitating his mother. His sister Patricia, called "Tish" has opted for no further contact with him since she filed a restraining order on him in 1972.

Judge Mark L. Wolf, who is mentioned near constantly in Kosilek's tome, always in a flattering ass-kissing way, has adjudicated nearly all of Robert's jailhouse lawyering suits for the last twenty years. Suits against sheriffs. Suits against his own lawyers. Suits for hormones. Suits for therapy. Suits for name change. Suits against the therapists provided by the court. Suits against the doctors providing court-ordered hormones. Suits for mammograms for his hormone-induced breast growth. Suits for laser hair removal. Suits against prison officials for not calling him by female pronouns. Suits for electrolysis to remove trace facial hair left after laser treatment. Suits for the right to lipstick use. Suits for prison lingerie. Suits against the chief of corrections. Too many suits to list. Kosilek has 16 hours a day, seven days a week, 52 weeks a year, for the rest of his life to do nothing but file suits in Judge Wolf's court. And now: An 8th amendment suit based on the precedent of "Sexually Dangerous Person" Battista which demands the surgical "right" to invert Kosilek's penis into a penetrable cavity, such penetrable cavity conferring womanhood on Massachusetts wife-killing men, apparently.

Judge Wolf has spent twenty years with Kosilek, week in and week out. He is married to Kosilek for as long as he holds his appointment. On September 5, 2012 Wolf issued a ruling granting Kosilek the tax-payer funded right to "sex-change surgery" and outlined a subsequent plan for his transfer to MCI Framingham medium security Women's Prison from his MCI Norfolk maximum security men's housing. The majority of Framingham inmates are jailed for non-violent offenses. 75% are mothers.

In "Grace's Daughter" Kosilek claims precedent: that a man named Debbie Moccia has already been housed at Framingham even though that man still had his penis intact. According to Kosilek, Debbie was "released" from the women's facility in August of 2005. This seems unlikely, since Moccia's current level 3 sex offender listing (denoting the highest possible risk of re-offending and an ongoing threat to public safety) still lists him as male. Then again, Moccia, 57, has been arrested under dozens of male and female aliases and has been arraigned nearly 250 times, at least 40 involving crimes of violence. Charges include rape, indecent assault, open and gross lewd and lascivious behavior against minors, stalking, harassing obscene phone calls, failing to register as a sex offender, criminal harassment, and on and on. In 2011 he smuggled a razor blade into a courtroom in his mouth. It was the second time he had done so. Maybe Moccia accidentally ended up at Framingham at one point or perhaps was placed in isolation there. Perhaps not.

On "April Fools Day" Monday April 1, 2013 the State of Massachusetts began presenting arguments appealing Judge Wolf's decision as well as his ruling for tax-payer reimbursement of $500,000 for Kosilek's legal costs. Included in the physician recommendations for treatment in Kosilek's case are authorization of further surgical procedures including facial feminization surgery, tracheal shave to remove his adam's apple, and breast implants. In his memoir Robert says at his advanced age he will probably forego many of the recommended cosmetic surgical procedures, although he "might need a nose job".

Kosilek closes his memoir by notifying the reader he has obtained a new pro-bono lawyer to review his case and seek the overturn of his current sentence of life in prison without parole. He is also writing a fictional trilogy titled "Ghosts of Our Mothers", a "saga that celebrates the universality of female experience, regardless of disparate circumstances".

Kosilek's ruling was overturned after the original publication of this article on April 9, 2013, Gendertrender.wordpress.com. Republished with permission.

CHAPTER 46

THE WANTED PROJECT

Nedra Johnson

Mothers and daughters, womyn born womyn
and we gather in the light of the August Moon
Amazon womyn and we're out in the woods
and we heal by the light of the August moon.
Powerful womyn, creative womyn!
Dancing in the light of the August Moon.
Girls and womyn in the Michigan woods.
And we love by the August Moon.

~ FROM A SONG BY NEDRA JOHNSON

THE WANTED PROJECT is a group of womyn who are reaching out to "whom it may concern." It is our hope that through The WANTED Project podcast series we are producing that we will gain community, celebrate our uniqueness as well as our commonalities, heal, and end our isolation. We hope that we will see ourselves reflected over and over through the power of example — by sharing our lives, our experience, strength, and hope for a future where we can be womyn without "qualifiers."

That doesn't mean that we might not individually enjoy qualifiers such as "butch" or "gender nonconforming." It means we understand that when we transgress the socially determined and enforced limitations and expectations forced on us because we are female, that such transgressions do *not* determine us as somehow "not women." Instead, they betray the social construct of gender as a falsehood and a tool of patriarchy meant to keep human females subjugated to human males.

There is no wrong way to be female.
We *see* you.
You are WANTED.

I'm going to start off with a little backstory to give people who are unfamiliar with the project a sense of our origins, and touch on what I see as a vision for our future. One important point is that the women involved in this project have a connection to the Michigan Womyn's Music Festival. The connection is not in any kind of official capacity, but the project was created by and for participants in that festival community.

The Michigan festival, for me, was a place where for the first time, I saw so many different kinds of ways to be female. For example, I really had no idea how hairy women could be. Looking back now, twenty-eight years later, I think, "Why didn't I know that? It just seems like common knowledge." But, I'm not a hairy person, so my reaction was, "Oh, wow – I didn't know that!" And that's because it's *so* common for women to shave, pluck, wax, and laser. Hair removal is a four-billion-dollar industry aimed mostly at women. What's funny is that it's so common for women to remove their body hair that we think of *that* as "natural." Women *not* having body hair is considered "natural" and women *having* body hair is considered "unnatural."

My assumptions got challenged the very first time I went to the Michigan festival. I saw womyn with full-on beards or mustaches or very hairy legs, and as I walked along the path, I thought to myself, "Oh my god! This is a way that women can be!" So much that I was seeing, even our different sizes and shapes, just enchanted me. I think that most women have issues with their body and think, "Oh, I'm not very pretty" or "I'm not very shapely in a way that's acceptable, out and about." I mean, you never see women who look like me on TV being portrayed as if they are beautiful, or even not repulsive.

I feel like my personal goal was indifference. I really didn't want people to have an opinion about my body, my presentation, or my clothes. I didn't want the kind of attention that you get from men if they find you attractive. Some people do – but I didn't.

So, Michigan was mind-blowing – it was a place where I fit in. There was a level of safety and a sense that you could be vulnerable; you turned off your daily instincts to be vigilant. I don't think women realize how *on* we are all of the time. We have this fear factor that's always making us conscious about where we are and who's around us. At the Michigan festival we didn't have to, because there were only females there. Or at least it was supposed to be that way.

I don't think that I'm someone who is seen as male in my presentation. Maybe here and there some people "sir" me, but it doesn't happen all that much, although you might think that it would because of the way I dress. I think it might if I were less curvy – if I were not as fat as I am, and able to hide my curves. Then maybe it would happen. It certainly did happen when I was younger and smaller. When I was a kid, I was someone whom people mistook for a boy. I always thought it was weird that they thought I looked like a boy, because I didn't think I looked like a boy.

Bathrooms have always been a big issue, with somebody telling me that I'm in the wrong bathroom. "This is the women's room – this is the *girl's* room." I'd just reply, "I know," and go on in. And sometimes it *really* upset people to the point that they called security, only to find themselves embarrassed by having gotten it wrong. I know that a lot of women themselves feel embarrassed about it. And you know, that can go either way. You can end up feeling embarrassed that people get it wrong and you're subject to dealing with security, but I always thought it was more embarrassing for them. I can see why women would be concerned with men in the bathroom. I don't think it takes much to really look at somebody – to look them in their eyes. Stop looking at their hat or their shirt or pants or whatever outfit they've got on. Look at *them*! You can generally spot someone who is just a gender nonconforming woman.

Michigan was a place where, as a female, you were seen as a woman. It was the one place that I know where women could be fully bearded, hairy, and muscular and all kinds of different presentations, and not be questioned. For one week, it was a place where no one was saying, "Are you *going* in the right place? Are you *in* the right place?" This is one of the things that was a real perk at Michigan for years and years.

What changed the festival from being a place for different presentations of women were advocates of trans inclusion challenging the festival's intention that it be for females only. So women got really paranoid. They stopped being able to trust that the intention for womyn-only space was being respected. That mistrust had an impact on many different women.

It got to be a really hard and sad thing. And that's not just for the women who were suddenly not being recognized as women. It was hard for the women who really need female-only space for what*ever* reason so that they could be vulnerable and feel safe in a way that they don't get to feel in spaces that are not female-only. That might mean they feel safe to take their shirt off in a way that they wouldn't in a space that included males. It might mean they feel comfortable talking about trauma in a workshop. But if those boundaries are being challenged and disrespected, you're quite certain that anybody who would do that is not somebody you feel safe around.

So, we were talking among ourselves about how we could change *that* – as we were also considering how to fight the effort to frame the festival's intention for female space as being "hateful" towards people who are not female. We talked about how we could also start working to make the festival go back to what it was – a welcoming space for women born female who didn't present in socially common ways.

Somebody suggested that we should make WANTED posters for males who were known to be attending the festival. But the unanimous response to that from *everybody* in that conversation was, "Oh no, no, no – that's not the way we do things." So I suggested that we make WANTED posters for what we actually *do* want. We discussed some things, tweaked some language, and we made a fake WANTED poster in the style of an old Wild West- style "Wanted" poster.

Below a photograph of a woman's face, it said…

WANTED: Women like Nedra - who have been disappeared by assumptions. Women who were born and assigned female, but who present in ways that the world determines as masculine/not womanly, women who are assumed to be trans men when they do not identify as men or trans men. Women who expand the possibilities of what it means to be born in this life, female. You are wanted. You are loved, and we want you to know it.

That was the first version. We also had a girl's version:

WANTED: Girls like Nedra - whose nature may or may not conform to what the world says a girl should be or can be. Girls who just want to be themselves and are still figuring out what the means. Girls who won't accept the limitations that are projected on them just because they are girls. Girls who define girl and who refuse to let it define them. You are wanted, you are loved, and we want you to know it.

Those were the basic two types of posters. There were a few variations for women who felt a little bit differently about the language. But it was basically the same intention across the board. Women assumed that the adults who participated were butch-identified, but that wasn't true. I don't think that we were all lesbians either, though most of us were. It was just an attempt to get people to look – and a hope that when they saw the posters, that they would *think* before suggesting to a woman that she didn't belong there, or asking a woman if she belonged there, or whether she was actually a woman.

There are many women who identify as women but are assumed to be trans men just because they are gender nonconforming women. And yeah, that can happen in "Area 51" (the world outside of the festival space), but the one place it shouldn't happen is in the space specifically determined to be for womyn who were born female.

So the festival was the one place where for one week, they didn't have to deal with that kind of bullshit. That's where the WANTED Project came from. We made eighty posters total for the first go-round. Seeing the posters seemed to be a powerful and moving experience for many women. We laminated the posters and hung them up in an area of the festival where you could display original artwork. I also made smaller versions and taped them up in the portable outhouses, which we called the porta "Janes." Part of festival culture was to communicate through flyers posted in the "Janes." I made a lot of these and had some extras, which was good because they kept going missing. At the time, because there was hostility from people who thought that the intention of female space should change, we thought, "OMG – this is not even hateful! Why are they taking down our posters?" As it turned out, we heard from women that they were so moved by the posters that they were collecting them like baseball cards.

Any posters we had left at the end of festival were taken by women who wanted to collect them. It was a very powerful experience, and interesting for me, because I'm not a visual artist. It was interesting to put something visual together that women were moved by, and I think it did work. It did help women to not be asked if they belonged there.

The Michigan Womyn's Music Festival was built on many intentions, *not* only the intention for female-only space. We were to assume that everyone who was there was female.

There were other intentions honored there – not necessarily even spoken aloud.

For example, if you smoked, you carried an Altoids tin and put your butts out in the tin and collected them. You didn't walk around the land after a concert and see thousands of cigarette butts. It wasn't like any other place in that regard. We didn't have a concert end and then find garbage everywhere. And it's not that people didn't have snacks and drinks – they just cleaned up. Whatever they brought and was garbage afterwards, they took it with them. There was an intention to do work shifts and women did them.

That's just the way we were as a community.

The reason it wasn't a "don't ask, don't tell" kind of thing, like outsiders often projected, was more that we understood the value of *not* asking women if they were female. Not questioning women about their gender in that space was held at a higher value than whether or not somebody was actually violating the festival's intention for female space.

Yes, it was *possible* to attend the festival as someone who was not female and get away with it. And you *could* interpret that as "don't ask don't tell." But "don't ask don't tell" in the military was a little more "it's ok to be gay in the military, we're just not gonna talk about it." For the festival, it was "we'd like you to respect this intention for female space," and there were people who chose *not* to respect it. This is probably the best way I can put it: Not enforcing a boundary is not the same as inviting you to violate it. And if you think it is, who thinks like that? That we didn't want to enforce the boundaries, but that we wanted them to be respected, was *not* an invitation to violate them. But that was often what some people thought. The value in allowing women the experience of *not* having to answer questions about how they look; of *not* being told in some implied way that they are outside of "woman" because they do not conform to social stereotypes, was held at a higher value.

We valued giving women that space, more so than we worried about whether some people might exploit that. The focus was always on women – females – and on creating space for females. So, the festival community did not try to keep out those who disrespected the intention. We focused on what we wanted – just like in this WANTED Project. And again, when I talk about intentions, I think it's really significant how much the community was built on intention. For example, I'm sure if you go to any major music festival, especially one that costs as much as $500, you will see armed security and twelve-foot fences with razor wire. We literally had a wire fence no higher than three feet tall. You could *easily* step over it, and yet people really didn't do that. That's amazing!

The festival organizers also worked at making the event accessible to women of different means. Some women paid more if they could and others paid less if they couldn't – it was a "more if/less if" practice. You could apply for a scholarship, where instead of paying $500, you'd pay $300 or $200. Depending on your needs, you could just ask for what you needed. I think all of this is important when we talk about the community that was being built and the intention for female space – and especially what it meant for women who maybe didn't fit in with "woman" in the larger world because of stereotypes and social expectations that didn't fit them.

The Michigan Womyn's Music Festival closed in August 2015, after celebrating its fortieth anniversary. The vision for the podcast project post-festival is to either interview women or allow us the space to tell our stories, to bear witness for each other in whatever ways we're comfortable doing within this medium. Basically, we're going to be talking about our lives. Maybe we'll tell how we came to be where we are now. Maybe we'll share our baby pictures and compare them to what we look like now. You don't have to be butch or femme, or have any kind of label on yourself. You don't have to be a lesbian. You just have to identify with what we're talking about being a female who doesn't fit society's expectations for "woman," beyond the fact that you're biologically female.

We know that society has a prescription for what we're supposed to do and be as women, for what we're supposed to like and be good at. A lot of us don't fit that. That doesn't put us outside of "woman." That puts *society's* expectations outside of reality.

So, I want to say welcome! If you identify, and you feel like you want to share your story, you can get in touch with us and we'll work out a way to make you a part of it. In a Michigan festival tradition in this new medium, we're planting acorns, and I'm here to tell you, "Welcome Home."

Contact the WANTED Project through http://www.wantedpodcast.com/

CHAPTER 47

THE UNIVERSE IS HER FORM

Vajra Ma

IF WE ASSUME the title of this essay to be true, all form in the universe is the form of Woman. This plainly establishes a non-separation. It explains why in Tantra, "He is She," which actually makes gender otherization impossible, let alone the notion of "identity." It removes any foundation from the patriarchal separation, erasure, and men lording over women and life resources in general. Most importantly, it unmasks the dogmatized devaluing of Woman as a mere issue of jealousy: the "sour grapes" principle, which tries to establish that women are inferior and therefore men can own, use, exploit and erase them.

The politicized trans narrative at issue here – which is to be seen totally separate from individual choices by individual people – actually depends on that patriarchal sour grapes principle. In reality, the grapes are luscious and sweet.

A VISION OF TOTALITY

Imagine you are standing before a towering ancient temple embellished with images carved in golden-hued stone of nude women and men in various positions of amorous engagement. The women have large, round breasts and full, curved hips that sway to one side or the other. They are adorned with ornate jewelry, necklaces, hair ornaments, earrings, bracelets, anklets, hip belts and sometimes a gossamer fabric delicately drapes across their figures. The men look a lot like the women. Though their breasts are not full and round and their hips not as full, they are as gracefully rendered and stand in hip-swayed stance as the women and they are adorned with similar jewelry. Yet, the men are unambiguously male and they exude virility in their sinuous gracefulness.

What are we seeing here? Or actually, what are we *not seeing*?

What we are not seeing is the Western hard-bodied male ideal, with six-pack abs, bulging biceps, and legs planted wide in the stance of challenge and, most of all, dominance. And yet, these men are unambiguously male and virile as they gently cup their female companion's breast or tenderly pluck the gossamer garment that flows over her hips. Both men and women gaze into each other's doe-like eyes; both women and men's voluptuous lips are delicately curved in serene smiles of sensual delight.

We also see that there is no rigid binary division between women and men. In these exquisitely rendered carvings both the female and male are *feminine* as per the Western stereotype of feminine. He is not pronouncedly *other* than She. Male and female are not depicted as polar opposites. There is no binary, no "otherization" in these images. Instead, the men and women share a spiritually grounded sensuality, expressed in fluid, serpentine curves, gentle smiles, and tender touches.

What *is* going on, on the other hand, is a quality of sensuous male-female love play that is utterly foreign to objectification of women's bodies, coercive acts of misogyny, or the loveless banging, thrashing and pounding reflected in today's pornographic culture. These couples and groups of women and men who are united in caresses, embraces and sometimes explicit sexual intercourse have absolutely nothing in common with misogyny or pornography. They are fully engaged with each other physically, sexually, emotionally and — this is a temple — spiritually. Their gazes, gestures and postures evoke both the spiritual, transcendent Beloved and the human, here-and-now Beloved. Their smiles, touches and embraces convey mutual reverence and respect, harmony and reciprocity of feeling and awareness.

In these images, I recognize the nuanced sexual-sensual sensibilities that I personally have found in my nearly thirty years of working with women to be natural to women, sensibilities that seamlessly interweave heart and body, sexuality and spirituality. What exudes from these temple carvings is reverence for the human body, the non-division of spirit and flesh. In the tantric view such divisions are not real. Instead, Tantra offers an illuminating view and a liberating path through and beyond conceptual distortions and divisions. *There is no moralistic judgment in tantra. There is only the inquiry into "what is here."*

The description above is based on a tantric temple in India.[1]

These tantric people glory in the common ground of the Feminine, a Feminine of a different order than the commodified Western stereotype, a Feminine that encompasses both female and male and points us to our inherent totality.

SHAKTI, THE PRIMAL CREATIVE POWER

The totality referred to here is based in the tangible experience of Shakti, the primal feminine creative power that underlies reality, the animating force of all that exists. She is the Great

Goddess, the Cosmic Womb that creates and encompasses all that is. She is Divine Love. Shaktism, or Shakta Tantra, is that tantric view which regards the Feminine as the Supreme Reality and esteems Woman, who carries the enfoldment of the cosmic womb within her, as the particular embodiment of Shakti, Goddess.[2] We see this expressed in the Shakti-sangama Tantra: *Woman is the creator of the universe, the universe is her form.*[3]

The primacy of the female stood without question in the ancient world, millennia before the onset of patriarchal-dominator societies, a mere six thousand years ago. The historical reality of Woman as spiritual and societal leader is globally evident in cultures on every continent. The modern-day Mosuo society in China is an intact matriarchal culture that knows no marriage, where there is no such thing as an "illegitimate child," and where women are highly respected and free to be sexual with whomever they invite into their "flower room" in their mother's home. In Aboriginal Australia, the myths recount the men's admission that they stole the power from the women when they weren't looking. The attempt to not just steal but appropriate power by force is a core issue of this essay.

Feminine Power under Siege

Tantra,[4] the philosophy, cosmology and science of consciousness, (not a religion!) has long recognized the inherent and advantageous powers of female embodiment.[5] It is in India-originated Tantra, as well as in its tantric Tibetan Buddhist iteration, that I have found my greatest inspiration as I have explored women's and my own *bodyknowing* (defined later) and originated the subtle body moving meditation I have taught since 1992, The Tantric Dance of Feminine Power,® the Womb-Sourced Yoga of Feminine Wisdom. This has opened for me many of the insights that weave through this essay. It is through this female embodiment practice that I have cultivated direct, conscious awareness of Shakti and deep reverence for the powers and qualities of the female body. Or more accurately, of the female *bodymind*, for science has shown conclusively that the body and the mind are not separate, but function as a unified, interactive, and interdependent system. This fact of bodymind[6] unity and that Woman carries source, the cosmic womb enfolded within her, illuminates why Woman has, until patriarchy, been revered, and, conversely, why patriarchy, which is based on the illusory division of flesh and spirit, does all it can to erase this reverence. Thus, extrapolating from the Shakti-sangama Tantra, *woman is the foundation of the world;* the foundation of patriarchy is the erasure of Woman.

To restore reverence and respect for Woman is central to ending this erasure. It is key to dismantling patriarchy and its countless erasures, distortions and divisions, which include the current trans narrative and particularly its dogma[7] of "gender identity" which, while purportedly trying to provide wholeness to gender-dysphoric people, actually perpetuates the erasures, distortions and divisions at the root of their suffering. Though rarely overtly spoken today, this reverence still lives in the depths of the heart and body; it is the original spirituality of humanity. I would therefore like to frame the trans narrative in the (pre-patriarchal) historical context of respect and reverence for Woman, to engage and stimulate an awareness of the reality of the unique nature and powers of the female bodymind. It is my desire to give the reader, trans and non-trans alike, a way to "hold" the trans narrative that points the way back to humanity's common ground. I will do this by sharing aspects of the Shakta Tantra view and my direct experience in working extensively with female subtle bodyknowing.

To recognize and respect the reality of women's bodies would make female erasure impossible.

THE TANTRIC DANCE OF FEMININE POWER

As a teacher, facilitator and ordained Priestess of the Goddess and Women's Mysteries, I have worked with women, and to a lesser degree men, in ritual, private healing sessions, devotional moving meditation, and subtle bodyknowing since the late 1980s. Bodyknowing is conscious awareness of and participation with the language of the body which is sensation, breath, sound, shape, motion and emotion.[8] *Subtle* bodyknowing is listening/feeling the body's language with highly refined and nuanced awareness.

In The Tantric Dance of Feminine Power, which is generally done unpartnered, the erotic is entirely internal, self-referenced, a dance of comingling energies of womb, heart, third eye[9] and countless inner *nadis* (energy channels)[10] tremoring with electromagnetic energy, pleasure and power, all of which suffuse the bodymind with a sense of being loved. The Dance[11] also awakens spiritual awareness or "wisdom streams" and in this way has been a kind of Rosetta stone by which, because I have already experienced directly in my body what they describe, I perceive the meaning of esoteric spiritual texts which I might not have otherwise understood.

The Dance is a dynamic, spontaneous, deeply internal moving meditation and is "dance" only in the sense of the cosmic play of energy. There are no steps or technique. However, there is a form. The form is based in the natural wave pattern of pleasure and discovered through feeling subtle sensations and emotions.[12]

The body's language, including erotic experiences, can be a portal into experiencing the all-pervading love of Shakti:

Love, enjoyed by the ignorant,
Becomes bondage.
That very same love, Tasted by one with
understanding,
Brings liberation.
[...]
Enjoy all the pleasures of love fearlessly,
For the sake of liberation.

~ CITTAVISUDDHIPRAKARANA[13]

The Tantric Dance of Feminine Power is simultaneously a prayer and the answer to the prayer.[14] We start with devotional intention, then let our awareness drop into the womb where we rest and wait for *spanda* to gather, the tremoring vibration that underlies reality, until we feel the impulse to movement. Movement arises from feeling subtle sensations of pleasure; that pleasure moves the body into shapes, or body *mudras/asanas*. (The pleasure can be as simple as the awareness of the stretch of a muscle or the warm quickening of an emotion.) Each body shape, from moment to moment, has its integral bio-circuitry which holds a particular frequency of power and knowledge. The Dance is a continuous, uninterrupted stream of *asanas*, a "streaming yoga." As we let our selves be affected by the feelings and shapes, they amplify and heighten; and rather than dissipate the intensity we continue to absorb and thus embody higher and higher frequencies.

These descriptions of The Dance convey the Source, how we literally revere and worship the pleasurable feelings as the subtle form of the Divine Mother herself. "Worship me as your innermost self," says the Goddess in the Tripura Rahasya. In The Dance we do this — *both women and men* — and this is how we can come to directly experience what is manifest in the women and men on those temple walls — *karuna*, the mystical blend of celestial, erotic, and mother love, of pleasure, sexuality, and compassion. Our heart is pierced with devotion, our body suffused with beauty, divine pride, feminine power, and love.

In view of this, it follows that the form of fluid wave pattern is the same for men as for women. The hard line between male and female tends to dissolve. Female and male alike source from the womb (I tell men to imagine a womb and they report it transforms their perception of their body and sexuality). Men undulate and move in circular, fluid shapes, moving through an array of feelings. We are, all of us, all of it. No concepts here, just direct experience of the bodymind and the Shakti that animates all. What is the difference between the men and women? The women access Shakti and manifest the wisdom level of The Dance much more easily and readily: "What a male tantrika realizes in one year, a female adept attains in one day."[15]

DIVIDE AND CONQUER THE FEMALE

Tantra has long recognized the power of Woman, the preeminence of female embodiment. It is considered auspicious to incarnate as a woman, a sentiment that amounts to heresy in patriarchal society, which is founded on patriarchal religion that trivializes, marginalizes, and ultimately demonizes Woman. Patriarchy is at battle with the body specifically, Woman's body. Woman must be controlled and the way to do that is by dividing the power and totality manifest in her body: Divide women internally from their distinctly female, womb-empowered bodies by denigrating menses, medicalizing pregnancy and birth (doctors, mostly male, "deliver" babies); by objectifying their bodies in the "beauty," fashion, media, and pornography industries; and by dividing women from each other and their collective female bodyknowing into nuclear, male-dominated family units.

The crux of patriarchal power is division and separation, based in erasure of reality through *concepts*. Patriarchy conceptualizes the physical as separate from the spiritual, profane from holy. In reality there is no division; the body and all matter is holy. Patriarchy divides man from woman by conceptualizing them as binary, polar "opposites." It conceptualizes and separates humanity from everything else, earth, plants, animals, cosmos, and from god. In this scenario, God is not our innermost self, but the first "*other*." This is followed by the concept that a man-god made a woman out of a man. Woman is not just the "second *sex*," but the second "*other*." Patriarchy denies reality, that Woman is primary for she creates man. It reverses this reality and, from these distortions, it makes up an identity (primacy and rulership over woman) for the male. We might consider this the beginnings of today's "gender identity" problem.

The trans narrative[16] perpetuates patriarchy's central violence, the battle with the body. It postulates "I was born in the wrong body" and plays out "gender identity" to its logical conclusion. Biology, nature, and cosmos got it wrong; Woman and her womb got it wrong, just as she did in the garden when she ate the apple. The trans narrative echoes the division of women from their bodies in complaints such as "to talk about menstruation or vaginas is misogynist because it excludes trans women." True misogyny, however, was exhibited when one high-profile trans activist derisively referred to a woman's child as a "womb turd."[17] Such complaints and epithets are unthinkable in the tantric view, or the view of anyone who respects women or the human body.

That "womb turd" slur also illustrates the true root and actual *nature* of misogyny: I don't have it; so I want to trivialize, marginalize, and devalue it by any means. It's the sour grapes principle referred to earlier.

The trans agenda takes separation even a step further. Rather than merely separate body and mind, one need not address body at all! Biology is erased from the definition of woman (and man) and replaced with the patriarchal concept "gender identity." The legal definition of "gender identity" in numerous US states is similar to what was proposed for federal legislation in July 2015.[18] It reads:

"The term 'gender identity' means the gender-related identity, appearance, mannerisms, or other gender-related characteristics of an individual, regardless of the individual's designated sex at birth."

Woman and man are reduced to concepts based in costumes and stereotypes. With Orwellian doublespeak and a convoluted distortion of biological reality, the trans agenda conceptualizes the body as "wrong," then imposes the concept of "gender identity" on it to make it "right." It declares "some women have penises" and "some men, vaginas" but "woman," "man," and "gender" are *never defined* and that vacuum of objective definition spins us round in a vortex of circular logic that says: "Anyone who feels like or identifies as a woman is one." "If you have a penis and you identify as a woman, then the penis is a female organ." Woman is now a concept, a "gender identity," completely separated from biology. Here, the patriarchal erasure of Woman through separation from her body reaches its zenith—any man can be a woman.

It is ironic that "gender identity," instead of liberating sincere trans-identified people from suffering, traps them in the very gender binary stereotypes – constructed by hetero-normative society – that makes them feel trapped in the first place. In constructing "gender identity" they look in exactly the wrong place for wholeness. Tragically, "identity" is not only a concept that limits fluidity, but it installs a steel fence of mutual *otherness* and separates oneself from the totality.

The aim of tantra is to *dissolve identity* so that we may be open to the totality. This does not mean we forget who we are; it simply means we do not cling to the roles we play in our life, or hold them rigidly.

The body does not care if we identify as gender queer, pansexual, gay, lesbian or hetero. It does not care if we identify as an athlete, professor, qi gong master, mother, politician or house painter. (It does, however, care about how much or how little reverence we treat it with.) Our identity means nothing to the body. Our *feelings* about our identity do, on the other hand, greatly impact our body chemistry and our physical and psychological health, and it is in this reality that bodyknowing resides. The body is biological. It is not a concept. It is real. It is self-intelligent. Cut the skin, it will heal itself. Put food in its stomach, it will digest it. While our thoughts and feelings *affect* healing and digestion, healing and digestion are *not dependent* upon them; the body will perform these processes whether or not we give effort or attention to them. The same self-intelligence goes for the miraculous capacity of Woman's body to gestate and birth a human being.

COMMON GROUND AND THE GREAT TANTRIC SECRET

There is a common ground upon which humanity can meet without conflict or debate. It is the body, the body *itself.* It requires neither coercive laws nor legalistic redefinition of tangible reality.

To refer back to our Beloveds on the temple walls, they love each other with such graceful reverence and tender respect because they love *the body itself.* Respect and receptivity to one's own body as sacred make it possible to love another's body as sacred. Conversely, reverence and respect for the body are exactly what is missing in the trans agenda and what must be missing to enable it, to enable the erasure required to act as if being a woman is no big deal: anybody can do it, just dress and act a certain way: But this missing (common) ground — the sacred body — is where humanity needs to meet to resolve the millennia of erasure of the female, an erasure which now, due to the drugs and surgery of modern medical intervention, can play out with a biological literalness that was not available before today's politicized trans agenda.

The body loves us. It is not the wrongdoer who traps us where we are not supposed to be, into who we are not. The anguish of feeling "I was born in the wrong body" is *felt* in the body. The suffering is real, but it does not *originate* from the body. It is, rather, a consequence of rigid, moralistic societal constructs and the society and people who enforce them driven by a fear that is based in their own rigid identity. No one is born in this anguish. What a terrible cruelty to impose it through external gender constructs. What is marvelous, on the other hand, is that the liberation we seek *does* originate from the body. To find it we need to surrender control and listen to/feel the body's own language — sensation, breath, sound, shape, motion and emotion.

In Tantra, "…the female embodies the power; the male, the capacity for wonder."[19] The current trans agenda is dominated by the battle between wonder and reverence before the Primal Feminine (and as it is embodied in Woman) and the resistance and attempt to control the uncontrollable (central to patriarchy). "A tantrika worships woman because he recognizes her power," says Daniel Odier in *Desire: The Tantric Path to Awakening*. "This recognition dissolves all obstacles, is the cornerstone of a deep relationship. The great masters of the past who sought the teachings of the yoginis totally melted […] and let themselves be led toward totality, the unsettling reunion of the body, mind, emotions and space."[20]

The attempt to control separates us from our deep soul-longing to melt into wholeness, to be immersed in the totality, to come home to the Great Round of the Great Mother. There is good reason that awe is defined as "a feeling of reverential respect mixed with fear or wonder." We have two choices in the face of the Primal Feminine: surrender in awe, or deny with control.

If a woman is to fully inhabit her body, she must stop fearing and hiding her innate power and surrender to it. If a man wants to be a woman, he cannot do so by imposing drugs or surgery or superficial imitation by way of dress and mannerisms. But there is something he *can* do; he can become a woman energetically, without drugs, without surgery, without political strong-arming and without trying to coerce others into giving him an untruthful reflection. *The aim of a male tantrika is to become a woman energetically.*

Some years ago, I had an extraordinary experience at the end of a six-week men-only Tantric Dance class series. As I sat with these seven men in the closing circle of the last class, I suddenly felt a peculiar sensation (peculiar only because it was in a circle of men); I felt exactly as I do in a circle of women! I felt and spoke the closing prayer of gratitude to the Goddess exactly as I would when I was sitting with women because these men had become women energetically.

What we see in the sensuously virile men on our temple walls is that they are women energetically. Being a woman energetically does not diminish masculine virility. To the contrary, the source of virility is Shakti, the Feminine Power. The Goddess speaks in the scripture:

"A weak man is declared to be without any Shakti, nobody says that he is without Shiva, or without Vishnu. Those who are timid, afraid, or under one's enemies they are all called Shakti-less; no one says that this man is Shiva-less and so forth."

(DEVI BHAGAVATA PURANA: 3.6)

It follows then that Woman initiates the male into experiencing her spherical totality "The universe is her form." She *is* the totality; she contains the womb. This does not separate her from man, because it is reality rather than concept or identity. That is the very ground of their union, as it is for the union of a couple of any sexual orientation. "*When a tantric man and woman lie down to make love, it is like two goddesses lying down to make love.*[21]

Woman is to man as Goddess is to humanity and all creation. Woman embodies and manifests the primal creative power of Shakti. It is for this reason that Tantra recognizes Woman as *the creator of the universe* and declares *the universe is her form*. Coming back to the Shakti-sangama Tantra:

[Woman] is the true form of the body.
Whatever form she takes,
Whether the form of a man or a woman,
Is the superior form.

What? Woman can take the form of a man? Where the trans narrative might grasp at that claiming "See! That's what a trans man is!" this would be a pathetic reduction indeed. The next few lines elaborate why:

In woman is the form of all things,
Of all that lives and moves in the world.

We are back to totality *all that lives and moves in the world*. The totality is infinitely diverse; it does not erase distinction—it *encompasses* it. A man is not a woman and a woman is not a frog or a palm tree. We do not erase the distinctions between woman, frog or palm tree; why should we erase the distinction between woman and man? What we need to appreciate is that just as all distinctions are encompassed in the Cosmic Womb, likewise, Woman encompasses man in her womb. *In woman is the form of all things.* She creates the male from her form and he emerges from her. *He* is a variation of *her*. In this way she takes *the form of a man*. This is the Great Tantric Secret stated earlier: He is She.

The desire of a man to be a woman is not new. In India the Hijra, men who dress and live as women, date far back (as does cross-sex living for both women and men in many cultures).[22] "Even the powerful [Hindu] gods crave to enter feminine form."[23] "According to Vaishnavitic doctrine, 'all souls are feminine to the Supreme Reality.'"[24] Many Purana legends describe males transforming into females. In one story, Shiva, a male god, was making love to his mate Parvati and took on the form of a woman to please her.

COMING FULL CIRCLE TO A VISION OF TOTALITY: THE FEMININE IS THE WHOLE

The Vedas are the oldest recorded religious texts of India's Hinduism, dating back to 1500 BCE, but they contain vestiges of the Shakta view that far predates them. That view originates in the ancient matriarchal cultures of India. Giti Thadani documents this with ten years of original on-site research in India as detailed in her book *Sakhiyani*. She documents that before the Vedas, the totality of divine power was viewed as two females, called the *jami* sisters or twins. The polarities of light and dark, day and night, dry and moist were not "feminine" and "masculine" but wholly Feminine. They transformed into each other by passing through a third space, the womb-shaped triadic space between them. Thadani says "[There is no] binary opposition between polarities, but rather moving passages, in between third spaces. This dynamic triad allows dual elements to coexist as a single unit." This is the cyclic wholeness of the Feminine Round depicted in so many tantric *yantras* (geometric mandalas) which contain the triangle within the circle. It is not unlike the awareness of love experienced as a third space or presence between two lovers.

If the Feminine is the whole, it cannot logically be dominated or appropriated. On the other hand, because it is the whole, those who envy Her for being the whole are intent on doing just that.

THE WONDROUS FEMALE BODY

In my experience, grounded to a large extent in The Tantric Dance of Feminine Power, conceptual conflict and paradox melt, dissolve in the direct reality of bodyknowing. In The Dance, I surrender my "head" and allow my heart to be pierced with reverence. I melt in the pleasure of Shakti as she tremors through me. It may be true that the populace at large is not likely to engage in a moving meditation like this, but we all have the ready capacity for wonder which dissolves conceptual conflict and opens the heart in endlessly nourishing awe. The gestating and birthing power of the womb is wondrous enough, but the female body displays even further marvelous qualities that inspire reason for reverence.

One of those qualities is that the womb is not only a portal for new life, but a portal for spiritual wisdom. At age thirty-eight, after learning that women used to collectively bleed in moon lodges to bring through wisdom to guide their community, I experimented with attuning to my own bleeding time. Instead of resisting – and thereby cramping – I surrendered into the initially uncomfortable, thick energy pulling me down into my womb. Soon, the congestion eased, spread out and diffused through my body a warm, nourishing elixir that permeated me with a euphoric, dreamy state. I felt literally fed by my womb. It was a wondrous experience that imprinted on me permanently so that during each monthly blood flow I was physically, emotionally and spiritu-ally nourished and often rode the accompanying surges of inspiration and creativity by writing or visioning creative projects. Multiply that by billions, and we can sense the enormity of humanity's loss by dividing women from their bodies and from their collective womb-sourced visioning.

Centuries of shaming and demonizing women about menses and their innate pleasure-spiritual connection are part of the central strategy of patriarchal erasure of Woman.

SWEET AND LUSCIOUS GRAPES

The resolution of all the envy and control-based violence and suffering lies in surrendering to the fact that we all long for the nectar, for connection, for union, for the embrace of totality, of our innermost self, and that we cannot buy it, legislate it, imitate it or coerce it by forcing others to affirm an identity that denies the very source of what we long for.

We have established that the title of this essay is true, that all form in the Universe is the form of Woman. We have also shown that "identity" separates us from any chance to fulfill that longing to meet our innermost self. After all, identity insists on prescribing how it has to happen, by dishonoring the body, its implicit wisdom and, most of all, by violating the reality that the Universe is Her Form, that

In woman is the form of all things,
Of all that lives and moves in the world.

The Shakti-sangama continues, inviting us to realize in wonder that:

There is no jewel rarer than a woman,
no condition superior to that of a woman.
There is not, nor has been, nor will be
any destiny to equal that of a woman;

there is no kingdom, no wealth,
to be compared with a woman;
there is not, nor has been, nor will be
any holy place like unto a woman.
There is no prayer to equal a woman.
There is not, nor has been, nor will be
any yoga to compare with a woman,
no mystical formula nor asceticis
to match a woman.
There are not, nor have been, nor will be
any riches more valuable than woman.

---

[1] The Khajuraho Temple is one of twenty-two surviving temples of a group of eighty-five built between 900 and 1130 CE. The group of temples covers nine square miles in central India and is a UNESCO World Heritage Site.

[2] Women who have had a hysterectomy retain their womb's energetic imprint in their body.

[3] Shakti-sangama Tantra (II.52), a tantric text.

[4] Not to be confused with neo-tantra, popular in the West, which focuses on relationship and sexual intimacy skills.

[5] For purposes of this essay, I will limit my historical references to the great East Indian tradition of the Divine Mother, rooted in the Shakta wisdom of ancient matriarchal cultures of India.

[6] I use body and bodymind interchangeably in this essay. "Bodyknowing" references the unity of body and mind (knowing).

[7] Dogma: a principle or set of principles laid down by an authority as incontrovertibly true. A belief or set of beliefs that is accepted by the members of a group without being questioned or doubted.

[8] Emotions *are* sensations but I explicitly include emotions because repression of them is central to our afflictions. I want to elevate them to the level of carriers of intelligence and information that is true of them.

[9] The third eye is the pineal gland in the center of the brain which translates chemical information into inner vision. It is also known as "the eye of the womb," active in the visionary wisdom streams of menses and menopause.

[10] Tantra "maps" them at 72,000.

[11] The Dance refers solely to The Tantric Dance of Feminine Power® and not to the many derivatives nor to other practices with a similar name.

[12] Since there is neither performance nor resistance involved, we do not engage in jerky, shaking, broad-stroked or beat-driven movement.

[13] As quoted in *Passionate Enlightenment: Women in Tantric Buddhism*, Miranda Shaw, Princeton University Press, 1994, P. 140. In her related footnote, Shaw points out that "love" could also be translated as "desire" or "erotic attraction."

[14] Phrase originated by Deena Booth, aka Kamala, an adept of the practice (now deceased).

[15] See *Tantric Quest: An Encounter with Absolute Love*, Daniel Odier, Inner Traditions, 1997, p. 21.

[16] When I speak in this essay of trans narrative or trans agenda, I am referring to the political and societal actions of the trans activists. By no means do all trans-identified people fit into this aggressive, misogynist narrative. However they are ultimately harmed by it.

[17] The woman at whom this epithet was thrown by trans activist Andrea James (a trans woman), was Alice Dreger. See http://alicedreger.com/in_fear. The term "womb turd" is included now in the online Urban Dictionary.

[18] As of July 2016, this definition has not changed.

[19] See *Tantric Quest*, p. 21.

[20] See *Desire: The Tantric Path to Awakening,* Daniel Odier, Inner Traditions, 2001, p. 163.

[21] Personal conversation with Amarananda Bhairavan, author of *Kali's Odiyya: A Shaman's True Story of Initiation* and holder of the Oti Vidya lineage of Kerala, India.

[22] The similarities and differences of how this configured in cultures then versus in the modern trans narrative is a worthwhile investigation but beyond the scope of this essay.

[23] See *Kali: The Feminine Force*, Ajit Mookerjee, Destiny Books, 1998, p. 41.

[24] Vaishnavism is a major branch of Hinduism.

CHAPTER 48

———— ～ ————

RADICAL FEMALE EMBODIMENT AND
REPRODUCTION OF RESISTANCE

Mary Ceallaigh

To My Sisters
Who, in seeking answers for today and tomorrow
Might pause, look for the wisdom of women who've gone before - and remember.
To My Elders
Who, in having lived their best lives
Might surge, ignite the hearts of women in the words of these pages – and bless our way.

INTRODUCTION

IT IS NOT an over-estimation to call the journey of women's development and social liberation a "Heroine's Journey." When we confront the difficulty of undoing eight to ten thousand years of patriarchal empire's objective to ensure that women as a class forget that the human female of the species is the *source* and the *destination* of not only our bodies, but also the world's universal myths. This "forgetting" is not unintentional, and has served to separate woman from her body, from the power of her self-possession, and from her intimacy with the living land and natural laws. It has deeply established male-centered, domination-oriented culture upon women's bodies and the land itself and silenced the fact that 90% of human history was earth-based, mother-honoring, and more egalitarian.[1][2] "Homo sapiens" (in Latin, "wise persons") means anything but wise in an empire that uses and abuses everything in its path, seeking to control and manipulate the destinies of all vulnerable beings. Male supremacy is the social power structure all over the present industrial world - from the household level to the institutions of law, education, and medicine – glory in ritualizing human separation from the earth

550

and from our common origin: the body of the human female. This anti-female messaging starts happening even before birth and is imprinted heavily and in specific ways during and after birth, and in the enculturation of gender hierarchy and its sex-role stereotypes as "normal."

The misery called patriarchy, and its oppression of the natural world and its most vulnerable beings is reproducing itself, and it is doing so every moment of the day, in both external and internal ways. Systemic oppressions sexism, racism, and "biophobia"[3] among them are entangled with internalized oppression and a collective forgetting that hinders or obstructs feminist movements, and just seems to be getting worse. This source-hating, woman-hating culture has melted the Arctic and expedited social collapse. All the waterways on earth are now poisoned, as is the cultural river of life which streams toxic, male-catering porn culture 24/7 on every internet device, permeating mundane daily life and social interactions, to make the civilized world even more inhospitable to females and female reverence. The popular and patriarchal imagination of the cyborg based in the folly of industrial civilization's loathing and denial of the body and the Earth – is what remains in these conditions.[4]

Ironically, the constructs of the post-postmodernist "artificial futures" are touted as harbingers of radical progress and change. But in the reality of actual biology and a living planet, they are far more equivalent to late-night TV, having little to do with the ultimate and intimate processes of transmutation now occurring on the planet due to the disaster of the mad nuclear age and a global climate catastrophe that scientists say has no parallel in sixty-six million years.[5] [6] Currently, Greenland is losing about 8,300 tons of ice per second each day — ice that is melting on land as well as icebergs that are being discharged into Baffin Bay. This is a rapid, rapid mass loss that is just one of many related events that indicate a planetary emergency. The melted Arctic region is changing the Earth's gravity field so quickly that it is being observed via satellite.[7]

We have effectively entered an era for which there is no analogue.

This much is crystal-clear: Women who seek the fullest liberation and sustainable self-possession to meet these times have a map, and it is located within female embodiment its reproduction of resistance to social and ecological injustice and its creation of resilience. Indeed, as has been spoken, sung, and written by foremothers before us, there is no greater quest for women than to fully inhabit the power that is housed *within* our bodies, supported by the earth's gravity and our own gravitas capable of being very strategic, very tactical, and very fierce in defense of the defenseless, *and* in the dismantling of the oppressor.

WHAT ARE WE REPRODUCING?

From the biosphere level to the human cultural level, the life-death-life cycle is unleashing an uproar of change and keening ecological and social collapse on this earth – one that is strangely denied by many would-be activists focused instead on genderism/transgenderism, human supremacy, and individualism in a digital culture which deeply enshrines the unreal and unsustainable. The natural world of our one and only fertile planet is suffering greatly from geopolitical industrial domination. Devastatingly, in 2016 we see reports that there are less than one hundred orcas left in the Pacific Northwest and they are starving[8] [9] and a similar number of the iconic Mexican gray wolves on land[10]. Some 100-200 species a day are going extinct.[11] The magnificent ocean's coral colors are bleaching out in the Great Barrier Reef, never to return again.

Women's culture is being forgotten with great rapidity as high technology multiplies fantasy, and earth-based wisdom lineages have reached the point of being nearly wiped out. And so, female reproduction *in* patriarchy particularly at this late stage has a strong tendency to be the reproduction *of* patriarchy. A realistic, strategic assessment is necessary when we look at *how* we might multiply female power and bodily sovereignty as we meet what comes, *why* we might want to reproduce resistance, and *what* it is made of. This will lead us towards remembering matriarchal views of ourselves and our mothering power, but first we have to deconstruct and discern where we are and what we we've been taught to believe.

Women must frequently ask ourselves the sometimes uncomfortable and always enlightening question – both individually and as a class *what are we reproducing*? Of the women who are privileged enough to choose, women willingly conceive babies sometimes just because they feel like it, because they feel they should, or that they can. The most privileged women (those who are white-privileged, educated, affluent, and largely autonomous) may believe that creating a new human during the decline of this civilization and biosphere is morally and ethically sound because of a sense of family as a personal empire.

None of those reasons is a compelling argument for reproduction as a feminist act in conditions of class oppression. For those of who have the luxury to consider it, a feminist view of reproduction at this phase of planetary suffering might listen to the spoken word of women, the hushed stories, and the facts of life behind our oppression and ask *what* we're reproducing, *whose* power structure we're serving, and *how* we can effectively oppose this power structure in more strategic ways and higher numbers. Such questioning by the highly privileged among us (questioning which is, in itself, a form a privilege) steps outside our oppressed female socialization and wields powerful potentials for insight and vision. Though not very popular (in fact such questioning hardly ever happens in some female communities), this questioning is much needed if we are to multiply women's capacities for fighting back against sexual terrorism and structured oppression.

A recent article in *The Nation*, "How Do You Decide to Have a Baby When Climate Change Is Remaking Life on Earth?"[12] asks what more than a few environmentally empathic women asked themselves decades ago upon learning of the climate scientist reports in the early 1970s. These women have been grieving the dying ozone layer and the nightmares of patriarchal exploitation, genocide, and ecocide for a long time. It's a question that those of us privileged enough and/or insightful enough to discuss may find confronting or triggering – and in the individualism, identity politics, and materialism that provides a ready denial of reality and biology, it is easier not to think about it, and not to ask. However, just the facts as we know them, from a meta-analysis of our planetary plight, is that the future has already been stolen from the babies of many species. Human children of today are facing a global food crisis (wrought by industrial agriculture's wastelands combined with industrially-accelerated global warming's extreme weather effects on crops in the next few decades) and will see massive storms inundate coastal cities and the Great Plains turn to dust.[13]

Within an empire where the wild is held hostage, there is much misery being reproduced by male violence, the nuclear family disaster, social alienation, and emotional disconnection from the natural world. As Gerda Lerner has eloquently explained, female reproduction is now inseparable from capitalism.[14] Control of women's potential capacity for reproduction and sex(uality) has been commodified and politicized within what is now a global neo-patriarchal settlement.[15] If we care deeply about women (ourselves and other women as a class) there is new value to be found in seizing the means of our production – our bodies – from patriarchy and its internalized oppressions (i.e., betrayals among women as a barrier to a common language, shared power, and a feminist psychology of ethics).[16]

THE BODY POLITIC

"Be still," the men say. She continues to roar. "Why does she roar?" they ask. The roaring must be inside her, they conclude. They decide they must see the roaring inside her. They approach her in a group, six at her two front legs and six at her two back legs. They are trying to put her to sleep. She swings at one of the men. His own blood runs over him. "Why did she do that?" the men question. She has

no soul, they conclude, she does not know right from wrong. "Be still," they shout at her. "Be humble, trust us," they demand. "We have souls," they proclaim, "we know what is right," they approach her with their medicine, "for you." She does not understand this language. She devours them.

~ Susan Griffin, "The Lion in the Den of the Prophets," from
Woman And Nature[17]

Many ecofeminist and feminist spirituality writings in more recent decades originated from seeds planted by the feminist movement surge of the 1960s. This organic sensibility emerged within an exploration of the "embodied personal" or, a "body politic" highly relevant to the processes of revolution. Ecology, like the body, offers feminism an organic dimension by which to explore women's survival not as abstract "sisters in patriarchy," but as women addressing the concrete and visceral dimensions of social and ecological injustice.[18] Authentically feminist body politics contains a latent ecological sensibility that, in turn, invokes a "biological" dimension of social life, an ecological body that stands in direct relationship to the political, social world. Recognizing the interconnections between the body and the political and shifting our political discussions to include issues deemed "organic" or "embodied" reflects an implicit ecological impulse,[19] an affinity with the wild (or at least the feral) among women.

Gloria Steinem's famous pithy reply when questioned on why she refused to marry, was that she didn't "breed well" in captivity – a direct response to a fragmented culture which does everything it can to obstruct female self-possession. Indeed, mammalian breeding in captivity is highly dysfunctional, as seen by mammals in zoos, and in this culture's pathologizing of the human menstrual cycle, fertility, and birth and its many separation rituals performed on mothers and babies that imprint us with dissociation early, continued by the limiting the human child with gender and rewarding the sex-role stereotypes that perpetuate patriarchy. I think acknowledging this with empathetic sobriety, whether or not we have produced offspring, is really critical for a fuller-bodied feminist ethics.

A high degree of emotional embodiment is demanded to even be able to speak of our own shadows, as well as the intergenerational traumas and victim narratives passed down through our female lines that can obscure our birthright: new liberation stories. However, realistic assessment can and does unravel the patriarchal dictation of our destinies, encouraged by learning about the visionary foremothers and present-day women warriors of various kinds who've fought back in a variety of ways to thwart structured oppression. This includes doing their best to not reproduce children "in captivity," in order to multiply liberation in generation. These too, are our stories. These, too, are rich material for new women's narratives. Yet the childless woman's creative power is insultingly pathologized in patriarchal metaphors such as "barren, wasted land, or infertile" because defining and manipulating women's fertility is a divine right accorded to the dominant culture, its priestly male "experts" and their female accomplices. Patriarchy is a realm wherein the private lived experiences of "childless" women are considered matters for priestly discussion, and where it is projected by men that no woman could possibly want or welcome a life without genetic reproduction. In the last decade we've seen this become the booming business of high tech womb trafficking (aka "surrogacy"). How many trafficked "surrogate" mothers have ended up living out the rest of their lives in poverty or navigating various other severities in contrast to the trust-fund owning or ivy league track commmodified child that they gave life to? We will never know, but feminists are fighting for the criminalization of demand for surrogacy for this reason and more.[20]

When looking at woman from an absolute level, *no* woman is infertile, no woman is barren: women are pregnant all the time with their own power. We gestate and give birth to human beings as well as to insight, healing, wisdom, and leadership, Our collective action of self-care and female solidarity (our greatest weapon) is the practice of dismantling patriarchy both internally and externally, whether or not we have genetic offspring and in fact regardless of what form our "babies" take (such as gardens, students, business enterprises, artistic expression, community organizing, breakthrough inventions, and basically anything we can conceive of). The more women are willing to embrace highly-nuanced reflection on the patriarchal institution of motherhood, the more we are capable of powerful and real mothering: towards our children, all children, all beings, the living land that supports us, and in organized opposition to the hierarchical domination that haunts our lives. We are much more than physical reproduction of the power structure, but patriarchy doesn't want us to know that.

FEMALE-BODIED, RED-BLOODED

The figure of Great Goddess is not limited to the child bearer; as the Triple goddess she is also the youthful, wild, autonomous goddess, the Amazon, and the old, wise goddess, the master of art, philosophy, and all inventions.

~ DR. HEIDE GOTTNER-ABENDROTH[21]

Having recently become an official half-century woman of fifty years old, I've been reflecting on the self-healing journey I embarked on during college. The journey could be said to have begun with experimenting with taking radical analysis of social and political feminism into a lifelong practice of reconnecting body with mind, and reclaiming menstrual health and cycle wisdom long abandoned by Western industrialism. During my years of midwifery apprenticeships in my twenties and thirties, I assisted three different childless midwives along the way, women who helped other women transformational journeys of birth, breastfeeding, and newborn care. These midwives, who'd survived girlhood as a bleeding female in a "man's world," and had sought and learned from women's traditions and brought a female-bodied compassion and passion to their work with women. They also brought an ability to bear witness to women's realities with a presence unhindered by personal birth templates or stories that can significantly limit some care providers' service of laboring women. This offered me a unique vantage point on socially constructed motherhood and physiological mothering, and the biological femaleness that healthy women of varying reproductive statuses share: the uterine-heart connection (which remains in a "phantom" form with neural pathways even in cases of hysterectomy), the intuitive guidance system of glandular health (the pituitary-hypothalmic-ovarian axis) the tingling milk ducts of both childless women and grandmothers in postpartum retreat settings when an infant's urgent wail starts to rise for a feeding, and the ancestral songs that emerge out of our beings when we get in the flow of a soulful song for ourselves or those we care for.

Biological childlessness in a female is a realm of blood-rich and transformation-heavy experience that – when connected to emotional and spiritual solidarities, can offer a deep facilitation of women's ever-changing journeys of body and mind that no male can ever come close to. Men can't understand what it's like to be women because they are not female. However, through empathy, women – who are females have traveled through countless menstrual cycling realities and can indeed analyze and embody the ecology of being female within themselves and in facilitation of other women - and do so even when we weren't taught how by the culture at large or by our own female relatives. Such is the Heroine's Journey.

Female-centered worldviews defy male-centered limitations of the female body, and strike terror in the hearts of most men in a culture that continually seeks to control the female experience by extracting emotional, sexual, and reproductive labor from women and perpetuating vicious cycles of abuse and victimization. However, our courage builds as we remember what Simone Weil did when she wrote: "One should identify oneself with the universe itself.

Everything that is less than the universe is subjected to suffering..."[22] Even further into this understanding is the fact that the human body is composed of atoms, which are themselves mostly space. Technically and cosmically, there's no difference between inner space and outer space when it comes to embodiment – they are continuously in relationship.

In also takes courage to confront our internalized oppression the self-limiting identifying of ego with sex-role stereotypes, and that frequently and falsely polarize women into "mothers" and "non-mothers" in order to, as Joan C. Chisler, PhD, writes of in the anthology *From Menarche to Menopause: The Female Body in Feminist Therapy,* displace our shared experience of the two things *all* female humans experience: menarche and menopause. And with this, the floating anxieties we all share around the fact that we *could* experience other things at various points in our lives (like sexism, ageism, racial profiling and additional misogyny if we are women of color, miscarriage, stillbirth/perinatal loss, obstetric violence, postnatal depression, male pattern sexual harassment and/or rape, unwanted pregnancy, abandonment by partners, socially unsupported female economic struggle, the list goes on...) that also contribute to our potential solidarity as women[23] This, right here, is where the roots-oriented (radical) analysis of authentic feminism is so very powerful in forging a framework for understanding the false power structure that surrounds us and its sex-based oppressions that run through all female lives. It is the *being* female that is the key point of unity amidst so much diversity – at least as an overview. Patriarchy doesn't want women to be complex to this degree, nor to wield radical analysis in a biologically coherent way.

Doing so "radically" down to the roots, is a daily practice, a course of action from *within the female body* - not an external "identity." We begin by not changing the world, but by re-assessing ourselves, as Germaine Greer so thoroughly emboldened women to do by exposing the male denaturing of "woman," in her epic book The Female Eunuch.[24] Through dedicated feminist effort (and with self-compassion) we correct our mis-educations and learn through practice to re-embody ourselves. This helps us forge authentic compassion for other females of all species, and free ourselves from the bondage of man-made, manufactured choice. This leaves us with more options for creating matriarchally-rooted, biology-loving, informed choice in our present life journeys. We come to understand what the artificial, non-feminism of "male-stream" culture works so hard to obscure. With practice we can resist both the comfort of silence and the distress of *listening to what our bodies have to say about the truth of our experience.* Because, despite all this, no one knows us like our bodies know us, and if the body keeps the score on all our female trauma, returning *to* the body is a radical act par excellence.[25]

After all, we've all got scars just from having had a girlhood in patriarchy, the stuff that makes women warriors - especially multiply oppressed women, having sustained simultaneous battles in diverse terrains with a spiritual tenacity that only other multiply oppressed women can ever come close to knowing.

We have lost some of our mothers forever to this silence. We have found hatred in the mother for the daughter and in the daughter for the mother. Parts of our mothers are lost to us, our mothers come back to us dismembered, we have lost ourselves or parts of ourselves. We must let our voices live within us... we survive by hearing.

~ Susan Griffin[26]

Women have never been accorded human dignity and sexual ownership of their bodies.

~ Sheila Jeffreys[27]

We must resist the male effort to determine form (and name and claim all life for itself), which always ends with dissolving that form at will, in some combination of (nuclear) warfare, biophobia, and misogyny. The devaluation of female bodies is deeply entangled within neo-patriarchal culture. This devaluation powerfully influences the practice of medicine, the science that supports it, and our own beliefs about the power – or lack of power – within our bodies. In turn, these beliefs affect our female biology (i.e., the neurons that fire together, wire together) and what we believe can shape our experience. Without meaning to undermine any individual's positive experience, it can't be over-emphasized how transformational it can be to trust the wisdom coming from Mother Nature's millions of years of experimentation much more than the sixty-five years of biochemical wizardry from Father Pharmaceutical.[28]

In matriarchal spirituality, we concentrate on fostering the full development of inner power what Starhawk calls the "power from within" and vitality and joy of life. "Power from within" is the power women have to act without dominating others or allowing themselves to be dominated."[29] In other words, an autonomous feminist perspective, made "womanifest" through female sacred biology: embodiment and womancraft.[30]

A WOMAN'S PLACE IS... IN HER BODY

Your beliefs and thoughts are wired into your biology. They become your cells, tissues, and organs. There's no supplement, no diet, no medicine, and no exercise regimen that can compare with the power of your thoughts and beliefs. That's the very first place you need to look when anything goes wrong with your body.

~ CHRISTIANE NORTHRUP, MD[31]

What does female embodiment look like? What does it strengthen in a woman? And what does it mean for a woman to be embodied, sourced in her own power, when confronting the power structure at the crossroads of cataclysmic ecocide?

Radical female embodiment deeply knows that "a woman's place" is in her body, a body that, if lovingly returned to, speaks the truth of our experiences of navigating the sexual terrorism of men with the bondage of internalized oppression, giving us signs and symptoms to guide a radical self-care and remembering of all that's been lost by our mis-education. Radical embodiment in females is revolutionary and full-capacity (whether or not one has offspring). In anchors female liberation deep in the bodymind, undoing knots of trauma and colonization, and is an ideal prerequisite for reproduction of any kind.

Having safe spaces in which to learn how to be at home in our bodies, reclaim our sovereignty, practice daily self-care, know how to self-heal a variety of bodily conditions, and learn all levels of self-defense skills – many if not all these things are appealing to girls and women, though rarely accessible in full. Our feminist foremothers of several decades back made impressive efforts in articulating the need for women's centers, where females who'd survived girlhood could gather for a variety of resources and trainings that in turn effectively reproduce women's liberation rather than feminine gendering. Many of them had discovered that the word "feminine" is derived from the Latin *fe* meaning "faith", and *mina* meaning "less" - that somehow woman by definition has less faith; less than whom? Those church fathers who coined the word "feminine" to explain a host of female complaints and symptoms. Religious institutions as well as gynecologist offices have been churches wherein initiation, confession, sacrament, and sometimes sexual abuse take place.[32] Somewhere deep inside many women – and even those who long for feminist liberation is an apology for our very existence, as if the "original sin" of being born female is not redeemable by works, and as if women have less faith in the ability to heal ourselves.[33]

Women have been socialized to have less faith in ourselves and more faith in the experts – but who is a better expert about our bodies than ourselves? The abandonment and dishonoring of the body and its powers is an ontologically (developmentally) disastrous error. In her brilliant and heartfelt essay "The Woman I Love Is A Planet," Paula Gunn Allen writes that our bodies are the most precious "talismans" connecting us to the Earth: "Walking in balance, in harmony, and in a sacred manner requires staying in your body, accepting its discomforts, decayings, witherings, and blossomings – and respecting them."[34] In other words, one of the most politically radical and effective things that any of us can do is respect our bodies – and the bodies of others – in all of their biological manifestations and transformations. This includes respecting the gifts of aging, times of fatness and times of leanness, hairiness and baldness, female hardness, male softness, bodily waste-making, and even our sickness, and inevitable death.[35]

"Radical embodiment – the soul totally in the body – is the most exquisite experience available on Earth. The integrity of a woman with an open heart is always astounding."

~ CHRISTIANE NORTHRUP, MD[36]

The ground of female embodiment is a sacred one: a bleeding ground, inherently transformative. Only women bleed for reasons of normal physiology. Our bodies speak a language fluent with the truth of our experiences – the interpretation of which has largely been lost, but reclaimed in some realms of feminist inquiry and practice, particularly when our mutual destiny with the earth is fully understood. Bleeding grounds us. We are reminded, in all our humility, of our connection to this planet and our subsequent return to her womb. There is no time to waste. Women will show the way to love and defend this Earth; we know the balancing of life and death, growing and letting go.[37] And so we come to understand that reciprocity is necessary, that radical embodiment is not without sacrifice. The word "sacrifice" comes from *sacer*, meaning "sacred," "holy," and *facere* meaning "to make," "to do." Sacrifice makes something holy, and creative revolt is costly – but not as costly as compliance with a totalitarianism that is terrorizing the natural world, dismissing biology, and stealing the future of the babies of all species. The intrepid Brazilian liberation theologian Ivone Gebara – despite being "silenced" by the Vatican – wrote that women have to resist silence, that women have to speak up, to cry out like Susanna in the Old Testament, who spoke out against the elders even though she knew she would not be believed, and that it could cost her her life.[38]

It's no secret that we are stronger and more resilient than we may think - as patriarchy works incessantly to deny, through its lies and false mythologies. The campaign to erase women's physiological bodily powers and displace our blood mysteries has become distinctly dystopic and absurdly religious in its high tech fervor. Yet women's embodied capacity to give life to ourselves is a spiritual and mental agility - as so well sung by liberationist African American jazz singer Abbey Lincoln when she intones "walk like a lion and soar like an eagle."[39] When a woman truly comes home to herself, she re-gathers and re-members the parts of herself that were humiliated, denied, or stolen one way or another, and in the process multiplies a vital force of increasing inner peace and sovereign joy– regardless of circumstances and also determined to see circumstances change.

"Falling in love with life itself, whatever form it takes, is an experience so powerful that I've known it to cause even women who were well past menopause to start getting their periods again."

~ CHRISTIANE NORTHRUP, MD [40]

Women come home to the awareness of their bodies with many stories of sex-based injustices and serious violations, along with coping devices of artificial/gendered, male-catering identities that may run their lives for quite some time even after having navigated to safe relationships and spaces for self-discovery (which for many women means having female-only spaces). Our bodies *are* our selves in ways that reflect both our collective oppression and self-care liberation. Our bodies' messages and illness are wake-up calls in the language that best speaks through our particular mental and emotional barriers and to the issues we need to change in our lives. The wisdom of this language is very precise.[41] Once self-reverence is self-evident, we find that narratives of victimization and re-traumatization shift as if by natural law – and the more that self-hatred begins to evaporate.[42]

The work of deeply rooted embodiment gives a capacity to multiply joyful struggle. In the material conditions of surviving the war being waged against girls and women, we must not only reclaim our wholeness, we must learn how to defend ourselves with our whole heart, knowing that no one can steal our joy. Doing so, our inner lives are changed, our bodies befriended, and the capacity for social change becomes fierce, involving the decolonizing of delusions: human supremacy, white supremacy, and male supremacy.[43]

Closing

We can't keep sticking together women who have been broken into little pieces. Fighting back is as close to healing as we are going to come. It is important to understand that we will live with a fair amount of pain for most of our lives. If your first priority is to live a painless life, you will not be able to help yourself or other women. What matters is to be a warrior. Having a sense of honor about political power is healing. Discipline is necessary. Actions against men who hurt women must be real. We need to win. We are in a war. We need a political resistance. We need it above ground. We need it with our lawmakers. With our government officials. We need it with our professional women. We need it above ground. We need it underground too.[44]

~ Andrea Dworkin

We need feminist militancy on behalf of girls, women, all children, and all beings. Woman's revolution must entail the correction of false perspectives and assumptions about womanhood, sex, love, and society because what is at stake is a living plant and the liberation of women. The necessary challenge we all face is to reclaim our personal and community will to live in our sacred duty, to radically embody our female force.[45] It's not a question of telling women what to do next, or even what to want to do next – because the female, being a universal force, is no one's student: she is at the center of things, she teaches herself, and aligns with those whom she teaches with. This article was written in the hope that women will further remember a force forward, around, and through the trap of patriarchy. Once that happens, women will know how and what they plan to do with their "one wild and precious life"[46] because the force of our foremothers is with us. Hopefully these words are in service of the subversive and regenerative.

May we cherish ourselves as if we already live in a world safe for women in a matrifocal culture guided by the wisdom of wise elder women. May we long for, seek, and find the wise woman within. May we celebrate the precious and rare elder female mentors and healers in our lives while they are still with us in old age: elder women/womyn/wimmin/wims who continue to live their lives as an "ovamony"[47] of female resistance and share with us the gift of age. May all ages of women privileged enough to read feminist articles and lead various struggles in various places fight for informed choice, and also for "informed desire." May our understanding be expanded by an appreciation of women's herstory, roots-oriented analysis, and the essential ethics that can provide a compass for finding our way forward. May we navigate with alert, open eyes. May we fight strategically from the heart's love for life, and may we find ourselves response-able to our planetary and cultural crises with deeply rooted embodiment.[48]

> *I know I am made from this earth, as my mother's hands were made from this earth, as her dreams came from this earth and all that I know, I know in this earth, the body of the bird, this pen, this paper, these hands, this tongue speaking, all that I know speaks to me through this earth and I long to tell you, you who are earth too, and listen as we speak to each other of what we know:* **the light is in us**.[49]

~ SUSAN GRIFFIN

---

[1] Maureen Murdock, *The Heroine's Journey.* (Boston, MA: Shambhala, 1990).

[2] E. Pennisi, "Our Egalitarian Eden," *Science* 344, no. 6186 (May 23, 2014): 824–25, doi:10.1126/science.344.6186.824.

[3] The word "Biophobia" was coined by David W. Orr to mean "aversion to nature, discomfort in natural places," in the chapter "Love It or Lose It: The Coming Biophilia Revolution" in *Earth In Mind.* (Washington, DC: Island Press, 1994).

[4] Jane Caputi, *Gossips, Gorgons & Crones: The Fates of the Earth* (Santa Fe, NM: Bear & Co. Pub, 1993), p. 254.

[5] Ibid, p. 255.

[6] "What We're Doing to the Earth Has No Parallel in 66 Million Years, Scientists Say," Chris Mooney, *The Washington Post*, 3/21/ 2016, https://www.washingtonpost.com/news/energy-environment/wp/2016/03/21/what-were-doing-to-the-earth-has-no-parallel-in-66-million-years-scientists-say/.

[7] "Melting Greenland Ice Changing Earth's Gravity," CBC News, 2/8/2016, http://www.cbc.ca/news/canada/north/melting-greenland-ice-changing-ocean-circulation-earth-s-gravitational-field-1.3437904.

[8] National Oceanic and Atmospheric Administration of the U.S. Government, Species in the Spotlight: Southern Resident Killer Whale http://www.fisheries.noaa.gov/stories/2015/06/spotlight_srkw.html

[9] "The Orcas Are Starving" by David Niewart, Crosscut News, 6/24/2016 http://crosscut.com/2016/06/the-orcas-are-starving/

[10] Center For Biological Diversity, Saving The Mexican Gray Wolf, Key Documents Page http://www.biologicaldiversity.org/species/mammals/Mexican_gray_wolf

[11] The U.N. Environment Programme reports that scientists estimate that 150-*200 species* of plant, insect, bird and mammal become *extinct* every 24 hours. This is nearly 1,000 times the "natural" or "background" rate. 99% of currently threatened species are at risk from human activities. *Encyclopædia Britannica, Endangered Species. 2009.* http://www.britannica.com/EBchecked/topic/186738/endangered-species

[12] Madeline Ostrander, "How Do You Decide to Have a Baby When Climate Change Is Remaking Life on Earth?" *The Nation*, March 24, 2016, http://www.thenation.com/article/how-do-you-decide-to-have-a-baby-when-climate-change-is-remaking-life-on-earth/.

[13] "The Coming Food Crisis and What To Do About It," Greg Laden's Blog, April 13, 2015, http://scienceblogs.com/gregladen/2015/04/13/the-coming-food-crisis-and-what-to-do-about-it/.

[14] Gerda Lerner, *The Creation of Patriarchy* (Women and History, Vol. 1) (New York: Oxford Univ. Press, 1986).

[15] Beatrix Campbell, "Why We Need a New Women's Revolution | Beatrix Campbell," *The Guardian*, May 25, 2014, http://www.theguardian.com/commentisfree/2014/may/25/we-need-new-womens-revolution.

[16] For more on the subject of inter-feminist ethics, see the paper by Karen *Fite* and Nikola *Trumbo*, "*Betrayals among Women: Barriers to a Common Language*," Lesbian Ethics 1 (Fall 1984). Also see the last chapter of Phyllis Chesler's *Woman's Inhumanity to Woman* entitled "A Feminist Psychology of Ethics" Chicago Review Press, IL, 2009.

[17] *Woman And Nature: The Roaring Inside Her.* Griffin, Susan. Harper & Row: New York, NY. 1978.

[18] Chaia Heller, *Ecology Of Everyday Life: Rethinking The Desire For Nature.* Black Rose Books: Tonawanda, NY. 1999. p. 40.

[19] Ibid, p. 42.

[20] "All Surrogacy is Exploitation – the world should follow Sweden's ban." by Kajsa Ekis Ekman, The Guardian, 2/25/2016 https://www.theguardian.com/commentisfree/2016/feb/25/surrogacy-sweden-ban

[21] Heide Göttner-Abendroth, *The Dancing Goddess: Principles of a Matriarchal Aesthetic*, 1st English edition, Beacon Press, Boston, MA, 1991, p. 224.

[22] Simone Weil, *Notebooks, (Vols. 1 and 2),* Putnam Books, New York, NY, 1956

[23] Joan C. Chrisler, ed., *From Menarche to Menopause: The Female Body in Feminist Therapy* Routledge, New York, NY, 2011

[24] Greer, Germaine, The Female Eunuch, Book Club Associates, London. 1973. p. 14.

[25] Bessel A. Van der Kolk, *The Body Keeps the Score: Brain, Mind, and Body in the Healing of Trauma* (New York: Viking, 2014).

[26] Griffin, p. 202.

[27] Sheila Jeffreys, in interview on ABC Radio Australia: Asia Pacific "Call for prostitution in Australia to be totally illegal." October 17, 2011. Transcript available at Resources Prostitution: https://ressourcesprostitution.wordpress.com/2014/06/24/sheila-jeffreys-vs-the-pimp-government-of-australia/

[28] Christiane Northrup, M.D., *The Wisdom of Menopause: Creating Physical and Emotional Health during the Change*, (New York: Bantam Books, 2012), p. 141.

[29] Ibid, p. 220.

[30] I first heard the noun 'womancraft' and the verb 'womanifest' via my primary midwifery teacher, Jeannine Parvati (1945-2005). She was bicultural Ute First Nations and Jewish, a published author and public speaker who loved wordsmithing as well as etymology, especially within the framework of reclaiming women's realities from patriarchal colonization. She agreed with Chomsky that 'language is power' with the added emphasis of further defining that power as the truth of Female Source, female body as regenerative first earth, and the earth as everyone's planetary mother in the cosmos.

[31] Christiane Northrup, M.D., *Goddesses Never Age: The Secret Prescription for Radiance, Vitality, and Well-Being* (Carlsbad, California: Hay House, Inc., 2015).

[32] Malleus Maleficarum (The "Witch Hammer" treatise on the prosecution of witches, written in 1486 by Heinrich Kramer, a German Catholic clergyman submitted to the University of Cologne on May 9th, 1487 and used by the Church to harass and silence noncompliant females). Part I, Question VI, fourth paragraph from the end: "And it is clear in the case of the first woman that she had little faith; for when the serpent asked why they did not eat of every tree in Paradise, she answered: Of every tree, etc. - lest perchance we die. Thereby she showed that she doubted, and had little in the word of God. And all this is indicated by the etymology of the word; for *Femina* comes from *Fe* and *Minus*, since she is ever weaker to hold and preserve the faith. And this as regards faith is of her very nature; although both by grace and nature faith never failed in the Blessed Virgin, even at the time of Christ's Passion, when it failed in all men." http://www.sacred-texts.com/pag/mm/mm01_06a.htm

[33] Jeannine Parvati, *Hygieia: A Woman's Herbal*, 19[Th] edition, Pan American Books. 1994. p. 88.

[34] Paula Gunn Allen essay in *This Sacred Earth: Religion, Nature and Environment*. Edited by Roger S. Gottlieb. Routledge Books, New York, NY. 1996, p. 364.

[35] Christiane Northrup MD, *Women's Bodies, Women's Wisdom: Creating Physical And Emotional Health And Healing*, Bantam Books, New York, NY, 201, pp. 4-5.

[36] Christiane Northrup MD, *The Wisdom of Menopause*. Bantam Books, New York, NY. 2001. p. 455.

[37] Parvati, p.10.

[38] China Galland, *The Bond Between Women: A Journey to Fierce Compassion*, Riverhead Books, New York, NY. 1998. Pg. xiv

[39] Abbey Lincoln, Turtle's Dream album. Song entitled "Turtle's Dream." Polygram Records, 1995.

[40] Northrup, M.D., The Wisdom of Menopause. p. 265.

[41] Ibid. p. 20.

[42] As practiced in the internal observations of the silent sitting meditation called 'vipassana,' ('seeing reality-as-it-is') a focused and systematic inner exploration of the physical body with the natural breath, and training the mind to recognize constant change and the deep flow of life and natural law. Taught via non-sectarian, donation-based, 10-day silent retreats completely staffed by trained volunteers and offered at centers that have sex-segregated housing, dining, and hall seating. I have attended five of these retreats and served as a female student coordinator. https://www.dhamma.org/en-US/index

[43] "The Psychology of Supremacism: Whether White, Male or Human." by Darcia Narvaez, Professor of Psychology at the University of Notre Dame, *Psychology Today*, 1/24/2016

https://www.psychologytoday.com/blog/moral-landscapes/201601/the-psychology-supremacism-whether-white-male-or-human

[44] From American radical feminist Andrea Dworkin's keynote speech at the Canadian Mental Health Association's "Women and Mental Health Conference Women In a Violent Society," held in Banff, Alberta, May 1991. http://www.nostatusquo.com/ACLU/dworkin/TerrorTortureandResistance.html

[45] Germaine Greer, The Female Eunuch, Book Club Associates, London. 1973. pp.18-19.

[46] From Mary Oliver's Poem 133, "The Summer Day".

[47] A female embodied alternative to the word "testimony" that derives from "testes".

[48] Chaia Heller, *Ecology Of Everyday Life: Rethinking The Desire For Nature.* Black Rose Books: Tonawanda, NY, 1999, p. 9.

[49] Griffin, Pg. 227.

CHAPTER 49

YES ALL WOMEN

Sara St. Martin Lynne

SOMETIMES I WORRY that I will run out of words. That there are only so many ways to say, "There is a war on women and girls. If you refuse to acknowledge that, you are on the opposing side. Period. The end."

There was no way to avoid the news that a young man who was full of entitlement and unbridled misogyny went on a killing spree last weekend. And while not every man who kills or harms women has a chilling 140-page manifesto or a YouTube channel, we know that this kind of thing happens all too frequently. Multiple women and girls are killed or seriously harmed every day because a man or boy somewhere believes that she owes him access to her body. We are inundated with these stories. A teenage girl was stabbed in the face for declining an invitation to the prom, 236 girls were kidnapped from school and sold for sex, and two sisters were raped and hung from a tree in India. Witness the shaming and cyberbullying of Alyssa Funke, her subsequent suicide, and the mockery that continued after she took her own life. In Pakistan, pregnant Farzana Parveen was surrounded by a mob of thirty men, led by her father and brothers, and was bludgeoned to death in an "honor killing."

These are all just stories from recent weeks, some as recent as yesterday. These are the stories that break through and become "news" as opposed to the more ordinary rapes, deaths, abuses and cyberattacks that are never brought to our attention. What was most appalling (though not surprising) to me and multitudes of other women was the response of so many men claiming that Eliot Rodger was a victim who avenged himself and thereby became a hero. "If only some woman would have blown this guy, those people would still be alive." The only blessing here is that for a moment many women (some for the first time ever) acknowledged the flesh-and-bones experience of misogyny. I have been inspired, enraged and brought to tears by the voices that have been raised in the outcry of Yes All Women. Story after story, account after account, women are speaking. I've not been able to step in. I've been sitting in deep sadness and troubled reflection about the number of girls and women in my life alone who have died or are survivors of the war against females, myself included. My heart is too full, my chest is too heavy, my eyes too red and dry to think in 140-character articulations. I've been wishing that I could. I've been struck by a fear that by the time I actually process my thoughts and feelings and transmit them that the phenomena of women affirming this very important truth of our lives will have evaporated into the thin air of our collective twenty-four-hour attention span and that the room will have gone quiet, that I will have been too late, and that I will stand alone. I've been thinking about our bodies, about our psyches, our spirits. I've been thinking of blood, words, weapons and terror. I've been thinking about commercials and pop songs. I've been thinking about pornography, diet pills and plastic surgery. I've been thinking about what a dick Judd Apatow has been to Ann Hornaday. I've been thinking about smartphones and frat parties. I've been thinking about how women are perceived to lose dimension and become invisible as we age. I've been thinking about the message – the relentless message that women and girls are not our own, ever.

I woke up yesterday morning thinking about the biblical matriarch Rachel, "who would not be consoled for the loss of her children." There are a few biblical passages that I still know but that is one that landed in me as a young girl and tucked itself away. The first time I heard it something inside of me said, "listen to this story and remember." I have carried in me this image of a woman who refused to stop wailing about the murder of countless newborn babies. It was stirring to me and it felt like a protest of some sort, even before I had the language or experience to comprehend that concept. I understand that women don't hold a patent on grief, but no one will ever convince me that women and girls do not shoulder and mourn the destruction of all patriarchal violence acutely, devastatingly and in a way that is completely exclusive to women and girls. We have the authority to speak about that devastation because that is something that *all women and girls* know, including the ancient Rachel.

And so I've been holding vigil over our dead. Privately. Solemnly. And I've been thinking about and being amazed at the ways in which we survive. The way we rally and the power (and resistance) that comes from women naming the violence that is carried out against us by men and what happens when we witness it for one another. Like most people, I know more women who have survived some sort of complex psychological, physical or sexual violence in their lifetimes than those who have not. But I'm not just taking into account the adult women that I know who have found a way to talk about this. I'm very much thinking about the girls I grew up with. I'm thinking about that moment of shared revelation that we were being hunted, that the bounty on us was real and how the air around us began to smell like fear and watchfulness, and how eventually we stopped noticing it. I'm thinking about the rumors of "slutty" girls at school, the shame of girls whose rape stories were paraded around like victory marches for boys and cautionary tales for girls, I'm remembering the resignation and frustration of some of the adult women in my life, the stories they would only tell each other when they were sure that we weren't listening. I'm thinking about the suicides, the depression, the addictions, the hopelessness, the poverty, the PTSD, the rage. I'm thinking about the things that are witnessed, not spoken. I'm thinking of how rarely these things get spoken.

I'm thinking about a ten-year-old girl who told me last summer that "she just wants to be a girl, she doesn't want to have to think about rape and all that scary stuff." She is ten years old. She is already navigating an awareness and fear that the sacredness of her young, strong, girl body is subject to being taken against her will and that she may be powerless to stop it. The awareness of this danger will never leave her, though I can't help but wonder if her consciousness of it will. How long will she lament this? How long before she stops protesting that fear and it just becomes part of the air that she breathes with the rest of us? Hers was not a political statement out of the mouth of an "angry feminist," not a status update, or a meme floating by in your news feed. There was no hashtag attached to that moment. This was a ten-year-old girl, a child, sitting on a bench in the sun talking about rape. It's time to listen up. It's time to step up, sharpen the blades, and protect our young. It's time to evoke the ancient Rachel and refuse to shut the fuck up – refuse to be comforted into silence. In fact, I'm thinking it's time to make a sound so deafeningly loud that it gets inscribed in our own holy texts.

Republished with permission from http://fishwithoutabicycle.com/yesallwomen

A CREED FOR FREE WOMEN
Elsa Gidlow

I am.
I am from and of The Mother.
I am as I am.
Willfully harming none, none may question me.

As no free-growing tree serves another or requires to be served,
As no lion or lamb or mouse is bound or binds,
No plant or blade of grass nor ocean fish,
So I am not here to serve or be served.
I am Child of every Mother,
Mother of each daughter,
Sister of every woman,
And lover of whom I choose or chooses me.

Together or alone we dance Her Dance,
We do the work of The Mother,
She we have called Goddess for human comprehension,
She, the Source, never-to-be-grasped Mystery,
Terrible Cauldron, Womb,
Spinning out of her the unimaginably small
And the immeasurably vast –
Galaxies, worlds, flaming suns—
And our Earth, fertile with her beneficence,
Here, offering tenderest flowers.
(Yet flowers whose roots may split rock.)
I, we, Mothers, Sisters, Lovers,
Infinitely small out of her vastness,
Yet our roots too may split rock,
Rock of the rigid, the oppressive
In human affairs.

Thus is She
And being of Her
Thus am I.
Powered by Her,
As she gives, I may give,
Even of the blood and breath:
But none may require it;
And none may question me.

I am.
I am That I am.

Elsa Gidlow, "A Creed For Free Women" in Sapphic Songs, Druid Heights Books, 1982. Republished with permission from her estate.

For Anthology Endnotes, Suggested Readings, Resources, and Blogs

WWW.FEMALEERASURERESOURCES.ORG

This website provides the sources cited in this anthology and updated resources related to the topics of female erasure, gender identity politics, violence against women, and more. You are invited to help educate, share resources and articles on these topics by submitting them to the website.

The power to know, to will, to dare, is the power to make change.

About the Anthology Editor

Ruth Barrett, anthology editor and contributor, has dedicated her life to stopping gender oppression and providing safe, sacred, female-sovereign spaces for women and girls. She is an ordained elder priestess, ritualist, and teacher of the Dianic tradition.

Barrett graduated from the University of California at Santa Cruz with a degree in folklore. She went on to co-found the Temple of Diana, Inc., a nationally recognized Dianic temple, with her life partner, Falcon River.

Barrett received the L.A.C.E. Award for outstanding contributions in the area of spirituality from the Gay and Lesbian Center in Los Angeles. She has written *Women's Rites, Women's Mysteries: Intuitive Ritual Creation*, and she has contributed to multiple anthologies about women's spirituality.

Barrett is also a goddess-centered folk musician, mountain dulcimer artist, and singer. She received the Jane Schliessman Award for outstanding contributions to women's music. She directed the Candlelight Concert at the Michigan Womyn's Music Festival for twenty-two years.

ABOUT THE CONTRIBUTORS

(In alphabetical order)

Lane Anderson (pseudonym) is a practicing psychotherapist who has worked extensively with "trans teens" and their families. She shares with us her clinical insights into her clients, adolescent psychology, and the impact of the transgender phenomenon on our society as a whole.

Joan F. Archive (pseudonym) is a women's studies professor and writer whose work addresses the history of women's struggle for education and legal equality.

Temple Ardinger is a bisexual feminist witch. She is active in protecting female sovereign space and women's right to discuss and name our experience of womanhood. She shares the story of her journey from "daddy's girl" to "neighbor boy" and how finding her connection to Goddess and working within women-only circles helped heal those wounds.

Monica Asencio is a Mexican American environmental feminist, a radical homesteader, and co-parent of two teenage daughters, who were ages one and four when they came into her life. She co-owns a landscape company with her life partner that specializes in helping people grow their own food organically and cultivate for themselves a feeling of connectedness - where their life, and their time, means something real and important.

Ruth Barrett is spiritual feminist clergy (ordained elder Priestess), seasoned ritualist, and educator in the Dianic tradition where the Goddess and the female body is the central religious metaphor. Rituals exclusively celebrate the female life cycle and support healing and liberation from gender oppression. She is also an award winning pioneering goddess-centered musician/ singer and author of *Women's Rites, Women's Mysteries – Intuitive Ritual Creation* (Llewellyn, 2007), and has contributed to several anthologies, including *Foremothers Of The Women's*

Spirituality Movement: Elders and Visionaries (Taneo Press, 2015). Ruth has provided rituals, classes, and conferences held in sacred female-sovereign spaces for women and girls for four decades. www.guardiansofthegrove.org and www.dancingtreemusic.com.

Miriam Ben-Shalom began serving in the 84th U.S. Army Reserves Training Division in 1974, and became one of the first two female drill sergeants in the division. After publicly expressed her sexual identity as a lesbian, Ben-Shalom was subsequently discharged from the Army Reserves. Her suit for reinstatement was heard by the U.S. District Court in Chicago, that ruled Ben-Shalom's discharge violated the First, Fifth, and Ninth Amendments of the Constitution. The U.S. Army appealed the decision, then withdrew its appeal and simply refused to comply with the order. In 1987, the U.S. Court of Appeals in Chicago supported the lower court's ruling, and in September 1988 Ben-Shalom was reinstated. The Army appealed the decision and in August 1989 a federal appeals court ruled against Ben-Shalom. Ben-Shalom appealed her case to the U.S. Supreme Court where they declined to hear her case and let stand the previous court's ruling, effectively ending Ben-Shalom's military career. Ben-Shalom formed American Veterans for Equal Rights, and she has received several awards for her community activism.

Jennifer Bilek is a radical feminist and fine art painter living in NYC whose portraits are in private collections across the United States and Europe. In 2015 she exhibited her work at Art Basel Miami and the Salmagundi Club NYC. In Jennifer's words: "My work is bold and unapologetic. It does not lend itself to being demurely placed over a sofa to blend with the colors of someone's living room." Jennifer participated in and wrote about the Occupy Wall Street Movement at the time of it's inception in NYC and has recently taken up the fight against the corporately fueled politics of Transgenderism and GenderIdentity. http://jennifer-bilek.com/index.html, http://jenniferbilek.com/interviews.html, http://www.theupcoming.co.uk/?s=jennifer+bilek.

Cathy Brennan is a feminist activist, blogger of *Gender Identity Watch*, and attorney. Her essay explores how overbroad gender identity protections are negatively impacting the most vulnerable Women and Girls in our society - women who are incarcerated, girls who are housed in foster care or other protective facilities, homeless women and girls, and women and girls seeking support after sexual violence. It will detail legal developments that infringe on female bodily autonomy and discuss how such laws violate international human rights standards.

Mary Ceallaigh began feminist social justice activism in the Los Angeles area in the late 1980s. She is a graduate of Pacific Oaks College (B.A. Human Development) and Hygieia College Mystery School. Mary was co-author of NOW's 1999 *Resolution To Expand The Definition of Reproductive Rights to Include Homebirth and The Midwifery Model of Care*, and has apprenticed with radical midwives both in the U.S. and in Scotland. As a midwifery educator, she has been featured by ABC/NBC News, RTS Swiss National Radio, Radio Ireland, and others. Mary is a certified Kundalini yoga teacher and also practices Vipassana meditation & Ving Tsun kung fu.

Dominique Christina is a National Poetry Slam Champion, two-time winner of the Women of the World Slam Championship, and author of the poetry collections: "The Bones, The Breaking, The Balm" published by Penmanship Books, and "They Are All Me" by Swimming With Elephants Publishing. Her third book, "This is Woman's Work" by SoundsTrue Publishing received starred reviews in Library Journal and Publisher's Weekly. Her work has been featured in the Huffington Post and Upworthy and can also be found in numerous literary journals, magazines and anthologies.

Double XX Howl (pseudonym) is a published author who inhabits both the center and the margins. She is also a professor navigating the gender discourse wars.

Crash (pseudonym) is a radical butch dyke and aspiring farmer. She tries to draw insight from what she's lived through and writes to help other women, especially those healing from trauma, dysphoria and dissociation. She blogs at crashchaoscats.wordpress.com.

Kathy Crocco has participated in women's sports as an athlete, coach, official, and passionate spectator. She has dedicated the last forty years to volunteering with her local Special Olympics organization.

Maya Dillard Smith is a civil and human rights activist, legal scholar, political strategist, and news commentator. She is the Founder of FindingMiddleGround.org. and former Chief Executive of the ACLU of Georgia. Equipped with a degree from the UC Berkeley as a teen mom, a Master's from Harvard at age 23, and a law degree from UC Hastings while raising three daughters, Ms. Dillard Smith is a nationally recognized voice on controversial issues with a demonstrated track record of working with strange bedfellow, often acrimonious stakeholders across the political spectrum to problem solve value-based solutions for all. www.FindingMiddleGround.org

Alix Dobkin is a lesbian-feminist activist and musician. After a folk singing career in the 1960's, ALIX DOBKIN became a feminist, fell in love with a woman, and produced the groundbreaking 1973 "Lavender Jane Loves Women." Six albums and one songbook later Alix was a 2009 Lambda Literary Award finalist, *"MY RED BLOOD: A Memoir of Growing Up Communist, Coming Onto the Greenwich Village Folk Scene,* and published *Coming Out in the Feminist Movement.*

Carol Downer co-founded the nation's first women's self-help clinic in Los Angeles with Lorraine Rothman in 1972. Carol and Lorraine traveled the country to spread the idea of self-help, leaving in their wake a network of Feminist Women's Health Centers from California to Florida. The L.A. FWHC provided the full range of services for women's needs, including legal abortions, until it closed in 1984. Carol, an attorney specializing in civil law, has edited or co-authored numerous books and articles in the field of women's health. Recipient of the 2013 Margaret Sanger Award from the Veteran Feminists of America, Carol organizes the website: www.Womenshealthinwomenshands.org.

GallusMag (pseudonym) is the author of GenderTrender, a website focused on trends in gender and the most popular long-running gender website in history. One reviewer called GenderTrender "The motherlode of gender-critical analysis and opinion." Gallus Mag is a working class butch lesbian who spends her days moving boxes from one location to another when not minding the blog in her spare time: Gendertrender.wordpress.com

Elsa Gidlow (1898 – 1986) – A Creed For Free Women
The closing words of this anthology are spoken by English born, Elsa Gidlow, a poet who in 1923 published, *On A Grey Thread*, the first openly lesbian love poetry in the United States. She promoted alternative spiritualties including goddess worship, and her poetry expressed a deeply physical/spiritual understanding of powerful female realities. In the 1950s, Gidlow helped found Druid Heights, a bohemian community in Marin County, California. She was the author of thirteen books and appeared as herself in the documentary film, Word Is Out: Stories of Some of Our Lives (1977). Completed just before her death, her book *Elsa, I Come With My Songs* (1986), bccamc the first published lesbian autobiography.

Ila Suzanne Gray lives in Portland, Oregon where she is working on her fourth collection of poetry. Her poem *Then There Were the Wimmin* was produced as performance art at the Los Angeles Women's Building. She collaborated with Kay Gardner on the oratorio *Ouroboros: Seasons of Life, A Woman's Passage*. Her poems appear in in *We'Moon Calendars* and other pagan, lesbian and literary journals including *Gertrude* and *Windfall, A Journal of Poetry of Place*. She is a mixed media artist, a Dianic, a Buddhist and a Stone Crone. Her profound and unambiguous female aesthetic leaves an indelible impression.

Hypotaxis (pseudonym) is a radical feminist dyke blogger. Her sporadic musings on gender, feminism, and popular culture can be found at patheticfallacies.wordpress.com.

Elizabeth Hungerford is a feminist writer at sexnotgender.com and ehungerford.com. She is also the co-founder of a public discussion group about the contentious politics of gender. As an attorney, she is particularly interested in class-based analysis of gender, identity, women-only spaces, and the philosophical contradictions created by protecting "gender identity" as a matter of law.

Rachel Ivey organizes against male violence and in support of female autonomy. Having taken the long road toward radical feminist ideas, she speaks and writes from experience about the conflicts between radical and liberal conceptions of feminism. She currently splits her time between grassroots and mainstream feminist organizing, and learns much from the intersections and divergences between the two.

Sheila Jeffreys has been a feminist activist in UK and Australia for more than forty years. She is the author of nine books including *Gender Hurts*: a feminist analysis of the politics of transgenderism, (2014, Routledge). She is a Professorial Fellow in the School of Social and Political Sciences at the University of Melbourne and now lives in the UK. Jeffries submits on evidence to the transgender equality inquiry.

Nedra Johnson is a touring singer songwriter, multi-instrumentalist, blogger and podcast producer living in New York City. Her work, whether music, writing or podcasting centers women and our fight for autonomy. Her WANTED Project Podcast series seeks to connect women who are often made invisible by lack of conformity to the social expectations and limitations forced upon women. http://www.wantedpodcast.com

Lierre Keith is an American writer, radical feminist, and environmentalist, Lierre Keith is author six books, including the novels *Conditions of War* and *Skyler Gabriel*. Her non-fiction works include the highly acclaimed *The Vegetarian Myth: Food, Justice, and Sustainability*. She is coauthor, with Derrick Jensen and Aric McBay, of *Deep Green Resistance: Strategy to Save the Planet* (Seven Stories Press, 2011) and she's the editor of *The Derrick Jensen Reader: Writings on Environmental Revolution* (Seven Stories Press, 2012). She's been arrested six times for acts of civil disobedience. Her writing and lectures focus on civilization's violence against the planet, male violence against women, and the need for serious resistance to both. www.lierrekeith.com

Nuriddeen Knight *is an alumna of Teachers College, Columbia University, where she earned an MA in psychology with a focus on the child and the family.*

Mara Lake (pseudonym) is a spirited professional wombyn committed to confronting issues of systemic inequality and co-creating win-win solutions. For wombyn everywhere she stands up for their fundamental right to privacy in all matters and supports the right of wombyn to make individual choices for their lives. In this personal essay she offers a pristine analysis of the troubling impacts of a biological male's legally entitled intrusion upon an established wombyn's community.

Dr. Kathleen "Kelly" Levinstein, **PhD, LCSW, LMSW** is a Professor of Social Work at the University of Michigan, Flint. Among many other accomplishments, Dr. Levinstein was a Heilbein Scholar at the NYU School of Social Work, where she also taught, and has directed and provided clinical services for people with disabilities for many years, primarily in New York and New Jersey. Dr. Levinstein has been a clinical and research social worker for 40 years, and according to the International Federation of Social Workers the only out Autistic PhD level Social Worker, not just nationally but also globally. She worked as a consultant for the Archdiocese of NY and NJ, Amnesty International, Human Rights Watch, and at the nation's largest insurer authorizing care for Autistics and investigating fraud before beginning life as a full time academic and researcher. Her research and advocacy work includes human and civil rights violations against the autistic community.

Julia Long is a lesbian feminist who has been active in the women's movement for a number of years, particularly in campaigns against all forms of male violence: she loves protests that involve lots of feminist singing and chanting! She is committed to women-only organizing, and to helping to support and rebuild lesbian feminist community, culture and politics. She believes that a visible lesbian feminist community is vital to the survival of all women, and considers herself fortunate beyond words to have attended the final Michigan Womyn's Music Festival in 2015. Julia currently teaches Sociology at Anglia Ruskin University.

Sara St. Martin Lynne is a blogger and award winning film director and producer. She was an official videographer for the Michigan Womyn's Music Festival for nine consecutive years and is also the creator and curator for Voices From the Land - An Online Collective Memoir of the Michigan Womyn's Music Festival, a website where over 200 women and girls have shared their Festival experiences. Sara's popular blog fishwithoutabicycle.com is comprised of autobiographical essays all related to her own female experience, spirit, community and resilience under patriarchy.

Vajra Ma is the leading exponent of women's womb awakening in Feminist Spirituality. Based in her work with women's subtle bodyknowing since the mid-1980's, she originated the devotional moving meditation The Tantric Dance of Feminine Power®, the core practice of her mystery school and Priestess lineage Woman Mysteries of the Ancient Future Sisterhood®. Vajra Ma is author of *From a Hidden Stream: The Natural Spiritual Authority of Woman* and is published in numerous anthologies including *Foremothers of the Women's Spirituality Movement*. She is an ordained Dianic Priestess of Women's Mysteries with Temple of Diana, Inc.

Kathy Mandigo, M.D. is a general physician in Vancouver who has practiced medicine for over thirty years. She has worked in private practice and community health, including many years in Vancouver's Downtown Eastside. She also has a Master's degree in Health Care and Epidemiology, and has worked at the Canadian HIV Trials Network, the BC Centre for Excellence in HIV/AIDS, and Health Canada.

Patricia McFadden is a sociologist, activist, and radical African Feminist/Scholar, born in Swaziland. She lives and works in Zimbabwe as well as at the level of the regional and global women's movement (She considers the Women's Movement her home), and also conducts gender training for the United Nations system. She works particularly in conceptualising gender within the African context; making the distinction between Gender as a construct and Feminism as a political ideology/stance. She also works in Sexuality and Reproductive Rights/Health, and more recently she has been focusing on issues of citizenship and relations of property between African women and the state. Dr. McFadden was awarded the 1999 Hellman/Hammett Human Rights Award, an award that recognizes the courage of writers around the world who have been targets of political persecution.

Jackie Mearns is a radical lesbian feminist who lives in Scotland. She came to her feminist consciousness as a survivor of domestic abuse by a transgendered man. Her experience opened her eyes to the myriad ways that women's voices are silenced when they need to tell the truth about their lived experiences, how the very language that women need to define ourselves is being stripped from us, and how the precious bonds between us are being broken as the forces that forbid us to connect with each other in our own spaces grow in momentum. She is committed to raising women's voices in any way she can, and believes that defending women's right to define their own reality and to set their own boundaries is the ground zero of feminism. She says, "Being with a man who insisted that he was a lesbian helped me realize that the only *actual* lesbian in that relationship was me." She blogs at: https://naefearty.wordpress.com/2014/07/24/one-is-lonely-two-is-a-revolution/

Patricia Monaghan (1946-2012) - Mother
Visionary poet and scholar, Patricia Monaghan celebrated the mythic in the ordinary, the spiritual in the mundane, the sensuous in the scientific. Patricia was one of the pioneers of the contemporary women's spirituality movement and author of classic texts in the field of goddess scholarship. Her work focused on spirituality, peace, and environmental issues. Patricia was a Professor of Interdisciplinary Studies at DePaul University, and a Founding Fellow of The Black Earth Institute, a think-tank for artists seeking to connect social justice, environment and spirituality. Patricia was honored with a Pushcart Prize, the Paul Gruchow Nature Writing award, and the Friends of Literature award for poetry.

Barbara Mor (1936-2015) was an American poet, author, editor, and feminist of the twentieth-century Goddess movement. She became most widely known for *The Great Cosmic Mother*, (co-authored with Monica Sjöö), a cross-disciplinary study that cites numerous archaeological, anthropological, historical and mythological texts and artifacts as evidence of women's role as creators and first practitioners of humanity's earliest religious and cultural belief systems.

Ava Park is Founder and Presiding Priestess of The Goddess Temple of Orange County, founded in 2004, the only brick and mortar goddess temple of its kind in the world, serving as a spiritual center holding sacred space for women's mysteries and magic and *"empowering women to lead the world to goodness."* She is the creatrix of the new *Museum of Woman,* a public feminist museum of educational and entertaining exhibits of the hidden history of Goddess veneration on earth. Park is the author of *The Queen Teachings for Women* ©, *"empowering successful, self-actualized women to birth and lead a new civilization for humanity."*

Phonaesthetica (pseudonym) blogs from the American Southwest, where she keeps an eye out for the same old woman-hating derp disguised as progress. She looks like a salad, but identifies as a meatloaf. When it comes to television, she loves with a love that is more than love; just like Annabel Lee, except without all the chilling wind and sepulchers. She spent four happy Augusts at the Michigan Womyn's Music Festival.

Falcon River is a 60's vintage Butch woman from the southern United States. In 1978, she helped create and manage a women's bar called "Mother's Brew" that provided a feminist library, art gallery, and battered women's safe space. Falcon was an informant for *Baby, You're My Religion: Women, Gay Bars, and Theology Before Stonewall*, by Marie Cartier, Ph.D., (2013), and *The Michigan Womyn's Music Festival: An Amazon Matrix of Meaning*, by Laurie J. Kendall, Ph.D., (2008). She is also included in *Feminists Who Changed America 1963-1975*, editor Barbara J. Love (2006). Falcon is a storyteller, traditional archery instructor, teacher of magical arts, and co-founder of Temple of Diana, Inc., with life partner Ruth Barrett.

Max Robinson is a lesbian living with her girlfriend, her psychiatric service dog, and their four cats in Southern Oregon. She works in group homes, supporting developmentally disabled adults in foster care. Her recent novel, *Laika,* as well as other works are available at gumroad. com/wearethecatfish and wearethecatfish.com.

Kathy Scarbrough is a scientist, with a B.A. degree in biochemistry and a Ph.D. in physiology with specialization in the female reproductive neuroendocrinology. She was active in local women's liberation groups in the late 70s a member of Redstockings in the 1980s and became an associate editor of Carol Hanisch's publication Meeting Ground in the 1990s. She is currently an editor of MeetingGroundOnline, the webmaster for Hanisch's web site, a dues-paying feminist of Redstockings, National Women's Liberation and Women's Liberation Front. She agitates for other freedom struggles in addition to women's liberation because oppression due to race, class and sex all have to go.

Mary Lou Singleton is a radical feminist midwife, mother, and family nurse practitioner. She has served on the board of directors of the Midwives Alliance of North America and the advisory board of the Stop Patriarchy Abortion Rights Freedom Ride. She is the chair of the Reproductive Sovereignty task force of the Women's Liberation Front. http://womensliberationfront.org /

Monica Sjöö (1938 – 2005) Swedish born Monica Sjöö was a radical anarcho/eco-feminist and Goddess artist, writer and thinker involved in Earth spirituality. She co-authored the classic, *The Great Cosmic Mother: Rediscovering the Religion of the Earth* (1975) with Barbara Mor, and the first chapter opens this anthology. Monica's paintings were inspired by the veneration in ancient cultures of the Great Mother, the Earth and she exhibited throughout Europe and in America. Her most famous work is "God giving birth" (1968) became a feminist icon by depicting God as a Black woman and the human creation as a real birth.

Sally Tatnall is a life long activist working to combat racism, sexism, and classism. She is active locally with anti racism work. She works at a local abortion clinic she helped start in the 70s, and attends activities for lesbians over 50 where she raises feminist issues because some lesbians are not feminists. She works to preserve women-only space for women born women and has lived to see too many of the organizations she started in the 70s disappear.

Yeye Luisah Teish is an initiated elder and womanchief in the Ifa/Orisha tradition of the African diaspora. She is the author of Jambalaya: the Natural Woman's Book of Personal Charms and Practical Rituals and the Founding Mother of Ile Orunmila Oshun (the house of Destiny and Love). Yeye performs divinations, teaches classes in Spiritual Guidance, and conducts intensive workshops in Women's Rites of Passage, Sexual Abuse Recovery, and Women's Empowerment. She is a ritual theater director and mixed media artist. Her article addresses Sexual imperialism, spiritual culture appropriation/misrepresentation, and the impact of "patriarchy in drag" on the psyche and culture of African American women.

Sharon Thrace (pseudonym) is an artist, a software developer and a published writer on the topics of entertainment, politics, and feminism. Her essay details the rapid demise of her seemingly loving, stable 15-year marriage when her husband came out as transgender. She further details the experience on her blog at https://transwidow.wordpress.com.

Marie Verite (pseudonym) is the creator of the blog *4thWaveNow*. She is the mother of a teenaged daughter who suddenly announced she was a "trans man" after a few weeks of total immersion in YouTube transition videos. After much research and fruitless searching for an alternative online viewpoint, this mom began writing about her deepening skepticism of the ever-accelerating medical and media fascination with the phenomenon of "transgender children." 4thWaveNow has expanded to feature not only Marie's writing, but that of other parents, formerly trans-identified women, and people with professional experience with young people who are questioning their gender identity. www.4thwavenow.com

Devorah Zahav is a lesbian separatist who blogs at RedressAlert.tumblr.com about her experience of stopping ftm transition, the causes and meanings of dissociation from femaleness, and building paths toward integration and identification with all varieties of female reality. She founded Autotomous Womyn's Press, publisher of *Blood and Visions: Womyn Reconciling With Being Female.* She was honored to participate in the final Closing Ceremony of the final Michigan Womyn's Music Festival.

Additional Acknowledgements to the following quotation contributors: Ruth Barrett, Cathy Brennan, Karen Cayer, Kathy Crocco, Mary Daly, Hypotaxis, Parker Wolf, C.H, and Sheila Jeffreys.

79808827R00347

Made in the USA
Middletown, DE
12 July 2018